FOURTH EDITION

Language

INTRODUCTORY READINGS

FOURTH EDITION

Language

INTRODUCTORY READINGS

VIRGINIA P. CLARK
PAUL A. ESCHHOLZ
ALFRED F. ROSA

EDITORS

ST. MARTIN'S PRESS
NEW YORK

Library of Congress Catalog Card Number: 84-51144
Manufactured in the United States of America.
6543
nmlk

For information, write:
St. Martin's Press, Inc.
175 Fifth Avenue
New York, NY 10010

cover design: Darby Downey

ISBN: 0-312-46797-4

Acknowledgments
"Language: An Introduction" by W. F. Bolton. Condensed by permission of Random House, Inc. from *A Living Language: The History and Structure of English*, by W. F. Bolton. Copyright 1982 by Random House, Inc.
"Nine Ideas About Language" by Harvey A. Daniels. From *Famous Last Words: The American Language Crisis Reconsidered*, by Harvey A. Daniels. Copyright 1983 by Southern Illinois University Press. Reprinted by permission of the Southern Illinois University Press.
Excerpt from *Humankind* by Peter Farb. Copyright 1978 by Peter Farb. Reprinted by permission of Houghton Mifflin Company.
"The Acquisition of Language" by Breyne Arlene Moskowitz. Copyright © 1978 by Scientific American, Inc. All rights reserved.
"Developmental Milestones in Motor and Language Development" by Eric H. Lenneberg. From *Biological Foundations of Language* by Eric H. Lenneberg. Copyright 1967 by John Wiley & Sons. Reprinted by permission of John Wiley & Sons.
"Sounds" by Peter A. de Villiers and Jill G. de Villiers. Reprinted by permission of the publishers from *Early Language* by Peter A. de Villiers and Jill G. de Villiers, Cambridge, Mass.: Harvard University Press, Copyright © 1979 by Peter A. de Villiers and Jill G. de Villiers.
"Predestinate Grooves: Is There a Preordained Language 'Program'?" by Jean Aitchison. From *The Articulate Mammal: An Introduction to Psycholinguistics*, Second Edition, by Jean Aitchison. Copyright 1976, 1983 by Jean Aitchison. Reprinted by permission of Universe Books, New York, and Hutchison Publishing Group Ltd., London.
"The Development of Language in Genie: A Case of Language Acquisition Beyond the 'Critical Period'" by Victoria Fromkin, Stephen Krashen, Susan Curtiss, David Rigler, and Marilyn Rigler. From *Brain and Language*. Vol. 1, No. 1: 81–107. New York: Academic Press, Inc. January 1974.
"Genie: A Postscript" by Maya Pines. From "The Civilizing of Genie," from *Psychology Today*, September 1981.
"Creole Languages" by Derek Bickerton. Copyright © July 1983 by Scientific American, Inc. All rights reserved.
"Brain and Language" by Jeannine Heny. Copyright 1985 by Jeannine Heny. Figures 1 and 3 from *Language and Speech* by George Miller. W. H. Freeman and Company. Copyright © 1981. Figure 2 from *Brain and the Conscious Experience*, edited by John C. Eccles. Springer-Verlag, 1966. Figure 4 from "The Great Cerebral Commissure," in *Left Brain, Right Brain*, Springer and Deutsch, W. H. Freeman, 1981. Copyright © 1981.
"The Loss of Language" by Howard Gardner. From *Human Nature*, March 1978. Copyright 1978 by Human Nature, Inc. Reprinted by permission of the publisher.
"Phonetics" by Edward Callary. Copyright 1981 by R. E. Callary. Revised 1984 by R. E. Callary.

Acknowledgments and copyrights continue at the back of the book on pages 731–732, which constitute an extension of the copyright page.

Preface

The limits of my language mean the limits of my world.
—Ludwig Wittgenstein

Our language is central to everything we do. Language, more than any other human attribute, distinguishes us from all other forms of life on earth. Because we cannot function without our language, and because the language we use and how we use it set strict boundaries to what we can do, new discoveries and changes in linguistics can profoundly affect what we think of ourselves and our place in society. In appreciating the complexities of the medium through which we all communicate, we can understand more fully our humanity.

This fourth edition of *Language: Introductory Readings* has been re-organized to reflect the changing emphases in the study of language. For example, the third edition's Part Two, on language acquisition and the brain, has been divided into two parts, with one being devoted wholly to language acquisition. And, the third edition's Part Four, on phonology, morphology, and syntax, has also been split into two parts—one dealing with syntax and language processing (the latter a topic new to this edition) and the other a separate, expanded section encompassing phonetics, phonology, and morphology. Also treated more extensively are semantics and pragmatics, and new to this edition is a selection on natural language processing by computers (i.e., artificial intelligence). The two separate sections on animal communication and nonverbal communication that appeared in the third edition have been eliminated; each subject is treated here in one comprehensive survey article.

In addition to providing more focused and in-depth coverage, the selections are up-to-date. Twenty-one of the forty readings are new, and three—those by William Kemp and Roy Smith, by Jeannine Heny, and by Frank Heny—were especially prepared for this edition. Edward Callary has completely revised his article on phonetics, which was originally written for the third edition. Also, several selections that appeared in the third edition have since been published in revised form, and thus they are included here in their newer versions.

The new edition retains the teaching aids familiar from its predecessors: an introduction and discussion-and-review questions for each selection, an annotated bibliography and a variety of projects at the end of each part, and a general introduction for each part that describes the topics it covers and relates the readings to one another. In addition,

v

a glossary of frequently used terms and a complete topical index are provided for the first time.

The professional literature of linguistics and related fields ranges greatly in its demands on the reader's knowledge. We have therefore tried to choose selections that are consistent in level of difficulty and that are accessible to undergraduates who have no previous formal study of linguistics but have a serious interest in the subject. The sequence of the nine parts represents one possible syllabus for a course in language. However, instructors with other preferences will find that the order can easily be rearranged and that all sections may not be needed for some courses. Even so, we do recommend that Part One, "Language and Its Study," be assigned first, and that students read Edward Callary's "Phonetics" in Part Four before tackling any of the selections that make use of the phonetic alphabet (i.e., those by Peter A. de Villiers and Jill G. de Villiers, Morris Halle, H. A. Gleason, and Roger W. Shuy).

We are grateful to two colleagues for their constant encouragement and indispensable professional advice: Jinny Samuelson of the University of Akron and Frank Heny of the University of Vermont and Carleton College. Without their assistance, this edition would not have been possible. If any shortcomings remain, they are our responsibility. We also received valuable criticism of the third edition and advice toward the fourth from teachers around the country, who, in a real sense, were collaborators in setting the new proportions and coverage of this book: Barbara Abbott, Michigan State University; Wayne C. Anderson, University of North Carolina—Greensboro; Mark Aronoff, SUNY—Stony Brook; Anne Bolin, University of Colorado—Denver; Hagit Borer, University of California—Irvine; Robert Brown, University of Minnesota; Michael E. Connaughton, Saint Cloud State University; Joseph R. Cooke, University of Washington; Soren F. Cox, Brigham Young University; Kitty Chen Dean, Nassau Community College; Martha Dietz, Colgate University; Patricia J. Donegan, Ohio State University; Carol Eastman, University of Washington; Donald Ellis, Michigan State University; Robert J. Ewald, Findlay College; Richard A. Farland, Stetson University; Barbara Farnandis, Chicago State University; Graham S. Frear, Saint Olaf College; Richard Freed, Eastern Kentucky University; Robert Gates, Syracuse University; Francis G. Greco, Clarion State College; Ordelle G. Hill, Eastern Kentucky University; Nicholas Howe, Rutgers University; Charles Huff, Indiana University—Bloomington; Martin Huntley, Brown University; Valdon L. Johnson, University of Northern Iowa; Ellen M. Kaisse, University of Washington; Joseph Keller, Indiana University—Purdue University at Indianapolis; W. J. Vande Kopple, Calvin College; Stephen J. Korinko, Concordia College; E. C. Kyte, Northern Arizona University; Catherine P. Lewicke, Worchester State College; Thomas Liszka, DePaul University;

Vincent Lopresti, University of Wisconsin—Oshkosh; Michael Mates, Shoreline Community College; Virginia McDavid, Chicago State University; Cezary Mendelius, Saginaw Valley State College; Mildred C. Melendez, Sinclair Community College; Elaine Miller, Seton Hall University; Edward J. Milowicki, Mills College; Patricia Moody, Syracuse University; Marshall Myers, Kentucky Wesleyan College; John Nerbonne, Ohio State University; Klaus Obermeier, Ohio State University; Edward Y. Odisho, Loyola University—Lake Shore; Alexandra Olsen, University of Denver; Kenneth A. Robb, Bowling Green State University; Carol Rosen, Cornell University; Helen Scott, Grinnell College; Edward L. Smith, University of Texas—Austin; H. Stephen Straight, SUNY—Binghamton; L. J. Theismeyer, University of Notre Dame; Lynn F. Williams, Emerson College; Rita Yeasted, La Roche College; George Yule, University of Minnesota—Minneapolis; and Paul Zimansky, Boston University.

Finally, special thanks once again go to our students at the University of Vermont, whose continued enthusiasm for language study and whose responses to and evaluations of materials included in this edition, as well as in the first three, have been most helpful.

Virginia P. Clark
Paul A. Eschholz
Alfred F. Rosa

Contents

Part Seven/Language Variation: Regional and Social   461

Part Eight/Historical Linguistics and Language Change   579

Part Nine/Beyond Speech: Broader Perspectives 631

Part One

Language and Its Study

Language is not only the principal medium that human beings use to communicate with each other but also the bond that links people together and binds them to their culture. To understand our humanity, we must understand the language that makes us human. The study of language, then, is a very practical, as well as a very challenging, pursuit. In beginning this study, we must consider some fundamental questions: What is language? What are its unique characteristics? Are there some commonly held misconceptions that impede our understanding of language—and if so, what are they? What effect does language have on people and on their culture? The selections in Part One raise these basic questions and suggest some answers.

Most people take their language ability for granted; speaking and understanding speech seem as natural as breathing or sleeping. But human language is extremely complex and has unique characteristics. In the first selection in this section, W. F. Bolton discusses the properties of human language that make it species-specific and explains the intricate physiological adaptations that make speech and hearing possible. He also points out that all languages are systematic and that no language is "simple" or "primitive," and he alerts us to the harm of ethnocentric attitudes.

Following this definition of human language and introduction to the physiology of speech and hearing, Harvey A. Daniels discusses nine "facts" about human language that most contemporary linguists

1

believe to be demonstrably true. These ideas are important in their own right; in addition, understanding them will make the selections in other parts of this book more enjoyable and meaningful.

The selections in Part One provide an introduction to the study of language: its physiology and unique properties, and facts that refute nine commonly held misconceptions about language. Reading these articles should help us begin to understand the complexity of both human language and the problems involved in studying it. Moreover, doing so should make it impossible to take for granted the unique and complicated phenomenon that is human language.

1/Language: An Introduction

W. F. BOLTON

The ability to use language is the most distinctive human character-istic, and yet most people take this ability for granted, never consid-ering its richness and complexity. In the following selection, W. F. Bolton, Professor of English at Douglass College, analyzes the intri-cate physiological mechanisms involved in speech production and in speech reception, or hearing. Especially interesting is his discussion of the differences between "speech breathing" and "quiet breathing." Professor Bolton also explains the "design features" that characterize human language; this explanation is important for understanding many of the later selections in this book. His concluding warning against ethnocentricity is particularly important today.

Language is so built into the way people live that it has become an axiom of being human. It is the attribute that most clearly distinguishes our species from all others; it is what makes possible much of what we do, and perhaps even what we think. Without language we could not specify our wishes, our needs, the practical instructions that make possible cooperative endeavor ("You hold it while I hit it"). Without language we would have to grunt and gesture and touch rather than tell. And through writing systems or word of mouth we are in touch with distant places we will never visit, people we will never meet, a past and a future of which we can have no direct experience. Without language we would live in isolation from our ancestors and our des-cendants, condemned to learn only from our own experiences and to take our knowledge to the grave.

Of course other species communicate too, sometimes in ways that seem almost human. A pet dog or cat can make its needs and wishes known quite effectively, not only to others of its own species but to its human owner. But is this language? Porpoises make extremely com-plex sequences of sounds that may suggest equally complex messages, but so far no way has been found to verify the suggestion. Chimpan-zees have been taught several humanly understandable languages, notably AMESLAN (American Sign Language) and a computer lan-guage, but there has been heated debate whether their uses of these languages are like ours or merely learned performances of rather

3

greater subtlety than those of trained circus animals. If the accomplishments of dolphins and chimpanzees remain open questions, however, there is no question but that human uses of language, both everyday and in the building of human cultures, are of a scope and power unequaled on our planet.

It seems likely that language arose in humans about a hundred thousand years ago. How this happened is at least as unknowable as how the universe began, and for the same reason: there was nobody there capable of writing us a report of the great event. Language, like the universe, has its creation myths; indeed, in St. John's Gospel both come together in the grand formulation, "In the beginning was the Word, and the Word was with God, and the Word was God." Modern linguists, like modern cosmologists, have adopted an evolutionary hypothesis. Somehow, over the millennia, both the human brain and those parts of the human body now loosely classed as the organs of speech have evolved so that speech is now a part of human nature. Babies start to talk at a certain stage of their development, whether or not their parents consciously try to teach them; only prolonged isolation from the sounds of speech can keep them from learning.

Writing is another matter. When the topic of language comes up, our first thoughts are likely to be of written words. But the majority of the world's languages have never been reduced to writing (though they all could be), and illiteracy is a natural state: we learn to write only laboriously and with much instruction. This is hardly surprising, since compared with speech writing is a very recent invention—within the past 5,000 years. Still more recently there have been invented complex languages of gesture for use by and with people unable to hear or speak; these too must be painstakingly learned. What do the spoken, written, and sign languages have in common that distinguishes them from other ways to communicate?

Properties of Language

Perhaps the most distinctive property of language is that its users can create sentences never before known, and yet perfectly understandable to their hearers and readers. We don't have to be able to say "I've heard that one before!" in order to be able to say, "I see what you mean." And so language can meet our expressive needs virtually without limit, no matter how little we have read or heard before, or what our new experiences call on us to express. Another way of describing this property is to say that language is **productive**. We take this productivity for granted in our uses of language, but in fact it is one of the things that make human communication unique.

Less obvious is the fact that language is **arbitrary:** the word for something seldom has any necessary connection with the thing itself. We say *one, two, three*—but the Chinese say *yi, er, san.* Neither language has the "right" word for the numerals, because there is no such thing. (It might seem that a dog's barking, or a blackbird's call, were equally arbitrary, as both might be translated into various languages as "Go away!" or "Allez-vous-en!"—but within the species the sound is universally understandable. A chow and a German shepherd understand each other without translation—unlike speakers of Chinese and German).

Even the sounds of a language are arbitrary. English can be spoken using only 36 significantly different sounds, and these are not all the same as the sounds needed to speak other languages. These 36 sounds are in turn arbitrarily represented by 26 letters, some standing for two or more sounds, others overlapping. (Consider *c, s,* and *k.*) And the patterns into which these sounds, and indeed words, may be arranged are also arbitrary. We all know too well what *tax* means but, in English at least, there is no such word as *xat.* In English we usually put an adjective before its noun—*fat man;* in French it's the other way around, *homme gros.* This patterning is the key to the productivity of language. If we use intelligible words in proper patterns, we can be sure of being understood by others who speak our language. Indeed, we seem to understand nonsense, provided it is fitted into proper patterns—the silly nonsense of doubletalk, the impressive nonsense of much bureaucratese.

This ability to attach meaning to arbitrary clusters of sounds or words is like the use and understanding of symbolism in literature and art. The word *one* does not somehow represent the numeral, somehow embody its essence the way a three-sided plane figure represents the essence of triangularity. Rather, *one* merely stands for the prime numeral 1, giving a physical form to the concept, just as the word *rosebuds* gives a physical form to the concept "the pleasures of youth" in the poetic line, "Gather ye rosebuds while ye may." Thus the sound /wʌn/, spelled *one,* has a dual quality as a sound and as a concept. This can be seen from the fact that /wʌn/, spelled *won,* matches the identical sound to a wholly different concept. This feature of **duality** is both characteristic of and apparently unique in human communication, and so linguists use it as a test to distinguish language from other kinds of communication in which a sound can have only a single meaning. (Such sounds are called signs, to distinguish them from the symbols that are human words.)

Sounds can be made into meaningful combinations, such as language, only if they are first perceived as meaningfully distinct, or **discrete.** We can find an analogy in music. Musical pitch rises continuously without steps from the lowest frequency we can hear to the highest, sliding upward like the sound of a siren. But most of music is not continuous; it consists of notes that move upwards in discrete steps, as in a scale (from *scalae*, the Latin for "stairs"). This is why we can talk about notes being the same or different, as we could not easily do if all possible tones from low to high were distributed along a continuous line. Similarly, in speech we can slide through all the vowels from "ee" in the front of the mouth to "aw" in the throat—but then how could we tell *key* from *Kay* from *coo* from *caw*? Likewise we distinguish between *v* and *f*, so that *view* is different from *few*. But these distinctions are arbitrary. They are not even common to all languages. For example, in German the letters *v* and *f* both represent the sound /f/, the letter *w* represents the sound /v/—and there is no sound /w/. What all languages do have in common, however, is the property of discreteness.

These four properties, or "design features," of language were first set down by Charles Hockett in 1958 as part of an attempt to see how human language differs from animal communication systems. There are of course other design features—their number has varied from seven to sixteen—but these four (discreteness, arbitrariness, duality, and productivity) appear to be the most important. Among the others:

Human language uses the *channel of sound*, generated by the vocal organs and perceived by the ear, as its primary mode. As a consequence, speech is *nondirectional*: anyone within hearing can pick it up, and we can hear from sources which we cannot see. Our hearing, being stereophonic, can also tell from what direction the sound is coming. Also, our language acts *fade rapidly* (unless recorded on tape or in writing). We do not, as a rule, repeat these acts the way animals often do their signals.

In human language, *any speaker can be a listener and any listener can be a speaker*, at least normally. Some kinds of animal communication, such as courtship behavior, are one-way. And we get *feedback* of our own utterances through our ears and through bone conduction. Non-sound animal communication, like the dances of bees, can often only be invisible to the originator of the message.

Our language acts are *specialized*. That is to say, they have to do only with communication; they do not serve any other function. For example, speech is not necessary for breathing, nor is it the same as other sounds we make, such as a laugh or a cry of pain or fear. Of course, such sounds can communicate, but only by accident to those within earshot. Their main purpose is a reflexive one: they happen more or less involuntarily, like the jerk of a tapped knee.

Italian children grow up speaking Italian; Chinese children learn Chinese. *Human language is transmitted by the cultures we live in*, not by our parentage: if the Chinese infant is adopted by an Italian couple living in Italy, he or she will grow up speaking perfect Italian. But a kitten growing up among human beings speaks neither Italian nor Chinese; it says *meow*. Its communication is determined by its genetic makeup, not by its cultural context.

Nonlanguages

Other kinds of human communication are sometimes called language: body language, or *kinesics*, is one example. The way we use our bodies in sitting, standing, walking, is said to be expressive of things we do not say. It probably is, but that does not make it language. Body language lacks duality, in that it is not symbolic but rather a direct representation of a feeling; discreteness, in that there is no "alphabet" of distinctive movements or postures; and productivity, in that "original" expressions are likely not to be understood. Moreover, it appears to be only partly arbitrary, for the movement or posture is often selected by its "meaning" as representational, not arbitrary; "barrier signs" such as crossing one's arms or legs need no dictionary. Try testing body language against the other design features.

The Physiology of Speech

Speech is a kind of specialized exhalation, so it follows that we breathe while we speak. But the two sorts of breathing are not at all the same. "Quiet" breathing is more rapid and shallow than breathing during speech. Quiet breathing is also more even and restful than speech breathing, for during speech the air is taken in quickly and then expelled slowly against the resistance of the speech organs. Quiet breathing is mostly through the nose, speech breathing through the mouth. These differences, and others, would normally affect the accumulation of carbon dioxide (CO_2) in the blood, and the level of CO_2 is the main regulator of breathing—the rate or volume of breathing responds to the level of CO_2 so as to keep us from getting too uncomfortable. If we consciously use "speech" breathing but remain silent, we resist this response and our discomfort grows rapidly. That discomfort does not take place during actual speech, however; some other mechanism comes into play.

Thus, it is quite clear that breathing undergoes peculiar changes during speech. What is astonishing is that man can tolerate these modifications for an apparently unlimited period of time without experiencing respiratory distress, as is well demonstrated by the interminable speech with which many a statesman embellishes his political existence. Cloture is dictated by motor fatigue and limited receptivity in the audience—never by respiratory demands.[1]

Our neural and biochemical makeup is in fact specially adapted so that we can sustain the speech act. Other animal species are equally adapted to their systems of communication, but none of them can be taught ours because ours is species-specific, a set of abilities that have evolved in humankind over a very long time. The evolution has included the most intricate adaptations of the body and its workings, particularly the neural system (including, above all, the brain); the motor system (especially the muscles that the neural system controls); and the sensory system (especially hearing, of course, but also touch).

The speech act involves an input of meaning and an output of sound on the part of the speaker, the reverse on the part of the listener. But a great deal takes place between the input and the output, and it takes place in the brain. That means that the organ for thinking, the brain, is by definition the seat of language. And the brain is also the control center for the intricate virtuoso muscular performance we call speech, commanding the vocal activities and—most important—ensuring their coordination and sequencing.

The brain is not just an undifferentiated mass in which the whole organ does all of its tasks. The different tasks that the brain does are localized, and in a more general way, the whole brain is lateralized. In most people, the right half (or hemisphere) controls the left half of the body and vice versa, and many brain functions are also lateralized. Language is one of them; it is localized in several areas of the left hemisphere. The language centers are not motor control centers for the production of speech. Instead, they are "boardrooms" in which decisions are made, decisions that motor control centers in both hemispheres of the brain implement by issuing the orders to the body. The orders are carried by electric impulses from the central nervous system (brain and spinal cord) into the peripheral nervous system (activating the muscles).

Wernicke's area lies in the left hemisphere of the brain, just above the ear. It takes its name from the German Carl Wernicke (1848–1905), who in 1874 showed that damage to that part of the brain leads to a disrupted flow of meaning in speech. A decade earlier the Frenchman Paul Broca (1824–1880) had shown that damage to another area of the left hemisphere, several inches further downward, led instead to disrupted pronunciation and grammar. There are also differences in the areas when it comes to receptive ability: damage to Broca's area does not much affect comprehension, but damage to Wernicke's area disrupts it seriously.

---

[1] Eric H. Lenneberg, *Biological Foundations of Language* (New York: John Wiley & Sons, Inc., 1967), p. 80.

These differences suggest that the two chief language areas of the brain have functions that are distinct but complementary. It seems that the utterance gets its basic structure in Wernicke's area, which sends it on to Broca's area through a bundle of nerve fibers called the *arcuate fasciculus*. In Broca's area the basic structure is translated into the orders of the speech act itself, which go on to the appropriate motor control area for implementation. In reverse order, a signal from the hearing or the visual system (speech or writing) is relayed to Wernicke's area for decoding from language to linguistic meaning. Broca's area, which seems to write the program for the speech act, is not so important to listening or reading as Wernicke's area is.

All of this, naturally, is inferential: the evidence as we know it points to these conclusions, but no one has ever actually seen these brain activities taking place. The conclusions are also incredible. It is difficult to imagine all that activity for a simple "Hi!" But those conclusions are the simplest ones that will account adequately for the evidence.

All sound, whether a cat's meow, a runner's "Hi!," or a sonar beep, is a disturbance of the air or other medium (water, for example) in which it is produced. When the sound is speech it can be studied in terms of its production (articulatory phonetics), its physical properties in the air (acoustic phonetics), or its reception by the ear and other organs of hearing (auditory phonetics). The first of these is the easiest to study without special instruments, and it is the only one of the three that directly involves the motor system.

The vocal organs are those that produce speech. They form an irregular tube from the lungs, the windpipe, the larynx (and the vocal cords it contains), and the throat, to the mouth (including the tongue and lips) and nose (Fig. 1). All the organs except the larynx have other functions, so not all their activities are speech activities. The lungs are central to breathing, for example, to provide oxygen to the blood, and so many animals that cannot speak have lungs. In that sense speech is a secondary function of the lungs and of all the vocal organs; it has been said that they are "vocal organs" only in the sense that the knees are prayer organs. The action of forming the sound we write with the letter *p* is very similar to that of spitting, but *p* is a part of a language system while spitting is not.

Nonetheless, to regard the speech function of these organs as secondary is to overlook the profound language adaptation of the whole human anatomy. The language functions of the motor system are not simply "overlaid" on their other functions, for the language functions in many ways conflict with the others: the tongue is far more agile than is needed for eating, the ear more sensitive than is needed for nonspeech sounds, and the esophagus much too close to the pharynx for safety (hence the need for the Heimlich maneuver). In human

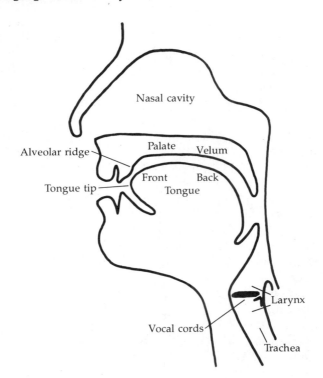

Figure 1

beings, there is nothing really secondary about the speech activities of the vocal organs.

The lungs produce a steady stream of exhaled air which the other speech organs specialize into speech. For vowels and for many consonants, the air is set into rapid vibration by the vocal cords in the larynx or "Adam's apple." The more rapid the vibration, the higher the pitch of the speech. The air can also be set in motion by a partial constriction farther up the vocal tract in the mouth, or by a complete stoppage followed by an abrupt release. The vocal cords produce a buzzlike vibration, constriction produces a hissing sound, stoppage and release produce a small explosion. A buzz alone gives us one or another of the vowels, such as the *u* in *buzz*. A stop without buzz will be like the *p* in *stoppage*, with buzz like the *b* in *buzz*.

Whether buzzing or not, the column of air driven by the lungs next passes through the pharynx, a tube that extends from the larynx through the back of the mouth as far as the rear opening of the nasal cavity. The nasal cavity itself is a chamber about four inches long, opening in front at the nostrils and at the rear into the pharynx. The nasal cavity is divided in two by the septum. The nostrils cannot open and close, but the entrance into the pharynx is controlled by the soft palate or velum. The velum is open for *n* and *m* (and often for sounds adjacent to them), closed for other sounds. You can probably feel, or with a mirror even see, the velum open at the end of a word like *hang*.

Within the mouth, the air column is molded by the tongue and the lips. The lips can cause constriction or stoppage; they constrict the air when the upper teeth touch the lower lip to make an *f* or *v* sound, and they stop the air when they close to make a *p* or *b* sound. They also close for the *m* sound, which is emitted through the nose, not the mouth. The lips can further mold the air by rounding, as they do when making the vowel sound in *do* or the consonant sound in *we*, among others.

The tongue—which has a surprising shape for those familiar only with the tip and the upper surface of it—can cause constriction or stoppage of the airflow at any point from the back of the teeth to the roof of the mouth near the velum. Like the lips, the tongue is involved in making both vowel sounds and consonant sounds. It makes both with the tip in a word like *eat*. Or the rear of the tongue can arch up toward the roof of the mouth to make a "back" consonant or vowel. It makes both in a word like *goo*. The tongue can approach the roof of the mouth in other positions farther forward as well, and it can change the shape of the oral cavity in other ways without actually approaching or touching the roof of the mouth.

So the speech sounds are formed in the larynx, in the mouth, and in the nasal cavity. They are formed by the action of the larynx, the velum, the tongue, and the lips. The lips may touch the teeth, and the tongue may touch the teeth or the roof of the mouth. That sounds a trifle complicated, but it is only a small part of what goes on in the motor system. To begin with, all the vocal organs are controlled by muscles, from those that cause the lungs to inhale and exhale air to those that shape the lips in speech. These muscles are not single—a lung muscle, a lip muscle, and so forth—but arranged in intricate groups. In reality, the vocal organs are not only those that articulate but those that activate the articulators.

Other parts of the anatomy too are involved in articulation although we do not usually think of them as vocal organs. The pharynx changes shape as we talk, and so do the cheeks. Some of the vocal organs move in ways that coordinate with articulation but do not seem to be part of it: the larynx moves up and down, for example, in speaking as it does more obviously in swallowing.

Finally, all the vocal organs are in constant motion during speech. The vowels in *house* and in *white* are formed by a change of position in the mouth, not by a single position. And as the mouth moves from the first consonants in these words, through the complex vowel sound, to the final consonants, it is always in motion. What is more, these actions must be coordinated. To take a simple example, the buzz of the larynx must be "on" for the first sounds of *mat* but "off" for the *t*; meanwhile, the mouth closes and the velum opens for the *m*, but they reverse roles for the *a* and *t*. The whole performance adds up to a virtuoso display that far exceeds in complexity . . . the minute adjustments required for even the finest violinist's playing. To observe that "The cat is on the mat" is, from the standpoint of the motor skills required, so demanding that we would think it impossible if we paused to analyze it. We usually do not.

The Sensory System

In a way, the main sensory system of language, hearing, is the reverse of speech. Speech turns meaning into sound, while hearing turns sound into meaning. Speech encodes meaning as language in the brain, and the brain sends neural messages to the motor system for action; the motor system produces speech. Hearing turns the speech sounds back into neural messages which go to the brain where they are decoded into language and interpreted for meaning.

Sound, as we have seen, is a disturbance of the air—a kind of applied energy. The ear is designed to pick up and process that energy, often in incredibly small amounts. The ear is good not only at amplifying small sounds but at damping loud ones, within limits: a very sudden, very loud noise, or even sound that is not sudden (if it is loud enough), can cause damage to the sensitive sound-gathering mechanisms of the ear, damage which if severe or prolonged can be permanent.

What we usually mean by *ear* is the appendage earrings hang from, but that is only the ear's most visible part. In fact it has three divisions: the outer ear, which extends into the eardrum; the middle ear; and the inner ear. The outer ear collects the sound, passes it through the ear canal, and focuses it on the eardrum. The eardrum is a tightly stretched membrane which is set into motion by the vibrations of sound energy; it is really a "drum" in reverse, for while the bass drum in a marching band converts the energy of motion (a blow from a drumstick) into sound waves, the eardrum converts sound waves into motion energy which is picked up in the middle ear. That motion is carried through the middle ear by three tiny bones; here weak sounds are amplified and very strong sounds are damped. The last of the three bones delivers the sound motion to a membrane called the oval window, which is smaller than the eardrum; the difference in size helps to concentrate the sound energy.

The oval window divides the middle ear from the inner ear. The inner ear is composed of several cavities in the bones of the skull; in one of these, the cochlea, the energy that arrived at the outer ear as sound, and is now motion, will be converted by a set of intricate organs into electrical impulses and fed into the central nervous system for delivery to the auditory center of the brain. The remaining steps in the process are then neural, not sensory.

The process here described, and our idea of hearing in general, relates to sound that reaches us from outside by conduction through the air, water, or other medium. But there is another way in which we can receive sound. A vibrating tuning fork held against the skull will be "heard" by conduction through the bone itself, even if the ear-hole is effectively plugged. Bone-conduction helps us monitor our own speech by providing continuous feedback; thus we can pick out our own words even when surrounded by loud conversation or noise. Bone-conduction has a different sound quality from air-conduction, which is why your voice sounds to you one way when you are speaking and another when you hear it played back from a tape. And bone-conduction can sometimes substitute for air-conduction—for example, when a hearing aid "plays" sound waves directly into the bones of the skull.

Language and Culture

Language is species-specific to humankind. By *humankind* we mean the genus *Homo*, species *sapiens*—no other species of this genus survives. Any smaller subdivisions, such as sex or race, may differ among themselves in other very visible ways, but the neural, motor, and sensory equipment necessary to language is common to all. Not that the equipment is identical; otherwise everyone would speak at about the same pitch. But racial, sexual, or individual differences in the shape and size of the nose and lips, or of the internal speech organs, do not override the structural similarity of the vocal organs among all human groups, and they definitely do not result in any functional differences. The members of any group, that is, have the vocal organs to articulate any human language with complete mastery. The same is true of other genetic factors: the intellectual ability to use language is the same in all the varieties of humankind and in all normal individuals.

That is not the same as saying that adult individuals can learn a foreign language as easily as they learned their own in childhood. The physiological habits of the speech organs are complex, and they are learned early. We observe that a native speaker of Chinese has difficulty with the sound of r in *very*, a native speaker of Japanese with the sound of l in *hello*. That is because their native languages have given them no opportunity to practice those sounds. On the contrary, the languages have reinforced other sounds that tend to crop up when the Chinese speaker attempts English r or the Japanese speaker English l. The problem, however, is one of habit and not heredity. An American of Chinese ancestry has no trouble with the sounds of English, including *r*, while a person of European ancestry raised to speak Chinese would.

Our virtuosity in our own language carries with it other commitments, some easily understandable and some less so. Speakers of English easily handle a system of pronouns that distinguishes among masculine (*he*), feminine (*she*), and neuter (*it*) forms. They may have trouble with a language like German, however, where the nouns, adjectives, and articles (equivalents of *the* and *a*) make a similar three-way distinction, often in apparent disregard of the sex of the noun—a *maiden* (*das Mädchen*) is neuter, [but changes to feminine] when she becomes a *wife* (*die Frau*)—or with a language like French which makes only a two-way distinction between masculine and feminine, so that *table* is feminine (*la table*) but *floor* is masculine (*le plancher*).

We should not rush to conclude, however, that the Germans and the French see sexual characteristics in inanimate objects or concepts, or do not see them in people. Rather, their languages have grammatical features that English lacks. True, words like *he, she*, and *it* do reflect the sex of their antecedent (except for a few oddities, like referring to a ship as "she"). But their equivalents in French and German refer not to sex but to *gender*, which is an entirely linguistic, and therefore arbitrary, matter. No French speaker regards a table as having any feminine properties other than grammatical ones.

In more remote languages the differences are still greater. When a Chinese speaker counts items, he or she puts a "measure word" between the number and the item: "one [measure word] book," and so forth. There is nothing quite like this in English, although when we arrange numbers in order we signify that we are ordering rather than counting by inserting expressions like *number, No.,* or #: "We're number 1," "Love Potion No. Nine," and the like. But our practice is invariable, while the Chinese measure word is not; it varies according to the thing being counted. The most common one is *ga*, "one *ga* book." But for flat objects it is *zhang*, "one *zhang* table"; and for other kinds of objects there are many other measure words. Sometimes it is far from obvious what the objects have in common that makes them take a common measure word: the measure word *ba* is used for both chairs and umbrellas!

This all sounds formidably difficult, but only to us—not to the Chinese. The Mandarin variety of Chinese is the native language of over half a billion people in the world today, and they all master their language at the same rate and by the same age as English speakers do. No language, no matter how strange and difficult it may seem to outsiders, is too hard for its native speakers to master. All languages are systematic, which makes their complexities intelligible to their native speakers, but each system is arbitrary in its own way, which makes it something of a closed book to others.

Equally, no language is especially "simple," if by that word we mean lacking complexity in its phonological and grammatical systems. More likely, people who speak of simplicity in language have a restricted vocabulary in mind. But even this judgment needs to be well-informed if it is to be at all valid. Of course, some languages have larger vocabularies than others; English may comprise half a million words, depending on your manner of counting, while a small tribal group out of touch with the complexities of industrial and urban civilization would probably have a markedly smaller vocabulary. But that vocabulary might be more subtle than English in those areas of thought and experience vital to its users. For example, Eskimos have many different words for different kinds of snow. Moreover, the tribal vocabulary could rapidly expand to deal with new needs as they come along, by borrowing or creating new words. Borrowing, indeed, is one of the most important ways that the English vocabulary has grown to such size. (And, of course, no individual speaker of English has all its half-million words at his or her disposal.)

So the equation of language with culture, one we tend to make, has two possibilities of misleading us. First, we are likely to judge another culture as "simple" because we do not understand it or even know much about it; cultural anthropologists would quickly remedy that error for us. Second, we are likely to think that a "primitive" culture has a primitive language. Yet such remote languages, we now know, seem forbiddingly complex to outsiders who try to learn them.

These attitudes are forms of **ethnocentricity**—a point of view in which one culture is at the center of things and all others are more or less "off the target," either because they never got on target (they are too primitive or they have wandered away from it (they are decadent). Language is very fertile ground for ethnocentricity. We are quick to judge even small differences from our own variety of English as "wrong," either laughably or disgustingly. When another people's language is different in more than just small ways, we are inclined to doubt the native intelligence of those who use it, its adequacy for serious purposes, or both.

A more enlightened and indeed more realistic view is the opposite of ethnocentricity. It often goes by the name of "cultural relativism," but learning the name is not the same thing as adopting the view. Only an objective eye on the facts, and a careful eye on our own attitudes, will raise us above ethnocentricity.

To compare linguistics with the study of other forms of human behavior is instructive, but a still grander comparison comes to mind: In many ways the study of language is like the study of life itself. Languages, like species, come into being, grow, change, are sometimes grafted to each other, and occasionally become extinct; they have their histories and, in the written record, their fossils. The origins of both life and language, and their processes, are mysteries that can be penetrated (if at all) by reasoning from incomplete and perhaps ultimately inadequate evidence. And linguists, the scientists of language, study language and its environment with a biologist's care and intensity in order to approach an understanding of the nature of language itself— the most characteristic attribute of all humanity.

In the following pages you can read about the tools and methods of that study, and about the current state of linguistic knowledge. The nature of language and its internal laws, how we learn it, how languages and dialects differ and why, how to reconstruct the linguistic past, how people and animals communicate without words: these are some of the topics discussed in the rest of this book. Its essays offer a compact résumé of the science of linguistics.

FOR DISCUSSION AND REVIEW

1. Why is the fact that human language is *productive* one of its most distinctive properties? In answering this question, consider both your ability to create sentences you have never seen or heard before and also your ability to understand such sentences.

2. Another important property of human language is that it is *arbitrary*. Discuss the several aspects of language characterized by this property.

3. Two other significant "design features" of human language are *duality* and *discreteness*. One way to be sure that you understand these concepts is to try to explain them in your own words to someone else. Write brief explanations of these two concepts, and ask a friend to evaluate their clarity.

4. Review the seven additional "design features" discussed by Bolton. Do they seem to you to be of equal importance? Why or why not?

5. According to Bolton, body language (*kinesics*) lacks the distinctive properties of human language. Discuss this statement in terms of the design features he describes.

6. In what ways does human physiology support the conclusion that speech is not simply an "overlaid function"?

7. Summarize the differences between "quiet" breathing and "speech" breathing. *Without speaking,* use "speech" breathing for at least a minute. Write a brief description of your physical sensations.

8. Explain the functions in the hearing process of (a) the outer ear, (b) the middle ear, and (c) the inner ear.

9. For what reasons does Bolton insist that "all languages are systematic" and that "no language is especially 'simple'"? In what way is an un-

derstanding of these principles important to our understanding of different cultures and their peoples? What is *ethnocentricity*?

10. In the preface to this book, we quote the philosopher Ludwig Wittgenstein: "The limits of my language mean the limits of my world." Discuss the implications of this statement, considering the points Bolton makes and paying particular attention to the concepts of *ethnocentricity* and *cultural relativism*.

11. Bolton asserts that "we seem to understand nonsense, provided it is fitted into proper patterns." Consider the following "nonsense," the opening stanza of "Jabberwocky" by Lewis Carroll (Charles Lutwidge Dodgson [1832–1898]):

> 'Twas brillig, and the slithy toves
>   Did gyre and gimble in the wabe;
> All mimsy were the borogroves,
>   And the mome raths outgrabe.

What do you "know" about the meaning of this stanza? For example, can you identify any nouns? Any verbs? Do you know that something will or did happen? If so, what is that something? Try to describe *how* you "understand" these and other aspects of the stanza.

2/Nine Ideas About Language

HARVEY A. DANIELS

In the following chapter adapted from his book Famous Last Words:
The American Language Crisis Reconsidered, *Harvey A. Daniels, a director of the Illinois Writing Project and a professor at the National College of Education, presents nine fundamental ideas about language that are widely accepted by contemporary linguists. In doing so, he dispels a number of myths about language that are all too prevalent among Americans. The ideas introduced here provide a foundation for readings in later parts of this book, where they are discussed in more detail.*

Assuming we agree that the English language has in fact survived all of the predictions of doom which have been prevalent since at least the early eighteenth century, we also have reason to believe that current reports of the death of our language are similarly exaggerated. The managers of the present crisis of course disagree, and their efforts may even result in the reinstatement of the linguistic loyalty oath of the 1920s or of some updated equivalent ("I promise to use good American unsplit infinitives") in our schools. But it won't make much difference. The English language, if history is any guide at all, will remain useful and vibrant as long as it is spoken, whether we eagerly try to tend and nurture and prune its growth or if we just leave it alone.

Contemporary language critics recognize that language is changing, that people use a lot of jargon, that few people consistently speak the standard dialect, that much writing done in our society is ineffective, and so forth—but they have no other way of viewing these phenomena except with alarm. But most of the uses of and apparent changes in language which worry the critics *can* be explained and understood in unalarming ways. Such explanations have been provided by linguists during the past seventy-five years.

I have said that in order to understand the errors and misrepresentations of the language critics, we need to examine not only history but also "the facts." Of course, facts about language are a somewhat elusive commodity, and we may never be able to answer all of our questions about this wonderfully complex activity. But linguists have made a good start during this century toward describing some of the basic features, structures, and operations of human speech. This section presents a series of nine fundamental ideas about language that form, if not exactly a list of facts, at least a fair summary of the consensus of most linguistic scholars.

1. Children learn their native language swiftly, efficiently, and largely without instruction. Language is a species-specific trait of human beings. All children, unless they are severely retarded or completely deprived of exposure to speech, will acquire their oral language as naturally as they learn to walk. Many linguists even assert that the human brain is prewired for language, and some have also postulated that the underlying linguistic features which are common to all languages are present in the brain at birth. This latter theory comes from the discovery that all languages have certain procedures in common: ways of making statements, questions, and commands; ways of referring to past time; the ability to negate, and so on.[1] In spite of the underlying similarities of all languages, though, it is important to remember that children will acquire the language which they hear around them—whether that is Ukrainian, Swahili, Cantonese, or Appalachian American English.

In spite of the commonsense notions of parents, they do not "teach" their children to talk. Children *learn* to talk, using the language of their parents, siblings, friends, and others as sources and examples—and by using other speakers as testing devices for their own emerging ideas about language. When we acknowledge the complexity of adult speech, with its ability to generate an unlimited number of new, meaningful utterances, it is clear that this skill cannot be the end result of simple instruction. Parents do not explain to their children, for example, that adjectives generally precede the noun in English, nor do they lecture them on the rules governing formation of the past participle. While parents do correct some kinds of mistakes on a piecemeal basis, discovering the underlying rules which make up the language is the child's job.

From what we know, children appear to learn language partly by imitation but even more by hypothesis-testing. Consider a child who is just beginning to form past tenses. In the earliest efforts, the child is likely to produce such incorrect and unheard forms as *I goed to the store* or *I seed a dog*, along with other conventional uses of the past tense: *I walked to Grandma's*. This process reveals that the child has learned the basic, general rule about the formation of the past tense— you add *-ed* to the verb—but has not yet mastered the other rules, the exceptions and irregularities. The production of forms that the child

---

[1] Victoria Fromkin and Robert Rodman, *An Introduction to Language* (New York: Holt, Rinehart and Winston, 1978), pp. 329–342.

has never heard suggests that imitation is not central in language learning and that the child's main strategy is hypothesizing—deducing from the language she hears an idea about the underlying rule, and then trying it out.

My own son, who is now two-and-a-half, has just been working on the -*ed* problem. Until recently, he used present tense verb forms for all situations: *Daddy go work?* (for: *Did Daddy go to work?*) and *We take a bath today?* (for: *Will we take a bath today?*). Once he discovered that wonderful past tag, he attached it with gusto to any verb he could think up and produced, predictably enough, *goed, eated, flied,* and many other overgeneralizations of his initial hypothetical rule for the formation of past tenses. He was so exicted about his new discovery, in fact, that he would often give extra emphasis to the marker: *Dad, I swallow-ed the cookie.* Nicky will soon learn to deemphasize the sound of -*ed* (as well as to master all those irregular past forms) by listening to more language and by revising and expanding his own internal set of language rules.

Linguists and educators sometimes debate about what percentage of adult forms is learned by a given age. A common estimate is that 90 percent of adult structures are acquired by the time a child is seven. Obviously, it is quite difficult to attach proportions to such a complex process, but the central point is clear: schoolchildren of primary age have already learned the great majority of the rules governing their native language, and can produce virtually all the kinds of sentences that it permits. With the passing years, all children will add some additional capabilities, but the main growth from this point forward will not so much be in acquiring new rules as in using new combinations of them to express increasingly sophisticated ideas, and in learning how to use language effectively in a widening variety of social settings.

It is important to reiterate that we are talking here about the child's acquisition of her native language. It may be that the child has been born into a community of standard English or French or Urdu speakers, or into a community of nonstandard English, French, or Urdu speakers. But the language of the child's home and community *is* the native language, and it would be impossible for her to somehow grow up speaking a language to which she was never, or rarely, exposed.

2. Language operates by rules. As the -*ed* saga suggests, when a child begins learning his native language, what he is doing is acquiring a vast system of mostly subconscious rules which allow him to make meaningful and increasingly complex utterances. These rules concern sounds, words, the arrangement of strings of words, and aspects of the social act of speaking. Obviously, children who grow up speaking different languages will acquire generally different sets of rules. This fact reminds us that human language is, in an important sense, arbitrary.

Except for a few onomatopoetic words (*bang, hiss, grunt*), the assignment of meanings to certain combinations of sounds is arbitrary. We English speakers might just as well call a chair a *glotz* or a *blurg*, as long as we all agreed that these combinations of sounds meant *chair*. In fact, not just the words but the individual sounds used in English have been arbitrarily selected from a much larger inventory of sounds which the human vocal organs are capable of producing. The existence of African languages employing musical tones or clicks reminds us that the forty phonemes used in English represent an arbitrary selection from hundreds of available sounds. Grammar, too, is arbitrary. We have a rule in English which requires most adjectives to appear before the noun which they modify (*the blue chair*). In French, the syntax is reversed (*la chaise bleue*), and in some languages, like Latin, either order is allowed.

Given that any language requires a complex set of arbitrary choices regarding sounds, words, and syntax, it is clear that the foundation of a language lies not in any "natural" meaning or appropriateness of its features, but in its system of rules—the implicit agreement among speakers that they will use certain sounds consistently, that certain combinations of sounds will mean the same thing over and over, and that they will observe certain grammatical patterns in order to convey messages. It takes thousands of such rules to make up a language. Many linguists believe that when each of us learned these countless rules, as very young children, we accomplished the most complex cognitive task of our lives.

Our agreement about the rules of language, of course, is only a general one. Every speaker of a language is unique; no one sounds exactly like anyone else. The language differs from region to region, between social, occupational and ethnic groups, and even from one speech situation to the next. These variations are not mistakes or deviations from some basic tongue, but are simply the rule-governed alternatives which make up any language. Still, in America our assorted variations of English are mostly mutually intelligible, reflecting the fact that most of our language rules do overlap, whatever group we belong to, or whatever situation we are in.

3. All languages have three major components: a sound system, a vocabulary, and a system of grammar. This statement underscores what has already been suggested: that any human speaker makes meaning by manipulating sounds, words, and their order according to an internalized system of rules which other speakers of that language largely share.

The sound system of a language—its phonology—is the inventory of vocal noises, and combinations of noises, that it employs. Children learn the selected sounds of their own language in the same way they learn the other elements: by listening, hypothesizing, testing, and listening again. They do not, though it may seem logical, learn the sounds first (after all, English has only forty) and then go on to words and then to grammar. My son, for example, can say nearly anything he needs to say, in sentences of eight or ten or fourteen words, but he couldn't utter the sound of *th* to save his life.

The vocabulary, or lexicon, of a language is the individual's storehouse of words. Obviously, one of the young child's most conspicuous efforts is aimed at expanding his lexical inventory. Two- and three-year-olds are notorious for asking "What's that?" a good deal more often than even the most doting parents can tolerate. And not only do children constantly and spontaneously try to enlarge their vocabularies, but they are always working to build categories, to establish classes of words, to add connotative meanings, to hone and refine their sense of the semantic properties—the meanings—of the words they are learning. My awareness of these latter processes was heightened a few months ago as we were driving home from a trip in the country during which Nicky had delighted in learning the names of various features of the rural landscape. As we drove past the Chicago skyline, Nicky looked up at the tall buildings and announced "Look at those silos, Dad!" I asked him what he thought they kept in the Sears Tower, and he replied confidently, "Animal food." His parents' laughter presumably helped him to begin reevaluating his lexical hypothesis that any tall narrow structure was a silo.

Linguists, who look at language descriptively rather than prescriptively, use two different definitions of *grammar*. The first, which I am using, says that grammar is the system of rules we use to arrange words into meaningful English sentences. For example, my lexicon and my phonology may provide me with the appropriate strings of sounds to say the words: *eat four yesterday cat crocodile the*. It is my knowledge of grammar which allows me to arrange these elements into a sentence: *Yesterday the crocodile ate four cats*. Not only does my grammar arrange these elements in a meaningful order, it also provides me with the necessary markers of plurality, tense, and agreement. Explaining the series of rules by which I subconsciously constructed this sentence describes some of my "grammar" in this sense.

The second definition of *grammar* often used by linguists refers to the whole system of rules which makes up a language—not just the rules for the arrangement and appropriate marking of elements in a sentence, but all of the lexical, phonological, and syntactic patterns which a language uses. In this sense, *everything* I know about my language, all the conscious and unconscious operations I can perform when speaking or listening, constitutes my grammar. It is this second definition of grammar to which linguists sometimes refer when they speak of describing a language in terms of its grammar.

4. Everyone speaks a dialect. Among linguists the term *dialect* simply designates a variety of a particular language which has a certain set of lexical, phonological, and grammatical rules that distinguish it from other dialects. The most familiar definition of dialects in America is geographical: we recognize, for example, that some features of New England language—the dropping *r*'s (*pahk the cah in Hahvahd yahd*) and the use of *bubbler* for *drinking fountain*—distinguish the speech of this region. The native speaker of Bostonian English is not making mistakes, of course; he or she simply observes systematic rules which happen to differ from those observed in other regions.

Where do these different varieties of a language come from and how are they maintained? The underlying factors are isolation and language change. Imagine a group of people which lives, works, and talks together constantly. Among them, there is a good deal of natural pressure to keep the language relatively uniform. But if one part of the group moves away to a remote location, and has no further contact with the other, the language of the two groups will gradually diverge. This will happen not just because of the differing needs of the two different environments, but also because of the inexorable and sometimes arbitrary process of language change itself. In other words, there is no likelihood that the language of these two groups, though identical at the beginning, will now change in the same ways. Ultimately, if the isolation is lengthy and complete, the two hypothetical groups will probably develop separate, mutually unintelligible languages. If the isolation is only partial, if interchange occurs between the two groups, and if they have some need to continue communicating (as with the American and British peoples) less divergence will occur.

This same principle of isolation also applies, in a less dramatic way, to contemporary American dialects. New England speakers are partially isolated from southern speakers, and so some of the differences between these two dialects are maintained. Other factors, such as travel and the mass media, bring them into contact with each other and tend to prevent drastic divergences. But the isolation that produces or maintains language differences may not be only geographical. In many American cities we find people living within miles, or even blocks of each other who speak markedly different and quite enduring dialects. Black English and midwestern English are examples of such pairs. Here, the isolation is partially spatial, but more importantly it is social, economic, occupational, educational, and political. And as long as this effective separation of speech communities persists, so will the differences in their dialects.

Many of the world's languages have a "standard" dialect. In some countries, the term *standard* refers more to a *lingua franca* than to an indigenous dialect. In Nigeria, for example, where there are more than 150 mostly mutually unintelligible languages and dialects, English was selected as the official standard. In America, we enjoy this kind of national standardization because the vast majority of us speak some mutually intelligible dialect of English. But we also have ideas about a standard English which is not just a *lingua franca* but a prestige or preferred dialect. Similarly, the British have Received Pronunciation, the Germans have High German, and the French, backed by the authority of the Académie Française, have "Le Vrai Français." These languages are typically defined as the speech of the upper, or at least educated, classes of the society, are the predominant dialect of written communication, and are commonly taught to schoolchildren. In the past, these prestige dialects have sometimes been markers which conveniently set the ruling classes apart from the rabble—as once was the case with Mandarin Chinese or in medieval times when the English aristocracy adopted Norman French. But in most modern societies the standard dialect is a mutually intelligible version of the country's common tongue which is accorded a special status.

A standard dialect is not *inherently* superior to any other dialect of the same language. It may, however, confer considerable social, political, and economic power on its users, because of prevailing attitudes about the dialect's worthiness.

Recently, American linguists have been working to describe some of the nonstandard dialects of English, and we now seem to have a better description of some of these dialects than of our shadowy standard. Black English is a case in point. The most important finding of all this research has been that Black English is just as "logical" and "ordered" as any other English dialect, in spite of the fact that it is commonly viewed by white speakers as being somehow inferior, deformed, or limited.

5. Speakers of all languages employ a range of styles and a set of subdialects or jargons. Just as soon as we accept the notion that we all speak a dialect, it is necessary to complicate things further. We may realize that we do belong to a speech community, although we may not like to call it a dialect, but we often forget that our speech patterns vary greatly during the course of our everyday routine. In the morning, at home, communication with our spouses may consist of grumbled fragments of a private code:

Uhhh.
Yeah.
More?

Um-hmm.
You gonna . . .?
Yeah, if . . .
'Kay.

Yet half an hour later, we may be standing in a meeting and talking quite differently: "The cost-effectiveness curve of the Peoria facility has declined to the point at which management is compelled to consider terminating production." These two samples of speech suggest that we constantly range between formal and informal styles of speech— and this is an adjustment which speakers of all languages constantly make. Learning the sociolinguistic rules which tell us what sort of speech is appropriate in differing social situations is as much a part of language acquisition as learning how to produce the sound of /b/ or /t/. We talk differently to our acquaintances than to strangers, differently to our bosses than to our subordinates, differently to children than to adults. We speak in one way on the racquetball court and in another way in the courtroom; we perhaps talk differently to stewardesses than to stewards.

The ability to adjust our language forms to the social context is something which we acquire as children, along with sounds, words, and syntax. We learn, in other words, not just to say things, but also how and when and to whom. Children discover, for example, that while the purpose of most language is to communicate meaning (if it weren't they could never learn it in the first place) we sometimes use words as mere acknowledgments. (Hi. How are you doing? Fine. Bye.) Youngsters also learn that to get what you want, you have to address people as your social relation with them dictates (Miss Jones, may I please feed the hamster today?). And, of course, children learn that in some situations one doesn't use certain words at all—though such learning may sometimes seem cruelly delayed to parents whose off-spring loudly announce in restaurants: 'I hafta go toilet!''

Interestingly, these sociolinguistic rules are learned quite late in the game. While a child of seven or eight does command a remarkably sophisticated array of sentence types, for example, he has a great deal left to learn about the social regulations governing language use. This seems logical, given that children *do* learn language mostly by listening and experimenting. Only as a child grows old enough to encounter a widening range of social relationships and roles will he have the ex-perience necessary to help him discover the sociolinguistic dimensions of them.

While there are many ways of describing the different styles, or registers, of language which all speakers learn, it is helpful to consider them in terms of levels of formality. One well-known example of such a scheme was developed by Martin Joos, who posited five basic styles, which he called *intimate, casual, consultative, formal,* and *frozen.*[2] While Joos's model is only one of many attempts to find a scale for the range of human speech styles, and is certainly not the final word on the subject, it does illuminate some of the ways in which day-to-day language varies. At the bottom of Joos's model is the *intimate* style, a kind of language which "fuses two separate personalities" and can only occur between individuals with a close personal relationship. A husband and wife, for example, may sometimes speak to each other in what sounds like a very fragmentary and clipped code that they alone understand. Such utterances are characterized by their "extraction"— the use of extracts of potentially complete sentences, made possible by an intricate, personal, shared system of private symbols. The *intimate* style, in sum, is personal, fragmentary, and implicit.

The *casual* style also depends on social groupings. When people share understandings and meanings which are not complete enough to be called intimate, they tend to employ the *casual* style. The earmarks of this pattern are ellipsis and slang. Ellipsis is the shorthand of shared meaning; slang often expresses these meanings in a way that defines the group and excludes others. The *casual* style is reserved for friends and insiders, or those whom we choose to make friends and insiders. The *consultative* style "produces cooperation without the integration, profiting from the lack of it."[3] In this style, the speaker provides more explicit background information because the listener may not understand without it. This is the style used by strangers or near-strangers in routine transactions: co-workers dealing with a problem, a buyer making a purchase from a clerk, and so forth. An important feature of this style is the participation of the listener, who uses frequent interjections such as *Yeah, Uh-huh* or *I see* to signal understanding.

This element of listener participation disappears in the *formal* style. Speech in this mode is defined by the listener's lack of participation, as well as by the speaker's opportunity to plan his utterances ahead of time and in detail. The *formal* style is most often found in speeches, lectures, sermons, television newscasts, and the like. The *frozen* style is reserved for print, and particularly for literature. This style can be densely packed and repacked with meanings by its "speaker," and it can be read and reread by its "listener." The immediacy of interaction between the participants is sacrificed in the interests of permanance, elegance, and precision.

Whether or not we accept Joos's scheme to classify the different gradations of formality, we can probably sense the truth of the basic proposition: we do make such adjustments in our speech constantly, mostly unconsciously, and in response to the social situation in which

[2] Martin Joos, *The Five Clocks* (New York: Harcourt, Brace and World, 1962).
[3] Ibid., p. 40.

we are speaking. What we sometimes forget is that no one style can accurately be called better or worse than another, apart from the context in which it is used. Though we have much reverence for the formal and frozen styles, they can be utterly dysfunctional in certain circumstances. If I said to my wife: "Let us consider the possibility of driving our automobile into the central business district of Chicago in order to comtemplate the possible purchase of denim trousers," she would certainly find my way of speaking strange, if not positively disturbing. All of us need to shift between the intimate, casual, and consultative styles in everyday life, not because one or another of these is a better way of talking, but because each is required in certain contexts. Many of us also need to master the formal style for the talking and writing demanded by our jobs. But as Joos has pointed out, few of us actually need to control the frozen style, which is reserved primarily for literature.[4]

Besides having a range of speech styles, each speaker also uses a number of jargons based upon his or her affiliation with certain groups. The most familiar of these jargons are occupational: doctors, lawyers, accountants, farmers, electricians, plumbers, truckers, and social workers each have a job-related jargon into which they can shift when the situation demands it. Sometimes these special languages are a source of amusement or consternation to outsiders, but usually the outsiders also speak jargons of their own, though they may not recognize them. Jargons may also be based on other kinds of affiliations. Teenagers, it is often remarked by bemused parents, have a language of their own. So they do, and so do other age groups. Some of the games and chants of youngsters reflect a kind of childhood dialect, and much older persons may have a jargon of their own as well, reflecting concerns with aging, illness, and finances. Sports fans obviously use and understand various abstruse athletic terms, while people interested in needlecrafts use words that are equally impenetrable to the uninitiated. For every human enterprise we can think of, there will probably be a jargon attached to it.

But simply noting that all speakers control a range of styles and a set of jargons does not tell the whole story. For every time we speak, we do so not just in a social context, but for certain purposes of our own. When talking with a dialectologist, for example, I may use linguistic jargon simply to facilitate our sharing of information, or instead to convince him that I know enough technical linguistics to be taken seriously—or both. In other words, my purposes—the functions of my language—affect the way I talk. The British linguist M. A. K. Halliday has studied children in an attempt to determine how people's varying

4 Ibid., pp. 39–67.

purposes affect their speech.[5] Halliday *had* to consider children, in fact, because the purposes of any given adult utterance are usually so complex and overlapping that it is extremely difficult to isolate the individual purposes. By examining the relatively simpler language of children, he was able to discover seven main uses, functions, or purposes for talking: *instrumental, regulatory, interactional, personal, heuristic, imaginative,* and *representational.*

The *instrumental* function, Halliday explains, is for getting things done; it is the *I want* function. Close to it is the *regulatory* function, which seeks to control the actions of others around the speaker. The *interactional* function is used to define groups and relationships, to get along with others. The *personal* function allows people to express what they are and how they feel; Halliday calls this the *here I come* function. The *heuristic* function is in operation when the speaker is using language to learn, by asking questions and testing hypotheses. In the *imaginative* function, a speaker may use language to create a world just as he or she wants it, or may simply use it as a toy, making amusing combinations of sounds and words. In the *representational* function, the speaker uses language to express propositions, give information, or communicate subject matter.

Absent from Halliday's list of functions, interestingly, is one of the most common and enduring purposes of human language: lying. Perhaps lying could be included in the representational or interactional functions, in the sense that a person may deceive in order to be a more congenial companion. Or perhaps each of Halliday's seven functions could be assigned a reverse, false version. In any case, common sense, human history, and our own experience all tell us that lying—or misleading or covering up or shading the truth—is one of the main ends to which language is put.

As we look back over these three forms of language variation—styles, jargons, and functions—we may well marvel at the astounding complexity of language. For not only do all speakers master the intricate sound, lexical, and grammatical patterns of their native tongue, but they also learn countless, systematic alternative ways of applying their linguistic knowledge to varying situations and needs. We are reminded, in short, that language is as beautifully varied and fascinating as the creatures who use it.

6. Language change is normal. This fact, while often acknowledged by critics of contemporary English, has rarely been fully understood or accepted by them. It is easy enough to welcome into the language such innocent neologisms as *astronaut, transistor,* or *jet lag.*

[5] M. A. K. Halliday, *Explorations in the Functions of Language* (London: Edward Arnold, 1973).

These terms serve obvious needs, responding to certain changes in society which virtually require them. But language also changes in many ways that don't seem so logical or necessary. The dreaded dangling *hopefully*, which now attaches itself to the beginning of sentences with the meaning *I hope*, appears to be driving out the connotation *full of hope*. As Jean Stafford has angrily pointed out, the word *relevant* has broadened to denote almost any kind of "with-it-ness." But these kinds of lexical changes are not new, and simply demonstrate an age-old process at work in the present. The word *dog* (actually, *dogge*), for example, used to refer to one specific breed, but now serves as a general term for a quite varied family of animals. Perhaps similarly, *dialogue* has now broadened to include exchanges of views between (or among) any number of speakers. But word meanings can also narrow over time, as the word *deer* shrank from indicating any game animal to just one specific type.

The sounds of language also change, though usually in slower and less noticeable ways than vocabulary. Perhaps fifty years ago, the majority of American speakers produced distinctly different consonant sounds in the middle of *latter* and *ladder*. Today, most younger people and many adults pronounce the two words is if they were the same. Another sound change in progress is the weakening distinction between the vowel sounds in *dawn* and *Don*, or *hawk* and *hock*. Taking the longer view, of course, we realize that modern pronunciation is the product of centuries of gradual sound changes.

Shifts in grammar are more comparable to the slow process of sound change than the sometimes sudden one of lexical change. Today we find that the *shall/will* distinction, which is still maintained among some upper class Britishers, has effectively disappeared from spoken American English. A similar fate seems to await the *who/whom* contrast, which is upheld by fewer and fewer speakers. Our pronouns, as a matter of fact, seem to be a quite volatile corner of our grammar. In spite of the efforts of teachers, textbooks, style manuals, and the SAT tests, most American speakers now find nothing wrong with *Everyone should bring their books to class* or even *John and me went to the Cubs game*. And even the hoary old double negative (which is an obligatory feature of degraded tongues like French) seems to be making steady, if slow progress. We may be only a generation or two from the day when we will again say, with Shakespeare, "I will not budge for no man's pleasure."

While we may recognize that language does inexorably change, we cannot always explain the causes or the sequences of each individual change. Sometimes changes move toward simplification, as with the shedding of vowel distinctions. Other changes tend to regularize the language, as when we de-Latinize words like *medium/media* (The newspapers are one media of communication), or when we abandon *dreamt* and *burnt* in favor of the regular forms *dreamed* and *burned*. And some coinages will always reflect the need to represent new inventions, ideas, or events: *quark, simulcast, pulsar, stagflation*. Yet there is plenty of language change which seems to happen spontaneously, sporadically, and without apparent purpose. Why should *irregardless* substitute for *regardless*, meaning the same thing? Why should handy distinctions like that between *imply* and *infer* be lost? But even if we can never explain the reasons for such mysterious changes—or perhaps *because* we can't—we must accept the fact that language does change. Today, we would certainly be thought odd to call cattle *kine*, to pronounce *saw* as *saux*, or to ask about "thy health," however ordinary such language might have been centuries ago. Of course, the more recent changes, and especially the changes in progress, make us most uncomfortable.

But then our sense of the pace of language change is often exaggerated. When we cringe (as do so many of the language critics) at the sudden reassignment of the word *gay* to a new referent, we tend to forget that we can still read Shakespeare. In other words, even if many conspicuous (and almost invariably lexical) changes are in progress, this doesn't necessarily mean that the language as a whole is undergoing a rapid or wholesale transformation.

However, once we start looking for language change, it seems to be everywhere, and we are sorely tempted to overestimate its importance. Sometimes we even discover changes which aren't changes at all. Various language critics have propounded the notion that we are being inundated by a host of very new and particularly insidious coinages. Here are some of the most notorious ones, along with the date of their earliest citation in the *Oxford English Dictionary* for the meaning presently viewed as modern and dangerous: *you know* (1350); *anxious* for *eager* (1742); *between you and I* (1640); *super* for *good* (1850); *decimate* for *diminish* by other than one-tenth (1663); *inoperative* for nonmechanical phenomena (1631); *near-perfect* for *nearly perfect* (1635); *host* as in *to host a gathering* (1485); *gifted*, as in *He gifted his associates* (1660); *aggravate* for *annoy* (1611).[6]

If we find ourselves being aggravated (or annoyed) by any of these crotchety old neologisms, we can always look to the Mobil Oil Corporation for a comforting discussion of the problem. In one of its self-serving public service magazine ads, Mobil intoned: "Change upsets people. Always has. Disrupts routine and habit patterns. Demands constant adaptation. But change is inevitable. And essential. Inability to change can be fatal."[7] And Mobil inadvertently gives us one last

---

[6] With many thanks to Jim Quinn and his *American Tongue and Cheek* (New York: Pantheon, 1981).

[7] "Business Is Bound to Change," Mobil Oil advertisement, *Chicago Tribune*, January 5, 1977.

example of a language change currently in progress: the increasing use of sentence fragments in formal written English.

7. Languages are intimately related to the societies and individuals who use them. Every human language has been shaped by, and changes to meet, the needs of its speakers. In this limited sense, all human languages can be said to be both equal and perfect. Some Eskimo languages, for example, have many words for different types of snow: wet snow, powdery snow, blowing snow, and so forth. This extensive vocabulary obviously results from the importance of snow in the Eskimo environment and the need to be able to talk about it in detailed ways. In Chicago, where snow is just an occasional annoyance, we get along quite nicely with a few basic terms—snow, slush, and sleet—and a number of adjectival modifiers. Richard Mitchell has described a hypothetical primitive society where the main preoccupation is banging on tree-bark to harvest edible insects, and this particular people has developed a large, specialized vocabulary for talking about the different kinds of rocks and trees involved in this process. In each of these cases, the language in question is well adapted to the needs of its speakers. Each language allows its speakers to easily talk about whatever it is important to discuss in that society.

This does not mean, however, that any given language will work "perfectly" or be "equal" to any other in a cross-cultural setting. If I take my Chicago dialect to the tundra, I may have trouble conversing with people who distinguish, in Eskimo, ten more kinds of snow than I do. Or if one of Mitchell's tree-bangers came to Chicago, his elaborate rock-and-bark vocabulary would be of little use. Still, neither of these languages is inherently inferior or superior; inside its normal sphere of use, each is just what it needs to be.

There is a related question concerning the differences between languages. Many linguists have tried to determine the extent to which our native language conditions our thought processes. For all the talk of similarities between languages, there are also some quite remarkable differences from one language to another. The famous studies of American Indian languages by Benjamin Lee Whorf and Edward Sapir have suggested, for example, that Hopi speakers do not conceptualize time in the same way as speakers of English.[8] To the Hopi, time is a continuing process, an unfolding that cannot be segmented into chunks to be used or "wasted." The words and constructions of the Hopi language reflect this perception. Similarly, some languages do not describe the same color spectrum which we speakers of English normally regard as a given physical phenomenon. Some of these name only two,

[8] See Edward Sapir, *Culture, Language, and Personality* (Berkeley: University of California Press, 1949).

others three, and so on. Are we, then, hopelessly caught in the grasp of the language which we happen to grow up speaking? Are all our ideas about the world controlled by our language, so that our reality is what we *say* rather than what objectively, verifiably exists?

The best judgment of linguists on this subject comes down to this: we are conditioned to some degree by the language we speak, and our language does teach us habitual ways of looking at the world. But on the other hand, human adaptability enables us to transcend the limitations of a language—to learn to see the world in new ways and voice new concepts—when we must. While it is probably true that some ideas are easier to communicate in one language than another, both languages and speakers can change to meet new needs. The grip which language has on us is firm, but it does not strangle; we make language more than language makes us.

It is also important to realize that a language is not just an asset of a culture or group, but of individual human beings. Our native language is the speech of our parents, siblings, friends, and community. It is the code we use to communicate in the most powerful and intimate experiences of our lives. It is a central part of our personality, an expression and a mirror of what we are and wish to be. Our language is as personal and as integral to each of us as our bodies and our brains, and in our own unique ways, we all treasure it. And all of us, when we are honest, have to admit that criticism of the way we talk is hard not to take personally. This reaction is nothing to be ashamed of: it is simply a reflection of the natural and profound importance of language to every individual human being.

To summarize: all human languages and the concept systems which they embody are efficient in their native speech communities. The languages of the world also vary in some important ways, so that people sometimes falsely assume that certain tongues are inherently superior to others. Yet it is marvelous that these differences exist. It is good that the Eskimo language facilitates talk about snow, that the Hopi language supports that culture's view of time, and, I suppose, that Chicago speech has ample resources for discussing drizzle, wind, and inept baseball teams.

8. Value judgments about different languages or dialects are matters of taste. One of the things we seem to acquire right along with our native tongue is a set of attitudes about the value of other people's language. If we think for a moment about any of the world's major languages, we will find that we usually have some idea—usually a prejudice or stereotype—about it. French is the sweet music of love. German is harsh, martial, overbearing. The language of Spain is exotic, romantic. The Spanish of Latin Americans is alien, uneducated. Scandinavian tongues have a kind of silly rhythm, as the Muppet Show's

Swedish chef demonstrates weekly. British English is refined and intelligent. New York dialect (especially on Toity-Toid Street) is crude and loud. Almost all southern American speakers (especially rural sheriffs) are either cruelly crafty or just plain dumb. Oriental languages have a funny, high-pitched, singsong sound. And Black English, well, it just goes to show. None of these notions about different languages and dialects says anything about the way these tongues function in their native speech communities. By definition—by the biological and social order of things—they function efficiently. Each is a fully formed, logical, rule-governed variant of human speech.

It is easy enough to assert that all languages are equal and efficient in their own sphere of use. But most of us do not really believe in this idea, and certainly do not act as if we did. We constantly make judgments about other people and other nations on the basis of the language they use. Expecially when we consider the question of mutually intelligible American dialects, we are able to see that most ideas about language differences are purely matters of taste. It isn't that we cannot understand each other—Southerners, Northerners, Californians, New Yorkers, blacks, whites, Appalachian folk—with only the slightest effort we can communicate just fine. But because of our history of experiences with each other, or perhaps just out of perversity, we have developed prejudices toward other people's language which sometimes affect our behavior. Such prejudices, however irrational, generate much pressure for speakers of disfavored dialects to abandon their native speech for some approved pattern. But as the linguist Einar Haugen has warned:

> And yet, who are we to call for linguistic genocide in the name of efficiency? Let us recall that although a language is a tool and an instrument of communication, that is not all it is. A language is also a part of one's personality, a form of behavior that has its roots in our earliest experience. Whether it is a so-called rural or ghetto dialect, or a peasant language, or a "primitive" idiom, it fulfills exactly the same needs and performs the same services in the daily lives of its speakers as does the most advanced language of culture. Every language, dialect, patois, or lingo is a structurally complete framework into which can be poured any subtlety of emotion or thought that its users are capable of experiencing. Whatever it lacks at any given time or place in the way of vocabulary and syntax can be supplied in very short order by borrowing and imitation from other languages. *Any scorn for the language of others is scorn for those who use it, and as such is a form of social discrimination.* [Emphasis mine.][9]

It is not Haugen's purpose—nor is it mine—to deny that social acceptability and economic success in America may be linked in certain ways to the mastery of approved patterns of speech. Yet all of us must

[9] Einar Haugen, "The Curse of Babel," in Einar Haugen and Morton Bloomfield, *Language as a Human Problem* (New York: W. W. Norton, 1974), p. 41.

realize that the need for such mastery arises *only* out of the prejudices of the dominant speech community and not from any intrinsic shortcomings of nonstandard American dialects.

9. Writing is derivative of speech. Writing systems are always based upon systems of oral language which of necessity develop first. People have been talking for at least a half million years, but the earliest known writing system appeared fewer than 5,000 years ago. Of all the world's languages, only about 5 percent have developed indigenous writing systems. In other words, wherever there are human beings, we will always find language, but not necessarily writing. If language is indeed a biologically programmed trait of the species, writing does not seem to be part of the standard equipment.

Although the English writing system is essentially phonemic—an attempt to represent the sounds of language in graphic form—it is notoriously irregular and confusing. Some other languages, like Czech, Finnish, and Spanish, come close to having perfect sound-symbol correspondence: each letter in the writing system stands for one, and only one, sound. English, unfortunately, uses some 2,000 letters and combinations of letters to represent its forty or so separate sounds. This causes problems. For example, in the sentence: *Did he believe that Caesar could see the people seize the seas?* there are seven different spellings for the vowel sound /i/. The sentence: *The silly amoeba stole the key to the machine* yields four more spellings of the same vowel sound. George Bernard Shaw once noted that a reasonable spelling of the word *fish* might be *ghoti*: *gh* as in *enough, o* as in *women,* and *ti* as in *nation.* In spite of all its irregularities, however, the English spelling system is nevertheless phonemic at heart, as our ability to easily read and pronounce nonsense words like *mimsy* or *proat* demonstrates.

Writing, like speech, may be put to a whole range of often overlapping uses. And shifts in the level of formality occur in writing just as they do in talk. An author, like a speaker, must adjust the style of her message to the audience and the occasion. A woman composing a scholarly article, for example, makes some systematically different linguistic choices than those she makes when leaving a note for her husband on the refrigerator. Both writers and speakers (even good ones) employ various jargons or specialized vocabularies that seem comfortable and convenient to the people they are addressing. Rules change with time in both writing and speech. Most obviously, changes in speech habits are reflected in writing: today we readily pen words which weren't even invented ten or a hundred years ago. And even some of the rules which are enforced in writing after they have been abandoned in speech do eventually break down. Today, for example, split infinitives and sentence fragments are increasingly accepted in writing. Our personal tastes and social prejudices, which often guide our reactions to other people's speech, can also dictate our response to other people's writing.

Our beliefs about writing are also bound up with our literary tradition. We have come to revere certain works of literature and exposition which have "stood the test of time," which speak across the centuries to successive generations of readers. These masterpieces, like most enduring published writing, tend to employ what Joos would call formal and frozen styles of language. They were written in such language, of course, because their authors had to accommodate the subject, audience, and purpose at hand—and the making of sonnets and declarations of independence generally calls for considerable linguistic formality. Given our affection for these classics, we quite naturally admire not only their content but their form. We find ourselves feeling that only in the nineteenth or sixteenth century could writers "really use the language" correctly and beautifully. Frequently, we teach this notion in our schools, encouraging students to see the language of written literature as the only true and correct style of English. We require students not only to mimic the formal literary style in their writing, but even to transplant certain of its features into their speech— in both cases without reference to the *students'* subject, audience, or purpose. All of this is not meant to demean literature or the cultivation of its appreciation among teenagers. It simply reminds us of how the mere existence of a system of writing and a literature can be a conservative influence on the language. The study, occasionally the official worship, of language forms that are both old and formal may retard linguistic changes currently in progress, as well as reinforce our mistaken belief that one style of language is always and truly the best.

The preceding nine ideas about language are not entirely new. Many of them have been proclaimed by loud, if lonely, voices in centuries long past. It has only been in the last seventy or eighty years, however, that these ideas have begun to form a coherent picture of how language works, thanks to the work of the descriptive and historical linguists. It is their research which has been, I hope, accurately if broadly summarized here.

A look at the history of past crises offered a general kind of reassurance about the present language panic. It suggested that such spasms of insecurity and intolerance are a regular, cyclical feature of the human chronicle, and result more from social and political tensions than from actual changes in the language. The review of research presented in this section broadens that perspective and deflates the urgency of the 1983-model literary crisis in some other ways. It shows us that our language cannot "die" as long as people speak it; that language change is a healthy and inevitable process; that all human languages are rule governed, ordered, and logical; that variations between different groups of speakers are normal and predictable; that all speakers employ a variety of speech forms and styles in response to changing social settings; and that most of our attitudes about language are based upon social rather than linguistic judgments.

And so, if we are to believe the evidence of historical and linguistic research, our current language crisis seems rather curious. This is a crisis which is not critical, which does not actually pose the dangers widely attributed to it. If anything, the crisis is merely a description of linguistic business as usual, drawn by the critics in rather bizarre and hysterical strokes. It seems fair to ask at this point: What's the problem?*

FOR DISCUSSION AND REVIEW

1. In presenting his "nine ideas about language," Daniels attempts to dispel some commonly held but inaccurate beliefs about language. List as many of these myths as you can. How successful is Daniels in dispelling them?

2. As Daniels notes, children learn relatively late the "rules" about the kinds of speech that are appropriate in various circumstances. From your own experience, give some examples of children's use of language that, given the social context, was inappropriate.

3. You probably would describe a particular event—for example, a party, a camping trip, an evening with a friend—differently to different people. Jot down the way you would tell a good friend about some event. Then write down the way you would describe the same occurrence to your parents. When you compare the two accounts, what differences do you find? Are they the differences that Daniels leads you to expect?

4. Daniels believes that most people have "some idea—usually a prejudice or stereotype"—about different languages and dialects. Define the terms *prejudice* and *stereotype*. Then test Daniels's theory by asking five people what they think of (a) the languages and dialects, or (b) the speakers of the languages and dialects, that Daniels mentions on pp. 32–33. Study the responses and describe any prejudices or stereotypes that you find.

---

* Editors' note: Each of the nine ideas presented by Daniels is treated more extensively elsewhere in this book. For idea 1, see Part 2. For idea 2, see Parts 4, 5, and 6. For idea 3, see Parts 2, 4, 5, and 6. For idea 4, see Part 7. For idea 5, see Part 7. For idea 6, see Part 8. For idea 7, see Part 7. For idea 8, see Part 7. For idea 9, see Part 9.

Projects for "Language and Its Study"

1. In "Language: An Introduction," W. F. Bolton points out that "perhaps the most distinctive property of language is that its users can create sentences never before known, and yet perfectly understandable to their hearers and readers." He calls this property *productivity*. To illustrate Bolton's point, show a photograph or a cartoon to the members of your class, and ask each of them to describe in one sentence what they see. Write down the sentences, and have the class compare them. What conclusions can be drawn?

2. Discussing the origin of human language, Bolton writes: "How this happened is at least as unknowable as how the universe began." However, a number of theories (e.g., the ding-dong and bow-wow theories) about the origin of language that used to be taken seriously have now been discredited. Read about four of these early theories in your library, and prepare an oral or written report describing the theories and evaluating their adequacy. Good starting places for this research are such standard textbooks as *The Origins and Development of the English Language* (Thomas Pyles and John Algeo) and *A History of the English Language* (Albert C. Baugh and Thomas Cable).

3. In describing the vocal organs that produce speech, Bolton notes that all of them except the larynx have other functions. Although disease sometimes necessitates the removal of an individual's larynx, speech is not always impossible for such a person. Both the artificial larynx and a technique involving swallowing air and talking while the air is "exhaled" have made speech possible for many people who have had this surgery. Prepare a report on one of these techniques. A great deal of published material will be available in your library; you may also find it useful to interview a speech pathologist or a specialist in this kind of rehabilitative medicine.

4. As Bolton notes, the human esophagus is "much too close to the pharynx for safety (hence the need for the Heimlich maneuver)." Prepare a description and a demonstration of the Heimlich maneuver. Be prepared to describe the extent of its usefulness (ask at least five people if they have had any firsthand experience with it) and to make a recommendation about whether it should be taught and, if so, to whom.

5. In some cases of deafness, as Bolton indicates, "bone-conduction can sometimes substitute for air-conduction." Prepare a brief report describing how hearing aids work; you may want to pay particular attention to bone-conduction.

6. Harvey A. Daniels presents "nine fundamental ideas about language." List the nine one-sentence ideas, and show them to five people who are not in your class. Summarize their reactions. Are some of the ideas more controversial or less accepted than others?

7. On pp. 31–32, Daniels describes the Sapir-Whorf hypothesis that the structure and vocabulary of people's languages influence their cultural and social beliefs, as well as their view of the world. Prepare a written or oral report explaining and analyzing the Sapir-Whorf hypothesis. Be sure to include examples of the ways in which language allegedly conditions perceptions.

8. An interesting group project is to debate the validity of the Sapir-Whorf hypothesis. An excellent summary of the arguments pro and con can be found in Danny D. Steinberg's *Psycholinguistics: Language, Mind and World* (London and New York: Longman, 1982), pp. 101–120.

9. In his book *The Word-A-Day Vocabulary Builder*, lexicographer Bergen Evans states:

> Words are the tools for the job of saying what you want to say. And what you want to say are your thoughts and feelings, your desires and your dislikes, your hopes and your fears, your business and your pleasure— almost everything, indeed, that makes up you. Except for our vegetable-like growth and our animal-like impulses, almost all that we are is related to our use of words. Man has been defined as a tool-using animal, but his most important tool, the one that distinguishes him from all other animals, is his speech.

Do you agree with Evans's statement? Is it possible to think without language? Are there some creative activities for which people do not need speech? Write a brief essay in which you defend your position.

10. In his book *Humankind*, Peter Farb writes:

> Social scientists have long known that the way people perceive the world is influenced by the culture in which they are brought up. It has been noted, for example, that cultures give varying emphasis to round objects as distinct from rectangular ones. In Western cultures, rectangular objects tend to predominate, as witness the shapes of houses, furniture, television and movie screens, books, doorways, and numerous things constructed with carpenter's tools. Circular objects are much more common in many other cultures; thus the Zulus of South Africa live in circular houses inside circular compounds, keep their cattle in circular pens, and use circles in the imagery of their religious ceremonies. The way these traditional shapes affect perception has been formulated into what is known as the carpentered-world hypothesis, and has been tested by means of the optical illusion known as the Sander Parallelogram, shown [top of next page].

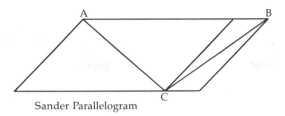

Sander Parallelogram

A person brought up in a Western culture who looks at this parallelogram tends to suppose that the diagonal line *AC* is longer than the diagonal *CB*. Measurement with a ruler, though, proves that *AC* is actually about fifteen percent shorter than *CB*. A moment's thought explains why a Westerner is likely to make this error. The carpentered world in which we live exposes us to rectangular surfaces, but these are rarely seen as right angles because objects are usually viewed from one side or another. We almost never see the rectangular top of a coffee table from directly overhead. Rather, we usually view it from one side and at an acute angle, which distorts it into the form of a parallelogram. Our everyday experience thus tells us that diagonal *AC* on a coffee table or any other three-dimensional rectangular object would be longer than diagonal *CB*, and so in a two-dimensional parallelogram we also automatically perceive *AC* as though it were longer. But people in rural Africa, who live in a circular world, are not hampered by any such preconception concerning rectangular forms. To them, that *CB* is longer is thus obvious. On the other hand, people in rural Africa are much more likely to be susceptible to various optical illusions involving circles. (pp. 304–305)

Using "Language Shapes Reality" as the thesis and title of a short paper, describe incidents from your own experience that clearly exemplify the shaping power of language. For example, consider some of the recent purchases you have made. Have any of them been influenced by brand names, advertisements, or language used by salespersons? Did you ever find yourself taking or avoiding a course primarily because of its name?

11. As Daniels notes, "Although the English writing system is essentially phonemic—an attempt to represent the sounds of language in graphic form—it is notoriously irregular and confusing." (Consider, for example, the various ways the vowel sound in the word *keep* can be spelled: k*ee*p, k*ey*, tr*ea*t, p*eo*ple, qu*ay*, am*oe*ba, th*ie*f, rec*ei*ve.) It is no wonder that there have been many attempts to reform the spelling of English to make it more closely reflect its actual pronunciation. From Benjamin Franklin to Noah Webster, from Theodore Roosevelt to George Bernard Shaw, many people have devised "improved" spelling systems for English. Prepare a report on (a) the proposals of one of the major would-be reformers, or (b) the history of the spelling-reform movement as a whole, summarizing both the arguments for and against spelling reform.

12. Daniels's book *Famous Last Words: The American Language Crisis Reconsidered*, from which "Nine Ideas About Language" is taken, disputes the idea that the English language is deteriorating and argues against what Daniels believes to be the trivializing attacks of such self-proclaimed experts as Edwin Newman, William Safire, John Simon, and the authors of usage handbooks. The subjects of just what is "correct usage" and of whether English is deteriorating are fascinating ones about which people have strong opinions.

Divide the class into three groups. Basing its arguments on facts, not opinions, each group should prepare a logical, well-documented position paper on one of the following: (a) the English language is deteriorating; (b) the English language is not deteriorating; and (c) there is an absolute standard for "correct" English and its basis is clear and defensible.

13. Consult at least four introductory linguistics texts (not dictionaries), and copy the definitions of *language* that each gives. After carefully comparing the definitions, write a paper discussing which points recur and explaining their significance. (If you decide to do this assignment as a class project, class members should collect as many different definitions of *language* as they can, being sure to identify the source of each. Copy and distribute the definitions; and discuss, as a group or in small groups, the significance of the similarities and differences among the definitions.)

Selected Bibliography

Akmajian, Adrian, Richard A. Demers, and Robert M. Harnish. *Linguistics: An Introduction to Language and Communication,* 2nd ed. Cambridge: The MIT Press, 1984. (Excellent introduction to the field of linguistics.)

Bloomfield, Leonard. *Language.* New York: Holt, Rinehart and Winston, 1933. (Still a classic work for students of linguistics.)

Bolinger, Dwight. *Aspects of Language,* 2nd ed. New York: Harcourt Brace Jovanovich, 1975. (Extensive and readable treatment of a wide variety of topics.)

————. *Language: The Loaded Weapon.* New York: Longman Group, 1980. (A short but insightful introduction to language, with an emphasis on the importance of meaning.)

Chase, Stuart. "How Language Shapes Our Thoughts," in *Harper's Magazine,* April 1954, pp. 76–82. (A discussion of language as a shaper of thought with examples drawn from many different cultures.)

Farb, Peter. *Humankind.* Boston: Houghton Mifflin, 1978. (Very readable discussion of all aspects of human behavior, including language.)

————. *Word Play: What Happens When People Talk.* New York: Alfred A. Knopf, 1973; rpt. New York: Bantam, 1975. (Entertaining, knowledgeable discussion.)

Fromkin, Victoria, and Robert Rodman. *An Introduction to Language,* 3rd ed. New York: Holt, Rinehart and Winston, 1983. (One of the most popular introductory books.)

Human Ancestors: Readings from "Scientific American." San Francisco: W. H. Freeman and Company, 1979. (Collection of eleven articles describing a number of aspects of the search for evidence regarding the origin and development of human beings.)

Kluckholm, Clyde. "The Gift of Tongues," in *Mirror for Man: The Relation of Anthropology to Modern Life.* New York: Whittlesey House, 1949. (An anthropologist's view of language, culture, and the Whorfian hypothesis.)

Langer, Suzanne K. *Philosophy in a New Key: A Study in the Symbolism of Reason, Rite, & Art,* 3rd ed. Cambridge: Harvard University Press, 1956. (A classic work on the human symbol-making process and its relationship to language.)

Lehmann, Winfred P. *Language: An Introduction.* New York: Random House, 1983. (A good, brief introduction to current areas of interest in linguistics.)

Lieberman, Philip. *On the Origins of Language.* New York: Macmillan, 1975. (Careful analysis of paleontological and archeological evidence.)

Michaels, Leonard and Christopher Ricks, eds. *The State of the Language.* Berkeley: University of California Press, 1980. (A collection of sixty-three short, interesting essays on topics of widespread interest.)

Nilsen, Don L. F., and Alleen Pace Nilsen. *Language Play: An Introduction to Linguistics.* Rowley, MA: Newbury House Publishers, 1978. (Interesting; includes topics often omitted. See Chapter 1, "What Is Language?")

Pei, Mario. *The Story of Language,* rev. ed. Philadelphia: J. B. Lippincott Company, 1965. (A popular and readable introduction.)

Quinn, Jim. *American Tongue and Cheek: A Populist Guide to Our Language.* New York: Penguin Books, 1982. (Delightful and informative; traces changing attitudes toward usage, takes on the current "usage experts," and demonstrates that the English language is alive and well.)

Sagan, Carl. *The Dragons of Eden: Speculations on the Evolution of Human Intelligence.* New York: Random House, 1977. (Controversial but fascinating.)

Salus, P. H., ed. *On Language: Plato to Von Humboldt.* New York: Holt, Rinehart and Winston, 1969. (Includes several essays on the nature and origin of language.)

Sapir, Edward. *Language: An Introduction to the Study of Speech.* 1921; rpt. New York: Harcourt Brace & World, 1949. (A classic book that explores the relationship between speech and culture.)

de Saussure, Ferdinand. *Course in General Linguistics.* Trans. by Wade Baskin; Charles Bally and Albert Sechehaye, eds. 1915; rpt. New York: Philosophical Library, 1959. (A classic; based on lecture notes collected by former students.)

Stam, J. *Inquiries in the Origin of Language: The Fate of a Question.* New York: Harper & Row, 1976. (Traces the history of theories about the origin of language.)

Ullmann, Stephen. *Words and Their Use.* New York: Philosophical Library, 1951. (Contains an excellent chapter on the symbol-making process in language.)

Whorf, Benjamin Lee. *Language, Thought, and Reality.* John B. Carroll, ed. Cambridge: The MIT Press, 1956. (A classic work on the relationship between language and culture.)

Wilson, Edward O. *On Human Nature.* Cambridge: Harvard University Press, 1978. (Difficult but rewarding; attempt to join biological thought to the social sciences and the humanities.)

Part Two

Language
Acquisition

A child is born, and grows, and learns to speak and to understand others when they speak. What could be more ordinary, more easily taken for granted? But that children—all children—master a large part of their native language(s) at as early an age as five is astonishing. We still do not fully understand how children learn language. However, once linguists and psychologists realized how extraordinary an accomplishment language acquisition is, they began to investigate and gain an understanding of the process. What they have discovered in recent years about language acquisition is the subject of the articles in this section.

In "The Acquisition of Language," Breyne Arlene Moskowitz provides an overview of the language acquisition process. She shows how children, in learning all the systems of grammar—phonology, syntax, lexicon, and pragmatics—use the same basic technique of developing a general rule and testing it, modifying the rule and narrowing its scope gradually, until near-mastery is achieved. Following this discussion, Eric H. Lenneberg juxtaposes, in chart format, a description of motor skills and language development for children aged twelve weeks to four years. Consideration of developmental milestones in these two areas and of the extent to which they are or are not parallel raises a number of important questions, some of which are addressed in the third selection, by Peter A. de Villiers and Jill G. de Villiers. They examine in detail one specific aspect of children's language acquisition—sounds. They describe the task children face in separating sounds first into speech and nonspeech, and then in identifying the units of speech, phonemes and words; and they explain how children are able to accomplish this so rapidly. Broadening the focus, Jean Aitchison, in "Predestinate Grooves," argues explicitly that language acquisition is a biologically triggered behavior which must occur during a specific critical period if it is to occur normally. She discusses the characteristics of biologically triggered behaviors—walking, for example—and explains in what ways speech shares these features.

Much can be learned about the language acquisition process from the study of a normal child who, for whatever reasons, has lived in a severely deficient linguistic environment, and Aitchison briefly describes several such cases. In the next article, "The Development of Language in Genie: A Case of Language Acquisition Beyond the 'Critical Period,'" Victoria Fromkin and her colleagues report in detail on the linguistic development of Genie, a thirteen-year-old girl found in 1970 who had suffered extreme isolation. Genie's case is particularly interesting because of its relevance to the idea that there is a "critical period" for language acquisition and because of the unusual amount of information that is available about Genie's linguistic development.

Additional light is shed on language acquisition by an examination of Creole languages by Derek Bickerton. There are many different creole languages spoken throughout the world, and they exhibit striking grammatical similarities. Bickerton suggests that these similarities exist because creoles, which were created by children whose parents spoke pidgins, reveal the children's innate universal grammar, the grammar that they had to use in the absence of an adequate, natural language model. He also suggests that the features of natural languages that are most like the features of creoles are acquired most rapidly and easily by children.

Much has been learned in recent years about the language acquisition process, but there is still much that we do not fully understand. The selections in Part Two suggest that future research will significantly increase our understanding of the unique phenomenon that most people take for granted—language acquisition.

1/The Acquisition of Language

BREYNE ARLENE MOSKOWITZ

The image of proud parents leaning over their young baby's crib, urging the infant to repeat such words as "mama" and "dada," is an American stereotype. The acquisition of language, however, follows quite a different path than such a picture suggests. Language acquisition occurs in all children in the same succession of stages, as linguistics professor Breyne Arlene Moskowitz describes in the following selection. Professor Moskowitz explores the prerequisites for language learning, the holophrastic stage (one-word utterances), the two-word stage, the telegraphic stage, the acquisition of function words, the process of rule formation, semantic processes, and the phonology and actual articulation of utterances. She shows that in all areas of language acquisition, children are active learners and follow the same basic procedure: hypothesizing rules, trying them out, and then modifying them. Children formulate the most general rules first and apply them across the board; narrower rules are added later, with exceptions and highly irregular forms. Although the examples discussed in this selection concern children who are learning English, the same process has been observed in children learning other languages. While reading the selection, reflect on the language development of any young children you know to see if you can identify the stages described by Moskowitz.

An adult who finds herself in a group of people speaking an unfamiliar foreign language may feel quite uncomfortable. The strange language sounds like gibberish: mysterious strings of sound, rising and falling in unpredictable patterns. Each person speaking the language knows when to speak, how to construct the strings and how to interpret other people's strings, but the individual who does not know anything about the language cannot pick out separate words or sounds, let alone discern meanings. She may feel overwhelmed, ignorant and even child-like. It is possible that she is returning to a vague memory from her very early childhood, because the experience of an adult listening to a foreign language comes close to duplicating the experience of an infant listening to the "foreign" language spoken by everyone around her. Like the adult, the child is confronted with the task of learning a language about which she knows nothing.

The task of acquiring language is one for which the adult has lost most of her aptitude but one the child will perform with remarkable skill. Within a short span of time and with almost no direct instruction the child will analyze the language completely. In fact, although many subtle refinements are added between the ages of five and ten, most children have completed the greater part of the basic language-acquisition process by the age of five. By that time a child will have dissected the language into its minimal separable units of sound and meaning; she will have discovered the rules for recombining sounds into words, the meanings of individual words and the rules for recombining words into meaningful sentences, and she will have internalized the intricate patterns of taking turns in dialogue. All in all she will have established herself linguistically as a full-fledged member of a social community, informed about the most subtle details of her native language as it is spoken in a wide variety of situations.

The speed with which children accomplish the complex process of language acquisition is particularly impressive. Ten linguists working full time for ten years to analyze the structure of the English language could not program a computer with the ability for language acquired by an average child in the first ten or even five years of life. In spite of the scale of the task and even in spite of adverse conditions—emotional instability, physical disability and so on—children learn to speak. How do they go about it? By what process does a child learn language?

What Is Language?

In order to understand how language is learned it is necessary to understand what language is. The issue is confused by two factors. First, language is learned in early childhood, and adults have few memories of the intense effort that went into the learning process, just as they do not remember the process of learning to walk. Second, adults do have conscious memories of being taught the few grammatical rules that are prescribed as "correct" usage, or the norms of "standard" language. It is difficult for adults to dissociate their memories of school lessons from those of true language learning, but the rules learned in school are only the conventions of an educated society. They are arbitrary finishing touches of embroidery on a thick fabric of language that each child weaves for herself before arriving in the English teacher's classroom. The fabric is grammar: the set of rules that describe how to structure language.

The grammar of language includes rules of phonology, which describe how to put sounds together to form words; rules of syntax, which describe how to put words together to form sentences; rules of semantics, which describe how to interpret the meaning of words and sentences; and rules of pragmatics, which describe how to participate in a conversation, how to sequence sentences and how to anticipate the information needed by an interlocutor. The internal grammar each adult has constructed is identical with that of every other adult in all but a few superficial details. Therefore each adult can create or understand an infinite number of sentences she has never heard before. She knows what is acceptable as a word or a sentence and what is not acceptable, and her judgments on these issues concur with those of other adults. For example, speakers of English generally agree that the sentence "Ideas green sleep colorless furiously" is ungrammatical and that the sentence "Colorless green ideas sleep furiously" is grammatical but makes no sense semantically. There is similar agreement on the grammatical relations represented by word order. For example, it is clear that the sentences "John hit Mary" and "Mary hit John" have different meanings although they consist of the same words, and that the sentence "Flying planes can be dangerous" has two possible meanings. At the level of individual words all adult speakers can agree that "brick" is an English word, that "blick" is not an English word but could be one (that is, there is an accidental gap in the adult lexicon, or internal vocabulary) and that "bnick" is not an English word and could not be one.

How children go about learning the grammar that makes communication possible has always fascinated adults, particularly parents, psychologists, and investigators of language. Until recently diary keeping was the primary method of study in this area. For example, in 1877 Charles Darwin published an account of his son's development that includes notes on language learning. Unfortunately most of the diarists used inconsistent or incomplete notations to record what they heard (or what they thought they heard), and most of the diaries were only partial listings of emerging types of sentences with inadequate information on developing word meanings. Although the very best of them, such as W. F. Leopold's classic *Speech Development of a Bilingual Child*, continue to be a rich resource of contemporary investigators, advances in audio and video recording equipment have made modern diaries generally much more valuable. In the 1960s, however, new discoveries inspired linguists and psychologists to approach the study of language acquisition in a new, systematic way, oriented less toward long-term diary keeping and more toward a search for the patterns in a child's speech at any given time.

An event that revolutionized linguistics was the publication in 1957 of Noam Chomsky's *Syntactic Structures*. Chomsky's investigation of the structure of grammars revealed that language systems were far deeper and more complex than had been suspected. And of course if linguistics was more complicated, then language learning had to be more complicated. In the . . . years since the publication of *Syntactic Structures* the disciplines of linguistics and child language have come of age. The study of the acquisition of language has benefited not only from the increasingly sophisticated understanding of linguistics but also from the improved understanding of cognitive development as it is related to language. The improvements in recording technology have made experimentation in this area more reliable and more detailed, so that investigators framing new and deeper questions are able to accurately capture both rare occurrences and developing structures.

The picture that is emerging from the more sophisticated investigations reveals the child as an active language learner, continually analyzing what she hears and proceeding in a methodical, predictable way to put together the jigsaw puzzle of language. Different children learn language in similar ways. It is not known how many processes are involved in language learning, but the few that have been observed appear repeatedly, from child to child and from language to language. All the examples I shall discuss here concern children who are learning English, but identical processes have been observed in children learning French, Russian, Finnish, Chinese, Zulu and many other languages.

Children learn the systems of grammar—phonology, syntax, semantics, lexicon and pragmatics—by breaking each system down into its smallest combinable parts and then developing rules for combining the parts. In the first two years of life a child spends much time working on one part of the task, disassembling the language to find the separate sounds that can be put together to form words and the separate words that can be put together to form sentences. After the age of two the basic process continues to be refined, and many more sounds and words are produced. The other part of language acquisition—developing rules for combining the basic elements of language—is carried out in a very methodical way: the most general rules are hypothesized first, and as time passes they are successively narrowed down by the addition of more precise rules applying to a more restricted set of sentences. The procedure is the same in any area of language learning, whether the child is acquiring syntax or phonology or semantics. For example, at the earliest stage of acquiring negatives a child does not have at her command the same range of negative structures that an adult does. She has constructed only a single very general rule: Attach "no" to the beginning of any sentence constructed by the other rules of grammar. At this stage all negative sentences will be formed according to that rule.

(1)	(2)	(3)	(4)	(5)	(6)
boy		boys	boysəz	boys	boys
cat		cats	catsəz	cats	cats
			catəz		
man	men	mans	mansəz	mans	men
			menəz		
house		house	housəz	houses	houses
foot		foots	footsəz	feets	feet
feet		feets	feetsəz		

Sorting out of competing pronunciations that result in the correct plural forms of nouns takes place in the six stages shown in this illustration. Children usually learn the singular forms of nouns first (1), although in some cases an irregular plural form such as "feet" may be learned as a singular or as a free variant of a singular. Other irregular plurals may appear for a brief period (2), but soon they are replaced by plurals made according to the most general rule possible: To make a noun plural add the sound "s" or "z" to it (3). Words such as "house" or "rose," which already end in an "s"- or "z"- like sound, are usually left in their singular forms at this stage. When words of this type do not have irregular plural forms, adults make them plural by adding an "əz" sound. (The vowel "ə" is pronounced like the unstressed word "a.") Some children demonstrate their mastery of this usage by tacking "əz" endings indiscriminately onto nouns (4). That stage is brief and use of the ending is quickly narrowed down (5). At this point only irregular plurals remain to be learned, and since no new rule-making is needed, children may go on to harder problems and leave final stage (6) for later.

Throughout the acquisition process a child continually revises and refines the rules of her internal grammar, learning increasingly detailed subrules until she achieves a set of rules that enables her to create the full array of complex, adult sentences. The process of refinement continues at least until the age of ten and probably considerably longer for most children. By the time a child is six or seven, however, the changes in her grammar may be so subtle and sophisticated that they go unnoticed. In general children approach language learning economically, devoting their energy to broad issues before dealing with specific ones. They cope with clear-cut questions first and sort out the details later, and they may adopt any one of a variety of methods for circumventing details of a language system they have not yet dealt with.

Prerequisites for Language

Although some children verbalize much more than others and some increase the length of their utterances much faster than others, all children overgeneralize a single rule before learning to apply it more narrowly and before constructing other less widely applicable rules, and all children speak in one-word sentences before they speak in two-word sentences. The similarities in language learning for different children and different languages are so great that many linguists have believed at one time or another that the human brain is preprogrammed for language learning. Some linguists continue to believe language is innate and only the surface details of the particular language spoken in a child's environment need to be learned. The speed with which children learn language gives this view much appeal. As more parallels between language and other areas of cognition are revealed, however, there is greater reason to believe any language specialization that exists in the child is only one aspect of more general cognitive abilities of the brain.

Whatever the built-in properties the brain brings to the task of language learning may be, it is now known that a child who hears no language learns no language, and that a child learns only the language spoken in her environment. Most infants coo and babble during the first six months of life, but congenitally deaf children have been observed to cease babbling after six months, whereas normal infants continue to babble. A child does not learn language, however, simply by hearing it spoken. A boy with normal hearing but with deaf parents who communicated by the American Sign Language was exposed to television every day so that he would learn English. Because the child was asthmatic and was confined to his home he interacted only with people at home, where his family and all their visitors communicated in sign language. By the age of three he was fluent in sign language but neither understood nor spoke English. It appears that in order to learn a language a child must also be able to interact with real people in that language. A television set does not suffice as the sole medium for language learning because, even though it can ask questions, it cannot respond to a child's answers. A child, then, can develop language only if there is language in her environment and if she can employ that language to communicate with other people in her immediate environment.

Caretaker Speech

In constructing a grammar children have only a limited amount of information available to them, namely the language they hear spoken around them. (Until about the age of three a child models her language on that of her parents; afterward the language of her peer group tends to become more important.) There is no question, however, that the language environments children inhabit are restructured, usually unintentionally, by the adults who take care of them. Recent studies show that there are several ways caretakers systematically modify the child's environment, making the task of language acquisition simpler.

Caretaker speech is a distinct speech register that differs from others in its simplified vocabulary, the systematic phonological simplification of some words, higher pitch, exaggerated intonation, short, simple sentences and a high proportion of questions (among mothers) or imperatives (among fathers). Speech with the first two characteristics is formally designated Baby Talk. Baby Talk is a subsystem of caretaker speech that has been studied over a wide range of languages and cultures. Its characteristics appear to be universal: in languages as diverse as English, Arabic, Comanche, and Gilyak (a Paleo-Siberian language) there are simplified vocabulary items for terms relating to food, toys, animals and body functions. Some words are phonologically simplified, frequently by the duplication of syllables, as in "wawa" for "water" and "choo-choo" for "train," or by the reduction of consonant clusters, as in "tummy" for "stomach" and "scambled eggs" for "scrambled eggs." (Many types of phonological simplification seem to mimic the phonological structure of an infant's own early vocabulary.)

Perhaps the most pervasive characteristic of caretaker speech is its syntactic simplification. While a child is still babbling, adults may address long, complex sentences to her, but as soon as she begins to utter meaningful, identifiable words they almost invariably speak to her in very simple sentences. Over the next few years of the child's language development the speech addressed to her by her caretakers may well be describable by a grammar only six months in advance of her own.

The functions of the various language modifications in caretaker speech are not equally apparent. It is possible that higher pitch and exaggerated intonation serve to alert a child to pay attention to what she is hearing. As for Baby Talk, there is no reason to believe the use of phonologically simplified words in any way affects a child's learning of pronunciation. Baby Talk may have only a psychological function, marking speech as being affectionate. On the other hand, syntactic simplification has a clear function. Consider the speech adults address to other adults; it is full of false starts and long, rambling, highly complex sentences. It is not surprising that elaborate theories of innate language ability arose during the years when linguists examined the speech adults addressed to adults and assumed that the speech addressed to children was similar. Indeed, it is hard to imagine how a child could derive the rules of language from such input. The wide study of caretaker speech conducted over the past eight years has shown that children do not face this problem. Rather it appears they construct their initial grammars on the basis of the short, simple, grammatical sentences that are addressed to them in the first year or two they speak.

(1)	(2)	(3)	(4)	(5)	(6)
walk		walked	walkedəd	walked	walked
play		played	playedəd	played	played
need		need	needəd	needed	needed
			camedəd		
come	came	comed	comedəd	comed	came
			goed		
go	went	goed	wentəd	goed	went

Development of past-tense forms of verbs also takes place in six stages. After the present-tense forms are learned (1) irregular past-tense forms may appear briefly (2). The first and most general rule that is postulated is: To put a verb into the past tense, add a "t" or "d" sound (3). In adult speech, verbs such as "want" or "need," which already end in a "t" or "d" sound, are put into the past tense by adding "əd" sound. Many children go through a brief stage in which they add "əd" endings to any existing verb forms (4). Once the use of "əd" ending has been narrowed down (5), only irregular past-tense forms remain to be learned (6).

Correcting Language

Caretakers simplify children's language-analysis task in other ways. For example, adults talk with other adults about complex ideas, but they talk with children about the here and now, minimizing discussion of feelings, displaced events and so on. Adults accept children's syntactic and phonological "errors," which are a normal part of the acquisition process. It is important to understand that when children make such errors, they are not producing flawed or incomplete replicas of adult sentences; they are producing sentences that are correct and grammatical with respect to their own current internalized grammar. Indeed, children's errors are essential data for students of child language because it is the consistent departures from the adult model that indicate the nature of a child's current hypotheses about the grammar of language. There are a number of memorized, unanalyzed sentences in any child's output of language. If a child says, "Nobody likes me," there is no way of knowing whether she has memorized the sentence intact or has figured out the rules for constructing the sentence. On the other hand, a sentence such as "Nobody don't like me" is clearly not a memorized form but one that reflects an intermediate stage of a developing grammar.

Since each child's utterances at a particular stage are from her own point of view grammatically correct, it is not surprising that children are fairly impervious to the correction of their language by adults, indeed to any attempts to teach them language. Consider the boy who lamented to his mother, "Nobody don't like me." His mother seized the opportunity to correct him, replying, "Nobody likes me." The child repeated his original version and the mother her modified one a total

of eight times until in desperation the mother said, "Now listen carefully! Nobody likes me." Finally her son got the idea and dutifully
replied, "Oh! Nobody don't likes me." As the example demonstrates,
children do not always understand exactly what it is the adult is correcting. The information the adult is trying to impart may be at odds
with the information in the child's head, namely the rules the child is
postulating for producing language. The surface correction of a sentence does not give the child a clue about how to revise the rule that
produced the sentence.

It seems to be virtually impossible to speed up the language-learning process. Experiments conducted by Russian investigators show
that it is extremely difficult to teach children a detail of language more
than a few days before they would learn it themselves. Adults sometimes do, of course, attempt to teach children rules of language, ex-
pecting them to learn by imitation, but Courtney B. Cazden of Harvard
University found that children benefit less from frequent adult correction of their errors than from true conversational interaction. Indeed, correcting errors can interrupt that interaction, which is, after
all, the function of language. (One way children may try to secure such
interaction is by asking "Why?" Children go through a stage of asking
a question repeatedly. It serves to keep the conversation going, which
may be the child's real aim. For example, a two-and-a-half-year-old
named Stanford asked "Why?" and was given the nonsense answer:
"Because the moon is made of green cheese." Although the response
was not at all germane to the conversation, Stanford was happy with
it and again asked "Why?" Many silly answers later the adult had tired
of the conversation but Stanford had not. He was clearly not seeking
information. What he needed was to practice the form of social conversation before dealing with its function. Asking "Why?" served that
purpose well.)

In point of fact adults rarely correct children's ungrammatical sentences. For example, one mother, on hearing "Tommy fall my truck
down," turned to Tommy with "Did you fall Stevie's truck down?"
Since imitation seems to have little role in the language-acquisition
process, however, it is probably just as well that most adults are either
too charmed by children's errors or too busy to correct them.

Practice does appear to have an important function in the child's
language learning process. Many children have been observed pur-
posefully practicing language when they are alone, for example in a
crib or a playpen. Ruth H. Weir of Stanford University hid a tape
recorder in her son's bedroom and recorded his talk after he was put
to bed. She found that he played with words and phrases, stringing
together sequences of similar sounds and of variations on a phrase or
on the use of a word: "What color . . . what color blanket . . . what
color mop . . . what color glass . . . what color TV . . . red ant . . . fire

. . . like lipstick . . . blanket . . . now the blue blanket . . . what color TV . . . what color horse . . . then what color table . . . then what color fire . . . here yellow spoon." Children who do not have much opportunity to be alone may use dialogue in a similar fashion. When Weir tried to record the bedtime monologues of her second child, whose room adjoined that of the first, she obtained through-the-wall conversations instead.

The One-Word Stage

The first stage of child language is one in which the maximum sentence length is one word; it is followed by a stage in which the maximum sentence length is two words. Early in the one-word stage there are only a few words in a child's vocabulary, but as months go by her lexicon expands with increasing rapidity. The early words are primarily concrete nouns and verbs; more abstract words such as adjectives are acquired later. By the time the child is uttering two-word sentences with some regularity, her lexicon may include hundreds of words.

When a child can say only one word at a time and knows only five words in all, choosing which one to say may not be a complex task. But how does she decide which word to say when she knows 100 words or more? Patricia M. Greenfield of the University of California at Los Angeles and Joshua H. Smith of Stanford have suggested that an important criterion is informativeness, that is, the child selects a word reflecting what is new in a particular situation. Greenfield and Smith also found that a newly acquired word is first used for naming and only later for asking for something.

Superficially the one-word stage seems easy to understand: a child says one word at a time, and so each word is a complete sentence with its own sentence intonation. Ten years ago a child in the one-word stage was thought to be learning word meanings but not syntax. Recently, however, students of child language have seen less of a distinction between the one-word stage as a period of word learning and the subsequent period, beginning with the two-word stage, as one of syntax acquisition. It now seems clear that the infant is engaged in an enormous amount of syntactic analysis in the one-word stage, and indeed that her syntactic abilities are reflected in her utterances and in her accurate perception of multiword sentences addressed to her.

Ronald Scollon of the University of Hawaii and Lois Bloom of Columbia University have pointed out independently that important patterns in word choice in the one-word stage can be found by examining larger segments of children's speech. Scollon observed that a nineteen-month-old named Brenda was able to use a vertical construction (a series of one-word sentences) to express what an adult might say with a horizontal construction (a multiword sentence). Brenda's pronunciation, which is represented phonetically below, was imperfect and Scollon did not understand her words at the time. Later, when he transcribed the tape of their conversation, he heard the sound of a passing car immediately preceding the conversation and was able to identify Brenda's words as follows:

> Brenda: "Car [pronounced 'ka']. Car. Car. Car."
> Scollon: "What?"
> Brenda: "Go. Go."
> Scollon: [Undecipherable.]
> Brenda: "Bus [pronounced 'baish']. Bus. Bus. Bus. Bus. Bus. Bus.
>   Bus. Bus."
> Scollon: "What? Oh, bicycle? Is that what you said?"
> Brenda: "Not ['na']."
> Scollon: "No?"
> Brenda: "Not."
> Scollon: "No. I got it wrong."

Brenda was not yet able to combine two words syntactically to express "Hearing that car reminds me that we went on the bus yesterday. No, not on a bicycle." She could express that concept, however, by combining words sequentially. Thus the one-word stage is not just a time for learning the meaning of words. In that period a child is developing hypotheses about putting words together in sentences, and she is already putting sentences together in meaningful groups. The next step will be to put two words together to form a single sentence.

The Two-Word Stage

The two-word stage is a time for experimenting with many binary semantic-syntactic relations such as possessor-possessed ("Mommy sock"), actor-action ("Cat sleeping") and action-object ("Drink soup"). When two-word sentences first began to appear in Brenda's speech, they were primarily of the following forms: subject noun and verb (as in "Monster go"), verb and object (as in "Read it") and verb or noun and location (as in "Bring home" and "Tree down"). She also continued to use vertical constructions in the two-word stage, providing herself with a means of expressing ideas that were still too advanced for her syntax. Therefore once again a description of Brenda's isolated sentences does not show her full abilities at this point in her linguistic development. Consider a later conversation Scollon had with Brenda:

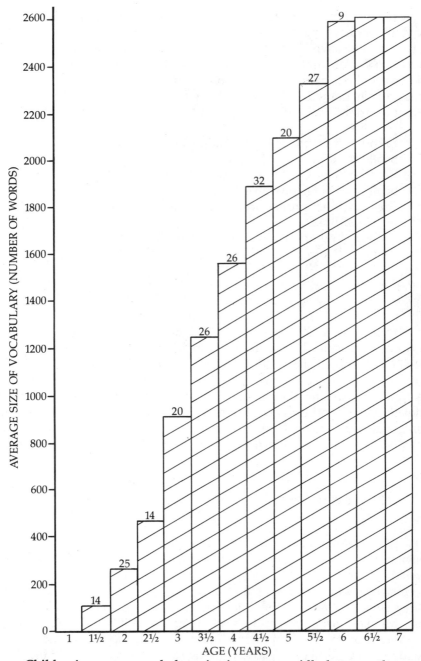

Children's average vocabulary size increases rapidly between the ages of one-and-a-half and six-and-a-half. The numbers over the first ten columns indicate the number of children tested in each sample age group. Data are based on work done by Madorah E. Smith of the University of Hawaii.

Brenda: "Tape corder. Use it. Use it."
Scollon: "Use it for what?"
Brenda: "Talk. Corder talk. Brenda talk."

Brenda's use of vertical constructions to express concepts she is still unable to encode syntactically is just one example of a strategy employed by children in all areas of cognitive development. As Jean Piaget of the University of Geneva and Dan I. Slobin of the University of California at Berkeley put it, new forms are used for old functions and new functions are expressed by old forms. Long before Brenda acquired the complex syntactic form "Use the tape recorder to record me talking" she was able to use her old forms—two-word sentences and vertical construction—to express the new function. Later, when that function was old, she would develop new forms to express it. The controlled dovetailing of form and function can be observed in all areas of language acquisition. For example, before children acquire the past tense they may employ adverbs of time such as "yesterday" with present-tense verbs to express past time, saying "I do it yesterday" before "I dood it."

Bloom has provided a rare view of an intermediate stage between the one-word and the two-word stages in which the two-word construction—a new form—served only an old function. For several weeks Bloom's daughter Alison uttered two-word sentences all of which included the word "wida." Bloom tried hard to find the meaning of "wida" before realizing that it had no meaning. It was, she concluded, simply a placeholder. This case is the clearest ever reported of a new form preceding new functions. The two-word stage is an important time for practicing functions that will later have expanded forms and practicing forms that will later expand their functions.

Telegraphic Speech

There is no three-word stage in child language. For a few years after the end of the two-word stage children do produce rather short sentences, but the almost inviolable length constraints that characterized the first two stages have disappeared. The absence of a three-word stage has not been satisfactorily explained as yet; the answer may have to do with the fact that many basic semantic relations are binary and few are ternary. In any case a great deal is known about the sequential development in the language of the period following the two-word stage. Roger Brown of Harvard has named that language telegraphic speech. (It should be noted that there is no specific age at which a child enters any of these stages of language acquisition and further that there is no particular correlation between intelligence and speed of acquisition.)

Early telegraphic speech is characterized by short, simple sentences made up primarily of content words: words that are rich in semantic content, usually nouns and verbs. The speech is called telegraphic because the sentences lack function "words": tense endings on verbs and plural endings on nouns, prepositions, conjunctions, articles and so on. As the telegraphic-speech stage progresses, function words are gradually added to sentences. This process has possibly been studied more thoroughly than any other in language acquisition, and a fairly predictable order in the addition of function words has been observed. The same principles that govern the order of acquisition of function words in English have been shown to operate in many other languages, including some, such as Finnish and Russian, that express the same grammatical relations with particularly rich systems of noun and verb suffixes.

In English many grammatical relations are represented by a fixed word order. For example, in the sentence "The dog followed Jamie to school" it is clear it is the dog that did the following. Normal word order in English requires that the subject come before the verb, and so people who speak English recognize "the dog" as the subject of the sentence. In other languages a noun may be marked as a subject not by its position with respect to the other words in the sentence but by a noun suffix, so that in adult sentences word order may be quite flexible. Until children begin to acquire suffixes and other function words, however, they employ fixed word order to express grammatical relations no matter how flexible adult word order may be. In English the strong propensity to follow word order rigidly shows up in children's interpretations of passive sentences such as "Jamie was followed by the dog." At an early age children may interpret some passive sentences correctly, but by age three they begin to ignore the function words such as "was" and "by" in passive sentences and adopt the fixed word-order interpretation. In other words, since "Jamie" appears before the verb, Jamie is assumed to be the actor, or the noun doing the following.

Function Words

In spite of its grammatical dependence on word order, the English language makes use of enough function words to illustrate the basic principles that determine the order in which such words are acquired. The progressive tense ending "-ing," as in "He going," is acquired first, long before the present-tense third-person singular ending "-s," as in "He goes." The "-s" itself is acquired long before the past tense endings, as in "He goed." Once again the child proves to be a sensible linguist, learning first the tense that exhibits the least variation in form.

(1) Laura (2:2)	(4) Andrew (2:0)
Her want some more.	Put that on.
Her want some more candy.	Andrew put that on.
(2) Laura (2:2)	(5) Andrew (2:1)
Where my tiger?	All wet.
Where my tiger book?	This shoe all wet.
(3) Laura (2:2)	(6) Benjy (2:3)
Let's dooz this.	Broke it.
Let's do this.	Broke it.
Let's do this puzzle.	Broke it I did.

Children correct their speech in ways that reflect the improvements they are currently making on their internal grammar. For example, Laura (1–3) is increasing the length of her sentences, encoding more information by embellishing a noun phrase. Andrew (4, 5) and Benjy (6) appear to be adding subjects to familiar verb-phrase sentences.

(7) Jamie (6:0)

Jamie: Why are you doing that?
Mother: What?
Jamie: Why are you writing what I say down?
Mother: What?
Jamie: Why are you writing down what I say?

(8) Jamie (6:3)

Jamie: Who do you think is the importantest kid in the world except me?
Mother: What did you say, Jamie?
Jamie: Who do you think is the specialest kid in the world not counting me?

(9) Jamie (6:6)

Jamie: Who are you versing?
Mother: What?
Jamie: I wanted to know who he was playing against.

(10) Jamie (6:10)

Jamie: I figured something you might like out.
Mother: What did you say?
Jamie: I figured out something you might like.

Jamie (7–10) seems to be working on much more subtle refinements such as the placement of verb particles, for example the "down" of "writing down." (Each child's age at time of correction is given in years and months.) Corrections shown here were recorded by Judy S. Reilly of University of California at Los Angeles.

The "-ing" ending is pronounced only one way, regardless of the pronunciation of the verb to which it is attached. The verb endings "-s" and "-ed," however, vary in their pronunciation: compare "cuts (s)," "cuddles (z)," "crushes (əz)," "walked (t)," "played (d)" and "halted (əd)." (The vowel "ə," called "schwa," is pronounced like the unstressed word "a.") Furthermore, present progressive ("-ing") forms are used with greater frequency than any other tense in the speech children hear. Finally, no verb has an irregular "-ing" form, but some verbs do have irregular third-person present-tense singular forms and many have irregular past-tense forms. (The same pattern of learning earliest those forms that exhibit the least variation shows up much more dramatically in languages such as Finnish and Russian, where the paradigms of inflection are much richer.)

The past tense is acquired after the progressive and present tenses, because the relative time it represents is conceptually more difficult. The future tense ("will" and a verb) is formed regularly in English and is as predictable as the progressive tense, but it is a much more abstract concept than the past tense. Therefore it is acquired much later. In the same way the prepositions "in" and "on" appear earlier than any others, at about the same time as "-ing," but prepositions such as "behind" and "in front of," whose correct usage depends on the speaker's frame of reference, are acquired much later.

It is particularly interesting to note that there are three English morphemes that are pronounced identically but are acquired at different times. They are the plural "-s," the possessive "-s" and the third-person singular tense ending "-s," and they are acquired in the order of listing. Roman Jakobson of Harvard has suggested that the explanation of this phenomenon has to do with the complexity of the different relations the morphemes signal: the singular-plural distinction is at the word level, the possessive relates two nouns at the phrase level and the tense ending relates a noun and a verb at the clause level.

The forms of the verb "to be"—"is," "are" and so on—are among the last of the function words to be acquired, particularly in their present-tense forms. Past- and future-tense forms of "to be" carry tense information, of course, but present-tense forms are essentially meaningless, and omitting them is a very sensible strategy for a child who must maximize the information content of a sentence and place priorities on linguistic structures still to be tackled.

Plurals

When there are competing pronunciations available, as in the case of the plural and past tenses, the process of sorting them out also follows a predictable pattern. Consider the acquisition of the English plural, in which six distinct stages can be observed. In English, as in many other (but not all) languages, nouns have both singular and plural forms. Children usually use the singular forms first, both in situations where the singular form would be appropriate and in situations where the plural form would be appropriate. In instances where the plural form is irregular in the adult model, however, a child may not recognize it as such and may use it in place of the singular or as a free variant of the singular. Thus in the first stage of acquisition, before either the concept of a plural or the linguistic devices for expressing a plural are acquired, a child may say "two cat" or point to "one feet."

When plurals begin to appear regularly, the child forms them according to the most general rule of English plural formation. At this point it is the child's overgeneralization of the rule, resulting in words such as "mans," "foots" or "feets," that shows she has hypothesized the rule: Add the sound /s/ or /z/ to the end of a word to make it plural. (The slashes indicate pronounced sounds, which are not to be confused with the letters used in spelling.)

For many children the overgeneralized forms of the irregular nouns are actually the earliest /s/ and /z/ plurals to appear, preceding "boys," "cats" and other regular forms by hours or days. The period of overgeneralization is considered to be the third stage in the acquisition of plurals because for many children there is an intermediate second stage in which irregular plurals such as "men" actually do appear. Concerned parents may regard the change from the second-stage "men" to the third-stage "mans" as a regression, but in reality it demonstrates progress from an individual memorized item to the application of a general rule.

In the third stage the small number of words that already end in a sound resembling /s/ or /z/, such as "house," "rose" and "bush," are used without any plural ending. Adults normally make such words plural by adding the suffix /əz/. Children usually relegate this detail to the remainder pile, to be dealt with at a later time. When they return to the problem, there is often a short fourth stage of perhaps a day, in which the child delightedly demonstrates her solution by tacking /əz/ endings indiscriminately onto nouns no matter what sound they end in and no matter how many other plural markings they may already have. A child may wake up one morning and throw herself into this stage with all the zeal of a kitten playing with its first ball of string.

Within a few days the novelty wears off and the child enters a less flamboyant fifth stage, in which only irregular plurals still deviate from the model forms. The rapid progression through the fourth stage does not mean that she suddenly focused her attention on the problem of /əz/ plurals. It is more likely that she had the problem at the back of her mind throughout the third stage. She was probably silently formulating hypotheses about the occurrence of /əz/ and testing them against the plurals she was hearing. Finding the right rule required discovering the phonological specification of the class of nouns that take /əz/ plurals.

Arriving at the sixth and final stage in the acquisition of plurals does not require the formulation of any new rules. All that is needed is the simple memorizing of irregular forms. Being rational, the child relegates such minor details to the lowest-priority remainder pile and turns her attention to more interesting linguistic questions. Hence a five-year-old may still not have entered the last stage. In fact, a child in the penultimate stage may not be at all receptive to being taught irregular plurals. For example, a child named Erica pointed to a picture of some "mouses," and her mother corrected her by saying "mice." Erica and her mother each repeated their own version two more times, and then Erica resolved the standoff by turning to a picture of "ducks." She avoided the picture of the mice for several days. Two years later, of course, Erica was perfectly able to say "mice."

Negative Sentences

One of the pioneering language-acquisition studies of the 1960s was undertaken at Harvard by a research group headed by Brown. The group studied the development in the language of three children over a period of several years. Two members of the group, Ursula Bellugi and Edward S. Klima, looked specifically at the changes in the children's negative sentences over the course of the project. They found that negative structures, like other subsystems of the syntactic component of grammar, are acquired in an orderly, rule-governed way.

When the project began, the forms of negative sentences the children employed were quite simple. It appeared that they had incorporated the following rule into their grammar: To make a sentence negative attach "no" or "not" to the beginning of it. On rare occasions, possibly when a child had forgotten to anticipate the negative, "no" could be attached to the end of a sentence, but negative words could not appear inside a sentence.

In the next stage the children continued to follow this rule, but they had also hypothesized and incorporated into their grammars more complex rules that allowed them to generate sentences in which the negatives "no," "not," "can't" and "don't" appeared after the subject and before the verb. These rules constituted quite an advance over attaching a negative word externally to a sentence. Furthermore, some of the primitive imperative sentences constructed at this stage began with "don't" rather than "no." On the other hand, "can't" never appeared at the beginning of a sentence, and neither "can" nor "do" appeared as an auxiliary, as they do in adult speech: "I can do it." These facts suggest that at this point "can't" and "don't" were unanalyzed negative forms rather than contractions of "cannot" and "do not," but that although "can't" and "don't" each seemed to be interchangeable with "no," they were no longer interchangeable with each other.

In the third stage of acquiring negatives many more details of the negative system had appeared in the children's speech. The main feature of the system that still remained to be worked out was the use of pronouns in negative sentences. At this stage the children said "I didn't see something" and "I don't want somebody to wake me up." The pronouns "somebody" and "something" were later replaced with "nobody" and "nothing" and ultimately with the properly concorded forms "anybody" and "anything."

Many features of telegraphic speech were still evident in the third stage. The form "is" of the verb "to be" was frequently omitted, as in "This no good." In adult speech the auxiliary "do" often functions as a dummy verb to carry tense and other markings; for example, in "I didn't see it," "do" carries the tense and the negative. In the children's speech at this stage "do" appeared occasionally, but the children had not yet figured out its entire function. Therefore in some sentences the auxiliary "do" was omitted and the negative "not" appeared alone, as in "I not hurt him." In other sentences, such as "I didn't did it," the negative auxiliary form of "do" appears to be correct but is actually an unanalyzed, memorized item; at this stage the tense is regularly marked on the main verb, which in this example happens also to be "do."

Many children acquire negatives in the same way that the children in the Harvard study did, but subsequent investigations have shown that there is more than one way to learn a language. Carol B. Lord of U.C.L.A. identified a quite different strategy employed by a two-year-old named Jennifer. From twenty-four to twenty-eight months Jennifer used "no" only as a single-word utterance. In order to produce a negative sentence she simply spoke an ordinary sentence with a higher pitch. For example, "I want put it on" spoken with a high pitch meant "I don't want to put it on." Lord noticed that many of the negative sentences adults addressed to Jennifer were spoken with an elevated pitch. Children tend to pay more attention to the beginning and ending of sentences, and in adult speech negative words usually appear in the middle of sentences. With good reason, then, Jennifer seemed to have hypothesized that one makes a sentence negative by uttering it with a higher pitch. Other children have been found to follow the same strategy. There are clearly variations in the hypotheses children make in the process of constructing grammar.

Stage 1	Stage 2	Stage 3
No . . . wipe finger.	I can't catch you.	We can't make another
No a boy bed.	I can't see you.	broom.
No singing song.	We can't talk.	I don't want cover on it.
No the sun shining.	You can't dance.	I gave him some so he
No money.	I don't want it.	won't cry.
No sit there.	I don't like him.	No, I don't have a book.
No play that.	I don't know his name.	I am not a doctor.
No fall!	No pinch me.	It's not cold.
Not . . . fit.	Book say no.	Don't put the two wings
Not a teddy bear.	Touch the snow no.	on.
More . . . no.	This a radiator no.	
Wear mitten no.	No square . . . is clown.	**A**
	Don't bite me yet.	I didn't did it.
	Don't leave me.	You didn't caught me.
	Don't wake me up . . .	I not hurt him.
	again.	Ask me if I not made
	He not little, he big.	mistake.
	That no fish school.	**B**
	That no Mommy.	Because I don't want
	There no squirrels.	somebody to wake
	He no bite you.	me up.
	I no want envelope.	I didn't see something.
	I no taste them.	**C**
		I isn't . . . I not sad.
		This not ice cream.
		This no good.
		I not crying.
		That not turning.
		He not taking the walls
		down.

Three stages in the acquisition of negative sentences were studied by Ursula Bellugi of the Salk Institute for Biological Studies and Edward S. Klima of the University of California at San Diego. They observed that in the first stage almost all negative sentences appear to be formulated according to the rule: Attach "no" or "not" to the beginning of a sentence to make it negative. In the second stage additional rules are postulated that allow the formation of sentences in which "no," "not," "can't" and "don't" appear after the subject and before the verb. In the third stage several issues remain to be worked out, in particular the agreement of pronouns in negative sentences (B), the inclusion of the forms of the verb "to be" (C), and the correct use of the auxiliary "do" (A). In adult speech the auxiliary "do" often carries tense and other functional markings such as the negative; children in the third stage may replace it by "not" or use it redundantly to mark tense that is already marked on the main verb.

Semantics

Up to this point I have mainly discussed the acquisition of syntactic rules, in part because in the years following the publication of Chomsky's *Syntactic Structures* child-language research in this area flourished. Syntactic rules, which govern the ordering of words in a sentence, are

Child's Lexical Item	First Referents	Other Referents in Order of Occurrence	General Area of Semantic Extension
mooi	moon	cake round marks on windows writing on windows and in books round shapes in books tooling on leather book covers round postmarks letter "o"	shape
bow-wow	dog	fur piece with glass eyes father's cufflinks pearl buttons on dress bath thermometer	shape
kotibaiz	bars of cot	large toy abacus toast rack with parallel bars picture of building with columns	shape
bébé	reflection of child (self) in mirror	photograph of self all photographs all pictures all books with pictures all books	shape
vov-vov	dog	kittens hens all animals at a zoo picture of pigs dancing	shape
ass	goat with rough hide on wheels	things that move: animals, sister, wagon . . . all moving things all things with a rough surface	movement texture
tutu	train	engine moving train journey	movement
fly	fly	specks of dirt dust all small insects child's own toes crumbs of bread a toad	size
quack	ducks on water	all birds and insects all coins (after seeing an eagle on the face of a coin)	size
koko	cockerel's crowing	tunes played on a violin tunes played on a piano tunes played on an accordion tunes played on a phonograph all music merry-go-round	sound
dany	sound of a bell	clock telephone doorbells	sound

Children overgeneralize word meanings, using words they acquire early in place of words they have not yet acquired. Eve V. Clark of Stanford University has observed that when a word first appears in a child's lexicon, it refers to a specific object but the child quickly extends semantic domain of word, using it to refer to many other things. Eventually meaning of the word is narrowed down until it coincides with adult usage. Clark found that children most frequently base the semantic extension of a word on shape of its first referent.

not all a child needs to know about language, however, and after the first flush of excitement over Chomsky's work investigators began to ask questions about other areas of language acquisition. Consider the development of the rules of semantics, which govern the way words are interpreted. Eve V. Clark of Stanford reexamined old diary studies and noticed that the development in the meaning of words during the first several months of the one-word stage seemed to follow a basic pattern.

The first time children in the studies used a word, Clark noted, it seemed to be as a proper noun, as the name of a specific object. Almost immediately, however, the children generalized the word based on some feature of the original object and used it to refer to many other objects. For example, a child named Hildegard first used "tick-tock" as the name for her father's watch, but she quickly broadened the meaning of the word, first to include all clocks, then all watches, then a gas meter, then a firehose wound on a spool and then a bathroom scale with a round dial. Her generalizations appear to be based on her observation of common features of shape: roundness, dials and so on. In general the children in the diary studies overextended meanings based on similarities of movement, texture, size and, most frequently, shape.

As the children progressed, the meanings of words were narrowed down until eventually they more or less coincided with the meanings accepted by adult speakers of the language. The narrowing-down process has not been studied intensively, but it seems likely that the process has no fixed end point. Rather it appears that the meanings of words continue to expand and contract through adulthood, long after other types of language acquisition have ceased.

One of the problems encountered in trying to understand the acquisition of semantics is that it is often difficult to determine the precise meaning a child has constructed for a word. Some interesting observations have been made, however, concerning the development of the meanings of the pairs of words that function as opposites in adult language. Margaret Donaldson and George Balfour of the University of Edinburgh asked children from three to five years old which one of two cardboard trees had "more" apples on it. They asked other children of the same age which tree had "less" apples. (Each child was interviewed individually.) Almost all the children in both groups responded by pointing to the tree with more apples on it. Moreover, the children who had been asked to point to the tree with "less" apples showed no hesitation in choosing the tree with more apples. They did not act as though they did not know the meaning of "less"; rather they acted as if they did know the meaning and "less" meant "more."

Subsequent studies have revealed similar systematic error making in the acquisition of other pairs of opposites such as "same" and "different," "big" and "little," "wide" and "narrow" and "tall" and "short." In every case the pattern of learning is the same: one word of the pair is learned first and its meaning is overextended to apply to the other word in the pair. The first word learned is always the unmarked word of the pair, that is, the word adults use when they do not want to indicate either one of the opposites. (For example, in the case of "wide" and "narrow," "wide" is the unmarked word: asking "How wide is the road?" does not suggest that the road is wide, but asking "How narrow is the road?" does suggest that the road is narrow.).

Clark observed a more intricate pattern of error production in the acquisition of the words "before" and "after." Consider the four different types of sentence represented by (1) "He jumped the gate before he patted the dog," (2) "Before he patted the dog he jumped the gate," (3) "He patted the dog after he jumped the gate" and (4) "After he jumped the gate he patted the dog." Clark found that the way the children she observed interpreted sentences such as these could be divided into four stages.

In the first stage the children disregarded the words "before" and "after" in all four of these sentence types and assumed that the event of the first clause took place before the event of the second clause. With this order-of-mention strategy the first and fourth sentence types were interpreted correctly but the second and third sentence types were not. In the second stage sentences using "before" were interpreted correctly but an order-of-mention strategy was still adopted for sentences that used "after." Hence sentences of the fourth type were interpreted correctly but sentences of the third type were not. In the next stage both the third and the fourth sentence types were interpreted incorrectly, suggesting that the children had adopted the strategy that "after" actually meant "before." Finally, in the fourth stage both "before" and "after" were interpreted appropriately.

It appears, then, that in learning the meaning of a pair of words such as "more" and "less" or "before" and "after" children acquire first the part of the meaning that is common to both words and only later the part of the meaning that distinguishes the two. Linguists have not yet developed satisfactory ways of separating the components of meaning that make up a single word, but it seems clear that when such components can be identified, it will be established that, for example, "more" and "less" have a large number of components in common and differ only in a single component specifying the pole of the dimension. Beyond the studies of opposites there has been little investigation of the period of semantic acquisition that follows the early period of rampant overgeneralization. How children past the early stage learn the meanings of other kinds of words is still not well understood.

Phonology

Just as children overgeneralize word meanings and sentence structures, so do they overgeneralize sounds, using sounds they have learned in place of sounds they have not yet acquired. Just as a child may use the word "not" correctly in one sentence but instead of another negative word in a second sentence, so may she correctly contrast /p/ and /b/ at the beginnings of words but employ /p/ at the ends of words, regardless of whether the adult models end with /p/ or /b/. Children also acquire the details of the phonological system in very regular ways. The ways in which they acquire individual sounds, however, are highly idiosyncratic, and so for many years the patterns eluded diarists, who tended to look only at the order in which sounds were acquired. Jakobson made a major advance in this area by suggesting that it was not individual sounds children acquire in an orderly way but the distinctive features of sound, that is, the minimal differences, or contrasts, between sounds. In other words, when a child begins to contrast /p/ and /b/, she also begins to contrast all the other pairs of sounds that, like /p/ and /b/, differ only in the absence or presence of vocal-cord vibration. In English these pairs include /t/ and /d/, and /k/ and the hard /g/. It is the acquisition of this contrast and not of the six individual sounds that is predictable. Jakobson's extensive examination of the diary data for a wide variety of languages supported his theory. Almost all current work in phonological theory rests on the theory of distinctive features that grew out of his work.

My own recent work suggests that phonological units even more basic than the distinctive features play an important part in the early acquisition process. At an early stage, when there are relatively few words in a child's repertory, unanalyzed syllables appear to be the basic unit of the sound system. By designating these syllables as unanalyzed I mean that the child is not able to separate them into their component consonants and vowels. Only later in the acquisition process does such division into smaller units become possible. The gradual discovery of successively smaller units that can form the basis of the phonological system is an important part of the process.

At an even earlier stage, before a child has uttered any words, she is accomplishing a great deal of linguistic learning, working with a unit of phonological organization even more primitive than the syllable. That unit can be defined in terms of pitch contours. By the late babbling period children already control the intonation, or pitch modulation, contours of the language they are learning. At that stage the child sounds as if she is uttering reasonably long sentences, and adult listeners may have the impression they are not quite catching the child's words. There are no words to catch, only random strings of babbled sounds with recognizable, correctly produced question or statement intonation contours. The sounds may accidentally be similar to some of those found in adult English. These sentence-length utterances are called sentence units, and in the phonological system of the child at this stage they are comparable to the consonant-and-vowel segments, syllables and distinctive features that appear in the phonological systems of later stages. The syllables and segments that appear when the period of word learning begins are in no way related to the vast repertory of babbling sounds. Only the intonation contours are carried over from the babbling stage into the later period.

No matter what language environment a child grows up in, the intonation contours characteristic of adult speech in that environment are the linguistic information learned earliest. Some recent studies suggest that it is possible to identify the language environment of a child from her babbling intonation during the second year of life. Other studies suggest that children can be distinguished at an even earlier age on the basis of whether or not their language environment is a tone language, that is, a language in which words spoken with different pitches are identifiable as different words, even though they may have the same sequence of consonants and vowels. To put it another way, "ma" spoken with a high pitch and "ma" spoken with a low pitch can be as different to someone speaking a tone language as "ma" and "pa" are to someone speaking English. (Many African and Asian languages are tone languages.) Tones are learned very early, and entire tone systems are mastered long before other areas of phonology. The extremely early acquisition of pitch patterns may help to explain the difficulty adults have in learning the intonation of a second language.

Phonetics

There is one significant way in which the acquisition of phonology differs from the acquisition of other language systems. As a child is acquiring the phonological system she must also learn the phonetic realization of the system: the actual details of physiological and acoustic phonetics, which call for the coordination of a complex set of muscle movements. Some children complete the process of learning how to pronounce things earlier than others, but differences of this kind are usually not related to the learning of the phonological system. Brown had what has become a classic conversation with a child who referred to a "fis." Brown repeated "fis," and the child indignantly corrected him, saying "fis." After several such exchanges Brown tried "fish," and the child, finally satisfied, replied, "Yes, fis." It is clear that although the child was still not able to pronounce the distinction between the sounds "s" and "sh," he knew such a systematic phonological distinction existed. Such phonetic muddying of the phonological waters complicates the study of this area of acquisition. Since the child's knowledge of the phonological system may not show up in her speech, it is not easy to determine what a child knows about the system without engaging in complex experimentation and creative hypothesizing.

Children whose phonological system produces only simple words such as "mama" and "papa" actually have a greater phonetic repertory than their utterances suggest. Evidence of that repertory is found in the late babbling stage, when children are working with sentence units and are making a large array of sounds. They do not lose their phonetic ability overnight, but they must constrain it systematically. Going on to the next-higher stage of language learning, the phonological system, is more important to the child than the details of facile pronunciation. Much later, after the phonological system has been acquired, the details of pronunciation receive more attention.

In the period following the babbling period the persisting phonetic facility gets less and less exercise. The vast majority of a child's utterances fail to reflect her real ability to pronounce things accurately; they do, however, reflect her growing ability to pronounce things systematically. (For a child who grows up learning only one language the movements of the muscles of the vocal tract ultimately become so overpracticed that it is difficult to learn new pronunciations during adulthood. On the other hand, people who learn at least two languages in early childhood appear to retain a greater flexibility of the vocal musculature and are more likely to learn to speak an additional language in their adult years without the "accent" of their native language.)

In learning to pronounce, then, a child must acquire a sound system that includes the divergent systems of phonology and phonetics. The acquisition of phonology differs from that of phonetics in requiring the creation of a representation of language in the mind of the child. This representation is necessary because of the abstract nature of the units of phonological structure. From only the acoustic signal of adult language the child must derive successively more abstract phonological units: first intonations, then syllables, then distinctive features and finally consonant-and-vowel segments. There are, for example, few clear segment boundaries in the acoustic signal the child receives, and so the consonant-and-vowel units could hardly be derived if the child had no internal representation of language.

At the same time that a child is building a phonological representation of language she is learning to manipulate all the phonetic variations of language, learning to produce each one precisely and automatically. The dual process of phonetics and phonology acquisition is one of the most difficult in all of language learning. Indeed, although a great deal of syntactic and semantic acquisition has yet to take place, it is usually at the completion of the process of learning to pronounce that adults consider a child to be a full-fledged language speaker and stop using any form of caretaker speech.

Abnormal Language Development

There seems to be little question that the human brain is best suited to language learning before puberty. Foreign languages are certainly learned most easily at that time. Furthermore, it has been observed that people who learn more than one language in childhood have an easier time learning additional languages in later years. It seems to be extremely important for a child to exercise the language-learning faculty. Children who are not exposed to any learnable language during the crucial years, for example children who are deaf before they can speak, generally grow up with the handicap of having little or no language. The handicap is unnecessary: deaf children of deaf parents who communicate by means of the American Sign Language do not grow up without language. They live in an environment where they can make full use of their language-learning abilities, and they are reasonably fluent in sign language by age three, right on the developmental schedule. Deaf children who grow up communicating by means of sign language have a much easier time learning English as a second language than deaf children in oral-speech programs learning English as a first language.

The study of child language acquisition has made important contributions to the study of abnormal speech development. Some investigators of child language have looked at children whose language development is abnormal in the hope of finding the conditions that are necessary and sufficient for normal development; others have looked at the development of language in normal children in the hope of helping children whose language development is abnormal. It now appears that many of the severe language abnormalities found in children can in some way be traced to interruptions of the normal acquisition process. The improved understanding of the normal process is being exploited to create treatment programs for children with such problems. In the past therapeutic methods for children with language problems have emphasized the memorizing of language routines, but methods now being developed would allow a child to work with her own language-learning abilities. For example, the American Sign Language has been taught successfully to several autistic children. Many of these nonverbal and antisocial children have learned in this way to communicate with therapists, in some cases becoming more socially responsive. (Why sign language should be so successful with some autistic children is unclear; it may have to do with the fact that a sign lasts longer than an auditory signal.)

There are still many questions to be answered in the various areas I have discussed, but in general a great deal of progress has been made in understanding child language over the past 20 years. The study of the acquisition of language has come of age. It is now a genuinely interdisciplinary field where psychologists, neurosurgeons and linguists work together to penetrate the mechanisms of perception and cognition as well as the mechanisms of language.

Bibliography

Bloom, Lois. *One Word at a Time.* The Hague: Mouton, 1975.

Brown, Roger. *A First Language: The Early Stages.* Cambridge, Mass.: Harvard University Press, 1973.

Dil, Anwar S., ed. *Language Structure and Language Use: Essays by Charles A. Ferguson.* Stanford, Calif.: Stanford University Press, 1971.

McNeill, David. *The Acquisition of Language: The Study of Developmental Psycholinguistics.* New York: Harper & Row, 1970.

FOR DISCUSSION AND REVIEW

1. Explain how the tables showing the development of correct noun plural forms and of correct past tense forms of verbs illustrate and support the claim that "children approach language learning economically, devoting their energy to broad issues before dealing with specific ones."

2. What are the characteristics of "caretaker speech"? Why is its use important to children in their acquisition of language? How has the recognition of caretaker speech modified linguists' thinking about the process of language acquisition?

3. Explain how and why children in the one-word and two-word stages of language acquisition use vertical constructions. In what sense is this linguistic strategy an example of a technique that children use in all areas of cognitive development?

4. Children's acquisition of function words (including inflectional affixes such as noun plurals and the *-ing* and past-tense forms of verbs) in English and in other languages follows a very predictable order. Using examples from English, explain what principles govern the sequence of function-word acquisition.

5. Discuss how children expand their semantic understanding and use of a word. What features of the referent are most important? Although less is known about the narrowing-down process, consider what the results of semantic overgeneralization and subsequent narrowing-down may be in the communication process—both among older children and adults, especially since "the meanings of words continue to expand and contract through adulthood."

6. With regard to the manner in which children learn the meanings of pairs of words with opposite meanings (e.g., *more* vs. *less*), explain the statement that "children acquire first the part of the meaning that is common to both words and only later the part that distinguishes the two."

7. What part of the language system do children learn first? What are some implications of this very early learning for adults who are trying to learn a new language?

8. Explain the statement that "learning to pronounce . . . , a child must acquire a sound system that includes the divergent systems of phonology and phonetics."

2/Developmental Milestones in Motor and Language Development

ERIC H. LENNEBERG

All normal children, whatever their native language, go through the same stages of language acquisition in nearly the same order, although not all progress at the same rate. All normal children also move through the same stages of motor development—though again at different rates. However, the relationship between language acquisition and sensorimotor development is not clear. Some researchers believe that some level of sensorimotor knowledge must be present in order for language acquisition to proceed; others argue that it is cortical maturation itself which is the essential prerequisite both for the development of language and for sensorimotor development. The issue is whether language is an autonomous cognitive system or whether it is only one way of many in which development of general cognitive ability is manifested. A further question is whether and to what extent children possess an innate capacity specifically for language acquisition. The following chart juxtaposes the stages of motor and language development typically reached by children from twelve weeks through four years of age.

At the completion of:	Motor Development	Vocalization and Language
12 weeks	Supports head when in prone position; weight is on elbows; hands mostly open; no grasp reflex	Markedly less crying than at 8 weeks; when talked to and nodded at, smiles, followed by squealing-gurgling sounds usually called *cooing*, which is vowel-like in character and pitch-modulated; sustains cooing for 15–20 seconds

At the completion of:	Motor Development	Vocalization and Language
16 weeks	Plays with a rattle placed in his hands (by shaking it and staring at it), head self-supported; tonic neck reflex subsiding	Responds to human sounds more definitely; turns head; eyes seem to search for speaker; occasionally some chuckling sounds
20 weeks	Sits with props	The vowel-like cooing sounds begin to be interspersed with more consonantal sounds; labial fricatives, spirants, and nasals are common; acoustically, all vocalizations are very different from the sounds of the mature language of the environment
6 months	Sitting: bends forward and uses hands for support; can bear weight when put into standing position, but cannot yet stand with holding on; reaching: unilateral; grasp: no thumb apposition yet; releases cube when given another	Cooing changing into babbling resembling one-syllable utterances; neither vowels nor consonants have very fixed recurrences; most common utterances sound somewhat like *ma, mu, da,* or *di*
8 months	Stands holding on; grasps with thumb apposition; picks up pellet with thumb and finger tips	Reduplication (or more continuous repetitions) becomes frequent; intonation patterns become distinct; utterances can signal emphasis and emotions
10 months	Creeps efficiently; takes side-steps, holding on; pulls to standing position	Vocalizations are mixed with sound-play such as gurgling or bubble-blowing; appears to wish to imitate sounds, but the imitations are never quite successful; beginning to differentiate between words heard by making differential adjustment
12 months	Walks when held by one hand; walks on feet and hands—knees in air; mouthing of objects almost stopped; seats self on floor	Identical sound sequences are replicated with higher relative frequency of occurrence and words (*mamma* or *dadda*) are emerging; definite signs of understanding some words and simple commands (show me your eyes)
18 months	Grasp, prehension, and release fully developed; gait stiff, propulsive, and precipitated; sits on child's chair with only fair aim; creeps downstairs backward; has difficulty building tower of 3 cubes	Has a definite repertoire of words—more than three, but less than fifty; still much babbling but now of several syllables with intricate intonation pattern; no attempt at communicating information and no frustration for not being understood; words may include items such as *thank you*

At the completion of:	Motor Development	Vocalization and Language
		or *come here*, but there is little ability to join any of the lexical items into spontaneous two-item phrases; understanding is progressing rapidly
24 months	Runs, but falls in sudden turns; can quickly alternate between sitting and stance; walks stairs up or down, one foot forward only	Vocabulary of more than 50 items (some children seem to be able to name everything in environment); begins spontaneously to join vocabulary items into two-word phrases; all phrases appear to be own creations; definite increase in communicative behavior and interest in language
30 months	Jumps up into air with both feet; stands on one foot for about two seconds; takes few steps on tip-toe; jumps from chair; good hand and finger coordination; can move digits independently; manipulation of objects much improved; builds tower of six cubes	Fastest increase in vocabulary with many new additions every day; no babbling at all; utterances have communicative intent; frustrated if not understood by adults; utterances consist of at least two words, many have three or even five words; sentences and phrases have characteristic child grammar, that is, they are rarely verbatim repetitions of an adult utterance; intelligibility is not very good yet, though there is great variation among children; seems to understand everything that is said to him
3 years	Tiptoes three yards; runs smoothly with acceleration and deceleration; negotiates sharp and fast curves without difficulty; walks stairs by alternating feet; jumps 12 inches; can operate tricycle	Vocabulary of some 1000 words; about 80% of utterances are intelligible even to strangers; grammatical complexity of utterances is roughly that of colloquial adult language, although mistakes still occur
4 years	Jumps over rope; hops on right foot; catches ball in arms; walks line	Language is well-established; deviations from adult norm tend to be more in style than in grammar

FOR DISCUSSION AND REVIEW

1. **Study Lenneberg's table showing typical stages of motor and language development for young children. Do motor development and language development seem to progress at similar rates—that is, do children develop more rapidly in one area than in the other?**

2. Jean Piaget has argued that children acquire meanings as an extension of sensorimotor intelligence and that the development of vocabulary categories, for example, depends upon motor development (things can be "graspable" or "suckable"). Thus, abilities in different areas (e.g., motor skills and language) that appear at the same age should be similar because they are based on the same cognitive knowledge. Can you support or refute this argument on the basis of Lenneberg's table, or do you need additional information? If you believe that you need additional information, describe the kind(s) of data that you would want to have.

3/Sounds

PETER A. DE VILLIERS
AND JILL G. DE VILLIERS

*The following selection by Peter A. de Villiers and Jill G. de Villiers
focuses on one aspect of children's language acquisition—sounds. The
task confronting children regarding sounds is complicated: not only
must they learn to distinguish speech from other kinds of noise, but
they must also learn to break down continuous streams of speech
sounds into units—phonemes and words—that are appropriate for
the language(s) they are learning. As the authors point out, different
languages use different phonemes and combine them into words according to rules that vary from language to language. Children's ability to acquire language rapidly depends on their innate predisposition
to perceive small but important variations in speech sounds. It is
important to realize that all children, no matter what language(s) they
are learning, use essentially the same principles or strategies as they
develop their ability to perceive and to produce speech and speech
sounds and as they progress from cooing to babbling (about which
there are many unanswered questions) to uttering words.*

In the first two years the child is transformed from a helpless, self-
absorbed infant, whose waking life seems dominated by the acquisition
and elimination of food and drink, into a mobile, inquisitive, and communicative toddler who has developed a mind of his own and is now
preoccupied with exploring his social and physical environment. The
two most striking changes in this period are the onset of walking and
the emergence of speech, events that are typically quite closely meshed
in time. The child usually takes his first hesitant steps and utters his
first understandable words toward the end of the first year or early in
the second. A major factor in advances in locomotion and vocalization
seems to be the physical maturity of the child. Malnutrition and various
types of mental retardation that slow the maturation of the child's brain
tend to slow down his progress through the motor milestones of sitting,
crawling, standing, and walking, and the development of vocal communication to about the same degree. Nevertheless, it is not too remarkable to find a chatty one-year-old who still spends more time on
his bottom than on his feet, or a budding sprinter at fifteen months
who has little to say for himself.

In [this selection] we shall examine the emergence of the first words, considering how physical maturation and the child's environment affect the rate and pattern of word learning. Three major questions about children's first words will concern us:

1. What do the first words sound like and how do they relate to the child's preverbal vocalizations?
2. What do the first terms of reference mean, for the child and for the adult, and how does the adult's speech to the child influence which words are learned first?
3. What functions do the early words serve in communication, and how do they relate to the nonverbal interaction between parent and child?

Hearing Speech Sounds

We begin with the sounds of speech, for it is here that the child must also begin. From the first he is exposed to a wide variety of noises from his environment, including the complex sounds directed at him by other people. To decipher the messages that those sounds contain the child must separate the noises he hears into speech and nonspeech, and then divide up the speech into words and the individual sounds that form them. Most of the coos, grunts, clicks, and wheezes that may accompany speech, and some of the variation in the speech sounds themselves, can be ignored, for they do not affect the messages being communicated; but other subtle differences in sound alter the meaning of words and sentences. For example, many words in English are distinguished by just one consonant or vowel sound. Consider the set: *bin, din, fin, gin, kin, pin, sin, shin, tin, thin,* and *win*; these words differ only by their initial consonants. The set *pan, pen, pin, pun,* and *pawn* differs only by the vowels. The speech sounds of a language that contrast with one another in this way indicate changes in meaning and are called *phonemes*. Linguists place them inside slashed lines (/b/, /d/, /g/) to distinguish them from the letters of the alphabet and from speech-sound changes that do not affect the meaning of words. The child must learn to hear and pronounce the phonemes of his language with reasonable accuracy in order to be understood.

To complicate the task for the child, the sound changes that distinguish between phonemes, and hence between words, vary from language to language. Pronunciation of the /t/ sound in English varies in breathiness (aspiration) depending on the word in which it appears. In *stop* there is comparatively little air expelled with the /t/, but in *top* there is more—the reader can verify this by saying the two words up against the back of the hand. Yet differences in aspiration do not contrast words in English; *stop* pronounced with the breathy /t/ of *top* still has the same meaning. In contrast, the degree of aspiration of /t/, /p/, and /k/ is crucial for distinguishing between words in languages like Zulu, Hindi, and Arabic. The Zulu word *tusa* means "to praise," but *tʰusa* with a breathy /t/ means "to frighten."

On the other hand, English makes some distinctions between phonemes that are not made in other languages. Words such as *zip* and *sip* contrast in meaning, so /z/ and /s/ are separate phonemes in English. But in Spanish there is no contrast in meaning carried by /z/ and /s/ so they are not different phonemes. Similarly, Japanese native speakers do not distinguish between sounds in the range of our /r/ and /l/, although they do produce speech sounds that approximate those consonants. The child learning a particular language comes to hear and produce with accuracy the sound differences that change meaning and ignores those variations that are nonfunctional in his language. Adult English speakers come to ignore aspiration so well that they have difficulty in learning to hear and produce the different /t/, /k/, and /p/ phonemes in Zulu. Similarly, a failure to distinguish /r/ and /l/ is part of our stereotype of Japanese speakers learning English.

Children do not come to the task of discriminating between speech sounds completely unprepared, however. Within a matter of days after birth, they are highly responsive to speech or other sounds of similar pitch to the human voice. In fact, speech seems to be rewarding to the infant in a way that other sounds are not. Newborns will learn to suck on an artificial nipple hooked to a switch that turns on a brief portion of recorded speech or vocal music, but they will not suck as readily in order to hear instrumental music or other rhythmical sound.[1] In the first few months of life, speech elicits greater electrical activity in the left half of the child's brain and music elicits greater activity in the right half of the brain, as is the case with adults.[2] This suggests that at a very early age the two hemispheres of the brain are already specialized for dealing with the different kinds of sound. So from the beginning of infancy children are able to discriminate speech from nonspeech, and they seem to pay particular attention to speech.

Still more important, young infants are especially sensitive to some sound differences that distinguish between words in many languages. For example, one way that English speakers produce different phonemes is by varying the time between moving the lips and vibrating the vocal cords. In speaking a /b/, for instance, the vocal cords vibrate

[1] E. C. Butterfield and G. N. Siperstein, "Influence of Contingent Auditory Stimulation Upon Non-nutritional Suckle." In *Proceedings of the Third Symposium on Oral Sensation and Perception: The Mouth of the Infant* (Springfield, Ill.: Charles C. Thomas, 1974).

[2] D. L. Molfese, "Cerebral Asymmetry in Infants, Children and Adults: Auditory Evoked Responses to Speech and Musical Stimuli," *Journal of the Acoustical Society of America*, 1973, 53, 363.

just as the lips open, but in the case of /p/ the lips move fractions of a second before the vocal cords are set in motion. The time at which the vocal cords vibrate is known as the voice-onset-time or VOT: /b/ has a VOT of 0 milliseconds, because there is no delay, /p/ has a VOT of +40 milliseconds. In all other respects the two sounds are highly similar. The same time difference distinguishes /d/ from /t/ and /g/ from /k/.

Does it require lengthy exposure to a language to hear this minute difference between consonants, or are we innately equipped to hear it? Studies with preverbal infants disclose that they can discriminate sounds like /b/ and /p/ at a very early age.[3] The most effective demonstration takes advantage of the finding that infants will suck on a nipple to hear speech. Provided that the baby sucks with sufficient force he is played a tape of the syllable /ba/ following each suck. After a few minutes of this he appears to tire of the sound and the rate of sucking declines rapidly. At this point the syllable is changed to /pa/. If the child cannot tell the difference between the two sounds the rate of sucking should continue to decline, as it does if one continues to play the /ba/ syllable. But with infants as young as a few weeks old the rate of sucking jumps to high levels immediately following the change, indicating that the child can distinguish between the old /ba/ and the new /pa/.

Infants and English-speaking adults can readily detect small differences in VOT in the region of +25 to +40 milliseconds, but they are insensitive to larger differences in VOT at other points along the time continuum. For example, if one sound has a VOT of +40 milliseconds and another has a VOT of +100 milliseconds, we hear them both as /p/, and so do infants. This suggests that the human ear has a region of special sensitivity in the region of +25 to +40 milliseconds of VOT, and many languages have taken advantage of that sensitivity by placing the boundaries between several consonants at that point. The child embarks upon the task of language learning innately prepared to distinguish small variations in sound that will change the meanings of many words.

Nevertheless, a few languages place phoneme boundaries outside this region of special sensitivity. Thai, for instance, has a /b/ like that of English; but it also has a prevoiced /ᵐb/, for which the vocal cords are vibrated some 50 milliseconds before the mouth is opened (that is, the boundary between /b/ and /ᵐb/ is around a VOT of *minus* 50 mil-

---

[3] P. D. Eimas, "Linguistic Processing of Speech by Young Infants." In R. L. Schiefelbusch and L. L. Lloyd, eds., *Language Perspectives: Acquisition, Retardation and Intervention* (Baltimore: University Park Press, 1974). E. C. Butterfield and G. F. Cairns, "Discussion Summary: Infant Reception Research." In R. L. Schiefelbusch and L. L. Lloyd, eds., *Language Perspectives: Acquisition, Retardation and Intervention* (Baltimore: University Park Press, 1974).

liseconds). Infants cannot distinguish the prevoiced /^{m}b/ from a /b/ until they have had considerable exposure to the Thai language.

The delicate timing of the ear in making these distinctions is worth noting. Delays no longer than 40 milliseconds in the onset of voicing distinguish /b/ from /p/, /d/ from /t/, and /g/ from /k/. Similarly, rapid changes in sound frequency that last for only 25 to 50 milliseconds separate /b/ from /d/ and /d/ from /g/. Unfortunately some children experience great difficulty in hearing brief changes in sound or detecting small differences in time intervals, although by other measures they do not appear to be deaf.[4] Dysphasic children [children whose speech and comprehension of language are impaired] may include those who are severely hampered in their acquisition of English because they cannot distinguish between many consonant sounds like the above.

Although the normal infant is very sensitive to voice-onset-time differences between /b/ and /p/, /d/ and /t/, and so on, he must still learn that these differences are important for distinguishing between words in his native language. Only toward the end of the second year, when the child understands several words and even has a few in his own productive vocabulary, can he use differences in voicing to contrast words that label objects. We can demonstrate this by presenting the child with two funny toys made up to look like people. Each object is given a nonsense-syllable name, such as *bok* and *pok*, chosen so that they differ only by the initial consonant. The child is then invited to do things with each object, such as "Let pok take a ride on the wagon" or "Put the hat on bok." Although one-month-old infants can detect the sound difference between /b/ and /p/, children under eighteen months have little success in picking out the correct object in the *bok-pok* task.[5] It is not that they cannot associate a nonsense-syllable level with an object or cannot carry out the actions, because they have no problem when the difference between labels is made more distinct, for example, *bok* and *zav*. They simply have not yet learned that a difference in VOT like that between /b/ and /p/ signals a difference in reference.

To summarize, infants are responsive to speech at a remarkably early age and can make fine discriminations between a number of speech sounds. However, the child must learn which of the many discriminable differences in speech sounds actually function to mark differences in reference in his native language. This requires consid-

[4] P. Tallal and M. Piercy, "Development Aphasia: Rate of Auditory Processing and Selective Impairment of Consonant Perception," *Neuropsychologia*, 1974, 12, 83–93.

[5] O.K. Garnica, "The Development of Phonemic Speech Perception." In T. E. Moore, ed., *Cognitive Development and the Acquisition of Language* (New York: Academic Press, 1973).

erable exposure to the language and is not complete even at the end of the second year.

Producing Speech Sounds

At three or four months of age babies begin cooing and babbling sounds that approximate speech. The babbling increases in frequency until it peaks between nine and twelve months. Although it often occurs in sentencelike sequences with rising and falling intonations, babbling remains uninterpretable to parents. At about a year children produce their first understandable words, often reduplicated syllables like *mama, dada,* or *papa,* or single consonant-vowel syllables like *da* for *dog* or *ba* for *baby.* For some children babbling ceases when the first words appear, but other children continue to produce long babbled sentences even while their intelligible vocabulary grows. We observed a delightful instance of this while making a movie on language acquisition for the Canadian Broadcasting Corporation. We were filming an eighteen-month-old girl, Katie, to illustrate the one-word stage of speech. Katie obligingly produced with great clarity and apparent effort the single words *book* and *look* while leafing through a large picture book with her mother. But then she picked up her own little book and began to "read" it, uttering long sentences of nonsense complete with elaborate intonation. To our amusement the cameraman then zoomed in on Katie, to reveal to the viewers that all the time her book had been upside down. Katie clearly knew that there was more involved in reading than uttering single words, no matter how precisely they were pronounced.

But children's use of babbled sentences is not confined to imitations of reading. Some children seem determined not to let their desire to communicate be frustrated by their lack of words. It can be most disconcerting to have a fifteen-month-old, who you know can only manage a handful of English words come through from an adjoining room, look you in the eye, point back into the other room, and say: "Gonggong dingdong baba da?" You cannot escape the feeling that the child has created a language of his own and if you possessed an English-Childish dictionary he would tell you something quite profound.

Surprisingly, there has been almost no study of the babbled sentences of children who can already say a few words even though such study might illuminate the child's early mastery of speech. For example, is any aspect of the babbling consistent across similar circumstances? Do the same wordlike sequences turn up in the same eliciting situations? This kind of consistency would suggest that the child constructs his own words for objects and events at the same time that he learns words from the adults around him. A few children do seem to do this; it is not uncommon to hear parents say something like "That's Sam's word for spaghetti" after the child has uttered something that sounds to the naive listener more like a burp than a word.

Even if the speech sounds vary from occasion to occasion, does the intonation pattern of the babbled sentences seem to be appropriate to their apparent communicative intent? Are questions distinguishable from statements, for example? Infants as young as six to eight months old notice the difference between a rising and falling intonation pattern over a syllable or phrase,[6] but there is no evidence that those patterns function to distinguish a query from a statement until much later. In the one-word stage children do come to use intonation to signal different intentions—demands, questions, statements, and so on—but the intonation patterns [they use] do not always correspond to those used by adults in their simple sentences to [children]. One wonders if some children use intonation in their babbled sentences before they apply them to their single-word utterances.

These questions are part of a larger issue: What is the relationship between babbling and the child's first words? The child babbles a wide variety of speech sounds, some of which do not occur in the language he is learning, although they may be found in other languages. Thus a child who hears only English may nevertheless produce a click sound that is used extensively in Southern African languages but never appears in English. Or he may make a sound by blowing through his lips like a cross between a /p/ and an /f/; this appears in Japanese but is decidedly not English. On the other hand, the child may not babble many sounds that are quite frequent in his native language. Some sounds therefore drop out while others appear for the first time in the transition from babbling to words.

One theory of speech development suggests that the child's language comes to approach that of adult speakers by two processes. First, parents selectively reward those sounds that approximate the speech sounds of their language by paying attention, smiling, or responding verbally to them and not to other sounds. Second, the child imitates the speech he hears from others. A more sophisticated version of this theory argues that the child associates his mother's voice with the good feelings of comfort, warmth, and food. Thereafter his own speech is rewarding to him to the extent that it sounds like his mother's.[7] Hence imitation is itself rewarding. There are elements of truth in this theory. Children clearly learn to pronounce words correctly by comparing their own productions with those of the adults around them. Furthermore, young children are accomplished mimics of the behavior and speech

[6] E. L. Kaplan, "The Role of Intonation in the Acquisition of Language" (diss., Cornell University, 1969).

[7] D. L. Olmsted, *Out of the Mouth of Babes* (The Hague: Mouton, 1971).

of their parents and do attempt to imitate the words they hear. Even the pitch of a child's voice shifts to match that of the person to whom he is talking; it is higher when he interacts with a woman and lower when he interacts with a man.[8] Finally, social and vocal reward does increase the frequency of babbling.[9] Even deaf children babble for longer if they can see an adult responding to their vocalizations, although they cannot hear their own sounds or the adult's vocal response.

Nevertheless, such a theory is at best incomplete, for it leaves out important determinants of speech development in children. There are constraints on the rate and pattern of sound development in babbling and in the early words which depend more on the maturing control of the child over his articulatory organs than on the frequency of the speech sounds in parental speech or on any rewards the child receives for producing those sounds. The onset of babbling seems to be a matter of physical maturation rather than exposure to speech, since deaf children begin to babble at about the same age as hearing children. However, continuation of babbling past eight or nine months of age depends on being able to hear oneself and others. Profoundly deaf children usually stop babbling at about that age and seldom learn to produce words.

The developmental pattern of babbling is also very similar across different languages, so that French, Japanese, and English babies all sound alike at this stage.[10] The child begins by producing guttural consonant sounds like /g/ and /k/ at the back of the mouth, and vowels like /a/ near the middle of the mouth. The range of babbled vowels then expands to include those pronounced near the front or back of the mouth, but the guttural consonants tend to disappear and be replaced by sounds like /b/, /p/, and /d/, which are produced at the teeth and lips. This change in the dominant consonant sounds cannot be explained by selective reward or imitation because there would be no reason for the perfectly appropriate /g/ and /k/ sounds to drop out of the child's repertoire if he were learning English, for example. Social and vocal rewards increase the amount of babbling, but they have little, if any, effect on the range of sounds babbled. Even when nine-month-old children are exposed to a concentrated input of syllables containing a wider variety of consonants than they themselves produce, they do not immediately broaden the range of consonants that they babble,

[8] P. Lieberman, *Intonation, Perception, and Language* (Cambridge: MIT Press, 1967).
[9] H. L. Rheingold, J. L. Gerwitz, and H. W. Ross, "Social Conditioning of Vocalizations in the Infant," *Journal of Comparative and Physiological Psychology*, 1959, 52, 68–73. G. Todd and B. Palmer, "Social Reinforcement of Infant Babbling," *Child Development*, 1968, 39, 591–596.
[10] S. Nakazima, "A Comparative Study of the Speech Developments of Japanese and American English in Childhood," *Studies in Phonology*, 1962, 2, 27–39.

although they babble more frequently.[11] It is only at the very end of the period of babbling that language input begins to influence the child's speech, and here the different languages begin to be distinguished.

Emergence of the first words at ten to fifteen months is determined as much by the child's control of articulation as by his ability to associate labels with objects. Most children can understand and respond appropriately to a number of words before they can produce any. Furthermore, the few deaf children who have been studied learning sign language from their parents produced their first signed words for objects around eight months, somewhat earlier than speaking children, presumably because gestural signs are easier to make than words are to articulate at that age. But the consistency of the speech input can also be an important influence on the age at which a child utters his first words and the speed at which he learns words. Children exposed to two or more languages from the beginning tend to be a little slower in their early vocabulary development because each object and event is paired with more than one word. However, they soon catch up with children learning a single language.

The change from babbling to words represents a shift from unconstrained practice or play with sounds (where there is no necessity for the child to produce any particular sound following any other) to planned, controlled speech. The child must produce particular speech sounds in sequence to make the words intelligible to his hearer. In fact children greatly simplify the pronunciation of their early words. For a while many children regularize all multisyllable words to reduplicated syllables—for example, a child might say *bubba* for *button, butter, bubble,* and *baby,* making use of context vital for understanding what he is referring to. At the same time, all single-syllable words may be reduced to a consonant plus a vowel: *du* for *duck, be* for *bed,* and so on. To some extent adults' baby talk to children provides simplified models that fit this mold, words like *mama, dada, weewee, booboo,* and *choochoo.*

Nevertheless, amid the fragmented early words there may be the isolated word that the child pronounces flawlessly. At fifteen months our son Nicholas produced a perfect *turtle* for the various toy turtles that swam with him in his bathtub. Later on, when the child begins to form systematic strategies or rules for the pronunciation of words, these "progressive idioms" are brought into line with the new patterns of pronunciation. So at eighteen months Nicholas' *turtle* became *kurka.* Another example is provided by Hildegard, the daughter of the linguist Werner Leopold.[12] Between ten and sixteen months Hildegard pro-

[11] B. J. Dodd, "Effects of Social and Vocal Stimulation on Infant Babbling," *Developmental Psychology,* 1972, 7, 80–83.
[12] W. Leopold, *Speech Development of a Bilingual Child: A Linguist's Record. Volume 2: Sound Learning in the First Two Years* (Evanston: Northwestern University Press, 1947).

nounced the word *pretty* in a remarkably adult manner; but at eighteen months *pretty* became *biddy*, in keeping with the way she said other words at that time.

Sometimes the child understands several words beginning with or containing a particular type of speech sound, but for a period of time he makes no attempt to produce them. Since there is nothing that the words have in common besides the sounds they share, the child appears to be actively avoiding words containing certain speech sounds and selectively producing those sounds he has mastered.

Some of the pronunciation errors that children make in their first words may arise from mishearing the adult words, especially in the case of multisyllable words. The accurate perception of speech sounds develops over the second and third years, and misperceptions of similar-sounding words occasionally occur, especially if the child knows the meaning of only one of the words. Nicholas at fourteen months had learned what *comb* meant and, whenever he came across one, would attempt to comb the precious few strands of hair he possessed at the time. One day he found a pine cone outside and brought it to his mother. "What a lovely cone," she said to him, whereupon he tried to comb his hair with it. At about the same age he confused the words *rape* and *grape*, but we will leave the details of that incident to the reader's imagination. Generally, however, the child's perception of words seems to be much better than his production of them. A child might use the word *maus* for both *mouth* and *mouse*, or *guck* for both *truck* and *duck*, yet quite easily pick out the appropriate referents for those words.

When the child has acquired about fifty words he begins to adopt quite regular patterns of pronunciation, some of which are found in children learning any language. This leads to consistent errors in pronunciation, some arising from the systematic deletion of parts of the adult word, others taking the form of the substitution of certain sounds for the correct adult sounds. For example, it is fairly universal that children in the early stages of language development reduce the consonant clusters that begin words, usually to a single consonant. So *spoon* becomes *poon*, *smack* is reduced to *mack*, and so on. Consonant clusters are one of the last aspects of the sound system of English to be mastered, and some children continue to experience difficulty with them until four or five years of age.

Another common strategy that children employ to simplify the pronunciation of words is the assimilation of all the consonants or vowels in a word to the same place of articulation in the mouth. This process can operate in either direction, with the initial consonant being changed to correspond to the place of articulation of the final consonant, as in *goggy* for *doggy*, or the opposite, *doddy* for *doggy*.

Finally, young children have a preference for initial consonants that are accompanied by vibration of the vocal cords (voicing) and for final consonants that are not voiced. They therefore tend to replace unvoiced consonants like /p/, /t/, and /k/ with their voiced counterparts /b/, /d/, and /g/ at the beginning of words, but do just the opposite at the ends of words. So a child will say *bie* for *pie*, *doe* for *toe*, and *bop* for *pop*; but at the same time pronouce *knob* as *knop* and *dog* as *dok*. Frequently several of the simplifying principles will operate at once in the child's pronunciation of a word. The use of *guck* for *truck* and *beep* for *creep* represents the combination of all three of the above principles. The initial consonant cluster is reduced from two consonants to one, the first and last consonants are produced at the same point in the mouth (/g/ and /k/ at the back of the mouth, /b/ and /p/ at the lips), and the first consonant is voiced.

In short, the errors of omission and substitution that two-year-olds make in their attempts to produce adult words are not random, but follow systematic patterns. Many other simplifying principles have been observed,[13] and individual children may differ as to which of the principles they adopt or which of them predominate at different stages of language development. But the principles we have looked at here are widespread across children and across languages, and all children may demonstrate one or more of them.

A close relationship exists between babbling and the pronunciation of the early words. Many of the simplifying principles used by children reflect the preferences for certain sounds or sound combinations that develop in the latter part of the period of babbling.[14] In babbling, there are very few consonant clusters, reduplicated syllables are common, and initial consonants outnumber final ones two to one. Further, initial consonants tend to be voiced but final consonants are unvoiced. All of these are common patterns in the early words as well. The maturing control of the child over his speech organs may therefore not only determine the sound preferences that emerge in later babbling but also constrain the types of errors and substitutions the child makes in his first words.

One final observation is worth making about the sound of the early words. It is tempting to assume that the child's pronunciation of words differs from that of adults because he is unable to produce certain sounds or particular sound combinations. To some extent this is true, but it is not always correct. The speech of Amahl, the son of the English linguist Nils Smith, illustrates how this assumption can be mislead-

[13] D. Ingram, "Current Issues in Child Phonology." In D. M. Morehead and A. E. Morehead, eds., *Normal and Deficient Language* (Baltimore: University Park Press, 1976).
[14] D. K. Oller, L. A. Wieman, W. J. Doyle, and C. Ross, "Infant Babbling and Speech," *Journal of Child Language*, 1976, 3, 1–12.

ing.[15] At twenty-five months Amahl consistently pronounced *puddle* as *puggle*. At the same time, however, *puzzle* came out as *puddle*, so it was certainly not the case that Amahl could not say the word. At a later stage Amahl systematically replaced *s* by *th* when it began a word. So he pronounced the word *sick* as *thick*. But at the same time he substituted *f* when he was aiming at *th*, so when he tried to say *thick* it came out *fick*. The crucial determinants of what the child says seem to be what he is aiming at and his regular patterns of producing those sounds. The child progresses by closing the gap between what he says and what he means to say.

FOR DISCUSSION AND REVIEW

1. Describe the complications that children face in learning to hear and pronounce the phonemes of their native language(s).

2. What reasons do we have to believe that young infants "pay particular attention to speech"? How can one test very young infants in a valid and reliable way?

3. In what ways does the ability of infants to distinguish among phonemes support the existence of an innate predisposition for language acquisition?

4. Children's babbling has a number of unusual characteristics; describe them. What are two unresolved questions about babbling and its role in language acquisition?

5. Children's perception of sounds (phonemes) and individual words is better than their production of them. Identify two consequences of this.

6. What kinds of pronunciation errors are made by all normal children who are learning to speak, regardless of the language(s) they are learning? Why is it significant that these errors are systematic, not random?

7. Compare de Villiers and de Villiers's statements about children's development of comprehension and production of sounds with Lenneberg's chart (pp. 74–76). What are the major linkage points, or "milestones," in terms of language acquisition and motor development? Why are these milestones so important?

[15] N. V. Smith, *The Acquisition of Phonology: A Case Study* (Cambridge, Eng.: Cambridge University Press, 1973).

4/Predestinate Grooves: Is There a Preordained Language "Program"?

JEAN AITCHISON

One possible and increasingly accepted explanation why all children go through the same stages of language acquisition in the same order but at different rates is that language acquisition is biologically triggered. In the following chapter from her book The Articulate Mammal, *Jean Aitchison, a British linguist who teaches at the London School of Economics, describes the characteristics of biologically determined behaviors and considers whether and to what extent language acquisition fits this model. She also describes a "critical period" for language acquisition. In addition, using examples of specific children, Aitchison discusses certain aspects of language acquisition, such as crying, cooing, babbling, the acquisition order of various grammatical forms, and the significance of the mean length of utterance (MLU) measure.*

There once was a man who said, "Damn!"
It is born in upon me I am
An engine that moves
In predestinate grooves,
I'm not even a bus, I'm a tram.
                              MAURICE EVAN HARE

Language emerges at about the same time in children all over the world. "Why do children normally begin to speak between their eighteenth and twenty-eighth month?" asks one researcher. "Surely it is not because all mothers on earth initiate language training at that time. There is, in fact, no evidence that any conscious and systematic teaching of language takes place, just as there is no special training for stance or gait." (Lenneberg 1967, p. 125)

This regularity of onset suggests that language may be set in motion by a biological time-clock, similar to the one which causes kittens to open their eyes when they are a few days old, chrysalises to change into butterflies after several weeks, and humans to become sexually mature at around 13 years of age. However, until relatively recently, few people had considered language within the framework of biological maturation. But in 1967 E. H. Lenneberg, then a biologist at the Harvard Medical School, published an important book, entitled *The Biological Foundations of Language*. Much of what is said in this chapter is based on his pioneering work.

The Characteristics of Biologically Triggered Behavior

Behavior which is triggered off biologically has a number of special characteristics. In the following pages we shall list these features, and see to what extent they are present in language. If it can be shown that speech, like sexual activities and the ability to walk, falls into the category of biologically scheduled behavior, then we shall be rather clearer about what is meant by the claim that language is "innate."

Exactly how many "hallmarks" of biologically controlled behavior we should itemize is not clear. Lenneberg lists four. The six listed below were obtained mainly by subdividing Lenneberg's four:

1. The behavior emerges before it is necessary.
2. Its appearance is not the result of a conscious decision.
3. Its emergence is not triggered by external events (though the surrounding environment must be sufficiently "rich" for it to develop adequately).
4. There is likely to be a "critical period" for the acquisition of the behavior.
5. Direct teaching and intensive practice have relatively little effect.
6. There is a regular sequence of "milestones" as the behavior develops, and these can usually be correlated with age and other aspects of development.

Let us discuss these features in turn. Some of them seem fairly obvious. We hardly need to set about testing the first one, that "the behavior emerges before it is necessary"—a phenomenon sometimes pompously labeled the "law of anticipatory maturation." Language develops long before children need to communicate in order to survive.

Their parents still feed them, clothe them, and look after them. Without some type of inborn mechanism, language might develop only when parents left children to fend for themselves. It would emerge at different times in different cultures, and this would lead to vastly different levels of language skills. Although children differ enormously in their ability to knit or play the violin, their language proficiency varies to a much lesser extent.

Again, little explanation is needed for the second characteristic of biologically triggered behavior: "Its appearance is not the result of a conscious decision." Clearly, a child does not suddenly think to himself, "Tomorrow I am going to start to learn to talk." Children acquire language without making any conscious decision about it. This is quite unlike a decision to learn to jump a four-foot height, or hit a tennis ball, when a child sets himself a target, then organizes strenuous practice sessions as he strives toward his goal.

The first part of feature 3 also seems straightforward: "The emergence of the behavior is not triggered by external events." Children start to talk even when their surroundings remain unchanged. Most of them live in the same house, eat the same food, have the same parents, and follow the same routine. No specific event or feature in the child's surroundings suddenly sets him off talking. However, we must here digress briefly in order to point out an aspect of biologically scheduled behavior that is sometimes misunderstood: although no external event *causes* the behavior, the surrounding environment must be sufficiently "rich" for it to develop adequately. Biologically programmed behavior does not develop properly in impoverished or unnatural surroundings. We have the apparent paradox that some types of "natural" behavior require careful "nurturing." Just as Chris and Susie, two gorillas reared away from other gorillas in Sacramento Zoo, are unable to mate satisfactorily (according to an item in the *Evening Standard*)—so an impoverished linguistic environment is likely to retard language acquisition. Children brought up in institutions, for example, tend to be backward in speech development. Lenneberg notes that a child raised in an orphanage will begin to talk at the same time as other noninstitutionalized children. But his speech will gradually lag behind the norm, being less intelligible, and showing less variety of construction. . . .

Rather more discussion is needed to justify the existence in language of a fourth characteristic of biologically controlled behavior: "There is likely to be a critical period for the acquisition of the behavior." It is clear that there is a biologically scheduled starting point for language acquisition, but far less clear that there is a biologically scheduled finishing point.

We know for certain that language cannot emerge before it is programmed to emerge. Nobody has ever taught a young baby to talk—

though it seems that there is nothing much wrong with the vocal cords of a new-born infant, and from five or six months onwards it can "babble" a number of the sounds needed in speech. Yet children utter few words before the age of eighteen months. It is clear that they have to wait for some biological trigger. The "trigger" appears to be connected with brain growth. Two-word utterances, which are usually regarded as the beginning of "true language," begin just as a massive spurt in brain growth slows down. Children do not manufacture any new brain cells after birth. They are born with millions, perhaps billions. At first the cells are not all interconnected, and the brain is relatively light (about 300 g). From birth to around two years, many more cells interconnect, and brain weight increases rapidly. By the age of two, it weighs nearly 1000 g (Lenneberg 1967).

It is not nearly so easy to tell when a child has finished acquiring a language. Nevertheless, there are a number of indications that, after the onset of adolescence, humans can acquire a new language only after a considerable struggle.

First of all, almost everybody can remember how difficult it was to learn French at school. Even the best pupils had a slightly odd accent, and made numerous grammatical mistakes. The difficulty was not that one was learning a second language, since children who are brought up speaking French and English as equal "mother tongues" do not experience similar problems. Nor is there much difficulty for children who emigrate to France around the age of five or six, when they already speak fluent English. Moreover, the failure to learn perfect French cannot be due simply to lack of exposure to the language. There are numerous people who have emigrated to France as adults, and converse only in French—yet few, if any acquire a mastery of the new language equivalent to that of their native tongue. It seems that the brain loses its "plasticity" for language learning after a certain age.

However, evidence concerning difficulties with French at school is mainly anecdotal. Perhaps the most impressive evidence for the existence of a critical period comes from comparing the case histories of two socially isolated children, Isabelle and Genie. Both these children were cut off from language until long after the time they would have acquired it, had they been brought up in normal circumstances.

Isabelle was the illegitimate child of a deaf mute. She had no speech, and made only a croaking sound when she was found in Ohio in the 1930s at the age of six and a half. Mother and child had spent most of the time alone in a darkened room. But once found, Isabelle's progress was remarkable: "Isabelle passed through the usual stages of linguistic development at a greatly accelerated rate. She covered in two years the learning that ordinarily occupies six years. By the age of eight and one half Isabelle was not easily distinguishable from ordinary children of her age" (Brown 1958, p. 192).

Genie, however, was not so lucky.* She was not found until she was nearly fourteen. Born in April 1957, she had lived most of her life in bizarre and inhuman conditions. "From the age of twenty months, Genie had been confined to a small room. . . . She was physically punished by her father if she made any sounds. Most of the time she was kept harnessed into an infant's potty chair; otherwise she was confined in a home-made sleeping bag in an infant's crib covered with wire mesh" (Curtiss et al., 1974, p. 529). When found, she was totally without language. She began acquiring speech well after the onset of adolescence—after the apparent "critical period."

Although she learnt to speak in a rudimentary fashion, she progressed more slowly than normal children (Curtiss 1977). For example, ordinary children go through a stage in which they utter two words at a time ("want milk," "Mummy play"), which normally lasts a matter of weeks.

Genie's two-word stage lasted for more than five months. Again, ordinary children briefly pass through a phase in which they form negative sentences by putting the word *no* in front of the rest of the utterance, as in "no Mummy go," "no want apple." Genie used this primitive form of negation for over two years. Normal children start asking questions beginning with words such as *where, what*, at the two-word stage ("where Teddy?"). Genie finds this kind of question impossible to grasp, occasionally making inappropriate attempts such as "where is stop spitting?" The only aspect of speech in which Genie outstripped normal children was her ability to learn vocabulary. She knew many more words than ordinary children at a comparable stage of grammatical development. However, the ability to memorize lists of items is not evidence of language capacity—even the chimps Washoe and Sarah found this relatively easy. It is the rules of grammar which are the important part, and this is what Genie finds difficult. Her slow progress compared with that of Isabelle seems to provide evidence in favor of there being a "cut-off" point for language acquisition. We must be cautious however. Two individual cases cannot provide firm proof, especially as each is problematical. Isabelle was not studied by linguists, so her speech may have been more deficient than was reported. Genie, on the other hand, shows some evidence of brain damage. Tests suggest that her left hemisphere is atrophied, which means that she may be functioning with only one half of her brain, the half not usually associated with language (Curtiss 1977; Curtiss et al. 1974).

According to Lenneberg, further evidence in favor of a critical period is provided by mentally handicapped children, such as "mongols" (Down's syndrome cases) (Lenneberg 1967). These follow the same

* Editors' note: Genie is discussed in more detail in the following selection (pp. 112–133).

general path of development as normal children, but much more slowly. Lenneberg claims that they never catch up because their ability to learn language slows down dramatically at puberty. But some researchers have disputed this claim, arguing that the children's language ceases to develop through lack of stimulation, not lack of ability.

The recovery possibilities of brain-damaged patients give further support, and in addition, indicate that the critical period coincides with the period of lateralization—the gradual specialization of language to one side of the brain. Lenneberg suggests that this process occurs between the ages of 2 and 14, though . . . others have suggested that its completion occurs around the age of 5 or 6. If a child under the age of 2 sustains severe damage to the left (language) hemisphere of the brain, his speech will develop normally, though it will be controlled by the right hemisphere. But as the child gets older, the likelihood of left hemisphere damage causing permanent impairment gets progressively greater. At the age of 7 or 8, the damage is usually long-lasting, whereas in an adolescent or adult it often results in lifelong speech disturbance. When lateralization is complete, the brain seems to have lost a natural "bent" for learning languages.

We have now considered several pieces of indirect evidence for the existence of a "critical period." They all suggest (though do not conclusively prove) that toddler time to adolescence is a time set aside by nature for the acquisition of language. Lenneberg notes:

> Between the ages of two and three years language emerges by an interaction of maturation and self-programmed learning. Between the ages of three and the early teens the possibility for primary language acquisition continues to be good; the individual appears to be most sensitive to stimuli at this time and to preserve some innate flexibility for the organization of brain functions to carry out the complete integration of subprocesses necessary for the smooth elaboration of speech and language. After puberty, the ability for self-organization and adjustment to the physiological demands of verbal behavior quickly declines. The brain behaves as if it had become set in its ways and primary, basic skills not acquired by that time usually remain deficient for life. [Lenneberg 1967, p. 158]

A similar critical period is found for the acquisition of their song by some species of birds. A chaffinch's song, for example, becomes fixed and unalterable when it is around fifteen months old. If the chaffinch has not been exposed to chaffinch song before that time, it never learns to sing normally (Thorpe 1972).

Let us now turn to the fifth characteristic of biologically triggered behavior, "Direct teaching and intensive practice have relatively little effect." In activities such as typing or playing tennis, a person's achievement is often directly related to the amount of teaching he receives and the hours of practice he puts in. Even people who are not "naturally" superb athletes can sometimes win tennis tournaments through sheer hard work and good coaching. But the same is not true of language, where direct teaching seems to be a failure. Let us consider the evidence for this.

When one says that "direct teaching is a failure," people smile and say, "Of course—whoever tries to *teach* a child to speak?" Yet many parents, often without realizing it, try to persuade their children to imitate them. They do this in two ways: firstly, by means of overt correction, secondly, by means of unconscious "expansions."

The pointlessness of overt correction has been noted by numerous researchers. One psychologist attempted over a period of several weeks to persuade his daughter to say *other* + noun instead of *other one* + noun. The interchanges went somewhat as follows:

Child: Want other one spoon, Daddy.
Father: You mean, you want the other spoon.
Child: Yes, I want other one spoon, please Daddy.
Father: Can you say "the other spoon"?
Child: Other . . . one . . . spoon.
Father: Say "other".
Child: Other.
Father: "Spoon."
Child: Spoon.
Father: "Other spoon."
Child: Other . . . spoon. Now give me other one spoon?

[Braine 1971, p. 161]

Another researcher tried vainly to coax a child into saying the past tense form *held*:

Child: My teacher holded the baby rabbits and we patted them.
Adult: Did you say your teacher held the baby rabbits?
Child: Yes.
Adult: What did you say she did?
Child: She holded the baby rabbits and we patted them.
Adult: Did you say she held them tightly?
Child: No, she holded them loosely.

[Cazden 1972, p. 92]

In fact, repeated corrections are not merely pointless: they may even hinder a child's progress. The mother of seventeen-month-old Paul had high expectations, and repeatedly corrected his attempts at speech. He lacked confidence, and his progress was slow. But the mother of fourteen-month-old Jane was an accepting person who responded uncritically to everything Jane said. Jane made exceptionally fast progress, and knew eighty words by the age of fifteen months (Nelson 1973, p. 105).

So forcing children to imitate is a dismal failure. Children cannot be trained like parrots. Equally unsuccessful is the second type of coaching often unconsciously adopted by parents—the use of "expansions." When talking to a child an adult continuously "expands" the youngster's utterances. If the child says, "There go one," a mother is likely to expand this to "Yes, there goes one." "Mommy eggnog" becomes "Mommy had her eggnog," and "Throw Daddy" is expanded to "Throw it to Daddy." Children are exposed to an enormous number of these expansions. They account for perhaps a third of parental responses. Brown and Bellugi note:

> The mothers of Adam and Eve responded to the speech of their children with expansions about 30 percent of the time. We did it ourselves when we talked with the children. Indeed, we found it very difficult to withhold expansions. A reduced or incomplete English sentence seems to constrain the English-speaking adult to expand it into the nearest properly formed complete sentence. [Brown and Bellugi 1964, p. 144]

At first researchers were uncertain about the role of expansions. Then Courtney Cazden carried out an ingenious experiment using two groups of children, all under three and a half (Cazden 1972). She exposed one group to intensive and deliberate expansions, and the other group to well-formed sentences which were *not* expansions. For example, if a child said, "Dog bark," an expanding adult would say, "Yes, the dog is barking." An adult who replied with a nonexpanded sentence might say "Yes, he's trying to frighten the cat" or "Yes, but he won't bite," or "Yes, tell him to be quiet." After three months the rate of progress of each group was measured. Amazingly, the expansion group were *less advanced* than the other group, both in average length of utterance and grammatical complexity.

Several explanations of this unexpected result have been put forward. Perhaps adults misinterpret the child's intended meaning when they expand. Erroneous expansions could hinder his learning. Several "wrong" expansions have been noted. For example:

Child: What time it is?
Adult: Uh huh, it tells what time it is.

Alternatively, a certain degree of novelty may be needed in order to capture a child's attention, since he may not listen to apparent repetitions of his own utterances. Or it may be that expansions overrestrict the data the child hears. His speech may be impoverished because of an insufficiently rich verbal environment. As we noted earlier, the child *needs* copious and varied samples of speech.

The last two explanations seem to be supported by a Russian experiment (Slobin 1966, p. 144). One group of infants was shown a doll, and three phrases were repeatedly uttered, "Here is a doll . . . Take the doll . . . Give me the doll." Another group of infants was shown the doll, but instead, *thirty* different phrases were uttered, such as "Rock the doll . . . Look for the doll." The total number of words heard by both groups was the same, only the composition differed. Then the experimenters showed the children a selection of toys, and asked them to pick out the dolls. To their surprise, the children in the second group, the ones who had heard a richer variety of speech, were considerably better at this task.

We may conclude then that parents who consciously try to "coach" their children by simplifying and repeating may be actually *interfering* with their progress. It does not pay to talk to children as if one was telling a foreign tourist how to get to the zoo. Language that is impoverished is harder to learn, not simpler. Children appear to be naturally "set" to extract a grammar for themselves, provided they have sufficient data at their disposal. Direct teaching is irrelevant, and those who get on best are those who are exposed to a rich variety of language—in other words, those whose parents talk to them in a normal way.

But what does "talk in a normal way" mean? Before we go on to discuss the role of practice, this is perhaps the best place to clear up a misunderstanding which seems to have originated with Chomsky. He claims that what children hear "consists to a large extent of utterances that break rules, since a good deal of normal speech consists of false starts, disconnected phrases and other deviations" (Chomsky 1967, p. 441). Certainly, children are likely to hear *some* deviant sentences. But recent research indicates that the speech children are exposed to is not particularly substandard. Adults tend to speak in shorter sentences and make fewer mistakes when they address children. There is a considerable difference between the way a mother talks to another adult, and the way she talks to her child. One researcher recorded a mother talking to an adult friend. Her sentences were an average fourteen to fifteen words long, and she used several polysyllabic medical terms:

> I was on a inhalation series routine. We wen' aroun' from ward to ward. People, are, y'know, that get all this mucus in their chest, and it's very important to breathe properly an' to be able to cough this mucus up and out an' through your chest, y'know as soon as possible. And we couldn't sterilize the instruments 'cause they were plastic.

But when she spoke to her child the same mother used five- or six-word sentences. The words were shorter, and referred to things the child could see or do:

> Come look at Momma's colorin' book.
> You wanna see my coloring book?

Look at my coloring book.
Lookit, that's an Indian, huh?
Is that an Indian?
Can you say Indian?
Talk to me.
[Drach, quoted in Ervin-Tripp 1971]

It seems that parents automatically simplify both the content and syntax when they talk to children. This is not particularly surprising—after all, we do not address bus conductors and boyfriends in the same way. The use of language appropriate to the circumstances is a normal part of a human's language ability. "Motherese," as it is sometimes called, consists of short, well-formed sentences spoken slowly and clearly. . . . Direct teaching, in the sense of correction and [expansion], does not accelerate the speed of learning and might even be a hindrance.

Let us now return to the question of practice. What is being claimed here is that practice alone cannot account for language acquisition. Children do not learn language simply by repetition and imitation. Two types of evidence support this view.

The first concerns the development of "inflections" or word endings. English has a number of very common verbs which have an "irregular" past tense form (e.g., *came, saw, went*) as opposed to the "regular" forms such as *loved, worked, played*. It also has a number of irregular plurals such as *feet* and *mice*, as well as the far more numerous plurals ending in -*s* such as *cats, giraffes*, and *pythons*. Quite early on, children learn correct past tense and plural forms for common words such as *came, saw*, and *feet*. Later, they abandon these correct forms and replace them with overgeneralized "regular" forms such as *comed, seed*, and *foots* (Ervin 1964). The significance of this apparent regression is immense. It means that language acquisition cannot possibly be a straightforward case of "practice makes perfect" or of simple imitation. If it were, children would never replace common forms such as *came* and *saw*, which they hear and use all the time, with odd forms such as *comed, seed*, and *foots* which they are unlikely to have come across.

The second type of practice which turns out to be unimportant for language acquisition is spontaneous imitation. Just as adults subconsciously imitate and expand their children's utterances, so children appear to imitate and "reduce" sentences uttered by their parents. If an adult says "I shall take an umbrella," a child is likely to say "Take rella." Or "Put the strap under her chin" is likely to be repeated and reduced to "Strap chin." At first sight, it looks as if this might be an important mechanism in the development of language. But Susan Ervin of the University of California at Berkeley came to the opposite conclusion when she recorded the spontaneous utterances of a small group of toddlers (Ervin 1964). To her surprise she found that when a child spontaneously imitates an adult, her imitations are not any more advanced than her normal speech. She shortens the adult utterance to fit in with her current average length of sentence and includes the same number of endings and "little" words as in her nonimitated utterances. Not a single child produced imitations which were more advanced. And one child, Holly, actually produced imitations that were less complex than her spontaneous sentences! Susan Ervin notes: "There is not a shred of evidence supporting a view that progress toward adult norms of grammar arises merely from practice in overt imitation of adult sentences" [Ervin 1964, p. 172].

We may conclude, then, that mere practice—in the sense of direct repetition and imitation—does not affect the acquisition of language in a significant way. However, we must be careful that such a statement does not lead to misunderstandings. What is being said is that practice alone cannot account for language acquisition: children do not learn merely by constant repetition of items. In another sense, they do need to "practice" talking but even this requirement is not as extensive as might be expected. They can learn a surprising amount by just listening. It has been shown that the amount of talking a child needs to do in order to learn language varies considerably. Some children seem to speak very little. Others are constantly chattering, and playing with words. One researcher wrote a whole book on the presleep monologues of her first child Anthony, who murmured paradigms to himself as he prepared for sleep:

> Go for glasses
> Go for them
> Go to the top
> Go throw
> Go for blouse
> Pants
> Go for shoes
>   [Weir 1962]

To her disappointment, her second child, David, was nowhere near as talkative although he eventually learned to speak just as well. These repetitious murmurs do not seem to be essential for all children.

So far, then, we have considered five of the six characteristics of biologically triggered behavior which we listed at the beginning of this chapter. All these features seem to be present in language. We now come to the sixth and final feature, "There is a regular sequence of 'milestones' as the behavior develops, and these can usually be correlated with age and other aspects of development." We shall deal with this in a section by itself.

The Preordained Program

All children seem to pass through a series of more or less fixed "stages" as they acquire language. The age at which different children reach each stage or "milestone" varies considerably, but the relative chronology remains the same. The milestones are normally reached in the same order, though they may be nearer together for some children and farther apart for others.

Language Stage	Beginning Age
Crying	birth
Cooing	6 weeks
Babbling	6 months
Intonation patterns	8 months
1-word utterances	1 year
2-word utterances	18 months
Word inflections	2 years
Questions, negatives	2¼ years
Rare or complex constructions	5 years
Mature speech	10 years

Consequently, we can divide language development up into a number of approximate phases. The [accompanying table] is highly oversimplified. The stages overlap, and the ages given are only a very rough guide—but it does give some idea of a child's likely progress.

In order to illustrate this progression we shall describe the successive phases which a typical (and nonexistent) English child is likely to go through as she learns to speak. Let us call this child *Barbara*—a name derived from the Greek word for "foreigner" and meaning literally "someone who says bar-bar, who talks gibberish."

Barbara's first recognizable vocal activity was *crying*. During the first four weeks of her life, she was truly:

> An infant crying in the night:
> An infant crying for the light:
> And with no language but a cry.
> [Tennyson]

A number of different types of cry could be detected. She cried with hunger when she wanted to be fed. She cried with pain when she had a tummyache, and she cried with pleasure when she was fed, comfortable, and lying in her mother's arms. However, strictly speaking, it is perhaps inaccurate to speak of crying as a "language phase," because crying seems to be instinctive communication and may be more like an animal call system than a true language. This seems to be confirmed by some research which suggests that the different "messages" contained in the crying of babies may be universal, since English parents could identify the "messages" of a foreign baby as easily as those of English babies (Ricks 1975). So although crying may help to strengthen the lungs and vocal cords (both of which are needed for speech), crying itself perhaps should not be regarded as part of true language development.

Barbara then passed through two reasonably distinct prelanguage phases, a *cooing* phase and a *babbling* phase. Early researchers confused these stages and sometimes likened them to bird song. . . .

The first of these two phases, *cooing*, began when Barbara was approximately six weeks old. To a casual observer, she sounded as if she was saying, "goo goo." But cooing is difficult to describe. Some textbooks call it "gurgling" or "mewing." The sound is superficially vowel-like, but the tracings produced on a sound spectogram show that it is quite unlike the vowels produced by adults. Cooing seems to be universal. It may be the vocal equivalent of arm and leg waving. That is, just as babies automatically strengthen their muscles by kicking their legs and moving their arms about, so cooing may help them to gain control over their vocal apparatus.

Gradually, consonant-type sounds become interspersed in the cooing. By around six months, Barbara had reached the *babbling* stage. She gave the impression of uttering consonants and vowels together, at first as single syllables—but later strung together. The consonants were often made with the lips, or the teeth, so that the sequences sounded like *mama, dididi,* or *papapa.* On hearing these sounds, Barbara's parents confidently but wrongly assumed that she was addressing them. Such wishful thinking accounts for the fact that *mama, papa,* and *dada* are found as nursery words for mother and father all over the world (Jakobson 1962). Barbara soon learned that a cry of *mama* meant immediate attention—though she often used it to mean, "I am hungry" rather than to refer to a parent. This phenomenon has been noted by numerous researchers. . . .

Throughout the babbling period Barbara seemed to enjoy experimenting with her mouth and tongue. She not only babbled, she blew bubbles, gurgled and spluttered. Superficially, she appeared to be uttering an enormous variety of exotic sounds. At one time, researchers wrongly assumed that children are naturally capable of producing every possible speech sound. . . . More recent investigators have noted that the variety of sounds used in babbling is not particularly great. But because the child does not yet have complete control over his vocal organs, the noises are often unlike adult sounds, and seem exotic to an untrained observer. In general, babbling seems to be a period when a child experiments and gradually gains muscular control over his vocal organs. Many people claim that babbling is universal. But there are a few puzzling records of children who did not babble, which provide problems for this point of view. All we can say at the moment is that babbling is sufficiently widespread to be regarded as a normal stage of development.

Some investigators have tried to compare babbling babies who have been exposed to different languages. It has been reported that Chinese babbles are distinguishable from American, Russian, and Arabic ones (Weir 1966). Because Chinese is a language which distinguishes words by means of a change in "tone" or "pitch," Chinese babies tend to produce monosyllabic utterances with much tonal variation. American babies produce polysyllabic babbles with intonation spread over the whole sequence. The nontone babies sound superficially similar—though American mothers could often pick out the American baby, Russians the Russian baby, and Arabs the Arab baby. But the mothers could not distinguish between the babies babbling the other two languages. This research supports the notion of a "babbling drift," in which a child's babbling gradually moves in the direction of the sounds he hears around him. In this respect babbling is clearly distinct from crying, which has no discernible relationship with any one language.

A question which perhaps should be asked at this stage is the following: how much can children actually distinguish of their parents' speech? It is sometimes assumed that babies hear merely a general mish-mash of sound, and only gradually notice the difference between say p and b. However, recent research indicates that infants are capable of discriminating a lot more than we realize. Eimas and his colleagues (1971), for example, have shown that babies between one and four months old *can* distinguish between p and b. They started by playing a repeated b sound to selected infants. They they switched to p. A clear change in the babies' sucking behavior showed that they had noticed the alteration. So even though infants may not listen carefully to everything their parents say, they may well be capable of hearing a considerable amount from a very young age. Somewhat surprisingly, these results of Eimas have been replicated with rhesus and chinchilla monkeys (Morse 1976; Kuhl and Miller 1974, 1975), and so may be due to the hearing mechanisms in certain types of mammals, and not just humans alone. In brief, a child's perception may be much sharper than had previously been supposed, even though it may not be equivalent to an adult's for some time (Fourcin 1978).

Simultaneously with babbling, and from around eight or nine months, Barbara began to imitate *intonation patterns*. These made her output sound so like speech that her mother sometimes said, "I'm sure she's talking, I just can't catch what she's saying. . . ." English mothers have noted that their children often use a "question" intonation, with a rise in tone at the end of the sentence. This may be due to a normal parent's tendency to bend over the child, asking, "What are you trying to say then?" "Do you want some milk?" "Do you know who this is?" and so on.

Somewhere between one year and eighteen months Barbara began to utter *single words*. She continued to babble as well, though her babbling gradually diminished as true language developed. The number of single words acquired at around this time varies from child to child. Some have only four or five, others have around fifty. As an average child Barbara acquired about fifteen. Many of them were names of people and things, such as *uf* (woof) "dog," *daba* "grandma," *da* "doll." Then as she neared her second birthday, she reached the more impressive *two-word stage*.

From the time Barbara started to put words together she seemed to be in a state of "language readiness," and mopped up language like a sponge. The most noticeable feature of this process was a dramatic increase in her vocabulary. By the time she was 2½-years-old, she knew several hundred words. Meanwhile, there was a gradual but steady increase in her average or mean length of utterance—usually abbreviated to MLU. MLU is calculated in terms of grammatical items or "morphemes": plural -*s* and past tense -*d*, for example, each count as one item and so do ordinary words such as *mummy* and *bath*. Compound words such as *birthday* and *quack-quack* also count as a single item (Brown 1973, p. 54). Many (but not all) researchers accept this as a useful gauge of progress—though the child with the longest utterances does not necessarily have the most grammatically advanced, or even the most grammatically correct utterances (Garman 1979).

The fact that a steady increase in MLU occurs from the age of around 2 onwards has been shown by Roger Brown of Harvard University, who carried out a detailed study of the speech development of three unacquainted children, Adam, Eve, and Sarah—though he found that the chronological age at which different children reached an MLU stage differed considerably (Brown, Cazden, and Bellugi 1968; Brown 1973). A comparison of Adam and Eve showed that Eve outstripped Adam by far. Eve's MLU was two items at around twenty months, three at twenty-two months, and four at twenty-eight months. Adam was over twenty-six months old before he achieved an MLU of two items. He was nearly 3 years old before his MLU reached three items and 3½ before it reached four items—a whole year behind Eve. [See the accompanying figure.]

If we assume that Barbara is not as advanced as Eve, but ahead of Adam, she possibly had an MLU of two items a little before her second birthday, an MLU of three items at 2½, and four items around her third birthday.

In the early part of the two-word stage, when she was around 2 years old, Barbara's speech was "telegraphic." She sounded as if she

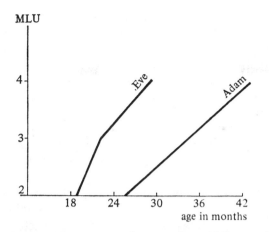

was sending urgent telegrams to her mother: "Want milk," "Where duck?" As in a real telegram, she tended to preserve the nouns and verbs in the correct order, but omitted the "little" words such as *the, a, has, his, and.* She also left out word endings, such as the plural *-s* or past tense *-d,* as in *two shoe* and *milk spill.*

Then, gradually, the "little" words and *inflections* were added. "All these, like an intricate work of ivy, began to grow up between and upon the major construction blocks, the nouns and verbs" (Brown 1973, p. 249).

In this aspect of language, Barbara is following the same path of development as the Harvard child Adam, but at a slightly earlier age (Brown 1973, p. 271). Between the ages of 2 and 3½, Barbara acquired the following grammatical forms:

Age 2

Progressive *-ing*	I singing
Plural *-s*	Blue shoes
Copula *am, is, are*	He is asleep
Articles *a, the*	He is a doctor

Age 3

3rd person singular *-s*	He wants an apple
Past tense *-d*	I helped Mummy
Full progressive *am, is, are* + *-ing*	I am singing
Shortened copula	He's a doctor
Shortened progressive	I'm singing

Note that it is important to distinguish between the *emergence,* or first appearance of an ending, and its *acquisition,* its reliable use in the places where an adult would expect to find it. An ending can be considered acquired if it occurs in at least 90 percent of the contexts where it is needed (Brown 1973, p. 258).

The actual age at which Barbara acquired each form is not significant because it varies widely from child to child. What is important and interesting is the *order* of acquisition. The sequence seems surprisingly similar among English-speaking children. Roger Brown notes that in the unacquainted Harvard children, the developmental order of these grammatical forms was "amazingly consistent." There were one or two minor variations: Sarah, for example, acquired the progressive *-ing* after the plural, whereas Adam and Eve acquired it before. But in all the children, both the progressive *-ing* and the plural *-s* occurred before the past tense, the third person singular *-s*, and the copula *am, is, are*.

Perhaps even more surprising, is the fact that in all the Harvard children the copula *am, is, are* as in *I am a doctor* developed before *am, is, are* when it was part of the progressive construction, for example, *I am singing*. And the shortened copula as in *He's a bear* came before the shortened progressive, for example *He's walking*. This is really quite an astonishing discovery. Although we might expect children to go through similar general lines of development, there seems to be no obvious reason why a variety of English children should correspond so closely in their acquisition of specific items.

A similar consistency of order is found in the acquisition of more complicated constructions, such as *questions* and *negatives*. For example, in the acquisition of *wh-* questions (questions beginning with *what, why, where, who*, etc), we can safely assume that Barbara, like Adam, Eve, and Sarah, went through three intermediate stages before she acquired them perfectly (Klima and Bellugi 1966). First of all, soon after her second birthday, she placed the *wh-* word in front of the rest of the sentence:

What	Mummy doing?
Why	you singing?
Where	Daddy go?

A second stage occurred three or four months later when she added an auxiliary verb such as *can* or *will* to the main verb:

Where	you	will go?
Why	kitty	can't see?
Why	you	don't know?

Finally, before she was 3, she realized that the subject noun must change places with the auxiliary and produced correct sentences such as:

Where	will you	go?
Why	can't kitty	see?
Why	don't you	know?

Once again [we have] the rather surprising finding that all English children tend to follow the same pattern. . . . As already noted, the actual *age* at which each stage is reached is irrelevant. It is the order which matters.

By the age of 3½, Barbara, like most children, was able to form most grammatical constructions—and her speech was reasonably intelligible to strangers. Her constructions were, however, less varied than those of an adult. For example, she tended not to use the "full" passive such as *The man was hit by a bus.* But she was able to converse quite adequately on most topics.

By 5, she gave the superficial impression of having acquired language more or less perfectly. But this was an illusion. Language acquisition was still continuing, though more slowly. The grammar of a child of 5 differs to a perhaps surprising degree from adult grammar. But the 5-year-old is not usually aware of his shortcomings. In comprehension tests, children readily assign interpretations to the structures presented to them—but they are often the wrong ones. "They do not, as they see it, fail to understand our sentences. They understand them, but they understand them wrongly" (Carol Chomsky 1969, p. 2). To demonstrate this point, the researcher (Chomsky's wife) showed a group of 5- to 8-year-olds a blindfolded doll, and said: "Is this doll hard to see or easy to see?" All the 5- and 6-year-olds said *hard to see,* and so did some of the 7- and 8-year-olds. The response of 6-year-old Lisa was typical:

> Chomsky: Is this doll easy to see or hard to see?
> Lisa: Hard to see.
> Chomsky: Will you make her easy to see?
> Lisa: If I can get this untied.
> Chomsky: Will you explain why she was hard to see?
> Lisa: (to doll): Because you had a blindfold over your eyes.

Some psychologists have criticized this particular test. A child sometimes believes, ostrich-fashion, that if his own eyes are covered, others will not be able to see him. And he may be partly switching to the doll's viewpoint when he says a blindfolded doll is hard to see. But a rerun of this experiment using wolf and duck puppets, and sentences such as:

> *The wolf is hard to bite.*
> *The duck is anxious to bite.*

confirmed the original results (Cromer 1970). Children of 5 and 6 just do not realize that pairs of sentences such as *The rabbit is nice to eat* and *The rabbit is eager to eat* have completely different underlying meanings.

In fact, the gap between child and adult speech lasts longer than was once realized. More recently, detailed experiments on French children's understanding and use of the articles *le/la* "the" and *un/une* "a" have shown quite surprising differences between child and adult usage, which remained in some cases up till the age of 12 (Karmiloff-Smith 1979).

But the discrepancies between Barbara's speech and that of the adults around her gradually disappeared over the next few years. By the age of about 11, Barbara exhibited a command of the structure of her language comparable to that of an adult. At the age of puberty, her language development was essentially complete. She would continue to add individual vocabulary items all her life, but her grammatical rules were unlikely to change except in trivial respects. The "critical period" set by nature for the acquisition of language was over.

Note, incidentally, that language milestones tend to run parallel with physical development. Clearly, there is no essential correlation between language and motor development, since there are numerous examples of children who learn to talk, but never walk, and vice versa. However, rsearchers are agreed that in normal children the two often go together. Language milestones are often loosely linked to physical milestones. For example, the gradual change of cooing to babbling occurs around the time an infant begins to sit up. A child utters single words just before he starts to walk. Grammar becomes complex as hand and finger coordination develops.

Let us now summarize our conclusions. . . . [We] have shown that language seems to have all the characteristics of biologically programmed behavior. It emerges before it is necessary, and its emergence cannot be accounted for either by an external event, or by a sudden decision taken by the child. There seems to be a "critical period" set aside by nature for its acquisition, and direct teaching and intensive practice have relatively little effect. Language acquisition follows a regular sequence of milestones in its development, which can be loosely correlated with other aspects of the child's development. In other words, there is an internal mechanism both to trigger it off and to regulate it.

However, it would be wrong to think of language as something which is governed *only* by internal mechanisms. These mechanisms require external stimulation in order to work properly. The child needs a rich verbal environment during the critical acquisition period.

This suggests that the so-called nature-nurture controversy . . . may be misconceived. Both sides are right: nature triggers off the behavior, and lays down the framework, but careful nurture is needed for it to reach its full potential. The dividing line between "natural" and "nurtured" behavior is by no means as clear-cut as was once thought. In other words, language is "natural" behavior—but it still has to be carefully "nurtured" in order to reach its full potential. . . .

Bibliography

Bernstein, B. (1972), "Social class, language, and socialisation," in P. P. Giglioli (ed.), *Language and Social Context*, Harmondsworth: Penguin.

Braine, M. D. S. (1971), "The acquisition of language in infant and child," in C. E. Reed (ed.), *The Learning of Language*, New York: Appleton-Century-Crofts.

Brown, R. (1958), *Words and Things*, New York: The Free Press.

———. (1973), *A First Language*. London: Allen & Unwin.

Brown, R., and Bellugi, U. (1964), "Three processes in the child's acquisition of syntax," in E. H. Lenneberg (ed.) (1964), *New Directions in the Study of Language*, Cambridge, Mass.: MIT Press. Also in R. Brown (ed.), *Psycholinguistics: Selected Papers*, New York: The Free Press.

Brown, R., Cazden, C., and Bellugi, U. (1968). "The child's grammar from I to III," in J. P. Hill (ed.), *Minnesota Symposium on Child Psychology*, vol. II, Minneapolis: University of Minnesota Press.

Cazden, C. (1972), *Child Language and Education*, New York: Holt, Rinehart and Winston.

Chomsky, C. (1969), *The Acquisition of Syntax in Children from 5 to 10*, Cambridge, Mass: MIT Press.

Chomsky, N. (1967), "The formal nature of language," in E. H. Lenneberg, *Biological Foundations of Language*, New York: Wiley.

Curtiss, S. (1977), *Genie: A Psycholinguistic Study of a Modern-Day "Wild Child,"* New York: Academic Press.

Curtiss, S., Fromkin, V., Krashen, S., Rigler, D., and Rigler, M. (1974), "The linguistic development of Genie," *Language*, 50, pp. 528–554.

Eimas, P., Siqueland, E., Jusczyk, P., and Vigorito, J. (1971), "Speech perception in infants," *Science* 171, pp. 303–306.

Ervin, S. M (1964), "Imitation and structural change in children's language," in E. H. Lenneberg (ed.) (1964), *New Directions in the Study of Language*, Cambridge, Mass.: MIT Press.

Ervin-Tripp, S. (1971), "An overview of theories of grammatical development," in D. I. Slobin (ed.), *The Ontogenesis of Grammar*, New York: Academic Press.

Fourcin, A. J. (1978), "Acoustic patterns and speech acquisition," in N. Waterson and C. Snow (eds.), *The Development of Communication*, Chichester: John Wiley & Sons.

Garman, M. (1979), "Early grammatical development," in P. Fletcher and M. Garman (eds.), *Language Acquisition*, Cambridge: Cambridge University Press.

Jakobson, R. (1962), "Why 'Mama' and 'Papa'?" in A. Bar-Adon and W. F. Leopold (eds.) (1971), *Child Language: A Book of Readings*, Englewood Cliffs, N.J.: Prentice-Hall.

Karmiloff-Smith, A. (1979), *A Functional Approach to Child Language: A Study of Determiners and Reference*, Cambridge: Cambridge University Press.

Klima, E., and Bellugi, U. (1966), "Syntactic regularities in the speech of children," in J. Lyons and R. J. Wales (eds.), *Psycholinguistics Papers*, Edinburgh: Edinburgh University Press. Revised version in A. Bar-Adon and W. F. Leopold (eds.) (1971), *Child Language: A Book of Readings*, Englewood Cliffs, N.J.: Prentice-Hall.

Kuhl, P., and Miller, J. D. (1974), "Discrimination of speech sounds by the chinchilla: /t/ vs /d/ in CV syllables," *Journal of the Acoustical Society of America* 57, series 41 (abstract).

———. (1975). "Speech perception by the chinchilla: phonetic boundaries for synthetic VOT stimuli," *Journal of the Acoustical Society of America* 57, series 49 (abstract).

Lenneberg, E. H. (1967), *The Biological Foundations of Language*, New York: Wiley.

Morse, P. A. (1976), "Speech perception in the human infant and rhesus monkey," in S. Harnad, H. Steklis, and J. Lancaster (eds.), *Origins and Evolution of Language and Speech, Annals of the New York Academy of Sciences*, vol. 280.

Nelson, K. (1973), "Structure and strategy in learning to talk," *Monograph of the Society for Research in Child Development* 38, pp. 1–2.

Ricks, D. M. (1975), "Vocal communication in pre-verbal normal and autistic children," in N. O'Connor (ed.), *Language, Cognitive Deficits, and Retardation*, London: Butterworth.

Slobin, D. I. (1966), "The acquisition of Russian as a native language," in F. Smith and G. A. Miller (eds.), (1966), *The Genesis of Language*, Cambridge, Mass.: MIT Press.

Thorpe, W. H. (1972), "Vocal communication in birds," in R. A. Hinde (ed.), *Non-Verbal Communication*, Cambridge: Cambridge University Press.

Weir, R. H. (1962), *Language in the Crib*, The Hague: Mouton.

———. (1966), "Some questions on the child's learning of phonology," in F. Smith and G. A. Miller (1966), *The Genesis of Language*, Cambridge, Mass.: MIT Press.

FOR DISCUSSION AND REVIEW

1. What does Aitchison mean by "a biological time-clock"? Give four examples of its effects in animals that are not mentioned by Aitchison.

2. Aitchison discusses six features of biologically scheduled behavior in addition to its one predominant characteristic. Consider each of these seven in turn. To what extent is each actually a characteristic of human language? Are there any qualifications or caveats that need to be added? What are they?

3. Discuss the importance of the interaction of a child's environment and his or her biological predisposition for language acquisition. What conclusions, if any, can you draw concerning the function of day care centers, nursery schools, and kindergartens?

4. Explain the term "critical period." Summarize the arguments for both a biologically controlled starting point and a similarly controlled finishing point for language acquisition.

5. Reread the two examples of parent-child dialogue and the paragraph that follows them. How do the dialogues support the concept of language acquisition as biologically determined behavior? Consider outright correction, attempts to force imitation, and adult expansions of children's utterances.

6. Compare and contrast Aitchison's description of the way that parents talk to young children with Moskowitz's description of "caretaker speech." What similarities do you find? What differences?

7. What is the significance, in terms of theories of language acquisition, of the fact that children learn and use correct plural forms of some irregular nouns and correct past tense forms of some irregular verbs, but subsequently "regress"—i.e., cease using the correct irregular forms, replacing, for example, *went* with *goed* or *feet* with *foots*?

8. Explain the apparent paradox that practice is in one sense unimportant for language acquisition, but that in another sense children need to practice.

9. Moskowitz, de Villiers and de Villiers, and Aitchison all discuss the stages of normal language acquisition, although they do so in different ways. (For example, Moskowitz deals in generalizations, whereas Aitchison discusses specific children, both real and imaginary, and de Villiers and de Villiers focus on one aspect of language acquisition.) Compare and contrast the three discussions, looking especially for similarities and differences. Summarize your conclusions in a chart or table.

10. Review Lenneberg's "Developmental Milestones in Motor and Language Development" in light of Aitchison's discussion and examples of the fact that "Language milestones are often closely linked to physical milestones." Are her examples persuasive? What about the linkage between cognitive development and language milestones?

5/The Development of Language in Genie: A Case of Language Acquisition Beyond the "Critical Period"

VICTORIA FROMKIN, STEPHEN KRASHEN,
SUSAN CURTISS, DAVID RIGLER, AND
MARILYN RIGLER

Genie's story is tragic, involving, as it does, the irretrievable loss of human potential. For most of the first fourteen years of her life, Genie was isolated in a small, dark room, where she suffered extreme physical and emotional neglect. Out of this tragedy, linguists, psychologists, neurologists, and others have learned a great deal from careful study of Genie's development beginning almost immediately after she was discovered in 1970 and continuing until 1979. During this time, she was evaluated regularly, and as a result, our understanding of many aspects of language acquisition, cognitive development, the critical age theory, and brain lateralization and function has advanced enormously.

In this selection, adapted from Fromkin et al., first published in 1974, the development of Genie's linguistic abilities is examined in detail. As you read, keep in mind the normal stages of language acquisition described in earlier selections in Part Two. When the following article first appeared, the authors were guardedly optimistic about the possibility of Genie's further linguistic development. Unfortunately, by 1979 it had become clear that her progress in language

Notes: The research reported on in this paper was supported in part by a grant from the National Institutes of Mental Health, U.S. Department of Health, Education and Welfare, No. MH-21191-03.

This is a combined and expanded version of a number of papers presented before the American Psychological Association, the Linguistic Society of America, the Acoustical Society of America, and the American Speech and Hearing Association, including S. Curtiss (1972); Curtiss et al. (1972, 1973); Krashen et al. (1972a, 1972b); Fromkin (1972); D. Rigler (1972).

112

development had slowed dramatically and that a 1974 prediction of permanent dysphasia had been correct. However, Genie continued to be far more advanced cognitively than linguistically, and she could communicate effectively using a variety of nonverbal techniques, including her own drawings. In 1977, Susan Curtiss published a study, Genie: A Psycholinguistic Study of a Modern-Day "Wild Child" *(New York: Academic Press), which presented background material on Genie's personality, especially her interactions with Curtiss, and detailed her linguistic development and the ways in which she was evaluated.*

According to Maya Pines, "within a few months of [Genie's] arrival at Children's Hospital [in 1970] she began going to nursery classes for normal children. She soon transferred to a special elementary school for handicapped children. Next, she spent several years in a city high school for the mentally retarded. Outside school, a speech therapist worked with her consistently for many years" (Psychology Today, *September 1981, p. 31). The postscript to this article by Pines describes how and why the work with Genie ended.*

Genie, the subject of this study, is an adolescent girl who for most of her life underwent a degree of social isolation and experiential deprivation not previously reported in contemporary scientific history. It is a unique case because the other children reported on in contemporary literature were isolated for much shorter periods and emerged from their isolation at much younger ages than did Genie. The only studies of children isolated for periods of time somewhat comparable to that of this case are those of Victor (Itard, 1962) and Kaspar Hauser (Singh and Zingg, 1966).

All cases of such children reveal that experiential deprivation results in a retarded state of development. An important question for scientists of many disciplines is whether a child so deprived can "catch up" wholly or in part. The answer to this question depends on many factors including the developmental state achieved prior to deprivation, the duration, quality, and intensity of the deprivation, and the early biological adequacy of the isolated child. In addition, the ability of such "recuperation" is closely tied to whether there is a "critical period" beyond which learning cannot take place. The concept of a "critical period" during which certain innately determined faculties can develop derived from experimental embryology. It is hypothesized that should the necessary internal or external conditions be absent during this period, certain developmental abilities will be impossible.

Lenneberg (1967) presents the most specific statement about critical periods in man as it concerns the acquisition of language. He starts with the assumption that language is innately determined, that its acquisition is dependent upon both necessary neurological events and some unspecified minimal exposure to language. He suggests that this critical period lasts from about age two to puberty: language acquisition is impossible before two due to maturational factors, and after puberty because of the loss of "cerebral plasticity" caused by the completion of the development of cerebral dominance, or lateralized specialization of the language function.

The case of Genie is directly related to this question, since Genie was already pubescent at the time of her discovery, and it is to this question that the discussion is primarily directed. The case also has relevance for other linguistic questions such as those concerning distinctions between the comprehension and production of language, between linguistic competence and performance, and between cognition and language.

There are many questions for which we still have no answers. Some we may never have. Other must await the future developments of this remarkable child. The case history as presented is therefore an interim report.

Case History

Genie was first encountered when she was thirteen years, nine months. At the time of her discovery and hospitalization she was an unsocialized, primitive human being, emotionally disturbed, unlearned, and without language. She had been taken into protective custody by the police and, on November 4, 1970, was admitted into the Children's Hospital of Los Angeles for evaluation with a tentative diagnosis of severe malnutrition. She remained in the Rehabilitation Center of the hospital until August 13, 1971. At that time she entered a foster home, where she has been living ever since as a member of the family.

When admitted to the hospital, Genie was a painfully thin child with a distended abdomen who appeared to be six or seven years younger than her age. She was 54.5 inches tall and weighed 62.25 pounds. She was unable to stand erect, could not chew solid or even semisolid foods, had great difficulty in swallowing, was incontinent of feces and urine, and was mute.

The tragic and bizarre story which was uncovered revealed that for most of her life Genie suffered physical and social restriction, nutritional neglect, and extreme experiential deprivation. There is evidence that from about the age of twenty months until shortly before admission to the hospital Genie had been isolated in a small closed room, tied into a potty chair where she remained most or all hours of the day, sometimes overnight. A cloth harness, constructed to keep her from handling her feces, was her only apparel of wear. When not strapped into the chair she was kept in a covered infant crib, also confined from the waist down. The door to the room was kept closed, and the windows were curtained. She was hurriedly fed (only cereal and baby food) and minimally cared for by her mother, who was almost blind during most of the years of Genie's isolation. There was no radio or TV in the house and the father's intolerance of noise of any kind kept any acoustic stimuli which she received behind the closed door to a minimum. (The first child born to this family died from pneumonia when three months old after being put in the garage because of noisy crying.) Genie was physically punished by the father if she made any sounds. According to the mother, the father and older brother never spoke to Genie although they barked at her like dogs. The mother was forbidden to spend more than a few minutes with Genie during feeding.

It is not the purpose of this paper to attempt to explain the psychotic behavior of the parents which created this tragic life for Genie, nor to relate the circumstances which led to the discovery. (See Hansen, 1972; D. Rigler, 1972). It is reported that Genie's father regarded her as a hopelessly retarded child who was destined to die at a young age and convinced the mother of this. His prediction was based at least in part on Genie's failure to walk at a normal age. Genie was born with a congenital dislocation of the hips which was treated in the first year by the application of a Frejka pillow splint to hold both legs in abduction, and the father placed the blame for her "retardation" on this device.

On the basis of what is known about the early history, and what has been observed so far, it appears that Genie was normal at the time of birth and that the retardation observed at the time of discovery was due principally to the extreme isolation to which she was subjected, with its accompanying social, perceptual, and sensory deprivation. Very little evidence exists to support a diagnosis of early brain damage, primary mental deficiency, or infantile autism. On the other hand, there is abundant evidence of gross environmental impoverishment and of psychopathological behavior on the part of the parents. This is revealed to some extent in Genie's history and equally by the dramatic changes that have occurred since her emergence. (See D. Rigler, 1972; M. Rigler, 1972.)

Genie's birth was relatively normal. She was born in April, 1957, delivered by Caesarian section. Her birth problems included an Rh negative incompatibility for which she was exchange transfused (no sequelae were noted), and the hip dislocation spoken of above. Genie's development was otherwise initially normal. At birth she weighed 7 pounds, 7.5 ounces. By three months she had gained 4.5 pounds. According to the pediatrician's report, at six months she was doing well and taking food well. At eleven months she was still within normal limits. At fourteen months Genie developed an acute illness and was seen by another pediatrician. The only other medical visit occurred when Genie was just over 3.5 years of age.

From the meager medical records at our disposal, then, there is no indication of early retardation. After admission to the hospital, Genie underwent a number of medical diagnostic tests. Radiology reported a "moderate coxa valga deformity of both hips and a narrow rib cage" but no abnormality of the skull. The bone age was reported as approximately eleven years. Simple metabolic disorders were ruled out. The neurologist found no evidence of neurological disease. The electroencephalographic records reported a "normal waking record." A chromosomal analysis was summarized as being "apparently normal."

During the first few months of her hospitalization additional consultations were undertaken. The conclusion from among all of these evaluative efforts may be summarized briefly. Functionally Genie was an extremely retarded child, but her behavior was unlike that of other mentally defective children. Neither, apparently, was she autistic. Although emotionally disturbed behavior was evident there was no discernible evidence of physical or mental disease that would otherwise account for her retarded behavior. It therefore seems plausible to explain her retardation as due to the intensity and duration of her psychosocial and physical deprivation.

The dramatic changes that have occurred since Genie's emergence reinforce this conclusion. Approximately four weeks after her admission to the hospital a consultant described a contrast between her admission status and what he later observed (Shurley, personal communication). He wrote that on admission Genie

> . . . was pale, thin, ghost-like, apathetic, mute, and socially unresponsive. But now she had become alert, bright-eyed, engaged readily in simple social play with balloons, flashlight, and toys, with familiar and unfamiliar adults. . . . She exhibits a lively curiosity, good eye-hand coordination, adequate hearing and vision, and emotional responsivity. . . . She reveals much stimulus hunger. . . . Despite her muteness . . . Genie does not otherwise use autistic defenses, but has ample latent affect and responses. There is no obvious evidence of cerebral damage or intellectual stenosis— only severe (extreme) and prolonged experiential, social, and sensory isolation and deprivation during her infancy and childhood . . . Genie may be regarded as one of the most extreme and prolonged cases of such deprivation to come to light in this century, and as such she is an "experiment in nature."

Genie's Linguistic Development

Important elements in Genie's history are still unknown and may never be known. We have no reliable information about early linguistic developments or even the extent of language input. One version has it that Genie began to speak words prior to her isolation and then ceased. Another is that she simply never acquired language at all beyond the level observed on hospital entry. One thing is definite: when Genie was discovered she did not speak. On the day after admission to the hospital she was seen by Dr. James Kent who reports (Kent, 1972):

> Throughout this period she retained saliva and frequently spit it out into a paper towel or into her pajama top. *She made no other sounds except for a kind of throaty whimper*. . . . (Later in the session) . . . she imitated "back" several times, as well as "fall" when I said "The puppet will fall." . . . She could communicate (her) needs nonverbally, at least to a limited extent. . . . Apart from a peculiar laugh, frustration was the only other clear affective behavior we could discern. . . . When very angry she would scratch at her own face, blow her nose violently into her clothes and often void urine. During these tantrums *there was no vocalization*. . . . We felt that the eerie silence that accompanied these reactions was probably due to the fact that she had been whipped by her father when she made noise.

At the outset of our linguistic observations, it was not clear whether Genie's inability to talk was the result solely of physiological and/or emotional factors. We were unable to determine the extent of her language comprehension during the early periods. Within a few days she began to respond to the speech of others and also to imitate single words. Her responses did not however reveal how heavily she was dependent on nonverbal, extralinguistic cues such as "tone of voice, gestures, hints, guidance, facial and bodily expressions" (Belugi and Klima, 1971). To determine the extent of her language comprehension it was necessary to devise tests in which all extralinguistic cues were eliminated.[1] If the comprehension tests administered showed that Genie did comprehend what was said to her, using linguistic information alone, we could assume that she had some knowledge of English, or had acquired some linguistic "competence." In that case, the task facing Genie would not be one of language learning but of learning how to use that knowledge—adding a performance modality—to produce speech. If the tests, on the other hand, in addition to her inability to speak, showed that she had little ability to understand what was said to her when all extralinguistic cues were eliminated, she would be faced with true first-language acquisition.

---

[1] The tests were designed, administered, and analyzed by S. Curtiss.

Linguistic Comprehension

The administration of the comprehension tests which we constructed had to wait until Genie was willing and able to cooperate. It was necessary to develop tests which would not require verbal responses since it was her comprehension not her active production of speech to be tested at this stage. The first controlled test was administered in September, 1971, almost eleven months after Genie's emergence. Prior to these tests Genie revealed a growing ability to understand and produce individual words and names. This ability was a necessary precursor to an investigation of her comprehension of grammatical structure, but did not in itself reveal how much language she knew since the ability to relate the sounds and meanings of individual lexical items, while necessary, is not a sufficient criterion for language competence.

It was quite evident that at the beginning of the testing period Genie could understand individual words which she did not utter herself, but, except for such words, she had little if any comprehension of grammatical structures. Genie was thus faced with the complex task of primary language acquisition with a postpubescent brain. There was no way that a prediction could be made as to whether she could or would accomplish this task. Furthermore, if she did not learn language it would be impossible to determine the reasons. One cannot draw conclusions about children of this kind who fail to develop. One can, however, draw at least some conclusions from the fact that Genie has been acquiring language at this late age. The evidence for this fact is revealed in the results of the seventeen different comprehension tests which have been administered almost weekly over the last two years. A slow but steady development is taking place. We are still, of course, unable to predict how much of the adult grammar she will acquire.

Among the grammatical structures that Genie now comprehends are singular-plural contrasts of nouns, negative-affirmative sentence distinctions, possessive constructions, modifications, a number of prepositions (including *under, next to, beside, over*, and probably *on* and *in*), conjunction with *and*, and the comparative and superlative forms of adjectives. (For further details on the comprehension tests, see Curtiss et al., 1973.)

The comprehension tests which are now regularly administered were designed by Susan Curtiss who has been most directly involved in the research of Genie's linguistic development. (New tests are constantly being added.) The nouns, verbs, and adjectives used in all of the tests are used by Genie in her own utterances (see below for discussion on Genie's spontaneous speech production). The response required was primarily a "pointing" response. Genie was familiar with this gesture prior to the onset of testing. One example can illustrate the kinds of tests and the procedures used.

To test Genie's singular/plural distinction in nouns, pairs of pictures are used—a single object on one picture, three of the identical objects on the other. The test sentences differ only by absence or presence of plural markers on the nouns. Genie is asked to point to the appropriate picture. The words used are: balloon(s), pail(s), turtle(s), nose(s), horse(s), dish(es), pot(s), boat(s). Until July, 1972, the responses were no better than chance. Since July, 1972, Genie gives 100 percent correct responses. It is important to note that at the time when she was not responding correctly to the linguistically marked distinction, she could appropriately use and understand utterances including numbers ("one," "two," "three," etc.) and "many," "more," and "lots of."

Speech Production and Phonological Development

Genie's ability to comprehend spoken language is a better indication of her linguistic competence than is her production of speech because of the physical difficulties Genie has in speaking. At the age when normal children are learning the necessary neuromuscular controls over their vocal organs to enable them to produce the sounds of language, Genie was learning to repress any and all sounds because of the physical punishment which accompanied any sounds produced. This can explain why her earliest imitative and spontaneous utterances were often produced as silent articulations or whispered. Her inability to control the laryngeal mechanisms involved in speech resulted in monotonic speech. Her whole body tensed as she struggled to speak, revealing the difficulties she had in the control of air volume and air flow. The intensity of the acoustic signal produced was very low. The strange voice quality of her vocalized utterances is at least partially explainable in reference to these problems.

Because of her speech difficulties, one cannot assess her language competence by her productive utterances alone. But despite the problems which still remain, there has been dramatic improvement in Genie's speech production. Her supraglottal articulations have been more or less normal, and her phonological development does not deviate sharply from that observed in normal children. In addition, she is beginning, both in imitations and in spontaneous utterances, to show some intonation and her speech is now being produced with greater intensity.

Like normal children, Genie's first one-word utterances consisted of Consonant-Vowel (CV) monosyllables. These soon expanded into a more complex syllable structure which can be diagrammed as (C) (L/G) V (C), where L stands for liquid, G, glide, and the parenthesized elements optional.

Words of two and three syllables entered into her productive vocabulary and in these words stress was correctly marked by intensity and/or duration of the vowel as well as vowel quality (with the unstressed vowel being ə). To date, all of the consonants of Standard American English are included in her utterances (with the interdental fricatives occurring only in imitations, and the affricates occurring inconsistently). She still deletes final consonants more often than not. Their correct sporadic presence, however, shows them to be part of her stored representation of the words in which they occur. Consonant clusters were first simplified by the deletion of the /s/ in initial /sp/ /sk/ /st/ clusters; at the present time, in addition to this method of preserving the CV syllable structure, she sometimes adds an epenthetic schwa between the two consonants.

Other changes in Genie's phonological system continue to be observed. At an earlier stage a regular substitution of /t/ for /k/, /n/, and /s/ occurred in all word positions: this now occurs only word medially. /s/ plus nasal clusters are now being produced.

What is of particular interest is that in imitation Genie can produce any English sound and many sound sequences not found in her spontaneous speech. It has been noted by many researchers on child language that children have greater phonetic abilities than are revealed in their utterances. This is also true of Genie; her output reflects phonological constraints rather than her inability to articulate sounds and sound sequences.

Neither Genie nor a normal child learns the sound system of a language totally independent from the syntactic and semantic systems. In fact, the analysis of the syntactic and semantic development of Genie's spontaneous utterances reveals that her performance on the expressive side is paralleling (although lagging behind) her comprehension.

As stated above, within a few weeks after admission to the hospital Genie began to imitate words used to her, and her comprehension of individual words and names increased dramatically. She began to produce single words spontaneously after about five months.

Sentence Structure

For normal children perception or comprehension of syntactic structures exceeds production; this is even more true in Genie's case possibly for the reasons given above. But even in production it is clear that Genie is acquiring language. Eight months after her emergence

Genie began to produce utterances, two words (or morphemes) in length. The structures of her earliest two-word "sentences" were Modifier + Noun and Noun + Noun genitive constructions. These included sentences like "more soup," "yellow car," "Genie purse" and "Mark mouth." After about two months she began to produce strings with verbs—both Noun (subject) + Verb, and Verb + Noun (object), e.g., "Mark paint" (N + V), "Curtiss cough" (N + V), "want milk" (V + N) and "wash car" (V + N). Sentences with a noun followed by a predicate adjective soon followed, e.g., "Dave sick."

In November, 1971, Genie began to produce three- and four-word strings, including subject + verb + object strings, like "Tori chew glove," modified noun phrases like "little white clear box," subject-object strings, like "big elephant long trunk," and four word predications like "Marilyn car red car." Some of these longer strings are of interest because the syntactic relations which were only assumed to be present in her two-word utterances were now overtly expressed. For example, many of Genie's two-word strings did not contain any expressed subject, but the three-word sentences included both the subject and object: "Love Marilyn" became "Genie love Marilyn." In addition, Modifier-noun Noun Phrases and possessive phrases which were complete utterances at the two-word sentence stage are now used as constituents of her longer strings, e.g., "more soup" occurred in "want more soup" and "Mark mouth" became a constituent in "Mark mouth hurt."

In February, 1972, Genie began to produce negative sentences. The comprehension test involving negative/affirmative distinctions showed that such a distinction was understood many months earlier. (In the tests she had no difficulty in pointing to the correct picture when asked to "show me 'The girl is wearing shoes'" or "Show me the bunny that has a carrot" vs. "Show me the bunny that does not/doesn't have a carrot.") The first negative morpheme used by Genie was "no more." Later she began to use "no" and "not." To date, Genie continues to negate a sentence by attaching the negative morpheme to the beginning of the string. She has not yet acquired the "Negative movement transformation" which inserts the Negative morpheme inside the sentence in English.

About the same time that the negative sentences were produced, Genie began to produce strings with locative-nouns, such as "Cereal kitchen" and "play gym." In recent months prepositions are occurring in her utterances. In answer to the question "Where is your toy radio?" she answered "On chair." She has also produced sentences such as "Like horse behind fence" and "Like good Harry at hospital."

In July, 1972, Verb plus Verb-phrase strings were produced: "Want go shopping," "Like chew meat." Such complex VPs began to emerge in sentences that included both a complex Noun-phrase and a complex

Verb-phrase, e.g., "Want buy toy refrigerator" and "Want go walk (to) Ralph." Genie has also begun to add the progressive aspect marker "ing" to verbs, always appropriately to denote ongoing action: "Genie laughing," "Tori eating bone."

Grammatical morphemes that are phonologically marked are now used, e.g., plurals as in "bears," "noses," "swings," and possessives such as "Joel's room," "I like Dave's car."

While no definite-indefinite distinction has appeared, Genie now produces the definite article in imitation, and uses the determiner "another" spontaneously, as in "Another house have dog."

At an earlier stage, possession was marked solely by word order; Genie now also expresses possession by the verb "have," as in "bears have sharp claw," "bathroom have big mirror."

A most important syntactic development is revealed by Genie's use of compound NPs. Prior to December, 1971, she would only name one thing at a time, and would produce two sentences such as: "Cat hurt" followed by "dog hurt." More recently she produced these two strings, and then said "Cat dog hurt." This use of a "recursive" element is also shown by the sentence "Curtiss, Genie, swimming pool" in describing a snapshot.

Genie's ability to combine a finite set of linguistic elements to form new combinations, and the ability to produce sentences consisting of conjoined sentences, shows that she has acquired two essential elements of language that permit the generation of an infinite set of sentences.

This is of course an overly sketchy view of the syntactic development evidence in Genie's utterances. (For further details see Curtiss et al., 1973.) It is clear even from this summary that Genie is learning language. Her speech is rule-governed—she has fixed word-order of basic sentence elements and constituents, and systematic ways of expressing syntactic and semantic relations.

Linguistic Development in Relation to Normals

Furthermore it is obvious that her development in many ways parallels that of normal first-language acquisition. There are, however, interesting differences between Genie's emerging language and that of normal children. Her vocabulary is much larger than that of normal children whose language exhibits syntactic complexity parallel to Genie's. She has less difficulty in storing lists than she does learning the rules of the grammar. This illustrates very sharply that language acquisition is not simply the ability to store a large number of items in memory.

Genie's performance on the active/passive comprehension test also appears to deviate from that of normal children. Bever (1970) reports on experiments aimed at testing the capacity in young children "to recognize explicitly the concept of predication as exemplified in the appreciation of the difference between subject-action and action-object relations." The children in these experiments were requested to act out using both simple active sentences and reversible passive sentences, such as "The cow kisses the horse" and simple passives such as "The horse is kissed by the cow." He reports that "children from 2.0 to 3.0 act out simple active sentences 95 percent correctly, (and) . . . do far better than 5 percent on simple passives." He concludes that "since they perform almost randomly on passives . . . they can at least distinguish sentences they can understand from sentences they cannot understand. Thus, the basic linguistic capacity evidenced by the two-year-old child includes the notion of reference for objects and actions, the notion of basic functional internal relations, and at least a primitive notion of different sentence structures." Genie was similarly tested but with the "point to" response rather than the "acting out" response. That is she was asked to point to "The boy pulls/is pulling the girl" or "The girl is pulled by the boy." For each such test sentence she was presented with two pictures, one depicting the boy as agent, the other with the girl as agent. Unlike the children tested by Bever, Genie's responses to both active and passive sentences have been random, with no better than a chance level of correct responses for either the active or the passive sentences. This is particularly strange when compared with Genie's own utterances which show a consistent word order to indicate Subject Verb Object relations. While she never produces passive constructions, her active sentences always place the object after the verb and the subject before the verb (when they are expressed).

Another difference between Genie and normal children is in the area of linguistic performance. Genie's linguistic competence (her grammar, if we can speak of a grammar at such an early stage of development) is in many ways on a par with a two or two and a half year old child. Her performance—particularly as related to expressive speech—is much poorer than normal children at this level. Because of her particular difficulties in producing speech, however, a number of relatively successful efforts have been directed to teaching her written language. At this point she recognizes, names, and can print the letters of the alphabet, can read a large number of printed words, can assemble printed words into grammatically correct sentences, and can understand sentences (and questions) constructed of these printed words. On this level of performance, then, she seems to exceed normal children at a similar stage of language development.

Genie's progress is much slower than that of normals. Few syntactic markers occur in her utterances; there are no question words, no demonstratives, no particles, no rejoinders. In addition, no movement transformations are revealed. Such rules exist in the adult grammar and in normal children's grammars as early as two years. Transformational rules are those which, for example, would move a negative element from the beginning of the sentence to the position after an auxiliary verb. Such a transformational rule would change *I can go* in its negative form from *Neg + I + can + go* to *I + can + neg* (can't) + *go*. As stated above, Genie continues to produce negative sentences only by the addition of the negative element to the beginning of the sentence, e.g., *No more ear hurt, No stay hospital, No can go*.

Cognitively, however, she seems to be in advance of what would be expected at this syntactic stage. Her earliest productive vocabulary included words cognitively more sophisticated than one usually finds in the descriptions of first vocabulary words. Color words and numbers, for example, were used which usually enter a child's vocabulary at a much later grammatical stage (Castner, 1940; Denckla, 1972).

At the time that Genie began to produce utterances of two words (June 1971) she had an active vocabulary of over 200 words, which far exceeds the size of the normal children's lexicon at this stage (about fifty words). This development seems to parallel that found in aphasic children (Eisenson and Ingram, 1972). She comprehends all the *wh*-questions; normal children ordinarily learn *how, why,* and *when* questions later than *who, what,* and *where* (Brown, 1968), although syntactically such questions are similar. Her comprehension of the comparative and superlative, and the differences between *more* and *less* also indicate cognitive sophistication not revealed by her syntax, suggesting at least a partial independence of cognition and language.

Cognitive Development

The attempt to assess Genie's cognitive development is extremely difficult. All tests purported to measure cognitive abilities, in fact, measure knowledge that has been acquired through experience. In addition, many tests are substantially dependent on verbal response and comprehension. The distinction between cognition and language development is therefore not always possible. A number of tests have, however, been utilized.

Genie could not easily be psychologically tested by standard instruments at the time of her admission. It is still difficult to administer many of the standard tests. On the Vineland Social Maturity Scale, however, she averaged about fifteen months at the time of admission, and on a Gesell Developmental Evaluation, a month and a half later, scores ranged from about one to about three years of age. There was a very high degree of scatter when compared to normal developmental patterns. Consistently, language-related behavior was observed to occur at the lower end of the range of her performance and was judged (by the psychologists at the hospital) to be at about the fifteen months level.

Her cognitive growth, however, seemed to be quite rapid. In a seven month span her score had increased from fifteen to forty-two months, and six months after admission, on the Leiter International Performance Scale (which depends relatively little on culturally based, specific knowledge, and requires no speech) she passed all the items at the four year level, two at the five year level, and two out of four at the seven year level. In May 1973 her score on this test was on the six to eight year level. At the same time, the Stanford Binet Intelligence Scale elicited a mental age of five to eight. In all the tests, the subsets which involved language were considerably lower than those assessing other abilities.

From this brief summary of Genie's linguistic development we can conclude the following: (1) When she first emerged from isolation, Genie, a child of thirteen years, nine months had not acquired language; (2) Since there is no evidence of any biological deficiencies, one may assume this was due to the social and linguistic isolation which occurred during eleven years of her life; (3) Since her emergence she has been acquiring her first language primarily by "exposure" alone (this is revealed both by her own speech and by her comprehension of spoken language); (4) Her cognitive development has exceeded her linguistic development.

The "Critical Age" Hypothesis and Language Lateralization

As mentioned above, Genie's ongoing language acquisition is the most direct test of Lenneberg's critical age hypothesis seen thus far. Lenneberg (1967) has presented the view that the ability to acquire primary language (and the acquisition of second languages "by mere exposure") terminates with the completion of the development of cerebral dominance, or lateralization, an event which he argues occurs at around puberty. As we have demonstrated above, however, while Genie's language acquisition differs to some extent from that of normal children, she is in fact in the process of learning language, as shown by the results of tests and by the observations of her spontaneous and elicited speech. Thus, at least some degree of first language acquisition seems to be possible beyond the critical period.

Genie also affords us the opportunity to study the relationship of the development of lateralization and language acquisition.

Lateralization refers to the fact that each hemisphere appears to be specialized for different cognitive functions; that is, some functions seem to be "localized" primarily on one side of the brain. . . . [The various monaural and dichotic listening tests given to Genie suggested a pronounced right-hemisphere dominance for language as well as for environmental sounds.]

In trying to assess this unusual situation it is important to note that Genie seems very proficient in what are considered right hemisphere functions. . . . [In] psychological tests her development can be comprehended more meaningfully when performances on two kinds of test tasks are distinguished: those that require analytic or sequential use of symbols, such as language and number; and those that involve perception of spatial configurations or Gestalts. On the first group of tasks Genie's performance is consistently in the low range, presently approximating an age of two-and-a-half to three years, approximately the age level of her linguistic performance using comparative linguistic criteria. On configurational tests, however, her performance ranges upwards, lying somewhere between eight years and the adult level, depending on the test. . . . The rate of growth on these tests has been very rapid. . . .

It would appear then that Genie is lateralized to the right for both language and nonlanguage functions. This assumes that these nonlinguistic abilities, which have been shown to be right-hemisphere lateralized, are indeed functions of Genie's right hemisphere. We are now in the process of designing tests involving other modalities which will hopefully provide more conclusive evidence on this question.

If this proves to be the case, one tentative hypothesis to explain how this developed is as follows: At the time of her isolation, Genie was a "normal" right handed child with potential left hemisphere dominance. The inadequate language stimulation during her early life inhibited or interfered with language aspects of left hemisphere development. This would be tantamount to a kind of functional atrophy of the usual language centers, brought about by disuse or suppression. Apparently, what meager stimulation she did receive was sufficient for normal right hemisphere development. (One can imagine her sitting, day after day, week after week, year after year, absorbing every visual stimulus, every crack in the paint, every nuance of color and form.) This is consistent with the suggestion (Carmon et al., 1972) that the right hemisphere is the first to develop since it is more involved with the perception of the environment. Genie's current achievements in language acquisition, according to this reasoning, are occurring in that hemisphere which somehow did mature more normally.

The hypothesis that Genie is using a developed right hemisphere for language also predicts the dichotic listening results. The undeveloped language areas in the left hemisphere prevent the flow of (just language) impulses from the left primary auditory receiving areas to the right hemisphere. This explains why Genie's scores are so similar to split-brain and hemispherectomized subjects; the only auditory pathways that are functional for *verbal* stimuli are the right ipsilateral and left contralateral. The low right score is due to the suppression that occurs under the dichotic condition. Her perfect monotic scores are predicted, since suppression only takes place dichotically.

If this hypothesis is true it modifies the theory of the critical period: while the normal development of lateralization may not play a role in the critical period, lateralization may be involved in a different way; the left hemisphere must perhaps be linguistically stimulated during a specific period of time for it to participate in normal language acquisition. If such stimulation does not take place during this time, normal language acquisition must depend on other cortical areas and will proceed less efficiently due to the previous specialization of these areas for other functions.

A comparison of Genie's case with other instances of right (minor) hemisphere speech in adults implies that Genie's capacity for language acquisition is limited and will cease at some time in the near future. Such cases are rare and not well described from a linguistic point of view. A. Smith's (1966) description of a left hemispherectomized man is the best of these. This man could not speak at all after his left hemisphere was removed but did begin to communicate in "propositional language" ten weeks later. The patient continued to make linguistic progress but remained severely aphasic eight months after surgery (see also Bogen, 1969). Similarly, Hillier (1954) reported a left hemispherectomy performed on a 14 year old boy for a tumor whose onset was one year previous to surgery. Again, there was early progress in language learning but after 19 months progress ceased and the deficit became stable.

It is unfortunate that there is no information concerning cerebral dominance for other cases of isolated children—those that acquired language as well as those that didn't. Itard suggests that Victor was about twelve years of age when he was found in the woods of Aveyron, and that "It is . . . almost proved that he had been abandoned at the age of four or five years" (Itard, 1962). If, in those first years he was not genetically deficient, lateralization should have been complete and language should have been acquired. Itard states further that "if, at this time, he already owed some ideas and some words to the beginning of an education, this would all have been effaced from his memory in consequence of his isolation." How, why, and if such "memory effacement" occurs are questions open to speculation. Despite this "effacement," Victor "did acquire a very considerable reading vocabulary, learning, by means of printed phrases, to execute such simple commands as to pick up a key" (Itard, 1962, p. xii), but he never learned to speak. The scar "which (was) visible on his throat" may have damaged his larynx. It is impossible to tell from Itard's reports the exact extent of Victor's comprehension of spoken language.

Another case, similar to some extent to that of Genie, is that of a child who was not exposed to language until she was six-and-a-half years old because of her imprisonment with a mute and totally uneducated aphasic mother (Mason, 1942). Within twenty-two months, she progressed from her first spoken words ("ball," "car," "bye," "baby") to asking such questions as "Why does the paste come out if one upsets the jar?" The rapidity with which she acquired the complex grammar of English provides some support for the hypothesis that the language learning mechanism is more specific than general.

This case is also consistent with a two-to-puberty critical period theory. The language learning capacity of the right hemisphere, then, may be limited either in time or amount of learning. Because we have no grammatical descriptions of right hemisphere speech, we cannot predict how far Genie will progress from comparisons with such cases. On the other hand, Genie's progress in language acquisition impressionistically seems to have far exceeded that of the other reported cases. We intend to continue administering dichotic listening tests to see if the left hemisphere begins to show increasing language function. If this occurs, one plausible conclusion would be that language acquisition and use are a precondition for such lateralization to occur. We note, of course, that this would be contrary to the Krashen and Harshman position that lateralization *precedes* language acquisition. There is also some evidence of laterality differences in neonates (Wada, quoted in Geschwind, 1970; Molfese, 1972).

It is clear from this report that we have more questions than answers. We are hopeful that Genie's development will provide some of these answers.

As humanists we are hopeful that our tentative prognosis of a slowing down of language and permanent dysphasia will prove to be wrong. For despite the predictions of our hypothesis, Genie continues to make modest but steady progress in language acquisition and is providing us with data in an unexplored area, first language acquisition beyond the "critical period." After all, a discarded hypothesis is a small price to pay for confirmation of the astonishing capabilities and adaptability of the human mind. (See postscript by Maya Pines on pp. 131–132.)

Bibliography

Bellugi, U., and Klima, E. 1971. Consultation Report. March.

Bever, T. G. 1970. The cognitive basis for linguistic structures. In J. R. Hayes (Ed.) *Cognition and the Development of Language*. New York: John Wiley. Pp. 279–362.

Bogen, J. E. 1969. The other side of the brain I: Dysgraphia and dyscopia following cerebral commissurotomy. *Bulletin of the Los Angeles Neurological Societies 34*, July, 73–105.

Brown, R. 1968. The development of WH questions in child speech. *Journal of Verbal Learning and Verbal Behavior 7*, 279–290.

Carmon, A., Harishanu, Y., Lowinger, R., and Levy, S. 1972. Asymmetries in hemispheric blood volume and cerebral dominance. *Behavioral Biology*.

Castner, B. M. 1940. *Language Development in the First Five Years of Life*. Ed. A. Gesell, New York: Harper & Row.

Chomsky, N. 1962. Explanatory models in linguistics. In E. Nagel, P. Suppes, and A. Taiski (Eds.) *Logic, Methodology, and the Philosophy of Science*. Stanford University Press.

Clarke, A. D. B. and Clarke, A. M. 1960. Some recent advances in the study of early deprivation. *Child Psychology and Psychiatry 1*.

Curtiss, S. 1972. The development of language in Genie. Paper presented to the 1972 Annual Convention of the American Speech and Hearing Association, San Francisco, Calif. Nov. 18–20.

Curtiss, S., Fromkin, V., and Krashen, S. 1972. The syntactic development of Genie. Paper presented to the Dec., 1972 annual meeting of the Linguistic Society of America, Atlanta, Georgia.

Davis, K. 1940. Extreme social isolation of a child. *American Journal of Sociology 45*, 554–565.

———. 1947. Final note on a case of extreme isolation. *American Journal of Sociology 52*, 432–437.

Denckla, M. B. 1972. Performance on color tasks in kindergarten children. *Cortex 8*, 177–190.

Dennis, W., and Najarian, P. 1957. Infant development under developmental handicap. *Psychological Monographs 71*, No. 7.

Eisenson, J. and Ingram, D. 1972. Childhood aphasia—an updated concept based on recent research. *Papers and Reports on Child Language Development*. Stanford University, 103–120.

Fraiberg, S., and Freedman, D. A. 1964. Studies in the ego development of the congenitally blind child. *The Psychoanalytic Study of the Child 19*, 113–169.

Fromkin, V. 1972. The development of language in Genie. Paper presented at the 80th Annual Convention of the American Psychological Association, Honolulu, Hawaii, Sept. 1–8.

Geschwind, N. 1970. The organization of language and the brain. *Science 170*, 940–944.

Haggard, M. and Parkinson, A. 1971. Stimulus and task factors as determinants of ear advantage. *Quarterly Journal of Experimental Psychology 23*, 168–177.

Hansen, H. 1972. The first experiences and the emergence of "Genie." Paper presented at the 80th Annual Convention of the American Psychological Association, Honolulu, Hawaii, Sept. 1–8.

Hillier, F. 1954. Total left hemispherectomy for malignant glaucoma. *Neurology 4*, 718–721.

Howe, M. and Hall, F. G. 1903. *Laura Bridgeman*. Boston: Little, Brown and Co.

Itard, J. 1962. *The Wild Boy of Aveyron.* New York: Appleton-Century-Crofts.

Kent, J. 1972. Eight months in the hospital. Paper presented at the 80th Annual Convention of the American Psychological Association, Honolulu, Hawaii, Sept. 1–8.

Koluchova, J. 1972. Severe deprivation in twins. *Child Psychology and Psychiatry* 13.

Krashen, S. 1972. Language and the left hemisphere. *Working Papers in Phonetics* 24, UCLA.

———. 1973a. Lateralization, language learning, and the critical period: Some new evidence. *Language Learning* 23, 63–74.

———. 1973b. Mental abilities underlying linguistic and non-linguistic functions. *Linguistics.*

Krashen, S., Fromkin, V., Curtiss, S., Rigler, D., and Spitz, S. 1972a. Language lateralization in a case of extreme psychological deprivation. Paper presented to the 84th meeting of the Acoustical Society of America.

Krashen, S., Fromkin, V. and Curtiss, S. 1972b. A neurolinguistic investigation of language acquisition in the case of an isolated child. Paper presented to the Linguistic Society of America. Winter meeting, Atlanta, Georgia, Dec. 27–29.

Krashen, S. and Harshman, R. 1972. Lateralization and the critical period. *Working Papers in Phonetics* 23, 13–21. UCLA (Abstract in *Journal of the Acoustical Society of America* 52, 174).

Lenneberg, E. H. 1967. *Biological Foundations of Language.* New York: Wiley.

Mason, M. K. 1942. Learning to speak after six and one-half years. *Journal of Speech Disorders* 7, 295–304.

Milner, B., Taylor, L., and Sperry, R. 1968. Lateralized suppression of dichotically presented digits after commissural section in man. *Science 161*, 184–186.

Molfese, D. L. 1972. Cerebral asymmetry in infants, children and adults: Auditory evoked responses to speech and musical stimuli. *Journal of the Acoustical Society of America 53*, 363 (A).

Rigler, D. 1972. The Case of Genie. Paper presented to the 1972 Annual Convention of the American Speech and Hearing Association, San Francisco, Calif. Nov. 18–20.

Rigler, M. 1972. Adventure: At Home with Genie. Paper presented at the 80th Annual Convention of the American Psychological Association, Honolulu, Hawaii, Sept. 1–8.

Singh, J. A. L., and Zingg, R. M. 1966. *Wolf-Children and Feral Man.* Archon Books.

Skinner, B. F. 1957. *Verbal Behavior.* New York: Appleton-Century-Crofts.

Smith, A. 1966. Speech and other functions after left (dominant) hemispherectomy. *Journal of Neurology, Neurosurgery and Psychiatry 29*, 467–471.

Spitz, R. A. 1949. The role of ecological factors in emotional development. *Child Development 20*, 145–155.

Von Feuerbach, A. 1833. *Kasper Hauser.* (Translated from the German) London: Simpkin and Marshall.

Zurif, E. B. and Mendelsohn, M. 1972. Hemispheric specialization for the perception of speech sounds: the influences of intonation and structure. *Perception and Psychophysics 11*, 329–332.

Genie: A Postscript

In 1978, Genie's mother became her legal guardian. During all the years of Genie's rehabilitation, her mother had also received help. An eye operation restored her sight, and a social worker tried to improve her behavior toward Genie. Genie's mother had never been held legally responsible for the child's inhuman treatment. Charges of child abuse were dismissed in 1970, when her lawyer argued that she "was, herself, a victim of the same psychotic individual"—her husband. There was "nothing to show purposeful or willful cruelty," he said.

Nevertheless, for many years the court assigned a guardian for Genie. Shortly after Genie's mother was named guardian, she astounded the therapists and researchers who had worked with Genie by filing a suit against Curtiss and the Children's Hospital among others—on behalf of herself and her daughter—in which she charged that they had disclosed private and confidential information concerning Genie and her mother for "prestige and profit" and had subjected Genie to "unreasonable and outrageous" testing, not for treatment, but to exploit Genie for personal and economic benefits. According to the *Los Angeles Times*, the lawyer who represents Genie's mother estimated that the actual damages could have totaled $500,000. [*Editor's note:* The case was settled out of court, with no damages awarded.]

[In the years since the case] was filed, Genie has been completely cut off from the professionals at Children's Hospital and UCLA. Since she is too old to be in a foster home, she apparently is living in a board-and-care home for adults who cannot live alone. The *Los Angeles Times* reported that as of 1979 her mother was working as a domestic servant. All research on Genie's language and intellectual development has come to a halt. However, the research Genie stimulated goes on. Much of it concerns the relationship between linguistic ability and cognitive development, a subject to which Genie has made a significant contribution.

Apart from Chomsky and his followers, who believe that fundamental language ability is innate and unrelated to intelligence, most psychologists assume that the development of language is tied to—and emerges from—the development of nonverbal intelligence, as described by Piaget. However, Genie's obvious nonverbal intelligence—her use of tools, her drawings, her knowledge of causality, her mental maps of space—did not lead her to an equivalent competence in the grammar normal children acquire by the age of five.

Puzzled by the discrepancy between Genie's cognitive abilities and her language deficits, Curtiss and Fromkin wondered whether they

From Maya Pines, "The Civilizing of Genie," *Psychology Today*, September 1981.

could find people with the opposite pattern—who have normal language ability despite cognitive deficits. That would be further evidence of the independence of language from certain aspects of cognition.

In recent months, they have found several such persons among the mentally retarded, as well as among victims of Turner's syndrome, a chromosomal defect that produces short stature, cardiac problems, infertility, and specific learning difficulties in females. With help from the National Science Foundation (which had also funded some of Curtiss's research on Genie), Fromkin and Curtiss have identified and started working with some children and adolescents who combine normal grammatical ability with serious defects in logical reasoning, sequential ability, or other areas of thinking.

"You can't explain their unimpaired syntax on the basis of their impaired cognitive development," says Curtiss, who is greatly excited by this new developmental profile. She points out that in the youngsters studied, the purely grammatical aspect of language—which reflects Chomsky's language universals—seems to be isolated from the semantic aspect of language, which is more tied to cognition. "Language no longer looks like a uniform package," she declares. "This is the first experimental data on the subject." Thus the ordeal of an abused child may help us understand some of the most puzzling but important aspects of our humanity.

FOR DISCUSSION AND REVIEW

1. Noting that all children who suffer serious experiential deprivation show retarded development, Fromkin et al. state that "An important question for scientists of many disciplines is whether a child so deprived can 'catch up' wholly or in part." List the various factors on which the answer to this question depends.

2. Describe as fully as you can the condition (physical, developmental, etc.) of Genie at the time she was discovered and hospitalized. Summarize the conditions under which she had lived prior to her discovery, and consider the possible effect on her of each.

3. On what basis do the authors conclude that although "functionally, Genie was an extremely retarded child," the most plausible explanation of this retardation was "the intensity and duration of her psychosocial and physical deprivation"?

4. Explain the importance of devising at the outset tests to use with Genie to ascertain the extent (if any) of her language comprehension.

5. Explain the following statement: "the ability to relate the sounds and meanings of individual lexical items, while necessary, is not a sufficient criterion for language competence."

6. The authors state, "Genie's ability to comprehend spoken language is a better indication of her linguistic competence than is her production

of speech because of the physical difficulties Genie has in speaking." What does this fact suggest about the importance of such early stages of language discussed by Aitchison as crying, cooing, babbling, and intonation patterns, and of practice?

7. After stating that Genie is learning language, the authors point out differences in her linguistic development from that of "normals." What are these differences, and what is their significance? What stage has Genie reached in the acquisition of negative sentences? What are the implications of this fact?

8. Review the earlier discussions in this section of the relationship between cognitive development and language acquisition. What is the significance of the fact that "cognitively, . . . she [Genie] seems to be in advance of what would be expected at this syntactic stage"? Note, too, that the *rate* of Genie's cognitive growth exceeded that of her language acquisition.

9. Explain how Genie's linguistic development has been a test of Lenneberg's critical age hypothesis. Discuss the results of this "test."

10. What has Genie taught us about the relationship between language acquisition and brain lateralization? How do these findings relate to the critical age hypothesis?

11. Explain the tentative hypothesis developed by the authors to account for Genie's being "lateralized to the right for both language and non-language functions." How does this hypothesis, if correct, modify the critical period theory?

6/Creole Languages

DEREK BICKERTON

Typically used for trading by speakers of two or more different languages, pidgins *are rudimentary languages with simplified grammars and limited lexicons. They are auxiliary languages; people do not learn them as native speakers. In contrast,* creoles, *which develop from pidgins, are learned by native speakers and are considered fully developed languages.*

Children born into a society in which a pidgin language is spoken are in a unique situation. The pidgin used by their parents is unsuitable for use as their primary *language; because of its extreme variability from speaker to speaker, it does not provide children with a language model from which they can derive systematic rules. Lacking interaction with parents whose speech is suitably modeled to the youngsters' needs—that is, appropriately simplified and well-formed—the children cannot compare their own utterances with those of older speakers and thus master increasingly complex structures of a natural language. Rather, they must rely on an innate "bioprogram" for language acquisition, a universal grammar that is usually modified by children's language environment (e.g., English, German, Russian, Persian, Hindi, or Shona). Reliance on this universal innate grammar by such children has resulted in the development of creole languages whose basic structures differ from those of other languages. Apparently, these children do not use the structural grammatical input available to them—that is, pidgin languages—in their development of creoles.*

In the following selection, Derek Bickerton, professor of linguistics at the University of Hawaii, focuses on the development of Hawaiian Creole and points out that creole languages throughout the world exhibit remarkable structural uniformities. His work is of great importance to our understanding of the process of language acquisition.

The ancient Greek historian Herodotus records the story of Psamtik I, pharaoh of Egypt in the seventh century B.C., who set out to discover the original language of humanity. On royal decree two infants were taken away from their parents and put in the care of a mute shepherd, who was instructed to raise the children in isolation from other people. The shepherd was to take note of the first word uttered by the children;

"uncorrupted" by the language of their forefathers, Psamtik reasoned, they would begin to speak in the pure tongue from which all other languages were derived. The first intelligible sound the children made was "bekos," which meant bread in the ancient language Phrygian. Therefore, Psamtik maintained, the original language of humanity is Phrygian.

The story has amused generations of linguistics students. Most linguists, who have taken it for granted that no such experiment should ever be carried out, have dismissed the Psamtik experiment as being defective in design and unlikely to yield any useful result. Indeed, the assumption that an "original" vocabulary can be recovered is over-optimistic, and linguistic isolation of the individual, which has been documented in a few cases of severe child abuse, usually results in the absence of language. Nevertheless, a modified form of the experiment has been repeated many times over the past 500 years among the children of slaves and laborers who were pressed into service by the European colonial powers.

These laborers, who were shipped from many parts of the world to tend and harvest crops in Africa, the Indian Ocean region, the Orient, the Caribbean, and Hawaii, were obliged to communicate within their polyglot community by means of the rudimentary speech system called pidgin. Pidgin speech is extremely impoverished in syntax and vocabulary, but for the children born into the colonial community it was the only common language available. From these modest beginnings new native languages evolved among the children, which are generically called creole languages. It can be shown that they exhibit the complexity, nuance and expressive power universally found in the more established languages of the world.

Taken at face value, the development of many different creole languages suggests that the search for a single, original language is misguided. For many years, however, scholars have noted a remarkable similarity of structure among all the creole languages. It can now be demonstrated, by considering the origin of creole language in Hawaii, that similarities among creoles cannot be accounted for by contact with other languages, either indigenous or imported. The finding suggests that what is common to creole languages may indeed form the basis of the acquisition of language by children everywhere. There is now an impressive body of evidence to support this hypothesis: between the ages of two and four the child born into a community of linguistically competent adults speaks a variety of language whose structure bears a deep resemblance to the structure of creole languages. Hence, by an ironic stroke of justice, the surviving linguistic remnants of colonialism may offer indispensable keys to the study of our own linguistic heritage.

The historical conditions that favored the development of creole languages are well known. Between 1500 and 1900 England, France, the Netherlands, Portugal, and Spain established numerous labor-intensive, agricultural economies on isolated littorals and underpopulated tropical islands throughout the world. The colonies were engaged primarily in monoculture, usually sugar, and their economic viability depended on an abundance of cheap labor imported from distant regions under conditions of chattel slavery. Workers were drawn first from West Africa and later from East Africa, India and the Orient, and they spoke a variety of mutually incomprehensible languages.

Under more salutary conditions of immigration the workers or their children would eventually have learned the language of the local colonial power, but two factors combined to keep them from doing so. First, the number of speakers of the colonial languages rarely exceeded 20 percent of the total population, and it was often less than 10 percent. In other words, there were relatively few people from whom the dominant language could have been learned. Second, the colonial societies were small, autocratic and rigidly stratified. There were few chances for prolonged linguistic contact between field laborers and speakers of the dominant language.

Except in Hawaii, there is little reliable documentary evidence concerning the early linguistic history of the colonial societies. It has generally been assumed that pidgin developed as a contact language solely to allow communication between masters and workers and among workers from various immigrant groups. Creole languages then arose among the children of the workers through the "expansion" of pidgin; there was little occasion for the children to use the ancestral languages of their parents, and they still lacked access to the language of the dominant culture. What is meant by the term "expansion" has remained obscure until my colleagues and I began our studies in Hawaii.

The unique advantage for the study of creole language in Hawaii is that the details of its formation can be reconstructed at least in part from the speech of people still living. Although Hawaiian contact with Europeans goes back to 1778, it was not until 1876 that a revision in the U.S. tariff laws, allowing the free importation of Hawaiian sugar, enabled Hawaiian sugar plantations to increase their output by several hundred percent. A polyglot force of indentured laborers, made up of Chinese, Filipinos, Japanese, Koreans, Portuguese, Puerto Ricans, and others, began to be assembled, and by 1900 it outnumbered the other groups in Hawaii, both native and European, by a ratio of two to one.

A pidgin based on the Polynesian language Hawaiian initially served as a means of communication between immigrants and the locally born, but the annexation of Hawaii by the U.S. in 1898 eventually led to the replacement of Hawaiian by English. After 1900 the Hawaiian language declined, and pidgin Hawaiian was replaced as a lingua franca by a pidgin based on English. By the time we began our intensive study of language variation in Hawaii in the early 1970's there were still many survivors, both immigrant and locally born, from the years 1900 until 1920.

Our recordings of locally born people make it clear that the process of creolization was under way by 1900 and was certainly complete by 1920. Most of the linguistic features that characterize Hawaiian Creole English are present in the speech of working-class people born in Hawaii since 1905; before that date the proportion of Creole speakers to the rest of the population falls off rapidly. On the other hand, the speech of immigrants is always some form of pidgin, although just what form it takes depends on the date of the immigrant's arrival in Hawaii as well as the immigrant's language background. The pidgin spoken by the earliest immigrants among our subjects is much more rudimentary than that spoken by the later ones, probably because the latter were exposed to Creole as well as pidgin. Nevertheless, the distinction between pidgin and Creole remains fundamental: anyone familiar with Hawaii can quickly identify the ethnic origins of any immigrant on the basis of speech patterns alone. Without a conversational topic or a person's physical appearance as a guide, however, no one can reliably identify the ethnic origins of any locally born speaker solely on the basis of the speaker's pronunciation or the grammatical structure of the utterances.

One of the main characteristics of pidgin, therefore, is its variability from speaker to speaker. Each immigrant seems to have gone about the task of inventing a makeshift language in some individual way. For example, pidgin speakers of Japanese ancestry generally place the verb at the end of a sentence, as in "The poor people all potato eat" ("All that the poor people ate were potatoes"). Filipino pidgin, however, places the verb before the subject: "Work hard these people" ("These people work hard"). More often word order follows no fixed principle except the pragmatic one that old, shared information is stated near the beginning of a sentence and new information near the end.

It is probably the case that anything expressible in Creole, or in English for that matter, can also be expressed in pidgin. Nevertheless, the pidgin speaker is at a great disadvantage, because pidgin lacks many of the building blocks possessed by all native languages. Such everyday necessities of language as articles, prepositions and auxiliary verbs are either absent or appear sporadically in a quite unpredictable fashion. Pidgin sentences have no subordinate clauses, and single-clause utterances frequently lack verbs.

The first of the following examples was recorded from a pidgin-speaking Korean; omitted words are bracketed in the translation: "And a too much children, small children, house money pay" ("And [I had] too many children, small children, [I had] to pay the rent"). The second example was recorded from a Japanese speaker: "Before mill no more Filipino no nothing" ("Before the mill [was built, there were] no Filipinos here at all"). The third example, recorded from the speech of a retired bus driver, illustrates the heroic measures needed to say anything out of the ordinary in pidgin: "Sometime good road get, sometime, all same bend get, enguru [angle] get, no? Any kind same. All same human life, all same" ("Sometimes there's a good road, sometimes there's, like, bends, corners, right? Everything's like that. Human life's just like that").

The language-learning task confronted by the child born into a community of such speakers is far different from the task imposed on the child who is surrounded by linguistically competent adults. The children of English or Chinese parents, for example, are presented with accurate models to follow. Although their mistakes are seldom overtly corrected, they can almost constantly check their own utterances against those of older speakers and adapt them where necessary. When they have mastered the simpler structures of their language, more complex structures are readily available.

For the Hawaiian-born child of immigrant parents, however, there was no consistent linguistic model for the basic word order of simple sentences and often no model at all for the more complicated structures of language. Many such children were born of interethnic or interracial marriages, and so even at home there was little occasion to speak the native language of either parent. Moreover, even among the children not born of linguistically mixed parents there was considerable incentive to abandon the parents' native language and adopt some version of pidgin in the company of peers and neighboring adults. Like first-generation immigrant children elsewhere, the children of Hawaiian immigrants often became bilingual or even trilingual, and they adopted the common language of their peers as a native language in spite of considerable efforts by their parents to maintain the ancestral tongue.

The historical evidence is consistent with the view that the structure of Creole arose without significant borrowing from other languages. Bilingual or trilingual children of school age need not (and usually do not) mix up the structural features of the languages they speak, and there is no reason to suppose such crossovers were common in Hawaii. The most compelling argument for the autonomous emergence of Creole, however, is its observed uniformity. How, within a single generation, did such a consistent and uniform language develop out of the linguistic free-for-all that was pidgin in Hawaii? Even if all the children of various immigrant groups had begun by learning the languages of their parents, and even if the differences among the various pidgins had been smoothed by interaction and contact among the children, the homogeneity of the language that developed remains in need of explanation. Fifty years of contact among pidgin-speaking

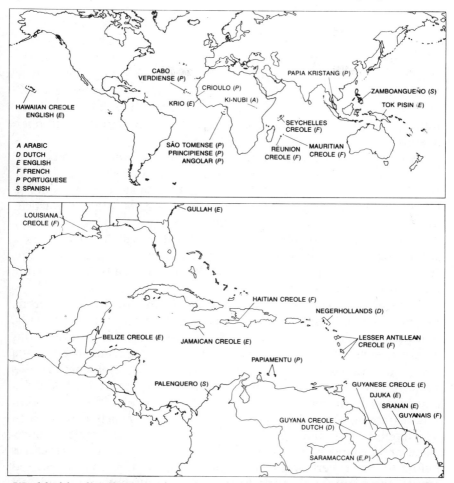

Worldwide distribution of creole languages reflects the historical circumstances of their development. Almost all creoles arose on isolated tropical littorals or islands, where colonial powers had established agricultural economies based on cheap immigrant labor. The geographic dispersion of the colonies suggests that creole languages developed independently of one another. The letters in parentheses after the name of each language indicate the colonial language from which most of the vocabulary of the creole is borrowed.

adults were not enough to erase the differences among the national language groups; the homogeneity must have resulted from the differences between children and adults.

One might still suppose the structural uniformity of Creole is derived from certain structures of one of the ancestral languages or perhaps from certain structures of English, the language of the plantation owners. There are numerous differences, however, between the structure of Creole and the structure of any of the languages with which

Creole speakers might have been in contact. In English, for example, it is possible to refer to an object or a group of objects in a nonspecific way, but English grammar forces the speaker to state in advance whether the number of unspecified objects is one or many, singular or plural. One must say either "I am going to the store to buy a shirt" or "I am going to the store to buy shirts," even though one may not want to commit oneself in advance to buying any particular number of shirts.

In Creole a grammatically neutral marker for number can be employed on the noun "shirt" in order to avoid specifying number: "I stay go da store for buy shirt" ("I am going to the store to buy shirt"). Moreover, in Creole the addition of a definite or an indefinite article to "shirt" changes the meaning of the sentence. In saying "I stay go da store for buy one shirt" the Creole speaker asserts the shirt is a specific one; in the sentence "I stay go da store for buy da shirt" the speaker further presupposes that the listener is already familiar with the shirt the speaker is going to buy.

There are many other features of Creole that distinguish it from English. Whereas in English there is a past tense, which is usually marked with the suffix "-ed," in Creole there is a tense called the anterior tense, which is marked with "bin" for older speakers and with "wen" for younger speakers. The anterior tense is somewhat like the English past perfect: "had walked" in English is "bin walk" in Creole, and "walked" in English is simply "walk" in Creole. In order to distinguish irreal, or possible, actions or processes from actual ones, English employs the conditional or the future tense. In Creole all such irreal circumstances are expressed by the particle "go," which is placed before the main verb and marks what linguists call modality. For example, the sentence "If I had a car, I would drive home" is rendered in Creole as "If I bin get car, I go drive home."

There is also a Creole auxiliary verb that marks what linguists call aspect; it too is placed before the main verb and indicates that the action expressed by the verb is nonpunctual, or in other words repeated, habitual, continuing or incomplete. In order to say "I run in Kapiolani Park every evening" in Creole one must say "I stay run in Kapiolani Park every evening." If the particle "stay" is omitted by the Creole speaker, the action is understood to be completed or nonrepetitive.

In English there is no straightforward way to distinguish purposes that have been accomplished from those that have not. The sentence "John went to Honolulu to see Mary" does not specify whether or not John actually saw Mary. In Creole grammar the ambiguity must be resolved. If John saw Mary and the Creole speaker knows that John saw Mary, the speaker must say, "John bin go Honolulu go see Mary." If John did not see Mary or if the speaker does not know whether or

Pidgin	Hawaiian Creole English
Building—high place—wall part—time—nowtime—and then—now temperature every time give you.	Get one [There is an] electric sign high up on da wall of da building show you what time an' temperature get [it is] right now.
Now days, ah, house, ah, inside, washi clothes machine get, no? Before time, ah, no more, see? And then pipe no more, water pipe no more.	Those days bin get [there were] no more washing machine, no more pipe water like get [there is] inside house nowadays, ah?
No, the men, ah—pau [finished] work—they go, make garden. Plant this, ah, cabbage, like that. Plant potato, like that. And then—all that one—all right, sit down. Make lilly bit story.	When work pau [is finished] da guys they stay go make [are going to make] garden for plant potato an' cabbage an' after little while they go sit down talk story ["shoot the breeze"].
Good, this one. Kaukau [food] any kind this one. Pilipin island no good. No more money.	Hawaii more better than Philippines, over here get [there is] plenty kaukau [food], over there no can, bra [brother], you no more money for buy kaukau [food], 'a'swhy [that's why].

PIDGIN AND CREOLE versions of identical sentences illustrate the structural differences between pidgin and Creole in Hawaii. Pidgin, which is spoken only by immigrants, varies widely from speaker to speaker. Although one can probably say anything in pidgin that can be said in English or Creole, the structure of pidgin is extremely rudimentary. Pidgin sentences are little more than strings of nouns, verbs and adjectives, often arranged to place old, shared information first and new information later in the sentence. Creole arose in Hawaii only among the children of immigrants, and it is much richer in grammatical structure than pidgin. Moreover, the rules of Creole grammar are uniform from speaker to speaker, and they resemble the structural rules of other creoles. English versions of words and phrases are given in brackets.

not John saw Mary, the speaker must say, "John bin go Honolulu for see Mary."

Similar distinctions could be drawn between the grammatical structure of Creole and the structure of other contact languages, such as Hawaiian, Ilocano (the language spoken in the north of the Philippine island of Luzon), and Japanese. There are also resemblances, but most of them are confined to idiomatic expressions. For example, the Creole expression "O the pretty," which means "How pretty he [she/it] is," is a literal translation of the Hawaiian-language idiom "O ka nani." In the main, however, our investigations strongly suggest that the basic structures of Creole differ from those of other languages. Although it might seem that some children of immigrants could transfer the structures of their parents' native languages onto the evolving Creole language, they did not do so. The structural linguistic input

English	Hawaiian Creole English
The two of us had a hard time raising dogs.	Us two bin get hard time raising dog.
John and his friends are stealing the food.	John-them stay cockroach the kaukau.
He doesn't want to play because he's lazy.	He lazy, 'a'swhy he no like play.
How do you expect to finish your house?	How you expect for make pau you house?
It would have been better if I'd gone to Honolulu to buy it.	More better I bin go Honolulu for buy om.
The one who falls first is the loser.	Who go down first is loser.
The man who was going to lay the vinyl had quoted me a price.	The guy gon' lay the vinyl bin quote me price.
There was a woman who had three daughters.	Bin get one wahine she get three daughter.
She can't go because she hasn't any money.	She no can go, she no more money, 'a'swhy.

STRUCTURAL DIFFERENCES between sentences in Hawaiian Creole and their English equivalents show that the grammar of Creole did not originate as a grammar borrowed from English. For example, the past perfect tense of a verb in Creole is expressed by the particles "bin" or "wen," which precede the main verb, instead of by the suffix "-ed." Nonpunctual, or progressive, aspect is expressed by the word "stay" instead of by the suffix "-ing." In the English sentence "The two of us had a hard time raising dogs" the rules of grammar oblige the speaker to indicate that the noun "dog" is either singular or plural. In the Creole version of the sentence, however, neither singular nor plural is implied. There are also relatively insignificant lexical differences between the two languages: "cockroach" is picturesquely employed as a verb, and "kaukau," which may be derived from the Chinese pidgin term "chow-chow," is a common word for "food." Equally striking structural differences are found between Hawaiian Creole and other languages, such as Chinese, Hawaiian, Japanese, Korean, Portuguese, Spanish, or the Philippine languages, with which speakers of Hawaiian Creole might have been in contact.

that was available to the children was apparently not used in the development of Creole.

Even if it could be demonstrated that all the grammatical structures of Creole were borrowed, cafeteria-style, from one contact language or another, the uniformity of Creole would present a difficult question: How did the speakers who invented Creole come to agree on which structure to borrow from which language? Without such agreement Creole could not be as uniform as it is. Yet it seems highly implausible that the agreement could have been reached so quickly. If there had been massive borrowing from ancestral languages, differences in the version of Creole spoken by various groups would have persisted at least one generation beyond the first generation of speakers.

There is another dimension to the problem of the uniformity of Hawaiian Creole. It turns out that creole languages throughout the world exhibit the same uniformity and even the same grammatical structures that are observed in Hawaii. The finding is all the more remarkable when it is compared with the rather poor correspondence in structure I have noted between Hawaiian Creole and other contact languages in Hawaii. For example, the distinction made in Hawaiian Creole between singular, plural, and neutral number is also made in all other creole languages. Similarly, in all other creole languages there are three invariant particles that act as auxiliary verbs and play the roles that "bin," "go" and "stay" play in Hawaiian Creole.

In Haitian Creole, for example, the word "té" marks the anterior tense of the verb, the word "av(a)" marks irreal modality, and the word "ap" marks the aspect of the verb as nonpunctual. Thus in Haitian Creole the phrase "I have been walking" is rendered "m [I] t'ap [té + ap] maché." Similarly, in Sranan, an English-based creole found in Surinam (formerly Netherlands Guiana), the anterior tense marker is "ben," the irreal modality marker is "sa" and the nonpunctual aspect marker is "e." The phrase "He would have been walking" is rendered "A[he] ben sa e waka." Most important, there is a strict order that must be followed in all creole languages when more than one of these markers is present in a sentence. The particle for tense precedes the particle for modality, and the particle for modality precedes the particle for aspect.

Finally, consider the grammatical distinction I have noted between purposes accomplished and unaccomplished. The same distinction, absent in English, is found in all creoles. In Mauritian Creole, a creole based on the French vocabulary that is used on the island of Mauritius, a sentence such as "He decided to eat meat" can be expressed in two ways. If the subject of the sentence carried out his decision, the sentence is rendered "Li ti desid al mâz lavian," which literally means "He decided go eat meat." If the decision was not carried out, the sentence is rendered as "Li ti desid pu mâz lavian," or literally "He decided for eat meat." In Jamaican Creole the sentence "He went to wash" must be rendered either as "Im gaan fi bied" ("He went with the intention of washing") or as "Im gaan go bied" ("He went to wash and completed the task").

These examples only suggest the extent of the structural similarities among creole languages. The similarities seem unaffected by the wide geographic dispersion of the creoles and the variation among the languages such as Dutch, English, and French from which they draw the greatest part of their vocabulary. . . .

The linguist's first reaction to such a finding is to look for a common ancestor of the similar languages. For example, it has been conjectured

Verb Form	Nonstative Verbs			Stative Verbs		
	Hawaiian Creole	*Haitian Creole*	*Sranan*	*Hawaiian Creole*	*Haitian Creole*	*Sranan*
Base form ("He walked"; "He loves")	He walk	Li maché	A waka	He love	Li rêmê	A lobi
Anterior ("He had walked"; "He loved")	He bin walk	Li té maché	A ben waka	He bin love	Li té rêmê	A ben lobi
Irreal ("He will/would walk"; "He will/would love")	He go walk	L'av(a) maché	A sa waka	He go love	L'av(a) rêmê	A sa lobi
Nonpunctual ("He is/was walking")	He stay walk	L'ap maché	A e waka	—	—	—
Anterior + irreal ("He would have walked"; "He would have loved")	He bin go walk	Li t'av(a) maché	A ben sa waka	He bin go love	Li t'av(a) rêmê	A ben sa lobi

Anterior + nonpunctual ("He was/had been walking")	He bin stay walk	Li t'ap maché	A ben e waka	—	—	—
Irreal + nonpunctual ("He will/would be walking")	He go stay walk	L'av ap maché	A sa e waka	—	—	—
Anterior + irreal + nonpunctual ("He would have been walking")	He bin go stay walk	Li t'av ap maché	A ben sa e waka	—	—	—

CONJUGATION OF THE VERB is similar in all creole languages, in spite of superficial lexical differences. Moreover, the creole system is quite distinct from the one encountered in English and in most other languages. The table gives conjugations in Hawaiian Creole, Haitian Creole, and Sranan (an English-based creole spoken in Surinam, the former Netherlands Guiana) for stative and nonstative verbs. Stative verbs are verbs such as "like," "want," and "love," which cannot form the nonpunctual aspect; in English, for example, one cannot add "-ing" to a finite stative verb. The base form of the verb refers to the present for stative verbs and to the past for nonstative verbs. The anterior tense is roughly equivalent to the English past tense for stative verbs and to the English past perfect tense for nonstative verbs. The irreal mode includes the English future, conditional and subjunctive. In all the creole languages the anterior particle precedes the irreal particle, and the irreal particle precedes the nonpunctual particle. In Hawaiian Creole, however, "He bin go walk" has come to mean "He walked" instead of "He would have walked," and the forms "He bin stay walk," "He go stay walk" and "He bin go stay walk," although they were widespread before World War II, are now almost extinct because of the growing influence of English in Hawaii. The bracketed English translations are provided only as a rough guide to the meaning.

that the linguistic ancestor was a contact language that grew out of Portuguese and certain West African languages in the course of the first Portuguese explorations of Africa in the 15th and 16th centuries. According to the hypothesis, this contact language was subsequently spread around the world by Portuguese sailors, changing its vocabulary but not its syntax or semantics as it entered the sphere of influence of another colonial power. Superficially such an explanation might seem to be consistent with the development of Creole in Hawaii, because Portuguese laborers were brought to the islands in large numbers during the late 19th and early 20th centuries.

There are several serious flaws in the account. First, Hawaiian Creole bears scant resemblance to any of the contact languages, including Portuguese. Second, the claims of linguistic similarity between creoles and Portuguese or between creoles and West African languages are grossly exaggerated. Most important, our study of hundreds of Hawaiian speakers has made it clear that Hawaiian Creole almost certainly originated in Hawaii. We found no surviving immigrant who speaks anything approximating a creole language; instead every immigrant we surveyed speaks some variety of pidgin. If Hawaiian Creole was primarily an imported language, it would have been carried by immigrants, and presumably it would have been learned by others among the immigrant population. One must therefore conclude that Hawaiian Creole arose among the children of immigrants, where it is now found. Moreover, if a creole language could develop in Hawaii without ancestry, it can arise anywhere else in a similar way.

The implications of these findings are far-reaching. Because the grammatical structures of creole languages are more similar to one another than they are to the structures of any other language, it is reasonable to suppose most if not all creoles were invented by the children of pidgin-speaking immigrants. Moreover, since creoles must have been invented in isolation, it is likely that some general ability, common to all people, is responsible for the linguistic similarities.

The suggestion that people are biologically predisposed to use language is not a new one: for more than two decades Noam Chomsky of the Massachusetts Institute of Technology has argued that there is an innate universal grammar underlying all human languages. The universal grammar is postulated largely on the grounds that only by its means could children acquire a system as enormously complex as a human language in the short time they do. Studies by the late Eric H. Lenneberg tend to confirm Chomsky's hypothesis. The acquisition of language resembles the acquisition of other complex and flexible aspects of the child's behavior, such as walking, which are undoubtedly controlled to some degree by neurophysiological development. The universal grammar conjectured by Chomsky is a computing device, somehow realized neurologically, that makes a wide range of grammatical models available to the child. According to Chomsky, the child must then "select" which of the available grammatical models matches the grammar of the language into which the child is born.

The evidence from creole languages suggests that first-language acquisition is mediated by an innate device of a rather different kind. Instead of making a range of grammatical models available, the device provides the child with a single and fairly specific grammatical model. It was only in pidgin-speaking communities, where there was no grammatical model that could compete with the child's innate grammar, that the innate grammatical model was not eventually suppressed. The innate grammar was then clothed in whatever vocabulary was locally available and gave rise to the creole languages heard today.

The implications of this hypothesis call into question an idea that most linguists, including Chomsky, have tacitly accepted for many years, namely that no one of the world's languages is easier or harder for the child to acquire than any other. If there is a creole grammar somehow imprinted in the mind, creole languages should be easier to acquire than other languages. How is it, then, that not all children grow up speaking a creole language? The answer is they do their best to do just that. People around them, however, persist in speaking English or French or some other language, and so the child must modify the grammar of the native creole until it conforms to that of the local language.

Two kinds of linguistic evidence are relevant for testing the hypothesis. First, if some grammatical structure of creole is at variance with the corresponding grammatical structure of the local language, one should find that children make systematic errors with respect to the structure of the local language. On the other hand, if the two grammatical structures tend to agree, one should find extremely early, rapid, and errorless acquisition of the local-language structure.

Consider the systematic error observed by David McNeill of the University of Michigan in the speech of a four-year-old boy. In one of McNeill's observing sessions the boy complained, "Nobody don't like me," and the boy's mother responded by correcting the sentence: "Nobody likes me." The boy then repeated his sentence and the mother repeated her correction no fewer than eight times. Finally, the child altered his sentence and shouted in exasperation, "Nobody don't likes me."

The error is found in many English-speaking children between three-and-a half and four years old, including children who are not exposed to dialects of English that employ double negatives. There are many languages, such as French and Spanish, that also employ double negatives, but the only languages that allow negative subjects with negative verbs are creoles. For example, in Papia Kristang, the Portuguese-based creole language of the Malay Peninsula, one can say,

Child Language	English Creoles
Where I can put it?	Where I can put om? (Hawaii)
Daddy throw the nother rock.	Daddy t'row one neda rock'tone. (Jamaica)
I go full Angela bucket.	I go full Angela bucket. (Guyana)
Lookit a boy play ball.	Luku one boy a play ball. (Jamaica)
Nobody don't like me.	Nobody no like me. (Guyana)
I no like do that.	I no like do that. (Hawaii)
Johnny big more than me.	Johnny big more than me. (Jamaica)
Let Daddy get pen write it.	Make Daddy get pen write am. (Guyana)
I more better than Johnny.	I more better than Johnny. (Hawaii)

SENTENCES SPOKEN BY CHILDREN between two and four years old, all born of English-speaking parents, are strikingly similar to sentences in English-based creole languages. The similarities among creole languages and the likelihood that the languages arose independently of one another suggest that creoles develop among children whenever there is no adequate native language to serve as a model. The author conjectures that if children were removed from their native English-language community at the age of about two, they would grow up speaking a language whose vocabulary would be primarily English but whose grammar would be a creole.

"Angkosa nte mersimentu," or literally, "Nothing not-have value." In Guyanese Creole, which is based on English and found in Guyana (formerly British Guiana), one can say, "Non dag na bait non kyat," or literally, "No dog did not bite no cat."

A second instance of systematic error is found in the formation of children's questions. Children learning English often indicate questions only by their intonation; the subject and the auxiliary verb are almost never reversed. For example, children repeatedly say things such as "You can fix this?" even though they have heard countless questions such as "Can you fix this?" Similarly, no creole language distinguishes questions and statements on the basis of word order; the difference is marked by intonation alone.

Consider the sentence "A gon' full Angela bucket." Although such a sentence is unacceptable in English, it is perfectly acceptable in Hawaiian Creole, Guyanese Creole, or any of several other creoles related to English. It is synonymous with the sentence "I'm going to fill Angela's bucket," but it differs from the structure of the English sentence in the following ways. First, the first-person pronoun "I" is reduced to "A"; second, the auxiliary verb "am" is omitted; third, the forms "go" or "gon" are used to mark the future tense; fourth, the word "to" in the infinitive is omitted; fifth, the adjective "full" is employed as if it were a transitive verb, and sixth, the possessive marker "-'s" is omitted. All these features are characteristics of creoles, but this sentence was not uttered by a creole speaker. It was spoken by the three-year-old daughter of an English-speaking linguist.

When a feature of the local language matches the structure of creole, children avoid making errors that would otherwise seem quite natural. For example, children learning English acquire the suffix "-ing," which expresses duration, at a very early age. Even before the age of two many children say things such as "I sitting high chair," where the verb expresses a continuing action. One would expect that as soon as the suffix was acquired it would be applied to every possible verb, just as the suffix "-s" that marks the English plural is frequently overgeneralized to nouns such as "foot" and "sheep."

One would therefore expect children to utter ungrammatical sentences such as "I liking Mommy" and "I wanting candy." Remarkably, such errors are almost never heard. Children seem to know implicitly that English verbs such as "like" and "want," which are called stative verbs, cannot be marked by the suffix "-ing" to indicate duration. The distinction between stative and nonstative verbs is fundamental to creole languages, however, and no marker of continuing action can be employed with a stative verb in creoles either.

The distinction between specific and nonspecific reference, which I have already discussed, is an important feature of creole languages. In English the distinction can be subtle, but young children nonetheless acquire it with ease. Michael P. Maratsos of the University of Minnesota constructed a series of sentences for children to complete, for which the completions depended on the distinction between specific and nonspecific reference. For example, the sentence "John has never read a book," which makes nonspecific reference to the noun "book," can be completed by the phrase "and he never will read a book"; it cannot be completed by the phrase "and he never will read the book." Similarly, the sentence "John read a book yesterday," in which a specific book is presupposed, can be completed by the phrase "and he enjoyed the book"; it cannot be completed by the phrase "and he enjoyed a book." Children as young as three years were able to make such distinctions correctly about 90 percent of the time.

Many more studies of language acquisition will have to be carried out before the structure of creole languages can be firmly accepted as the basis of first-language acquisition. Daniel Isaac Slobin of the University of California at Berkeley has suggested that there is a set of processes children apply to any language they hear, which he calls basic child grammar. [Slobin] cites evidence from several languages for the hypothesis, and it now appears that basic child grammar and creole languages may have much in common.

If creole languages represent the manifestation of a neurologically determined program of child development, then Psamtik was by no means the fool he has been taken for. It may be possible to discover, at least in general outline, the structure of human language in the early stages of its development. Moreover, in attempting to reconstruct such a language linguists may be able to answer questions the pharaoh did not even ask: How did human language originate? What are the minimum prerequisites for such a thing as language to arise in a species? If such questions can be answered or even formulated in a precise and coherent way, we shall be much closer to understanding what makes the human species different from others.

Bibliography

Baker, Philip, and Chris Corne. *Isle de France Creole*. Ann Arbor, MI: Karoma Publishers, 1982.

Bickerton, Derek. *Roots of Language*. Ann Arbor, MI: Karoma Publishers, 1981.

Chomsky, Noam. *Rules and Representations*. New York: Columbia University Press, 1980.

Lenneberg, Eric H. *Biological Foundations of Language*. New York: John Wiley & Sons, 1967.

FOR DISCUSSION AND REVIEW

1. In what sense has the experience of the children of pidgin-speaking laborers in various colonial outposts constituted a replication of the seventh-century-B.C. pharaoh Psamtik's experiment?

2. Bickerton states his central hypothesis as follows: "Between the ages of two and four the child born into a community of linguistically competent adults speaks a variety of language whose structure bears a deep resemblance to the structure of creole languages. Hence, by an ironic stroke of justice, the surviving linguistic remnants of colonialism may offer indispensable keys to the study of our own linguistic heritage." Make up a list summarizing the evidence that Bickerton offers to support this hypothesis. Then consider from which aspect(s) of language his evidence is taken (rules of phonology, syntax, semantics, and/or pragmatics). What conclusions can you draw?

3. Give three reasons why Hawaii is especially well-suited for the study of creole languages.

4. Bickerton describes the distinction between pidgin and creole as "fundamental." Write brief descriptions of pidgin and of creole that clarify this fundamental distinction.

5. List three ways in which the process of language acquisition for a child born into a pidgin-speaking community differs significantly from that for a child surrounded by native speakers of any "natural" language. Be sure to include specific details and examples.

6. Bickerton writes of the "observed uniformity" of Hawaiian Creole and asks, rhetorically, "How, within a single generation, did such a consistent and uniform language develop out of the linguistic free-for-all that was pidgin in Hawaii?" Summarize his answer. What "straw man" explanations does he suggest and then dismiss?

7. Explain how Bickerton's ideas support, refute, and/or modify Noam Chomsky's ideas about "an innate universal grammar underlying all human languages."

8. What evidence does Bickerton give to support his arguments that "there is a creole grammar somehow imprinted in the mind" and that "creole languages represent the manifestation of a neurologically determined program of child development?"

9. List four important grammatical features shared by creole languages.

Projects for "Language Acquisition"

1. Examine the following conversation between Eve, a 24-month-old child, and her mother:

Eve: Have that?
Mother: No, you may not have it.
Eve: Mom, where my tapioca?
Mother: It's getting cool. You'll have it in just a minute.
Eve: Let me have it.
Mother: Would you like to have your lunch right now?
Eve: Yeah. My tapioca cool?
Mother: Yes, it's cool.
Eve: You gonna watch me eat my lunch?
Mother: Yeah, I'm gonna watch you eat your lunch.
Eve: I eating it.
Mother: I know you are.
Eve: It time Sarah take a nap.
Mother: It's time for Sarah to have some milk, yeah. And then she's gonna take a nap and you're gonna take a nap.
Eve: And you?
Mother: And me too, yeah.[1]

Compare the grammar of Eve's speech with that of her mother. What elements are systematically missing from the child's speech? Now, look at Eve's speech in a conversation with her mother that was taped only three months later:

Mother: Come and sit over here.
Eve: You can sit down by me. That will make me happy. Ready to turn it.
Mother: We're not quite ready to turn the page.
Eve: Yep, we are.
Mother: Shut the door, we won't hear her then.
Eve: Then Fraser won't hear her too. Where he's going? Did you make a great big hole there?
Mother: Yes, we made a great big hole in here; we have to get a new one.
Eve: Could I get some other piece of paper?
Mother: You ask Fraser.
Eve: Could I use this one?
Mother: I suppose so.
Eve: Is Fraser goin take his pencil home when he goes?
Mother: Yes, he is.[2]

What changes do you note in Eve's speech? Try to describe the "grammatical rules" that govern her speech in each passage. Although

---

[1] A transcription of a taped conversation from Ursula Bellugi, "Learning the Language," *Psychology Today* 4 (December 1970), 33.
[2] Ibid., 33–34.

Eve could not tell us of the rules she learned during the three-month interval, what rules, as evidenced implicitly by her speech, has she internalized? What conclusions can you draw about the process of language learning among children? Write a short paper dealing with these questions.

2. Read Noam Chomsky's well-known review article "Review of B. F. Skinner's *Verbal Behavior*" (*Language* 35 [1959], 26–58). Prepare a report explaining the objections of Chomsky, a linguist, to the views of Skinner, a behaviorist psychologist, about language acquisition.

3. Prepare a report on how children acquire social skills in the use of language simultaneously with their acquisition of other language skills. Use as one source Susan Ervin-Tripp's "Social Backgrounds and Verbal Skills" in Renira Huxley and Elisabeth Ingram, eds., *Language Acquisition: Models and Methods* (New York: Academic Press, 1971).

4. One of the best texts on language acquisition is Jill G. de Villiers and Peter A. de Villiers, *Language Acquisition* (Cambridge, MA: Harvard University Press, 1978). Any single chapter in the book would provide enough material for a more detailed look at some stage or aspect of language acquisition than we could provide in this anthology, and the extensive bibliography will suggest additional topics.

5. Using the bibliography given in Fromkin et al.'s "The Development of Language in Genie . . ." (see pp. 127–128) and the selected bibliography on pp. 154–156, prepare a report on a particular feral or isolated child. Comparing the various cases with your classmates should clarify some of the problems earlier investigators have encountered.

6. As noted in "Genie: A Postscript," Susan Curtiss and Victoria Fromkin's recent research has focused on "people with the opposite pattern [from Genie]—who have normal language ability despite cognitive deficits." Using the resources available in your college library, especially journals, prepare a report describing what they have learned. You will find it helpful to check for recent journal publications by Curtiss.

7. We know that young children who are learning two or more languages at the same time use similar strategies to acquire the different languages. But it is not clear what effect, if any, being bilingual has on people. Using library resources, prepare a report in which you summarize opinions about the advantages or disadvantages of being bilingual.

8. The process of learning a second language is usually different for adults (and older children) than it is for young children, if only because the former group is likely to learn in a classroom setting. Using library resources, prepare a report in which you describe the difficulties that adult second-language learners encounter and the learning strategies they employ.

9. Throughout much of the world, people need to speak at least two languages in order to function in their societies. In the United States, however, only about ten percent of Americans speak a language in addition to English. Proposals for curriculum reform in American schools often call for an increase in the teaching of foreign languages. As a group project, hold a debate on the subject, "American high-school graduates should be fluent in at least one language besides English."

Selected Bibliography

Note: Five of the six articles in this section include bibliographies (Moskowitz, de Villiers and de Villiers, Aitchison, Fromkin et al., and Bickerton). The reader should consult these for a more exhaustive listing of sources.

Bain, Bruce, ed. *The Sociogenesis of Language and Human Conduct.* New York: Plenum Press, 1983. (A large and eclectic collection of interesting essays.)

Bar-Adon, A., and Leopold, W. F. *Child Language: A Book of Readings.* Englewood Cliffs, NJ: Prentice-Hall, 1971.

Bates, Elizabeth. *Language and Context: The Acquisition of Pragmatics.* New York: Academic Press, 1976. (Describes the development in children of knowledge of pragmatics.)

Bellugi, Ursula. "Learning the Language." *Psychology Today*, 4 (December 1970), 32–35, 66. (A nontechnical description of language acquisition and the grammar of children.)

Bickerton, Derek. *Roots of Language.* Ann Arbor: Karoma Publishers, 1981. (Develops the argument that Creole languages provide the key to understanding the nature of all human languages.)

Brown, Roger. *A First Language.* Cambridge, MA: Harvard University Press, 1973. (An important and classic work.)

——. "How Shall a Thing Be Called?" *Psychological Review*, 85 (1958), 145–154. (A discussion of how adults teach children the names of objects.)

Curtiss, Susan. *Genie: A Psycholinguistic Study of a Modern-Day "Wild Child."* New York: Academic Press, 1977. (Detailed analysis of Genie's linguistic and cognitive development.)

——. "Genie: Language and Cognition," *UCLA Working Papers in Cognitive Linguistics* 1 (1979), 15–62. (Genie's cognitive development and its relationship to her linguistic ability.)

——. "The Critical Period and Feral Children," *UCLA Working Papers in Cognitive Linguistics*, 2 (1980), 21–36. (Complete description of known cases of feral children; argues for the existence of a specific language faculty.)

de Villiers, Jill G., and Peter A. de Villiers. *Language Acquisition.* Cambridge, MA: Harvard University Press, 1978. (If you read only one book about language acquisition, choose this one. Thorough, complete, balanced; includes discussion of the language problems of deaf, retarded, dysphasic, and autistic children.)

Ferguson, Charles A., and Daniel I. Slobin, eds. *Studies of Child Language Development*. New York: Holt, Rinehart and Winston, 1973. (Valuable collection of hard-to-find papers; covers the acquisition by children of a number of different languages.)

Ferguson, Charles A., and Catherine E. Snow, eds. *Talking to Children: Language Input and Acquisition*. Cambridge: Cambridge University Press, 1977. (Focuses on the importance of mothers' speech to children; covers a number of different languages.)

Heatherington, Madelon E. *How Language Works*. Cambridge, MA: Winthrop Publishers, 1980. (Excellent introduction to the study of language; see Chapter 2 about language acquisition.)

Kagan, Jerome. "Do Infants Think?" *Scientific American*, 226 (1972), 74–82. (Argues that cognitive development is under way as early as nine months of age.)

Kess, Joseph F. *Psycholinguistics: Introductory Perspectives*. New York: Academic Press, 1976. (See Chapter 3 for a detailed description of language acquisition.)

Lenneberg, Eric H. *Biological Foundations of Language*. New York: John Wiley & Sons, 1967. (A seminal and now classic work; technical investigation of the biological aspects of language.)

McNeill, David. *The Acquisition of Language: The Study of Developmental Psycholinguistics*. New York: Harper & Row, 1970. (Brief but technical discussion of language acquisition.)

Morehead, Donald M., and Ann E. Morehead, eds. *Normal and Deficient Language*. Baltimore: University Park Press, 1976. (Excellent studies of language acquisition by normal, deaf, dysphasic, and retarded children.)

Nilson, Don L. F., and Alleen Pace Nilsen. *Language Play: An Introduction to Linguistics*. Rowley, MA: Newbury House Publishers, 1978. (A thoroughly readable book; see especially Chapters 2 and 4 for discussions of the behaviorist and innatist hypotheses of language acquisition and of the important role of playing with language.)

Schiefelbusch, Richard L., and Lyle L. Lloyd, eds. *Language Perspectives: Acquisition, Retardation and Intervention*. Baltimore: University Park Press, 1974. (An important collection; deals with a number of aspects of language acquisition by normal, deaf, retarded, and autistic children.)

Shipley, Elizabeth F., Carlota S. Smith, and Lila R. Gleitman. "A Study in the Acquisition of Language: Free Responses to Commands." *Language*, 45 (1969), 322–342. (Comprehension of speech exceeds ability to produce speech in children who are at certain stages of language development.)

Slobin, Dan I. *Psycholinguistics*. Glenview, IL: Scott, Foresman, 1971. (Still a good, brief introduction, especially helpful concerning language acquisition in children.)

———. "Children and Language: They Learn the Same Way All Around the World." *Psychology Today*, 6 (July 1972), 71–74, 82. (A nontechnical description of language acquisition by children of different cultures.)

Smith, Frank, and George A. Miller, eds. *The Genesis of Language: A Psycholinguistic Approach*. Cambridge, MA: The MIT Press, 1966. (Essays dealing with language development in children.)

Steinberg, Danny D. *Psycholinguistics: Language, Mind, and World.* New York: Longman, 1982. (Focuses on reading and second language teaching; see especially Chapters 8 and 9.)

Teller, Virginia, and Sheila J. White, eds. "Studies in Child Language and Multilingualism," *Annals of the New York Academy of Sciences,* 365 (1980). (Contains four interesting articles on language acquisition.)

Walker, Edward, ed. *Explorations in the Biology of Language.* Montgomery, VT: Bradford Books, 1978. (Six difficult but important essays focusing on language as a biological manifestation of universal cognitive structure.)

Part Three

Language and the Brain

During the last two decades, stimulated by what was learned from the split-brain operations of the 1960s, interest in and research about brain lateralization have increased dramatically. A number of popular books have appeared, most of them enthusiastic but not all of them entirely accurate. And, the field has attracted specialists from a variety of disciplines—psychology, philosophy, neurology, history, art, education, and most important from our point of view, linguistics. By the early 1980s, it had become clear that earlier ideas about the total dominance of the left hemisphere for language functions were major oversimplifications. The situation is far more complicated than early researchers believed, and we now know that the right hemisphere plays an important role in language processing.

In "Brain and Language," the first selection in Part Three, Jeannine Heny traces the development of research on the relationship of the brain to language and explores probable reasons for the development of brain lateralization. She then describes a variety of methods for measuring which hemisphere does what, and identifies the limitations of each method. The right hemisphere, Professor Heny explains, has a number of important functions, including some that are crucial to normal language-processing. In addition, she notes that linguistic tasks are not assigned identically in terms of hemispheres in all people, a point she makes clear in her discussion of bilinguals, deaf users of American Sign Language, literate people, speakers of certain languages, lefthanders, and women.

Aphasia, or language impairment due to brain injury, is the subject of the second selection, Howard Gardner's "The Loss of Language." Approximately 400,000 Americans have a stroke every year. According to Gardner, because the probability of having a stroke increases with age, "if other causes do not intervene, it is from this condition that most of us will eventually die" (*The Shattered Mind*, p. 12). Although people do not usually survive severe strokes that destroy large parts of the brain, some strokes are so mild that individuals may not even be aware of them or may recover completely within a few days. Many strokes, however, fall between these extremes—they are "insufficient to kill the individual or reduce him to a vegetable state, yet serious enough to permanently affect his functioning" (ibid.). In "The Loss of Language," Gardner, who has worked extensively with brain-damaged patients, describes two major kinds of aphasia and suggests that further research in this area can yield valuable insight into how the human brain processes language.

There are still a great many questions about the relationships among the human brain, language, and cognition. It is clear, however, that research will continue and that, as it does, we will learn more about the functioning of the brain.

1/Brain and Language

JEANNINE HENY

In the following selection, Jeannine Heny of Middlebury College examines the evolution of the human brain and some possible causes of brain lateralization. She traces the sometimes halting progress of early research involving aphasia and the attempts to "map out" the language functions of the cortex. Describing the many contemporary methods of measuring hemispheric activity, Professor Heny demonstrates that both the left and right hemispheres of the brain are important in language processing, and that it is probably the type of processing, rather than the material being processed, that differentiates the two hemispheres. Curiously, though, people do not all use the same hemisphere for language tasks; in fact, the same person may process identical material differently at different times. As Professor Heny points out, our understanding of the complex relationship between language and the brain has increased enormously in recent years, but it is still tantalizingly incomplete.

About five million years ago, the brain size of humanity's ancestors began to increase dramatically. During this evolutionary era, the human brain as we know it more than tripled in volume, after about ten million years of relatively stable size. Five million years may seem very long; but, as Figure 1 shows, on an evolutionary scale such a time span can mean a remarkably fast rate of change.

Gradually, other changes took place: our hominid forebears became predominantly righthanded, made use of increasingly sophisticated tools, and organized their culture in ever more complex ways. The result of this evolution, *homo sapiens*, looked rather unimpressive: puny and almost hairless, with a bent windpipe that reduced his breathing efficiency to nearly half its original capacity. Worse yet, his teeth were practically useless as chewing tools: he had nothing to match the sharp incisors of rats or the long canine teeth of wolves, lions, and other primates. But he did have at least one feature that more than compensated for all he lacked: the most highly developed communication system on earth, human language. In fact, the changes in the human brain involved much more than increased size, as Figure 2 reveals. In lower mammals such as the rat, the brain is almost wholly taken up with sensory and motor functions. In contrast, the primate brain has a greatly enlarged outer layer or *cortex*, resulting in a dramatic increase

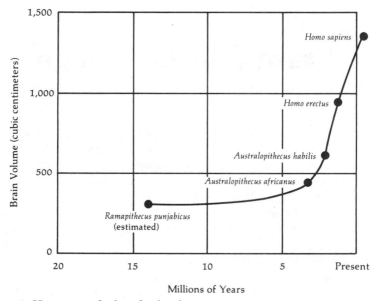

Figure 1. Human evolution: brain size.

in "uncommitted" cortical tissue not needed for basic functions. This article focuses on the brain, and especially on the parts of this "uncommitted cortex" that underlie human linguistic ability.

Discovering the Brain

For centuries, the nature of the brain was shrouded in mystery. Aristotle is said to have thought it was a cold sponge, whose main task was to cool the blood.[1] Later, Leonardo Da Vinci represented the brain as a curious void filled by three tiny bulbous structures arranged in a straight line behind the eyeball, whose functions he defined according to commonly held assumptions of his time.[2]

Not all early theories were quite so misguided, however. From the first studies on language deficits in the Greco-Roman era, it was suspected that the brain played some direct part in language use. Still, modern scholarship on this question began only in the nineteenth century.

In 1836, an obscure French country doctor, Marc Dax, attended a medical conference in Montpelier, France, and presented the only scientific paper of his life. Dax claimed that, in forty aphasic patients he

---

[1] Comment (cited from work by Clarke and O'Mally) in Arbib, Caplan, and Marshall (1982), p. 6; this article provides an interesting overview of neurolinguistic history.
[2] Harth (1982), pp. 37–42. A copy of Leonardo's sketch appears on p. 43.

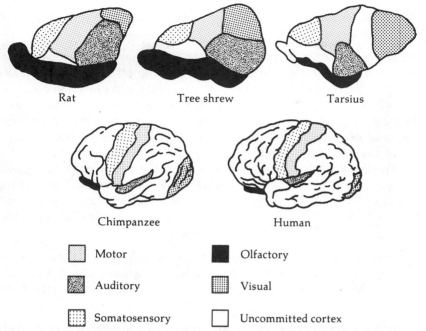

Rat   Tree shrew   Tarsius

Chimpanzee   Human

☐ Motor   ■ Olfactory

▨ Auditory   ▦ Visual

▥ Somatosensory   ☐ Uncommitted cortex

Figure 2. Human evolution: brain function. These figures show the approximate space devoted to sensory and motor functions in various mammalian brains. The white areas, called *association* **cortex, represent neural tissue not committed to basic functions. As shown, the increase in brain size is accompanied by a dramatic increase in the proportion of association cortex in humans.**

had seen in his practice, loss of language ability always correlated with damage to the left half of the brain. The paper went unnoticed at the time, and its remarkable insight was soon forgotten.

It was the French surgeon Paul Broca who, in 1864, dramatically proved Dax's original claim (about which, by the way, he knew nothing). For three years, he had studied aphasic symptoms in patients who, at autopsy, were found to have brain damage to the left frontal lobe. Broca was struck by the contrast with right hemisphere damage, which seemed to have little effect on speech. The area Broca isolated, and the aphasia associated with it, now bear his name: "Broca's aphasia" has come to stand for a complex of symptoms, ranging from extreme difficulty in articulation to "agrammatic" speech, where a patient produces halting strings of words without grammatical markers (e.g., inflections on verbs) or function words (such as articles and prepositions). The passage below gives an example of speech by a patient with Broca's aphasia. The patient is trying to describe a picture showing a little boy stealing cookies from a cookie jar while his chair is tipping over; a little girl is helping him. Their mother stands at the window staring into space while the sink in front of her overflows.

Cookie jar . . . fall over . . . chair . . . water . . . empty . . . ov . . . ov
. . . [Examiner: "overflow?"] Yeah.[3]

Ten years after Broca's discovery, Karl Wernicke, a twenty-six-year-old researcher in Germany, made yet another startling break-through. The patients who especially attracted his interest had no damage to Broca's area. In fact, in some sense, they were fluent speakers. They could produce a stream of speech with no trouble in pronunciation and no significant loss of grammatical morphemes. But the content of their utterances ranged from puzzling to meaningless.

The Wernicke's aphasic who produced the following passage was trying to describe the same picture as the Broca's aphasic. His flowing speech contrasts sharply with the hesitant ungrammatical answer of the first patient. Yet, despite his fluency, he seems to make very little sense of the situation he sees:

> Well, this is . . . mother is away here working out o'here to get her better, but when she's working, the two boys looking in the other part. One their small tile into her time here. She's working another time because she's getting, too.[4]

Broca's aphasic seemed to understand language, whereas Wernicke noted severe comprehension problems with this new complex of symptoms. Ultimately, Wernicke's research led him to propose not just a new language area, but an overall theory of how language is handled in the brain. Wernicke's area, located near the primary auditory cortex, just above and behind the left ear, seemed to be responsible for the storage of words. It was there, Wernicke claimed, that the mind chooses words to convey its thoughts. Once that is done, the message has to be transmitted to Broca's area, near the precentral motor cortex, where the movements of speech originate. There, the message is encoded into commands to the tongue, lips, and other articulators, and emerges as speech. Wernicke's model, summarized in Figure 3, still stands at the center of brain research.

The discovery of these classical language areas in the left hemisphere soon spurred researchers to look for the remaining pieces of the neurolinguistic puzzle. Science seemed on the brink of understanding just how the brain handled language; only the details of subsidiary language areas needed to be spelled out. Yet, despite Broca's and Wernicke's striking discoveries, efforts to map the rest of the brain's cortex in terms of language function have met with little success. On the one hand, it does seem that specific areas in the brain control discrete language functions. Spectacular cases of this have been documented, such as the discovery of the French neurologist Dejerine in 1892. Dejerine

---

[3] Cited from earlier work by Goodglass and Kaplan, in Blumstein (1982), p. 205.
[4] Blumstein, p. 205.

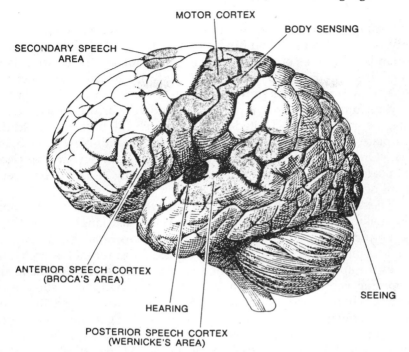

MOTOR CORTEX

BODY SENSING

SECONDARY SPEECH
AREA

ANTERIOR SPEECH CORTEX
(BROCA'S AREA)

SEEING

HEARING

POSTERIOR SPEECH CORTEX
(WERNICKE'S AREA)

Figure 3. The classical language areas of the brain. Note the proximity of Broca's area to the "motor cortex," where instructions to speech articulators originate. The proximity of Wernicke's area to neural centers for sight and hearing is also important, because this arrangement seems to allow the spoken and written word to be available for semantic processing in Wernicke's area as soon as they are perceived.

observed a patient who could not read although his visual skills, writing, and speech were normal. On autopsy, it was found that the left visual area was destroyed, along with the nerves connecting visual regions in the two hemispheres. Thus, only the right, nonverbal hemisphere could "see"—and it could not perceive what it saw as *language*. Hence, of course, it could not "read" what it saw. Nor could it transmit the image it received to the language centers on the left for interpretation. Encouraged by this and other cases where highly circumscribed damage caused specific, clearly identifiable deficiencies, one school of scientists (informally called the "diagram makers") devoted their energies to the search for a precise map of the brain.

But the diagram-makers ran into problems from the outset. For one thing, it had long been known that severe aphasics, with extensive left hemisphere lesions and with no ability to produce a normal spontaneous utterance, can often sing, curse, and produce fixed expressions such as "How are you?" This suggested that, at the least, the right hemisphere (despite its absence on the neurolinguistic "map") may have some linguistic potential. More serious, however, was the inability of researchers to identify any consistent set of symptoms corresponding to areas of lesions (i.e., injuries) outside the classical language areas of Figure 3. Exhaustive study by neurologists such as Henry Head in the 1920s showed that, at best, only a rough correlation could be found between symptom types and very broad cortical areas. (Imagine a map of the United States in which the best one could do was place Boston "somewhere in the New England–New York State area." One could indeed capture the distinction between San Francisco and Boston with such a picture, but it could hardly be said to be a very useful device for getting to Boston!)

These puzzling phenomena led many researchers to abandon map-making altogether, in favor of the claim that language involves higher cognitive processes in a way that makes breaking down linguistic abilities into discrete units impossible. Most recent research embodies the spirit of both approaches: scientists still search for the locus of specific verbal capacities; in fact, they have had some success in locating where certain words seem to be stored in memory. But neurologists now generally agree that a patient with a general impairment affecting, for example, memory or the ability to carry out purposeful actions, will suffer from verbal deficits as well. The cortical areas that handle higher cognitive activity are too closely intertwined to be easily teased apart and mapped out.

Two Brains or One: Hemispheric Asymmetries

With the discovery that one important mental faculty seemed to be housed in only one side of the brain came a host of intriguing questions. Does a human being have two consciousnesses or one? Is the mute right half teeming with unsatisfied desires and ideas that will never be expressed due to the dominant, talkative left half? If the connections between the two halves were severed, would the result be a creature with two quite distinct personalities, each having its own thoughts, world view, and feelings? The famous nineteenth-century psychologist Gustav Fechner thought not. In fact, so deep was his conviction that he offered to have his brain anatomically split should he develop a terminal illness. He never did, and the experiment was left undone in his lifetime.[5]

To the more prosaic, however, other questions arose: if the left hemisphere handles language, what else does it do? And what, if anything, does the right hemisphere specialize in? Hypotheses meant to

[5] Springer and Deutsch (1981), p. 26.

Left Brain	Right Brain
Analytic processing	Holistic processing, (dealing with overall patterns, or "gestalt" forms)
Temporal relations	Spatial relations
Speech sounds	Nonspeech sounds
Mathematics	Music
Intellectual	Emotional

Table 1. The two brains and what they do.

capture the brain's left-right dichotomy have sprung up in abundance, especially in the past fifteen years. They include the short list of oppositions given in Table 1.

At its most fanciful, the asymmetry implied in the last pair of terms has led to global claims about Eastern and Western modes of thought, which, interesting as they may be, are unsubstantiated. They have even caused the study of the brain to be viewed as suspect by many who recall the now-discounted claims of phrenologists in the early nineteenth century that bumps on each person's skull mirror "bumps on the brain," which in turn reveal personality traits.

But serious scientific questions come from this list as well. First of all, what counts as language and what doesn't? Most would agree that the word *cow*, printed on a card, should be perceived as language; but what about the single letter *c*? Or for that matter, what about groups of letters that don't spell a word? There is some evidence that we perceive sequences like *kug, zeb,* or *bem* as language, while sequences like *nku, lke,* and *okl* are perceived more as though they were simply geometrical shapes (Young et al., 1984). Pronounceability seems to be the cue here: one could imagine Dr. Seuss creating a character called a *Zeb*, if he hasn't already done so; but a name like *Lke* would take some getting used to, even for an imaginative child.

Even more puzzling is that the very same linguistic material presented in two forms may be handled differently. Subjects seem to use the left hemisphere to read text in standard printed characters, but the right hemisphere for elaborate lettering styles that presumably require more visual skill (Bryden and Allard, 1976). Likewise, mirror-image writing or writing that is blurred or incomplete seems to be processed on the right.

In fact, subtleties of this sort abound. Japanese readers show some tendency for right-hemisphere activity when reading in the *kanji* script, where each character represents one word. But in the phonetically based *kana* script, where a letter represents a sound sequence (usually a syllable), the expected left-hemisphere dominance for language re-emerges. Aphasia types distinguish between the two writing systems as well. Japanese aphasics often seem to retain some ability to read in the *kanji* script while no longer able to comprehend the sound-based system. This again suggests that the processing of *kanji* characters can be mediated by neural areas outside the normal language areas on the left.

Thus, some seemingly verbal tasks can in fact be handled by the right hemisphere. To further complicate matters, some spatial work seems to be done on the left side, especially if it involves comparison or association between pairs of shapes. In an interesting study done in 1980, Gur and Reivich found no hemispheric advantage for a spatial (gestalt completion) test, suggesting it can be handled by either hemisphere. But there was a significant difference in how well the job was done; subjects who "chose" to use the right, "spatially adept" hemisphere performed with significantly greater efficiency. But those who didn't use the right hemisphere also achieved reasonable results, suggesting that in some cases the unspecialized hemisphere may be like an untrained worker who manages to succeed at a job although he may not be the ideal person to do it.

In the light of these and similar findings, researchers now believe that it is the type of *processing*, not the type of *material processed*, that distinguishes the two hemispheres; in other words, the first entry in Table 1 can be thought of as the only true difference between left and right hemisphere activity. The left hemisphere is called upon whenever detailed analysis is in order, whereas the right hemisphere goes into action if holistic processing is involved. Language and mathematics typically involve sequential analysis (analytical thinking), whereas pictures and faces are usually taken in all at once, as are musical patterns.

Under this new view of lateralization, the Gur and Reivich results can be more plausibly explained. If, for some reason, a task does not clearly identify itself as requiring a right or left hemisphere approach, the job might be shunted off to different halves of the brain in different people—or even in the same person at different times, depending on which hemisphere is more active at any given time. But it is quite reasonable to expect that the hemisphere with a more appropriate approach to processing a certain task will get better results.

Interesting support for this "processing strategy" approach comes from several experiments showing that trained musicians (who analyze as they listen) actually process music in the *left* hemisphere. It is only the musically unsophisticated person who hears music as holistic patterns, and thus shows the expected right-hemisphere dominance for music.

Finally, once lateralization is seen in this more abstract way, another seemingly unrelated fact may tie in as well: the ability for fine, sequenced hand movements (called *manual praxis*) is mediated in the left hemisphere. Although hand movement and language are quite different types of activities on the surface, it is reasonable to suppose that the type of mental activity needed to orchestrate fine hand movements might be similar to the cerebral organization needed to fashion complex sentence patterns.

This last point brings us back to the opening theme by leading us to ask: Where did brain asymmetry come from? Was language the first activity to move into the analytical left hemisphere? Some think not. As a species, we surely developed fine manual coordination before we developed language as we know it. Perhaps our ability to analyze linguistic structures with the left hemisphere arose from a need to plan the flaking techniques to make a rock into a sharp tool. In other words, the left hemisphere's first specialization may have been for coordinating fingers, wrist, and hand movements for complex tool use and manufacture. Language may have been drawn to the left hemisphere simply because the neural circuitry already developed there for these unrelated tasks was somehow suited to take on linguistic work.

The extent to which language and tool use share neurological mechanisms is still a matter of debate. But we do know that in aphasia, fine hand coordination as well as language is often impaired. And we also know that the human species has been overwhelmingly right-handed for a long time: Cro-Magnon hand-tracings were virtually always of the left hand; thus, the artists must have been drawing with the right. The skulls of prehistoric animals provide mute evidence as well; archeologists tell us that the earliest hunting hominids must have used tools held in their right hand to slay game, judging from the position of fractures and marks on the skulls of ancient animals.

Other hints lie scattered along our evolutionary trail as well, not all of them relating to tool use. Brain asymmetry has been found elsewhere in the animal kingdom: in rodents, in other primates, and especially in birds. Even the most imaginative of scientists has yet to suspect a song sparrow of being an effective tool user; yet sparrows (and chaffinches) *do* have song strongly lateralized in the left hemisphere. For some species, and perhaps even for humans, the right hemisphere's visual and emotional roles may have taken their place *before* left hemisphere functions. In the struggle for survival, even a rat can use an acute eye to spot a potential predator, and then a quick emotional response to avoid becoming dinner for a hungry hawk.

Testing the Brain

The careful reader will by now wonder how all the claims in Table 1 can be made with certainty. How do we know what a single hemisphere is doing? There are, of course, the aphasia studies, but studies of brain malfunction are less useful than one might think. Consider

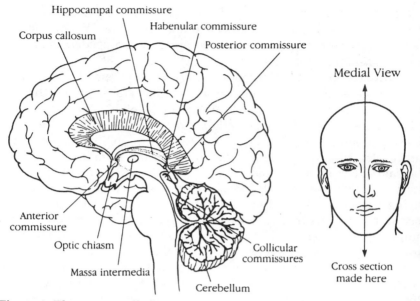

Figure 4. The corpus callosum.

the following analogy: Suppose you wanted to find out what a certain transistor in a radio does. You would learn very little if your only approach was to remove or damage that transistor, then turn the radio on to see what it would do!

A second problem involves the nature of the mechanism being studied. It is well known that brain tissue (unlike radio components) can "reorganize"; that is, if one area of tissue is damaged, especially at an early age, other areas may take over the original tissue's function. Thus, simple correlations between symptoms and areas of injured tissue may be very misleading.

THE "SPLIT BRAIN"

A surgical technique known as *commissurotomy*, used to treat severe cases of epilepsy, seems at first sight to provide ideal subjects for studying brain lateralization. Commissurotomy involves severing the *corpus callosum*, the main bundle of fibers connecting the brain's two hemispheres, as shown in Figure 4. With patients who have undergone this operation, neurologists can limit input to one hemisphere of the brain. Thus, one can show a picture or a written text to a single hemisphere of the brain to see how it responds. Or one can simply "talk" to one half of the brain at a time.

These patients have been studied intensely, and with interesting results, but the general implications of these studies are controversial. These patients have clearly had abnormal brain activity resulting from epilepsy, usually for many years. Thus, like aphasics, their brain tissue may have reorganized in ways that make them far from representative examples of normal brain function. Because of these problems, there has been great interest in developing tests for hemispheric lateralization that can be used with normal subjects.

BEHAVIORAL TESTS

A widely used technique called *tachistoscopic presentation* represents one attempt to ask what one half of the brain does more efficiently or more accurately than the other. A subject is asked to fix his gaze on a central point, directly in front of him. An image is then flashed to his right or left visual field. The subject does not know which side will come next, and the flash is too brief (less than one-fifth of a second) to allow eye movement to one side or the other. Because of the human nervous system's organization, the image is perceived primarily by one hemisphere of the brain—the one *opposite* the visual field involved. If a subject handles a stimulus presented on the right side of the screen notably well, he is assumed to be using the left hemisphere more efficiently for the task.

Doreen Kimura at the Montreal Neurological Institute has adapted this principle to auditory stimuli in the *dichotic listening test* she developed. The ear, like the eye, conveys messages most effectively via the so-called contralateral nerve pathway to the opposite hemisphere of the brain. Thus, if two different words are played to a subject's two ears, his left hemisphere will hear the word played to the right ear, and vice versa. As it turns out, many subjects consistently hear words more accurately with their right ear, but identify tunes more accurately if they are played to the left ear. This test has played a major role in setting up the list given in Table 1.

The LEM, or lateral eye movement, provides yet another test of brain activity via behavior. It is claimed that activity on one side of the brain triggers an automatic response in eye movement—in the opposite direction from the locus of mental activity. In fact, when answering a question, we do tend to look left or right, rather than looking directly at the asker of the question. And it seems that, for some people in some situations, an emotional question triggers an automatic glance to the left, whereas a verbal or intellectual question makes their gaze drift to the right, while the analytical left hemisphere computes the necessary answer.

Unfortunately, behavioral tests have their drawbacks. A single subject tested twice by one of these measures may show different lateralization for the same task with only one week intervening between the first and second test. It seems that hemispheric choice for many tasks is fickle enough to be disrupted by seemingly minor factors. In a phenomenon called "priming," subjects are asked to memorize a list of words, thus presumably turning on the left hemisphere's circuits. If they are immediately asked to perform some spatial task that normally yields right-hemisphere dominance, they will often fail to show the expected result. They will perform the task with the left hemisphere. To use a rough analogy, they seem to use the calculator which is already turned on, rather than the one specialized to do the work they want done. Obviously, the reliability of tests like these depends on the ability to control such outside factors on choice of processing strategy, and that is no simple matter.

PHYSIOLOGICAL MEASURES

Instead of watching how a subject behaves in various situations, one can look directly to the brain's physical properties for evidence of lateralization. However, the simplest physical facts about the brain are difficult to interpret. In the majority of brains, there is a physical enlargement of the left central area called the *planum temporale*, which should include Wernicke's area. But despite a long and heated debate in the nineteenth century about the relationship between brain size and intelligence (Broca believed a large brain meant high intelligence), no conclusions can be drawn from gross measurement of brain tissue. More subtle methods are needed to deal with the brain in physiological terms.

Scientists have learned to observe chemical and electrical activity in different regions of the brain. Sophisticated devices for accomplishing this include computerized axial tomography (CT or CAT) scan, positron emission tomography (PET) scan, electroencephalogram (EEG), and regional cerebral bloodflow (rCBF). Also useful is the famous Wada test, named after its developer, Juhn Wada.

In the Wada test, the powerful barbiturate sodium amytal is injected into the carotid artery leading to one hemisphere in patients about to undergo brain surgery, to determine whether language is affected. When the drug enters the language hemisphere, the patient's speech is arrested within seconds; thus, the surgeon can be sure which hemisphere he should try to protect from injury during the operation. Yet another surgical technique involves direct stimulation of the brain; pioneered in the 1950s by the surgeons Penfield and Wilder, this method has recently attracted renewed interest with the advent of improved techniques.

Language on the Right Side

So far, we have seen that language (or whatever we do when using language) lies largely in the domain of the left hemisphere. But, given the many complexities of human language, one cannot help but ask whether the right hemisphere's special capacities don't contribute somewhere along the way. Oddly enough, because of the brain's remarkable plasticity, in extraordinary circumstances the right hemisphere can mimic the left and take on primary responsibility for linguistic matters, although probably using quite different methods.

In rare cases, for instance, one hemisphere of an infant's brain must be removed shortly after birth. It is a startling tribute to the brain's adaptability that a ten-year-old child who has lost the left hemisphere from such an operation uses language just as a normal child in most situations. Only special testing methods can reveal subtle deficiencies in such children (Dennis, 1980). The child without a left hemisphere cannot, it seems, effectively handle rhyme. If context does not help him, he may not be able to tell the difference between an active and a passive sentence (*the boy kissed the girl* versus *the boy was kissed by the girl*). He may be baffled by or unaware of the ambiguity in the following sentence: "He gave her dog biscuits." (To see the ambiguity, insert *the* before *dog*, then before *biscuits*.)

In short, it would seem that the right hemisphere, if it gets an early enough start, can take over many linguistic responsibilities. But these extraordinary cases can be misleading: once lateralization patterns are established, at least by age twelve (some say five), the right hemisphere is highly limited in its formal linguistic capacity.

Overall, research suggests that the right hemisphere in adults is mute; it usually cannot speak. Nor can it write. It can learn to read, but it cannot use phoneme-to-letter correspondences to do so. That is, it must learn each word as a separate entity; given knowledge of the words *pan* and *cat*, it cannot make a guess at how to read the word represented by the letters *c-a-n*.

The right hemisphere may also be able to store some words, in what linguists call a mental *lexicon*. But, unlike the left brain, its word store is largely limited to fixed expressions and frequent, concrete, image-related words. In sharp contrast, it may well be less able to handle words like *claim* or *independence*, which embody abstract concepts.

But the right hemisphere has a primary role of its own in some areas related to language; it is not simply relegated to the role of doing what the left hemisphere does, only less effectively. The right hemisphere helps us understand whether or not an utterance is a question, and whether or not the speaker is angry: these tasks rely on the right brain's specialty in handling intonation contours and emotional tone.

Contrary to earlier claims, it has now been found that even the most severe Broca's aphasic speaks with a correct intonation contour, although his "sentences" may be labored and consist of only two words. In contrast, a patient with right hemisphere damage typically speaks in a monotone.

The right hemisphere also seems to play an important, if mystifying, role in mediating reading, especially when a child is first learning to read. But the most important language-related work of the right hemisphere seems to lie outside the realm of language as a formal system. To use language properly, we need more than rules of grammar, sound correspondences, etc. While speaking or writing in any real situation, we are constantly checking information about the world, our audience, and the overall situation. These are the *pragmatic* aspects of language use. Recent studies show that these "practical" issues of language use may be the right hemisphere's most important linguistic task.

LANGUAGE AND THE WORLD: A VIEW FROM THE RIGHT

In 1976, Alfonso Caramazza and his associates devised a test to find out whether people use spatial imagery to solve problems involving comparisons of this sort:

Type 1: John is taller than Bill; who is taller?
Type 2: John is taller than Bill; who is shorter?

The issue is how people deal with this problem; do we "imagine" a picture of John and Bill and then answer the question by comparing their height in our mental picture?

The subjects chosen were right-hemisphere-damaged patients and normal controls. Following accepted theory (language on the left, imagery on the right), the experimenters reasoned that, if the right-hemisphere patients did poorly on the test, it would show that this kind of linear syllogism required the use of imagery. If the patients performed the same as normals, the solution must be available via purely linguistic means, since these participants all had intact left-hemisphere processing ability.

The results were quite unexpected. On the first type of wording, involving repetition of the same adjective, right hemisphere patients performed as well as normals. But in type two, involving opposite adjectives (*taller* and *shorter*), the accuracy of the right-hemisphere group dropped dramatically, far more than that of the normals. One possible explanation, the researchers admitted, was that the linguistic ability to handle *antonyms*, or opposites, was impaired in their brain-damaged subjects.

Two years later, working with colleagues, Howard Gardner took up the notion of antonymy for its own sake. This new study tested a wide range of people, with or without neural injuries, on their ability to manipulate pairs of opposites (e.g., *difficult-easy* and *prince-princess*). Right-hemisphere patients performed significantly below normals in all tests. When the types of errors were tabulated, another surprise emerged. Asked to provide opposites to a set of words, right-hemisphere patients made the same kinds of mistakes as Wernicke's aphasics, who suffer severe semantic difficulties. In fact, the right-hemisphere group was more likely than any other group to choose a synonym or an associated word, rather than an opposite word. For *prince*, that is, they would be likely to produce *ruler* or *knight*, rather than the correct antonym *princess*. This kind of performance seems to reflect a basic lack of understanding of what an opposite is.

Antonymy is not the only concept that gives right hemisphere patients trouble. A scene reconstructed from research by Winner and Gardner (1977) illustrates yet another area in which the left half of the brain needs help from the right if it is to function properly. An aphasic is given two pictures: one of a very sad person, the other of a man struggling under the weight of a huge heart-shaped object. Asked to find a pictorial match for the expression "he has a heavy heart," the aphasic patient chooses the first picture, laughing at the second, which he clearly regards as absurd. Not so for his right-hemisphere damaged counterpart: this patient finds nothing funny about either picture. Asked the same question, he is as likely to choose one as the other. Again, it seems to be the right hemisphere that decides when a figurative, indirect, or humorous interpretation is called for in a given context.

It has been repeatedly shown in the past few years that, wherever contextual cues are needed to function well in a linguistic situation, aphasics with left-hemisphere damage perform surprisingly better than patients with right-hemisphere damage. The skills involved in understanding stories provide an example. Right-hemisphere patients seem unable to draw an abstract moral from a story. Asked to retell a story, they may deliberately reject plausible elements and interject irrelevant episodes, sometimes insisting that they improve the story (Wapner et al., 1981). Asked to retell a routine story about the theft of money from a grocery store, one patient insisted that a grocery store could not have been on a side street, as claimed in the original version. But despite rejecting this unobtrusive detail, the subject saw no problem in claiming that the robber stole all the groceries (instead of money). In the patient's confabulated version, the story ends with the robber's attempted escape: "[He] tripped over a bad sidewalk, fell down and broke all the eggs."

I am inclined to conclude this section in agreement with the authors of the last study who claim that efficient language use involves far more than the "linguistic computer" lodged in the left half of the brain. In their words, "While the left hemisphere might appreciate some of Groucho's puns, and the right hemisphere might be entertained by the antics of Harpo, only the two hemispheres unified can appreciate a whole Marx Brothers routine."

Are We All Alike?

What, the reader may ask, about *my* brain? Where do I store math, physics, music, or for that matter, language? Can one make a reliable guess for an individual in answer to these questions? Well, reliable to some degree, especially if you are dealing with a healthy, monolingual, English-speaking, righthanded, hearing adult male who can read. But beyond this class, special caution must be advised. The following sections are devoted to some groups that have proven to be different.

BABIES

The adult is not alone in having left-hemisphere language areas that are physically larger than those on the right. Babies have the same configuration, and even the unborn fetus shares the typical asymmetrical pattern. Experimental testing shows that behavioral asymmetries can be found in the very young as well. Lateralization effects have been found with infants as soon after birth as testing has been done. Using measures such as sucking response and changed heartbeat, one can measure the responses of infants to stimuli around them; studies using such measures have claimed to show clear lateralization for speech sounds in the left hemisphere of infant brains, as opposed to chirps or nonspeech sounds, which the babies seem to process in the right hemisphere. This lateralization effect has been shown, even in preterm babies born in about the thirty-sixth week of gestation.

The question of infant asymmetry raises interesting questions. How can a brain that has no language be lateralized for language? What kind of processing is the infant brain doing, and how does it assign the processing it does to a given hemisphere? Research on this intriguing topic may ultimately show which prelinguistic faculties lead to the development of language in children.

BILINGUALS

Perhaps the brain of the child represents an organ that is not rigidly wired; rather, it may be like a sort of electronic board with only some minimal (albeit highly significant) circuits provided at the outset. The details of the remaining circuitry may be up to the user to determine. If so, different users may wire their neural boards in quite different ways; provided, that is, they stay within the bounds of the conditions imposed by those initial connections (which will ensure that all systems end up with the needed wiring for human language, and not binary code or bird song).

Seen via this analogy, a bilingual speaker might be like a computer buff trying to do with one central processing unit the job normally done by two. Hence, one would expect the details of his processing machinery to be quite different. In fact, for some time, it has been noted that polyglot speakers (people with more than one language) produce unexpected aphasia types, perhaps because their experiences have led to different neural patterns than those of monolingual speakers. In about half the reported cases of aphasia in polyglot speakers, any recovery that takes place affects both (or all) languages at the same rate. Still, many patients recover one language earlier or more perfectly than others, and about one fourth of all polyglot patients never regain one or more of their languages.[6] Physicians cannot predict which language will be recovered first or more adequately, although some generalization is possible. The language best recovered is likely to be the last one used before injury, or the best known of the languages, or the one that is heard most during the recovery period. At any rate, all this suggests that, at the very least, the neural base for the two languages in some bilinguals is different; or that brain tissue which can take over the use of one language is quite incapable of handling another, for reasons which are poorly understood.

Some rare cases pose especially perplexing challenges. One such case reported in 1980 involved a French-Arabic bilingual nun in Morocco who had a moped accident and became totally aphasic. Four days later, she could speak a few words of Arabic, but no French. Two weeks later, she could speak French again fluently; but in the space of one day, her French fluency quite disappeared. She astounded observers by being able to converse fluently only in Arabic.[7]

Intriguing recovery patterns are not the only neurolinguistic challenge offered by the bilingual: the occurrence of language deficits in the first place is also significant. It has been shown that aphasia is about five times more likely to result from right-hemisphere damage in a polyglot speaker than in a monolingual. This suggests that some

[6] Grosjean (1982), p. 259.
[7] Grosjean, p. 260.

of a bilingual's linguistic ability may be stored on the right side of the brain, or at least in areas not affected by damage to the classical language areas on the left. Electrical stimulation of brain sites also suggests differential storage for two languages in a single brain. In bilinguals, naming of the same object in the two languages is disrupted by stimulating the cortex at different points. Scientists have noted that the cerebral anatomy of multilingual speakers is distinctive as well, although the relation between gross anatomy and brain function is far from understood.

At any rate, it is suspected that the right hemisphere plays a major role in second-language learning; in fact, learning a second language may alter patterns of cerebral dominance in unexpected ways. After a second language is acquired, dominance for the first language in some cases seems to switch from the left to the right hemisphere. The experience of learning and handling two languages may be enough to produce a very different neurological pattern than what would have emerged had the speaker learned only one language. Multilingual cases may be telling us that the cerebral cortex is like a computer in some respects: highly complex and rigid in its basic setup, yet also versatile, and subject to "programming" by the user.

SPEAKERS VERSUS SIGNERS

Speakers of American Sign Language (ASL or AMESLAN) use a language in which manual activity, not speech, is the basic carrier of meaning. If different life experiences result in different neural patterns, then the very nature of ASL raises some fascinating questions. Do the deaf generate and process signs using their left hemisphere? Can Broca's area, with its ability to interface with commands to the tongue and lips, also manage to spell out a program based on hand signals?

Concerning lateralization, early studies showed conflicting results; some seemed to show that asymmetries in the deaf were just the opposite from those of oral speakers; still others claimed to show that signers had no cerebral asymmetry at all.

One problem may lie in the nature of sign language itself. Most studies have used various kinds of static photographs to test asymmetry. But ASL signers do not communicate by flashing pictures at one another. In normal situations, signers deal with a number of parameters at once: hand position, movement, and orientation. At least some researchers claim that signers in action do indeed make crucial use of the traditional left-brain language centers in processing their language.

Using another measure to assess lateralization, recent studies of impaired signers (see Bellugi 1983) yield important evidence for the claim that signers may process language as oral speakers do: injury to the classical language areas on the left has been found to produce strikingly similar aphasia types in ASL and oral languages.

Finally, neurological patterning based on experience may be important. Deaf people whose schools used different training methods show consistently different patterns of asymmetry on various tests. In fact, one startling finding about signers suggests that the brain may be even more flexible than previously suspected. Neville (1977) reported that he observed evoked potential (electrical activity) in the auditory cortex of native signers in response to flashes of light. In oral speakers, the auditory cortex is the area where sound is first perceived in the brain: the hearing center, so to speak. If Neville's claim is substantiated, the term "auditory cortex" may prove quite inappropriate for users of ASL. Only time and further study may tell.

READERS, JAPANESE, AND OTHERS

Bilinguals and signers are not the only groups who are suspected of having distinctive neurological patterns. Anyone reading this selection falls into a third group: there is some evidence that experience with written language may have a significant effect in establishing left-hemisphere language dominance.

Illiterates show a much lower incidence of aphasia following left-hemisphere brain damage. Indeed, for illiterates, aphasic symptoms are as likely to result from right-hemisphere injury as from left-hemisphere lesions. The only reasonable explanation seems to be that language abilities are more symmetrical in this group. Perhaps dealing with the written word involves the left hemisphere's analytical techniques in such a way as to greatly strengthen the ties between language and the left side of the brain. People who do not learn to read and write do not have this reinforcing experience, and thus do not show the degree of cerebral asymmetry for language found in literate speakers.

Why should certain experiences (like reading, or signing, or speaking two languages) cause the brain to forge distinctive neural pathways? Perhaps a clearer statement of the facts is needed before this question can even be meaningfully asked. Additional clues are beginning to surface suggesting more ways in which an individual's early experience may help determine his cerebral circuitry. Two of these clues are particularly interesting.

Japanese speakers seem to process single-vowel sounds on the left, as normal linguistic material. This is in contrast to English speakers (among others), who hear these sounds better with the right hemisphere. (Sounds like *ah* and *ooooh* are likely to be interpreted as emotional utterances rather than as words). Professor Tadanoku Tsunoda of Tokyo's Medical and Dental University blames this on the "vowel dominant" nature of his language, which may influence the way Japanese children perceive the boundary between language and other sounds.[8]

This Japanese case recalls a widely accepted claim about tone languages, based on lateralization for tone in Thai. Native speakers of Thai, who must make use of the pitch levels in a sentence to understand its meaning, tend to perceive tone as linguistic material. To most English speakers, the complex pitch patterns of a tone language like Thai or Vietnamese simply sound like some kind of puzzling singsong effect overlayed on speech; hence, they are likely to filter out the tone and send it off to the right hemisphere. Given this, it is not surprising that English speakers have substantial difficulty in learning tone languages!

LEFT-HANDERS AND WOMEN

Two more groups stand out as neurologically "different"; this time, the difference cannot be traced entirely to experience, as genetic makeup is important as well.

The history of left-handers is fraught with myths and misleading ideas. In some societies, left-handed people have been viewed as clumsy and awkward, if not downright sinister. (In China, India, and Arab countries, they are said to have been banned from the dinner table.) To many, however, reversed hand preference is seen as a sign of eminence. (Michelangelo, Benjamin Franklin, Alexander the Great, and Einstein are cited as examples.)

In the first edition of their widely read book *Left Brain, Right Brain*, Sally Springer and Georg Deutsch entitled one chapter "The Puzzle of the Left-Hander." They pointed out that it is difficult to clearly identify a left-handed person. Many people use the left hand for some activities and the right for others.

Springer and Deutsch trace theories that relate familial history and writing position to brain asymmetry in left-handers. One interesting claim they report is that the characteristic "inverted" writing position found in some left-handers may indicate left-hemisphere language, and that this may be part of a more general pattern for detecting "like-hemisphere" language. In other words, the inverted writing position may be a sign that language lateralization and hand choice for an individual are the same. Supporters of this idea have pointed out that one very rare right-handed "inverter" actually showed right-hemisphere dominance for language. Since inverted writing position and right-hemisphere language are highly unusual in a right-hander, the fact that both have shown up in a single individual is important evidence.

[8] Brabyn (1982), p. 11.

But Springer and Deutsch's "puzzle" remains. Scientists have discarded the original misconception that the left-handed person is simply a mirror-image of a right-hander in favor of the claim that 70 percent of left-handed people have a dominant left hemisphere for speech, just as right-handers do. Of the rest, half were thought to have speech on the right, and half (about 15 percent of the total) were said to be bilateral for language, having no clearly dominant hemisphere. But recent studies reanalyzing data from aphasia have put even this second schema in doubt: at least one researcher has concluded that bilateral speech representation in this population may be more common than previously believed, perhaps as high as 40 percent (cited in Segalowitz and Bryden 1983, p. 348).

For one thing, left-handed speakers are eight times more likely than right-handers to suffer from aphasia after damage to the right hemisphere only. For right-handers, the incidence of such aphasia is 3 percent, compared to 25 percent in their left-handed counterparts. This could only mean that, in some sense, left-handers store more language ability in the nondominant hemisphere than do right-handers. Since there is no clear evidence for any bilateral speech in right-handed monolinguals, this new idea may identify a significant difference between the two handedness groups.

In 1879, the eminent social psychologist Gustave LeBon wrote:

> In the most intelligent races, as among the Parisians, there are a large number of women whose brains are closer in size to those of gorillas than to the most developed male brains. . . . All psychologists who have studied the intelligence of women . . . recognize that they . . . represent the most inferior form of human evolution and that they are closer to children and savages than to an adult, civilized man.[9]

LeBon, following Broca, felt that bigger meant better in cerebral terms, and thus justified his sexist views by biological argument.

None but the most irrational antifeminist would today accept LeBon's comments. But we do know that women's brains are distinctive. For one thing, the gross physiological differences noted between the hemispheres are less obvious in women than in men. And other strong indicators of cerebral asymmetry are equally hard to come by in women.

Like left-handers, women may tend toward symmetrical, evenly balanced, language capacities in the two hemispheres. Again, the aphasia statistics are revealing. Women are far less likely than men to become aphasic from unilateral damage to the left hemisphere. This suggests that, at the very least, the right hemisphere in women can take over language functions readily if the language centers on the left

[9] Gould (1980), p. 155.

become disabled: more plausible is the notion that there is some language-processing ordinarily taking place on the right in women.

Behavioral tests also yield evidence for bilateral speech in women. In dichotic listening tests, men outnumber women nearly 2–1 in showing right-ear advantage for verbal material. In fact, some early attempts to find asymmetries in the human brain seem to have failed simply because they included too many female subjects!

Hopefully, the interpretation of all this will emerge from further scientific work. Perhaps the strategic (spatial or holistic) habits associated with the right hemisphere are adapted by women for use in language processing. This almost surely reflects some biological difference between the sexes—but whether it is in actual brain tissue is quite unclear at this time.

Where Do We Go from Here?

The human brain still shelters the fundamental mystery of our existence: what does it mean to be human? Clearly, language must be an important part of the answer, and we have come a long way from the Egyptian physicians who attributed language disorders to "the breath of an outside god" (Arbib et al., 1982). As this article shows, much progress has been made in finding the answers to an ancient and fundamental question: how does *homo sapiens* of Figure 1 differ from his Australopithecine ancestors? How does this creature manage to handle such a highly complex communication system in the three pounds or so of gray matter lodged in the human skull?

To understand the biology of language, one would have to answer many questions not even hinted at here. How is language related to other cognitive skills? What goes on behind the scenes, in the subcortical tissue under the uncommitted cortex? (It is clear that the thalamus, for instance, plays an important role in language.)

The complexity of the issues involved, and the way they touch on many disciplines at once, is clearly reflected in the titles of recent books: two collections published in 1983 on language issues include the terms *neuropsychology* and *psychobiology* in their titles. *Neurolinguistics* as a discipline in its own right has been known only for the past decade or so. *Biolinguistics* has, to my knowledge, yet to be sanctioned by official usage; perhaps it has missed its chance, outdistanced by the more precise blends just cited. But the next decade is sure to see a new crop of titles like these, as scholars from many different areas together probe the mysteries of language, brain, and cognition in humans.

Bibliography

Arbib, M. A., Caplan, D., and Marshall, J. C. "Neurolinguistics in Historical Perspective." In *Neural Models of Language Processes*, eds. M. Arbib, D. Caplan, and J. Marshall. New York: Academic Press, 1982.

Bellugi, U. "Language Structure and Language Breakdown in American Sign Language." In *Psychobiology of Language*, ed. M. Studdert-Kennedy. Cambridge, MA: MIT Press, 1983.

Blumstein, S. E. "Language Dissolution in Aphasia: Evidence for Linguistic Theory." In *Exceptional Language and Linguistics*, eds. L. Obler and L. Menn. New York: Academic Press, 1982.

Brabyn, H. "Mother Tongue and the Brain." *UNESCO Courier*, Feb. 1982, pp. 10–13.

Bryden, M. P. and Allard, F. "Visual Hemifield Differences Depend on Typeface." *Brain and Language* 3, 191–200, 1976.

Caramazza, A., Gordon, J., Zurif, E. B., and DeLuca, D. "Right-Hemisphere Damage and Verbal Problem Solving Behavior." *Brain and Language* 3, 41–46, 1976.

Dennis, M. "Language Acquisition in a Single Hemisphere: Semantic Organization." In *Biological Studies of Mental Processes*, ed. D. Caplan. Cambridge, MA: MIT Press, 1980.

Gardner, H., Silverman, J., Wapner, W., and Zurif, E. "The Appreciation of Antonymic Contrasts in Aphasia." *Brain and Language* 6, 301–317, 1978.

Gould, S. J. *The Panda's Thumb: More Reflections in Natural History*. New York: Norton and Company, 1980.

Grosjean, F. *Life With Two Languages*. Cambridge, MA: Harvard University Press, 1982.

Gur, R. C. and Reivich, N. "Cognitive Task Effects on Hemispheric Blood Flow in Humans: Evidence for Individual Differences in Hemispheric Activation." *Brain and Language* 9, 78–92, 1980.

Harth, E. *Windows on the Mind: Reflections on the Physical Basis of Consciousness*. New York: Morrow, 1982.

Neville, H. J. "Electroencephalographic Testing of Cerebral Specialization in Normal and Congenitally Deaf Children: A Preliminary Report." In *Language Development and Neurological Theory*, eds. S. Segalowitz and F. Gruber. New York: Academic Press, 1977.

Segalowitz, S. and Bryden, M. "Individual Differences in Hemispheric Representation of Language." In *Language Functions and Brain Organization*, ed. S. Segalowitz. New York: Academic Press, 1983.

Springer, S. P. and Deutsch, G. *Left Brain, Right Brain*. San Francisco: W. H. Freeman and Company, 1981.

Wapner, W., Hamby, S. and Gardner, H. 1981. "The Role of the Right Hemisphere in the Apprehension of Complex Linguistic Materials." *Brain and Language* 14, 15–33, 1981.

Winner, E., and Gardner, H. "The Comprehension of Metaphor in Brain-Damaged Patients." *Brain* 100, 719–727, 1977.

Young, A. W., Ellis, A. W., and Birn, P. L. "Left Hemisphere Superiority for Pronounceable Nonwords, but Not for Unpronounceable Letter Strings." *Brain and Language* 22, 14–23, 1984.

FOR DISCUSSION AND REVIEW

1. What is the difference between Broca's area and Wernicke's area? How does each area seem to contribute to language production or understanding? How do relationships between these areas and cortical centers for sight, hearing, and motor function play an important role in Wernicke's overall model of how the brain works in terms of language?

2. Why might studies done on aphasics and split-brain subjects yield misleading information on brain lateralization?

3. Why is it difficult to clearly label a person as left- or right-handed? Do you know of any people who use different hands for different tasks? If so, list which hand is used for specific tasks. What pattern(s), if any, can you suggest?

4. Divide the following activities into two columns (*left* and *right*), according to which hemisphere you think is likely to be dominant for performing each. In cases where you are unsure, explain the aspects of the task that led you to list it tentatively on one side rather than the other:
   a. distinguishing between the syllables *ba* and *pa*
   b. choosing the right answer in a multiplication problem
   c. defining the word *independence*
   d. recognizing a friend's face
   e. singing the "Star Spangled Banner"
   f. deciding whether your employer is in a good mood
   g. recognizing the string of letters *ZBQ*
   h. playing the guitar
   i. recognizing a grasshopper's chirp
   j. understanding the utterance: "The girl was bitten by the dog."
   k. finding a word to rhyme with *inch*

5. There is some uncertainty about how blind people process Braille characters. In tests, it seems that subjects with good vision, when they first encounter the raised characters, can make them out best with their left hand. But it is very difficult to get clear-cut results for experienced Braille readers. How do you explain this? Discuss how this situation might be comparable to how trained and untrained people process music. What is the relationship to Heny's discussion of sign language? How would nonsigners be likely to process signs?

6. Would you expect a measure of electrical impulses from the brain of a sleeping person during an active dreaming session to reveal left or right hemispheric activity? Why? What kind of mental activity seems to be going on when a person dreams?

7. How do dichotic listening and tachistoscopic tests work? If a subject sees or hears more accurately on the left, which cerebral hemisphere must be involved? Why?

8. In general terms, how do women and left-handers seem to differ from other individuals in terms of brain asymmetry?

9. Suppose you constructed an experiment in which you asked people to choose a picture that matches the sentence: "He's really gotten himself into a nice pickle now!" Their choices include illustrations of:
   a. A man who has just dug his way into a giant pickle.
   b. A man with a bewildered look on his face standing near a disabled car on an isolated road. His clothes are covered with grease, and strewn around him on the ground are what appear to be the parts of his engine.
   c. A man sitting in an armchair reading a book.
What performance would you expect on this test from each of the following groups, and why?
   a. Broca's aphasics
   b. Wernicke's aphasics
   c. right-hemisphere–damaged patients
   d. normal "control" subjects

2/The Loss of Language

HOWARD GARDNER

*The limitations of handicapped people often give us a better under-
standing of the normal. We can also learn a great deal from the many
people who suffer from* aphasia, *the loss of language skills resulting
from damage to the brain, usually from a stroke or traumatic head
injury. In the following selection, Howard Gardner, author of* The
Shattered Mind, The Quest for Mind, Frames of Mind, *and* Art,
Mind, and Brain, *describes the symptoms of two major kinds of
aphasia. The first is* Wernicke's aphasia, *whose victims speak fluent
nonsense and have great difficulty both in uttering words that refer
to specific objects and people and in understanding others' speech; the
second is* Broca's aphasia, *whose victims can speak only slowly and
imperfectly and have difficulty understanding speech in which word
order, inflections, and other grammatical signals are especially important. Gardner suggests that linguists, as well as physicians and
psychologists, have an important role to play in understanding
aphasia, and that aphasia in turn can test linguists' assumptions about
their subject, perhaps even offering an approach to some long-standing
psychological and philosophical questions about language and thought.*

Skill in language develops so quickly and operates so smoothly that
we take our linguistic capacities largely for granted. Most three-year-
olds can speak simple grammatical sentences and execute simple commands. Nearly every 10-year-old in our society can read and write at
the primer level and most adults can read a novel in an afternoon or
write several letters in an evening.

Our linguistic potentials are even more impressive. Placed in a
foreign culture, particularly as children, we readily learn the basic
phrases of another language; and all of us, bilingual or not, have mastered various language-related codes—the number system (Arabic or
Roman), musical notation, Morse code, or the familiar trademarks for
commercial products.

The loss of various language abilities in the otherwise normal adult
is tragic, and the consequences are as devastating as those of blindness,
deafness, or paralysis (which often accompanies it). Deprived of the
power to communicate through language and language-like channels,
the individual is cut off from the world of meaning. . . . Though loss
of language is relatively rare among young persons, it becomes in-

creasingly common with age—about one quarter of a million individuals suffer linguistic impairment each year. The extent and duration of language disability vary greatly, but a significant proportion of the afflicted individuals are left with a permanent impairment. Those who suffer language loss as a consequence of damage to their brains are victims of the strange condition called aphasia.

Aphasic individuals are not always immediately recognizable. One patient whom I recently interviewed appeared to be normal when he entered the room: a nice-looking, well-groomed, sixty-two-year-old, retired bookkeeper. He answered my first questions appropriately and with a speed that suggested nothing was amiss. Asked his name, the gentleman responded, "Oh, my name, that's easy, it is Tuh, Tom Johnson and I. . . ." It was only when I gave Mr. Johnson a chance to speak a bit more that the extent and nature of his aphasia became clear:

"What kind of work have you done, Mr. Johnson?" I asked.

"We, the kids, all of us, and I, we were working for a long time in the . . . you know . . . it's the kind of space, I mean place rear to the spedwan. . . ."

At this point I interjected, "Excuse me, but I wanted to know what work you have been doing."

"If you had said that, we had said that, poomer, near the fortunate, forpunate, tamppoo, all around the fourth of martz. Oh, I get all confused," he replied, looking somewhat puzzled that the stream of language did not appear to satisfy me.

Mr. Johnson was suffering from a relatively common language disorder called Wernicke's aphasia. Patients with this disorder have no trouble producing language—if anything, the words flow out too freely and it sometimes proves difficult to silence them. Nor do Wernicke's aphasics have any trouble producing the words that structure and modulate speech—"if," "and," "of," and the like. But when they try to come up with specific substantives—nouns, verbs, and adjectives that specify persons, objects, events, and properties—these patients have great difficulty. As Mr. Johnson exhibited several times, aphasics frequently cannot issue the precise words they want to say, and they frequently wander from the stated topic to another, the meaning of which remains obscure to the listener.

From my description of the interview, it may seem that Mr. Johnson understood what I was saying but was simply encountering trouble in responding appropriately. This supposition was quickly and dramatically dispelled when I took a key and a pencil from my pocket and asked him to point in turn to each one. These two simple words, known to any child, eluded him. When asked to point to other objects and to body parts, he also fared poorly, as he had when trying to name certain objects. He could not read words aloud correctly, nor could he understand most written commands, though he did read letters and numbers aloud. Any bystander would have inferred that Mr. Johnson's understanding was very limited (as indeed it was).

One fascinating island of preserved comprehension remained, however. Toward the close of the interview I said, almost out of the blue, "Oh, Mr. Johnson, would you please stand up and turn around twice?" Suddenly, as if his comprehension had been magically restored, Mr. Johnson stood up and proceeded to rotate in just the way I requested. He was also able to carry out several commands that involved his whole body (like "Lean forward" or "Stand at ease"). However, this preserved comprehension could not be elicited in any other manner.

Mr. Johnson, a Wernicke's aphasic, can be instructively contrasted with another patient whom I recently met. Mr. Cooper, a forty-seven-year-old former Army officer, was seated in a wheelchair, obviously paralyzed on the entire right side of his body. A slight droop on the right side of his face became more noticeable when he opened his mouth or smiled. When I asked what was wrong with him, Mr. Cooper immediately pointed to his arm, his leg, and his mouth. He appeared reluctant to speak at all. Only when I pressed him did he point again to his mouth and with obvious effort blurt out the sound "Peech."

I posed Mr. Cooper a number of questions that could be answered by "yes" or "no," and in each case he nodded appropriately. I then said that it was important that he try to speak. Noting his wedding ring, I asked, "How many children do you have?" Mr. Cooper looked blank for a time. Then he peered at his fingers and began to raise them, accompanying the motion with low and strained sounds: "one, two, tree, pour, no pive . . . yes pive," he said triumphantly.

Next, I asked him to tell me about the kind of work he had been doing.

"Me . . . build—ing . . . chairs, no, no cab—in—nets." The words came out slowly, taking him forty seconds to finish.

"One more question," I said. "Can you tell me how you would go about building a cabinet?"

Mr. Cooper threw up his left hand in frustration, and after I gently insisted that he attempt a verbal explanation, he said, "One, saw . . . then, cutting wood . . . working. . . ." All of this was said with great effort and poor articulation, which left me (and Mr. Cooper) unprepared for a sudden oath, "Jesus Christ, oh boy." This was uttered effortlessly, as if another language mechanism—an island of preserved production—had temporarily been stimulated.

During the rest of our examination, Mr. Cooper performed well on tasks that required little language production. On request he pointed easily to objects around the room and even to a series of objects placed in front of him. He read simple commands silently and carried them out clumsily but properly. He could name some familiar objects and read aloud some names of objects, though he failed at reading aloud letters of the alphabet and small grammatical words such as articles and prepositions. He could read aloud the word "bee," but not "be," though the latter occurs more frequently in spoken and written language. He could carry a melody and sing lyrics to familiar songs more readily than he could recite those same lyrics.

But Mr. Cooper had definite difficulties in understanding. Although he could designate a series of two objects, he sometimes failed at three and he never succeeded at four—the level of success achieved by most normal adults. He caught the drift of nearly all questions in casual conversation, and could almost always produce at least a minimally appropriate response, but he experienced significant problems with questions that involved careful attention to word order and inflection. I could stump him with sentences like "Do you put on your shoes before you put on socks?" or "The lion was killed by the tiger: Which animal is dead?" or "With the pen touch the pencil." Just as Mr. Cooper's spontaneous speech was limited largely to nouns and verbs and virtually devoid of words that modulate meaning, so too he often failed on questions and commands that required him to note the order of words and the meanings of prefixes, suffixes, and other grammatical fixtures.

Mr. Johnson and Mr. Cooper illustrate two of the most common forms of aphasia. In six years of work with aphasic patients, I have seen dozens of patients whose symptoms closely resemble those of one or the other man. Mr. Johnson is a victim of Wernicke's aphasia; as a result of damage to the left temporal lobe of his brain his auditory comprehension has become severely impaired, but he remains able to produce long, often obscure, strings of speech. Mr. Cooper has Broca's aphasia, a condition caused by damage to the left frontal lobe. He understands language, although not perfectly; his chief difficulty is in producing words, specifically those that modify nouns and verbs. The language of the Broca's aphasic is called agrammatic (or telegrammatic), and such a patient's understanding suffers from some of the same limits that affect his spontaneous speech.

These and other aphasic syndromes are the regular and nearly inevitable consequences of significant damage to the left hemisphere of the brain in normal right-handed individuals. As a result of a stroke, head injury, or brain tumor, cortical (or surface) tissue is destroyed in this half of the brain. Such lesions impair linguistic functions and frequently cause paralysis and loss of sensation in the opposite (right) side of the body. (The situation is somewhat different, and much more complex, in left-handers.)

The precise location and extent of the brain damage determine the nature of the linguistic disorder. There are forms of aphasia (called alexia) in which an individual's ability to read is most severely im-

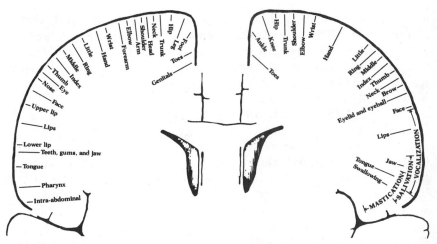

Once Paul Broca and Carl Wernicke had linked two varieties of aphasia to specific areas in the brain, neurologists began trying to locate all intellectual functions. Although they failed, they did succeed in identifying the areas connected with most motor and sensory functions. This figure locates the relative amount of brain space devoted to various functions. On the right are the areas that control motor functions; the fine muscles that control the lips and hands take up the most space. On the left are the areas that receive sensory input from skin receptors.

paired; agraphia, in which disorders of writing are most pronounced; anomia, in which most language functions are preserved but there is magnified difficulty in naming objects; conduction aphasia, in which speech and understanding are relatively intact but the patient experiences enormous difficulty in repetition; and a bizarre complementary condition called mixed transcortical aphasia, in which both conversational speech and comprehension are almost entirely destroyed, yet the patient retains the capacity to repeat, and even to echo, long strings of meaningful or meaningless words (it makes little difference which). The striking predictability of these syndromes reflects the uniformity with which language functions are organized in normal right-handed individuals.

Each of these conditions cries out for explanation. There are alexics who can read numbers, including Roman numerals, but not words or letters; transcortical aphasics who understand nothing but who will, in their repetitions, spontaneously correct ungrammatical phrases; anomic aphasics who cannot produce a familiar word (e.g., nose) but will readily produce a highly improbable substitute (proboscis). To be sure, not all aphasics show such clear syndromes; the syndromes are most likely to occur in individuals of middle age or older, who are fully right-handed, and who have suffered a stroke. Yet nearly every aphasic patient exhibits some bizarre combination of symptoms, and many exemplify the textbook descriptions in the preceding paragraph.

A first meeting with aphasic patients is often dramatic; their symptoms are frequently fantastic and disturbing. A person's first impulse is to aid these victims of brain disease in any way possible. But the study of their condition has an importance that goes beyond helping victims of aphasia; it holds the promise of clarifying a host of philosophical and psychological issues about the nature of language and the mind.

Reports of aphasia can be found in many classical writings and even in the Bible. Yet the serious scientific study of aphasia began just over a century ago when Pierre Paul Broca, a French anatomist, described two cases whose symptoms resembled Mr. Cooper's. Broca's cases were important not because of the way he described their behavior patterns but because he made an analytic leap. Noting that both of these cases had brain damage in the anterior portion of the left hemisphere, Broca proposed that this part of the brain played a special role in language. Besides immortalizing his name (Broca's aphasia, Broca's area), this discovery laid the groundwork for all aphasia research.

The reason for this breakthrough was simple but instructive. Until Broca's time, nearly all scientists assumed that the two halves of the brain, which on casual inspection look alike, carried out the same functions. It had often been observed that aphasia accompanied strokes and paralysis, but Broca was the first to argue publicly that language disorders are linked to the left portion of the brain. Though his announcement provoked controversy, supporting cases were quickly reported. Thirteen years later Carl Wernicke, a German neuropsychiatrist, described another set of symptoms, this time primarily affecting comprehension. He linked them to the left posterior (particularly temporal) lobe of the brain, thereby contributing his name to another brain area and another type of aphasia. Even more than Broca's discoveries, Wernicke's work stimulated scientists to construct models of language based on the behavior of brain-injured patients. [See Figure 3, p. 163.]

Broca and Wernicke gave impetus to a group of neurologists who have been called localizers. Adherents of this approach carefully investigated the anatomy of the human brain, the structure of the cortical tissue, and the connections between the different parts of the nervous system. Building on this refined knowledge of human neuroanatomy, they sought to discover the functions that were governed by each part of the brain. Their first step was to locate the motor functions (or voluntary actions), which are associated with sites in the frontal lobe, and the sensory functions, associated with sites in the parietal, temporal, and occipital lobes. But the localizers went beyond these relatively elementary processes and tried to apportion even the highest intellectual and emotional functions to specific regions of the brain.

Findings about language function spurred them on. Researchers had discovered an indisputable "high" human function—one denied all other animals—occupying specific regions in the brain. The type of aphasia discovered by Broca and the startlingly different one described by Wernicke were but the first manifestations of this line of analysis. Within twenty years, a gaggle of aphasias had been described, each traced to a specific area in the brain, each exhibiting its own enigmatic symptoms.

Researchers transcended these correlations between brain and behavior to propose models of language function. In one popular version the language signal entered Wernicke's area, where it was comprehended; then a return message was fired forward to Broca's area, where it was fitted out with grammatical trimmings and ultimately spewed forth to the world. It naturally followed that a lesion confined to Broca's area allowed comprehension at the cost of grammatical speech, whereas destruction of Wernicke's area impaired comprehension but allowed a stream of grammatically rich, but often meaningless speech.

The localizers probably went too far in their approach. In the early part of this century, a rival school reanalyzed Broca's original cases and announced that there was but one type of aphasia, the form stemming from lesions in and around Wernicke's area. Broca's aphasics, they said, were linguistically intact individuals who suffered only from problems in articulating their speech. Followers of this theory pointed out that not even textbook cases of Broca's aphasia showed all the observed symptoms and that some displayed additional symptoms. In their view, lesions anywhere in the left hemisphere could produce aphasia, and its severity reflected primarily the size of the lesion rather than its site. These partisans went on to argue that every aphasic exhibits difficulties in all language functions. Differences among the so-called syndromes, they said, are differences in degree (a little more reading difficulty in one case, a little more repetition difficulty in another) rather than in kind.

Today, after a century of research, there is little sympathy for either of the conflicting theories. Due in large measure to the efforts of Norman Geschwind, professor of neurology at the Harvard Medical School, the genuine contributions of the localizers are again appreciated. At the same time, a range of factors that modulate the classic syndromes—such as the nature of the brain disease, the age of the patient, or the situation of testing—are also recognized. The classic syndromes are seen as useful signposts for describing patients rather than as fixed descriptions of what a patient with a given lesion can and cannot do.

Progress has been stimulated by a number of factors. In the wake of this century's wars, researchers have seen hundreds of patients with aphasia. The publication of numerous cases and countercases has clarified our knowledge of the incidence of full-blown examples of the classic syndromes and produced precise descriptions of the symptoms of aphasia.

But perhaps the biggest contribution has come from interactions among specialists from diverse disciplines, each of whom had approached aphasia from a different perspective. In my own view, the most important infusions have come from linguists, who have brought to the study of aphasia logical and well-conceived categories for the analysis of language, and from psychologists, whose accurate experimental techniques have supplemented the important but necessarily superficial methods of bedside examination evolved by attending physicians.

Issues raised by routine bedside testing often stimulate research by interdisciplinary teams. Consider, for instance, Mr. Cooper's apparent success at understanding spontaneous conversation. Such observations have led many neurologists to conclude that a patient with Broca's aphasia has no difficulties in comprehending language. Teams of linguists and psychologists noted, however, that when such patients were tested, they received multiple cues from the context in which a question was posed and from redundancies within the message. Accordingly, they devised questions that could be understood only if one were processing grammatical inflections and exploiting cues of word order. Deprived of the redundancy of ordinary conversational speech, individuals with Broca's aphasia showed only meager comprehension.

Turning to issues raised by Mr. Johnson, experimenters have also clarified the nature of the comprehension defect in Wernicke's aphasia. Because these patients have difficulty understanding auditory messages and decoding single isolated words, some aphasiologists concluded that the primary impediment for the Wernicke's aphasic lay in his inability to decipher individual phonemes—the smallest discrete sounds of language, such as "th," "p," and "b." Careful experimental studies have documented, however, that Wernicke's aphasics can readily discriminate between individual phonemes; they may surpass Broca's aphasics at this task. Their difficulty in understanding occurs at a higher level of semantic interpretation.

Not all the contributions have come from research scientists. Demonstrations by clinicians sometimes challenge—and even undermine— the workaday categories embraced by researchers. None of the categorical distinctions honored by psychologists or linguists can explain Mr. Johnson's curious ability to carry out commands that use the whole body. If, however, one takes into account certain anatomical considerations, this behavior becomes clarified. Unlike commands using the face or individual limbs, which are carried out by the major pyramidal motor pathways running from the cortex to the spinal cord, these commands are executed by the alternative nonpyramidal tracts of the nervous system. A lesion in Wernicke's area usually spares these tracts. Here is a case where an anatomical point of view advances the explanation of aphasic behavior.

Constant interplay between bedside testing and experimental work proves crucial, since experimenters tend to devise careful but artificial test situations. When a patient fails on such a test, it becomes difficult to determine whether the patient lacks the ability in question or is simply confused by the instructions or by the task itself. Sometimes a patient fails on an experimenter's test only to demonstrate the skill in question when a natural situation arises in his life. A patient may fail to repeat an arbitrary set of phrases spoken by an experimenter and yet produce just these phrases in situations where they are warranted. Thus, in a curiously productive way, clinicians and experimenters keep one another honest.

It is impossible to understand the mind without considering its linguistic capacities. Yet both linguists and psychologists face a fundamental problem: the categories, distinctions, terminology, and levels of linguistic competence are based on the study of individuals in whom all linguistic capacities are operating efficiently. These individuals can produce the proper sounds, combine words according to the structure of a language, understand the meaning of the words they use, and use language appropriately in natural situations. Scholars have divided the study of language in the same way, analyzing it in terms of its phonological, syntactic, semantic, and pragmatic levels. No independent means exists for examining the validity of these categories, for determining whether another means of slicing the linguistic pie might not prove more comprehensive and accurate.

Here is where aphasia can make a unique contribution. Were it the case, as some researchers once implied, that all language skills break down simultaneously in aphasia, this pathological condition would hold little scientific interest. But aphasia proves remarkably selective in its damage. A patient may have an impaired ability to read while still being able to write, fail to comprehend and yet speak, fail to understand and yet repeat accurately. These and numerous other dissociations can demonstrate the validity of certain categories of analysis. For example, both Broca's aphasia and transcortical aphasia provide evidence for a separate level of syntactic analysis in the brain.

At other times the dissociations call into question some of the distinctions made by linguists. Aphasia gives little support for the linguist's distinction between competence and performance. Symptoms that violate our expectations can suggest new distinctions and categorization that linguists have ignored, as in the case of the dichotomy in the brain's response to "whole-body" and other kinds of commands.

Aphasia provides a testing laboratory for the distinctions made by those who study human languages—the primary window to the mind.

The study of aphasia may help to clarify several long-standing philosophical questions. Is language the ultimate symbol system on which all other modes of symbolization are parasitic? Or do other symbol systems exist that are relatively autonomous of language? Results from the study of aphasia indicate that language is but one of man's symbolic competences. Once a person's language ability is impaired, he ordinarily shows a lessened capacity to "read" other symbols. Yet this is not always the case. Many severely aphasic patients can carry out calculations, gesture meaningfully, or read musical notation.

Research on aphasia also pertains to another philosophical chestnut: the extent to which thought depends upon language. Aphasia exacts tolls on performance in various concept-formation tasks, as do all forms of brain damage. Yet it is by no means uncommon to encounter a severely aphasic individual who can solve a difficult maze or puzzle, play a game of chess or bridge, or score above normal on the nonverbal section of the Wechsler Adult Intelligence Scale. Other aphasic individuals have continued to paint, compose, or conduct music at a professionally competent level.

Mental functioning in aphasia is relevant to an issue of great current interest: the functions of the left and right hemispheres of the brain. In nearly all right-handers, the left hemisphere of the brain is specialized for language; lesions there will result in significant impairment of language. Such an injury spares right-hemisphere functioning and the aphasic patient remains relatively skilled in those functions for which the right hemisphere is superior—visual-spatial orientation, musical understanding, recognition of faces, and emotional balance.

In working with hundreds of aphasic patients I have been struck by the extent to which they seem to be well oriented, generally aware of what is going on around them, and appropriately attuned to emotional situations. And I have been struck, in contrast, by the frequently inappropriate and disoriented behavior of patients with right-hemisphere lesions, individuals whose language remains essentially intact but whose intuitive understanding of the world seems to have gone awry. In these areas, which have remained recalcitrant to formal testing, one may secure the best evidence that common sense does not depend on competence in language.

Anyone who has spent time with aphasic individuals will recognize the need to help these victims; their personal frustration is so glaring. In the wake of experiments by aphasiologists, speech pathologists have been able to begin rehabilitation with a greater understanding of the processes (and limitations) of language function, and with a heightened ability to exploit those mental powers ordinarily spared in aphasia. To be sure, no rehabilitation can fully compensate for destroyed brain tissue; the best healers are still time, youth, and—at least in matters of language—the degree of left-handedness in one's family.

Research on brain function has led to certain significant breakthroughs in aphasia therapy. Speech pathologists at the Boston Veterans Administration Hospital have devised a training program that significantly boosts language output. Their work is based on the clinical observation that Broca's aphasics can often sing well, and on experimental findings that musical and intonational patterns are mediated by structures in the right hemisphere. During the first phase of this rehabilitation program, called Melodic Intonation Therapy, patients sing simple phrases; in ensuing phases, they learn to delete the melody, leaving only the words. Mr. Cooper, who could sing lyrics to songs but had difficulty reciting them, would seem a likely candidate for this therapy. If he succeeds as well as other patients, in about three months he should be able to produce short but grammatical and appropriate sentences.

The study of aphasia is still in its infancy, but interest in this field has grown so rapidly that advances in understanding and rehabilitation are likely. Few areas of study feature as close a linkage between the medical and the scientific, the clinical and the experimental, the concerns of the theorist and the practitioner. And the mysteries to be solved are inextricably linked with the vast enigmas of language, brain, and mind. It is paradoxical—yet in a strange way heartening—that those who can say little may help us answer questions that have until now eluded even the most eloquent philosophers.

Bibliography

Gardner, Howard, *The Shattered Mind*. New York: Knopf, 1975.

Goldstein, Kurt. *Language and Language Disturbances*. New York: Grune & Stratton, 1948.

Goodglass, Harold, and Norman Geschwind. "Language Disorders, Aphasia." *Handbook of Perception*, Vol. 7, ed. Edward Carterette and Morton Friedman. New York: Academic Press, 1976.

Goodglass, Harold, and Edith Kaplan. *The Assessment of Aphasia and Related Disorders*. Philadelphia: Lea & Febiger, 1972.

Luria, A. R. *Traumatic Aphasia: Its Syndromes, Psychology, and Treatment*. New York: Humanities Press, 1970

FOR DISCUSSION AND REVIEW

1. What is the general definition of aphasia? How common a phenomenon is it? Who are its most frequent victims?

2. Describe the symptoms of Wernicke's aphasia. Reread the interview with Mr. Johnson, and give specific examples of these symptoms. Is he

equally capable of dealing with nouns, verbs, and adjectives (content words) and with words like *if* and *of* (function words)? Note that Gardner states that "Mr. Johnson's understanding was very limited."

3. Examine the chart of the homunculus on p. 188, and consider the relative amount of brain space devoted to various motor functions and to sensory input reception from the skin. What conclusions can you draw? (Compare, for example, the amount of brain space devoted to motor functions of the mouth and that devoted to the trunk of the body, or compare the space allocated to the hands versus the feet. In terms of sensory input, which body areas use the most brain space? Why?)

4. Describe the symptoms of Wernicke's aphasia, and show how they are manifested in Mr. Cooper's behavior. Note the extent of his ability to deal with function words and with complex syntactic constructions (e.g., the passive). What similarities, if any, do you see with certain stages of language acquisition?

5. Compare and contrast Mr. Johnson and Mr. Cooper (or the symptoms of Broca's aphasia and Wernicke's aphasia).

6. There is not complete agreement on the names for all types of aphasia. Explain each of the following, which are in general use, as Gardner defines them: *alexia, agraphia, anomia, conduction aphasia,* and *mixed transcortical aphasia.*

7. Drawing on the previous article by Jeannine Heny (pp. 159–183), explain Gardner's statement that "The striking predictability of [the various types of aphasia] reflects the uniformity with which language functions are organized in normal right-handers."

8. How, today, have the extreme forms of the "localizers'" theory been modified? Describe four specific contributions to the understanding of aphasia made by linguists and psychologists (e.g., comprehension in Broca's aphasia, decipherment problems in Wernicke's aphasia).

9. What are three important implications of the fact that "aphasia proves remarkably selective in its damage," that not all language skills are damaged equally or simultaneously?

10. How can the study of aphasia increase our understanding (1) of the human use of symbols; (2) of *what* thought, if any, is possible without language; and (3) of hemispheric specialization?

Projects for "Language and the Brain"

1. Some recent findings on neural asymmetry suggest that the kind of notation or code used in a given task influences how the task may be done. (Recall the comments in "Brain and Language" by Jeannine Heny on the two types of Japanese script, for example.) Using examples from your own experience, think of how using different codes might influence how you do a task. One example might be the use of Roman numerals versus Arabic numerals in multiplication: which can you process faster: "XIX times III" or "19 times 3"? Another example, if you know German, might be the use of familiar modern printing as opposed to the more elaborate script used in earlier German texts. Write a short essay in which you discuss how codes might affect your efficiency or the way you approach one specific task.

2. Lateral eye movement (LEM) is perhaps the most controversial and difficult to control of all behavioral tests for brain asymmetry. But it is also the most accessible to the lay person. Construct a list of six questions, each of which is either clearly emotional or clearly intellectual. Such questions might be expected to elicit left- or right-eye movements, respectively. An emotional (right-hemisphere) question might be, "What would you do if you saw a poisonous snake?" An intellectual (left-hemisphere) question might involve defining an abstract word or explaining how to compute taxes. Ask four people your questions, and watch their eyes as they answer. Do their LEMs seem to vary with question type? Or do you find (as some suspect) that each person looks relatively consistently in one direction? (Don't forget that a left-eye movement means right-hemisphere activity; you may find this confusing when facing a person in normal conversation.)

3. The nature and extent of therapy available to aphasics often make the difference between at least partial recovery and continued, severe language disability. Prepare a report on one of the different rehabilitation techniques now in use. You may wish to supplement library research by interviews with speech therapists and others who work with aphasic patients.

You may find particularly interesting a program called "Melodic Intonation Therapy," in which aphasics are first taught to sing phrases. Information about this technique can be found in the following two articles: (1) Albert, M. L., Sparks, R. W., and Helm, N. A. "Melodic intonation therapy for aphasia." *Archives of Neurology* 29 (1973), 130–31. (2) Sparks, R., Helm, N., and Albert, M. "Aphasia rehabilitation resulting from melodic intonation therapy." *Cortex* 10 (1974), 303–16. If you prepare your report on melodic intonation therapy, explain why it is helpful. If you know someone who has been helped by this technique, see whether he or she would be willing to discuss it with you.

A different therapy, designed for patients with another kind of aphasia, has been suggested by A. R. Luria. It is discussed in his book *Higher Cortical Functions* (New York: Basic Books, 1966).

4. In a recent journal article (*Neuropsychologia* 21, [1983], 669–678), a Japanese researcher, Takeshi Hatta, described an experiment in which he asked people to look at pairs of digits, comparing their relative physical sizes and their relative numerical values to see if they matched. If the subject saw a large 7 and a small 2, he was to say "yes." On the other hand, a large 4 and a small 8 required a negative answer. As expected, because the task involved analytical thinking (comparison and mathematics), the left hemisphere showed superior performance. But interestingly, even when he translated the task into some rare Ming-era *kanji* characters, the left dominance remained. This occurred despite the high visual complexity of the figures and the fact that people seldom use them (they did not even appear in an official *kanji* list published in 1850). His two types of pairs are illustrated here:

Arabic numeral pairs:

(A)   (B)

Kanji pairs:

(TWO)(ONE)   (HUNDRED MILLION)(THREE)

(A)   (B)

In an earlier study, Hatta had found that subjects read a watch (presumably a familiar "holistic" object) with the right hemisphere. Yet, when warned that the watch would be one hour slow or fast, the results reversed, and he found left hemisphere superiority.

In both cases, the type of task seems more important than the visual stimulus: in the first case, the stimulus changes and hemispherical preference remains the same; in the second, the stimulus stays the same but hemispheric choice changes. What do the two tasks in the first experiment and the second time-telling task have in common that make them demand left-hemisphere processing space?

Design a hypothetical experiment similar in spirit and goal to one of those just cited. For example, think of a situation in which you see or hear the same material, but do two different things with it.

Selected Bibliography

Note: The article by Jeannine Heny in Part Three contains an extensive bibliography, as do two of the books listed here: Segalowitz's Two Sides of the Brain *and Springer and Deutsch's* Left Brain, Right Brain. *The reader should consult these for a more exhaustive listing of sources.*

Blakeslee, Thomas R. *The Right Brain: A New Understanding of the Unconscious Mind and Its Creative Powers.* Garden City, NY: Anchor Press/Doubleday, 1980. (The title is accurate. Thorough exploration of the functions of the right hemisphere; excellent bibliography.)

Buck, Craig. "Knowing the Left from the Right." *Human Behavior,* 5 (June), 329–335, 1976. (Interesting collection of specific examples about what each side of the brain can do.)

Campbell, Jeremy. *Grammatical Man: Information, Entropy, Language, and Life.* New York: Simon and Schuster, 1982. (An extraordinary and fascinating book; see especially Parts Three and Four.)

Farb, Peter. *Humankind.* Boston: Houghton Mifflin, 1978. (Readable and informative; see Chapter 15 for a broad discussion of a variety of aspects of the brain and its functioning.)

Fromkin, Victoria. "Slips of the Tongue." *Scientific American,* 229, 110–117, 1973. (Interesting in themselves, slips of the tongue offer clues to language processing in the brain.)

Gardner, Howard. *The Shattered Mind: The Person After Brain Damage.* New York: Alfred Knopf, 1975. (Chapters 2, on aphasia, and 9, on the brain's two hemispheres, are especially interesting.)

———. *Art, Mind, and Brain: A Cognitive Approach to Creativity.* NY: Basic Books, 1982. (A consistently interesting collection of thirty-one essays, almost all of which were originally published elsewhere.)

———. *Frames of Mind: The Theory of Multiple Intelligences.* New York: Basic Books, 1983. (An interesting synthesizing work; see especially II, 5, "Linguistic Intelligence," and II, 8, "Spatial Intelligence.")

Gazzaniga, Michael S. "The Split Brain in Man." *Scientific American,* 217, 24–29, 1967. (A readable early report on the effects of split-brain surgery [commissurotomy].)

Geschwind, Norman. "Language and the Brain." *Scientific American,* 226, 76–83, 1972. (Discusses how aphasias and other kinds of brain damage help us understand how language is organized in the brain.)

———. "Specializations of the Human Brain." *Scientific American,* 241, 180–182, 186–187, 189–192, 196, 198–199, 1979. (Discussion of hemisphere specialization and of the specialization of particular areas of the brain.)

Jones, Gerald. "Clues to Behavior from a Divided Brain." In 1978 *Nature/Science Annual,* ed. Jane D. Alexander. Alexandria, VA: Time/Life Books, 1977. (A nontechnical summary.)

Ornstein, Robert E., ed. *The Nature of Human Consciousness: A Book of Readings.* San Francisco: W. H. Freeman and Company, 1973. (An interesting collection of forty-one articles; see especially Part II.)

Penfield, Wilder. *The Mystery of the Mind.* Princeton, NJ: Princeton University Press, 1975. (A personal account of the work of this renowned neurosurgeon.)

Perkins, William H. *Speech Pathology: An Applied Behavioral Science*, 2nd ed. St. Louis: C. V. Mosby, 1977. (Somewhat technical but very informative analysis of aphasia on pp. 131–133, 241–247, and 384–387.)

Pines, Maya. *The Brain Changers: Scientists and the New Mind Control.* New York: Harcourt Brace Jovanovich, 1973. (Fascinating chapters on many aspects of the brain; see especially Chapter 7, "What Half of Your Brain is Dominant—and Can You Change It?")

Restak, Richard M., M.D. *The Brain: The Last Frontier.* Garden City, NY: Doubleday & Company, 1979. (Readable, intriguing, and authoritative; hemispheric specialization, language acquisition, and much more. Good bibliography.)

Rieber, R. W., ed. *The Neuropsychology of Language: Essays in Honor of Eric Lenneberg.* New York: Plenum Press, 1976. (Although technical, the nine chapters are packed with information.)

Sagan, Carl. *The Dragons of Eden: Speculations on the Evolution of Human Intelligence.* New York: Random House, 1977. (Controversial but fascinating; worth reading.)

Sage, Wayne. "The Split Brain Lab." *Human Behavior*, 5 (June), 24–28, 1976. (Interesting and very readable summary of split-brain research.)

Samples, Robert E. "Learning With the Whole Brain." *Human Behavior*, 4 (February), 17–23, 1975. (Possible implications for education of our emphasis on the left half of the human brain.)

Scientific American, *The Brain.* San Francisco: W. H. Freeman, and Company, 1979. (The eleven articles originally appeared in the September 1979 issue of *Scientific American* and deal with a variety of topics related to the brain.)

Scientific American, *Mind and Behavior.* San Francisco: W. H. Freeman and Company, 1980. (Twenty-eight articles, mostly by psychologists, covering a diversity of interesting topics.)

Segalowitz, Sid J. *Two Sides of the Brain: Brain Lateralization Explored.* Englewood Cliffs, NJ: Prentice-Hall, 1983. (A very readable text by a distinguished researcher that discusses "the uses of the left-right distinction between the brain hemispheres" and gives "some perspective on the limitations of [this] construct." Excellent bibliography.)

Smith, Adam. *Powers of Mind.* New York: Random House, 1975. (Popular and interesting account of the workings of the brain, TM, EST, Rolfing, and much more. See especially "II. Hemispheres," pp. 59–182.)

Spring, Sally P., and Deutsch, Georg. *Left Brain, Right Brain:* San Francisco: W. H. Freeman and Company, 1981. (An outstanding book that discusses most of the important research into the nature of hemispheric asymmetries. Excellent bibliography.)

Walker, Edward, ed. *Explorations in the Biology of Language.* Montgomery, VT: Bradford Books, 1978. (Six difficult but important essays focusing on language as a biological manifestation of universal cognitive structure. The second essay deals with aphasia.)

Part Four

Phonetics, Phonology, and Morphology

The basic questions asked by any discipline vary over time. Such variation is taken for granted in a field such as chemistry, but it is less accepted in the study of language, or linguistics. And yet, in a mere seventy-five years, traditional grammar, largely unquestioned for centuries, has been fundamentally challenged, first by the proponents of structural grammar, and more recently by linguists advocating a generative approach to studying language. The basic goal of the latter group, who now dominate serious linguistic work in the United States, is to explain just what the speaker of a language, any language, knows. What does it mean, they ask, to know a language?

Most linguists agree that languages are best described in terms of their basic systems, or divisions:

1. *phonetics and phonology:* the sounds of a language, and the rules describing how they are combined
2. *morphology:* the ways in which the words of a language are built up from smaller units, and the nature of these units
3. *syntax:* the finite set of rules that enables native speakers to combine words in order to form phrases and sentences

4. *semantics:* the analysis of the meaning of individual words and of such larger units as phrases and sentences
5. *pragmatics:* the study of speech acts or of how language is used in various contexts

Each of these language components can be analyzed in terms of (1) the units that composed it and (2) the rules or patterns of each system that human beings follow when they speak.

Parts Four through Six deal with these basic systems of language. Part Four discusses the first two systems: phonetics and phonology, and morphology. There are good reasons to treat phonetics and phonology first. It is often helpful, for example, to use phonetic transcriptions or to refer to phonemes and phonological processes when discussing subjects such as syntax.

The first selection, "Phonetics," by Professor Edward Callary, deals with the important topic of phonetics, both articulatory and acoustic, and also with principles of phonetic transcription. Phonology is the subject of the next selection, "The Rules of Language," by Morris Halle. Professor Halle uses examples from a variety of languages to show that native speakers of a language possess a great deal of unconscious knowledge about the phonological rules of that language, knowledge that can be explained only by the existence of a genetic disposition to learn such rules. As he says, "our command of a language is genetically predetermined." Furthermore, the phonological rules of unrelated languages share a number of similarities, again pointing to our natural tendency to use rules and to the similarity of these genetically based rules.

Next, we turn to morphology. "The Minimal Units of Meaning: Morphemes," from the Ohio State University *Language Files*, focuses on the kinds of morphemes in English and the hierarchical way in which they combine to form words. The following selection, H. A. Gleason's "The Identification of Morphemes," uses data primarily from Hebrew to describe the analytical process for identifying morphemes. This discussion precedes "Morphology: Three Exercises," prepared by Professor Gleason, which involve the morphological analysis of samples of Swahili, Ilocano, and Dinka. In the final selection, Professor W. Nelson Francis examines the processes of word formation in English and explains which ones have been most important at different times. The concept of language as a rule-governed system recurs frequently in this anthology. It is stressed in Part Four, and it will be dealt with more extensively in Part Five. This repetition is warranted, for the concept is central to contemporary linguistics.

1/Phonetics

EDWARD CALLARY

Phonetics, which has been studied for many years, is one of the best known subfields of linguistics. Some knowledge of phonetics is an essential basis for further work in linguistics. In the following selection, written especially for this book, Professor Edward Callary of Northern Illinois University discusses some of the applications of current research in phonetics and clearly explains articulatory and acoustic phonetics. Then he explores two aspects of the "grammar of phonetics," aspects that are "known" by all native speakers of English: (1) some of the permissible sequences of sounds in English and how they can be described in terms of general rules, and (2) the regular changes in sounds made by speakers, changes that depend on the contexts in which the sounds occur. The exercises that appear throughout the article reinforce and clarify the author's points.

Phonetics—the study of speech sounds—is one of the best known areas of linguistics, and perhaps the oldest as well. Recorded studies of the sounds of speech date from at least the fifth century B.C. when Pānini, a Sanskrit grammarian, wrote a complicated series of rules describing the correct way to pronounce the Vedic hymns.

Phonetics is also an area of language study with immediate practical value. For example, a knowledge of phonetics is generally recognized as necessary in foreign-language teaching and learning; in identifying and remediating communication disorders such as certain kinds of aphasia (loss of language abilities) and stuttering; and in developing appropriate pedagogical and curricular materials for elementary- and secondary-school English and English-as-a-second-language classes.

During the past several decades, we have seen many more practical applications of phonetic research. Work like that done at Bell and Haskins Laboratories has been applied to the development and production of advanced telephone and other communications systems, where phonetic knowledge has been crucial in determining which aspects of speech sounds are essential and in eliminating redundant information, thus resulting in more efficient and less expensive communication. In the near future, we may well see phonetic investigations making important contributions to voice-operated (rather than keyboard-operated) typewriters and to security systems using voice analysis and recognition. Without fundamental knowledge of phonetics, these technological marvels would be impossible.

In this selection, we will be looking at several aspects of phonetics: first, the physiology of sound production, or how speech sounds are produced by the human vocal mechanism; second, sounds as physical objects; and third, using this common background, how phonetics "fits" within the larger system of grammar. Finally, we will briefly consider a thorny but perennial question: what is "correct" pronunciation?

The first goal of phonetics is to identify and describe the sounds that occur in a particular language, or in languages in general. Since speech sounds are used to convey information from one person to another, there are conceivably three perspectives from which we could view these sounds: first, as they are produced by a speaker; second, as they are transmitted through the air as sound waves; and third, as they are perceived and identified by a listener. These three perspectives are called *articulatory, acoustic,* and *perceptual phonetics,* respectively. They are complementary rather than contradictory points of view, and a full discussion of phonetics deals with all three. Here, however, following the usual practice in introductory material, we will consider only the first two—articulatory phonetics and acoustic phonetics.

Articulatory Phonetics

Probably the most obvious, and surely the oldest, approach to the study of speech sounds is articulatory phonetics, so called because it deals with how the human vocal apparatus is manipulated to produce sounds. The basic assumption of articulatory phonetics is that different sounds result from, and are best described in terms of, the configurations of the vocal tract necessary to utter the sounds. Therefore, in order to understand the bases upon which articulatory phonetics is built, we must have at least a rudimentary knowledge of the anatomy and physiology of the human vocal tract.

Before we examine the vocal tract in detail, however, we need to introduce one of the most important concepts in phonetics: when we talk about the sounds of speech, we are interested in the *sounds* themselves, and not the way they happen to be represented on a printed page. Phonetics is concerned with sound, not writing: to confuse the two, or to take the one for the other, is to confuse speech with its written representation. As literate people, we all too often mistakenly assume that writing is somehow the "real" language and that speech is an attempt (often a degenerate one) to express the sounds that letters inherently possess. The notion that letters have sound values (e.g., "the letter c has the sound of s or of k") is not only mistaken but terribly misleading. When we realize that, in the history of both the individual and the species, speech develops and has developed long before writing, we can see that writing is an attempt to represent the transient sounds of language, and not the other way around. Rather than saying that the letter c has sometimes the sound of s and sometimes the sound of k, it is truer to the facts of language to say that, in the English spelling system, the sound [s] as well as the sound [k] is sometimes represented by the letter c.[1]

> **Exercise 1.** In English spelling, the character (letter) c is ambiguous, representing sometimes one sound, sometimes another. Several other letters are ambiguous as well. Identify the different sound values represented by the following English letters or pairs of letters by listing words in which the letters represent different sounds (e.g., c is [k] in cat, but [s] in nice): x, d, s, g, th, ch.

While the sound and the spelling systems of many languages do not correspond exactly, the degree of misfit between sound and spelling in English is especially great. If you have studied a language such as Swahili or Spanish, you will remember that the chances of correctly pronouncing a word upon seeing it written for the first time are pretty good; furthermore, upon hearing a word in Swahili or Spanish for the first time, you have a good chance of spelling it correctly. Such, however, is not necessarily the case in English. Due to historical and cultural factors, the relationship between sounds and their customary orthography (spelling) is often tenuous. As a result, we have become so accustomed to such phenomena as the spelling bee, long lists of "spelling demons," and words with "silent letters" that we often think in terms of letters rather than sounds.

Most spelling inconsistencies in English are one of three types: (1) there may be more (or fewer) sounds in a word than the spelling leads us to believe; (2) a single sound may be represented by a variety of spellings; and (3) a given spelling may represent several different sounds.

Most of the notorious "silent letters" of English fall into category 1, and the majority of these can be explained by the history of the language. At one time in the past (although this is little consolation to the student struggling to master them now), most of the contemporary

---

[1] To avoid confusion between sounds and letters, phoneticians have adopted the convention of using square brackets (and occasionally slanted lines) to enclose sound values. Thus, [s] refers to a sound, while s refers to the letter.

silent letters were pronounced. The now silent *gh* of *light*, *night*, and *fight* was once pronounced in English, as was the initial *k* of *knee* and *know*. Following the invention of the printing press in the late fifteenth century, the English spelling system was gradually formalized and standardized. Changes in pronunciation continued, however, and as the years passed, spelling became ever more removed from pronunciation, and "silent letters" kept piling up in the historical spelling baggage that we continue to carry around today.[2]

Exercise 2.

a. Identify the number of *sounds* in each of the following words (e.g., *lamb* consists of three sounds):

night	tax	knee	judge
shack	receipt	change	thought
watch	check	weigh	yacht

b. The sound [e] (as in the name of the letter *a*) has several different spellings. List six words that illustrate six different ways of spelling the sound [e] in English.
c. The letter *o* is ambiguous; it represents different sound values. List five sounds represented by *o* (used singly and not doubly) along with illustrative words.

In order to overcome the limitations imposed by the regular alphabet, phoneticians use a special phonetic alphabet, one in which one-to-one correspondences between sounds and symbols are maintained. There is no such thing as *the* phonetic alphabet; many such alphabets have been devised over the years, each slightly different from the others. In fact, several phonetic alphabets, each using a different set of phonetic symbols, are currently in use. In this discussion, we will be using a modified version of the *International Phonetic Alphabet (IPA)*. While phonetic alphabets differ from one another in terms of the number and nature of their symbols, all have three characteristics in common: each symbol consistently represents one and only one sound; each sound is consistently represented by one and only one symbol; and the number of sounds is equal to the number of symbols.

---

[2] In order to narrow the gap between speech and writing, there have been various attempts at spelling reform. However, with few exceptions, these have had no lasting effect. One of the more outspoken critics of English spelling was the dramatist George Bernard Shaw, who pointed out that English spelling is so confused that one might spell *fish* as *ghoti* (take the *gh* of *laugh*, the *o* of *women*, and the *ti* of *nation*). Shaw provided in his will for an endowment to support research in spelling reform. Many revised spelling systems were proposed, and one was finally accepted. Although several literary works, including Shaw's own play *Androcles and the Lion*, were published using the "reformed" spelling system, the net effect in English has been negligible. English speakers are apparently just as reluctant to join the rest of the world in improved spelling as they are in adopting the metric system.

Symbols for the consonant sounds of English, along with some key words illustrating their sound values, follow.

Phonetic Symbol	As in:	Phonetic Symbol	As in:
p	pit, tip, stop	l	lit, till, slit
b	bat, tab	č	chew, hitch
m	mitt, ham, smoke	ǰ	gem, badge
f	fig, gift, muff	š	show, chaperon
v	vat, save	ž	treasure, garage
θ	thin, bath	r	right, tire, shrimp
ð	thus, bathe	y	you, yew
t	tip, putt, stick	w	win, when
d	dip, pad	k	catch, back, skin
n	know, pan, snow	g	give, plague
s	sun, bus	ŋ	thing, tongue
z	zoom, fuzz	h	hot, who

Seventeen of the twenty-four consonant symbols are familiar to you because they also occur in the regular alphabet; seven are unusual. Since the combination of letters *th* usually represents one or another of two different sounds (for example, the first sound of *thick* as opposed to the first sound of *then*), we need two unique symbols. We will represent the initial sound of *thick* with the Greek symbol theta [θ] and the initial sound of *then* with the Old English symbol called *eth* [ð].

Note the special uses in our phonetic alphabet of the modified letters *č*, *ǰ*, *š*, and *ž*. The symbol [č] represents the initial and final sounds of *church*, and [ǰ] represents the initial sound of *gem* or *Jim*. Without the diacritic wedge, [s] and [z] represent the medial consonants of *Bessie* and *busy*; with the wedges, they represent the medial consonants of *masher* and *azure*.

The final sound of words such as *sing* and *thong* is usually spelled *ng*. But since this is a single sound, we want to represent it with a single symbol. We do this by using [ŋ], an *n* with a tail.

Because most of the consonant symbols are taken directly from the traditional alphabet and because their sound values vary so little across dialects and across speakers, they shouldn't give you much trouble. The vowels, however, may pose some problems. They vary considerably from speaker to speaker and from one part of the country to another, so you should pay careful attention to the illustrations and be aware of any differences between your normal pronunciation and the key words given. The phonetic vowel symbols and some words illustrating their sound values follow.

Phonetic Symbol	As in:	Phonetic Symbol	As in:
i	see, each, machine	ʊ	book, full, could, wolf
I	it, myth	o	flow, road, no, open
e	able, weigh, great	ɔ	raw, fought, pause, fall, taught
ɛ	set, said, guest, says	a	hot, father
æ	at, plaid	ay	my, eye, ice, buy
ə	about, son, cup, system, easily	aw	out, cow, bough
u	fruit, ooze, move	oy	toy, boil, lawyer

When a word is written in phonetic symbols, we say that it is transcribed phonetically. When doing phonetic transcription, it is important to remember to transcribe the word as you actually say it in normal, everyday speech, not as you think it should be pronounced or as it is written in the regular alphabet. After you have determined your normal pronunciation, you must then select from the phonetic alphabet the symbols representing that pronunciation. Note from the list of key words that a distinction has been made between the vowels of *tot* and *taught*: the first would be transcribed [tat], and the second, [tɔt]. Many people do not make the same distinction; for them, the two words are pronounced identically and would be transcribed identically: that is, [tat]. Do you make this distinction?

On the other hand, while the author does not merge [a] and [ɔ], he does merge *wail* and *whale*, *witch* and *which*, and other similar pairs. Again, many speakers do not merge them. While the author would transcribe both *whine* and *wine* as [wayn], speakers who distinguish them would probably transcribe the first as [hwayn] and the second as [wayn]. Neither pattern is right or wrong; you must recognize your own pronunciation and transcribe the words accordingly.

Before we continue the discussion of articulatory phonetics, you should practice using the phonetic alphabet.

Exercise 3. Using the list of phonetic symbols as your reference, transcribe each of the following words:

ought	quick	friend
pigeon	tease	night
chief	thing	wrote
foot	scene	shook
boy	cough	many

appoint	been	gauge
shoot	school	gnat
bruise	was	ledge
business	moist	should
whose	laugh	suite
telephone	question	concise
extra	medicate	regional
analysis	foundation	language
English	gradual	explosion
enthusiasm	student	passion
anthropology	consonant	symphony
relaxed	resident	screams
clothes	initiate	ambiguous
ancient	checked	seconds
musical	immediately	chaperon

Exercise 4. Transcribe your name and address.

Exercise 5. Transcribe the names of the letters of the regular alphabet ([a], [bi], [si], and so on).

Now that you have had some experience with the phonetic alphabet, you will be better able to appreciate the use of phonetic symbols as we consider how sounds are produced by the human speech mechanism.

The Articulation of Speech Sounds

Figure 1 shows an outline of the vocal tract indicating those areas that are especially important in speech production. Refer to this outline as often as necessary; you should be able to locate these anatomical reference points and explain their role in articulation.

Speech sounds result from modifying a stream of air. In English, all speech sounds are made on the outgoing breath (this is true for the vast majority of speech sounds in other languages as well). Air is pushed from the lungs through the trachea and into the oral or nasal cavity, or in some cases both cavities. Modifying this flow of air causes different sounds to be articulated. Therefore, speech sounds can be described in terms of their characteristic *point* and *manner* of articulation. We will consider first the *points of articulation* and then the various *manners of articulation*.

The first point at which the airstream may be modified is at the *larynx*.[3] (Locate the larynx and all other points of articulation both on

---

[3] The scientific pronunciation of this word is [larɪŋks], but it is often pronounced [larnɪks], with the [ɪ] and the [n] interchanged (or *metathesized*, to use the technical term). Why do you think this happens? Is [larnɪks] easier to say than [larɪŋks]? Why or why not?

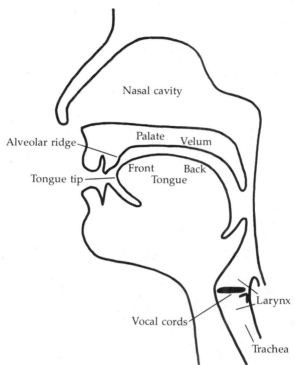

Figure 1

the diagram and on your own vocal tract.) Lying within the larynx are two sheets of elastic tissue called *vocal cords* (also called *vocal bands* or *vocal folds*). For speech, the vocal cords assume one of two basic positions: they are either relaxed and spread apart, or they are tensed and drawn together so that there is only a narrow opening between them. This opening is called the *glottis*. The vocal cords are in the relaxed position when we make sounds such as [s] or [f], and in the tensed position when we produce the corresponding [z] and [v]. Furthermore, when we articulate [s] or [f], the vocal cords remain relatively still; but for [z] and [v], they vibrate and, in so doing, lend a characteristic quality to the sound being uttered. This vocal cord vibration is called *voice*, and sounds produced with the vocal cords vibrating are called *voiced sounds*. (Note that the only significant difference between [s] and [z], or between [f] and [v], is the vocal cord vibration for [z] and [v].) You can check for the presence of voice quite easily by placing your little fingers in your ears and articulating a sound. The buzzing you hear with some sounds but not with others is vocal cord vibration. Try this first with [s], then with [z], and then with [f] and [v].

Exercise 6. Which of the following sounds are voiced: [θ], [n], [s], [r], [y]?

The distinction between voiced and voiceless sounds is fundamental in phonetics, as it is a feature found in all human languages. Most languages have pairs of sounds, such as [s] and [z], that differ primarily only in that one is voiced and the other is voiceless. English, for example, has eight such pairs:

Voiceless: θ f s š p t k č
Voiced: ð v z ž b d g ǰ

Voiced or voiceless is one important criterion by which we may classify speech sounds. Another is by the point of articulation. Since consonant sounds are produced by obstructing the flow of air, the location of this obstruction can be used to describe and classify sounds. For English consonants, there are six major points of articulation:

1. *Bilabial* (literally, "two lips") consonants are [p], [b], and [m].
2. *Labio-dental* sounds are made by bringing the lower lip into contact with the upper teeth. They are [f] and [v].
3. *Interdental* sounds are made, as the name implies, by placing the tongue tip between the teeth. There are two interdental sounds, both spelled *th*. The *th* of *thin* is voiceless, and its phonetic symbol is [θ]. The *th* of *then* is voiced, and its phonetic symbol is [ð]. Words having an initial voiceless interdental sound include *think, thong,* and *thorn;* words having an initial voiced interdental sound include *the, this,* and *though.*
4. *Alveolar.* The *alveolar ridge* is the bony protuberance located where the upper teeth join the palate. In English, six consonants are articulated in the alveolar area: [t] and [s] (both voiceless), and [d], [z], [n], and [l] (all voiced).
5. *Palatal.* The roof of the mouth consists of two distinct parts: the hard front part, called the *palate,* and the softer back part, called the *velum.* (By sliding the tip of your tongue back over the roof of your mouth, you will notice a sharp line dividing the palatal and velar areas.) Six sounds are articulated in the palatal area: the voiceless [č] and [š], and the voiced [ǰ], [ž], [r], and [y].
6. *Velar.* The velum is the soft, fleshy area lying directly in back of the palate. Velar sounds are articulated by bringing the back of the tongue into contact with the velum. There are three velars: the voiceless [k], and the voiced [g], and [ŋ].

We now have two ways to refer to a speech sound. We may identify its point of articulation or describe the condition of the glottis (i.e., whether the sound is voiced or voiceless). In order to describe a speech sound uniquely, however, we must refer to a third dimension—the *manner of articulation.* This term refers to the action of the vocal mechanism as a sound is articulated. Several actions are possible at most points of articulation. We have already said that consonants are formed by obstructing the airstream; the manner of articulation describes the way the airstream is obstructed. For English consonants there are six manners of articulation:

1. *Stops.* A stop is produced by completely blocking the breath stream, then releasing it abruptly. There are six stops, voiced/voiceless pairs evenly divided among three points of articulation: the bilabials [p] and [b], the alveolars [t] and [d], and the velars [k] and [g].
2. *Fricatives.* To produce fricative sounds, one of the articulators is brought close enough to one of the points of articulation to create a narrow opening. When the airstream is forced through this opening, a turbulence or friction is set up. Fricatives are therefore noisy sounds. As with stops, fricatives occur in voiced/voiceless pairs: interdental [θ] and [ð], labio-dental [f] and [v], alveolar [s] and [z], and palatal [š] and [ž].
3. *Nasals.* The velum serves two major functions in speech. As we have seen, it provides the point of articulation for [k], [g], and [ŋ]. Its second function results from its mobility. The velum can be raised and brought into contact with the pharyngeal wall, thus closing off the nasal cavity, or it can be lowered, thereby opening the nasal cavity. When the velum is lowered, air resonates in the nasal as well as in the oral cavities, and the airstream flows out of the vocal tract through the nose rather than through the mouth. Sounds made with the velum lowered are called *nasals.* Since the actions of the tongue and the velum are independent of one another, we may have nasals at various points of articulation within the oral cavity. The sound [m] is a bilabial nasal, [n] is an alveolar nasal, and [ŋ] is a velar nasal.
4. *Liquids.* The liquids are [l] and [r]. The word *liquid* is not a descriptive term such as *stop* or *nasal.* Rather, it is a cover term used to group together two sounds that are similar in many respects. The sound [l] is sometimes called a *lateral,* since air flows around one or both sides of the tongue as the sound is uttered; [r] is sometimes called a *retroflex,* since the tongue tip is turned upward during the sound's production. Although the specific place of articulation of both [l] and [r] varies quite a bit depending upon the preceding or following sounds, we will call [l] an alveolar liquid and [r] a palatal liquid.
5. *Affricates.* Affricates are complex sounds that result from the rapid succession of two manners of articulation: a stop followed by a fricative. Affricates appear initially in *chin* and *gin,* and finally in *itch* and *edge.* In *chin,* the affricate consists of the al-

veolar stop [t] closely followed by the palatal fricative [š]. Similarly, the affricate of *gin* consists of the stop [d] plus the fricative [ž]. (If you say [t + š] and [d + ž] rapidly, these sounds will lose their identities and become the affricates [č] and [ǰ], respectively.)

6. *Glides.* Glides are sounds that provide transitions to or from other sounds. At times they act like vowels, and at other times they act more like consonants. While we can clearly hear [y] and [w] initially in words such as *yet* and *wet*, it is less obvious that they occur finally in words such as *my* and *cow*. Note, however, the action, the movement, of the vocal mechanism as in pronouncing first *my* and then *cow*. With *my*, we end with a [y]-like articulation, and with *cow*, we end with a [w]-like articulation.

Sounds such as [y] and [w] are difficult to classify and describe. Over the years, they have been referred to variously as *semivowels*, *semiconsonants*, or *approximants*, the last term being descriptive of their manner of articulation. In producing a glide, we normally bring one articulator close to a certain point of articulation, but not so close as to create friction; we approximate rather than attain a specific point of articulation. Since the approximation for [y] is in the palatal area, we call [y] a palatal glide; [w] is a velar glide.

We can describe any consonant by referring to its point of articulation, its manner of articulation, and the presence or absence of voice. A summary of English consonants according to these characteristics is given in Table 1.

The points of articulation are those that we have been referring to, with several minor differences. First, the bilabials and the labiodentals (the "lip" sounds) have been brought together in the *labial* category. This allows greater flexibility of reference. If we want to refer to [p b m f v] as a group, we can use the more general term labial. We can also refer to subgroups when necessary: [p b m] are bilabial; [f] and [v] are labio-dental. Similarly, the interdentals and alveolars can be described as separate groups, or they can be identified together as the larger class *dentals.*

Second, [h] has not been assigned a point of articulation. Although some phoneticians call [h] a *glottal fricative* or a *glottal glide*, it appears that [h] has no unique point of articulation; rather, it assumes the same point of articulation as the vowel that follows it. We have not yet discussed the articulation of vowels, but note that in a word such as *heat*, [h] is articulated with the tongue in the forward part of the mouth and with the lips spread, whereas in *hoot*, it is produced with a retracted tongue and rounded lips. These tongue and lip positions are characteristic of the vowels [i] and [u]. Perhaps rather than saying that [h]

Manner	Point	Labial		Dental		Palatal	Velar
		Bilabial	Labiodental	Interdental	Alveolar		
Stop	Voiceless	p			t		k
	Voiced	b			d		g
Fricative	Voiceless		f	θ	s	š	
	Voiced		v	ð	z	ž	
Affricate	Voiceless					č	
	Voiced					ǰ	
Nasal		m			n		ŋ
Liquid					l	r	
Glide						y	w

Table 1. Consonants Arranged by Point and Manner of Articulation and Voice.

has no point of articulation, it would be more descriptive to say that [h] has as many different points of articulation as the number of vowels that may follow it.

Third, the description voiced/voiceless is relevant only for the stops, fricatives, and affricates. All the nasals and liquids, as well as [y] and [w], are voiced. These latter sounds and groups of sounds have no voiceless counterparts.

Finally, you will note that there are more unfilled than filled cells in Table 1, which at first glance may suggest that our classification is at best uneconomical and at worst misleading. But such is not the case. The empty cells result primarily from the fact that we have illustrated point and manner of articulation with English sounds only. If we had included sounds found in other languages (but not in English), more of the cells would be filled.

Knowledge such as that summarized in Table 1 is useful in many ways. One obvious application is helping to learn the correct pronunciation of a foreign language. Once you realize just what *fricative* or *voiceless* or *affricate* means, you can readily understand how these terms are combined in a language to describe a particular sound. Those of you who have studied Spanish, for example, may have had difficulty in correctly pronouncing the medial sound of *lobo* or *Cuba*, since this sound does not occur in English. However, if you know that it is a voiced bilabial fricative, you will have gone a long way toward learning its correct articulation.

Similarly, modern Chinese has a pair of sounds that do not occur in English. In the Chinese Pinyin (phonetic) writing system, they are spelled *c* and *z*. In learning the language, however, it is more helpful to know that these are, respectively, voiceless and voiced alveolar affricates.

To sum up, any consonant sound can be described by indicating its point of articulation, its manner of articulation, and whether it is voiced or voiceless. For instance, [p] is a voiceless bilabial stop, [n] is an alveolar nasal (it is not necessary to specify *voiced* because all nasals are voiced), [ž] is a voiced palatal fricative, and so on. Conventionally, in describing a speech sound, the voiced/voiceless feature is given first, the point of articulation feature second, and the manner of articulation last.

Exercise 7. Give the phonetic description of each of the following sounds: [m], [ǰ], [ŋ], [f], [k], [θ], [l], [z], [t], [ð]. Use the descriptions of [p], [n], and [z] in the preceding paragraph as models.

Exercise 8. Descriptions of sounds can often be used to explain phonetic behavior. The data shown in the following list illustrate frequent consonant substitutions by English-speaking children. Note that the substitutions are not random but follow definable patterns that can be characterized by using the phonetic descriptions we have just developed. Examine the intended sounds and the children's actual utterances, and for each case, describe the pattern of substitution the children used. (Data from K. Snow, "A Descriptive and Comparative Study of the Articulation of First Grade Children," reported in John Locke, *Phonological Acquisition and Change.* New York: Academic Press, 1983, p. 136.)

Intended Sound	Children's Substitution	Intended Sound	Children's Substitution
p	t, k	t	k
b	v, p	d	g, t
f	v	v	b
z	s	θ	f

Vowel Articulations

Vowels and consonants are produced in fundamentally different ways. Whereas consonants are articulated with a substantial degree of obstruction in the oral cavity, vowels are produced with a relatively free airflow. Vowels are open rather than closed sounds, made largely by shaping the vocal tract rather than by interfering with the flow of the airstream. Because the tongue is the main instrument used to change the shape of the oral cavity, vowels are most usefully described in terms of the position of the tongue as they are articulated.

Again, unlike consonants, vowels have no discrete physical points of reference, nothing as definite as *bilabial* or *alveolar*. Rather, vowels exist on a continuum and are best characterized as articulated with a greater or lesser degree of tongue placement along a given dimension. Basically, the tongue can move along two dimensions: high to low (toward or away from the palate) and front to back. A vowel articulated with the body of the tongue relatively forward is classified as a *front vowel*; one made with the tongue body relatively high is a *high vowel*; and so forth. Vowels produced with the body of the tongue neither high nor low are called *mid vowels*, and those made with the tongue body neither front nor back are called *central vowels*. Table 2 uses the high-low and front-back dimensions to schematize the relative articulations of English vowels.

Using the information presented in the table, we can describe any English vowel in terms of its relative tongue height and tongue "backness." For example, [I] is a low-high front vowel, [a] is a low back vowel, and [ə], called *schwa*, is a low-mid central vowel.

The vowels shown in Table 2 are all *simple vowels*; that is, they retain their basic quality throughout their duration. Simple vowels contrast with *diphthongs*, which are complex vowel sounds having one

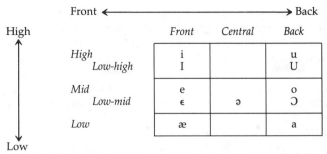

Table 2. **Vowels Arranged According to Tongue Height and Backness.**

beginning point and a different ending point. (The word *diphthong* itself comes from Greek *di*, meaning "twice" or "double," and *phthongos*, meaning "sound" or "voice." So diphthongs are literally "two sounds.") Diphthongs are combinations of sounds, and they are represented with a sequence of symbols in the phonetic alphabet. The first symbol represents the approximate phonetic quality of the beginning sound, and the second represents the approximate ending quality. There are three regular diphthongs in English: one occurs in words such as *my* and *sigh*, another in *now* and *out*, and a third in *hoist* and *void*. The phonetic symbol for the diphthong of *my* is [ay], indicating a sound close to [a] for the beginning element and close to [y] for the ending element. If you position your vocal apparatus for [a] and then glide immediately into [y], you will approximate the vowel of *my*. Similarly, if you start with [a] and glide toward [w], you will approximate the diphthong of *now* and *out*. One of the main reasons for calling [y] and [w] "glides" is the way they function in diphthongs.

The diphthong of *hoist* and *void* is symbolized [oy], indicating that this complex vowel begins with an [o]-like sound and glides to [y]. The three English diphthongs are all "rising" diphthongs—they glide from a low onset (or nucleus) toward a high position—high-front in the case of [oy] and [ay], and high-back in the case of [aw].[4]

Exercise 9. An inventory of sounds, such as the one presented here, gives the impression that all sounds are pretty much equal in the role they play within a language. But some sounds are more frequent than others, some sounds carry more information than others, and some are easier to articulate than others.

a. The low-back vowel [a] is a true universal; it is present in all known languages; [i] and [u] are nearly universal. In fact, some languages have only these three vowels; many other languages have a five-vowel system

---

[4] In describing English diphthongs, some phoneticians symbolize the high-front glide with [i] and the high-back glide with [u]. But the sound is the same, whether *my* is transcribed [may] or [mai]. The sounds [y] and [i] are articulated in the same palatal area, and [w] and [u] in the same velar area.

consisting of [i], [u], [a], [e], and [o]. Other vowels, such as [I] and [ɔ], are much less frequent. Using the information in Table 2, explain why [i], [u], and [a] would be a "better" vowel system, from the point of view of both the speaker and the hearer, than one consisting only of [I], [e], and [ɛ].

Assuming that a language has only the three vowels [i], [u], and [a], why would it be more natural to add next the vowels [e] and [o] rather than [I] and [ɛ]?

b. Within a given language, the frequency of occurrence of sounds in normal, "running" speech varies considerably. In English, for instance, consonants are nearly twice as frequent as vowels. Even among the consonants there are great variations in the frequencies of occurrence of individual sounds. In one study reported by S. R. and M. A. Faircloth (*Phonetic Science* [Englewood Cliffs, NJ: Prentice-Hall, 1973], p. 57), the four most frequently occurring consonants were, in descending order of frequency: [n], [t], [d], and [s]. The five least frequently occurring consonants were [š], [y], [č], [ž], and [ǰ]. By using phonetic descriptions, determine the common features of the most frequent sounds and those of the least frequent sounds. Using arguments based on phonetic data, explain why [n], [t], [d], and [s] occur much more frequently than [š], [y], [č], [ž], and [ǰ].

c. Language acquisition by children often gives us insights into the nature of phonetics. For example, some sounds are learned much more quickly than others, and therefore may be thought of as "easier" than others (perhaps they are less complex in some way). One study found that by the age of thirty-two months, ninety percent of children acquiring English could correctly articulate the following sounds: [n], [m], [p], [h], [t], [k], and [y]. However, even by the age of forty-eight months, the following sounds (among others) were still not correctly articulated by ninety percent of the children tested: [š], [č], [v], [z], [ž], [θ], and [ð]. (Data from E. Prather et al., "Articulation Development in Children Aged Two to Four Years." Reported in Locke, *Phonological Acquisition and Change* [New York: Academic Press, 1983], pp. 72–73.)

Using phonetic descriptions, describe and comment upon the group of easily acquired sounds and the group of sounds with which the children had difficulty. Also comment upon the relationship between the frequency of occurrence of sounds in adult speech (from part b) and children's patterns of phonetic acquisition.

Acoustic Phonetics

In recent years, the science of articulatory phonetics has been enhanced by investigations into the physical properties of speech sounds. Such studies, called *acoustic phonetics*, have led to a variety of technological advances, including improved radio and telephone communications and synthesized speech. (Synthesized speech, usually generated by computer, is the disembodied voice you hear when your

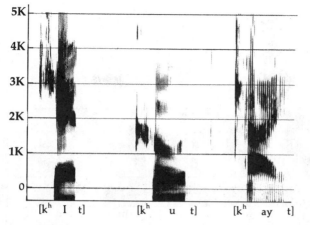

Figure 2. Spectrogram. The words *kit, coot,* and *kite,* spoken in isolation by an adult male. Note the differences among the vowels [I] and [u] and the diphthong [ay], keeping in mind that acoustically, vowels are the most clearly delineated class of sounds. In fact, the stops [p t k b d g] have no sound and do not usually show up in a spectrogram; we "hear" them because they affect the pronunciation of adjoining vowels. Since the dark areas of the spectrogram indicate the frequencies at which acoustic energy occurs, we can see that the front vowel [I] has two formants quite far apart, while the back vowel [u] has two formants that are much closer together.

car tells you that the seat belt hasn't been fastened; when the copy machine tells you, in its monotonous machine dialect, "Don't forget your original"; or when computerized games ask, "How much is six times nine?") Our knowledge of acoustic phonetics has grown so rapidly in the past few years that good computer-generated speech is now virtually indistinguishable from human speech.

Acoustic phonetics relies on sophisticated equipment that analyzes a speech signal into its three primary components: frequency (usually expressed in *Hertz* or cycles per second), intensity, and duration. The most frequently used instrument is the *sound spectrograph*; its output is a visual representation of speech called a *sound spectrogram.* Two spectrograms are shown in Figures 2 and 3. The first displays the isolated words *kit, coot,* and *kite.* Frequency is indicated along the vertical axis, duration along the horizontal axis (a single spectrogram can display approximately 2.5 seconds of speech), and intensity by the relative darkness of the markings. These markings are the most important elements of acoustic analysis; they represent bands of energy and are called *formants.* Listeners rely primarily upon the information contained in formant one (the formant closest to zero frequency) and formant two (the next closest) in identifying sounds.

Acoustically, vowels are the most clearly delineated class of speech sounds; their formant structure is the clearest and the easiest to identify,

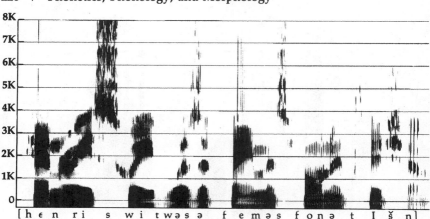

Figure 3. Spectrogram. The sentence, "Henry Sweet was a famous phonetician," spoken by an adult male. What are the acoustic characteristics of the fricatives? How do these differ from the characteristics of the stops?

as we can see in these examples. In contrast, the consonants are quite difficult to make out. Recent studies have indicated that not only do we identify particular vowels by the shape and relationship of the formants, we also use the vowel formants to determine which consonants precede or follow the vowel. Thus, for example, we apparently identify the initial consonant of *tea* not on the basis of any acoustic property of [t], but rather on the shape of the formants of [i].

Acoustic phonetics and articulatory phonetics give us slightly different perspectives on the nature of speech sounds. However, both are needed if we are to fully understand the role of speech sounds in human language.

Phonetics and Grammar

Now that we have identified the phonetic inventory of English and have seen how sounds can be described by their manner and place of articulation and the presence or absence of voicing, we are ready to examine several of the ways in which these sounds are employed by English grammar.[5] We will consider two aspects of this "grammar of phonetics": the permissible sequences of sounds, and the regular changes that sounds undergo when they occur in certain contexts. We will see that English grammar places severe restrictions on the number and kinds of sounds that can occur in sequence, and it also determines

[5] Although we will continue to use the more traditional articulatory descriptions of speech sounds, we could just as well use acoustic descriptions. As phonetics progresses as a science, we may well find more and more phonetic phenomena being described in acoustic terms.

and specifies the different ways in which a sound must be pronounced to speak English without an accent. Native speakers of English acquired this "grammar of English phonetics" as infants and very young children, without formal instruction. This ability is part of the innate human predisposition to acquire language.

Sequence Constraints

If all possible combinations of one, two, or three consonants were allowed at the beginning of an English word, there would be more than 12,000 different possibilities. However, the number actually found is fewer than 60; the other 11,040-some clusters are prohibited by the rules of English. We are interested first in determining which clusters are possible in English and which are not. In addition, we would like to go beyond a listing of the combinations that can and cannot occur and state the principles upon which these observations are based. For instance, as the linguist Noam Chomsky has pointed out, of the words *brick*, *blick*, and *bnick*, only the first actually occurs in English. However, and more important, the second could occur (it could be a scientific term, a new detergent, or the name of a snack cracker), but *bnick* can never occur as an English word. We learned this "rule" when we learned the language.

We will begin by listing some of the possible initial consonant clusters in English; then we will attempt to determine the rules of English that determine which consonants may cluster together in which order, and which are prohibited.

Consider for the moment all possible word-initial, two-consonant clusters, the second of the two consonants being [r]. Only nine different clusters are permitted. (Remember, we're dealing with sounds and not with spelling.)

[pr] as in *prank*	[gr] as in *grain*
[br] as in *break*	[fr] as in *front*
[tr] as in *train*	[θr] as in *three*
[dr] as in *drain*	[šr] as in *shrimp*
[kr] as in *crane*	

Having identified these clusters, we could merely list the sounds that can occur before [r] at the beginning of an English word: [p b t d k g f θ š]. Such a list tells us which sounds may occur in this position, but it says nothing about what, if anything, they have in common; nor does it explain why sounds such as [v], [l], or [m] cannot occur in this position.

If, however, we further examine these nine permissible sounds, we see that they divide neatly into two large groups: stops and fricatives. No nasals, liquids, glides, or affricates are permitted. Initial sequences of [lr] or [mr] are thus ruled out because they do not fall into one of the two permitted classes. Initial [vr], however, presents an apparent problem, because [v] is a member of a permitted class ([v] is a fricative). Note, however, that while *any* stop can precede [r] in this position, only certain fricatives can. We may have sequences of [fr], [θr], or [šr], but not [sr], [vr], [ðr], [zr], or [žr]. We need then to restate our initial hypothesis to include [f], [θ], and [š], but to exclude the other fricatives. To do this, we must refer to the phonetic descriptions of the sounds involved. When we do this, we see that the permitted fricatives are all voiceless. In contrast, the fricatives [v], [ð], [z], and [ž] are voiced; we may hypothesize that they are prohibited on the basis of this feature. We are still, however, left with a problem: [s], a voiceless fricative, does not pattern with the other voiceless fricatives—no English word can begin with the consonant cluster [sr] followed by a vowel sound. Since both manner of articulation and voicing have already been identified as prohibiting certain consonants from clustering with [r], it is logical to consider the point of articulation feature to see if it explains the exclusion of [s]. What we discover is that apparently the rules of English will allow any voiceless fricative to precede [r] word-initially, as long as it is not alveolar; [s], being alveolar, is thus prohibited. Therefore, a general statement concerning the sounds that may cluster with [r] word-initially would be something like, "Any sound that is a stop may precede [r] at the beginning of an English word. So, too, may a fricative, provided that it is voiceless and not alveolar."

Exercise 10.

a. Only six different consonants can precede [l] at the beginning of an English word. List them along with at least one example of each (i.e., an existing English word beginning with that cluster). Then group together the sounds that can precede initial [l] and describe the groups phonetically, just as we did for those sounds that can precede [r] word-initially.

b. Follow the same procedure as in part a and describe those sounds that can precede initial [w] (*twice, switch,* and so on).

c. An English word may begin with a maximum of three consonants. List several different examples. (Note: [spl] as in *split* and *splash* is a three-consonant cluster; *sch* as in *school* is not [skul].) After making a list with an many different clusters as you can, answer the following questions:

1. What must the first consonant be?
2. Which two phonetic characteristics must the second member have?
3. Which phonetic characteristics must the third member have?

Variation in Sounds

In addition to determining permissible sequences of sounds, the rules of language also prescribe how a sound will be pronounced. At first, this point may seem trivial, because we believe that [t] is pronounced [t], [n] is pronounced [n], [s] is pronounced [s], and so on. But if we pay careful attention to English pronunciation, we will find that such is not the case.

It is a curious fact of phonetics that we consistently recognize and interpret physically different sounds as the "same" sound. Because it is practically impossible to pronounce the same word twice in exactly the same way, an incredible variety of speech sounds reaches our ears every day. Why? One reason is that the size and shape of the vocal tract vary from one speaker to the next: because speech sounds derive from anatomical functions, different anatomies produce different sounds. Due to differences in vocal-tract size alone, the word *me* will be pronounced differently by an adult male, an adult female, and a child. However, native speakers ignore these differences when it comes to interpreting speech, and easily recognize *me* as *me*, and not as *see*, or *tea*, or something else.

More important than differences caused by anatomy are differences that are part of the phonetic system and are therefore consistent from one speaker to the next. These variations within sounds are generally determined by the phonetic environment in which the sound occurs. A given sound will have several pronunciations, called *variants*. As speakers, we know which variant to use in a certain context.

For example, consider the sound [t] as it occurs in *top, stop, pit, mutton, eighth, startle,* and *city.* Functionally, each of these occurrences of [t] is the same as the others but physically, each is different. The [t] of *top* is produced with an accompanying puff of air (called *aspiration*), while the [t] of *stop* is *unaspirated.* (You can easily demonstrate this for yourself by placing your fingertips against your lips and alternately pronouncing *top* and *stop.* The small burst of air that you feel with the [t] of *top* is aspiration.) The final sound of *pit* may be aspirated, unaspirated, or even *unreleased.* (A [t] is unreleased when we make closure between the tongue tip and alveolar ridge but stop articulating before the sound is released. We have the option of nonrelease at the ends of words.)

During speech, the airstream may exit through either the oral or the nasal cavity. Usually, [m], [n], and [ŋ] are the only sounds released through the nose. All other sounds have an oral release, except when they precede a nasal consonant. For example, the [t] of *mutton* has a nasal rather than an oral release. In articulating *mutton*, we close for [t] at the alveolar ridge, but before breaking the contact, we drop the velum and releases both [t] and the following nasal through the nasal cavity. Other words having a nasally released [t] include *rotten, tighten, shorten, Latin,* and *bitten.*

The four varieties of [t] that we have considered so far are distinguished from each other by manner-of-articulation differences (aspiration, no aspiration, unrelease, nasal release). The [t] of *eighth* differs from these four in its point of articulation.[6] This [t] is made not at the alveolar ridge as are the [t]s of *top, stop, pit,* and *mutton,* but with the tongue tip between the teeth. Because the teeth are involved, this sound has a dental articulation.

Another pronunciation of [t] occurs in *startle.* The second [t] of *startle* has two characteristic features: (1) it is voiced rather than voiceless, making it more like a [d] than a [t]; and (2) it is released through the position of the following [l]. In articulating this [t], we make contact between the tongue tip and the alveolar ridge, and without breaking contact, drop one or both sides of the tongue. This manner of articulation, called *lateral release,* occurs in normal speech whenever [t] precedes [l] (*little, battle, turtle, bottle,* and *metal*).

The [t] of *city* illustrates a seventh pronunciation; it is voiced, but its manner of articulation is different from that of the [t] in *startle.* In *city* (and also in *party, water, notice, ready,* and *butter*), the medial consonant (*t, d,* or *tt*) is produced by bouncing the tip of the tongue off the alveolar ridge. Sounds articulated in this manner are called *flaps,* or one-tap *trills.* In English, taps are always voiced. They occur most often between vowels and are usually spelled with *t* or *d.* Frequently, we have pairs of words, one spelled with medial *t* and the other with medial *d,* which are *homophones.* In American English, for instance, the pair *latter* and *ladder* are for most speakers pronounced exactly alike, as are the pairs *atom–Adam* and *petal–pedal.*

> **Exercise 11.** True homophones are sets of words with different meanings but identical pronunciations (such as *son* and *sun,* or *latter* and *ladder*). English also has sets of *near homophones*—words with different meanings but nearly identical pronunciations, the only phonetic difference being found in an unusual feature. For instance, most speakers distinguish the words *writer* and *rider,* but the difference is found in the length of the vowel rather than in the medial consonant. The [ay] of *rider* is quite a bit longer than the [ay] of *writer.* Check your normal pronunciation of the following pairs of words.
>
> | | | |
> |---|---|---|
> | raider–rater | udder–utter | bleeding–bleating |
> | medal–metal | madder–matter | padding–patting |
> | wading–waiting | alder–altar | bedding–betting |
> | wedding–wetting | sordid–sorted | carder–carter |

---

[6] *Eighth* has two regular pronunciations: [etθ] and [eθ]. This discussion is relevant to the [etθ] pronunciation only.

Are they true homophones? If not, is the difference in the length of the vowel or in some other area? Be specific.

We have seen that [t] has at least seven different pronunciations in English: it is aspirated in *stop*, unaspirated in *top*, released through the nose in *button*, released through the [l] position in *little*, possibly unreleased in *cut*, has a dental articulation in *mutton*, and is a voiced flap in *city*. This variation is not unique to [t]; all sounds have variant pronunciations.[7]

> **Exercise 12.** Pronounce several times each of the vowels in the following words: *go, coat, code, open, coal, robe, rope, core.* How many are different? In what ways do they differ?

Native speakers of a language know "intuitively" when to use each variant of a sound. This skill is part of our linguistic ability, something we learned just as we learned that a voiced labio-dental fricative is a sound of English but a voiced bilabial fricative is not. (This knowledge, of course, remains unconscious—certainly most people can't describe it—unless one studies linguistics, especially phonetics.)

Even though a given sound has several distinct pronunciations, we still believe, deep in our linguistic minds, that each of these different sounds is, in an important sense, the "same sound." Even though we can easily demonstrate that the medial sound of *atom* is voiced, thus making it more like a [d] than a [t], a part of our phonetic knowledge says, "It's still [t]," thus raising an apparent contradiction—that different sounds are the same sound.

The contradiction is more apparent than real, however, but to resolve it we must go beyond the physical description of speech sounds and into the minds of language users, specifically into the intentions of speakers and the interpretations of sounds by hearers. We will see that the sounds intended by speakers do not always correspond to what they actually utter and, conversely, that the sounds listeners actually hear are not always the sounds that they think they hear.

A basic tenet of modern linguistics is the notion that language exists on at least two levels. In phonetics, one level is the obvious physical phonetic fact that we can describe sounds, either articulatorily or acoustically, as they are actually produced. This is what we have been doing up to this point. The second level, which is more abstract and less obvious, is the psychological or mental level, where speech sounds are intended and interpreted.

[7] Using the wrong variant results in a stilted, overcorrect, artificial speech, or in a "foreign" accent. Pronounce the following words using an aspirated [t]: *butter, brittle, turtle, stir, pot, parting.* Note that, although the pronunciation is recognizable as English, it is a nonidiomatic, forced pronunciation.

We can identify and describe the sound units of either level. In some instances, the two levels correspond quite closely, while in others they vary considerably. Thus, we may well have a mental picture of a sound that is quite different from its physical reality.

Suppose that an English speaker wanted to utter the words *top button* (not a phrase you hear every day, to be sure, but a good illustration). Speakers would believe (at the mental level) that they were producing [t] in each word—not any particular kind of [t], just [t]. At this point, one [t] is the same as any other [t]. However, the rules of English phonetics require that each of these [t]s be different. As you will remember, the [t] of *top* must be aspirated; the [t] of *button*, to be idiomatic English, must not be aspirated and must be released through the nose. English speakers, knowing these rules, unconsciously aspirate the first [t] and nasally release the second [t] (physical level). Further along the speech chain, listeners hear different [t]s in *top* and in *button* (physical level), but ignore these differences and identify each sound as just [t] (mental level).

Note that the hearer's mental level corresponds to the speaker's mental level; similarly, the speaker's and hearer's physical levels also correspond. Between these two levels lie the rules of phonetics that, for a speaker, in effect "change" an intended sound into a physical fact or, for a hearer, change a physical fact into a mental fact. When we intend or interpret sounds, we apparently ignore such phonetic niceties as aspiration, nasal or lateral release, and dental articulation. However, the rules of English phonetics force us to observe them (although we are not conscious of doing so) whenever we articulate speech sounds.

As we have seen, sound units exist on the mental and the physical levels. A single mental unit may have one or more than one corresponding physical units. The mental unit /t/ in English, for example, has at least the following physical units corresponding to it: aspirated [t], unaspirated [t], nasally released [t], laterally released [t], dental [t], flap [t], and unreleased [t]. The technical term for the mental unit is *phoneme*, and that for the physical unit is *allophone*. We can say, then, that in English there is one /t/ phoneme but at least seven [t] allophones.[8]

These two sets of units, phonemes and allophones, play different roles within the phonetic system of all languages. Phonemes are contrastive units; they serve to distinguish words with different meanings. Substituting one phoneme for another will usually result in a different word, but substituting one allophone of a phoneme for another allophone of that phoneme will not; although the resulting pronunciation

---

[8] Note how the distinction between phoneme and allophone is reflected in our notation system. Phonemes are enclosed in slant lines (/ /), while allophones are enclosed in brackets ([ ]).

might strike you as a bit strange, the word would still be identifiable. Thus, *city* spoken with an aspirated [t] will be recognized as *city* and not as *sissy* or *sicky* or some other word.

Furthermore, allophones of a single phoneme are usually predictable, while phonemes are not; that is, we can usually predict when a particular allophone will occur. For example, nasally released [t] is found only when /t/ occurs immediately before a nasal; it cannot occur elsewhere. Similarly, nonaspirated [t] occurs immediately following [s]; it is non-English to pronounce a word such as *step* with an aspirated or flap /t/.

When a series of allophones occur only in restricted environments (as they do in this example), they are in *complementary distribution;* that is, certain allophones will occur only in certain positions within a word, and other allophones will occur only in other positions. In this way, they complement one another.

Now that we have seen that sounds (i.e., phonemes) normally and regularly assume a variety of forms according to where they occur within a word, we are ready to ask one of the fundamental questions of phonetics: Why are phonemes so variable? Is it merely caprice or perversity on the part of the English language, or are there good reasons for their variability? Furthermore, can we use descriptions of sounds to move toward an explanation of why the phonetic system of a language works the way it does? While there are still many unexplained phonetic phenomena, we do find the same kinds of things happening over and over in language after language. This indicates that many phonetic processes must have a basis not in one or another individual language, but rather in the human language faculty itself. In the remainder of this selection, we will examine several of these processes.

Let's return for a moment to the English /t/ phoneme.[9] By this time, you should be familiar with many of the /t/ allophones and their distributions:

- Aspirated [t] occurs word-initially or (optionally) word-finally.
- Dental [t] occurs before interdentals.
- Lateral release [t] occurs before [l].
- Unreleased [t] occurs before stops and (optionally) word-finally.
- Flap [t] occurs medially, usually between vowels.

To explain why these allophones are distributed as they are, we must introduce a new concept: *assimilation.* In phonetics, assimilation

[9] Because all phonemes have multiple allophones, we could actually use any phoneme from any language for illustration. However, the English /t/ phoneme is a particularly good choice as it has a wide variety of allophones, and the allophones are clearly and neatly distributed.

refers to a change a sound undergoes in order to become more like another, often adjacent, sound. Note from the distribution of the allophones of /t/ that a great deal of overlap exists between the phonetic description of the allophones and their environments (e.g., dental [t] before dentals, nasally-released [t] before nasals). These are cases in which the /t/ phoneme takes on articulation features from a following sound in order to become more like (i.e., assimilate itself to) the following sound. This is typical of assimilation in English; a sound usually changes to become more like a following sound rather than the other way around. The /t/ phoneme effectively changes its points of articulation to more closely agree with the point of articulation of the following sound.

Assimilation is a natural process found in all languages. As speakers, we find that it's easier to pronounce some sequences of sounds and more difficult to pronounce others. In order to increase the ease of articulation, we try whenever possible to reduce the number of articulatory movements or "gestures." One simple way to do this is to extend one articulatory feature over as many sounds as possible. For example, instead of articulating the /t/ of *button* with an oral gesture and the following /n/ with a nasal gesture, we anticipate the upcoming /n/ and pronounce the /t/ and the /n/ with nasal articulations.[10] Thus, the assimilation of /t/ to /n/ in *button* is an instance of assimilation in manner of articulation, because nasal is a manner feature.

Now let's consider the /t/ of *city, butter, water*, and the like. This /t/ allophone, you will remember, was described as a voiced flap. While the flapping is somewhat difficult to explain, the voicing is not. Some further data should make the nature of this assimilation clear. Consider the verbs *wait, sit*, and *put*, all of which end in the voiceless stop /t/. Note, however, what happens to these words when we add a suffix beginning with a vowel, such as *-er* or *-ing*. The voiceless /t/ of *wait, sit*, and *put* becomes the *voiced* flap of *waiter, sitting*, and *putting*. Again, this change is motivated by the desire to decrease the articulatory effort. In these instances, instead of turning the vocal-cord vibration alternately off and on, we extend voicing over a sequence of sounds and considerably reduce the effort required. To pronounce *waiter* with a medial voiceless sound would require us to activate the vocal cords for the first vowel (all vowels are voiced in English), deactivate them for the medial consonant, and then activate them again for the suffixal

[10] As an analogous case, consider assimilation in another physical domain—typing. When typing, we generally reduce finger movements to a minimum; we anticipate upcoming keys and, wherever possible, cheat slightly in their direction. Also, those fingers not being used usually approach their next striking position while, or even before, a preceding key is struck. This phenomenon is so frequent and regular that many typing errors can be explained, and even predicted, by its operation. Like the fingers, parts of the vocal tract that will be used in sounds yet to be uttered try, whenever possible, to get into phonating position before they are actually used.

vowel. The timing needed for these movements is tricky, and we find it much easier to let the vocal cords vibrate through the articulation of the medial consonant as well as the vowels. This, then, is an instance of assimilation in voice, because /t/, which is phonemically voiceless, becomes phonetically voiced and thus more like its surroundings.

Exercise 13. The English phoneme /k/ has several variants, among them a front allophone (pronounced more in the palatal region) and a back allophone (pronounced more in the velar region). Examine the following data and identify the environments in which each allophone is found. You will need to determine the phonetic characteristics of the sounds that "cause" /k/ to be pronounced first with one allophone and then with another. Be specific in your answer; refer to the vowel chart as necessary.

Palatal /k/ found in:	Velar /k/ found in:
keep	cool
king	cook
cane	coat
cabin	cot
Kent	caught

Do these data show assimilation? If so, determine whether it is in voice, in place of articulation, or in manner of articulation.

Exercise 14. Like /k/, the English phoneme /l/ has two major allophones, but they are distributed somewhat differently than the /k/ allophones. There is a front or "clear" /l/ ([l]) and a back or "dark" /l/ (symbolized [ɫ]). Transcribe the following words phonetically.

Clear /l/ found in:	Dark /l/ found in:
lean	feel
lit	loot
lane	low
let	tell
latch	all
late	law

1. In which *two* environments is back /l/ ([ɫ]) found?
2. Where is front /l/ ([l]) found?
3. Which occurrence(s) of these allophones can be predicted as a result of assimilation?

To summarize briefly, we have seen that abstract units called *phonemes* appear in actual speech as a series of allophones. We have also seen that the occurrence of many of the allophones of a given phoneme can be predicted, because they result from assimilation. Thus, we know where the back allophone of /k/, the nasally released allophone of /t/, and so on, will occur. These phonetic facts are relatively easy to apprehend, because the allophones represent relatively minor deviations from one basic phoneme. To a considerable degree, the allophones are phonetically similar to one another, and nowhere (at least in English) would we find a case where, for instance, aspirated and unreleased /t/ constituted the only difference between words. Yet, if we examine the phonetics of English or any other language in greater detail, we would find many instances where we would want to include as allophones of the same phoneme sounds that in other instances constitute independent phonemes. For example, consider the final sounds of the words *five, twelve, broad,* and *describe.* Note what happens to these voiced sounds when a suffix beginning with a voiceless consonant is added: the /v/ of *five* and *twelve* becomes the [f] of *fifth* and *twelfth*; the /d/ of *broad* becomes the [t] of *breadth*; and the /b/ of *describe* becomes the [p] of *description.* Since we recognize that *five* and *fif, twelve* and *twelf,* and the other variants are different forms of the same word, we also want to recognize that the [v] of *five* and the [f] of *fifth* are variants of the same sound, or allophones of the same phoneme. Whereas /f/ and /v/ contrast in some environments (e.g., word-initially), in other environments no contrast is possible. From such evidence, we can determine that English has a phonetic rule that changes a voiced sound to the corresponding voiceless sound whenever it appears before an affix beginning with a voiceless sound. This is, of course, another example of assimilation in voice. By the way, the rule that changes /v/ to [f] in *five–fifth* (and *fifty*), as well as in many other words, has been in English for so long that, unlike many assimilations, it is reflected in the regular orthography.[11]

Exercise 15. Following are some variant forms of one of the English prefixes meaning "not." Examine them, and try to explain the instances of assimilation.

Variant	*Found in:*	
[Im]	immature	immaterial
	imperfect	implausible
	imbalance	improper
[In]	inoperative	indecent
	inedible	intolerant
	innocent	indelicate
	interminable	
[Iŋ][12]	incorrigible	inglorious
	ingrate	incompetent

---

[11] This example, of course, is directly contrasted with the flap voicing of *wait–waiter.* There—and generally in English—/t/ and flaps never contrast; /v/ and /f/ regularly do.

[12] The variant [Iŋ] occurs more frequently in some people's speech than in that of others. And, although it is found more frequently in casual speech than in formal, it is certainly not uncommon in American English.

[Ir]   irresponsible   irreverent

[Il]   illegal   illegible

Dissimilation

As we have seen, assimilation tends to make neighboring sounds more alike, thereby contributing to greater ease of articulation. Many phonetic rules operate in such a way as to increase assimilation. Assimilation is probably the most widespread phonetic process known; it is found in languages throughout the world.

Given what we know about the reasons for assimilation, it would seem that sequences of sounds that are most alike would be the easiest to pronounce. This does not seem to be true, however; sounds can be so much alike that they are very difficult to pronounce (e.g., the tongue-twister, "The sixth sick sheik's sixth sheep's sick"). When faced with such situations, speakers frequently alter one or more of the sounds in order to ease the articulatory burden. Examples abound in English, and not only in tongue-twisters.

Sometime in the early sixteenth century, English speakers got the novel idea of giving a name to the closet in which they stored drinking vessels. They combined the name of the drinking vessel and the name of the material of the storage cabinet, and coined the word, *cupboard*. But this act of compounding juxtaposed two sounds with very similar phonetic characteristics: [b] and [p] are bilabial and stop. This combination of sounds proved difficult for English speakers, who facilitated their articulation by first voicing the [p], giving [bb], and then simplifying [bb] to [b], yielding a pronunciation that has been with us ever since. Deletions of this sort are found throughout the language.

As a general rule, English speakers easily tolerate a cluster of two consonants in word-final position, even if they do share a number of phonetic characteristics. However, when affixation or compounding adds a third consonant, speakers tend to break up the three-consonant cluster, most often by deleting the middle consonant. We have no difficulty in pronouncing the final [nd]s in *friend* or *kind* or *second*, even though [n] and [d] share both voicing and point of articulation. However, when another element is added, as in *friendship, kindness*, and *second base*, we have a problem. Our usual response is to delete the [d] (e.g., [frenšIp]).

Some phoneticians have called the process we have just described "complete assimilation," arguing that the [d] accommodated itself to the following sound so completely that, in effect, it has become that sound. This argument is suspect on several grounds. A more revealing explanation would view the resulting sequences of sounds as having been made different from their original forms: *-nds-* has become *-ns-*,

-*ndn*- has become -*nn*-, and -*ndb*- has become -*nb*-. If assimilation makes a sequence of items more similar, then the reduction of the consonant clusters we have just examined should perhaps be called *dissimilation*, because it serves to make a string of similar items less similar.

Exercise 16. Examine the following words, and then transcribe each word twice phonetically, first in formal style, making a special effort to indicate all the sounds, and second in informal, more conversational style. For each word, identify the sounds that are present in formal but not in informal style. Explain why these sounds have dropped out.

months	arctic	obvious	handball
bestseller	sandpaper	sounds	pumpkin
postman	width	fifths	hands

Taken together, asssimilation and dissimilation can often explain why a certain word will appear in one phonetic form on one occasion and in other phonetic forms on other occasions. *Hand*, for instance, regularly has at least three phonetic variants: it appears as [hænd] in *hand, handout,* and *handle,* as [hæn] in *handbag, handful,* and *handstand,* and as [hæŋ] in *handkerchief.* By taking into account the effects of assimilation and dissimilation, we can gain a better understanding of how [hænd] evolves into its various forms. Of course, [hænd] needs no explanation, and [hæn] is apparently the result of dissimilation, because we have the final [nd] of *hand* immediately preceding a consonant in *handbag* and *handful.* The phonetic form of *handkerchief* requires a two-part explanation, because assimilation and dissimilation are both at work. Compounding *hand* and *kerchief* gives us three consonants in sequence, with interlocking phonetic characteristics. The sounds [n] and [d] are voiced alveolars, while [d] and [k] are nonbilabial stops. The [d] is then dissimilated (dropped), leaving the intermediate form [hænkərčIf]. The [n] is now free to assimilate to the point of articulation of the following [k], becoming in the process the velar nasal [ŋ]. These two steps result in the usual phonetic form [hæŋkərčIf]. The steps must be taken in this order; dissimilation must precede assimilation in this instance. The change of [n] to [ŋ] cannot precede the deletion of [d], because, before [d] is deleted, [n] is adjacent to an alveolar and not a velar.

Exercise 17. Explain, in terms of assimilation and/or dissimilation, the changes the items in the first column undergo when they are combined with the words or affixes in the second column.
    Transcribe (phonetically) the combined forms into casual, idiomatic English.

1	2
grand	pa
Christ	mass
clothe	s
govern	ment
this	year
have	to
six	ths

Although they cannot explain every phonetic process, assimilation and dissimilation, working separately or together, can account for many of the variant pronunciations of words. Assimilation and dissimilation are fundamental concepts in understanding how phonetic systems work.

The notion that the "correct" pronunciation of an item might well differ from one environment to the next was implicit in the discussions of assimilation and dissimilation. Many people find this idea disturbing; they believe that there is (or at least should be) one and only one way to pronounce a word, a way that is correct for all times and all places. For them, a particular pronunciation is either right or wrong, not right on some occasions and wrong on others. They might argue, for instance, that the word *West* has only the pronunciation [wɛst]. To pronounce it without the final [t] would demonstrate either one's ignorance or one's stupidity (or perhaps both). However, what such well-intentioned purists don't realize is that the language itself will ultimately define right and wrong pronunciation, just as it ultimately defines right and wrong syntax. The rules for correct pronunciation must come from inside the language; they cannot be imposed from without. For example, in English, the final [θ] of *north* and *south* becomes the [ð] of *northern* and *southern,* and no amount of social persuasion will change that fact.

Furthermore, purists do not appreciate the effects of change on pronunciation—either historical or contemporary change. Surely, no one would seriously propose that we return to an earlier time in English when initial [k] was pronounced in *knee, knight,* and so on. But there must have been a time when equally well-intentioned people were warning against the "mispronunciation" of *knee* as [ni] and *knight* as [nayt].

Just as there is historical change in language, there is contemporary change, which we have called "variation." Much as we have different speech styles for different social occasions, we have different word forms and different pronunciations for different phonetic environments. Unlike the variations caused by social situations, these latter variations are defined by the language. To return for a moment to the example of [wɛst], most English speakers regularly use at least two forms of this word: [wɛs] and [wɛst]. The rules of English tell us when each form is correct. We have learned that at the end of a word group or preceding a vowel, *west* is pronounced [wɛst]—for example, *The Girl of the Golden West* or *West Australia*—but when preceding a consonant, the final [t] is deleted, especially in less formal speech situations—for example, *West Texas* or *West Virginia.* (The pronunciation [wɛst tɛksəs] would be bizarre, especially in Amarillo!)

Assimilations in particular are frequently seized upon as indicating sloppy or careless speech. After the citation of some examples, speakers are usually admonished to give each sound its "true value" whenever it occurs. But the admonishers do not realize that to do so would run contrary to the nature of language. Learning to use assimilations and dissimilations is just as much a part of learning a language as is learning individual words and sounds. To be effective users of a language, we must know the sounds that occur, and the rules that define their pronunciations in particular environments. Although it is true that the number of assimilations and dissimilations varies according to the social context of speech (the less formal the context, the greater the number of assimilations, and vice versa), they are found to some extent in all situations. Far from being careless and sloppy, people who make grammatical use of assimilations and dissimilations are demonstrating their mastery of the phonetic component of their language.

Conclusion

In this discussion, we have sketched only the barest outlines of phonetics and given only a small sample of the kinds of things that must be considered if we are to describe fully the sound patterns of language. While phoneticians sometimes disagree on the best way to describe phonetic phenomena, they generally agree that phonetics has two levels: (1) an abstract, or psychological, level and (2) a concrete physical level. Operating between these levels are the phonetic rules of a language, which specify exactly how the abstract units are to be pronounced. Although phoneticians have different ideas of the best way to present these rules, all presentations have as their primary goal the description of speakers' knowledge of the sound system of their language.

FOR DISCUSSION AND REVIEW

1. Identify and explain the importance of the three characteristics shared by all phonetic alphabets.

2. Define the terms *point of articulation, manner of articulation,* and

voiced (*sound*). Give two original examples of ways in which an understanding of these concepts could be helpful to you.

3. Examine the charts of English consonant and vowel phonemes. Explain why it is significant that not every slot (or cell) is filled.

4. Explain the relationship between phonemes and allophones and their differing roles within a language.

5. The terms *free variation* and *complementary distribution* are used to describe the occurrence of allophones. Define each term, and give two examples of each.

6. Both *assimilation* and *dissimilation* are important phonetic processes. Define each term, and give two original examples of each.

2/The Rules of Language

MORRIS HALLE

When you talk, what do you say? When you listen to someone else talk, what do you hear? Words, of course—or so all speakers and listeners believe. But they are mistaken, according to Professor Morris Halle of the Massachusetts Institute of Technology. Native speakers do, however, share a great deal of largely unconscious knowledge about their language, and they acquire this knowledge without formal instruction. Drawing examples from a number of different languages, Halle illustrates some of the phonological rules and principles of various languages as well as some similarities among these rules and principles. Every language has its own set of rules, and all human beings have a natural tendency to look for and use rules when processing language. Our ability to learn these rules as very young children and without instruction, and our persistence in using them, are attributable to the uniquely human genetic endowment.

The sounds that we hear when spoken to and that we emit when speaking are produced by complex gymnastics executed by our lips, tongue, velum, larynx, and lungs. The activities of these independent anatomical structures are coordinated with a precision that should be the envy of the most highly trained ballet dancer; yet this truly remarkable exercise is performed at the drop of a hat by even the clumsiest person. In contrast, even the most adroit primates have never been able to master it, despite intensive training. These facts suggest that the ability to speak is linked to our genetic endowment, that it is one of the aspects in which humans differ from all other mammals.

The gymnastic feats involved in speaking are clearly not the whole story. Speech is not just some noise that humans are capable of emitting; it is a noise that is produced to convey meaning. And how speech conveys meaning is surely one of the great puzzles that has intrigued thinkers for centuries.

Once the question of meaning is introduced, it is clear that we have to go beyond an analysis of vocal organ movements and of the acoustic signals these movements elicit. Such an analysis can tell us how the sounds of English differ from those of Finnish or Kwakiutl, but it cannot tell us why a sequence of sounds uttered by a speaker of English means something to us, whereas a sequence of sounds uttered by a speaker of Kwakiutl, or Finnish, usually means nothing. If we ask ourselves why most of us are able to understand a speaker of English but not a speaker of Finnish or Kwakiutl, the trivially obvious answer is that we know English but we don't know Finnish or Kwakiutl. But that answer leads naturally to a question with a much less obvious answer: What is the character of the specific knowledge that speakers of a particular language possess through which they are able to understand one another? Although not all linguists might choose to formulate it precisely in this fashion, this question has always been central to the science of linguistics.

Words: To Say and to Hear

A striking fact about all speech is that all speakers—no matter in what language—are sure that they produce words, and all hearers are certain that they perceive utterances as sequences of words. When we pay attention to our own speech, we observe at once that we do not normally break up our utterances into words; rather, we run words together without intervening pauses. One can readily convince oneself of this fact by reading a text in a way so—as—to—pause—after—every—word and observing that the result is highly unnatural. The acoustical speech signal of an utterance thus differs from its representation in writing: the spaces between the written words are generally missing in speech. Does this mean that, because we do not pronounce utterances word by word, our perception that utterances are made up of words is a kind of illusion—that we perceive words even though they are not actually there?

I would argue that this is indeed the case, for what we hear is only partly determined by the physical signal that strikes our ears. For instance, we generally hear words in utterances of only our own language; we fail to hear words in equally clear utterances in an unfamiliar language. Moreover, many utterances, even when pronounced perfectly clearly, are ambiguous, in the sense that they can be perceived as either of two (or sometimes more) distinctly different sequences of words.

A recent incident illustrates this quite well. Somebody reported to me that he had met a person with the interesting name:

Me [lbə] tory,

in which ə represents the sound of *a* in *about*. "Oh, yes," said I, "this person has the same last name as a sixteenth-century Polish king, Stefan Batory, who fought against the Turks." As I began a minilecture on Turkey's role as a major military power for many centuries, I was interrupted with the information that the person in question was female and that her first name was *Melba* and her last name *Torrey*. Although this name also provided the basis for an erudite disquisition,

Some English "Nonwords"

thrim	lgal	dramp	pfin
platch	gnet	shripe	bdit
snork	vrag	chride	nsip

Table 1. Readers whose mother tongue is English will recognize that some of these letter strings *might* be English words but some could not be. Abstract principles of word structure guide us subconsciously in our evaluation and use of these "nonwords."

the opportunity somehow had passed. Be that as it may, the point of the anecdote is that the utterance was ambiguous, and that its ambiguity was not located in the acoustical signal nor in the intention of the speaker. The hearer's misapprehension thus was due to the assumption (or illusion) that a particular sequence of sounds was divided into words in a way that did not coincide with the division intended by the speaker. Since knowing words is an essential component of every fluent speaker's command of language, an obvious topic to investigate is the form in which this knowledge is internalized by speakers: What do they know about the words of their language? At first blush it may appear that the answer is trivially simple. Speakers know that certain sound sequences have particular meanings; for example, the sound sequence [dɔg] refers to the animal otherwise known as man's best friend, whereas the sound sequence [tɔk] refers to the activity of speaking.

There is more to it, however. Speakers know not only the words of their language; they also know whether a given sound sequence could or could not be a word in their language. Consider the strings of letters in Table 1. Most readers have never encountered any of these "words" before. Yet there will be widespread agreement that some of these *might* be English words whereas others could not possibly be English. Furthermore, most readers will agree as to which "words" belong where; i.e., *thrim, snork, dramp, platch,* and *shripe* are likely to be judged English words, while *gnet, lgal, vrag, pfin, bdit,* and *nsip* are not English. Since none of the "words" was previously encountered, the judgment cannot be the result of checking through a list of memorized words. The explanation must be that we all share some basic information about the structural properties of English words—for example, that English words never begin with the consonant clusters *gn* and *lg,* whereas *sn* and *pl* are allowed. In other words, we all share some abstract principles of word structure such as those in the illustration.

It is unlikely that any readers will recall working out such principles in the course of learning English; in fact, few speakers will claim that they are even aware of knowing such principles. Yet their ability

Some Principles of English Word Structure

1	m n	do not figure in any clusters except *sn* and *ʒm*; *snail* and *small* are words, *gnet* is not a possible word.
2	m n l r w y	do not occupy the first position in a cluster; *platch* and *frith* are possible words, *lpatch* is not.
3	b d g	do not occupy the last position in a cluster; *bdit* is not a possible word.
4	p t k f o	may occupy either the first or the last position in a cluster, but not both; *thrim, sphere,* and *scare* are possible, but *pfin* is not.

Table 2. This list illustrates but a few of the abstract principles of English word structure. Although access to these (or similar) principles is necessary to account for English speakers' judgments about the "nonwords" above, few if any speakers will remember developing such principles in the course of learning the language.

to judge "words" such as those cited above as English or not can only be explained by the assumption that speakers of English possess this type of knowledge. In other words, this suggests that we have knowledge about our native tongue of which we are not conscious. Like Moliere's M. Jourdain, we all speak prose, but we are totally unaware of doing so.

Knowledge: Taught, Learned, and Innate

The existence of knowledge not directly accessible to our consciousness is not a particularly new discovery. One of the main purposes of Socrates' questions in Plato's writings was to demonstrate that even the most untutored among us possess knowledge of which we are totally unaware.

Many readers will accept this idea and yet be surprised that in passing on our language to our children we should be transmitting knowledge of which we ourselves are not consciously aware. Implicit in this surprise is the assumption that learning is always the result of overt teaching. But that assumption is false. Indeed, the acquisition of our mother tongue, I would argue, is a prime example of this kind of learning.

The fact that most of what we know about our native tongue is acquired without overt teaching raises a further question. All children are naturally interested in words and constantly inquire about them. But neither they nor their parents are the least bit curious about principles such as those illustrated in Table 2 that govern the distribution of initial consonant clusters. Yet somehow in the process of learning English we must have learned them. How can one explain this? How can one explain, in other words, that in the process of learning the words of English we incidentally learn principles of English word structure in which we have no conscious interest and to which nothing in our daily existence might plausibly draw our attention?

The only reasonable account of how speakers come to know these principles is to attribute them not to external factors but to innate mechanisms involved in memorizing words—that is, to assume that our minds are so constructed that when we memorize words, we automatically also abstract their structural principles. We might suppose that human memory for words is at a premium so that every word must be stored in a maximally economical form—i.e., in a form where every redundancy is eliminated. Since the principles noted in Table 2 capture an essential aspect of the redundancy inherent in English words, access to these principles is required to store English words in their most economical form. Different principles will, of course, be developed for different languages, but there is no language that lacks them altogether that does not place severe constraints on sequences of consonants and vowels in words. Thus the postulated mechanism that causes speakers to seek the abstract structural principles in their words will always produce a useful result.

It almost goes without saying that the propensity to search for structural regularities in the words we commit to memory is not something that we acquire from experience. Try to imagine, for instance, what sort of experiences might lead a child of average intelligence to grasp the fact that words contain redundancies that might be utilized for more economical coding. Moreover, these experiences must be common to children of all cultures, to Greenland Eskimos as well as to those whose parents are, for example, college professors. The only plausible explanation for the special way in which humans memorize words is innate: we do it in our particular way because for members of our species there is no other way.

There is of course nothing implausible in the suggestion that an organism is genetically constructed to perform particular tasks in particular ways. In fact, that is surely a major reason why a particular organism executes certain tasks very well and others poorly or not at all. Think, for example, of a kitten that shares a young child's every waking moment. At the end of a year or two the child will have acquired substantial mastery over its mother tongue, but the pet will fail to show any progress of this kind; instead, it will show great skill at catching mice and climbing trees. The reason for this is that humans are genetically different from cats, and part of that difference consists of the intellectual capacities that enable humans to acquire command of a language, presumably through special built-in features that determine, among other things, the way we memorize words.

The Special Roles of b, d, and g in Spanish

bajo	"low"	a[β]ajo	"below"
donde	"where"	a[ð]onde	"where to"
guardar	"to watch"	a[γ]uardar	"to wait for"

Table 3. The consonants b, d and g are the subject of special rules in English (*see Table 2*) and Spanish (*above*). Though the rules are very different in the two languages, the fact that the same group of sounds figures in the rules of two distantly related languages points toward a single set of principles governing sound groupings in all languages.

Universals of Language?

If the basis of our command of a language is genetically predetermined, then we should expect to find similarities among the principles and rules of all the different languages that are or have been spoken by humans. And we do.

In every language there are rules that affect groups of sounds rather than individual sounds, and the same groups of sounds figure in the rules of widely differing languages. For example, consider [b d g]. One of the most basic rules of Spanish phonetics states that these consonants are pronounced much as in English when they are the initial sound of a word and in certain other environments. However, they are pronounced very differently elsewhere, as shown in Table 3. We recall that clusters of consonants in this same class [b d g] are excluded from last position in English words (see Table 2). Thus, this class figures in rules of two such distantly related languages as English and Spanish.

Similarly, the class of consonants [m n l r w y] receives special treatment in the Papago language spoken by Indians native to Arizona, as shown in Table 4.; here those consonants figure in compound nouns, the second element of which is [ʔ o o ʔ o o], meaning "bone." In compounding, as the illustration shows, nouns are simply adjoined. However, adjoining consonants permute position, as in Table 4, when the first noun ends with a consonant from the set [m n l r w y] and the initial consonant of the second noun is a glottal stop [ʔ], a sound that in English we pronounce when we attempt to distinguish *an aim* from *a name*. Thus, when *wawuk* (racoon) is adjoined to *ʔooʔoo*, the result is *wawukʔooʔoo*, but when *ban* (coyote) is adjoined to *ʔooʔoo*, the result is not *banʔooʔoo* but *baʔnooʔoo*.

The same group [m n l r w y] that figures in the Papago rule of noun compounding plays a role in English; the group is excluded from initial-consonant clusters in English words (*see row 2 in Table 2*).

Some Special Roles of Consonants in Papago

1	wawuk[ʔ]oo[ʔ]oo	"racoon bone"
	[ʔ]u[ʔ]uhig[ʔ]oo[ʔ]oo	"bird bone"
	mawid[ʔ]oo[ʔ]oo	"mountain lion bone"
2	ba[ʔ]noo[ʔ]oo	"coyote bone"
	kaa[ʔ]woo[ʔ]oo	"badger bone"
	ceeko[ʔ]loo[ʔ]oo	"squirrel bone"

Table 4. In forming compounds, the Papago language of Indians native to Arizona treats nouns ending with m, n, l, r, w, and y differently (*see Table 2*) from other nouns (*see Table 1*). These consonants also figure in the principles of English (*Table 2*). That the same consonant groups—and few others—are involved in such rules in other languages suggests that to all humans, no matter what their linguistic heritage, certain sounds are naturally related and others unrelated.

These examples—and experienced linguists should have little difficulty in extending the list indefinitely—show that identical groups of consonants function in totally unrelated languages. Indeed, the same groupings of sounds reemerge in the rules of language after language, whereas other groupings of sounds—e.g., [n l b k] or [θ k r g m]—are never encountered. This observation suggests that to the human speaker there is something natural about certain groupings of sounds—that they somehow belong together—whereas other groupings are unnatural and therefore never encountered. The judgment as to what sounds naturally belong together probably derives from the design of our nervous system; and that, in turn, is determined by our genetic endowment.

Forming Words From Words

Rules and principles of language are not at all something esoteric that only linguists and other pedants enjoy splitting hairs over. On the contrary, rules are the very stuff of which language is made, and speakers use them with the greatest ease, even abandon. Indeed, the rules and principles that determine the shape of the words in a language make up only a fraction of those regularly mastered by fluent speakers of the language.

To convey some impression of the exuberance with which languages use rules, let me briefly discuss part of the system of plural rules in Kasem, a language spoken by about 80,000 people in West Africa, primarily in Ghana. For the class of nouns shown in Table 5, the singular forms end with the suffix *a* and the plural forms end with the suffix *i*. The suffixes appear in this form in row 1 (*bakada-bakadi* and *fala-fali*). The same suffixes are involved in the other examples, but their appearance there is masked by the effects of special rules.

The Plural Rules of Kasem

	Singular	Plural		Singular	Plural	
1	bakada	bakadi	"boy"	fala	fali	"white man"
2	kambia	kambi	"cooking pot"	pia	pi	"yam"
3	buga	bui	"river"	diga	di	"room"
4	mala	male	"chameleon"	kaba	kabe	"slave"
5	naga	ne	"leg"	la[ŋ]a	le	"song"

Table 5. For one class of nouns in Kasem, a language spoken by about 80,000 people in West Africa, the singular suffix is *a* and the plural suffix is *I* (*see rows 1 and 2*). But an elaborate set of rules obscures this simple state of affairs in many instances (*see rows 3, 4, and 5*).

For example, Kasem is subject to a rule that deletes the first in a sequence of identical vowels. Because of this Vowel Deletion Rule, the plural forms in row 2 are not *kambii* and *pii*, but *kambi* and *pi*.

A different rule—the Consonant Deletion Rule—accounts for the forms in row 3. This rule deletes stem-final [g] and [ŋ] in the plural. Consequently, in place of the expected *bugi* we get *bui*, and the plural of *diga* is not *digi* but *di*. The form *di* is somewhat more complicated than is first apparent. We know that the Consonant Deletion Rule would delete the *g* in *digi*, turning it into *dii*, but that is not the correct form; the correct form is *di*. There is, of course, no difficulty explaining how *di* arose: *dii* was subject to the Vowel Deletion Rule.

In the derivation of *di*, the two rules were applied in a specific order. If the rules had been applied in the reverse order, the result would have been *dii*. Since the basic form *digi* does not contain a sequence of identical vowels it could not be subject to Vowel Deletion. The subsequent application of Consonant Deletion would then produce *dii*, but to this form Vowel Deletion can no longer apply since this rule has been ordered before (not after) Consonant Deletion.

A further complication arises in the case of *mala*, chameleon (row 4). The plural form should be *malai*; instead we find *male*. To a linguist this is not strange, because linguists know numerous languages where, as a result of the Monophthongization Rule, the diphthong [ai] is replaced by the monophthong [e]. In fact, English spelling still shows traces of this development; the letter sequence *ai* is pronounced *e* as in *pain, maim,* and *gain*. This process is even more general in Kasem, with not only [ai] becoming [e] but also [au] becoming [o]. Now we are in a position to explain the forms in row 5 of Table 5: they are the result of the interaction of the Consonant Deletion Rule with the Monophthongization Rule. Specifically, the basic plural forms *nagi* and *la[ŋ]i* are transformed by the Consonant Deletion Rule into *nai* and *lai*, respectively. They are then turned into *ne* and *le* by the Monophthongization Rule.

The fact that Kasem speakers use special rules to generate the plural forms of their nouns should not seem strange in light of what we have said. What may strike the layperson as implausible is the relative complexity of the procedure—outlined only incompletely in Table 6—that appears to be involved in the inflection of Kasem words. We might well wonder whether we really go to all this trouble just to say a few words.

Implicit in this objection is the assumption that humans find it difficult to perform this sort of computation—that it would be easier to memorize such facts as the plural of *naga* is *ne* and that of *diga* is *di* than to postulate a single plural suffix *i* for all nouns in this class and to compute the different outputs according to the rules. The linguistic evidence suggests that the converse is much closer to the truth, for the Kasem example is the norm rather than the exception. Indeed, recourse to computation is so strongly favored over rote memory that speakers apparently do not have the option of foresaking rules for memorization.

Owhay Ancay Ouyay Eadray Isthay?

This natural bent for rules is expressed in a great many special uses of language. Children frequently use secret languages such as Ab-language or pig Latin, both of which are nothing but normal English to which one or two extra rules have been added. The rules for pig Latin, for instance, consist of a permutation that moves the initial consonant cluster from the beginning to the end of the word, to which the diphthong *ay* is then adjoined. Thus, *pig* becomes *igpay* and *Latin* becomes *atinlay*. These simple rules produce words so greatly at variance with standard English that children effectively possess a secret language quite impenetrable to their teachers and parents, which is, of course, the main purpose. Though to my knowledge the history of pig Latin has not been documented in detail, we know that it goes back many generations; today's speakers are not its inventors but have learned it from older children.

There are, however, numerous instances of secret languages invented by children. One such "language" was discovered about 20 years ago in Cambridge by Professor Joseph Applegate, then a member of the Department of Modern Languages at M.I.T.[1] A couple living in his building consulted Professor Applegate about their two younger boys who, they feared, were suffering from some neurological disorder. Although they appeared to understand English, the boys were

---

[1] Applegate, Joseph R., "Phonological Rules of a Subdialect of English," *Word* 17 (1961): 188–193.

Some Examples of Rules Operating on Kasem Plurals

Plural form:	Consonant Deletion Rule: Delete stem-final [g] and [ŋ]	Monophthongization Rule: [ai] becomes [e], [au] becomes [o]	Vowel Deletion Rule: Delete the first in a sequence of two identical vowels
bakad-i	→	→	→ bakadi
kambi-i	→	→	→ kambi
dig-i	→ dii	→	→ di
mala-i	→	→ male	→ male
nag-i	→ anai	→ ne	→ ne

Table 6. A flowchart illustrating the application of three rules in the formation of plurals in Kasem, a West African language spoken in parts of Ghana. The plurals of all words in this class are formed by adding the suffix *i* to the stem. But a Consonant Deletion Rule, which applies first, eliminates stem-final [g] and [ŋ] in the plural. Next Monophthongization turns [ai] and [au] into [e] and [o], respectively. Finally, Vowel Deletion eliminates one of two consecutive identical vowels. If the rules were applied in a different order, the outcome would be quite different for several forms. Unbroken arrows between rule blocks indicate that the rules are not applicable to the form in question.

Rules of a Language Invented by Children

	The Glottal Stop Rule		The Consonant Rule	
cake⟶	In words containing	⟶ca[ʔ]⟶	Eliminate sounds	⟶ca[ʔ]
full ⟶	two identical sounds from the group	⟶	in the group [f θ s č š γ ð z j ž],	⟶[p]ull
did ⟶	[p t k b d g], the second occurrence	⟶di[ʔ]⟶	replacing them with corresponding	⟶di[ʔ]
doze⟶	is replaced by a glottal stop[ʔ].	⟶	stops—[p] for [f], etc.	⟶do[d]

Table 7.

speaking a jargon that the parents found quite incomprehensible. The third child in the family, who was a few years older than the two problem children, had apparently no trouble understanding his brothers and often acted as their translator. After listening to the children for a few evenings, Professor Applegate discovered that the children were using a secret language of their own devising: by adding two rules to standard English, they were rendering their language quite impenetrable to their parents—although not to their brother.

Specifically, Professor Applegate found that the children's speech was modified by two rules absent from their parents' English. In words containing two identical stops—i.e., two occurrences of a sound from the set [p t k b d g]—the children's speech was subject to a Glottal Stop Rule that replaced the second stop by a glottal stop [ʔ]. The children therefore pronounced words such as *cake, daddy,* and *paper* as shown in group 1 of Table 8.

Second, the children's speech lacked affricates and fricatives—i.e., sounds belonging to the set [f θ s č š γ ð z j ž] were not used. In the children's language, a Consonant Rule replaced these with the corresponding stops—[f] by [p], [θ s č š] by [t], [γ] by [b], and [ð z ž] by [d]. As a result, the children pronounced alike words that are differentiated in adult speech, as shown in groups 2 and 3 of Table 8.

That was not all, however. The children differentiated the stop sound that arose by the Consonant Rule from all other stop sounds: only the latter were replaced by glottal stops as a result of the Glottal Stop Rule. (Additional examples are shown in group 3.) These rules, like those in the Kasem plural formation, were applied in a definite order, first the Glottal Stop Rule and then the Consonant Rule. Thus, *did* became *di*[ʔ] by the Glottal Stop Rule, and the Consonant Rule was not applicable. On the other hand, *doze,* to which the Glottal Stop Rule was not applicable, became *do*[d] by the Consonant Rule. Since the rules are ordered, it is impossible at this point to apply the Glottal Stop Rule again.

Some Words In a Language Invented by Children

1	cake	ca[ʔ]	daddy	da[ʔ]y	paper	pa[ʔ]er
2	full	[p]ull	pays	pay[d]	walks	walk[t]
	pull	[p]ull	paid	paid	walked	walk[t]
3	suit	[t]uit	doze	do[d]	fife	[p]i[p]
	toot	too[ʔ]	did	di[ʔ]	pipe	pi[ʔ]

Table 8. To give themselves a "secret" language, two children devised an elaborate set of transformations for common English words. Like the Kasem language of West Africa, the children's language was based on rules rather than rote memory—an indication, writes the author, that humans prefer even complex computation to rote memory. The relationship between the children's words and their cognates in adult varieties of American English is obvious in most instances, yet the differences were sufficient to block comprehension by adults. The [ʔ] is the phonetic symbol for a glottal stop, the sound that appears between the words *an aim* when the phrase is pronounced to differentiate it from the phrase *a name*.

While this system may seem surprisingly sophisticated, both it and the rules of Kasem are instances of the human tendency to use rules—with sometimes unexpected results. In the case of the Cambridge children, the tendency was used to obstruct rather than facilitate communication.

Language as Genetic Endowment

To summarize, the core of knowledge that fluent speakers have of their language has the form of rules, and these rules go well beyond what is directly observable in the movements executed by our vocal organs in speaking and the resulting acoustic signals. Each language has its own special set of rules, and these rules constitute the essence of what we learn when we acquire mastery of a given language. In learning these rules, young children require no special instruction, and much of what they—or, for that matter, any language students—learn never enters their consciousness. Underlying these rules is a set of highly abstract hypotheses about language, including such propositions as these: Speech is made up of words; words, in turn, are made up of sequences of sounds subject to definite rules; the rules affect specific groups of sounds; the same groups of sounds figure in other rules in English as well as in other languages; and the rules of any given language interact in the fashion shown by the Kasem plurals and the children's secret language.

The highly sophisticated character of these propositions excludes the possibility that they are acquired through experience. Yet the attainment of fluent command of a language by a native speaker crucially implies access to these and similar propositions. The conclusion, therefore, is that these propositions are a special aspect of the human genetic endowment, that they are part of what makes our species distinct from all others.

Bibliography

Chomsky, Noam, *Reflections on Language*. New York: Pantheon Books, 1975.
Chomsky, Noam, *Rules and Representations*. New York: Columbia University Press, 1980.
Halle, Morris, Joan Bresnan, and George A. Miller, eds. *Linguistic Theory and Psychological Reality*. Cambridge: M.I.T. Press, 1978.

FOR DISCUSSION AND REVIEW

1. How does Halle support his argument that "our perception that utterances are made up of words is a kind of illusion"?

2. Summarize four principles of English word structure. Describe when and how you learned them. If you know a language other than English, analyze whether or to what extent these same principles apply to it.

3. Why is it significant that the same groupings of sounds occur in the rules of many unrelated languages? Give two examples of such groupings. What kind of principle seems to govern the composition of these groupings? (Note: In answering the latter question, you may find it useful to review the preceding selection, "Phonetics" by Edward Callary.)

4. Halle refers to "the exuberance with which languages use rules" and illustrates his point with examples from Kasem, a language spoken in West Africa. Drawing on your own knowledge, give an example from another language. Explain how the Kasem example supports Halle's conclusion that "recourse to computation is so strongly favored over rote memory that speakers apparently do not have the option of foresaking rules for memorization."

5. Pig Latin and Ab-language are only two of the many secret languages that children have developed. If you know another such language, write out an explanation of its rules. Describe how you learned the language.

3/The Minimal Units of Meaning: Morphemes

OHIO STATE UNIVERSITY LANGUAGE FILES

Phonemes by themselves have no meaning. However, as we have seen, one of the distinguishing features of human language is its duality of patterning, its multilayered quality. Thus, phonemes, in themselves meaningless, are combined to form units that do have meaning— morphemes. Not all languages use the same kinds of morphemes, but all languages do use various kinds of morphemes as building blocks to construct words, *units larger than morphemes and harder to define. The first part of the following selection describes the* kinds *of morphemes that occur in English and identifies their various functions. The second part begins by examining the complex ways in which, in English, affixes combine with other units. It then explains the hierarchical internal structure of English words that results from these combinations.*

A morpheme is the minimal linguistic unit which has a meaning or grammatical function. Although many people think of words as the basic meaningful elements of a language, many words can be broken down into still smaller units, called *morphemes*. In English, for example, the word *ripens* consists of three morphemes: *ripe* plus *en* plus *s. -En* is a morpheme which changes adjectives into verbs: *ripe* is an adjective, but *ripen* is a verb. *Ripens* is still a verb: the morpheme *-s* indicates that the subject of the verb is third person singular and that the action is neither past nor future. . . .

Those morphemes which can stand alone as words are said to be *free morphemes*, e.g. *ripe* and *artichoke*. Those which are always attached to some other morpheme are said to be *bound*, e.g. *-en, -s, un-, pre-* (see below).

Notice that the term *morpheme* has been defined as "a minimal unit of *meaning* or *grammatical function*" to show that different morphemes serve different purposes. Some morphemes derive (create) new words by either changing the meaning (*happy* vs. *unhappy*, both adjectives) or the part of speech (syntactic category, e.g. *ripe*, an adjective, vs. *ripen*, a verb) or both. These are called *derivational morphemes*. Other morphemes change neither part of speech nor meaning, but only refine and give extra grammatical information about the already existing

249

Base	Suffix	Function	Example
wait	−s	3rd p sg present	She waits there at noon.
wait	−ed	past tense	She waited there yesterday.
wait	−ing	progressive	She is waiting there right now.
eat	−en	past participle	Jack has eaten all the Oreos.
chair	−s	plural marker	The chairs are set around the table.
chair	−'s	possessive	The chair's leg is broken.
fast	−er	comparative adj or adv	Billy Jean runs faster than Bobby.
fast	−est	superlative adj or adv	Valerie is the fastest runner of all.

Table 1. The Inflectional Suffixes of English

meaning of a word. Thus, *cat* and *cats* are both nouns and have the same meaning (refer to the same thing), but *cats*, with the plural morpheme -*s*, contains the additional information that there are more than one of these things. (Notice that the same information could be conveyed by including a number before the word—the plural -*s* marker then would not be needed at all.) These morphemes which serve a purely grammatical function, never creating a different word, but only a different *form* of the same word, are called *inflectional morphemes*.

Both derivational and inflectional morphemes are bound forms and are called *affixes*. When they are attached to other morphemes they change the meaning or the grammatical function of the word in some way, as just seen; when added to the beginning of a word or morpheme they are called *prefixes*, and when added to the end of a word or morpheme they are called *suffixes*. For example, *unpremeditatedly* has two prefixes (one added to the front of the other) and two suffixes (one added to the end of the other), all attached to the word *meditate*.

In English, the derivational morphemes are either prefixes or suffixes, but the inflectional morphemes are all suffixes. There are only eight of them in English. [See Table 1.] Below are listed four characteristics which separate inflectional and derivational affixes:

Inflectional Morphemes	*Derivational Morphemes*
1. Do not change meaning or part of speech, e.g. *big* and *bigger* are both adjectives.	1. Change meaning or part of speech, e.g. *-ment* forms nouns, such as *judgment*, from verbs, such as *judge*.
2. Typically indicate syntactic or semantic relations between different words in a sentence, e.g. the present tense morpheme -*s* in *waits* shows agreement with the subject of the verb (both are third person singular).	2. Typically indicate semantic relations within the word, e.g. the morpheme *-ful* in *painful* has no particular connection with any other morpheme beyond the word *painful*.

3. Typically occur with all members of some large class of morphemes, e.g., the plural morpheme -s occurs with most nouns.

3. Typically occur with only some members of a class of morphemes, e.g., the suffix -hood occurs with just a few nouns such as *brother, neighbor,* and *knight,* but not with most others, e.g., *friend, daughter, candle,* etc.

4. Typically occur at the margins of words, e.g., the plural morpheme -s always comes last in a word, as in *babysitters* or *rationalizations.*

4. Typically occur before inflectional suffixes, e.g., in *chillier,* the derivational suffix -y comes before the inflectional -er.

There is one more distinction between types of morphemes which it can be useful to make. Most morphemes have *semantic content,* that is, they either have some kind of independent, identifiable meaning or indicate a change in meaning when added to a word. Others serve only to provide information about *grammatical function* by relating certain words in a sentence to each other (see 2 under inflectional morphemes, above). The former are called *content morphemes,* the latter are called *function morphemes.* In English, all roots and derivational affixes are content morphemes, while inflectional affixes and such "function words" as prepositions, articles, pronouns, and conjunctions are function morphemes.

Many people confuse morphemes with syllables. A few examples will show that the numbers of morphemes and syllables in a word are independent of each other. *Ripe* is one morpheme which happens to consist of a single syllable. -S, however, is not even a syllable, though it is a morpheme. *Ripens* is a two syllable word composed of three morphemes, while *syllable* is a three syllable word composed of only one morpheme.

Morphemes are pairings of sounds with meanings. Some morphemes have one sound as their phonetic representation, e.g., [i] in *lucky* or [e] in *asexual.* Some morphemes consist of one syllable, e.g., [ən] in *unable* or [pri] in *preview.* Other morphemes are *polysyllabic* (have more than one syllable), e.g., *language, banana, Mississippi,* and the suffix -ity in *sanity.*

Sometimes different morphemes have the same phonetic representations, as in *ear* (for hearing) and *ear* (of corn). The same is true of affixes, e.g., the plural, possessive, and third person singular suffixes can all sound alike. There is a morpheme *in-* that means "not," e.g., *inoperable* or *intolerable,* and another *in-* that means "in," e.g., *intake* or *inside.* This same sequence [ɪn] is only part of [a] larger morpheme in [twɪn]. In the same way the [t] in [mɪst] can be either the past tense marker in *missed* or just part of the word *mist*, without any special morphemic content of its own.

Some morphemes have more than one phonetic representation depending on which sounds precede or follow them, but all meaning the same thing and serving the same purpose. For example, the phonetic representation of the plural morphemes is either [s] *cats*, [z] *dogs*, or [əz] *churches*. Each of these three different phonetic shapes is said to be an *allomorph* of the same morpheme. The plural, possessive, and third person singular morphemes all have three allomorphs apiece. Can you think of other morphemes which have more than one phonetic representation?

The Hierarchical Structure of Words

There are two important facts about the ways in which affixes join with other expressions. First, the expressions with which a given affix may combine normally belong to the same part of speech. For example, the suffix *-able* attaches freely to verbs, but not, for example, to adjectives or nouns; thus, we can add this suffix to the verbs *adjust, break, compare,* and *debate,* but not to the adjectives *asleep, lovely, happy,* and *strong,* nor to the nouns *anger, morning, student,* or *success.* Second, the expressions resulting from the addition of a given affix to some word or morpheme also normally belong to the same part of speech. For example, the expressions resulting from the addition of *-able* to a verb are always adjectives; thus *adjustable, breakable, comparable,* and *debatable* are all adjectives. An important consequence of these two facts is that in the formation of a word, the affixes aren't just strung together all at once; instead, they are put together step by step. That is, the internal structure of words is *hierarchical.*

To see this, consider the adjective *reusable* (as in *HandiWipes are reusable!*). This adjective consists of three morphemes: the free morpheme *use* and the derivational affixes *re-* and *-able.* As was noted above, *-able* is a suffix which joins with a verb to form an adjective:

(I) Verb   +   *-able*   =   Adjective
    adjust   *adjustable*
    break   *breakable*
    compare   *comparable*
    debate   *debatable*
    lock   *lockable*
    use   *usable*

The prefix *re-*, on the other hand, joins with a verb to form a new verb:

(II)   *re-*   +   Verb   =   Verb
             adjust   *readjust*
             appear   *reappear*
             consider   *reconsider*
             construct   *reconstruct*
             decorate   *redecorate*
             use   *reuse*

These facts allow us to see that the word *reusable* is formed in two steps: first, the prefix *re-* joins with the verb *use* to form the verb *reuse*, as in (II); second, the suffix *-able* attaches to the verb *reuse* to form the adjective *reusable*, just as it attaches to the verb *adjust* to form the adjective *adjustable* in (I). These steps in the formation of *reusable* can be schematically represented by means of a tree structure:

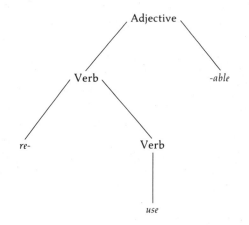

Notice that *reusable* cannot be regarded as the result of adding the prefix *re-* to the word *usable*. A little consideration reveals why this is so: since *use* is a verb, *-able* may attach to it to form the adjective *usable*, as in (I); but because *usable* is an adjective, *re-* cannot join with it, since *re-* only joins with verbs. Thus, our understanding of how the affixes *re-* and *-able* combine with other morphemes allows us to conclude that the verb *reuse*, but not the adjective *usable*, is a step in the formation of the adjective *reusable*.

Interestingly, some words are ambiguous (i.e. have more than one meaning) because their internal structure may be analyzed in more than one way. Consider, for example, the word *unlockable*; this could mean either "not able to be locked" or "able to be unlocked." If we consider the bound morphemes in this word very carefully, we can see why this ambiguity arises.

In English, there are not one but two prefixes *un-*: the first combines with an adjective to form a new adjective, and means simply "not";

(III) *un-*₁ + Adjective = Adjective
　　　　　　　　able　　　　　*unable* "not able"
　　　　　　　　aware　　　　*unaware* "not aware"
　　　　　　　　happy　　　　*unhappy* "not happy"
　　　　　　　　intelligent　　*unintelligent* "not intelligent"
　　　　　　　　lucky　　　　*unlucky* "not lucky"

The second *un-* combines with a verb to form a new verb, and means "to do the reverse of."

(IV) *un-*₂ + Verb = Verb
　　　　　　　do　　　　*undo* "to do the reverse of doing"
　　　　　　　dress　　*undress* "to do the reverse of dressing"
　　　　　　　load　　　*unload* "to do the reverse of loading"
　　　　　　　lock　　　*unlock* "to do the reverse of locking"
　　　　　　　tie　　　　*untie* "to do the reverse of tying"

Because of these two different sorts of *un-* in English, *unlockable* may be analyzed in two different ways. First, the suffix *-able* may join with the verb *lock* to form the adjective *lockable,* as in (I); *un-*₁ may then join with this adjective to form the new adjective *unlockable.* This way of forming *unlockable* is schematized in the following tree structure:

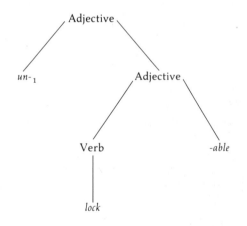

Since *un-*₁ just means "not," this tree structure represents the meaning "not able to be locked."

The second way of forming *unlockable* is as follows. The prefix *un-*₂ joins with the verb *lock* to form the verb *unlock,* as in (IV); the suffix *-able* then joins with this verb to form the adjective *unlockable.* This manner of forming *unlockable* is represented by the following tree.

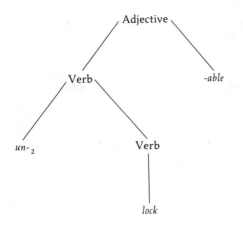

Since *un*-₂ means "to do the reverse of," as in the verb *unlock* "to do the reverse of locking," this tree represents the meaning "able to be unlocked."

Exercises

1. Consider each of the following suffixes; from the examples given, determine (i) the part of speech of the expressions with which the suffix combines, (ii) the part of speech of the expressions formed by the addition of the suffix, and (iii) the approximate meaning of the suffix.

   a. *-ify: clarify, intensify, purify, solidify, rarefy*
   b. *-ity: rigidity, stupidity, hostility, intensity, responsibility*
   c. *-ize: unionize, terrorize, hospitalize, crystallize, magnetize*
   d. *-ive: repressive, active, disruptive, abusive, explosive*
   e. *-ion: invention, injection, narration, expression, pollution*
   f. *-less: hopeless, penniless, useless, heartless, mindless*

2. Draw tree diagrams like those discussed above for each of the following words.

reconstruction	*impersonal*
unaffordable	*international*
un-American	*misunderstanding*
manliness	*irreplaceability*

FOR DISCUSSION AND REVIEW

1. **Explain the difference between derivational morphemes and inflectional morphemes. Illustrate each difference with an example not in the text.**

2. **What is the difference between content morphemes and function morphemes?**

3. **Describe the relationship between morphemes and syllables.**

4. Explain what an *allomorph* is. Give an example of an English morpheme, in addition to the regular noun plural, that has more than one phonetic representation.

5. Allomorphs, unlike allophones, need not be phonetically similar. The productive plural morpheme in English has the forms /-s/, /-z/, /-əz/; which one is used depends on the sound with which the noun to be made plural ends. These allomorphs are phonologically conditioned. Some nouns in English, however, do not form regular plurals. List as many "irregular" plurals as you can. Then try to divide them into groups (note: there are five types of morphologically conditioned plurals in English; four of them derive from Old English).

6. Explain the statement that "the internal structure of words is *hierarchical.*"

7. Explain the ambiguity of the words *bimonthly* and *biweekly*. Is it similar to or different from the ambiguity of *unlockable*? Explain.

4/The Identification of Morphemes

H. A. GLEASON, JR.

As native speakers of English, we usually do not find it difficult to identify the morphemes in English words. We are, of course, relying in part on our unconscious knowledge of the rules of English and in part on our familiarity with much of the English vocabulary. Therefore, in order to begin to understand the complexity of morphemic analysis, we need to examine data from a language that we do not know well. In the following excerpt from his book An Introduction to Descriptive Linguistics, *Professor H. A. Gleason uses some Hebrew verb forms to demonstrate the basic analytical technique for the identification of morphemes: comparing groups of utterances which are (1) partially* identical *in both expression and content and (2) partially* different *in both expression and content. Note that both conditions must be met: we are looking for the smallest change in content (i.e., structure) that results in a change in meaning (i.e., expression). At the end of his analysis of Hebrew verb forms, Professor Gleason introduces discontinuous morphemes, which do not occur in all languages; the type of morpheme known as an "infix"; "replacives," which do occur in English; and the zero affix (ø), which also occurs in English.*

The process of analysis [to identify morphemes] is best shown by detailed discussion of an actual example. For this purpose we will use a series of Hebrew verb forms. The data will be introduced a few words at a time. This is an artificial feature of the presentation. The preceding step is merely implied: namely that we have selected from the corpus those pairs or sets of items that can be profitably compared. The order of presentation is not necessarily that which is most efficient for the analysis of the data, but that which most effectively illustrates the methods used.

1. /zəkartíihuu/   "I remembered him"
2. /zəkartíihaa/   "I remembered her"
3. /zəkartíikaa/   "I remembered thee"

Comparison of items 1 and 2 reveals one contrast in expression, /-uu/:/-aa/, and one in meaning, as shown by translation, and hence presumably in content "him":"her." This may (tentatively!) be considered as a pair of morphemes. However, comparison of 1, 2, and 3 suggests that the first identification was wrong. The contrast now seems to be /-huu/ "him":/-haa/ "her":/-kaa/ "thee." We can be reasonably sure that the morpheme meaning "him" includes the sounds /-uu/ or /-huu/, but until we can identify the remaining parts of the word we cannot be sure how much else is included.

4. /zəkarnúuhuu/   "we remembered him"
5. /zəkarnúuhaa/   "we remembered her"
6. /zəkarnúukaa/   "we remembered thee"

Comparison of 4, 5, and 6 with 1, 2, and 3 reveals a contrast in expression and meaning between /-tíi-/ "I" and /-núu-/ "we." However, as before, we cannnot be sure how much is to be included until the remainders of the words are identified. It is conceivable that the morphemes might be /-rtíi-/ "I" and /-rnúu-/ "we". . . .

7. /qəṭaltíihuu/   "I killed him"
8. qəṭalnúuhuu/   "we killed him"

Comparison of 7 and 8 with the foregoing gives us a basis for identifying /zəkar-/ "remembered" and /qəṭal-/ "killed." By so doing we have tentatively assigned every portion of each word to a tentative morpheme. We have, however, no reason to be certain that each portion so isolated is only a single morpheme. We have only reasonable assurance that by dividing any of these words in a manner similar to /zəkar-tíi-huu/ we have divided between morphemes, so that each piece consists of one or more essentially complete morphemes; that is, each piece is probably either a morpheme or a morpheme sequence.

The problem is somewhat simpler if one sample is identical with another except for an additional item of meaning and of expression:

/koohéen/   "a priest"
/ləkoohéen/   "to a priest"

There can be little doubt as to the most likely place to divide, and we can be rather confident in identifying two tentative morphemes /lə-/ "to" and /koohéen/ "priest." Nevertheless, there are significant possibilities of error, so that this sort of division must also be considered tentative. Consider the following English example:

/hím/   "a song used in church"
/hímnəl/   "a book containing /hímz/"

The obvious division is into two morphemes /hím/ and /-nəl/. Reference to the spelling (which is, of course, never conclusive evidence for any thing in spoken language!), *hymn*:*hymnal* suggests that this is not very certain. Actually the two morphemes are /him ~ himn-/ and /-əli/, as may be shown by comparing additional data: *confession*:*confessional*, *hymnology*:*geology*, *hymnody*:*psalmody*.

9. zəkaarúuhuu/   "they remembered him"
10. /zəkaaráthuu/   "she remembered him"

If we compare 9 and 10 with the foregoing we find /-huu/ "him," /-úu-/ "they," and /-át-/ "she." But where 1–6 have /zəkar-/, 9 and 10 have /zəkaar-/. There is an obvious similarity of form between /zəkar-/ and /zəkaar-/ and the meaning seems to be identical. We may guess that they are two different allomorphs of one morpheme, and proceed to check whether this hypothesis is adequate. . . . We must leave the question . . . but must anticipate the result. /zəkar-/ and /zəkaar-/ will be shown to be variants of one tentative morpheme.

But though we will proceed on the basis that the hypothesis can be sustained, we must recognize that there are certain other possibilities. (1) /zəkar-/ and /zəkaar-/ may be different morphemes. This seems unlikely because of the similarity of meaning, but we must always remember that English translation may be misleading. (2) A somewhat less remote possibility is that /zəkar-/ and /zəkaar-/ are each sequences of morphemes and contain two contrasting morphemes. We can do nothing with this possibility from the data at hand, because there is no evidence of a contrast in meaning, but this may well be the kind of difference that does not show up clearly in translation. (3) We may have divided wrongly. Perhaps "I" is not /-tíi-/ but /-a-tíi-/ and "they" is similarly /-aa-úu-/. This would mean that the morpheme for "remembered" would have to be /zək-r-/. Our only present reason for rejecting this possibility is the comparative rarity of discontinuous morphemes. We would ordinarily assume that morphemes are continuous sequences of phonemes unless there is cogent reason to believe the contrary.

11. /zəkartúunii/   "you remembered me"

We have as yet no item which forms a wholly satisfactory comparison with 11. We may, however, tentatively divide it into /zəkar-/ + /-túu-/ "you" + /-nii/ "me." We do this because we have come to expect words similar to this to be divisible into three pieces, stem + actor + person acted upon, in that order. A division on such a basis is legitimate if done with caution, though obviously such an identification is not as certain as it would be if based on contrasts for each morpheme separately.

12. /sə̀martúuhaa/ , "you guarded him"
13. /ləqaaxúunii/ "they took me"

Even without providing minimal pairs, 12 and 13 pretty well corroborate the conclusion which was drawn from 11 [above]. They thus confirm the two morphemes /-túu-/ "you" and /-nii/ "me." Words 11, 12, and 13 would be rather unsatisfactory words from which to start an analysis. However, as the analysis proceeds, the requirements for satisfactory samples relax in some respects. This is because we are now able to make our comparisons within the framework of an emerging pattern. This pattern involves certain classes of elements, stems, actor affixes, and affixes stating the person acted upon. It involves certain regular types of arrangement of these elements. In short, the pattern we are uncovering is a portion of the structure of the language at a level a bit deeper than mere details of individual words.

14. /zəkaaróo/ "he remembered him"

This word cannot be analyzed by comparison with the foregoing only. We can easily identify the stem as /zəkaar-/, identical in form with that of 9 and 10. But the remainder /-óo/ neither seems to consist of the expected two parts (actor and person acted upon), nor to contain the morpheme /-huu/ "him" which meaning would lead us to expect. Since the pattern does not assist us here in the way it did with 11, we must seek some more direct type of evidence.

15. /zaakártii/ "I remembered"
16. /zaakárnuu/ "we remembered"
17. /zaakár/ "he remembered"

These three forms differ from all those examined before in that they do not express a person acted upon. If we compare these words with each other, and if we compare 15 and 16 with 1 and 4, we can easily identify the affixes expressing the actor. These are /-tii/ "I" and /-nuu/ "we," identical with those we found before except for a difference in the stress. In 17, however, there is no affix expressing actor. We will tentatively list ø (zero) "he" with the other actor affixes. This is intended merely as a convenient notation for our conclusion that the actor "he" is expressd by the absence of any affix indicating some other actor. These three forms also show another variant of the stem: /zaakár/; we shall proceed on the hypothesis that like

/zəkar-/ and /zəkaar-/, it is merely another conditioned variant. This proposal should be carefully checked by methods to be discussed later.

The analysis attained in the last paragraph suggests that item 14 can be considered as divisible as follows: /zəkaar-ø-óo/. The zero is, of course, a fiction, but it does serve to indicate that the form does show a rather closer parallelism with the others than we could see at first. That is, it contains a stem and a suffix expressing the person acted upon, and these are in the same order that we have found before. Whereas the pattern we had found did not seem to fit this word, closer examination shows that it does fit in with only slight modification. The pattern is therefore valid.

One problem posed by item 14 is taken care of in this way, but the other remains. We have identified two forms meaning "him," /-huu/ and /-óo/. These are not so obviously similar in form as /zəkar-/ and /zəkaar-/, so the hypothesis that they are allomorphs of one morpheme is not so attractive. Nevertheless, the similarity in meaning, and certain peculiarities in distribution which would be evident in a larger body of data, should induce us to check such a hypothesis. It will be sustained; /-huu ~ -óo/ is one morpheme.

In the course of the discussion we have found four stems: /zəkar-/ "remembered," /qətal-/ "killed," /šəmar-/ "guarded," and /ləqaax-/ "took." Comparison of these forms reveals that they all have the same vowels and differ only in consonants. /ləqaax-/ is not an exception, since it compares directly with /zəkaar-/. More data would yield a much longer list of such forms. This similarity in vowels could be a coincidence, but that possibility is slight. Another hypothesis is that these forms consist of two morphemes each. This is very attractive, but there is no means of checking it without a contrast. The following will provide such:

18. /šoonéer/   "watchman"
19. /zookéer/   "one who remembers"
20. /qootéel/   "killer"

By comparing these with some of the earlier samples we may identify the following morphemes: /z-k-r/ "remember," /q-ṭ-l/ "kill," /š-m-r/ "guard," /l-q-x/ "take," /-oo-ée-/ "one who," and /-ə-a- ~ -ə-aa- ~ -aa-á-/ "-ed." The first four of these are roots; the last two are some sort of affixes.

Note that we were wrong in considering /zəkar-/, /zəkaar-/, and /zaakár/ as allomorphs of a single morpheme. No damage was done, however, since these three forms, each composed of two morphemes, are distributed in exactly the same way as are allomorphs. What we assumed to condition the selection of one of these three (/zəkar-/ etc.) can just as well be considered as conditioning the selection of one of the allomorphs of the affix contained in these stems. Treating larger items as morphemes is, of course, wrong, but not seriously so at preliminary stages, provided the larger units consist of associated morphemes. Ultimate simplification is, however, attained by full analysis in any case like that just discussed.

That the [preceding] analysis . . . should yield morphemes such as /z-k-r/ and /-oo-ée-/ seems at first sight somewhat disconcerting. We expect morphemes to be sequences of phonemes. These, however, are discontinuous and interdigitated. Of course there is no reason why such morphemes cannot occur, as in fact our sample has indicated they do. They are much less common than compact sequences of phonemes, but they occur in a wide variety of languages and are quite common in some. Any combination of phonemes which regularly occur together and which as a group are associated with some point in the content structure is a morpheme. We need give no regard to any peculiarity of their arrangement relative to each other and to other phonemes. Rarely do morphemes consist of separate portions widely separated by intervening material. A linguist must always be prepared for such a phenomenon, however, rare as it may be.

Hebrew and related languages are unusual in the large number of discontinuous morphemes they contain. In fact the majority of the roots are similar to {zkr}, consisting of three consonants. Various allomorphs occur: /z-k-r/ in /zaakár/ "he remembered," /-zk-r/ in /yizkóor/ "he was remembering," and /z-kr-/ in /zikríi/ "my remembrance." The three consonants never occur contiguously in any utterance; such roots are discontinuous in all their occurrences.

In other languages, discontinuous allomorphs of otherwise quite usual morphemes occur. These commonly arise as a byproduct of a special type of affix not mentioned before, an infix. An infix is a morpheme which is inserted into the stem with which it is associated. In comparison with suffixes and prefixes, infixes are comparatively rare but of sufficiently frequent occurrence to warrant notice. An example is the common Greek stem formative /-m-/ in /lambanɔ·/ "I take" from the root /lab-/. Another is Quileute (Oregon) /-¢-/ "plural" in /ho¢kʷat'/ "white men" from /hokʷat'/ "white person." Such infixes produce discontinuous allomorphs /la-b-/ and /ho-kʷat'/ of the root morphemes with which they occur.

An affix should not be considered as an infix unless there is cogent reason to do so. Of course, any affix which actually interrupts another morpheme is an infix. In Tagalog *ginulay* "greenish blue" is formed from the root *gulay* "green vegetables." The *-in-* is clearly an infix. But it is not justifiable to consider English *-as-* in *reassign* as an infix. This word is made by two prefixes. First *as-* and *sign* form the stem *assign*. Then *re-* is added. The alternative would be to consider *re-* and *sign* as forming a stem *resign* to which an infix *-as-* is added. The latter would be immediately rejected by any native speaker of English, since he would sense that *reassign* has a much closer connection with *assign* than with *resign*. It is always better, unless there is good reason to the contrary, to consider words as being constructed of successive layers of affixes outward from the root.

Most English verbs have a form that is made by the addition of the suffix *-ed* /-d ~ -t ~ -ɨd/. This is usually known as the past. The verbs which lack this formation do, however, have some form which is used in all the same syntactic environments where we might expect such a form, and in comparable social and linguistic contexts. For example, in most of the places where *discover* /dɨskə́ver/ can be used, *find* /fáynd/ can also. Similarly, where *discovered* /dɨskə́vərd/ can be used, *found* /fáwnd/ generally can also. *Found* must therefore be considered as the past of *find* in the same sense that *discovered* is the past of *discover*.

Most of the past tenses which lack the *-ed* suffix are clearly differentiated from the base form by a difference of syllable nucleus. We may express the facts by the following equations:

> *discovered* = *discover* + suffix *-ed*
> *found*   = *find*   + difference of syllable nucleus

When it is so stated, it becomes evident that the difference of syllable nucleus functions in some ways like the suffix. We may consider such a difference in phonemes (they are not restricted to nuclei; consider *send*:*sent*) as a special type of morphemic element called a *replacive*.

We will use the following notation for a replacive: /aw ← (ay)/. This should be read as "/aw/ replaces /ay/." The equation above can be stated in the following form:

> *found* = *find* + *ou* ← (*i*)
> /fáwnd/ = /fáynd/ + /aw ← (ay)/

If this is done, then we must consider /aw ← (ay)/ as another allomorph of the morpheme whose most familiar form is *-ed* and which we can conveniently symbolize {-D$_1$}. This morpheme has a number of replacive allomorphs. . . . All of them are morphologically conditioned. {-Z$_1$}, the English noun plural affix, also has replacives among its allomorphs.

It is, of course, possible to describe a language like English without recourse to replacives. Thus, *geese* /gíys/ can be described as containing a root /g-s/ and an infix allomorph of the plural morpheme {-Z$_1$} of the form /-iy-/. Then the singular would have to be described as containing an infix /-uw-/, an allomorph of a singular morpheme *{X}. Except for the cases under consideration, there are no infixes, nor discontinuous morphemes in the language. To consider plurals like *geese* as formed by an infix turns out to involve many more complications than the alternative of describing replacives. As is often the case, the simpler explanation accords more closely with the native speaker's feeling about his language.

With replacives it is not easy to divide a word into its constituent morphemes. Obviously /giys/ is two morphemes, but the four phonemes cannot be neatly apportioned between them. A morpheme does not necessarily *consist* of phonemes, but all morphemes are statable in terms of phonemes. A replacive must be described in terms of two sets of phonemes: those that appear when it is present (/iy/ in *geese*) and those that appear when the replacive is absent (/uw/ in *goose*). A morpheme can consist of any recurring feature or features of the expression which can be described in terms of phonemes, without restriction of any sort.

A further, and in some respects more extreme, type of morphemic element can be seen in the past of some other English verbs. Words like *cut* and *hit* parallel such forms as *walked* in meaning and usage. There is, however, no phoneme difference of any kind between the past and the nonpast form. Nevertheless, it is in the interests of simplicity to consider all English past verb forms as consisting of a stem plus an affix. Moreover, the description must in some ways note the lack of any overt marker of the past. An expedient by which both can be done is to consider *cut* "past" as containing a root /kət/ plus a zero affix. (Zero is customarily symbolized ø to avoid confusion with the letter O.) ø is therefore another of the numerous allomorphs of {-D$_1$}.

The plural affix {-Z$_1$} also has a zero allomorph in *sheep*. The reason that it is necessary to describe these forms in this way rests ultimately in English content structure. Native speakers feel that the dichotomy between singular and plural is a basic characteristic of nouns. Every individual occurrence of any noun must be either singular or plural. *Sheep* is ambiguous, but not indifferent to the distinction. That is, in any given utterance the word is thought of by speaker and hearer as either singular or plural. Sometimes they may disagree, plural being intended and singular being perceived, or vice versa. It requires conscious effort for a person accustomed only to English patterns to conceive of noun referents without consideration of number. To attempt to do so impresses many people as being "too abstract." Yet they feel under no such compulsion to distinguish the exact number if it is more than two.

In other words, there is a covert difference between *sheep* "singular" and *sheep* "plural," and this is linguistically significant as may be seen from the fact that it controls the forms of certain other words in *This sheep is. . . . : These sheep are. . . .* The recognition of a ø allomorph of $\{-Z_1\}$ is merely a convenient device for entering all this into our description. . . .

FOR DISCUSSION AND REVIEW

Please see the following selection by Professor Gleason, "Morphology: Three Exercises."

5/Morphology: Three Exercises

H. A. GLEASON, JR.

The following selection by H. A. Gleason, Jr., provides practice in morphemic analysis and will help you to assess your understanding of the concepts introduced in "The Identification of Morphemes." Believing that students of linguistics need to work with problems drawn from a variety of languages, Professor Gleason prepared a Workbook in Descriptive Linguistics *to accompany his textbook* An Introduction to Descriptive Linguistics, *from which the previous selection was excerpted. The following exercises have been taken from that workbook. In the preface to the workbook, Professor Gleason notes that although there is some inevitable distortion in presenting short samples of languages, "All the problems represent real languages" and "the complexities are all genuine" (p. 2).*

SWAHILI (EAST AFRICA)

1.	atanipenda	he will like me
2.	atakupenda	he will like you
3.	atampenda	he will like him
4.	atatupenda	he will like us
5.	atawapenda	he will like them
6.	nitakupenda	I will like you
7.	nitampenda	I will like him
8.	nitawapenda	I will like them
9.	utanipenda	you will like me
10.	utampenda	you will like him
11.	tutampenda	we will like him
12.	watampenda	they will like him
13.	atakusumbua	he will annoy you
14.	unamsumbua	you are annoying him
15.	atanipiga	he will beat me
16.	atakupiga	he will beat you
17.	atampiga	he will beat him
18.	ananipiga	he is beating me
19.	anakupiga	he is beating you
20.	anampiga	he is beating him

21. amenipiga — he has beaten me
22. amekupiga — he has beaten you
23. amempiga — he has beaten him
24. alinipiga — he beat me
25. alikupiga — he beat you
26. alimpiga — he beat him
27. wametulipa — they have paid us
28. tulikulipa — we paid you

Note: The forms glossed "he" could as well be glossed "she." The forms glossed "you" are all singular. The plural "you" is omitted from this problem because of a minor complication.

Give the morphemes associated with each of the following meanings:

subjects: _____ I   *objects*: _____ me
          _____ you   _____ you
          _____ he   _____ him
          _____ we   _____ us
          _____ they   _____ them
tenses: _____ future   *stems*: _____ like
          _____ present   _____ beat
          _____ perfect   _____ annoy
          _____ past   _____ pay

What is the order of the morphemes in a word?

Supply the probable forms for the following meanings:

_____ I have beaten them   _____ you have beaten us
_____ they are beating me   _____ we beat them
_____ they have annoyed me_____ I am paying him

Supply the probable meanings for the following forms:

atanilipa _____   walikupenda _____
utawapiga _____   nimemsumbua _____

ILOCANO (PHILIPPINE ISLANDS)

1. píŋgan	dish	piŋpíŋgan	dishes
2. tálon	field	taltálon	fields
3. dálan	road	daldálan	roads
4. bíag	life	bibíag	lives
5. nuáŋ	carabao	nunuáŋ	caribao
6. úlo	head	ulúlo	heads

What type of affix is used to form the plural?

Describe its form and relationship to the stem. Be sure to make clear exactly how much is involved.

Given /múla/ "plant," what would be the most likely form meaning "plants"?

Given /tawtáwa/ "windows," what would be the most likely form meaning "window"?

DINKA (SUDAN)

1. pal	knife	paal	knives	_____
2. bit	spear	biit	spears	_____
3. γot	hut	γoot	huts	_____
4. čiin	hand	čin	hands	_____
5. agɔɔk	monkey	agɔk	monkeys	_____
6. kat	frame	kɛt	frames	_____
7. mač	fire	mɛ̆č	fires	_____
8. beñ	chief	bañ	chiefs	_____
9. dom	field	dum	fields	_____
10. dɔk	boy	dak	boys	_____
11. gɔl	clan	gal	clans	_____
12. tuɔŋ	egg	tɔŋ	eggs	_____
13. muɔr	bull	mior	bulls	_____
14. buɔl	rabbit	bial	rabbits	_____
15. met	child	miit	children	_____
16. ǰoŋ	dog	ǰɔk	dogs	_____
17. yič	ear	yit	ears	_____

What type of affix is shown in [these] data? List the forms of the affixes in the spaces provided opposite the stems with which they are found. Do not attempt to find conditioning factors; the distribution of allomorphs is morphologically conditioned. This is very frequently true of this type of affix.

6/Word-Making: Some Sources of New Words

W. NELSON FRANCIS

English has the largest vocabulary of any language in the world—over 600,000 words—in part, at least, because English has borrowed words from every language with which it has had any contact. (The rate of borrowing, interestingly, appears to be slowing; and English has become an exporter of words, much to the dismay of the French, among others.) But even without borrowing, English, like all other living languages, has a variety of ways of forming new words. Sometimes, of course, we use an old word with a new meaning, as when cool *("chilly") became* cool *("outstanding"). But many times we actually create new words; and when we do, we create them by very regular and predictable processes. In the following excerpt from his book* The English Language: An Introduction, *Professor W. Nelson Francis discusses the major ways, in addition to borrowing from other languages and semantic change, that new words are created and become a part of the vocabulary of English.*

Though borrowing has been the most prolific source of additions to the vocabulary of English, we acquire or create new words in several other ways. Those which will be discussed here, in descending order of importance, are *derivation, compounding, functional shift, back formation* and *clipping, proper names, imitation, blending,* and *original coinage.*

Derivation

The derivational process consists of using an existing word—or in some cases a bound morpheme* or morphemic structure—as a stem to which affixes are attached. Thus our imaginary word *pandle* might

---

*Editors' note: Francis earlier tells us: "The smallest meaningful units of language—those which cannot be subdivided into smaller meaningful units—are called *morphemes*. In combinations like *rooster, greenness, lucky, widen,* and *strongly,* all of which are made up of two morphemes, one morpheme carries the principal part of the meaning of the whole. This is called the *base* (or sometimes the *root*). The bases in the examples are *roost, green, luck, wide,* and *strong.* These . . . bases are capable of standing by themselves and of entering rather freely into grammatical combinations. For this reason they are called *free bases.* Other bases cannot stand alone or enter freely into grammatical combinations but must always appear in close affiliation with other morphemes. These are called *bound bases.* We can recognize a common base *turb* in such words as *disturb, perturb,* and *turbulent*; it never stands alone as the *green* of *greenness* does, so it is a bound base."

become the stem for such derivatives as *pandler, pandlette, depandle,* and *repandlize.* Affixes like these are called *productive*; all native speakers know their meanings and feel free to add them to various kinds of stems in accordance with analogy or the rules of English derivation. By this process any new word, whatever its source, may almost immediately become the nucleus of a cluster of derivatives. Thus *plane,* formed by clipping from *airplane,* has produced *emplane* and *deplane,* presumably by analogy with *entrain* and *detrain,* themselves formed by analogy with *embark* and *debark,* which were borrowed from French. When *telegraph* was formed by compounding of two Greek elements, it soon gave rise to *telegrapher, telegraphy, telegraphic,* and *telegraphist,* all of which were self-explaining derivatives.

So obvious is the process of forming derivatives with productive affixes that all of us probably do it much more frequently than we realize. The words we thus "create" in most cases have been frequently used before and are listed in the dictionary, but we may not know that. This process allows us to expand our vocabulary without specifically memorizing new words. But this reliance on analogical derivation may sometimes trap us into creating new words that are unnecessary because other derivatives already exist and have become standard. The student who wrote about Hamlet's *unableness to overcome his mental undecidedness* undoubtedly was familiar with *inability* and *indecision,* but under the pressure of an examination he forgot them and created his own derivatives instead.

Compounding

In a sense, compounding is a special form of derivation in which, instead of adding affixes (bound forms) to a stem, two or more words (or in some cases bound bases) are put together to make a new lexical unit. Compounding has been a source of new words in English since earliest times, and is particularly common in present-day English. Perusal of any daily paper will turn up countless examples of compounds that are new within the last few years or months: *launching pad, blast off, jet-port, freeway, ski-tow, freeloader, featherbedding, sit-in.* Our writing system does not indicate whether items like *weather satellite* are compounds or constructions. Many of them begin as constructions but then assume the characteristic stress patterns of compounds: some people still pronounce *ice cream* with the stress pattern of a construction (as in *iced tea*), but most treat it as a compound (as in *iceboat*). Some of the older compounds have gone through sound (and spelling) changes that have completely obscured their compound origin. Typical of these is *lord,* which began in early Old English as *hlāf-weard,* a compound of the ancestors of our *loaf* and *ward,* and passed through the stages of

OE *hlāford* and ME *loverd* to its present monosyllabic form. Other examples are *woman*, originally a compound of the ancestors of *wife* and *man*, and *hussy*, from *house* and *wife*, hence etymologically a doublet of *housewife*.

The semantic relationships between the parts of compounds are very varied. If compounds are thought of as the product of a transformation process, this variety can be revealed by reconstructing the phrase from which the compound might have been created. This may range from a simple modification, in which the transformation involves only a change in stress pattern (*hot dog, blackboard, bluebird*), to complete predication, where the transformation involves complicated reordering and deletion (as in *salesman* from *man who makes sales* or *movie camera* from *camera that takes movies*). Compounds may themselves enter into compounds to produce elaborate structures like *aircraft carrier* and *real estate salesman*. These must be considered compounds, since they have the characteristic stress pattern with the strongest stress on the first element (*aircràft càrrier, réal estàte sàlesman*), in contrast to the stress pattern of modification constructions (as in *aircràft desígner* or *rèal estàte invéstment*).

One special group of compounds, most of them of quite recent origin, includes those words—mostly technical and scientific terms—which are made up of morphemes borrowed from Greek. Many of the elements so used were free forms—words—in Greek, but must be considered bound bases in English. The practice of compounding them began in Greek: *philosophia* is compounded from *philos* "fond of" and *sophia* "wisdom." Words of this sort were borrowed into Latin in ancient times, and ultimately reached English by way of French. Renaissance scholars, who knew Greek and recognized the combining elements, began to make new combinations which did not exist in the original Greek. With the growth of scientific knowledge from the seventeenth century on, new technical and scientific terms were commonly invented this way.

Words created can be roughly divided into two groups. The first includes those which have wide circulation in the general vocabulary—like *telephone, photograph,* and *thermometer*. These are constructed out of a relatively small number of morphemes, whose meanings are well known:

tele	"far, distant"	*meter*	"measure"
phone	"sound"	*dyna*	"power"
photo	"light"	*hydro*	"water, moisture"
graph	"write, mark"	*bio*	"life"
thermo	"heat"	*morph*	"shape, form"

Inventors and manufacturers of new products often create names for their inventions from elements of this sort. Sometimes the Greek elements are combined with Latin ones, as in *automobile* (Greek *autos* "self," Latin *mobilis* "movable") and *television,* or even with native English elements, as in *dynaflow.* Recent creations in this group are *astronaut* and *cosmonaut,* from Greek *aster* "star," *kosmos* "universe," and *nautes* "sailor." Actually *cosmonaut* was first used in Russian, whence it was borrowed, but since both of its bases were already in use in English (as in *cosmology* and *aeronaut*), it might just as well have originated in English.

The second group of Greek-based compounds comprises the large number of technical and scientific terms whose use is almost wholly restricted to specialists. As in the case of *cosmonaut,* most of these words are readily interchangeable among the languages in which scientific publication is extensive. Since it is often difficult if not impossible to determine the language in which they were first used, the Merriam-Webster editors have recently made use of the term *International Scientific Vocabulary* (abbreviated ISV) to describe them. A few examples of wide enough circulation to be included in an abridged dictionary are the following:

hypsography: "recording (*graphy*) of elevation (*hypso*)"
telethermoscope: "instrument that perceives (*scope*) heat (*thermo*) at a distance (*tele*)"
electroencephalograph: "instrument that records (*graph*) electric current (*electro*) within (*en*) the head (*cephalo*)"
schizogenesis: "reproduction (*genesis*) by division (*schizo*)"

In all cases, since at least two of the combining elements are bases, these words must be considered compounds. They may also give rise to derivatives formed by the addition of affixes in regular patterns, such as *electroencephalography* and *schizogenetic.* It is in this way, rather than by direct borrowing, that Greek has made its great contribution to the English vocabulary.

Functional Shift

Since the late Middle English period, when most of the inflections surviving from Old English finally disappeared, it has been easy to shift a word from one part of speech to another without altering its form, at least in the unmarked base form. A verb like *walk* can be turned into a noun simply by using it in a syntactic position reserved for nouns, as in *he took a walk,* where the determiner *a* marks *walk* as a noun, direct object of *took.* This process, called *functional shift,* is an important concomitant of the historical change of English from a synthetic to an analytic language, and has greatly enlarged the vocabulary in a very economical way. Since the words so created belong to a different part of speech and hence have a different grammatical distribution from that of the original, they must be considered new words, homonymous in the base form with the words from which they were derived, rather than merely extensions of meaning. From another point of view, they may be thought of as derivatives with zero affixes. In some cases they may take a different stress pattern in their new use: the noun *implement,* with weak stress and the weak central vowel /ə/ in the last syllable, when shifted to a verb took secondary stress on the last syllable, whose vowel was changed to /ɛ/. Since there is overt change in pronunciation, this is true derivation rather than functional shift. But the two processes are obviously closely related.

Older instances of functional shift commonly produced nouns from verbs: in addition to *walk,* already cited, we might mention *run, steal, laugh, touch, buy, break,* and many others. In present-day English the shift from noun to verb is much in favor. In the past, short words like *brush* and *perch* were sometimes shifted from noun to verb, but today, longer nouns like *implement, position, process, contact* are often used as verbs. Even compound nouns get shifted to verbs; the secretary who said "I didn't back-file the letter, I waste-basketed it" was speaking twentieth-century English, however inelegant.

Back Formation and Clipping

Back formation and clipping are two modes of word creation which can be classed together as different types of *reduction.* In each case, a shorter word is made from a longer one, so that the effect is the opposite of derivation and compounding. Back formation makes use of analogy to produce a sort of reverse derivation. The existence of *creation, create,* and *donation* readily suggests that if there is not a verb *donate* there should be. This seems so natural to us that it is hard to believe that less than a century ago *donate* was considered an American barbarism by many puristically inclined British speakers of English.[1] Other words that have come into English by back formation are *edit* (from *editor*), *burgle* (from *burglar*), *enthuse* (from *enthusiasm*), *televise* (from *television,* by analogy with pairs like *supervise:supervision*), *automate* (from *automation*), *laze* (from *lazy*), and many more. Once pairs of words like these have become established, only the historical record proving prior use of the longer forms serves to distinguish them from normal derivational pairs.

Clippings, on the other hand, are shortenings without regard to derivational analogy. They are frequent in informal language, espe-

[1] See H. L. Mencken, *The American Language,* Fourth Edition (New York: Alfred A. Knopf, 1936), pp. 121, 165.

cially spoken, as in the campus and classroom use of *exam, lab, math,* and *dorm.* They are possible because often a single syllable, usually the one bearing the main stress, is sufficient to identify a word, especially in a rather closely restricted context, so that the remaining syllables are redundant and can be dropped. Most of them preserve a colloquial flavor and are limited to the special vocabularies of occupational groups. Others, however—often over the objections of purists—attain wide circulation and may ultimately replace the longer forms on most or all levels of usage. Some that have done so are *van* (from *caravan*), *bus* (from *omnibus*), *cello* (from *violoncello*), *mob* (from Latin *mobile vulgus* "unstable crowd"), *piano* (from *pianoforte*), and *fan* (in sense "ardent devotee," from *fanatic*). Others which are in acceptable, though perhaps characteristically informal, use alongside the longer unclipped words are *phone* (for *telephone*), *taxi* and *cab* (from *taxicab*) and *plane* (for *airplane* or older *aeroplane*). A rather special form of clipping is that which reduces long compounds or idiomatic fixed phrases to one of their elements—often the modifying element rather than the head— as in *express train, car* from *motor car,* and *outboard* from *outboard motor* (*boat*). This process often accounts for what otherwise seem strange transfers of meaning.

An extreme form of clipping is that which reduces words to their abbreviations and longer phrases to their initials. Abbreviation is, of course, a standard device of the writing system to save space by reducing the length of common or often repeated words. Usually it is confined to writing, and to rather informal writing at that. But some common abbreviations have been adopted in speech and ways have been found to pronounce them. The common abbreviations for the two halves of the day—A.M. and P.M.—which stand for the Latin phrases *ante meridiem* ("before noon") and *post meridiem* ("after noon") are frequently used in speech, where they are pronounced /é: + èm/ and /pí: èm/. These must indeed be considered words, though their spelling is that of abbreviations. The same is true of B.C. and A.D. in dates, O.K. (which has become an international word), U.S., G.I., L.P., TNT, TV, and DDT. In all these cases the pronunciation is simply the syllabic names of the letters, usually with the strongest stress on the last: /yù: + és/, /dì: + dì: + tí:/, and so on.

If the initial letters of a phrase, used as an abbreviation, happen to make a combination that is pronounceable, what results is an *acronym*—a word whose spelling represents the initial letters of a phrase. Though very popular in recent times, acryonyms are by no means an innovation of the twentieth century. The early Christians made a famous one when they took the initials of the Greek phrase {Ἰησοῦς Χριστὸς θεοῦ υἱὸς σωτήρ ("Jesus Christ, son of God, Savior") to make the Greek word ἰχθύς ("fish") and adopted the fish as a symbol of Christ. Acronyms have become more frequent in English since World

War II. Everyone talks about NATO, UNESCO, and NASA, often without being able to supply the longer title whose initials created the acronym. In fact, acronyms have become so popular that some longer titles have been created by a kind of back formation from the desired initials. It was certainly more than a happy accident that led the Navy in World War II to call its feminine branch "Women Assigned to Volunteer Emergency Service," or WAVES. More recently an organization devoted to finding foster parents for orphan children from foreign lands has called itself "World Adoption International Fund" so its initials would spell WAIF.

Proper Names

The giving of individual names to persons, geographic features, deities, and sometimes to animals is a universal human practice, apparently as old as language itself. A proper name, since it is closely restricted to a single specific referent, does not have the general and varied distribution and reference that characterize ordinary nouns. But there is frequent interchange across the line separating proper names from other words. Many proper names, such as *Taylor, Smith, Clark,* and *Wright,* are derived from common nouns describing occupations; others like *Brown, Strong,* and *Wild* derive from adjectives that may once have described the person so named. Placenames also frequently show their derivation from common nouns, as in *Northfield, Portsmouth,* and *Fairmount.*

There has also been interchange in the other direction, by which the proper name of a person or place becomes generalized in meaning, usually to refer to a product or activity connected with the referent of the proper name. One famous example is the name *Caesar,* originally a nickname coined from the Latin verb *caedo* "to cut" to describe Julius Caesar, who was cut from his mother's womb by the operation still called *Caesarian section.* The name was assumed by Julius's nephew Octavius, the first Roman emperor, and then by the subsequent emperors, so that it became virtually a synonym for *imperator* "emperor." In its later history it was borrowed into Germanic, ultimately becoming German *Kaiser* (there was also a Middle English word *kayser,* now obsolete), and into Slavonic, whence came *tsar.* Another interesting set of words derived from names are the adjectives *mercurial, saturnine,* and *jovial,* referring to temperaments supposed to be characteristic of people under the dominance of the planets Mercury, Saturn, and Jupiter. The corresponding *venereal* (from *Venus*) has been restricted in meaning almost entirely to medical use, but *venery* is still a rather high-flown word for love-making. Those supposed to derive instability from the changeable moon used to be called *lunatic* (from Latin *luna,* the moon). The punishment visited upon Tantalus, forever doomed to be within sight of food and water that receded when he reached for it, has given us the verb *tantalize,* formed by adding the productive suffix *-ize* (itself ultimately derived from Greek) to his name. Also ultimately Greek in origin are *hector* ("a bully, to bully") from the Trojan hero in the *Iliad* and *mentor* ("teacher"—now often used in the sports pages for "athletic coach") from the adviser of Telemachus in the *Odyssey.*

During the history of English since the beginning of the Middle English period, various words have been derived from proper names. Some earlier ones are *dunce* (from the scholastic philosopher Duns Scotus—used in ridicule of scholastic philosophy in the later sixteenth century), *pander* (from the character Pandarus in Chaucer's *Troilus and Criseyde, c.* 1385), *mawmet* (from Mahomet; at first it meant "idol," later "puppet, doll"). The Bible, widely read from Reformation times on and frequently discussed for its symbolic as well as its literal or historical meaning, has contributed many words of this sort, such as *jeremiad* ("a denunciatory tirade"), *babel, lazar* (from Lazarus; common for *leper* in Middle English), *maudlin* (from Mary Magdalen and her noted tears), and *simony* ("taking or giving money for church offices," from Simon Magus). On the border between proper and common nouns are names of Biblical and other personages taken in figurative meanings, though usually capitalized in writing, indicating that the transfer to common nouns is not complete: *the old Adam, raising Cain, a doubting Thomas, a Daniel come to judgment.*

Some proper names that have assumed general meanings have undergone pronunciation changes that obscure their origins. The adjective *tawdry* ("cheap and flashy") comes from a clipping of *Saint Audrey,* and presumably was first used to describe a kind of cheap lace sold at St. Audrey's Fair. *Bedlam,* which to us means "uproar, total confusion," was a proper name as late as the eighteenth century, when it was used as a short name for *St. Mary of Bethlehem,* a London insane asylum. The work *mawkin,* used dialectally in England for "scarecrow," comes from *Malkyn,* a girl's name, ultimately a nickname from *Mary.* The parallel nickname *Moll* gave rise to an American slang word for a criminal's girl. The history of *doll* is similar but more complicated; it passed from a clipped form of *Dorothy* to describe a miniature (usually female) figure, then to describe a small and pretty girl.

The names of historical characters—often those of unsavory reputation—have given us some rather common words. One of the most interesting of these is *guy,* from *Guy Fawkes,* used in England to describe the effigies of that notable traitor which are customarily carried in procession and burned on November 5, the anniversary of the discovery of his "Gunpowder Plot." The term came to mean "a figure of fun, a butt of scorn," and as a verb "to poke fun at, tease." In America it has become a universal colloquial term for any male not held in high respect. In phrases like *a nice guy* (when not used ironically) it has lost all of its original pejorative flavor.

Names of products derived from the names of their places of origin are rather plentiful in English. Textiles like *calico* (from *Calicut*, or *Calcutta*), *denim* (*serge de Nîmes*), *cashmere* (*Kashmir*), and *worsted* (from the name of a town in Norfolk, England) are well known. So are products like *china* (clipped from *chinaware* from *China ware*), *gin* (clipped from *Geneva*), *cognac*, and *cayenne*. Specialized and technical vocabularies are especially fond of words adapted from proper names. Skiing has its *telemark* and *christiania* (usually clipped to *christy*); librarians speak of *Dewey decimal classification* and *Cutter numbers*; horticulturalists of *fuchsia*, *dahlia*, and *wistaria*; physicists of *roentgen rays*, *curies*, and *angstrom units*; electricians of *ohms*, *watts*, and *amperes*; doctors of *rickettsia* and *Bright's disease*.

Imitation

A relatively small number of words in English apparently owe their origin to attempts to imitate natural sounds. *Bow-wow, meow, baa, moo,* and other words for animal cries are supposed to remind us of the noises made by dogs, cats, sheep, and cows. They are not accurate imitations, since they are pronounced with sounds characteristic of the sound-system of English, which these animals, not being native speakers of English, do not use. Other languages have other, often quite different imitative words. Both *cock-a-doodle-doo* and *kikiriki* are supposedly imitative of a rooster's crow; unless we assume that English and Greek roosters make quite different sounds, we must attribute the difference between these words to the differing sound-systems of the two languages.

Related to imitation is the phenomenon sometimes called *sound symbolism:* the habit of associating a certain type or class of meanings with a certain sound or cluster of sounds. There seems to be in English an association between the initial consonant cluster *sn-* and the nose (*snarl, sneer, sneeze, sniff, snivel, snore, snort, snout,* and *snuffle*). When slang words referring to or involving the nose are coined they may begin with this cluster, as in *snook* and *snoop*. English speakers associate the sound-combination spelled *-ash* (/æš/) with a sudden loud sound or rapid, turbulent, or destructive motion, as in *crash, dash, flash, smash,* and *splash*; and a final *-er* on verbs suggests rapidly repeated, often rhythmic motion, as in *flicker, flutter, hover, quiver, shimmer, waver*. This last example is perhaps a morpheme in its own right, though to call it one would give us a large number of bound bases that occur nowhere else. But it is well on the way to the morphemic status which certainly must be accorded to the *-le* or *-dle* of *handle, treadle,* and *spindle*.

Imitation was once considered so important as to be made the basis for a theory of the origin of language—the so-called "bow-wow theory." This theory is commonly discounted nowadays.

Blending

Blending is a combination of clipping and compounding, which makes new words by putting together fragments of existing words in new combinations. It differs from derivation in that the elements thus combined are not morphemes at the time the blends are made, though they may become so afterward as a result of the blending process, especially if several blends are made with the same element and the phenomenon of *false etymology* is present.

The poem "Jabberwocky'" in Lewis Carroll's *Through the Looking Glass* contains many ingenious blends, though only a few of them (called *portmanteau words* by Humpty Dumpty in the book) have passed into the general vocabulary. Thus *slithy* (from *lithe* and *slimy*) and *mimsy* (from *miserable* and *flimsy*) are not used outside the poem, but *chortle* (*chuckle* and *snort*) and *galumphing* (*galloping* and *triumphing*) are not uncommon words, though they are usually restricted to colloquial or facetious use.

The history of *-burger* illustrates the way in which blending can give rise to a new morpheme. The name *Hamburger steak* (varying with *Hamburg steak*) was given to a kind of ground beef in America in the 1880s. It was soon shortened by phrase-clipping to *hamburger*, losing its proper-name quality in the process. The *-er* here is simply the normal German suffix for making an adjective from a proper noun (as in *Brandenburger Tor* "Brandenburg Gate"). But to those who did not know German, the word looked (and sounded) like a compound of *ham* and *burger*. So the *-burger* part was clipped and combined with various words or parts of words to make *cheeseburger, deerburger, buffaloburger,* and many more. These have the form of compounds made up of one free base and a bound base *-burger*. Meanwhile by further clipping, *hamburger*, already short for *hamburger steak sandwich,* was cut down to *burger*, which now became a free form—a word. Thus what began as the last two syllables of a German proper adjective has become first a bound morpheme and then a full word in English.

Other morphemes which owe their origin to blending are *-rama*, *-orium*, *-teria*, and *-omat*. The first of these began with words of Greek origin like *panorama* and *cyclorama*.[2] The combining elements in Greek were *pan* "all," *kyklos* "circle, wheel," and *horama* "view," a noun derived from the verb *horan* "see." But the *-rama* part of these words was

---

[2] See John Lotz, "The Suffix '-rama,'" *American Speech,* 39 (1954), 156–158.

blended with *cine* (from *cinema*) to make *cinerama*, describing a type of wide-screen motion picture. Subsequently *-rama* was blended with various other elements to make new words like *colorama* and *vistarama*, as well as many trade and commercial names. It certainly must now be considered a separate morpheme, conveying a vague notion of grandeur and sweep (or so its users hope) to the words in which it is used. Similarly *-orium*, split off from *emporium* (a rather fancy Latin loan-word for "shop"), *-teria*, split off from the Spanish loan-word *cafeteria*, and *-omat*, split off from the trade name *Automat*, itself a clipping from *automatic*, have become separate morphemes, as in *lubritorium*, *valeteria*, and *laundromat*. The process of blending has thus produced not only new words but new morphemes capable of entering with some freedom into new compounds and derivatives. Many of the words thus coined never get any farther than their first application by an enterprising advertiser or proprietor, and those that do usually have a brief life. But a few seem to fill a real need and remain as part of the general vocabulary of English.

Coinage

Very few words are simply made up out of unrelated, meaningless elements. The other resources for making new words and the abundant vocabularies of other languages available for borrowing supply so many easy ways of producing new words that outright coinage seldom suggests itself. The outright coinage—unlike the compound, clipping, derivative, and blend—is also hard to remember because it has no familiar elements to aid the memory. So wholly new coinages are both harder to make and less likely to be remembered and used. It is no wonder that they are relatively rare. Some words, however, are indubitable coinages, and others for which etymologists have found no source may be tentatively assumed to be. Words like *quiz, pun, slang,* and *fun* have no cognates in other Germanic languages, cannot be traced to other languages as loan-words, and, since they are monosyllabic, are not compounds or derivatives, though they might be blends to which we have lost the key. One can imagine that *slang*—an eighteenth-century creation—combined elements from *slovenly* and *language*, but this is pure guesswork. These, together with more recent words, most of them facetious or slangy, like *hooch* and *pooch, snob* and *gob* ("sailor"), most probably originated as free coinages, sometimes involving sound symbolism.

More elaborate coinages, having more than one syllable, are likely to combine original elements with various other processes of word formation, especially derivation. Thus the stems of *segashuate, sockdologer,* and *spifflicated* seem to be coinages, but the suffixes are recognizable morphemes. In fact, it would be exceedingly unlikely for a native speaker to coin a word of more than one syllable without making use of one or more of the word-forming devices we have been discussing.

As even this brief chapter must have made obvious, the vocabulary of English is large, complex, highly diversified in origin, and constantly changing. No dictionary, however large, can contain it all. Or, if such a dictionary should be prepared, it would be out of date by the time it was printed, since new meanings, new borrowings, and new creations are being added every day. Nor can any single individual know it all. Speakers of English share a large vocabulary in common, it is true, but every individual speaker has his own unique inventory of the less commonly used words and meanings, reflecting his unique experience with language.

Many people—perhaps most people—go through life with a vocabulary adequate only to their daily needs, picking up new words when some new facet of life makes it necessary, but never indulging in curiosity and speculation about words. Others are wordlovers—collectors and connoisseurs. They like to measure one word against another, trace their etymologies and shifts of meaning, use them in new and exciting or amusing combinations. They play word-games like *Scrabble* and *Anagrams,* they do crossword puzzles, they make puns and rhymes and nonsense jingles. Some make poems, which are the highest form of word-game. But even those who aspire no further than to the writing of good clear expository prose must become at least amateur connoisseurs of words. Only this way—not by formal exercises or courses in vocabulary-building—will they learn to make the best possible use of the vast and remarkable lexicon of English.

FOR DISCUSSION AND REVIEW

1. Why is an understanding of morphology important in the study of word formation?

2. What role does analogy play in the process of forming words by derivation?

3. Compounding is of particular importance in areas involving extensive technological development. One study found that 19 percent of the words in a series of NASA reports were in nominal compounds, compared to only 3 percent in articles published in the *American Scholar*. Why might this situation exist?

4. Keep a list of nominal compounds that you encounter in your reading during the course of a week. Where are you most likely to find them? What is the longest one you found? (The author of the study referred to in question 3 found a nominal compound that contained 13 words!)

5. Consider the order of importance of the various methods of word formation listed by Francis in the first paragraph of this selection. Discuss the possible causes of this particular ordering or of some of its components. Why, for example, are derivation and compounding so important? Why are imitation and blending so relatively unimportant?

6. Identify the process of word formation in the following words: *gas, contrail, happenstance, spa, diesel, flu, laser, smog, meow, syphilis.*

Projects for "Phonetics, Phonology, and Morphology"

Note: Since a large number of exercises are included for the readings in Part Four, and since short exercises are particularly useful for these topics, we have suggested fewer long projects than usual.

1. An excellent project, if you speak another language, is to compare the significant units of sound of the two languages. For example, German does not have the sound with which the English word *judge* begins and ends. As a variation of this project, you could make a similar comparison for two different dialects of English. In either case, try to make your data as complete as possible.

2. Examine the following: "These *foser glipses* have *volbicly merfed* the *wheeple* their *preebs.*"[1] Although you do not know the meaning of any of the italicized words (How big is a "wheeple"? How does one "merf"? Are "glipses" good to eat?), you do know a great deal about them. What can you say about the form, function, and meaning of the words? On what basis?

3. Using either *The Barnhart Dictionary of New English Since 1963* or *The Second Barnhart Dictionary of New English*, choose a random sample of at least one hundred words and identify their source (e.g., borrowing, derivation, compounding). Prepare a report of your findings. Does your order of importance for processes of word formation coincide with that suggested by Francis? If not, try to suggest some reasons why it doesn't.

4. Read John Algeo's "Where Do All the New Words Come From?" in the Winter 1980 edition of *American Speech*. Prepare a report summarizing his findings. You may wish to compare them with what Francis says in his article in this section.

Selected Bibliography

Adams, V. *An Introduction to Modern English Word Formation*. London: Longman, 1973. (Very thorough analysis.)

Anderson, Stephen R. *The Organization of Phonology*. New York: Academic Press, 1974. (Technical and comprehensive.)

Aronoff, Mark. *Word Formation in Generative Grammar*. Cambridge, MA: The MIT Press, 1976. (Excellent but not for beginners.)

Chomsky, Noam, and Morris Halle. *The Sound Pattern of English*. New York: Harper & Row, 1968. (The first major application of transformational-generative theory to phonology.)

[1] This example comes from Kenneth G. Wilson, "English Grammars and the Grammar of English," which appears in the front matter of Funk & Wagnalls Standard College Dictionary: Text Edition (New York: Harcourt, Brace & World, 1963).

Cole, Ronald A., "Navigating the Slippery Stream of Speech," *Psychology Today* (April 1979).

Denes, Peter, and E. N. Pinson. *The Speech Chain*. Garden City, NY: Harper & Row, 1968. (A clear introduction to speech perception, speech production, and acoustic phonetics.)

Halle, Morris. "Knowledge Unlearned and Untaught: What Speakers Know About the Sounds of Their Language." In Morris Halle, Joan Bresnan, and George A. Miller (eds.), *Linguistic Theory and Psychological Reality*. Cambridge, MA: The MIT Press, 1978. (Very interesting; nontechnical.)

Halle, Morris, and G. N. Clements. *Problem Book in Phonology: A Workbook for Introductory Courses in Linguistics and in Modern Phonology*. Cambridge, MA: The MIT Press, 1983. (Contains an excellent introduction [pp. 2–25] and six sections with exercises based on a wide variety of languages.)

Hyman, Larry M. *Phonology: Theory and Analysis*. New York: Holt, Rinehart and Winston, 1975. (Important but difficult.)

Kenstowicz, M. and C. Kisseberth. *Generative Phonology: Description and Theory*. New York: Academic Press, 1979. (Technical but important.)

Ladefoged, Peter. *A Course in Phonetics*, 2nd ed. New York: Harcourt Brace Jovanovich, 1982. (An excellent introduction. The author writes, "This is a *course* in phonetics, not a book about phonetics.")

Matthews, P. H. *Morphology: An Introduction to the Theory of Word-Structure*. Cambridge: Cambridge University Press, 1974. (A comprehensive introductory textbook.)

Schane, S. A. *Generative Phonology*. Englewood Cliffs, NJ: Prentice-Hall, 1973. (An introduction, but technical.)

Sommerstein, A. *Modern Phonology*. Baltimore: University Park Press, 1977. (Another very good introduction.)

Part Five

Syntax and Language Processing

As we stated in the introduction to Part Four, most linguists agree that languages are best described in terms of their basic systems or divisions. In this part, we focus on syntax and language processing. Syntax involves the study of the largely unconscious finite set of rules that enables speakers to create and understand sentences, and of the relationships among the components of sentences. Although most people take it for granted, the ability of native speakers to comprehend sentences that they have never heard and to utter sentences that they have neither heard nor spoken previously is remarkable. We can do these things because all levels of language are rule-governed and because human beings are genetically predisposed to learn the kinds of rules characteristic of language. A discussion of syntax provides an excellent opportunity to reemphasize the concept of language as a rule-governed system.

Syntax is central to a description of a native speaker's knowledge of his or her language. What do native speakers know that enables them to create novel utterances and to understand sentences they have never heard? The first two selections in this part address this question directly. First, Roderick A. Jacobs and Peter S. Rosenbaum, in "What Do

Native Speakers Know About Their Language?" point out four apparently trivial but actually complex and crucial skills possessed by all native speakers. Next, Frank Heny examines some important syntactic structures and rules, using mainly English examples to try to show the kinds of structures that are found in language and how some of these might relate directly to the way in which language is learned.

The next selection, Neil Smith and Deirdre Wilson's "What Is a Language?" summarizes the aspects of language touched on by Heny, and at the same time introduces some new ideas. The authors emphasize the concept of human language as a rule-governed system and explain its implications. Thus, although every native speaker of English has his or her own unique grammar, all of these grammars have a great deal in common. These shared characteristics and the existence of so-called linguistic universals are attributable to the innate disposition of human beings to learn certain kinds of grammars but not others that, logically, should be equally possible.

In the next selection, Jean Aitchison's "The Cheshire Cat's Grin: How Do We Plan and Produce Speech?" the focus shifts to language processing. As David Lightfoot writes in *The Language Lottery*, "A grammar characterizes a person's linguistic knowledge, but something else characterizes how that knowledge is actually used when that person utters and hears sentences" (p. 192). It is this "something else" that Aitchison is interested in. On the basis of an analysis and categorization of a number of different kinds of speech errors, she suggests one possible model for the planning and carrying out of a speech utterance, including people's unit of planning, selection of a syntactic pattern, and actual choice of words.

The final selection is an interview with Noam Chomsky, the MIT linguist who has been the central figure in the development of generative grammar since the publication of his *Syntactic Structures* in 1957. In this interview, Chomsky emphasizes his belief that the development of human language depends upon genetically programmed mental structures. In his words, "language development really ought to be called language *growth*, because the language organ grows like any other body organ."

1/What Do Native Speakers Know About Their Language?

RODERICK A. JACOBS
AND PETER S. ROSENBAUM

In the following excerpt from their book English Transformational Grammar, *Professors Jacobs and Rosenbaum identify four kinds of knowledge that all native speakers of a language have about that language. These kinds of knowledge involve the ability to distinguish a grammatical utterance from an ungrammatical one, to understand utterances even though a portion or portions thereof may have been deleted, to recognize both lexical and syntactic ambiguity, and to recognize both lexical and syntactic synonymy. We take these abilities for granted; in fact, we usually do not even recognize that we have them. But trying to explain them, trying to account for these abilities of ours, raises fundamental questions. What is language? How is it learned? What is it that is learned? As the authors point out, "When we attempt to explain these skills, we are really seeking to explain an important part of what makes us human."*

The mysteries about language that will be discussed here [may] seem trivial and obvious at first sight. For example: Every normal human being is capable of distinguishing the sentences of his language from all other objects in the universe. Yet, how can this fact be explained? A sentence is a *string* of words, but not every string of words is a sentence. The following strings are English sentences:

1. the trains are most crowded during the holidays
2. aren't you thinking of a perambulator?
3. wash that car before breakfast!

Suppose the word order of these strings was reversed:

4. *holidays the during crowded most are trains the
5. *perambulator a of thinking you aren't
6. *breakfast before car that wash

Every speaker of English knows, without a moment's hesitation, that these strings are not English sentences, even though they contain English words. (An asterisk is always placed before a string which is syntactically or semantically deviant.) What is it that you know when you distinguish between strings of words which are sentences of your language and strings which are not sentences of your language? And where did you get this knowledge?

One possible answer to the latter question is that you memorized the possible sentences of your language while learning it in your infancy, much as you memorized the faces or names of classmates and friends. But this is not the way a human being learns his language. It is impossible to memorize *all* sentences possible in your language, and you frequently utter or hear sentences that do not duplicate any of your past experience. (In fact, the sentence you are reading now has probably not occurred previously in your experience.) Nonetheless, you have been able to distinguish between the grammatical strings and those strings made ungrammatical by reversal of word order. Obviously, you have not learned your language by memorizing its sentences. This, then, is one important human ability that needs to be investigated: How is a normal human being capable of deciding whether a string of words is a sentence in his language, and how is he able to do this for any of a potentially infinite number of strings he has never seen nor heard before?

But this is far from all that needs to be explained. For example, a speaker of a language can almost always tell whether a string is peculiar because of its meaning (i.e., its semantic interpretation) or because of its form (its "syntax"). In his first book on transformational grammar, Noam Chomsky pointed out that the following string is grammatical[1]:

*colorless green ideas sleep furiously.

However, it is nonsensical. It could be described as well-formed grammatically but ill-formed semantically.

Finally, the meaning of a string may be quite clear, but the string may be ungrammatical:

*John and I jumps over wall and we shoots he
*you don't can putting your feet on the table in here
*is reading your father this book.

Thus we are often able to understand foreigners and others who do not correctly use the rules of English.

---

[1] *Syntactic Structures* (Gravenhage, 1957), p. 15.

Furthermore, what is left unsaid may also be very important in a normal sentence of English. You would not be able to explain the full meaning of the following ungrammatical string:

*so was Norbert Wiener

but you would understand and be able to explain this string if it appeared as part of a grammatical string:

Yehudi Menuhin was a child prodigy and so was Norbert Wiener.

You understand the last four words to mean that Norbert Wiener was a child prodigy, although this is not stated in so many words. A speaker of a particular human language can often understand the full meaning of a sentence in his language without explicit statements in the words of the sentence. . . . Compare the following sentences:

1. Dr. Johnson asked someone to behave himself.
2. Dr. Johnson promised someone to behave himself.

When you read the first of these superficially similar sentences, you understood the person who was to behave to be "someone." But when you read the second sentence, you understood the person who was to behave to be "Dr. Johnson." In these two sentences, the items which you understood to refer to the person who was to behave were in different positions, although the sentences were identical on the surface except for one word. What is it that you know about English that enables you to understand the sentences correctly? How is it that you understand

finding the revolver in that drawer worried us

as meaning that *we* are the ones who found the revolver in that drawer? Your knowledge of your language includes the ability to reconstruct the full meaning of a sentence from a string of words which may not contain all the words necessary for an accurate interpretation if you were, say, a Thai learning English.

Frequently, a native speaker of English will understand a sentence as having more than one meaning, as being *ambiguous*. Sometimes just one word is ambiguous, as the word "bank" in

the police station was right by the bank.

Here "bank" could be either the bank where money may be deposited or the bank of a river. Sometimes, however, the ambiguity has to do with the grammatical structure of the sentence:

the lamb is too hot to eat.

This sentence means either that the lamb is so hot that it cannot eat anything or that the lamb is so hot that no one can eat it. Can you see the ambiguity in the following sentence:

visiting relatives can be a nuisance.

Sentences may be multiply ambiguous. Six possible interpretations of the following sentence are given below:

the seniors were told to stop demonstrating on campus.

1. The seniors were demonstrating on campus and were asked to desist.
2. The seniors were demonstrating and were asked, on campus, to desist.
3. The seniors were demonstrating and were asked to desist on campus (although they could demonstrate elsewhere).
4. People were demonstrating on campus, and seniors were asked to stop them.
5. People were demonstrating and seniors were asked, on campus, to stop them.
6. People were demonstrating and seniors were asked to stop them from doing this on the campus (although they could do it elsewhere).

This ability that you have to extract more than one meaning from some sentences of your language is matched by one other skill. You can usually tell when two or more sentences have the same meaning— when they are *synonymous*. Sometimes this synonymy arises from the existence of more than one word for a meaning, as in the joke translation of "Twinkle, twinkle, little star," which begins:

Scintillate, scintillate, diminutive asteroid,
How I speculate as to your identity.

Frequently the synonymy is a result of the way the sentences are structured, as demonstrated by the following sentences:

1. six out of seven salesmen agree that walruses have buck teeth.
2. that walruses have buck teeth is agreed by six out of seven salesmen.

3. it is agreed by six out of seven salesmen that walruses have buck teeth.

You have never seen nor heard these sentences before; yet you need little or no conscious thought to decide that all three of them have a common meaning—a meaning distinct from that of

six out of seven walruses believe that salesmen have buck teeth.

The simplest type of synonymy is word synonymy. As you saw in the alternative version of "Twinkle, twinkle, little star," different words may have the same meaning, though sometimes some alternatives may carry slightly differing connotations. Word synonymy is obviously responsible for the synonymy of the following pair of sentences:

oculists are expected to be well trained
eye doctors are expected to be well trained.

Anyone who speaks English as his native language understands these sentences to be synonymous because he has memorized the meanings of "oculist" and "eye doctor." Since these meanings are the same, he knows that the otherwise identical sentences must have the same meaning.

It is not as simple, however, to explain the native speaker's ability to detect synonymy in such sentences as:

1. the chicken crossed the expressway
   the expressway was crossed by the chicken
2. it is believed that the framers of the Constitution met in Philadelphia
   the framers of the Constitution are believed to have met in Philadelphia
3. economists claim that a recession is not inevitable, and economists are not noted for optimism
   economists, who are not noted for optimism, claim that a recession is not inevitable.

SUMMARY

When you use skills such as the four discussed in this article:

1. the ability to distinguish between the grammatical and ungrammatical strings of a potentially infinite set of utterances,

2. the ability to interpret certain grammatical strings even though elements of the interpretation may not be physically present in the string,
3. the ability to perceive ambiguity in a grammatical string,
4. the ability to perceive when two or more strings are synonymous,

you are making use of a kind of knowledge that can best be described as knowledge of the grammar of your language. This provides you with the grammatical information you need to understand and produce (or generate) the sentences of English. Although these four skills seem too obvious to bother with, they have never been satisfactorily explained. . . .

Language is a specifically human characteristic. Descartes noted in Part V of his *Discourse on Method:*

> It is a very remarkable fact that there are none so depraved and stupid, without even excepting idiots, that they cannot arrange different words together forming of them a statement by which they make known their thoughts; while, on the other hand, there is no other animal, however perfect and fortunately circumstanced it may be, which can do the same.[2]

The particular skills that human beings use when they speak and understand their own language are quite remarkable, especially when you realize that a language is basically an infinite set of sentences.

In a very real sense, then, the study of what a grammar must be like if it is to account for the sentences of our language is more than the study of the structure of English sentences and the processes which operate on these structures. The various linguistic skills reflect aspects of the intellectual abilities we possess by virtue of being human. When we attempt to explain these skills, we are really seeking to explain an important part of what makes us human.

FOR DISCUSSION AND REVIEW

1. Discuss the difference in the relationship between the italicized words in *a,* those in *b,* and those in *c* with respect to the phrase "to paint in Paris."
    a. *Whistler* persuaded *his mother* to paint in Paris.
    b. *Whistler* promised *his mother* to paint in Paris.
    c. *Whistler* left *his mother* to paint in Paris.
    Explain the ambiguity of *c.*

2. Explain the ambiguity in the following sentences:
    a. Eating apples can be enjoyable.
    b. She told me to leave at five o'clock.

[2] Quoted in N. Chomsky, *Cartesian Linguistics* (New York, 1966), p. 4.

    c. Could this be the invisible man's hair tonic?
    d. The old matron fed her dog biscuits.
    e. Every citizen may vote.

3. Describe the difference in the relationship of "Eberhart" to "please" in *a* and *b*:
    a. Eberhart is eager to please.
    b. Eberhart is easy to please.

4. Certain material has been deleted from the following sentences. Show what this deleted material must have been:
    a. She adopted forty-two cats simply because she wanted to.
    b. John likes Mary, Bill, and Sally.
    c. Oaks are taller than maples.
    d. Discovering the truth pleases scientists.
    e. Ladies wearing high heels are not welcome on tennis courts.

5. The following pairs of sentences are synonymous, but in a different way. Can you describe and explain the differences?
    a. My attorney specializes in copyright law.
       My lawyer specializes in copyright law.
    b. A proposal was made which bothered me.
       A proposal which bothered me was made.

2/Sentence Structure

FRANK HENY

A sentence is not just a string of words; it is a string of words in a certain order, a string that has structure. Thus, cat dog the the chased *is not a sentence; it is just a list of English words. But* the dog chased the cat *is a sentence (as is, for that matter,* the cat chased the dog*). A sentence, then, is more than the sum of its parts (i.e., its words); it is words ordered in a particular way, in this case according to the rules of English syntax. But how did we learn these rules, rules which to a large extent we don't know that we know? In the following article, Professor Frank Heny of Carleton College suggests an answer to this question, and then examines some of the basic syntactic rules of English that we all use every day of our lives. No single article can possibly treat English syntax in depth. But by drawing examples from two kinds of English questions and from several other familiar constructions, Professor Heny is able to illustrate some fundamental principles of syntax and to demonstrate that children come to language learning with an inborn mechanism that "severely limit[s] what the language learner needs to take into account." This same point, one of the crucial concepts in contemporary linguistic theory, will be made later in this section by Neil Smith and Deirdre Wilson, and again by Noam Chomsky.*

Learning Language Is Learning Structure

It is easy to imagine your language as a vast collection of words—such as *easy* and *think* and *language* and *vast*. But you know this can't be the whole truth as soon as you think about it. String together the words of the previous sentence in another order:

(1) truth be the about can't soon but it you as as whole this know think you

What makes the difference? The obvious difference between (1) and *But you know this can't be the whole truth as soon as you think about it* is the order of the words; and it is almost equally obvious that changing that order has an effect on how the words themselves interact with each other. Certain words now form coherent groups, like *the whole truth* or *as soon as you think about it*. Saying or writing the words in a

294

particular order gives them structure, and then they function as a part of language.

Learning a language must therefore be learning words organized into structures. Of course you have to learn the words, too, and what you probably remember about learning your language is limited to memories of learning new words—not the structures in which the words occur, the structures which make your language what it is. Think back as far as you can, and see if you can recall starting to learn English. I have memories of isolated incidents, feelings, and impressions from when I was about two years old. I can remember learning new words almost as far back as that. But I have no recollection whatsoever of learning a new *construction*—how to form passives or questions or relative clauses—or even how to form phrases like *the whole truth*.

Words themselves are familiar and comfortable objects that almost everyone can think about. Who doesn't, at least occasionally, notice someone else using a word in a way that strikes them as "strange"? We all come across new words in our daily lives, or new meanings for old ones, and these we can and do think and talk about. But we need special training to think consciously about constructions such as passives and questions and relative clauses, or even about the simplest ways in which words are put together to form sentences. Structure, although essential to our language, is not something we can easily manipulate consciously; it was learned unconsciously and remains inaccessible to conscious thought for the vast majority of language users throughout their lives.

Don't confuse learning the basic structure of your language (which took place before you were five years old) with the attempts of teachers, for example, to get you to write more effectively, or to say "It is I" instead of "It's me." What you learned about language from your teachers, you learned consciously, and you consciously applied what you had learned. But what you learned was facts or opinions about your language and how to use it effectively, which, compared to the language itself, were quite insignificant. The language itself was something you had already mastered, long before anyone tried to teach it to you. The basic English structures were all there well before you went to grade school. Quite unconsciously, and without any formal teaching, you had somehow developed a system so complex that linguists have still not figured out just how it works. How did you do it?

At present, no one really knows, although some very interesting ideas are now being explored. It seems likely that you developed the structures of your native language so easily simply because as a human being you began life already specially prepared to develop precisely this kind of structure. There was actually very little you had to *learn* about it. In other words, although you had to learn the *words* of your language from scratch, you did not really have to learn the *structures*.

They were already there—much as an embryo's eyes are there, with all the appropriate structure, waiting for the light and the sights they will see. The underlying patterns of language, any language, were waiting within you in some sense, and all you had to do was select from those internally stored structures the ones that best fit the patterns actually represented in the language you heard around you. By the time you were a year or two old, surrounded by English, the sounds of that language had already begun to form themselves into patterns in your mind—not because of your own attempts to discover English structure (surely too much for any toddler), but rather through a process in which those sounds began to clothe some of the preexisting structures, the ones matching English. Given this background, your learning English was no miracle. Indeed it would have been a miracle if you, as a normal human being, had not become a fluent English speaker.

To repeat: it was not so much that you *learned* your language as that it simply *developed*, fleshing out certain of a number of possible language structures that were in effect already waiting to develop. The language around you merely determined the particular choices made among those structures. Growing up exposed instead to French or Navajo or Japanese would have meant only that the language you heard around you would have forced the selection of entirely different options.

To see what this idea amounts to, we need to understand a little more about what kinds of systems languages are. Ideally that would mean looking at a number of languages. Because that would take too long, this account will be based almost entirely on English. However, it will be aimed at demonstrating not what *English* is like, but what *language* is like.

Structure Is More Than Just Word Order

Let us first be quite clear that English sentences are not just strings of words in a particular order, but really do have complex internal structures. I suggested in passing that a sentence is not just a string of words occurring in a particular order, but that, by being in that order, those words acquire a certain structure—and that it is this rather than mere word order that constitutes the sentence. To see that structure is indeed more than just order, look at example (2). Here is a single string of words that *without any change in order* can have two quite different meanings, each corresponding to a possible structure:

(2) a. I watched [the prisoner from the tower].
    b. I watched [the prisoner] [from the tower].

The first way of interpreting this string treats [*the prisoner from the tower*] as a unit: it is the [prisoner from the tower] who is seen by the speaker. This word group [*the prisoner from the tower*] functions as a single unit, a *constituent*, in other, similar sentences. In such sentences, the words *the prisoner from the tower* act together to characterize someone as a prisoner from some tower:

(3) a. [The prisoner from the tower] was what I saw.
    b. [The prisoner from the tower] was being watched carefully.
    c. [The prisoner from the tower], I watched carefully.

In each of these examples, the phrase [*the prisoner from the tower*] could be replaced by other constituents such as [*the prisoner from Siberia*] or [*a visitor from Mars*] or [*three men in dark glasses*]. Each of these, too, could act as a single unit in these sentences.

The second interpretation of the string *I watched the prisoner from the tower*, represented by (2b), does not at all connect the words *from the tower* to *the prisoner*. The two phrases act as separate units. This is suggested by the bracketing in (2b). This time, *from the tower* is much more closely associated with the verb *watched* or with the pronoun *I* than with the phrase *the prisoner*. The sentence is not about a prisoner from a tower at all, but reports that the speaker *watched from the tower*. Given this fact, it is not surprising that (2b) is very similar in meaning to another sentence in which the phrase *from the tower* occurs right at the beginning, next to *I*:

(4) [From the tower], I watched [the prisoner].

Constructed out of the same English words as (2), this string can only be taken as having a structure in which *the prisoner* and *from the tower* are separate, unrelated constituents.

Contrast the unambiguous interpretation of (4), in which *from the tower* is not linked to *the prisoner* in any way, with the equally unambiguous interpretation of all the sentences of (3)—in which the whole phrase [*the prisoner from the tower*] was always interpreted as a single constituent, i.e., where each sentence is about a prisoner from some tower.

In the examples of (3), the word order somehow forces us to interpret the words *the prisoner from the tower* as a single constituent, whereas in (4) the two parts of this string are split up and must be interpreted as two distinct, unrelated constituents. In contrast, the order of words in (2) permits either interpretation, depending on how we structure the words: as a single constituent or as two. The word order does not force us to choose, as it does in (3) or (4). In a particular instance, when we hear or utter a string of words like (2), we have to determine (generally unconsciously) which structure to assign to it and hence which sentence we will regard it as representing—(2a) or (2b).

All languages are built up in this way. They consist of small groups of words (phrases) interacting with each other in various ways to produce sentences. In English, the order of the words limits the ways in which words can interact to form phrases, although in (2), word order did not completely determine the phrase structure. In many languages word order plays little role; in Warlpiri, for example, spoken in Australia, the words from a single phrase can occur at many points in a sentence, almost as if one could say *The from watched I prisoner tower the*, and thus say what is meant by (2a). Which words go in which phrases is signaled by other means than word order in Warlpiri. Still, Warlpiri, just as much as English, constructs sentences out of phrases, and indeed phrases of much the same kinds as those found in English.

A child hearing English or Warlpiri will therefore need to "figure out" (unconsciously, of course) whether word order or something else signals which words group together into phrases, since that is one way languages differ. To put it another way, something will have to signal to the child's language learning device that it must select the option, in English, of determining the make-up of phrases in part by word order, and in Warlpiri's by some other option. On the other hand, since all languages consist of sentences structured into certain kinds of phrases, the child does not need to learn that both English and Warlpiri contain phrases. Since there is no alternative, there is nothing to learn; the only kinds of languages we humans learn are those consisting of phrases grouped into sentences.

Some Simple Phrases: NP and PP

Since the phrases that compose sentences are such a vital part of any human language, it is important to understand what they are like and how they interact. So far we have seen only that a string of words, like *the prisoner from the tower*, may act as a single phrase or may be two independent phrases, *the prisoner* and *from the tower*, each a constituent adding its own meaning to the sentence—as in (2b). We have seen that English words occurring together in a sentence are interpreted not just as *strings* of words, but as *structures* built up in some way out of those words. Their order may determine how they group into phrases, as in (3) and (4), or it may not, as in (2). It is the phrases rather than the words as such that form constituents of sentences: (2a) and (2b) contain the same words but different phrases—as suggested by the bracketing in those examples.

Now it is time to consider just what kinds of things those phrases are. They can be very complex, or very short and simple. We could replace *the prisoner* in (4) by similar phrases of increasing complexity, without altering the essential structure of the sentence as a whole:

(5) a. From the tower, I watched [*the prisoner with bare feet*].
   b. From the tower, I watched [*the prisoner in the yard with bare feet*].
   c. From the tower, I watched [*the prisoner in the yard with bare feet who was trying to run away*].

We could also replace these complex phrases by just a single word:

(5) d. From the tower, I watched [*John*].

A phrase does not have to be long, of course, and here it consists of just that one word, *John*. In each example of (5) the phrase in square brackets refers to the person who is said to be being watched, and this phrase plays the same role in the sentence as a whole.

Now let us look at the way these phrases are built up. Each one, no matter how complex or simple, contains at least one noun: *prisoner* in the first three, and *John* in the last. We may call such a unit a *noun phrase* (NP). It is a phrase built up around a noun.

Not every string of words containing a noun can be regarded as an NP, since in English the order of the words is significant. Whereas *the prisoner* is a perfectly fine NP, *prisoner the* is not, nor is *from the tower the prisoner*. Hence, a string like *From the tower the prisoner was watched carefully* can only be interpreted as a statement about how a prisoner, not further identified, was watched from the tower. Although right next to *the prisoner* and some distance away from the verb *watched*, the string *from the tower* goes unambiguously with *watched* and never with the NP *the prisoner*.

There are many restrictions on what can form an NP. Some strings simply cannot be rearranged in any way to form a single NP. For example, there is no way to rearrange the words in the string *the suddenly prisoner* and end up with a single well-formed NP. Similarly with strings like *the run prisoner,* or *that the three prisoner*. Noun phrases, like all the parts of a sentence, have a very precise *syntax*: they are constructed according to exact rules. Learning the language may consist in part of learning these rules, although it seems increasingly likely that many rules are in principle already "known" in some sense to the young child and hence do not actually have to be learned. How much of the syntax of NPs has to be learned we do not yet know. Certainly English speaking children have to learn something about word order, although it seems that, for example, once they learn that the *head* of the phrase, the noun around which it is constructed, comes at a certain point in an English NP, then a great deal about word order elsewhere in the NP follows from the general principles of human language they already possess, and they do not have to learn each fact about word order separately.

NPs do not constitute the only phrase-level building blocks of language. There are other phrases, like *from the tower*, which although not NPs, nevertheless contain noun phrases (*the tower*, in this instance). In addition they contain prepositions, like *from*. Prepositions vary greatly in behavior, just as there are many different kinds of nouns. But just as we may legitimately group together all the phrases built up around nouns as NPs, so we group together all the phrases that are constructed by adding an NP to a preposition. A phrase of this sort is generally called a *prepositional phrase* (PP). We will not deal in any detail with the syntax of prepositional phrases; nor will we examine any of the other, less important structural entities that can function on this level. We turn instead to the larger unit within which both PPs and NPs are always found in language: the sentence.

Basic English Sentence Patterns

Small units like NPs and PPs are very important constituents; they contribute a great deal to the structure of language. However, they do so only because of the way they interact with verbs. Verbs, and the phrases built up around them, are what really determine the essentials of sentence structure. Quite generally it seems that a language will have one or two "normal" or "unmarked" sentence patterns, which are embodied in many of the commonest, most ordinary sentences, and that it is the verbs of the language which are at the center of this structure, each verb having its own special variant of the basic pattern.

Here are some very simple examples of the English unmarked pattern:

(6) a. [The cat] slept.
 b. [A man] built this house.
 c. [The mouse] went down a hole.
 d. [The cat] put the mouse on the mat.

Each sentence contains an underlined verb and a phrase preceding the verb, the *subject* of the sentence, which is an NP. The subjects are enclosed in brackets.

Although every sentence in (6), and indeed every simple, "normal" English sentence, contains a verb and a preceding subject, there is a good deal of variation in what can *follow* the verb. Because of the way verbs work, each sentence in (6) is forced to differ a little in structure from all the others—and these differences always concern what can, must, or must not appear to the right of the verb. So, for example, the phrase *this house* cannot be incorporated into (6a) the way it is built into the following sentence (7a):

(7) a. *The cat slept this house.[1]

Unlike *build*, the verb *sleep* does not permit the phrase *this house* to appear to its right. In fact, it will not permit any other NP to appear there.

Conversely, the verb *build* cannot generally appear *without* an NP following it, as suggested by the ungrammaticality of (7b):

(7) b. *A man built.

What can, must, or must not appear to the right of the verb depends directly on that verb. After *sleep*, no phrase like *this house*, no NP, may appear at all, whereas after *build*, an NP *must* appear, at least in an "unmarked" sentence. (There are special cases like *We are building near Lake Tahoe*, where the implication in most contexts is that the speaker is building a house near Lake Tahoe. We will ignore such cases on this occasion.)

Those two verbs, *sleep* and *build*, represent the simplest cases. The first will not permit an NP to its right, an *object*, whereas the second requires one. Verbs like *sleep* are called *intransitive*. Verbs like *build* are called *transitive*. It is a little misleading that grammarians in the past noticed these two classes of verbs and a few more, and gave names to them, for there are many variations in the way English verbs require or permit the presence or absence of NPs and PPs to their right. For example, *put* requires both an NP and a PP. This is shown by the ungrammaticality of both (8a) and (8b). (Compare these two with the grammatical (6d).)

(8) a. *The cat *put* the mouse.
    b. *The cat *put* on the mat.

From observations like these it seems that each English verb is closely tied to any phrases that may appear to its right; these phrases are called its *complements*.

We can summarize what has been shown so far in this section by saying that English sentences "normally" consist of an NP before the verb (a subject), followed by the verb itself and then the complements of that verb, if it has any. Whether a verb has any complements, and if so precisely how many NPs and/or PPs must or may follow it, is a property of the verb itself. Comparing the sentences of (6) with each other shows how far the structure of each is directly dependent on the verb it contains and hence on the complements that must or may follow that verb.

Given this account of how the structure of an "unmarked" sentence is related to properties of the verb it contains, we can see how

---

[1] The asterisk (*) is used to indicate that the string, *The cat slept this house*, is not a well-formed English sentence.

a sentence will have certain general structural properties that will not vary with the verb, and certain properties that will vary, depending on the verb around which it is built.

If we put brackets around the verbs plus their complements in (6)—the *verb phrase* (VP)—then we see immediately that all four sentences have the same basic structure, an NP followed by a VP:

(6') a. [$_{NP}$ The cat] [$_{VP}$ *slept*].
   b. [$_{NP}$ A man] [$_{VP}$ *built* this house].
   c. [$_{NP}$ The mouse] [$_{VP}$ *went* down a hole].
   d. [$_{NP}$ The cat] [$_{VP}$ *put* the mouse on the mat].

It is important to emphasize that linguists believe they have found good evidence indicating that English sentences like those above really do have the kind of structure I have ascribed to them—in particular that there is a separate subject NP and then a VP, which excludes the subject and consists of the verb plus those NPs and PPs which are most closely associated with it—that is, those parts of the sentence which depend most directly on the verb, its complements. The evidence for this structure cannot be adequately dealt with here; but what is important is not so much the details of the arguments as an appreciation of the fact that every hypothesis about language structure that we use in our work must be carefully supported by systematic, coherent argumentation based on the facts. We are, after all, trying to understand how children develop language so easily, or to discover what it is about language that makes it easy for humans to learn, and, conversely, what it is about humans that makes their languages easy for them to learn. To carry out this research we must try to understand just what the central properties of language are, and there is no point inventing structures like those shown in (6') as a basis for further work unless they can be well supported by the facts. The VPs shown there do indeed seem to be well justified, even though no attempt will be made here to argue that the verb and its complements together form such a constituent.

A Phrase Structure Grammar for Basic English Sentences

If there is an "unmarked" pattern which English sentences follow, and especially if it is true that the main lines of this pattern develop more or less automatically as a child constructs his or her own version of English, then it must surely be true that each of us who has learned English has stored away unconsciously something corresponding to these basic sentence structures. To find out just what that stored knowledge of English is like, we need to formulate hypotheses about it and to build models representing these hypotheses in a precise manner, so that we can investigate them with rigor.

One of the most fruitful ways of modeling the basic structures of English is by means of a *phrase structure grammar*. This is a way of directly representing the structure of every basic sentence of the language as a tree—and doing so with the help of some very general tree-building rules. These rules, which we will look at presently, are a way of representing the properties that any sentence can possess; each tree corresponds to a particular sentence, being a model of the structure of that sentence constructed in accordance with the general rules. Some examples will help clarify this. The following trees might be assigned to the sentences of (6):

(9) a.

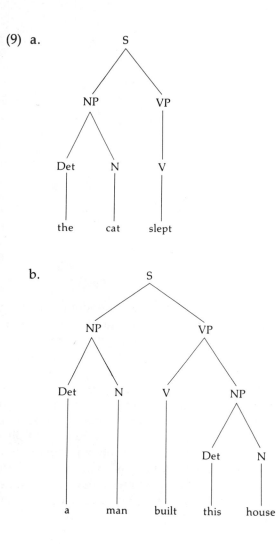

    b.

c.

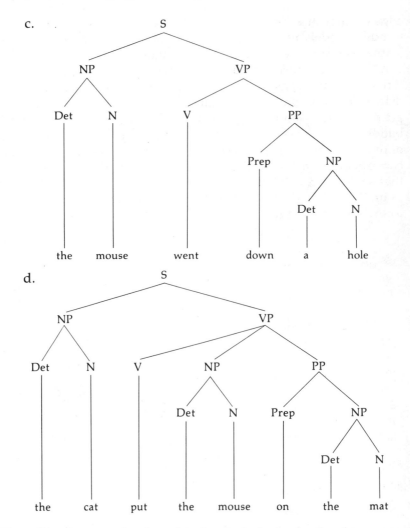

d.

Trees like these can be thought of quite independently of any general rules for constructing them. It is in principle possible to imagine that we might store each sentence of our language as a tree, thus representing the fact, frequently discussed above, that a sentence has structure. However, a little reflection should be enough to make it clear that English cannot be represented in that way.

Our knowledge of English cannot be thought of as simply a tree-like structure stored with each sentence. Our brains cannot store sentences individually. Apart from anything else, there are simply too many sentences in the language—in fact, an infinite number of possible sentences. Practically, what this amounts to is that each of us deals effortlessly every day with hundreds of sentences that we have never heard before—and every sentence is, as we have seen, not just a string of words but a structured string. Consequently, in learning English (or developing the structure of English), we must have acquired some way of assigning structure to *any* appropriate string of words. This aspect of our language is represented in a phrase structure grammar by a set of rules that captures the main aspects of English sentence structure in the form of trees, like those above, which it associates appropriately and automatically with every sentence of the language. For every possible sentence of English, the rules will construct a tree. The following set of rules would construct the trees of (9) and others like them:

(10) a. S   → NP VP
      b. VP → V (NP) (PP)
      c. PP → Prep NP
      d. NP → (Det) N

These rules provide a "recipe" for building a number of related structural skeletons that English sentences of the "normal" pattern will flesh out once appropriate words are linked to the end symbols N, V, Prep, and Det.

Each rule in (10) may be thought of as building part of a tree. Let us start with the part built by rule (10a): S → NP VP. In this tree (for each part of a tree is itself a tree), the S to the left of the arrow in the rule in question is drawn above the NP and VP appearing to the right of the arrow, and it is linked directly to each of them. The symbols to the right of the arrow (*NP* and *VP*) appear in precisely the same order from left to right as they do in the rule itself. So rule (10a) builds the following little piece of structure:

(11)

If you find it easier to think in terms of how *you* should interpret the rule, think of it as an instruction to write down the symbol to the left of the arrow, and then to write under that, and in the order in which they appear in the rule, all the symbols to the right of the arrow. And finally, link each of the lower symbols to the one above it. If you follow these instructions precisely, this should enable you to draw (11) as the structure (the *only* structure) resulting from the application of (10a) according to the interpretation we have just given that rule. First you write down the "S". Then under it you write "NP VP". And finally you link "NP" to "S", and "VP" to "S". The result is (11).

Now note carefully that this little tree forms a part of every one of the larger sentence trees in (9). Make sure you follow this before going further. Either make a tracing of (11) and lay it over each of the trees given in (9), or simply look carefully at those four earlier trees and satisfy yourself that you *could* lay a tracing of (11) over each of them. (It would cover the S node at the top of each tree, and the NP and VP which are joined to it.)

This is not trivial, although at first you may not see why it is important. The real significance of having a rule like (10a) in our grammar of English—a rule that draws the sub-tree (11) as a part of every sentence—is that it directly represents an aspect of English structure to which I have several times drawn attention: all "normal" English sentence patterns contain a subject NP followed by a VP. This rule, (10a), has NP VP on the right-hand side, and is the only rule for S in the grammar; so it forces every tree to contain, below the S and connected to it, NP followed by VP. In this way rule (10a) ensures that the language model of which it forms a central part will include only trees built with the structure NP + VP: every sentence will be associated with the structure NP + VP.

Although of itself quite a small point, it is a typical application of a basic methodology that is central to all current work in theoretical linguistics, and for that reason worth following closely. Let us look at it again from a slightly different angle. In order to discover just how language develops, we need to understand what kinds of structures may be included in a human language; in order to do that we formulate hypotheses about the structure of language, representing these hypotheses by means of some clear formalism such as a phrase structure grammar. Put this way, the grammar (i.e., the set of rules) in (10) is a step toward understanding how we learn language and must be thought of as an attempt to build a model of the kinds of structure that we, as children, eventually assign to English sentences.

So by using the grammar of (10) in our account of English, we are committed to the claim that the child ends up with a representation of English that is essentially like that set of rules, and that leads to representations for each of the sentences of (6) which are in essence those given in the trees drawn by those rules, namely (9a–d). Keep these underlying principles firmly in mind as we proceed. The formal details that we now turn to again are certainly important, for it is only by understanding them that you can really grasp the significance of theoretical work on language; but it is all too easy to get bogged down in these formal details and to lose sight of the goals that give them significance.

We can now fill in the rest of the picture, looking briefly at how the rules of (10b–d) provide "recipes" for drawing every aspect of the trees of (9). First, we must extend sub-tree (11). Look at that diagram once again. One branch ends in the symbol "VP", which is the symbol on the left of rule (10b). So when we apply the general instructions for tree-building to this particular rule, "VP" will be the symbol we write first, just as "S" was with respect to rule (10a). Then we will need to write under "VP" the symbols to the right of the arrow in the rule. And so on. In practice, since "VP" is already written down, in (11), we take that as our starting point. Any time the left-hand symbol of a rule we are applying is already part of an existing tree, we simply write down the symbols that are on the right of the arrow, placing them under the existing left-hand symbol. So in this case we may write down *V NP PP* (all of which appear on the right of the VP rule). We write them immediately under the existing VP in (11), and we obtain (12):

(12)

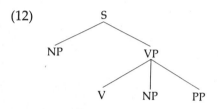

While it is perfectly true that application of rule (10b) to the VP in tree (11) does—and should—produce (12) (which is a sub-tree of the tree given earlier in (9c)), we have ignored a small but quite significant property of rule (10b), which makes (12) not the only tree drawn by that rule. In (10b), there are two symbols inside parentheses. These parentheses never appear in the drawings of trees; the parentheses are in fact not a part of the symbols themselves at all. They simply indicate, in the phrase structure rules, elements which *may*, but *need not*, appear in trees constructed by those rules.

Thus, when we applied (10a), we had no choice but to write down both "NP" and "VP". There was no choice because there were no parentheses around either symbol; and the rule was written without parentheses around these symbols in order to represent English as a language in which every sentence has a subject NP followed by a VP. Rule (10b), on the other hand, allows us a number of choices when we apply it. This reflects the fact that not every VP in every sentence has the same structure. In fact, as we emphasized early on, the structure of the VP of each sentence depends on which verb actually appears in it. Our general rules for constructing sentences must therefore permit the appropriate variation. The parentheses in rule (10b) are there because a VP may contain an NP, a PP, both, or neither. Both the NP and the PP are optional, and this is marked by enclosing both symbols in parentheses. When we apply the rule, we have to make a choice; we do not need to write down "V NP PP" under VP, but may leave out either NP or PP or both. So under the VP we may write down just "V NP", omitting the "PP". Or we may write down "V PP", or "V

NP PP". Or just "V". We cannot leave out the "V" since that is not inside parentheses. But since everything else is, we may omit any or all of the other symbols.

The operation of the rule may be easier to follow if we work through each of these possibilities one by one. First, here is the rule itself again:

$$VP \rightarrow V \ (NP) \ (PP)$$

Omit both elements in parentheses and we obtain the shortest version of the rule and the simplest trees:

(13) a. VP → V

Omit only the NP and we have:

b. VP → V PP

Omit the PP and we have:

c. VP → V NP

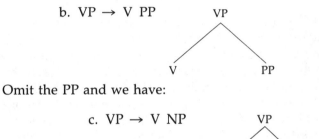

If both NP and PP are selected, in applying the rule, the longest possible version applies and the right-hand side includes the symbols "V NP PP", the result is a tree like the one already shown in (12), where the rule was applied to the VP of (11). Representing the longest version of the rule on its own, with the tree it produces, using the same format as (13a–c), we obtain:

d. V → V NP PP

(Compare this last tree with the one shown in [12].)

If, when we applied rule (10b) to the VP in tree (11), we had chosen just "V NP", instead of "V NP PP", the result would have been:

(14)

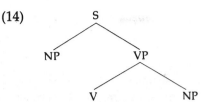

We could extend this figure so as to turn it into the tree shown in (9b). The structure we have in (14) is a subtree of (9b). To turn (14) into (9b) requires just two applications of rule (10d) to add the proper structure under NP—and then, of course, the right words have to be added at the ends of the branches. In a similar manner, all the sentences of (9) can be obtained from the rules of (10). It would be worth taking the time to try to derive each of these trees by applying those rules in proper order.

Note, as you do so, that a non-English string of English words like (*on the mat the cat the mouse put*) will not be assigned a structure by any possible combination of the rules. Why is that true? One way of looking at it is that rule (10a), which starts each derivation off by getting the "S" in position, forces every sentence to consist of an NP followed by a VP. And the rule for VP insists that the verb appear at the beginning of the verb phrase—*followed* by NP, PP, both, or neither. There is no rule that will get the verb to appear after a string consisting of *on the mat the cat the mouse*, since this string consists of PP (*on the mat*) + NP (*the cat*) + NP (*the mouse*). None of the subrules of (10) will place PP + NP + NP in that order, let alone place them before the verb. If English included sentences with such a pattern, we would need to add some rules to (10) to generate appropriate trees. For example we might assign to this non-English string a tree somewhat like the following:

(15)

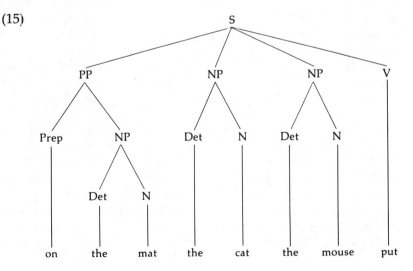

A rule that would generate (15) might, for example, be:

(16) S → PP NP NP V

Since English does not permit these structures, of course, we don't add this rule to (10) and hence our grammar just never generates strings like *on the mat the cat the mouse put*. Thus, the grammar properly represents the English native speaker's internalized language, generating the sentences of (9) while excluding strings like that shown in (15). We may therefore regard the rules of (10) as a reasonable first approximation to the sort of representation that must develop in the mind of the English learning child. Learning, or developing, a language is in part a matter of learning or developing a grammar like (10) that will construct appropriate structures for all the sentences of the language in question.

Children learning languages other than English may have to develop quite different rules from (10) in order to assign structures to the sentences of their language. If the verb goes last in the sentence, then they will end up with a rule more like the one given in (16), with the V at the end. Some aspects of the phrase structure of each language may just have to be learned. Whether the verb goes at the end or beginning of the sentence or, as in English, after the subject, is probably something that has to be learned, and then on the basis of this an appropriate phrase structure rule is constructed. On the other hand, as we suggested earlier in connection with NP structure, many aspects of the phrase structure rules may form part of those preexisting patterns which the child does not need to learn.

The verb, for example, cannot appear at just any point in a sentence; there are just a few positions where a verb can be expected to appear. It is likely that when children begin analyzing the language around them, this fact, coded into their own knowledge of what can constitute a language, greatly simplifies the task of discovering which are the verbs of the language to which the child is exposed.

Many other examples could be given of ways in which aspects of phrase structure may not need to be learned, but one more will suffice. There seems to be a link between the sentence position in which the verb appears in a language (first in the sentence, last, or after the subject) and the structure of PPs. A language with the verb in final position (having a phrase structure rule something like [16]), would not have PPs like those in English (preposition before the NP), but would place the "preposition" *after* the NP. (It would then be called a *postposition* by grammarians, but there is no real difference in the function of prepositions and postpositions.) Children exposed to a language in which the verb came last would quickly discover where the verb had to appear, and that to construct the sentences of the language they heard, they would need a rule with "V" on the far right, like (16), or perhaps a rule for VP such as VP → NP PP V. The children would not then need to learn, in addition, that the rule for PP in their language differed from the one given in (10c). There would be only one rule available for PP: PP → NP P. The P would come last in its phrase, just as the verb comes last.

Now, we are not certain whether this is indeed a case where the structure of human language is constrained by predetermined limitations, built into the human mind, on which of the possible phrase structure rules can combine to form a grammar for a human language. There may be another explanation for the fact that in any given language the form of the rule for the PP can be (in large measure) predicted from that of the rule introducing the verb. But it seems likely that this is an example of how learning language is simplified by the way in which variation is severely limited by constraints on how the human mind constructs grammars. Logically, one could have languages with verbs in final position, but with prepositions, as in English; but in trying to learn their language, children "know" that they need not take this logical possibility into account. As soon as the rule for the verb is discovered, this will supply the essentials of the rule for the PP.

Some Deviant Patterns: Auxiliaries in English Questions

Not all sentences of English follow patterns covered by the rules of (10). In some cases, we would need only to extend those rules. For example, our account of English makes no provision for NPs containing adjectives, such as *little* in *the little cat*. Nor does it allow us to introduce a PP inside an NP, such as [NP *the prisoner* [PP *from the tower*]], one of the first constructions we noticed, in (2). In both instances, it would be simple to add extra optional elements at the appropriate points in the rule for NP (10d). We might, for example, modify the present version, NP → (Det) N, to read NP → (Det) (Adj) N (PP), extending this rule even further to take care of complex NPs like *the man with a huge mouse in one of the three tiniest cages in the world*—and so on!

Among other words that must be introduced into the sentence in this way are *auxiliaries*. These are the little verb-like words that may appear between the subject NP and the VP in any ordinary English statement. When we introduced the idea that there are basic, unmarked patterns in English, we could perfectly well have added one or more auxiliaries to the sentences of (6), for auxiliary verbs are part of the basic sentence structure of the language. We could have used examples like the following (compare them with the corresponding sentences of (6)):

(17) a. [The cat] *has* [slept].
    b. [A man] *could* [build this house].
    c. [The mouse] *is* [going down a hole].
    d. [The cat] *will* [put the mouse on the mat].

In each case, one auxiliary verb appears between the subject and the VP. This is perfectly normal. In fact, up to three, and in passive sentences up to four, auxiliaries can appear in a fixed sequence in this position. The examples above could have been more complex: *The cat may have been sleeping*, or *The mouse could be going down a hole*, and so on.

    In a more exhaustive account of basic English structure, we would need to allow for these auxiliaries. Just as we suggested expanding the rule for NP (i.e., (10d)) to include adjectives, so we might add an extra symbol, say "AUX," between the NP and the VP of the rule (10a) to accommodate auxiliaries: S → NP AUX VP. Adding such a node would allow us to draw trees like the following:

(18)

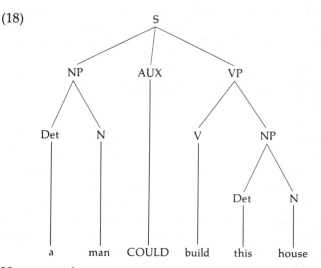

However, there is no point in going into more detail about how to modify the basic structures of English to accommodate auxiliaries. We are primarily concerned in this section with the fact that there are many English sentences whose structures differ from that of the "normal" patterns we have seen so far, and do so in ways which suggest that a grammar consisting only of rules like those of (10) does not adequately represent the full structure of a language like English— that human languages consist in part of other kinds of structure. The primary reason, therefore, for dealing with auxiliaries is that in certain kinds of sentences they lead us on to structures that deviate in an interesting way from the "normal" patterns we have seen thus far. Corresponding to each of (17a–d) is a sentence that we may think of as its question "counterpart." This question differs from the corresponding nonquestion only in that the first auxiliary precedes the subject NP:

(19) a. HAS the cat _____ slept?

b. COULD a man _____ build this house?

c. IS the mouse _____ going down a hole?

d. WILL the cat _____ put the mouse on the mat?

Questions like these are often called "Yes–no questions." As suggested by the gaps and arrows in (19), each Yes–no question is related to its nonquestion counterpart in a very regular fashion: the first auxiliary verb is not in its "normal" position, but appears to the left of the subject NP. (There is a single auxiliary in each of these, as there is in their statement counterparts; but it is clear from examination of pairs like *The mouse* could be *going down a hole*/could *the mouse* _____ be *going down a hole?* that only the *first* auxiliary occurs to the left of the subject.)

By using arrows and gaps suggesting the movement of the first auxiliary to a position to the left of the subject NP in (19), I am implying, of course, that the order SUBJECT + AUXILIARY is in some sense normal, and that when the first of the auxiliaries appears before the subject in questions, this is a "deviation" from the normal order. There are good reasons for thinking that this is so, but it goes beyond the scope of this discussion to explain in detail why that is so. On a purely intuitive level, it makes sense to think of all the auxiliary verbs as generated under the AUX node in the phrase structure rules, whether in statements or in questions, and then letting the first auxiliary "migrate" to the beginning of each sentence.

Rather than justifying this analysis, I will point out briefly some of the implications it would have for a theory of what kinds of structures may occur in human language. Instead of supposing that all human language could be represented in the mind by devices which were complex elaborations of the set of rules in (10), in other words, phrase structure grammars of some kind, we would be introducing a new kind of mechanism: a *movement rule*.

A sentence like (17a), *The cat has slept*, would be generated directly by phrase structure rules like those of (10). But its question counterpart, (19a), *Has the cat* _____ *slept*, would be defined in two steps. First, the phrase structure rules would yield a "normal" sentence, with the *has* in the position it occupies in (17a), and then this word would be moved to its eventual position at the front of the sentence. If we add a movement rule like this to our model of how English speakers analyze English sentences, we are immediately suggesting that humans pos-

314 / Syntax and Language Processing

sess in principle the ability to develop languages whose structure can be characterized by means of movement rules operating on the forms that the phrase structure grammar yields. If we want to understand how humans learn language, it is likely to be very important whether we are justified in supposing that there are such rules in the internalized grammars of human languages—and indeed this is a very important research question in theoretical syntax at the present time.

The "movement" of the first auxiliary to the beginning of the sentence, which is so characteristic of English questions of all kinds (and occurs in a few other very minor constructions such as, "Boy, *can he* drink beer!"), is actually very rare in other languages. There is probably no other language in which questions are marked by this auxiliary inversion rule—although the Germanic languages generally have the verb in initial position in Yes–no questions, making them look superficially very much like (19a–d). It would not do to introduce a new kind of device based on evidence drawn from such an apparently rare phenomenon. We will need to turn to other constructions for more compelling evidence. As we do so, we will build on this discussion of the structure of English Yes–no questions, since the English structures we will look at next also involve the auxiliary movement that we have examined here.

More Deviance: Wh-Movement

In addition to questions calling for "Yes" or "No" as an answer, there are questions that ask for more information; they are often called *information questions*. The following simple examples are quite typical:

> (20) a. Which cake *can* you make?
>   b. What *has* Joe put on the table?
>   c. Whose mouse *is* the boy looking for?

Like the examples of Yes–no questions given earlier, each of these sentences exhibits subject–auxiliary inversion—the auxiliary appears before the subject. This is perhaps easiest to see if we compare them to similar sentences that are statements. Here are some examples:

> (21) a. You *can* make this cake.
>   b. Joe *has* put the book on the table.
>   c. The boy *is* looking for his mouse.

In (20a) we find the sequence *can you* ("Which cake *can you* make?"); in the corresponding statement (21a), we find *you can* ("*You can* make this cake.") Similarly, we find *has Joe* in question (20b), but *Joe has* in the statement, (21b). In the third pair, we find *is the boy* in the question, but *the boy is* in the statement.

However, the really interesting property of these information questions is not that they exhibit the rather rare, perhaps uniquely English, phenomenon of auxiliary fronting, but that they begin with a phrase containing a question word—which does not correspond in any obvious fashion to anything at the beginning of their nonquestion counterparts. This characteristic of all the sentences of (20) allows us to investigate another kind of "movement" that is remarkably widespread in the languages of the world: the movement of a phrase containing a special question word to the very front of the sentence. In the following representation of (20) it is this "*Wh*-phrase," as it is often called, that has been italicized—and for clarity placed in brackets.

(20′) a. [*Which cake*] can you make _____ ?

     b. [*What*] has Joe put _____ on the table?

     c. [*Whose mouse*] is the boy looking for _____ ?

This representation of the sentences of (20) not only isolates the *Wh*-phrase for emphasis, but indicates by means of an arrow and a blank "gap" where that *Wh*-phrase originated. In these examples, this gap has been placed in the position that would be occupied by an ordinary NP in a corresponding statement. Compare the verb phrases of (20a) and (21a):

(22) a. [$_{VP}$ make _____]
     b. [$_{VP}$ make [$_{NP}$ *this cake*]]

What justification is there for representing question (20a) in this way? Specifically, why must we think of the *Wh*-phrase as linked to that position in the VP which in the statement (21a) contains the NP *this cake*? Why suppose there is a rule that in some sense "moves" it from that position?

Intuitively, it seems clear that *which cake* in (20a) is the object of *make*, just as *this cake* is in (21a). There is, in each case, a statement or question about some cake that can be made. But this is not a very clear argument for the representation given above. In fact there are clearer indications that the *Wh*-phrase must be regarded as in some sense a part of the VP even though it is not actually inside that phrase in any of these questions. Recall how the verb of a sentence determines what can appear in the VP. Examples (6)–(8) are relevant: whereas we can say *The cat slept*, we cannot say **The cat slept the milk*; and whereas we can say *A man built this house*, **A man built* is not acceptable. Now look again at the VPs of (20). This time we will represent them as if they had no gap at all corresponding to the *Wh*-phrase:

(20″) a. Which cake can you [vp make]?
   b. What has Joe [vp put on the table]?
   c. Whose mouse is the boy [vp looking for]?

If we treat each of these as a complete VP, as suggested by this last set of representations, then the VPs should be able to occur independently, forming acceptable sentences when they follow NP subjects. But this is simply not so, as illustrated by the following ungrammatical sentences:

(23) a. *You [vp made].
   b. *Joe [vp put on the table].
   c. *The boy [vp looked for].

If we try to use just the words *made, put on the table*, or *looked for* in an independent sentence without an initial *Wh*-phrase, the result is ungrammatical. This is quite comparable to ungrammatical examples like (7) and (8). It seems clear that in (20b), the verb phrase is not *put on the table*, but *put [what] on the table*, and that the word *what* is really acting as the NP object of *put*. Similarly for the other two examples. So the "real" structure of (20a) is *You can make [which cake]*. *Wh*-phrases, at least the ones we are considering, are simply special kinds of NPs, which generally have to appear at the front of the sentence rather than in their "normal" position (for example, as part of the VP).

One way of analyzing such sentences follows closely the lines suggested by the representation in (20′): the normal phrase structure rules (i.e., (10)) derive *Wh*-questions as if they were ordinary statements, with the *Wh*-phrase in the position it would occupy if it were an ordinary NP. In each of our examples it would be the object of the verb, inside the VP in the position indicated by the blank in (20′). Then a rule of *Wh-movement* moves the phrase to the front of the sentence, as suggested by the arrows in those examples. For example, *Which cake can you make* starts out as something like *You can make which cake* and then the phrase *which cake* moves to the front, as in (20′)—and the auxiliary moves, too. Since *Wh*-movement and other, similar cases of movement (where a phrase eventually appears some distance away from its original site as defined by the phrase structure rules and the requirements of the verbs, etc. of the language) are very common in the languages of the world, we must suppose that children are prepared to analyze language systems not only in terms of a phrase structure grammar (i.e. rules like those in (10)), but also in part through devices which have the effect of permitting such movement. So we must add movement rules to phrase structure rules when considering the devices available to the human language learner; a grammar developed by a child will contain both kinds of rules.

Constraints on Movement

Sentences that deviate from the unmarked structure of a subject NP followed by a VP because certain phrases have been moved to other positions could present a considerable challenge to young learners if they had to be learned entirely by trial and error, and if the moved phrase could in principle appear anywhere in a sentence rather than, for example, being constrained to appear only at the very beginning. Children learning English, or any of the many other languages with similar constructions, would somehow have to discover that a *Wh*-phrase belongs in its "real" position in the sentence—and must be interpreted as if it still remained there. Yet there is no audible sign of the gap in (20′); children simply have to use their knowledge of the language as a whole (and in particular of the basic sentence structures including the properties of verbs and what complements they permit or require) in order to determine where a gap exists. So far this might not seem too great a feat. The *Wh*-phrase corresponds to one or another of the places where an NP could appear: the subject of the sentence, or somewhere inside the VP. That is all learners need to discover. In one sense, this is perfectly true. However, note that in English, and in many other languages, it is possible for the gap to be virtually any distance away from the *Wh*-phrase.

This can easily come about because sentences can function as parts of other sentences—which can in turn be parts of other sentences. Look at the following example:

(24) a. Sam believes [$_{S1}$ (that) Bill can ride that horse].

The verb *believe* can appear with an ordinary NP object, as in *Sam believes* [*the child*], but it can also appear with a whole sentence as its object, as in (24a). There, the sentence *Bill can ride the horse* is the object of *believe*. (In [24a] the word *that* may precede the embedded sentence, but it need not. It is shown in parentheses to suggest this. In subsequent examples *that* will often be omitted. This makes the sentences sound more natural to me, although some speakers of English may prefer to put it back in.)

Now we can repeat the process of embedding, setting (24a) within another sentence as the object of yet another verb like *believe*. Let us use *think* in this case:

(24) b. Sue will think [$_{S2}$ that Sam believes
[$_{S1}$ that Bill can ride that horse]].

Now look at what happens when we take these complex sentences and replace one of the NPs with a gap, inserting a suitable *Wh*-phrase at the very beginning of the whole sentence:

(25) a. *Which horse* will Sue think [$_{S2}$ that Sam believes [$_{S1}$ Bill can
ride _____]]?
b. *Which girl* will Sue think [$_{S2}$ that Sam believes [$_{S1}$ _____
can ride that horse]]?

Having found some examples where *Wh*-phrases are associated with gaps inside sentences that are themselves embedded inside larger sentences, let us confirm that the process of embedding sentences can go on indefinitely. The following example consists of (24b) embedded as the object of the verb *hope*:

c. Your friend hopes [$_{S3}$ that Sue will think
[$_{S2}$ that Sam believes
[$_{S1}$ Bill can ride that horse]]].

We could go on: *I deny that my friend hopes that Sue will think that Sam believes that Bill can ride that horse.*
We can now try examples in which the *Wh*-phrase right at the beginning of the whole sentence is associated with a gap far down inside a deeply embedded sentence. Some of these examples may sound unnatural to you; if so, try to construct some long, complex sentences with a gap somewhere and a suitable *Wh*-phrase at the beginning. You will soon find many that are perfectly fine. (To make it easier to read the examples that follow, the sentence boundaries have not been marked. It would be a useful exercise to try to break them up into the smaller sentences out of which they are formed.)

(26) a. Which pen do you think it irritated Sam that his sister had
used _____ ?
b. Who do you think the teacher had told Mary that she believed Sam thought he had seen _____ ?
c. Which book did Andy say he had told Sue that Bill had
put _____ on the table?

These questions, and the earlier examples, are all formed in the same way; it is as if an NP containing a *Wh*-word had been taken from its original position, where it was either the subject of a sentence (as in [25b]) or in some position inside the VP, and moved to the very beginning of the whole sentence.

The ability of a *Wh*-phrase to appear far away from the position in the sentence it would occupy if it were an ordinary NP results in deviations from the unmarked NP AUX VP structure imposed by the phrase structure rules of (10) (as modified by the addition of AUX). One NP is not overtly present in its normal place, but appears at the beginning of some sentence, not necessarily even the one that it "really" belongs in.

It should be clear that children learning the language would be helped immensely in developing such sentences if they did not have to learn from scratch about *Wh*-movement—and better yet if there were only certain kinds of movement that could occur. There is reason to believe that children start out with both advantages: the potential for *Wh*-movement is one of the devices learners take for granted, and there are very strict constraints on how phrases can be moved around, which also seem to be limitations on the structure of human language that learners can take for granted. These, at any rate, are the tentative results of recent work.

We will now take a brief look at some of the limitations that appear to be placed on how a phrase can be moved. It is striking that the moved *Wh*-phrase always ends up at the edge of a sentence. This is true not only in English but also in other languages, many quite unrelated to English. It would be strange if all languages had developed this constraint by chance, and there is every reason to believe that it results instead from some essential property of the human mind. This is even more true of some of the other constraints, which although found in language after language, are very complex and, as we shall see, may even be in principle unlearnable.

Most of the other constraints on movement can be usefully thought of as limitations on the kinds of relations that can hold between a *Wh*-phrase and its gap, or *trace*. For example, although, as we have seen, a *wh*-trace (i.e., a gap) can occur in a deeply embedded sentence, this is impossible if that gap is inside a relative clause. A relative clause is a sentence-like constituent occurring inside an NP, playing a role within that NP. For example, the NP *the man who was reading the book* contains the relative clause *who was reading the book*. This relative clause is closely related to the sentence *He was reading the book*. In (27a) we have a well-formed relative clause (in square brackets) that is part of the subject NP; in (27b) we see the ungrammatical result of trying to extract a *Wh*-phrase from the relative clause:

(27) a.   {The man [*who is reading the book*]} will fall asleep.
     b.   *[*Which book*] will {the man who is reading _____} fall asleep?

In (27b) the *Wh*-phrase is meant to be the object of the verb *read*, just as *the book* is in (27a), as is suggested by the gap in that second example.

This is not an isolated case of an ungrammatical sentence resulting when the *Wh*-trace is inside a relative clause. Any sentence comparable in relevant ways to (27b) will be ungrammatical. Now notice a very important implication of this fact. Children cannot learn that such forms are ungrammatical by listening to the language around them, for English speakers simply do not use these forms. There is no way, short of asking their parents, in which children can discover that such forms fail to occur because they are ungrammatical. Yet it is perfectly clear to all of us that these forms are totally ungrammatical. And children of any age have no tendency to produce such forms as mistakes. It is quite impossible that every child learning English is successfully taught that such forms are not to be used; so the only possible explanation of the fact that we all feel them to be ungrammatical is that they are excluded by some part of the inborn mechanism with which we learn language. They reflect something quite deep, not learned but innate.

As a matter of fact, the position is a little more complicated, and even more interesting. Although many languages exclude forms like (27b), there are other languages that form questions, for example, without using *Wh*-movement, or that form relative clauses in some other way, in which such questions as (27b) are perfectly well formed. Thus, although as native speakers of English we might be tempted to think that such questions simply make no sense, they not only make sense but are perfectly normal in languages that use slightly different constructions to form either questions or relative clauses. They seem to be excluded from English and similar languages specifically because of the relationship between the *Wh*-phrase and its trace—or gap: the trace may not be inside a relative clause (of a particular kind) while the *Wh*-phrase is outside.

Constraints on Dependency

Recent research suggests that in general when two points in structure are linked to each other as the *Wh*-phrase is linked to its trace, the two may not stand in certain relationships. We have dealt in some detail with just one case in which a pair of points in structure are linked, and in which, apparently as a result, certain potential sentences are excluded from the language and felt to be ungrammatical by native speakers simply because in those sentences certain "impossible" structural relationships would hold between those two points. (In the present case, the trace of a *Wh*-phrase would have been inside a relative clause, while the *Wh*-phrase itself would have been outside the clause.)

There are many other constructions in which two items are linked in some way, and in many instances these constructions are subject to constraints bearing some similarity to the one that excludes *Wh*-questions such as (27b). Some of these constructions, like *Wh*-movement, seem to break up the basic sentence structure—at least on the surface— since one of the terms of the relationship (the trace in this instance) is not obviously present at all. Others are constructions in which two overtly occurring phrases are linked. In all these cases, one of the terms of the relation is dependent on the other, getting its meaning, so to speak, with the help of that other phrase. When, as in the case of *Wh*-movement, one of the terms is at least superficially not there at all, it is clear that this term (the trace) depends for meaning on the other term (the *Wh*-phrase). In most of the other examples which follow, it should be obvious which term is dependent on the other. (There are likely to be many aspects of these examples that will remain unclear. They are not meant to be studied in detail, but to provide an impression of the kinds of dependency that exist between terms.)

(28) a. *The trainer* said that *he* was sick.
   b. *Some small children* hurt *each other*.
   c. *Jane* hurt *herself*.
   d. *The elephants* wanted _____ to dance.
      [Compare: The elephants wanted *Mary* to dance.]
   e. *The book* that [I put _____ on the table] fell down.

The first example involves an ordinary definite personal *pronoun*, *he*; the second a *reciprocal, each other*; the third a *reflexive, herself*. In the fourth example, there is simply a gap, where an ordinary NP like *Mary* could otherwise occur, as the subject of an infinitive; and in the fifth example, a relative clause, there is also a gap, as suggested by its similarity to earlier examples involving *Wh*-movement—which may well be involved in the formation of English relative clauses.

One property that these examples have in common is that the dependent term occurs "lower down" in structure than the phrase on which it depends. That is to say if we reverse, in (28a), the pronoun and the phrase that is its *antecedent* (*the trainer*) to give *He said that the trainer was sick*, the phrase *the trainer* becomes the subject of the lower sentence (*the trainer was sick*), and *he* can no longer refer to the trainer, as it can in (28a).

Reflexives are even more constrained than ordinary pronouns. Not only is it impossible to say *Herself hurt Jane*, but we cannot substitute a reflexive for the pronoun *he* in the first sentence of (28): *The trainer said that himself was sick*. This leads to the observation that there is a further constraint on ordinary pronouns like *he*. A sentence like *Jane hurt her* is perfectly grammatical, but does not mean the same as (28c):

in *Jane hurt her, her* cannot refer to Jane. Whatever constraint operates in this case does not actually exclude the sentence in question, but simply excludes one particular interpretation of the pronoun.

Observations similar to these hold true for a wide variety of languages. Not that every language would exclude the equivalent of *The trainer said that* himself *was sick*. There is variation in this respect from language to language. However, everything that we know thus far suggests that even though languages can vary slightly in regard to the structural relationships that may hold between dependent terms and their antecedents, this variation itself is highly constrained: the permitted relationships between dependent terms and their antecedents may vary only a little, and along clearly defined parameters. Like the constraints on the relation between a *Wh*-phrase and its trace, constraints such as those limiting where a reflexive and its antecedent may appear relative to each other are very unlikely to have been learned— or indeed to be learnable in the usual sense. They, too, seem to hold out great promise as a means of gaining insight into what is actually involved in learning a language—and hence into what it means to be a member of the only species endowed with mechanisms that make this possible. From the few examples discussed in the last two sections, it may be clear that these mechanisms severely limit what language learners need to consider, thereby making it much easier to learn a language. If, for example, children "know" that the only place they need look for *Wh*-phrases is at the beginning of a sentence, and that a *Wh*-trace will never be found inside a relative clause, then that immediately narrows down what they have to learn about the language they happen to hear spoken around them.

One last question might occur to you: why should human language be so constrained with respect to the relationship between a dependent term and its antecedent? A little thought should now enable you to arrive at what seems the most likely answer: If there were no constraints on what could serve as a human language, one of the most difficult tasks for language learners would be discovering which terms could link together. Consider how totally baffling it would be if there could be any number of *Wh*-phrases in a complex sentence, each of them appearing anywhere at all, and each linked to an inaudible gap (or gaps) occurring anywhere else. Communication of the sort we are attempting right now would be impossible, and language would never have developed.

We may therefore with some confidence add constraints of various sorts to our model of the devices humans have available in learning a language. Children will develop a phrase structure grammar and some set of movement rules that together will define the language they acquire—and these rules will apply in conformity with various constraints. We have dealt with the phrase structure rules in some detail.

These, together with the properties of individual verbs (and other words), define the basic patterns of the language. Movement rules and constraints on dependency—including dependencies in the structures that result from movement—we have touched on only briefly. It seems likely, however, that an understanding of the precise nature of movement rules and constraints will throw much light on how humans develop language. They are the subject of much contemporary research in the field of linguistics.

FOR DISCUSSION AND REVIEW

1. Draw trees like those given in (9a–d) for the following sentences. As far as possible, use the same symbols as those used in the example trees (i.e., *P, N, NP, VP, Adj,* and so on), but where you believe that a word does not fall into any of the classes for which symbols have already been given, feel free to invent new ones.

    a. Two beetles crawled over a little leaf.
    b. I can see several old men on the docks.
    c. The goats may eat your straw hat.
    d. Jane drove the new tractor into the barn.
    e. Someone may be asking for assistance.

2.a. Try to give detailed trees for the two interpretations discussed in the text for the string *I watched the prisoner from the tower.* That is, turn the marked sentences (2a and 2b) into proper tree representations. Your two trees should reflect the crucial differences between the two readings that are discussed in the text. (How should you represent *the prisoner from the tower* in (2a)?)

    b. Do the rules given in (10) provide for trees like these you have constructed? If not, how do the rules need to be modified in order to do so? (Concentrate on [2a] and consider rule [10d], which draws NP trees.)

3. Your college library has introductory grammar texts for many languages, as do instructors in foreign-language departments. Look at the grammar of a language unfamiliar to you, preferably one very different from English. Where does the verb occur in statements? (At the end? At the beginning?) What is the structure of the NP? (Where does the N come, the Adj, and so on?) Try to formulate simple phrase structure rules for parts of the language you choose, along the lines of (10a–d) in the text, but with the symbols in the right place to draw appropriate trees for sentences in the language you have chosen. Draw a few trees for this language. Discuss problems that arise in deciding what the rules and trees should be like, and anything about language structure that this attempt has taught you.

4. Consider how information questions are formed in some language with which you are somewhat familiar. Use grammar books if necessary to supplement your knowledge, or ask a speaker of the language to help you find examples of these structures in it. Does the language use *Wh-*

movement (as English does) for forming these questions? Give detailed arguments for or against your conclusion. (You will have to consider both the form of the questions and the form of ordinary statements in the language.)

5. Consider how far the development of language in children results from the imitation of what they hear and how far it results from factors that are purely internal to the children. Be as specific as possible in your discussion.

6. Summarize the structure of the grammar that, according to Professor Heny, English-speaking children must have internalized as a representation of their language. What kinds of "rules" does this grammar contain? Comment on aspects of sentence structure that seem to have been left out of this selection and that would need to be added for a complete account.

3/What Is A Language?

NEIL SMITH AND DEIRDRE WILSON

In the following selection, Neil Smith and Deirdre Wilson of University College, London, focus on one of the fundamental ideas of contemporary linguistics—that of language as a rule-governed system. To claim that a language is rule-governed is also to claim that it can be described in terms of a grammar. Thus, the grammar of a language is a description of the rules of the language, rules of a kind that human beings are innately disposed to learn. These rules distinguish grammatical from ungrammatical sentences, and provide explicit descriptions of grammatical sentences, including their meaning and pronunciation. Although every individual has his or her unique grammar, all grammars have some things in common because of genetic constraints on the kinds of grammars, and hence languages, that human beings can learn.

At different times, different features of language have struck people as particularly significant, typical or worthy of attention. Any system as complex as a human language is bound to lend itself to a variety of independent approaches. For example, languages are used to communicate; one obvious line of research would be to compare human languages with other systems of communication, whether human or not: gestures, railway signals, traffic lights, or the languages of ants and bees. Languages are also used by social groups; another line of research would be to compare languages with other social systems, whether communicative or not: economic, political or religious, for example. Again, languages change through time: comparison of languages with other evolutionary systems, organic and inorganic, might also be pursued. While all of these approaches have undoubted appeal, there is an obvious logical point to be made: one must be able to describe a language, at least in part, before going on to compare it with other systems.

It seems to us that there is no way of describing or defining a given language without invoking the notion of a linguistic rule. If this is true, it is clearly important, since by investigating the nature and variety of linguistic rules we may be able to provide quite detailed evidence about points of comparison between human languages and other systems. It is for this reason that we have chosen [first] to . . . justify the claim that a language is definable in terms of a set of rules, arguing against some alternative conceptions of language, and examining the nature and status of linguistic rules.

Linguistic Rules

Within modern linguistic theory, to claim that a language is rule-governed is to claim that it can be described in terms of a grammar. A grammar is conceived of as a set of rules which have two main tasks. They separate grammatical from ungrammatical sentences, thus making explicit claims about what is "in the language" and what is not. They also provide a description of each of the grammatical sentences, stating how it should be pronounced and what it means. In other words, linguistic rules are not just the isolated and scattered maxims we memorized at school ("Prepositions are things you shouldn't end sentences with"); they combine with each other to form a system—a grammar—which gives an explicit and exhaustive description of every sentence which goes to make up a language. . . . We shall use "grammar" to mean a set of rules with this dual function.

It is easy to see that speakers of a language often behave as if their language were rule-governed. Fluent speakers may nonetheless make mistakes in speaking, and when they do, they have no hesitation in correcting themselves. Utterances like (1) and (2), for example, are commonplace:

(1) The thought of those poor children were really . . . *was* really . . . bothering me.
(2) Even though they told me to, I didn't sit down and be quiet . . . *was* quiet . . . I mean I didn't sit down and I wasn't quiet.

Such examples give clear evidence that speakers have some means of distinguishing grammatical from ungrammatical sentences, and are prepared to correct their mistakes even when no threat to communication is involved.

It is also possible for a speaker to feel that others around him are making mistakes—although his willingness to correct them will, in many cases, be tempered by considerations of politeness at least. An English speaker who hears (3), for example, will probably agree with the message it conveys, regardless of whether he interprets it as (4a) or (4b):

(3) Ze pound are worthless.
(4) a. The pound is worthless.
    b. The pound is worth less.

However, he will simultaneously recognize that the pronunciation of *the* is incorrect, and that *are* should have been *is*. In other words, he knows not just *that* a mistake has been made, but also *what* the mistake is.

When speakers of two different dialects of English meet, each is likely to feel that the other is making some mistakes. Readiness to correct what sounds like a mistake is affected here, not just by considerations of politeness, but also by the fact that certain dialects are generally considered superior to others, so that speakers of standard dialects will be more likely to correct those of nonstandard dialects than vice versa. In any case, the speaker of standard British English who hears (5a) and (5b) is likely to feel that they are incorrect:

(5) a. Mr Zed's done gone mental.
    b. Lord God, I done made a mess.

In most cases, he could also supply the standard equivalents (6a) and (6b):

(6) a. Mr Zed has gone mental (mad).
    b. Lord God, I've made a mess.

Similarly, speakers of the dialect which permits (5a) and (5b) would regard (6a) and (6b) as needing some correction. This case seems to show, not just that speakers of a language possess a set of rules, but that not all speakers of a language possess the same set of rules. In fact, as we shall show in the next section, it is probably quite fair to say that no two speakers of a language possess exactly the same set of rules: in other words, the rules which adequately describe a language are not the simple, prescriptive maxims of the classroom, but a far more complex and subtle set of constructs.

The speaker who is willing to correct himself and others gives evidence that there is, for him, a right and a wrong way of saying things. However, it does not necessarily follow that in making these corrections he is applying a set of linguistic rules. He might, for example, be following a set of linguistic conventions, or habits, or customs, which he dislikes seeing disrupted. In claiming that a language is rule-governed, we are also claiming that languages are not definable in terms of linguistic habits, conventions or customs; to see why, it is necessary to look a little more closely at what linguistic rules, embodied in grammars, actually do.

So far, we may have seemed to imply that a grammar simply provides a means of registering and correcting mistakes. This copy-editing function is an important one; however, grammars are also concerned with the description of sentences which contain no mistakes at all. As mentioned earlier, a grammar must provide a means of associating each sentence of a language with its correct pronunciation and meaning. Now speakers of a language are capable of pronouncing and understanding sentences which they have never heard before. For example, many readers of this book will be encountering at least one of the following for the first time:

(7) a. I can see a robin pecking around the ashes of the bonfire.
    b. Would you let us have poached egg for elevenses* please, Mummy?
    c. If you tell that joke again I shall divorce you.

However, none of these sentences is likely to present the slightest difficulty of understanding. It follows that one's ability to understand a sentence does not depend on custom, convention or habit, all of which would imply that repeated encounters with a sentence would be necessary before its correct interpretation could be established. Neither the ability to recognize a sentence as grammatical, nor the ability to produce or understand it, seems to depend on prior encounters in this way.

Conventions are social constructs: it takes at least two people to establish and operate a system of conventions. Rule-systems, on the other hand, could easily be constructed and operated by a single individual. There exist two main types of case where single individuals do seem to operate their own private linguistic rules: the case of children learning their first language, and the case of adults with idiosyncratic speech patterns. Both provide arguments against linguistic conventions, and in favor of linguistic rules.

Children learning their first language seem to construct rules for themselves—but they often get them wrong: they produce utterances which are ungrammatical from the adult point of view. The sentences in (8), produced by a three-year-old, are examples; the adult equivalent is given on the right:

(8) a. What that was? [What was that?]
    b. Where it is? [Where is it?]
    c. Where Amahl can write?[1] [Where can Amahl write?]

That many children pass through a similar phase is not surprising, since they will have heard adult sequences exactly parallel to their own, as in (9), for example:

(9) a. I don't know *what that was.*

* Editor's note: *Elevenses* is a British term for a late morning breakfast or snack.
[1] *Amahl* is the name of the child speaking.

    b. Tell me *where it is.*

    c. I think that is *where Amahl can write.*

However, the fact remains that the child who says one of the sentences in (8) is using a different grammatical rule from those of the adults around him, and which he seems to have made up for himself.

    Another case where the child's system may differ from the adult's is when the child has learned a linguistic rule, but has not yet learned that it has exceptions. On the analogy of (10), for example, children regularly produce forms such as those in (11):

(10) a. I talked, he danced, she moved, they waited, etc.

     b. One car, two cars; an elephant, lots of elephants, etc.

(11) a. I comed, John runned, they singed, she teached me, etc.

     b. Two sheeps, lots of tooths, some mouses, etc.

In other words, the child has overgeneralized the rules for regular past-tense and plural formation to cases where in the adult system they do not apply. This again indicates that the child makes up rules of his own, which only he actually follows.

    The number of verbs with an irregular past tense, and of nouns with exceptional plurals, is rather small: the resulting overgeneralizations are hardly surprising. However, children seem able to construct generalizations, make up rules, on the basis of extremely limited data. For example, *in newen times* for *nowadays* has been found on the sole analogy of *in olden times,* and *twoth* and *threeth,* with the sense of *second* and *third,* have been recorded from a child who could only count up to four. Moreover, examples of this kind are not limited to word-formation. On the analogy of such regular adult examples as (12), children will frequently supply the missing fourth item in (13):

(12) a. Pick the book up.

     b. Pick it up.

     c. Pick up the book.

(13)   Pick up it.

(13) is, of course, ungrammatical from the adult point of view, and the child is most unlikely ever to have heard it. Other examples of the creative use of language by children provide further evidence of their ability to control regularities: the following pairs were all taken from children aged between two and three:

(14) a. Pick me up. (and when the adult obliges)

     b. Pick me down.

(15) a. Plug the light in.

     b. Plug the light out.
(16) a. Amahl wakened up. (raising his head from the pillow)
     b. Amahl wakened down again. (putting his head back on
        the pillow)

Perhaps the clearest example, and the one most frequently commented on, is provided by the two-year-old who on seeing his uncle for the first time asked his mother:

(17) *What's that, Mummy?*,

using *what* as a cover term for both humans and things. Two days later he was addressing his uncle as "Mummy."

    As a last example of how children construct rules for themselves, consider the following solution to the problem of how to pronounce long words with an unstressed initial syllable, taken by one three-year-old. Observing that many such words were complex, consisting of a prefix *re-* and a stem, he generalized this pattern to all of them, with the result that while *recorder* and *remember*, for instance, were pronounced correctly, the following forms—which he clearly could not have imitated from those around him—also occurred:

(18) attack—pronounced *retack*
      disturb—pronounced *resterve*
      elastic—pronounced *relastic*
      enjoy—pronounced *rejoy*
      guitar—pronounced *retar*
      conductor—pronounced *reductor*, etc.

On this occasion, as on many others, the child's hypothesis is wildly out, but the regularity with which the forms appear shows that he is constructing rules. That they are the wrong ones merely makes it more obvious that linguistic rules are not always shared rules, and that the child can operate a rule-system which diverges markedly from the systems of those around him.

    Divergencies between rule-systems are not just found in the case of children who are still learning their language. Perfectly fluent adults may find idiosyncrasies in their own speech. The most common of these are in pronunciation and vocabulary. It seems clear that no two adults possess exactly the same set of vocabulary items, pronounced in exactly the same way. This is true of syntactic rules too. A very few readers may find that they regularly produce sentences like (19b), on the analogy of (19a) (as does one of the authors):

(19) a. He is happy, isn't he?
     b. I am happy, amn't I?

Others will find themselves reluctant to produce (19c), on the same analogy:

(19) c. He may leave, mayn't he?

Similar differences of opinion may arise over sentences like the following:

(20) a. What did you go out and do?
  b. What did you go out without doing?
  c. What did you go out before doing?
  d. What did you go out before you did?

Most people will find at least one of these sentences ungrammatical, but there may be disagreement about just how many should be rejected. These differences in rule systems do not appear to be geographically based, but they are nonetheless real. They indicate that languages are not entirely social constructs, possessed in the same form by all members of a social group, but that it is perfectly possible for an individual to possess a set of rules that he shares in its entirety with no one else.

A more extreme instance of adult idiosyncrasy is seen in the speech of people who have had a stroke, or have otherwise suffered damage to the brain, with resultant speech loss or aphasia. In fact the best defining criterion of aphasia is that the rules normally characteristic of speech have broken down, leading the patient to produce utterances which, depending on the severity of his case and the number and type of rules involved, may be complete nonsense (jargon), or merely inappropriate, e.g.:

(21) a. I was working with the shop is in the other room, dear.
  b. Have you got a match, I can't light my guitar. [= cigar]

In the case of (21b), we can recognize what should have been said, but in the case of (21a) it is clear that something has gone very seriously awry in the set of rules characterizing the linguistic system of the speaker.

What we have tried to show in this section is that a language is best described in terms of a grammar, or system of rules. For each speaker, there is a right and a wrong way of constructing and understanding sentences. This cannot be explained solely in terms of habit or custom, because of the case of novel utterances, which are produced and understood without having been heard before. It cannot be explained solely in terms of convention or social agreement, because each speaker has certain methods of construction and understanding which he shares with no one else. For the same reason, it cannot be seen as a prescriptive system, handed down by authority and imposed on each speaker from the outside. The only unitary way of describing the linguistic system of a speaker is to see it as governed by a set of rules which he may share, in part, with other speakers, but which he must ultimately have constructed for himself. We turn now to a closer examination of the nature and status of such rules.

The Psychological Reality of Rules

We have so far been assuming that speakers of a language actually know the grammars which they use in producing and understanding sentences, correcting mistakes, and so on. This assumption that speakers know grammars—usually expressed as a claim that grammars are *psychologically real*—pervades the whole of modern linguistic theory. Learning a language, as we have already seen, is equated with learning a grammar; knowing a language is equated with knowing a grammar. Linguistic differences between speakers are analysed as differences in their grammars. Linguistic change is analysed as the alteration of grammars through time. And a language itself is defined as the set of sentences described by a given grammar. Most of these definitions rest on the assumption that speakers actually know the grammar which describes their language: without this assumption, the postulation of grammars would contribute nothing to explaining linguistic behavior.

Clearly, the knowledge that speakers have of their own grammars is not conscious knowledge. This is obvious enough in the case of adults, but even more so in the case of children, who are normally completely unaware of the way in which they form relative clauses, for example, or the conditions under which they would use the word *come* rather than *go*. The linguistic knowledge that speakers have is unfortunately unconscious knowledge: the job of the linguist is to attempt an explicit, conscious formulation of the grammatical rules that speakers know. Linguistics conceived of this way is concerned with one aspect of the human mind and is therefore correctly classed as a branch of psychology.

Many people—most notably the philosopher Locke—feel unhappy about the idea of unconscious knowledge. These people have difficulty in explaining how speakers are able to produce, understand and form judgments about utterances that they have never heard before. The idea of a grammar which embodies the principles of sentence-formation and interpretation plays a crucial role in explaining how novel utterances are produced, understood and judged grammatical or ungrammatical. Someone who understands the principles of sentence-formation will be able to apply them to any sentence at all—even one he has never heard before. Someone who has no knowledge of such principles should not be able—as humans clearly are—to deal with utterances in this way. Moreover, those who believe that there is no such thing as unconscious knowledge have difficulty in explaining what goes on when an act of memory is performed. Memory is the classic case of unconscious knowledge: to remember something is to bring to consciousness an item of unconscious, stored knowledge. Thus it seems that, however repugnant the notion of unconscious knowledge may be, it is necessarily involved, both in linguistic and nonlinguistic behavior.

Sometimes those who object to the idea of unconscious knowledge and the notion of linguistic rules argue that novel utterances are produced and understood "by analogy" to sentences one has already heard and understood. This does not, of course, solve the problem of how these latter sentences themselves were produced and understood; but it also raises the much more serious question of how speakers know which is the correct analogy to draw. The following sentences, for example, are both grammatical and similar in meaning:

> (22) a. It is likely that John will leave.
> b. It is probable that John will leave.

By any normal notion of analogy, then, one might expect that (23a) and (23b) should also both be grammatical:

> (23) a. John is likely to leave.
> b. *John is probable to leave.[2]

But of course (23b) is ungrammatical. This raises the whole question of how the *correct* analogy is determined; now the notion of "correct analogy" seems itself to presuppose the existence of a set of rules distinguishing the correct from the incorrect analogies, returning us, by a slightly different route, to the idea of a grammar as a set of rules or principles for correct sentence-formation.

In looking at a set of linguistic facts, it is often fairly easy to find a pattern in them. For example, consider the following set of words from French:

> une balle—tennis ball
> un ballon—football
> une bille—billiard ball
> une boule—croquet ball

---

[2] From now on we shall follow the convention of indicating with an asterisk those sentences which we are judging ungrammatical.

un boulet—cannonball
une boulette—meatball

It is tempting to see the striking regularity of the appearance of *b* and *l* in these words as indication of some fixed relation between the sound and meaning of French words for *ball*. This might in turn have a natural historical explanation: for example if all the words evolved from a common root. However, if the job of the linguist is to reconstruct the grammar which speakers of a language actually know, it will be important for him to discover whether the patterns he finds are psychologically valid for speakers of the language, or whether they are there merely by accident or coincidence. The distinction between rule-governed regularities and fortuitous patterns in the language is usually treated in terms of a distinction between *accidental generalizations* and *significant generalizations*. The significant generalizations are those produced by the operation of rules; the accidental generalizations are the result of chance, or the effects of rules which applied at an earlier stage of the language, or of causes external to the language—anything except the operation of currently valid linguistic rules. Thus the search for linguistic rules has two aspects: first the search for patterns, and second, the rejection of those patterns which are judged accidental.

For example, there is a clear pattern in the occurrence of reflexive pronouns (*myself, herself,* etc.) in (24a–e):

(24) a. We washed ourselves.   *Ourselves washed us.
     b. John hurt himself.   *Himself hurt John.
     c. They surprised them-   *Themselves surprised them.
        selves.
     d. Your argument refutes   *Itself refutes your argument.
        itself.
     e. You behaved yourself.   *Yourself behaved you.

The pattern might be expressed as follows: a reflexive pronoun is the direct object of a verb, and agrees in number, person and gender with the subject noun-phrase of the same verb.[3] The resulting generalization relates subjects, verbs and reflexive direct objects. Is this a significant generalization about English? A little consideration shows that it is an accident of the limited data considered in (24), and that a more adequate formulation would contain no reference to subjects and direct objects. For example, in (25) the reflexive pronoun is not a direct object:

[3] In English, *number* involves a distinction between singular and plural: e.g., *I* versus *we; person* involves a distinction between speaker, hearer and a third party: e.g., *I* versus *you* versus *he;* gender involves a distinction between masculine, feminine and neuter: e.g., *he, she, it.* A *noun-phrase* is a group of words which contains a noun: e.g., *the little man;* the *subject* noun-phrase is normally the one which precedes the verb and the direct object noun-phrase is normally the one which immediately follows it.

(25) I talked to Mary about myself.

In (26), the reflexive pronoun does not agree with the subject:

(26) I talked to Mary about herself.

By considering (24)–(26), one might propose the following alternative generalization: a reflexive pronoun must agree in person, number and gender with *some* preceding noun-phrase. While this generalization is more adequate, consideration of still further data might show that it too was incorrect. For example, in (27a) the reflexive pronoun agrees with a preceding noun-phrase, but the result is ungrammatical; and in (27b) the reflexive pronoun agrees not with a preceding but with a following noun-phrase, and the result is nonetheless grammatical:

(27) a. *John said that himself was leaving.
     b. The story about himself that John told Mary was a pack of lies.

Gradual expansion of the data considered leads to successive rejection of accidental, incorrect generalizations and formulation of successively more adequate ones.

Cases like the above tend to show that it is easier to refute a proposed generalization than to show conclusively that it is correct. By the same token, it is easier to show that a proposed rule of grammar *cannot* be psychologically real than to show that it *must* be. Even when a proposed rule is consistent with all the data so far considered, there may be some further data not yet incorporated into the grammar which would either support it or conclusively refute it. One of the problems in writing grammars is thus to have some clear idea about the possible range of data which would have a bearing on the formulation of linguistic rules. The claim that rules of grammar are psychologically real extends the range of relevant data in important ways. For example, if rules are psychologically real, a consideration of how children learn them becomes relevant to decisions about their final form. If language change can be traced back to change in rules of grammar, then historical change in language may provide vital evidence about the form of rules before and after change. If dialect study is the study of similarity among grammars, then dialect comparison may provide valuable insights into the form of the grammars being compared; and finally if, as we shall argue, all languages are similar in certain respects, then even facts from totally unrelated languages may become relevant to the formulation of rules in a given language. Hence, although the claim that the rules of grammar are psychologically real is a strong, and seemingly unprovable one, it does allow for a considerable expansion in the range and type of data that become relevant to their formulation. . . .

In this section we have tried to show how the assumption that speakers of a language possess psychologically real grammars can be used to explain their command of language. The grammar that a speaker actually possesses will depend, at least in part, on the utterances he has heard in the past—mainly as a child learning his language for the first time. Since each speaker will have heard a different set of utterances, it is not surprising that he comes to possess a slightly different grammar from those of people around him. Strictly speaking, then, we cannot talk of *the* grammar of English, but only of the grammars of individual speakers of English.

However, what is surprising is how much agreement there is among the adult speakers of a language. We were able to assume, for example, that most of our readers would agree with our judgments about the grammaticality of the sentences in (24)–(27). In spite of the diversity of the utterances to which speakers are exposed in learning their language, there seems to be a remarkable similarity in the grammars which result from the learning process. Having emphasized the individual and idiosyncratic aspects of grammar, we now turn to its universal, common features.

Innateness and Universals

The work of Noam Chomsky, which provides one of the most coherent overall frameworks for the study of language ever seen, first came to the attention of the general public because, as part of that framework, he claimed that human beings were innately disposed to learn certain types of language. In other words, the languages that actually exist are the ones that children are predisposed to learn. This claim is supported by two further facts: first, that human languages do exhibit remarkable similarities; second, that children follow remarkably similar routes to learning the languages they learn. Both these facts would be explained on the assumption that children are innately equipped to learn only certain types of language, and that the form their linguistic development takes is genetically determined.

As an example of the similarities among languages, one might cite the two main strategies used in forming relative clauses. Certain languages, like English and French, use relative clause constructions like those italicized below:

(28) a. The man *that I saw* was your brother.
    b. I read the book *that you read.*

(29) a. L'homme *que j'ai vu* était ton frère.
  b. J'ai lu le livre *que tu as lu*.†

Other languages, for example Hebrew, use relative clauses which contain an extra pronoun: translated into English, these sentences would look as follows:

(30) a. *The man *that I saw him* was your brother.
  b. *I read the book *that you read it*.

The fact that most languages tend to adopt one of these two strategies for forming relative clauses is itself quite striking: logically speaking, there are thousands of alternative possibilities. What is even more striking is that languages which have opted for the same strategy as English and French usually turn out, on closer investigation, to possess traces of the Hebrew strategy too. So, for example, though standard French forms its relative clauses as in (29), many regional dialects of French adopt the Hebrew strategy. In these dialects, sentences like the following are perfectly grammatical:

(30) a. L'homme *que je l'ai vu* était ton frère.
  b. J'ai lu le livre *que tu l'as lu*.†

Moreover, although so far as we know there are no regional dialects of English which adopt this same strategy, there are certain complicated (and strictly ungrammatical) sentences of English in which it sounds fairly natural: for example, the following:

(31) a. *That's the kind of answer *that, when you come to think about it, you find you've forgotten it*.
  b. *This is the sort of book *that, having once read it, you feel you want to give it to all your friends*.

To see that these sentences are indeed ungrammatical, one simply has to omit the parenthetical clauses:

(32) a. *That's the kind of answer *that you find you've forgotten it*.
  b. *This is the sort of book *that you feel you want to give it to all your friends*.

Clearly (32a) and (32b) are ungrammatical, and we would not want to

† *Editors' note*: 29a is a translation of 28a, and 29b is a translation of 28b.
  † *Editors' note*: There is an extra pronoun in both of these sentences. Translated, they read:

(30) a. The man that I saw *him* was your brother.
  b. I read the book that you read *it*.

incorporate into English grammar the principles of relative clause formation that they share with (31). However, it seems that this strategy of forming relative clauses by leaving in an extra pronoun is so powerful that even those languages, like English and French, which do not explicitly adopt it, nonetheless show traces of it in certain ways: in regional dialects of French, and in long and complex constructions of English. In other words, relative clauses seem to be formed on broadly similar lines in many entirely unrelated languages. The assumption that human beings are predisposed to construct relative clauses along these lines would explain this striking similarity among languages.

The evidence that all children learning a language pass through similar stages is also compelling. For example, children learning English pass through a stage of producing two-word utterances like the following:

(33) a. Daddy gone.
b. Susie shoe.
c. Mummy play.

In their earliest attempts to form negative sentences, they merely put a *no* or a *not* in front of a sentence:

(34) a. No Daddy come.
b. Not Susie shoe.
c. No Mummy play.

Later, they incorporate the *not* into a sentence before a verb:

(35) a. Daddy not come.
b. Mummy not play.

Finally, the full complexity of the English verbal system is grasped, leading to the correct adult forms:

(36) a. Daddy didn't come; Daddy hasn't come; Daddy won't come.
b. Mummy didn't play; Mummy isn't playing; Mummy mustn't play; etc.

As with many other cases of language learning that we have seen, the sentences in (33)–(35) could not have been directly imitated from anything the children had heard around them, since they are ungrammatical in adult English. The assumption that the child's linguistic development is predetermined from birth to follow certain patterns would provide an attractive account of the clearly parallel linguistic development shown by all normal children.

The assumption that all languages are cut to the same pattern—that is, that there are *linguistic universals*—places an extra constraint on the search for linguistic rules. We have already argued for a distinction between accidental and significant generalizations, the latter being those that are psychologically real. We have also suggested that it is much easier to show that a proposed generalization is *not* significant than to show that it is. If there are linguistic universals, however, the domain of data that can be considered in formulating rules becomes much wider. First, a linguistic theory which incorporated explicit claims about the universal features of language would automatically disallow certain proposed rules as inconsistent with the known properties of language. Second, and more important, it would permit certain facts from other languages to have a bearing on—say—the formulation of the rule of relative clause formation in English, in the following way. Even though more than one possible generalization might be consistent with the facts of English, when relative clauses in other languages were considered, it might turn out that only one possible generalization was consistent with *all* the facts. If such a generalization could be found, and if it was a type permitted or favored by the theory of linguistic universals, then, within the framework we are considering, we would be justified in concluding that it was correct for English too. This is not, of course, to say that languages, like humans, do not have their own linguistic idiosyncrasies. However, it does say that even these idiosyncrasies will fall into universal patterns: languages do not vary without limit. . . .

. . . We have tried to give the following picture of a human language. It is a rule-governed system, definable in terms of a grammar which separates grammatical from ungrammatical sentences, assigning a pronunciation and a meaning to each grammatical sentence. This grammar is, in a minor sense, a construct of the linguist, in that linguists do attempt to construct grammars. However, in a much more important sense it is the construct of the child who has learned it, and the adult who knows it. We have expressed this as the claim that grammars are psychologically real. Each person has his own grammar—which is likely to change through time, and to differ in certain respects from the grammars of other speakers of the language. However, every grammar will have certain things in common with every other grammar, as a result of genetic constraints on the ability of human beings to learn languages. We have expressed this as the claim that all languages have an innately determined and universal structure. . . .

FOR DISCUSSION AND REVIEW

1. According to Smith and Wilson, what are the two functions of the grammar of any language?

2. What arguments support the claim that human language is "rule-governed"? Give some specific examples of such arguments.

3. Drawing on your own experience, list three examples illustrating the fact that "no two speakers of a language possess exactly the same set of rules."

4. Explain the significance of the observation that children "construct rules for themselves" and that, in so doing, they often get the rules "wrong."

5. In claiming that grammars are "psychologically real," linguists are also claiming that "speakers know grammars." In what sense do people "know" their own grammars?

6. Explain the difference between "accidental generalizations" and "significant generalizations." In principle, how can you tell which is which?

7. What kinds of data support Noam Chomsky's argument that human beings are "innately disposed to learn certain types of language"?

4/The Cheshire Cat's Grin: How Do We Plan and Produce Speech?

JEAN AITCHISON

In the following chapter from her book The Articulate Mammal, *Jean Aitchison addresses the question of how people plan and produce speech. It is clear even to a casual observer that, when speakers start to say something, they usually have not fully planned the utterance that follows. They must, then, be planning what to say next while they are already saying something else. Thus, speech production is obviously a complicated process. It is also a process that is not fully understood. In this selection, Aitchison describes various ways of investigating how people plan and produce speech, and suggests a possible model for speech production. This model, which is based in part on a rhythmic principle, involves a word-retrieval process that operates in several stages and that includes a sequential monitoring device.*

"I wish you wouldn't keep appearing and vanishing so suddenly," said Alice. "You make one quite giddy."

"All right," said the Cat; and this time it vanished quite slowly, beginning with the end of the tail, and ending with the grin, which remained some time after the rest of it had gone.

"Well! I've often seen a cat without a grin," thought Alice; "but a grin without a cat! It's the most curious thing I ever saw in all my life!"

LEWIS CARROLL
Alice in Wonderland

. . . **I**t is tantalizingly difficult to observe how anyone actually plans and produces speech. It is equally hard to devise experiments to test it. When somebody utters a sentence, we have very little idea how long it actually took to plan it, and what processes were involved. Consequently, we shall be very tentative over any conclusions we draw. As Fodor, Bever and Garrett comment: "Practically anything that one can say about speech production must be considered speculative, even by the standards current in psycholinguistics" (Fodor, Bever and Garrett 1974, p. 434).

Clues as to what is happening are infuriatingly elusive. In fact, there seems to be only one situation in which we can actually catch a speaker as he mentally prepares an utterance, and that is when someone is trying to recall a forgotten name. The name is often on "the tip of his tongue," but he cannot quite remember it. His mind is not completely blank as far as the word is concerned. A teasing and seemingly uncatchable wraith of it remains. He is left with a "kind of disembodied presence, a grin without the Cheshire Cat" (Brown 1970, p. 234).

Apart from this, we have to rely on indirect evidence. This is of two types. First of all, we can look at the pauses in spontaneous speech. The object of this is to try to detect patterns in the pausing which may give us clues as to when speech is planned. Secondly, we can examine speech errors, both the slips of the tongue found in the conversation of normal people (e.g., *hap-slappily* for "slap-happily," *cantankerous* for "contentious"), and the more severe disturbances of dysphasics—people whose speech is impaired due to some type of brain damage (e.g., *tarib* for "rabbit," *rabbit* for "apple"). Hopefully, breakdown of the normal patterns may give us vital information about the way we plan and produce what we say.

Pauses

It may seem rather paradoxical to investigate speech by studying nonspeech. But the idea is not as irrelevant as it may seem at first sight. Around 40 to 50 percent of an average spontaneous utterance consists of silence, although to the hearer the proportion does not seem as high because he is too busy listening to what is being said.

The pauses in speech are of two main types: *breathing* pauses and *hesitation* pauses of the "er . . . um" variety. The first type are relatively easy to cope with. There are relatively few of them (partly because we slow down our rate of breathing when we speak), and they account for only about 5 percent of the gaps in speech. They tend to come at grammatical boundaries, although they do not necessarily do so (Henderson *et al.* 1965).

Hesitation pauses are more promising. There are more of them, and they do not have any obvious physical purpose comparable to that of filling one's lungs with air. Normally they account for one third to one half of the time taken up in talking. Speech in which such pausing does not occur is "inferior" speech (Jackson 1932). Either it has been rehearsed beforehand, or the speaker is merely stringing together a number of standard phrases he habitually repeats, as when the mother of the seven-year-old who threw a stone through my window rattled off at top speed, "I do apologize, he's never done anything like that before, I can't think what came over him, he's such a good quiet little boy usually, I'm quite flabbergasted." (Unfortunately, we tend to overvalue the fluent, glib speaker who may not be thinking what he is saying, and often condemn a hesitant or stammering speaker who may be thinking very hard.)

Hesitation pauses are rather difficult to measure, because a long-drawn-out word such as *we . . . ell, in fa . . . act* may be substituted for a pause. This type of measurement problem may account for the extraordinary differences of view found among psycholinguists who have done research on this topic. The basic argument is about *where* exactly the pauses occur. One researcher claims that hesitations occur mainly after the first word in the clause or sentoid (Boomer 1965). But other psycholinguists, whose experiments seem equally convincing, find pauses mainly before important lexical items (Goldman-Eisler 1964; Butterworth 1980a). It seems impossible, from just reading about their experiments, to judge who is right.

But in spite of this seemingly radical disagreement we can glean one important piece of information. *All* researchers agree that speakers do not normally pause between clauses, they pause *inside* them. This means that there is overlapping in the planning and production of clauses. That is, instead of a simple sentence

Plan clause A	*Utter* clause A	*Plan* clause B	*Utter* clause B

we must set up a more complicated model:

Plan clause A	*Plan* clause B	
	Utter clause A	*Utter* clause B

In other words, it is quite clear that we do not cope with speech one clause at a time. We begin to plan the next clause while still uttering the present one.

Armed with this vital piece of information, we can now attempt to elaborate the picture by looking at the evidence from speech errors.

Speech Errors: The Nature of the Evidence

Linguists are interested in speech errors because they hope that language in a broken-down state may be more revealing than language which is working perfectly. It is possible that speech is like an ordinary household electrical system, which is composed of several relatively independent circuits. We cannot discover very much about these circuits when all the lamps and sockets are working perfectly. But if a mouse gnaws through a cable in the kitchen, and fuses one circuit, then we can immediately discover which lamps and sockets are linked together under normal working conditions. In the same way, it might be possible to find selective impairment of different aspects of speech.

The errors we shall be dealing with are, firstly, slips of the tongue, and, secondly, the speech of dysphasics—people with some more serious type of speech disturbance. Because the evidence is rather unusual, let us consider its nature a little more fully.

Everybody's tongue slips now and again, most often when the tongue's owner is tired, a bit drunk, or rather nervous. So errors of this type are common enough to be called normal. However, if you mention the topic of slips of the tongue to a group of people at least one of them is likely to smirk knowingly and say "Ah yes, tongue slips are sexual in origin, aren't they?" This fairly popular misconception has arisen because Sigmund Freud, the great Viennese psychologist, wrote a paper suggesting that words sometimes slipped out from a person's subconscious thoughts, which in his view were often concerned with sex. For example, he quotes the case of a woman who said her cottage was situated *on the hill-thigh (Berglende)* instead of "on the hillside" (Berglehne), after she had been trying to recall a childhood incident in which "part of her body had been grasped by a prying and lascivious hand" (Freud 1901). In fact, this type of example occurs only in a relatively small number of tongue slips. It is true, possibly, that a percentage of girls have the embarrassing experience of sinking rapturously into, say, Archibald's arms while inadvertently murmuring "Darling Algernon." It is also perhaps true that anyone talking about a sex-linked subject may get embarrassed and stumble over his words, like the anthropology professor, who red to the ears with confusion, talked about a *plenis-beeding ceremony* (penis-bleeding ceremony) in New Guinea. But otherwise there seems little to support the sexual origin myth. Perhaps one might add that people tend to notice and remember sexual slips more than any other type. During the anthropology lecture mentioned above, almost everybody heard and memorized the *plenis-beeding* example. But few people afterward, when questioned, had heard the lecturer say, *yam's book on young-growing* (Young's book on yam-growing). So laying aside the sex myth, we may say that slips of the tongue tell us more about the way a person plans and produces speech than about his or her sexual fantasies.

Dysphasia is rather different from slips of the tongue, in that it is far from "normal." The name *dysphasia* comes from a Greek word which means "bad speech," and so differs from *aphasia*, which means literally "without speech." Unfortunately, writers on the subject tend to use the two words almost interchangeably. They use both to mean "speech disturbance," though they often reserve the term aphasia for more severe varieties. Here we shall keep to the more strictly correct term dysphasia.

Dysphasia covers an enormous range of speech problems. At one end of the range we find people who can only say a single word such as *oh dear, oh dear, oh dear,* or more usually, a swear word such as *damn, damn, damn.* (One unproved theory is that people who have had a severe stroke sometimes find their speech "petrified" into the word they were uttering as the stroke occurred.) At the other end of the scale are people with only occasional word-finding difficulties—it is not always clear where true dysphasia ends and normal slips of the tongue begin. The fact that one merges into the other means that we can examine both types of error together in our search for clues about the planning and production of speech.

The typology of dysphasia (attempts to classify dysphasia into different kinds of disturbance) is a confused and controversial topic, and is beyond the scope of this book. Here we shall be looking mainly at name-finding difficulties, which is perhaps the most widespread of all dysphasic symptoms. Although it affects some patients more than others, it is usually present to some degree in most types of speech disturbance. A vivid description of this problem occurs in Kingsley Amis's novel *Ending Up* (1974). The fictional dysphasic is a retired university teacher, Professor George Zeyer, who had a stroke five months previously: "Well, anyway, to start with he must have a, a, thing, you know, you go about in it, it's got, er, they turn round. A very expensive one, you can be sure. You drive it, or someone else does in his case. Probably gold, gold on the outside. Like that other chap. A bar—no. And probably a gold, er, going to sleep on it. And the same in his . . . When he washes himself. If he ever does, of course. And eating off a gold—eating off it, you know. Not to speak of a private, um, uses it whenever he wants to go anywhere special, to one of those other places down there to see his pals. Engine. No. With a fellow to fly it for him. A plate. No, but you know what I mean. And the point is it's all because of us. Without us he'd be nothing, would he? But for us he'd still be living in his, ooh, made out of . . . with a black woman bringing him, off the—growing there, you know. And the swine's supposed to be some sort of hero. Father of his people and all that. A plane, a private plane, that's it."

It was not that George was out of his mind, merely that his stroke had afflicted him, not only with hemiplegia, but also with that condition in which the sufferer finds it difficult to remember nouns, common terms, the names of familiar objects. George was otherwise fluent and accurate and responded normally to others' speech. His fluency was especially notable; he was very good at not pausing at moments when a sympathetic hearer could have supplied the elusive word. Doctors, including Dr. Mainwaring, had stated that the defect might clear up altogether in time, or might stay as it was, and that there was nothing to be done about it.

Of course, not every dysphasic is as fluent as George. And some-times a patient is in the disquieting situation of thinking she has found the right word—only to discover to her dismay, when she utters it, that it is the wrong one. A description of this unnerving experience occurs in Nabokov's *Pale Fire:*

> She still could speak. She paused and groped and found
> What seemed at first a serviceable sound,
> But from adjacent cells imposters took
> The place of words she needed, and her look
> Spelt imploration as she sought in vain
> To reason with the monsters in her brain.

Perhaps the following two extracts will give a clearer picture of the problem. They are taken from tape-recordings of a severely dys-phasic patient in her seventies who had had a stroke two months ear-lier.

The patient (P) has been uttering the word *rhubarb*, apparently because she is worried about her garden which is going to rack and ruin while she is in hospital. The therapist (T) tries to comfort her, then says:

> T: Now then, what's this a picture of? (showing a picture of an apple).
> P: Ra- ra- rabbit.
> T: No, not a rabbit. It's a kind of fruit.
> P: Fruit.
> T: What kind of fruit is it?
> P: Oh this is a lovely rabbit.
> T: Not a rabbit, no. It's an apple.
> P: Apple, yes.
> T: Can you name any other pieces of fruit? What other kinds of fruit would you have in a dish with an apple?
> P: Beginning with an a?
> T: No, not necessarily.
> P: Oh well, rhubarb.
> T: Perhaps, yes.
> P: Or rhubarb.

In the second extract, the same type of phenomenon occurs, but in a different context.

> T: What's this boy doing? (showing a picture of a boy swimming).
> P: Oh he's in the sea.
> T: Yes.
> P: Driving . . . driving. It's not very deep. He's driving with his feet, his legs. Driving. Well driving, er diving.
> T: In fact he's . . .
> P: Swimming.
> T: Good, what about this one? (showing a picture of a boy climbing over a wall).

P: Driving, on a . . . on a wall.
T: He's what?
P: Dr . . . driving, he's climbing on a wall.

Most of the mistakes in these passages represent an extension of the selection problems seen in ordinary slips of the tongue. That is, the same kind of mistakes occur as in normal speech, but they occur more often and seem less obvious.

Broadly speaking, we may categorize speech errors into two basic types. First, we have those in which a wrong item (or items) is chosen, where something has gone wrong with the *selection* process. For example,

> Did you remember to buy some toothache? (Did you remember to buy some toothpaste?)

Note, by the way, that although generally classified as "slips of the tongue," selection errors are more accurately "slips of the brain."

Secondly, we find errors in which the correct choice of word has been made, but the *program* set up for utterance by the speaker has been faultily executed as in

> Someone's been writening threat letters (Someone's been writing threatening letters).

Let us look at these two categories, *selection errors* and *programming errors* more carefully, and attempt to subdivide them.

Errors in which wrong items have been chosen are most commonly whole word errors. There are three main types: *semantic errors* (or similar meaning errors), *malapropisms* (or similar sound errors), and *blends*.

So-called *semantic* or *similar meaning* errors are fairly common. In fact, they are so usual that they often pass unnoticed. We are talking about naming errors in which the speaker gets the general "semantic field" right, but uses the wrong word, as in

> Do you have any artichokes? I'm sorry, I mean aubergines.

This kind of mistake often affects pairs of words. People say *left* when they mean "right," *up* when they mean "down," and *early* instead of "late," as in

> It's six o'clock. Won't that be too early to buy bread?

Mistakes like this occur repeatedly in the speech of some dysphasics, and in its extreme form the general condition is sometimes rather pompously labelled "conceptual agrammatism" (Goodglass 1968). Such patients repeatedly confuse words like *yesterday, today* and *tomorrow*. They seem able to find names connected with the general area they are talking about, but unable to pinpoint particular words within it, so that a "garden roller" is likely to be called a *lawn mower*, a "spade" may be called a *fork*, and a "rake" may be called a *hoe*. A mistake like this occurred in one of the dysphasic passages quoted above: the patient said *diving* when she meant "swimming." At other times, a patient may use a paraphrase such as *water compartment* for "drinking trough," or *horse hut* for "stable."

The second type of word selection error, so-called *malapropisms* occur when a person confuses a word with another, similar sounding one. The name comes from Mrs. Malaprop, a character in Richard Sheridan's play *The Rivals*, who continually confused words which sounded alike, as in

> She's as headstrong as an allegory on the banks of the Nile (She's as headstrong as an alligator on the banks of the Nile).

and

> A nice derangement of epitaphs (a nice arrangement of epithets).

Not only in Sheridan's play, but in real life also, the results are sometimes hilarious, as when a lady lecturer claimed that

> You keep newborn chicks warm in an incinerator (You keep newborn chicks warm in an incubator.)

Equally funny was a man's statement that he had *nubile toes* instead of "mobile" ones.

So far, we have mentioned selection errors connected with meaning, and selection errors connected with the sound of the word. But it would be a mistake to assume that we can easily place mistakes into one or the other category. Often the two overlap. Although children's mistakes are usually purely phonetic ones, as in

> Mussolini pudding (semolina pudding)
> naughty story car park (multistory car park),

the majority of adult ones have some type of semantic as well as phonetic link. The malapropism *incinerator* for "incubator" is a case in point, since in addition to the phonetic similarity both words are connected with the idea of heat. Another example is the statement

You go under a runway bridge (You go under a railway bridge),

where, in addition to the similar sounds, both words describe a track for a means of transport. Yet another example is the error

compensation prize (consolation prize).

However, the semantic connection does not always have to be between the two words that are being confused. Sometimes the intruding idea comes in from the surrounding context, as in the statement

Learning to speak is not the same thing as learning to talk (Learning to speak is not the same thing as learning to walk).

Another example of this type of confusion was uttered by a nervous male involved in a discussion on BBC's *Woman's Hour* about a cat who never seemed to sleep, because it was perpetually chasing mice. He said:

How many sheep does the cat have in its house then? I'm sorry, I mean mice, not sheep.

The speaker correctly remembered that he was talking about an animal of some kind, but the animal had somehow become contaminated by the sound of the word *sleep*, resulting in *sheep*! He may also have been influenced by the fact that humans reputedly count sheep jumping over fences in order to get to sleep.

The third type of selection error, so-called *blends*, are an extension and variation of semantic errors. They are fairly rare, and occur when two words are "blended" together to form one new one. For example,

Not in the sleast

contains a mixture of "slightest and least." And

Please expland that

is a mixture of "explain and expand." A rather more bizzare example of a blend occurs in the first of the passages of dysphasic speech quoted on p. 346. The patient had been talking about *rhubarb*, and was trying to think of the word *apple*. What came out was a mixture of the two, *rabbit*! Such mixes are also known as *contaminations* since the two words involved "contaminate" one another. Often, in this kind of mistake, both the items chosen are equally appropriate. It is just that the speaker seems to have accidentally picked two together—or rather failed to choose between two equally appropriate words in time. He has not so much picked the wrong word, as not decided which of the right ones he needed.

Note, by the way, that two items are sometimes intentionally blended together in order to create a new word. Lewis Carroll makes Humpty Dumpty explain in *Alice Through the Looking Glass* that *slithy* means "lithe and slimy," commenting, "You see, it's like a portmanteau—there are two meanings packed up into one word"—though Lewis Carroll's made-up words may not be as intentional as they appear. Apparently, he suffered from severe migraine attacks, and it has been pointed out that many of his strange neologisms are uncannily like the kind of temporary dysphasia produced by some migraine sufferers (Livesley 1972). Perhaps better examples of intentional blends are *smog* from "smoke and fog," and *brunch* from "breakfast and lunch." There are sometimes interesting parallels of this type to be spotted between slips of the tongue and language change.

Let us now turn to *programming errors*—errors in which the correct word choice had been made, but the program set up has been faultily executed. There are three main types: transpositions, anticipations, and repetitions, which may affect words, syllables or sounds.

Transpositions are not, on the whole, very common (Cohen 1966; Nooteboom 1969). Whole words can switch places, as in

> Don't buy a car with its tail in the engine (Don't buy a car with its engine in the tail)
> I can't help the cat if it's deluded (I can't help it if the cat's deluded)

and so can syllables:

> I'd like a vienel schnitzer (I'd like a Viener Schnitzel).

But perhaps the best known are the sound transpositions known as spoonerisms. These are named after a real-life person, the Reverend William A. Spooner, who was Dean and Warden of New College, Oxford, around the turn of the century. Reputedly, he often transposed the initial sounds of words, resulting in preposterous sentences, such as

> The cat popped on its drawers (The cat dropped on its paws)
> You have hissed all my mystery lectures (You have missed all my history lectures)
> You have tasted the whole worm (You have wasted the whole term).

However, there is something distinctly odd about these original spoonerisms. One suspects that the utterances of the Reverend Spooner were carefully prepared for posterity. The odd features are that they always make sense, they affect only initial sounds, and there is no discernible phonetic reason for the transposed sounds. In real life, spoonerisms do not usually make sense, as in

tilver siller (silver tiller).

They can affect noninitial sounds, as in

a cop of cuffee (a cup of coffee).

And they frequently occur between phonetically similar sounds, as

leak wink (weak link).

Anticipations, particularly sound anticipations, are the most wide-spread type of programming error (Cohen 1966; Nooteboom 1969). Here, a speaker anticipates what he is going to say by bringing in an item too early. Note that it is not always possible to distinguish between anticipations and potential transpositions if the speaker stops himself halfway through, after realizing his error. This may partially account for the high recorded proportion of anticipations compared with trans-positions. For example, the following could be a prematurely cut off transposition:

I want you to tell Millicent . . . I mean, I want you to tell Mary what Millicent said.

But the following sound anticipations are clearly just simple antici-pations. A participant in a television discussion referred, much to his embarrassment, to:

The worst German chancellor (The West German Chancellor).

Here he had anticipated the vowel in *German*. The same thing hap-pened to the man, who interrupting overeagerly, begged to make

an impoitant point (an important point).

Repetitions (or *perseverations*) are rather rarer than anticipations, though commoner than transpositions. We find repeated words, as in:

A: Isn't it cold? More like a Sunday in February.
B: It's not too bad—more like a February in March I'd say. (It's not too bad—more like a Sunday in March).

An example of a repeated sound occurred when someone referred to:

the book by Chomsky and Challe (Chomsky and Halle)

—perhaps an indication of the mesmerizing effect of Chomsky on a number of linguists! Repetitions are relatively unusual because normal people have a very effective "wipe the slate clean "mechanism. As soon as they have uttered a word, the phonetic form no longer remains to clutter up the mind. This is perhaps the greatest single difference between ordinary people and dysphasics, who often, to their frustration and despair, repeatedly repeat sounds and words from the sentence before. A dysphasic had been shown a picture of an apple. After some prompting, she said the word *apple*. She was then shown a picture of a blue ball. When asked what it was, she replied without hesitation *apple*. The therapist pointed out that she was confusing the new object with the previous one. "Of course, how stupid of me," replied the patient. "This one's an *apple*. No, no, I didn't mean that, I mean *apple*!" A similar example occurs in the dialogue on p. 346 where the patient keeps repeating the word *rhubarb*.

We have now outlined the main types of selection and programming errors:

Selection Errors	*Programming Errors*
Semantic errors	Transpositions
Malapropisms	Anticipations
Blends	Repetitions

In the next section we shall see what kind of information we can glean from this disparate array of mistakes.

Planning and Producing Utterances

What (if anything) can we learn from this seemingly strange array of errors? In fact, quite a lot. First of all, we can suggest what are the units of planning—in other words, the size of chunk we prepare in advance ready for utterance. Secondly, we can make hypotheses as to how words and syntax are planned and assembled. Thirdly, we can look at the process of word selection.

Let us begin with the unit of planning. This appears to be what is sometimes called a *tone group* or *phonemic clause*—a short stretch of speech spoken with a single intonation contour. For example,

What time is it?
Deborah bought some snails

Max took a bath/before he went to the party.

Note, by the way, that a so-called *phonemic* clause (or tone group) should not be confused with a *syntactic* clause (or sentoid). The two quite often coincide, but do not necessarily do so. For example,

I want to buy some buns

is a single phonemic clause, though it is regarded in transformational grammar as containing two underlying syntactic clauses. In this chapter the word *clause* refers to a phonemic clause, unless otherwise stated.

The main reason for confidently asserting that the tone group is the unit of planning is that slips of the tongue usually occur within a single tone group. For example:

We'll go to taxi in a Chomsky (We'll go to Chomsky in a taxi)
We forged this congress . . . contract in our own congresses (We
    forged this contract in our own congresses).

This strongly suggests that each tone group is planned and executed as a whole. If larger units were prepared, we would expect to find frequent contamination between clauses. As it is, such interference is rare, so much so that Boomer and Laver (1968) regard it as a tongue slip "law" that "The target and the origin of a tongue-slip are both located in the same tone group" (with "law" to be understood in a statistical rather than in an absolute sense).

Assuming, then, that the tone group is the unit of planning, we now need to ask *when* each tone group is planned. We partially solved this problem in our discussion of hesitation pauses (pp. 342–343). There we noted that hesitation pauses (which may represent planning pauses) occur *within* clauses rather than between them. This indicates that speakers do not follow a simple sequence: *Pause and plan—utter. Pause and plan—utter.* Instead, they must prepare each new tone group while the previous one is being spoken.

But this vague assumption that we "plan in advance" is not very satisfactory. We need to be more precise. This leads us on to the second topic in this section—the planning and assemblage of words and syntax. Let us begin by making a fairly sweeping statement, and then justifying it. Briefly, we may divide the planning of an utterance into *two* main stages (Garrett 1976, 1980, 1980a): firstly, *outline planning*, which begins while the previous clause is being uttered. Secondly, *detailed planning*, which takes place while the clause is actually in progress. Outline planning means the choice of key words, syntax and intonation pattern, whereas detailed planning involves the fitting together of previously chosen words and syntax.

Let us look at outline planning first. The most straightforward evidence for the existence of this stage comes from anticipations and transpositions. If a person anticipates or transposes an item, clearly he is already thinking about it before it actually needs to be used. We note the general fact that the larger an item is, the further ahead it can be anticipated (Nooteboom 1969; Hotopf 1972). That is, the bigger the item, the bigger the gap between its actual occurrence and the place where it ought to be. The gap between confused words is normally greater than that between confused sound segments. However, the actual size of the gap is not the crucial point. The important thing to notice is this: although slips of the tongue normally occur within the tone group, on the rare occasions when this "law" is broken it is whole *words* which slip into the preceding clause, rather than sound segments. That is, words can cross clause boundaries, whereas sounds generally do not. For example:

> When you buy the laundry . . . (When you take the laundry, please buy me some cigarettes)
> When you take the roses out, admire . . . (When you take the garbage out, admire the roses)
> Extinguish your seatbelts . . . (Extinguish your cigarettes and fasten your seatbelts).

Compare these with the following sound transpositions and anticipations, which all occur within the same clause:

> She wrote me a yetter . . . (letter yesterday)
> Twapter chelve (chapter twelve)
> A cop of cuffee (a cup of coffee)
> Dog was . . . (Doug was a doctor)

The phenomenon described above indicates that key words are thought out while the preceding clause is being uttered—whereas the detailed organization of a tone group is left till later. Other types of advance planning are less easy to pin down. Of course, in many cases, common sense tells us that outline syntactic planning occurs well in advance of the actual utterance of a clause. In the sentence

> If he were to seduce Lolita, she would be delighted

the phrase *If he were* immediately indicates that the second clause has been thought about to some extent. However, this "common sense" notion is rather vague. Evidence that is somewhat more useful comes from looking at intonation patterns. Here, we find a surprising phenomenon: errors which occur within the tone group do not normally disrupt the intonation pattern. For example:

Take the freezes out of the steaker

has the same intonation pattern as the "target" sentence: "Take the steaks out of the freezer."

Assuming, then, that we are correct in saying that the planning of key words and outline syntax (including the intonation pattern) begins during the preceding clause, we are now faced with a tricky and much disputed question: which comes first, the words or the syntactic pattern? Those who argue that the words come first point out quite simply that it is "key" words which determine the choice of syntax, and by "key" words they mean above all nouns, verbs and sometimes adjectives. Clearly, verbs influence the choice of syntax more than the nouns—but the noun may, in some cases, influence the choice of verb.

Those who suggest that the syntax comes first put forward an equally strong argument. They note that when a speaker makes a word selection error, he almost always picks a wrong word belonging to the same word class as the target word. That is, nouns are confused with other nouns, verbs with other verbs, and adjectives with other adjectives. Even dysphasic speech, which is often quite garbled, tends to follow this pattern (though exceptions do occur). People say *up* instead of "down," *jelly* instead of "blancmange," *translation* instead of "transformation." But there is no reason for parts of speech to cling together like this. Why shouldn't verbs and nouns get confused? The fictional Mrs. Malaprop gets her word classes confused much of the time, which is why many of her malapropisms are essentially implausible. She says things such as:

You will promise to forget this fellow—to illiterate him, I say, quite from your memory (You will promise . . . to obliterate him . . . from your memory).

But in real life, it is extremely unusual to find adjective-verb confusions of the *illiterate* for "obliterate" type uttered by Mrs. Malaprop. Even malapropisms uttered by children generally follow this similar word-class pattern:

You take an antelope if you swallow poison (You take an antidote if you swallow poison)
I'm learning to play the elbow (I'm learning to play the oboe).

According to the "syntax first" supporters, the most likely explanation for this phenomenon is that the syntax has already been chosen, and the words are then slotted in: "Unless the syntactic structure is already constructed, word selection would not be constrained to proper word classes" (Fromkin 1973, p. 30). "The very fact that a mistakenly selected word always or nearly always belongs to the same word class as the intended word indicates that the grammatical structure of the phrase under construction imposes imperative restrictions on the selection of words" (Nooteboom 1969, p. 130).

How are we to solve this controversy between the "words first" and "syntax first" supporters? Who is right? Possibly both sides, to some extent. On the one hand, it is extremely unlikely that the key word advocates are entirely correct. There is no evidence whatsoever that we assemble *all* the key words, and then bind them together with joining words. On the other hand, it is quite impossible to plan the syntax with no idea of the lexical items which are going to be used. For example, the syntax of

John claimed to be able to eat a live frog

must depend to some extent on the word *claim*, since other words with a similar meaning take a different construction. We cannot say

*John asserted to be able to eat a live frog

or

*John declared to be able to eat a live frog.

It is possible then, that we start by picking perhaps *one* key verb or noun, and then build the syntax around it. Later we slot other words into the remaining gaps.

If one key word triggers off the syntax, then we must assume that words in storage are clearly marked with their word class or part of speech (e.g. noun, verb) as well as with information about the constructions they can enter into. For example:

| *eat* | Verb |
| | NP–eat–NP |

We are, therefore, hypothesizing that when people plan utterances they mentally set up syntactic trees which are built around selected key words:

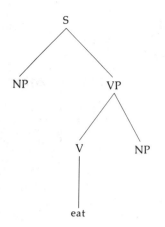

However, one problem remains. If we are correct in assuming that certain key words come first, how do we account for the fact that we often get the syntax right, but cannot remember key words, even though the forgotten item has clearly influenced the choice of syntax? For example:

He took a lot of . . . what's the word I want? . . . Persuasion.

This type of example suggests that we possibly plan with the "idea of a word" (for want of a better way of putting it), then only later fit it to a phonetic form. This is supported by slips of the tongue such as:

When is it going to be recovered by?

In this sentence the syntax was picked for "mend," but the phonetic form activated was *recovered*.

Note, by the way, that a "word idea" which (we are claiming) is selected before its phonetic form is not just an intangible "concept," but a definite and firmly packaged lexical item. It includes both an understanding of what is being referred to and a firm word class label (noun, verb, adjective, etc.), as well as information about the syntactic configurations it can enter into.

So far, then, we have dealt with outline planning. We have hypothesized that, while still uttering the previous clause, speakers begin to prepare key words (usually in nonphonetic form), then build the syntax around them, and this also involves selection of an intonation pattern. The second, detailed planning stage probably takes place while the clause is actually being uttered. One plausible suggestion is that we carry out the detailed planning during a hesitation pause which occurs near the beginning of a tone group. Boomer (1965) claims that he found a significantly high proportion of pauses *after* the first word of a clause. This suggests a picture like this:

Outline Plan A Detailed Plan A	Outline Plan B Detailed Plan B
Utter Clause A	Utter Clause B

By the detailed planning stage, we assume that the major lexical and syntactic choices have already been made. The items chosen now have to be correctly assembled. This involves at least two types of maneuver: on the one hand, lexical items have to be put into their correct slots in the sentence. This has been wrongly carried out in

> It's bad to have too much blood in the alcohol stream (It's bad to
> have too much alcohol in the bloodstream)
> A fifty-pound dog of bag food (A fifty-pound bag of dog food).

The slotting in of lexical items must also include the slotting in of negatives, since these can get disturbed as in

> It's the kind of furniture I never said I'd have (It's the kind of
> furniture I said I'd never have)
> I disregard this as precise (I regard this as imprecise).

In addition, detailed planning involves adding on word endings in the appropriate place. This has been done incorrectly in:

> She wash upped the dishes (She washed up the dishes)
> She come backs tomorrow (She comes back tomorrow)
> He became mentalier unhealthy (He became mentally unhealthier)

However, we can say rather more about the assemblage of words and endings than the vague comment that they are "slotted together." . . . Speakers seem to have an internal neural "pacemaker"—a biological "beat" which helps them to integrate and organize their utterances, and . . . this pacemaker may utilize the syllable as a basic unit. If we look more carefully, we find that syllables are organized into *feet*—a foot being a unit which includes a strong or stressed syllable. And we see that feet are organized into tone groups. In other words, we have a hierarchy of rhythmic units: tone groups made up of feet, and feet made up of syllables:

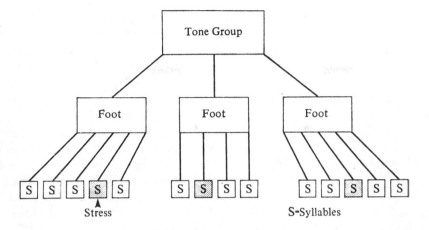

Stress   S-Syllables

So within each tone group an utterance is planned foot by foot. This is indicated by the fact that transposed words are normally similarly stressed, and occupy similar places in their respective feet. For example:

He found a wífe: for his jób (He found a job for his wife)
The Quáke caused: extensive válley: in the dámage (The quake
    caused extensive damage in the valley).

Within each foot, the stressed or "tonic" word may be activated first, since tonic words are statistically more likely to be involved in tongue slips than unstressed ones (Boomer and Laver 1968). Finally, the importance of the syllable as a "psychologically real" unit is shown by the fact that tongue slips "obey a structural law with regard to syllable place" (Boomer and Laver 1968, p. 7). That is, the initial sound of a syllable will affect another initial sound, a final sound will affect another final, and vowels affect vowels, as in:

jawfully loined (lawfully joined)
hass or grash (hash or grass)
bud begs (bed bugs).

Let us recapitulate: at the outline planning stage, the key words, syntax, and intonation of the tone group as a whole are set up. At the detailed planning stage, words and endings are slotted in foot by foot, with the stressed word in each foot possibly activated first. Finally, the remaining unstressed syllables are assembled.

Let us now turn to word selection and storage—our third major topic within this section. We can say rather more about this than merely noting the fact that the basic lexical item can be detached from its phonetic form (p. 357). We can, in addition, say something about how the "idea" or semantic form of a word is stored, as well as something about phonetic storage. We can also posit the existence of a "monitoring device" which checks to see that the two forms of the word, semantic and phonetic, have been correctly matched. Our most direct information comes from the "tip of the tongue" (TOT) experiment (Brown and McNeill 1966). Less direct evidence comes from word selection errors.

The TOT experiment was a simple one, which produced fascinating results. They assembled a group of students, and read them out definitions of relatively uncommon words. For example, when the "target" word was *sextant*, the students heard the definition: "A navigational instrument used in measuring angular distances, especially the altitude of sun, moon and stars at sea." Some of the students recognized the right word immediately. But others went into a TOT ("tip of the tongue") state. They felt they were on the verge of getting the word, but not quite there. In this state the researchers asked them to fill in a questionnaire about their mental search. To his surprise, he found that the students could provide quite a lot of information about the elusive missing name. Sometimes the information was semantic, and sometimes it was phonetic. For example, in response to the definition of *sextant*, several of them provided the similar meaning words *astrolabe, compass* and *protractor*. Others remembered that it had two syllables and began with an *s*, and made guesses such as *secant, sexton,* and *sextet*.

Semantically, this suggests that words are stored in "semantic fields"—that is, all words of a similar meaning are found together. When we select the "idea" of a word for utterance we enter the general area where it "lives," before pinpointing one word in particular. When errors occur we have been insufficiently precise in locating the exact one needed—as with *yesterday* instead of "tomorrow," *shirt* instead of "blouse," and (another example from the TOT experiment) *barge, houseboat, junk* instead of "sampan."

Phonetically, we find a similar picture. People seem to go to the general area where the word is stored before picking one word in particular. Malapropisms such as *competence* for "confidence," and *native ape* for "naked ape" suggest that people look for certain outline characteristics of the word, such as the initial consonant and number of syllables before they retrieve its full phonetic form (Fay and Cutler 1977). Adults give higher priority to the initial consonant than to the number of syllables, so that they often produce malapropisms such as *condescending* for "condensing," and *segregated* for "serrated." Children, on the other hand, seem to pay extra attention to the number of syllables, and produce comparatively more malapropisms with a wrong initial consonant, as in *ice cream toilet* for "ice cream cornet"

(cornet = cone), *mistake car* for "estate car," *leprechaun* for "unicorn" (Aitchison and Straf 1981). Of course, the situation is not quite as straightforward as suggested above, because a number of other factors play a role in memory, such as the presence of a rhyming suffix, as in *periscope* for "stethoscope," *porcupine* for "concubine." As with all psycholinguistic phenomena, there are a large number of intertwined variables to be considered, which it is not easy to separate out.

In general, the evidence suggests that words are retrieved in several stages, which follow one another very fast and may overlap: outline semantic form, detailed semantic form, outline phonetic form, detailed phonetic form. In addition, we can postulate the existence of a "monitoring device" which checks to see that each word has been fitted to the correct phonetic form:

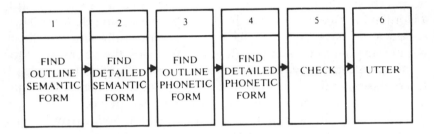

The existence of a monitoring device is indicated by the fact that in adult speech there is often both a phonetic and a semantic reason for a mistake, as in the malapropism *incinerator* for "incubator," where the speaker has uttered a noun that not only sounds similar to the intended one, but is also connected with heat. We can envisage the checking process working somewhat as follows. A speaker picks a word from storage, then looks up its phonetic form. He possibly selects outline characteristics first, in this case, a word consisting of several syllables beginning with *in-* and ending in *-ator*. If he is in too much of a hurry, he may then mistakenly pick a word similar to the one he wants, say *inculcator* or *incinerator* instead of "incubator." In order to stop too many wrong words being uttered, he probably makes a routine check to see that the phonetic form and word meaning fit together. If such a check did not exist, we would possibly find many more purely phonetic malapropisms which had no obvious connection with the topic under discussion. Presumably, many quite weird potential malapropisms are "caught" by the check barrier and never uttered. Most of those which are uttered have passed a check which was clearly not thorough enough. In other words, a speaker who is not concentrating may accidentally let through a word that has some phonetic and some semantic appropriateness, even when it is in fact the wrong one. In dysphasic speech especially, the check mechanism seems particularly weak. Dysphasics seem to let through a far wider range of inappropriate words, providing there is at least some sound and meaning link, however flimsy (as in *driving* for "swimming," caused by *driving* for "diving" and *diving* for "swimming"). Of course, even if the first "check" lets a word through, then there is a second "check" after a person has uttered it. If a speaker realizes his mistake, he says, "Sorry, I mean . . . ," and starts the phrase again.

The general picture of speech production which we form from word selection errors is of practiced behavior performed in a great hurry, such a hurry that the speaker does not have time to check the details of each word in full. Just as in the comprehension of speech, a listener employs perceptual strategies (short cuts which enable him to jump to conclusions about what he is hearing), so in the production of speech, production strategies are possibly utilized. A speaker finds a word in his mental store which has the correct outline characteristics. He does not have time to check each segment of the word in detail, but possibly relies on a monitoring device to stop the utterance of too many inappropriate words. If, however, a word happens to have both some phonetic and some semantic resemblance to the word he wants, it is likely to pass the monitoring device and be uttered.

Of course, this is only one of several theories about why we find so many errors with both a phonetic and a semantic similarity to the target. Another plausible suggestion is that speakers consider several possible candidates for utterance before they select the exact one they want. If there is another word which sounds similar to the target, and with a similar meaning, then it will be considered as a possibility, and might accidentally get included in the final utterance (Baars 1980).

Where does all this leave us? Still fairly much in the dark, compared with what we need to know. There are still enormous gaps in our knowledge, and much of what we have said is hypothetical. We have realized that, for every clause uttered, a human speaker must be carrying out a number of complex overlapping tasks, a feat he manages by relying on a rhythmic principle. Utterances are organized tone group by tone group. Within the tone group they are organized foot by foot, and within the foot syllable by syllable. As far as word storage and selection is concerned, the "idea" of a word is possibly selected first, then later attached to its phonetic form.

The question of how all this can be fitted into a coherent linguistic model is still to be solved. Perhaps, as an epilogue to the problems of speech planning and production, we can quote the words of a character in Oscar Wilde's play *The Importance of Being Earnest*, who commented that "Truth is never pure, and rarely simple."

Notes and Suggestions for Further Reading

Useful collections of papers which deal with slips of the tongue are Fromkin (1973), Fromkin (1980) and Cutler (1982). Lesser (1978) provides an introduction to the topic of dysphasia, while Goodglass and Blumstein (1973), Caramazza and Zurif (1978) contain a number of interesting papers. Butterworth (1980) deals with speech production in general, and contains papers both on slips of the tongue and on pauses.

The examples of slips of the tongue in this chapter are taken mainly from my own collection, supplemented by examples from Fromkin (1973). Note that the view taken in this chapter that the word-selection errors of dysphasics are quantitatively, not qualitatively, different from slips of the tongue in normal speakers, is not shared by all psycholinguists.

References

Aitchison, J., and Straf, M. (1981), "Lexical storage and retrieval: A developing skill?" *Linguistics 19*, pp. 751–95. Also in A. Cutler ed. (1982), *Slips of the Tongue and Speech Production*, Berlin: Mouton.

Baars, B. J. (1980), "The competing plans hypothesis: An heuristic viewpoint on the causes of errors in speech," in H. W. Dechert and M. Raupach eds. (1980), *Temporal Variables in Speech*, The Hague: Mouton.

Boomer, D. S. (1965), "Hesitation and grammatical encoding," *Language and Speech, 8*, pp. 148–58. Also in R. C. Oldfield and J. C. Marshall eds. (1968), *Language: Selected Readings*, Harmondsworth: Penguin.

Boomer, D. S. and Laver, J. D. M. (1968), "Slips of the tongue," *British Journal of Disorders of Communication, 3*, pp. 1–12. Also in V. A. Fromkin ed. (1973), *Speech Errors as Linguistic Evidence*, The Hague: Mouton.

Brown, R. (1970), *Psycholinguistics: Selected Papers*, New York: The Free Press.

Brown, R., and McNeill, D. (1966), "The 'Tip of the Tongue' phenomenon," *Journal of Verbal Learning and Verbal Behavior, 5*, pp. 325–37. Also in R. Brown ed. (1970), *Psycholinguistics: Selected Papers*, New York: The Free Press.

Butterworth, B. (1980), *Language Production*, vol. 1, New York: Academic Press.

———. (1980a), "Evidence from pauses in speech," in B. Butterworth ed. (1980), *Language Production*, vol. I, New York: Academic Press.

Caramazza, A., and Zurif, E. B. (1978), *Language Acquisition and Language Breakdown: Parallels and Divergencies*, Baltimore: Johns Hopkins.

Cohen, A. (1966), "Errors of speech and their implication for understanding the strategy of language users," in V. A. Fromkin ed. (1973), *Speech Errors as Linguistic Evidence*, The Hague: Mouton.

Cutler, A. (1982), *Slips of the Tongue and Speech Production*, Berlin: Mouton.

Fay, D. and Cutler A. (1977), "Malapropisms and the structure of mental lexicon," *Linguistic Inquiry, 8*, pp. 505–20.

Fodor, J. A., Bever, T. G., and Garrett, M. F. (1974), *The Psychology of Language*, New York: McGraw Hill.

Freud, S. (1901), "Slips of the tongue," in V. A. Fromkin ed. (1973), *Speech Errors as Linguistic Evidence*, The Hague: Mouton.

Fromkin, V. A. (1973), *Speech Errors as Linguistic Evidence*, The Hague: Mouton.

————. (1980), *Errors in Linguistic Performance: Slips of the Tongue, Ear, Pen and Hand*, New York: Academic Press.

Garrett, M. F. (1976), "Syntactic processes in sentence production," in R. J. Wales and E. Walker eds. (1976), *New Approaches to Language Mechanisms*, Amsterdam: North Holland.

————. (1980), "Levels of processing in sentence production," in B. Butterworth (1980), *Language Production*, vol. I, New York: Academic Press.

————. (1980a), "The limits of accommodation: Arguments for independent processing levels in sentence production," in V. A. Fromkin ed. (1980), *Errors in Linguistic Performance: Slips of the Tongue, Ear, Pen and Hand*, New York: Academic Press.

Goldman-Eisler, F. (1964) "Hesitation, information and levels of speech production," in A. V. S. De Reuck and M. O. O'Connor eds. (1964), *Disorders of Language*, London: Churchill Livingstone.

Goodglass, H. (1968), "Studies on the grammar of aphasics," in S. Rosenberg and J. H. Koplin eds. (1968), *Developments in Applied Psycholinguistics Research*, New York: Macmillan. Also in H. Goodglass and S. Blumstein eds. (1973), *Psycholinguistics and Aphasia*, Baltimore: Johns Hopkins University Press.

Goodglass, H., and Blumstein, S. (1973), *Psycholinguistics and Aphasia*, Baltimore: Johns Hopkins University Press.

Henderson, A., Goldman-Eisler, F., and Skarbek, A. (1965), "The common value of pausing time in spontaneous speech," *Quarterly Journal of Experimental Psychology*, 17, pp. 343–5.

Hotopf, N. (1972), "What light do slips of the tongue and of the pen throw on word production?," Unpublished research.

Jackson, H. J. (1932), *Selected Writings*, vol. II, London: Hodder and Stoughton.

Lesser, R. (1978), *Linguistic Investigations of Aphasia*, London: Edward Arnold.

Livesley, B. (1972), "The Alice in Wonderland syndrome," *Teach In*, 1, pp. 770–74.

Nooteboom, S. G. (1969), "The tongue slips into patterns," in A. G. Sciarone *et al.* eds. *Nomen: Leyden Studies in Linguistics and Phonetics*, The Hague: Mouton. Also in V. A. Fromkin ed. (1973), *Speech Errors as Linguistic Evidence*, The Hague: Mouton.

FOR DISCUSSION AND REVIEW

1. Why is it difficult to find out how people plan and produce speech? For example, why can't one just ask them?

2. Aitchison mentions the "tip of the tongue" (TOT) phenomenon, the situation in which someone says that a word or a name is "on the tip of my tongue, but I just can't quite remember it." Often, though, in this situation, we know that the elusive word "begins with *p*," for example,

or "sounds something like *roomer*" or "means ———." Based on your own experience, on information collected from others, or both, make lists of (a) at least five words that you or someone else couldn't at first remember and (b) what you or they *did* know about the words. Describe any patterns that you find.

3. Review what W. F. Bolton says about "quiet" breathing and "speech" breathing in "Language: An Introduction" in Part One. How are these two kinds of breathing related to the two kinds of pauses in speech described by Aitchison?

4. What is the significance of the fact that hesitation pauses usually occur *within*, not between, clauses?

5. Why are linguists interested in speech errors? What is *dysphasia*? Why is it useful to examine the name-finding problems of dysphasic individuals?

6. Based on your own experience, give an example of a selection error and a programming error. Into which of the subdivisions of these two main categories of speech errors does each of your examples fit?

7. Explain Aitchison's claim that the unit of planning for speech is "a tone group or phonemic clause." How does she support this assertion?

8. Explain *outline planning, detailed planning,* and the relationship between the two.

9. Both of the following statements assume "that the planning of key words and outline syntax (including the intonation pattern) begins during the preceding clause." Support or refute one of the statements. Use example sentences in your argument.
   a. In the planning of a speech utterance, the syntactic pattern is planned first.
   b. In the planning of a speech utterance, the words are selected first.

10. Explain why it seems reasonable to assume that "words in [mental] storage are clearly marked with their word class or part of speech."

11. To ensure that you understand the importance of the planning "hierarchy of rhythmic units: tone groups made up of feet, and feet made up of syllables," test your understanding by correctly explaining it to someone else.

5/An Interview With Noam Chomsky

JOHN GLIEDMAN

It is probably impossible to overstate the influence that Noam Chomsky has had on linguistics in the last twenty-five years, both through his own work and through that of his former students. Most of his books and articles about linguistics, however, are technical and highly specialized, making it difficult for nonlinguists to understand and appreciate his arguments. But in the following interview, originally published in Omni, *Chomsky addresses an audience of nonspecialists, and explains clearly and cogently his belief that "language depends upon a genetic endowment that's on a par with the ones that specify the structure of our visual or circulatory systems, or determine that we will have arms instead of wings."*

In 1953 a rickety old tub that had been sunk by the Germans and later salvaged was plodding its way across the Atlantic on the first voyage of its new life. Aboard that listing ship, a seasick young Philadelphian hit on an idea that would make him an internationally known scholar and would radically alter the way linguists view language.

"I remember exactly the moment when I finally felt convinced," Noam Chomsky recalls of the crossing. Sure of himself, he set about emphasizing the role of the mind, outlining the unconscious mechanisms that make human speech possible and insisting that a genetically programmed "language organ" in the brain primed the human infant to master the intricacies of his mother tongue. This language organ allows for the gift of speech that sets humans apart from the other animals. But it also defines and delimits the characteristics of all human languages, from Urdu to Navajo.

Before Chomsky's breakthrough in the mid-Fifties, American linguists did not believe that brain structure played any significant role in shaping language. They viewed the young child's mind as a blank slate, capable of learning virtually *any* conceivable kind of language. They had no concept then that certain languages might exist almost beyond human comprehension, just as X rays and ultraviolet radiation are invisible to the naked human eye.

Many of these linguists were searching for purely mechanical procedures—"discovery procedures"—that would objectively describe the structure of any human language. Chomsky himself started out as a structural linguist and published a technical paper on discovery procedures while he was a junior fellow at Harvard, in the early Fifties. He considered this work to be real linguistics, although he was exploring alternative ideas.

But by the time he set out on that fateful ocean voyage, he was ready to concede that "several years of intense effort devoted to improving discovery procedures had come to naught." His other efforts, carried out in almost complete isolation, were yielding consistently interesting results. This was Chomsky's pioneering research in generative grammars and explanatory theory. Chomsky expanded the definition of *grammar* to include all the elements and rules of each language that the child assimilates as he learns to speak and understand what is said to him, as well as the linguist's theory of what goes on in the speaker's/hearer's brain.

Chomsky believes that language, along with most other human abilities, depends upon genetically programmed mental structures. In other words, language learning during childhood is part of the body's preprogrammed pattern of growth. Just as heredity endows each infant with a heart and lungs that continue to develop after birth, it provides each newborn with a highly complex language organ. The accidents of evolution have shaped this language organ so that it is capable of learning only those languages within a relatively narrow range of logical structures. Other languages, no less suitable for intelligent communication but lacking these human hallmarks, would be virtually unlearnable, even for the most gifted linguist. Chomsky foresees the day when scientists will have constructed a kind of linguistic analogue to Mendeleyev's periodic table—a list of the linguistic "atoms" and their permissible combinations that defines *every possible* human language.

Chomsky's rise to scientific prominence was meteoric. After completing his undergraduate studies at the University of Pennsylvania, he went on to earn a doctorate there in 1955. That was the year he failed to find a publisher for his book *The Logical Structure of Linguistic Form*, and the prestigious journal *Word* rejected a paper summarizing his new ideas—practically by return mail. Yet, two years later his short monograph *Syntactic Structures* took the linguistic community by storm. Scarcely a decade passed before Chomsky was the world-renowned leader of an intellectual revolution in the field of linguistics.

Aside from the originality of his ideas, Chomsky owes his success to his awesome ability as a debater; he's famous for surgically dissecting the logical flaws in rival views. Then, too, he happened upon the linguistics scene during a period of growing dissatisfaction with traditional theories. His widely recognized gifts as a teacher also helped him. As University of California at Berkeley philosopher John Searle observed, Chomsky did not win over the established linguists in the Sixties: "He did something more important; he convinced their graduate students."

During the Sixties Chomsky achieved national recognition as a critic of the Vietnam War. He recalls that he sometimes made eight speeches a day while producing a torrent of documented critiques of American policy, as well as numerous technical books and papers in linguistics and philosophy. He was also a tax resister and withheld half of his federal income taxes as a protest against the war.

With changing political fashions, Chomsky has found it increasingly difficult to place his political essays in mainstream magazines, but he continues to be widely read and respected as a political commentator in Western Europe and Latin America. Since 1958 he has written 21 books and about 100 articles on linguistics, philosophy, and psychology. He has also found time to author or coauthor an additional 11 books and perhaps 1,000 articles on political and social themes.

Chomsky once said that "anybody who teaches at age fifty what he was teaching at age twenty-five had better find another profession." Over the last 25 years, his own linguistic theory has passed through four main stages, each differing in major ways from its predecessor. Chomsky is unique among contemporary scientists in that most of his opponents defend theories he either originated or profoundly influenced. Today he is a professor in the department of linguistics and philosophy at the Massachusetts Institute of Technology.

Psychologist and science journalist John Gliedman, who studied Chomsky's theories in the late Sixties at MIT, discussed ideas about language and mind in the linguist's austere campus office.

Omni: Why do you believe that language behavior critically depends on the existence of a genetically preprogrammed language organ in the brain?

Chomsky: There's a lot of linguistic evidence to support this contention. But even in advance of detailed linguistic research, we should expect heredity to play a major role in language because there is really no other way to account for the fact that children learn to speak in the first place.

Omni: What do you mean?

Chomsky: Consider something that everyone agrees is due to heredity—the fact that humans develop arms rather than wings. Why do we believe this? Well, since nothing in the fetal environments of the human or bird embryo can account for the differences between birds and men, we assume that heredity must be responsible. In fact, if someone came along and said that a bird embryo is somehow "trained" to grow wings, people would just laugh, even though embryologists lack anything like detailed understanding of how genes regulate embryological development.

Omni: Is the role of heredity as important for language as it is for embryology?

Chomsky: I think so. You have to laugh at claims that heredity plays no significant role in language learning, because exactly the same kinds of genetic arguments hold for language learning as hold for embryological development.

I'm very much interested in embryology, but I've got just a layman's knowledge of it. I think that recent work, primarily in molecular biology, however, is seeking to discover the ways that genes regulate embryological development. The gene-control problem is conceptually similar to the problem of accounting for language growth. In fact, language development really ought to be called language *growth,* because the language organ grows like any other body organ.

Omni: Is there a special place in the brain and a particular kind of neurological structure that comprises the language organ?

Chomsky: Little enough is known about cognitive systems and their neurological basis; so caution is necessary in making any direct claims. But it does seem that the representation and use of language involve specific neural structures, though their nature is not well understood.

Omni: But clearly, environment plays some role in language development. What's the relationship between heredity and environment for human language?

Chomsky: The language organ interacts with early experience and matures into the grammar of the language that the child speaks. If a human being with this fixed endowment grows up in Philadelphia, as I did, his brain will encode knowledge of the Philadelphia dialect of English. If that brain had grown up in Tokyo, it would have encoded the Tokyo dialect of Japanese. The brain's different linguistic experience—English versus Japanese—would modify the language organ's structure.

Roughly the same thing goes on in animal experiments, showing that different kinds of early visual experience can modify the part of the brain that processes visual information. As you may know, cats, monkeys, and humans have hierarchically organized brain-cell networks connected to the retina in such a way that certain cells fire only when there is a horizontal line in the visual field; other hierarchies respond only to vertical lines. But early experience can apparently change the relative numbers of horizontal- and vertical-line detectors. MIT psychologists Richard Held and Alan Hein showed some time ago, for example, that a kitten raised in a cage with walls covered by bold, black vertical lines will display good sensitivity to vertical lines as an adult but poor horizontal-line sensitivity. Lack of stimulation apparently causes the horizontal-line detectors to atrophy.

An even closer analogy exists between language growth and the growth that occurs in human beings *after* birth—for example, the onset of puberty. If someone came along and said, "Kids are trained to undergo puberty because they see other people," once again everybody would laugh. Would we laugh because we know in great detail the gene mechanisms that determine puberty? As far as I can tell, no one knows much of anything about that. Yet we all assume that puberty is genetically determined.

Omni: Still, as your own example shows, environmental factors do play a major role in physiological growth.

Chomsky: And it goes without saying that the onset of puberty may well vary over quite a range depending on childhood diet and all kinds of other environmental influences. Nonetheless, everyone takes for granted that the fundamental processes controlling puberty are genetically programmed. This is probably true of death as well. You may be genetically programmed to die at roughly a certain point; it's a reasonable theory.

Look, all through an organism's existence, from birth to death, it passes through a series of genetically programmed changes. Plainly language growth is simply one of these predetermined changes. Language depends upon a genetic endowment that's on a par with the ones that specify the structure of our visual or circulatory systems, or determine that we have arms instead of wings.

Omni: What about the linguistic evidence? What have you learned from studying human languages to corroborate your biological viewpoint?

Chomsky: The best evidence involves those aspects of a language's grammar that are so obvious, so intuitively self-evident to everyone, that they are quite rightly never mentioned in traditional grammars.

Omni: You mean that school grammars fill in the gaps left by heredity? They teach everything about French or Russian, for example, that can't be taken for granted by virtue of the fact that you're a human?

Chomsky: That's right. It is precisely what seems self-evident that is most likely to be part of our hereditary baggage. Some of the oddities of English pronoun behavior illustrate what I mean. Take the sentence, "John believes he is intelligent." Okay, we all know that *he* can refer either to John or to someone else; so the sentence is ambiguous. It can mean either that John thinks he, John, is intelligent, or that someone else is intelligent. In contrast, consider the sentence, "John believes him to be intelligent." Here the pronoun *him* can't refer to John; it can refer only to someone else.

Now, did anyone teach us this peculiarity about English pronouns when we were children? It would be hard to even imagine a training procedure that would convey such information to a person. Nevertheless, everybody knows it—knows it without experience, without training, and at quite an early age. There are any number of other examples that show that we humans have explicit and highly articulate linguistic knowledge that simply has no basis in linguistic experience.

Omni: There's just no way that children can pick up this kind of information by listening to the grown-ups around them?

Chomsky: Precisely. But let me give you another example. English contains grammatical constructions that are called parasitic gaps. In these constructions, you can drop a pronoun and still understand the sentence in the same way as when the sentence contains a pronoun. Consider the sentence, "Which article did you file without reading it?" Notice that you can drop the pronoun *it* without changing meaning or grammaticality. You can say, "Which article did you file without reading?" But you can't say, "John was killed by a rock falling on," when you mean, "John was killed by a rock falling on him." This time omitting the pronoun destroys both meaning and grammaticality.

Constructions of this type—where you can or cannot drop the pronoun—are very rare. In fact, they are so rare that it is quite likely that during the period a child masters his native language (the first five or six years of life), he never hears any of these constructions, or he hears them very sporadically. Nonetheless, every native speaker of English knows flawlessly when you can and can't drop pronouns in these kinds of sentences.

Omni: So we're faced with a mystery. How could anyone possibly learn enough about the English language to possess the rich and exotic grammatical knowledge that we all seem to possess by the time we are five or six years old?

Chomsky: There's an obvious answer to that: The knowledge is built in. You and I can learn English, as well as any other language, with all its richness because we are designed to learn languages based upon a common set of principles, which we may call universal grammar.

Omni: What is universal grammar?

Chomsky: It is the sum total of all the immutable principles that heredity builds into the language organ. These principles cover grammar, speech sounds, and meaning. Put differently, universal grammar is the inherited genetic endowment that makes it possible for us to speak and learn human languages.

Omni: Suppose that somewhere else in the universe intelligent life has evolved. Could we, with our specialized language organ, learn the aliens' language if we made contact with them?

Chomsky: Not if their language violated the principles of our universal grammar, which, given the myriad ways that languages can be organized, strikes me as highly likely.

Omni: Maybe we shouldn't call it *universal,* then. But please explain what you mean.

Chomsky: The same structures that make it possible to learn a human language make it impossible for us to learn a language that violates the principles of universal grammar. If a Martian landed from outer space and spoke a language that violated universal grammar, we simply would not be able to learn that language the way that we learn a human language like English or Swahili. We would have to approach the alien's language slowly and laboriously—the way that scientists study physics, where it takes generation after generation of labor to gain new understanding and to make significant progress. We're designed by nature for English, Chinese, and every other possible human language, but we're not designed to learn perfectly usable languages that violate universal grammar. These languages would simply not be within our range of abilities.

Omni: How would you assess current research about universal grammar?

Chomsky: In the last three or four years there's been a major conceptual change in the underlying theory. We now assume that universal grammar consists of a collection of preprogrammed subsystems that include, for example, one responsible for meaning, another responsible for stringing together phrases in a sentence, a third one that deals, among other things, with the kinds of relationships between nouns and pronouns that I discussed earlier. And there are a number of others.

These subsystems are not genetically preprogrammed down to the last detail. If they were, there would be only one human language. But heredity does set rather narrow limits on the possible ways that the rules governing each subsystem's function can vary. Languages like English and Italian, for example, differ in their choice of genetically permitted variations that exist as options in the universal grammar. You can think of these options as a kind of linguistic menu containing mutually exclusive grammatical possibilities.

For example, languages like Italian have chosen the "null subject" option from the universal-grammar menu: In Italian you can say *left* when you mean "He left" or "She left." English and French have passed up this option and chosen instead a rule that requires explicit mention of the subject.

Omni: What are some other grammatical options on the universal-grammar menu?

Chomsky: In English the most important element in every major grammatical category comes first in its phrase. In simple sentences, for example, we say *John hit Bill*, not *John Bill hit*. With adjectives we say *proud of John*, not *John of proud*; with nouns we say *habit of drinking wine*, not *drinking wine of habit*; and with prepositions we say *to John*, not *John to*. Because heads of grammatical categories always come first, English is what is called a head-initial language.

Japanese is a head-final language. In Japanese you say *John Bill hit*. And instead of prepositions, there are postpositions that follow nouns: *John to*, rather than *to John*. So here's another parameter the child's got to learn from experience: Is the language head-initial or head-final?

These grammatical parameters are interconnected. You can't pick them any more freely than, say, a wine fanatic who insists on white wine with fish and red wine with meat is free to choose any main dish once he's decided on his wine. But grammars are even more sensitive than this culinary example might suggest. A slight change in just one of the universal grammar's parameters can have enormous repercussions throughout the language. It can produce an entirely different language.

Again, there's a close parallel to embryology, where a slight shift in the gene mechanisms regulating growth may be all that separates a fertilized egg from developing into a lion rather than a whale.

Omni: So what exactly would you say *is* the grammar of English?

Chomsky: The grammar of English is the collection of choices—head-initial rather than head-final, and null subject forbidden, for example—that define one of a limited number of genetically permitted selections from the universal-grammar menu of grammatical options. And of course there are all the lexical facts. You just have to learn your language's vocabulary. The universal grammar doesn't tell you that *tree* means "tree" in English.

But once you've learned the vocabulary terms and fixed the grammatical parameters for English, the whole system is in place. And the general principles genetically programmed into the language organ just churn away to yield all the particular facts about English grammar.

Omni: It sounds as if your present research goal is to reach the point where you can define every human language's grammar simply by specifying its choices from the universal grammar's menu of options.

Chomsky: That's the kind of work you would hope would soon be done: to take a theory of universal grammar, fix the parameters one way or another, and then deduce from these parameters the grammar of a real human language—Japanese, Swahili, English, or whatnot.

This goal is only on the horizon. But I think that it is within our conceptual grasp. Undoubtedly the principles of universal grammar that we currently theorize are wrong. It would be a miracle if we were right this early along. But the principles *are* of the right type, and we can now begin to test our present system with complex examples to see what is wrong and to make changes that will improve our theory. . . .

Omni: Moving on to another controversial area in the behavioral sciences, how do you think your views differ from B. F. Skinner's behaviorist theory of language, learning, and mind?

Chomsky: Skinner used to take a relatively extreme position. At one point he held that, apart from the most rudimentary functions, essentially nothing of importance was genetically programmed in the human brain. Skinner agreed that humans were genetically programmed to see and hear, but that's about all. Accordingly he argued that all human behavior was simply a reflection of training and experience. This view can't possibly be correct. And, in fact, Skinner's approach has led absolutely nowhere in this area. It has yielded no theoretical knowledge, no nontrivial principles as far as I am aware—thus far, at any rate.

Omni: Why is that?

Chomsky: Because Skinnerian behaviorism is off the wall. It's as hopeless a project as trying to explain that the onset of puberty results from social training. But I really don't know whether Skinner still maintains this extreme position. [*He has since modified it.—Ed.*]

Omni: What about the late Jean Piaget? Where do you stand on his theories of the child's mental development?

Chomsky: Piaget's position is different; it's more complex than Skinner's. Piaget held that the child passes through cognitive states. According to my understanding of the Piagetian literature, Piaget and his supporters were never really clear about what produced a new stage of cognitive development. What they could have said—though they seemed to shy away from it—is that cognitive development is a genetically determined maturational process like puberty, for example. That's what the Piagetians *ought* to say. They don't like this formulation, but it seems right to me.

Omni: In other words, Piagetians place much more emphasis on the role of experience in cognitive development than you do. Are there other differences as well?

Chomsky: Yes. Piagetians maintain that the mind develops as a whole rather than as a modular structure with specific capacities developing in their own ways. This is a possible hypothesis, but in fact it seems to be extremely wrong.

Omni: How do you mean?

Chomsky: Well, consider the properties that determine the reference of pronouns that we talked about earlier. Once you ferret out these rules for pronouns, they seem to have nothing in common with the logical operations that Piagetians single out as being typical of the early stages of the child's mental development.

Omni: In other words, a four-year-old who may not realize that the amount of water stays the same when you pour the contents of a low, wide glass into a tall, thin container nevertheless displays sophisticated logical abilities in his grasp of the complex rules of English grammar?

Chomsky: Yes. And these abilities are independent of the logical capacities measured by tests. There's just no resemblance between what a child does with blocks and the kind of knowledge that he displays of English grammar at the same age. In fact, I think it's sort of quixotic to expect tight interconnections between language development and growth in other mental domains. By and large, body systems develop in their own ways at their own rates. They interact, but the circulatory system doesn't wait until the visual system reaches a certain stage of organization before proceeding to imitate the visual system's organizational complexity. Cognitive growth shouldn't be different in this respect either. As far as we know, it isn't. . . .

FOR DISCUSSION AND REVIEW

1. Describe Chomsky's view of the relationship between language and most other human abilities.

2. Explain the basis for Chomsky's statement that "we should expect heredity to play a major role in language." What arguments does he use to support this assertion?

3. According to Chomsky, what is the relationship between heredity and environment as far as language is concerned?

4. What kind of linguistic evidence does Chomsky cite to support his argument that language depends on a genetic "language organ"? Give an example of your own that illustrates the kind of unconscious knowledge we have about language.

5. In your own words, explain what Chomsky means by "universal grammar." Give three examples of "genetically permitted variations" that occur in the universal grammar. Why is universal grammar an important concept?

Projects for "Syntax and Language Processing"

1. Briefly define the term *grammar*. Then ask at least five people, other than those in your class, to define the term. Jot down their definitions. Prepare a brief report in which you summarize your findings and compare them with the definition of *grammar* used by Neil Smith and Deirdre Wilson in "What Is a Language?"

2. In "What Do Speakers Know About Their Language?" Roderick A. Jacobs and Peter S. Rosenbaum give examples of sentences illustrating native speakers' ability to recognize a grammatical English sentence, to interpret the meaning of a sentence, to perceive ambiguity, and to determine when sentences are synonymous. Using your own native-speaker knowledge, give at least one example of a sentence that illustrates each kind of knowledge, and write a brief explanation of how your example illustrates the knowledge.

3. This exercise is a class activity. Read the following paragraph:

> The hunter crept through the leaves. The leaves had fallen. The leaves were dry. The hunter was tired. The hunter had a gun. The gun was new. The hunter saw a deer. The deer had antlers. A tree partly hid the antlers. The deer was beautiful. The hunter shot at the deer. The hunter missed. The shot frightened the deer. The deer bounded away.

Without changing important words or the meaning, rewrite the paragraph so as to avoid the many short, choppy sentences. Then compare the rewritten versions prepared by the different members of the class. Are the paragraphs alike? If not, describe the differences and account for the fact that passages that appear in such varying forms have the same meaning.

4. Prepare and circulate among five to ten people a short questionnaire designed to reveal (a) their experiences with grammar during their school years and (b) their attitudes toward grammar. Some information that you may want to obtain includes the grade(s) in which they were taught grammar, what was taught, how much time was devoted to grammar (compared, for example, to literature), the attitudes of the teachers and the students toward grammar, and the kind of grammar that was taught. Prepare a report summarizing your data. What conclusions can you draw?

5. Did your previous study of grammar enhance your understanding of English? Of other languages? If so, explain how; if not, explain why not. Be specific.

6. The study of English grammar has a long and interesting history. Write a paper or prepare an oral report on one of the following topics: the first English grammars; changing attitudes toward teaching

grammar in schools; "prescriptive" versus "descriptive" grammars; the effect on students' writing abilities of studying grammar.

7. In "The Cheshire Cat's Grin . . .," Jean Aitchison divides errors occurring in normal speech into two principal types: selection errors and programming errors. She also gives several subdivisions for each type. Make a list of all speech errors of these kinds that you hear in the course of a week; then classify them, using Aitchison's categories. Which kind(s) are more frequent? Using Aitchison's model of speech production, explain your findings.

8. Based on library research, prepare a report analyzing the differing opinions of Jean Piaget and Noam Chomsky about children's mental development.

9. As a native speaker of English, you have an internalized knowledge of the language—call it a "native-speaker intuition" if you will. For example, you can recognize a grammatical English sentence, you can interpret a sentence, you can perceive ambiguity, and you can determine when strings are synonymous. Examine the following groups of sentences; what can you tell about each group?

a. 1. The bus station is near the bank.
   2. The soldiers were told to stop marching on the parade ground.
   3. The chicken is ready to eat.
b. 1. That student continually sleeps in class.
   2. Student in class continually that sleeps.
   3. In class that student continually sleeps.
c. 1. The Pittsburgh Pirates beat the Baltimore Orioles in the World Series.
   2. The ones that the Pittsburgh Pirates beat in the World Series were the Baltimore Orioles.
   3. The Baltimore Orioles were beaten by the Pittsburgh Pirates in the World Series.
d. 1. Sam asked the students to build a display.
   2. Sam promised the students to build a display.
   3. Sam told the students to build a display.

Write a short paper describing your conclusions.

Selected Bibliography

Note: Jean Aitchison's article, "The Cheshire Cat's Grin . . .," in this section contains an excellent bibliography of works dealing with language processing. Because of the many recent and rapid developments in syntactic theory, you should be particularly aware of the dates of publication of the books listed here.

Akmajian, Adrian, Richard A. Demers, and Robert M. Harnish, *Linguistics: An Introduction to Language and Communication*, 2nd ed. Cambridge, MA: M.I.T. Press, 1984. (A thoroughly revised edition of a very good text.)

Akmajian, Adrian, and F. W. Heny. *An Introduction to the Principles of Transformational Syntax*. Cambridge, MA: M.I.T. Press, 1975. (An excellent introductory text.)

Baker, C. L. *Introduction to Generative-Transformational Syntax*. Englewood Cliffs, NJ: Prentice-Hall, 1978. (Another excellent text; very thorough.)

Bolinger, Dwight. *Aspects of Language*, 2nd ed. New York: Harcourt Brace Jovanovich, 1975. (A readable introduction to the study of language.)

Caplan, David, ed. *Biological Studies of Mental Processes*. Cambridge, MA: M.I.T. Press, 1980. (Fifteen difficult but important essays.)

Chomsky, Noam. *Aspects of the Theory of Syntax*. Cambridge, MA: M.I.T. Press, 1965. (The first major revision of TG theory as originally described in *Syntactic Structures*.)

————. *Syntactic Structures*. The Hague: Mouton & Company, 1957. (Essential but difficult study; where it all began.)

Cole, Ronald A. "Navigating the Slippery Stream of Speech," *Psychology Today* (April 1979), pp. 77–78, 82–94. (Fascinating discussion of how people segment and understand the constantly changing stream of sound that constitutes speech.)

Culicover, Peter W. *Syntax*. New York: Academic Press, 1976. (An excellent introduction to the study of the formal syntax of natural language; presupposes some previous work in linguistics.)

Fromkin, Victoria, and Robert Rodman. *An Introduction to Language*, 3rd ed. New York: Holt, Rinehart and Winston, 1983. (An outstandingly readable text for introductory courses in linguistics.)

Grinder, John T., and Suzette Haden Elgin. *Guide to Transformational Grammar: History, Theory, Practice*. New York: Holt, Rinehart and Winston, 1973. (Marred by typographical errors, but still a valuable presentation.)

Halle, Morris, Joan Bresnan, and George A. Miller, eds. *Linguistic Theory and Psychological Reality*. Cambridge, MA: M.I.T. Press, 1978. (With nine main divisions that include material by eleven authors, this is a valuable collection; not for beginners.)

Huddleston, Rodney. *An Introduction to English Transformational Syntax*. London: Longman, 1976. (Emphasis on syntax; little about semantics and phonology.

Jacobs, Roderick A., and Peter S. Rosenbaum, eds. *Readings in English Transformational Grammar*. Waltham, MA: Ginn and Company, 1970. (Anthology of theoretical and descriptive articles; excellent bibliography.)

Johnson, Nancy Ainsworth: *Current Topics in Language: Introductory Readings*. Cambridge, MA: Winthrop Publishers, Inc., 1976. (Essays with a practical orientation.)

Joos, Martin, ed. *Readings in Linguistics*. Chicago: University of Chicago Press, 1966. (Traces the development of linguistics in the U.S. since 1925.)

Kayser, Samuel Jay, and Paul M. Postal. *Beginning English Grammar*. New York: Harper & Row, 1976. (Stresses syntactic argumentation, not just assertion.)

Langacker, Ronald W. *Language and Its Structure: Some Fundamental Linguistic Concepts*, 2nd ed. New York: Harcourt Brace Jovanovich, 1973. (Langacker cogently builds the case for universal principles of language organization in his chapter "The Universality of Language Design.")

Lenneberg, Eric H. *Biological Foundations of Language*. New York: John Wiley, 1967. (A classic work that every student of linguistics should be familiar with.)

Lester, Mark, ed. *Readings in Applied Transformational Grammar*. New York: Holt, Rinehart and Winston, 1970. (Intended for a nontechnical audience and including articles about psycholinguistic questions and the applications of transformational grammar.)

Lieber, Justin. *Noam Chomsky: A Philosophic Overview*. New York: St. Martin's Press, 1975. (Chomsky says of this book, "It is the book that I would recommend to people who ask me what I'm up to.")

Lightfoot, David. *The Language Lottery: Toward a Biology of Grammars*. Cambridge, MA: M.I.T. Press, 1982. (Highly recommended; not an introduction to the whole field of linguistics, but an exploration of the question "What is the genetic, internally prescribed basis of language structure?" Excellent bibliography.)

Lyons, John. *Introduction to Theoretical Linguistics*. Cambridge: Cambridge University Press, 1968. (Still very useful despite its date; unusually complete.)

Lyons, John. *Noam Chomsky* rev. ed. New York: The Viking Press, 1978. (Clear and complete account of Chomsky's central ideas. Contains a bibliography of Chomsky's works to 1976.)

Newmeyer, Frederick J. *Linguistic Theory in America: The First Quarter-Century of Transformational Generative Grammar*. New York: Academic Press, 1980. (An important work; traces chronologically and in detail the evolution of transformational-generative theory from the 1950s through the 1970s.)

Piattellini-Palmarini, M., ed. *Language and Learning: The Debate Between Jean Piaget and Noam Chomsky*. London: Routledge and Kegan Paul, 1980. (Fascinating presentation of Piaget's ideas about developmental stages and his belief that the mind develops as a whole, and of Chomsky's thesis that various aspects of the mind develop in their own ways.)

Postal, Paul M. "Underlying and Superficial Linguistic Structure." *Harvard Educational Review* 34 (1964), 246–66; reprinted in Reibel and Schane, eds. (see below). (A basic article.)

Radford, Andrew. *Transformational Syntax: A Student's Guide to Chomsky's Extended Standard Theory*. Cambridge: Cambridge University Press, 1981. (One of the most up-to-date specialized texts; useful chapter bibliographies.)

Reibel, David A., and Sanford A. Schane, eds. *Modern Studies in English: Readings in Transformational Grammar*. Englewood Cliffs, NJ: Prentice-Hall, 1969. (Anthology of articles on the transformational analysis of English.)

Soames, Scott, and David M. Perlmutter. *Syntactic Argumentation and the Structure of English*. Berkeley: University of California Press, 1979. (Difficult but valuable; focuses on syntactic argumentation and alternative hypothesis testing.)

Studdert-Kennedy, Michael, ed. *Psychobiology of Language*. Cambridge, MA: M.I.T. Press, 1983. (A collection of twenty essays; difficult but rewarding).

Part Six

Semantics and Pragmatics

Having looked at three of the basic systems of language (phonetics and phonology, morphology, and syntax) in Parts Four and Five, we now turn to semantics and pragmatics, the two other major divisions of language.

In the introduction to Part Four, we defined *semantics* as "the analysis of the meaning of individual words and of such larger units as phrases and sentences." However, this definition is too simple. As George L. Dillon writes in the first selection of Part Six, "Most writers on semantics would agree that it is the study of meaning. This is probably the only statement about the subject that all would subscribe to, and disagreement begins with what is properly meant by *meaning*." Part of this disagreement arises because linguists and logicians tend to use the word *semantics* differently. Also, although semantics is currently a field of much interest to linguists (and also one characterized by much controversy), this interest developed only within the last twenty years as linguists realized that a complete description of what native speakers know about their language must include semantics.

The first two selections in Part Six deal with semantics. In the first, George L. Dillon presents one model for a description of the knowledge that native speakers have about semantics: (1) words can be ambiguous and can make sentences in which they occur ambiguous; (2) some combinations of words are anomalous, some are contradictory, and some are redundant; (3) some words share parts of their meanings, and there are special kinds of such relationships; and (4) just as words can have special relationships to other words, so too can sentences have specific relationships to other sentences, such as entailment and equivalency in truth value. Finally, Dillon argues that the best analysis of these facts will probably be the one that is the most general and explicit—and that is a long way from being completed.

Following this general introduction, Mark Aronoff focuses on a specific semantic field, which he describes as "distinctly mundane": automobile semantics. He demonstrates that many words in this field can be understood only in relationship to one another; that aspects of the meaning of terms change rapidly and vary from person to person, although the changes themselves are regular; and that the changes in automobile semantics illustrate one common type of semantic change—that is, downgrading, or pejoration. (A familiar example involves the word *stench*, which was a common word in Old English and originally meant a strong smell, either pleasant or unpleasant. But it underwent downgrading, and thus has come to mean a strong and definitely unpleasant smell.)

The second basic system of language dealt with in Part Six is *pragmatics*, the study of speech acts or of how language is used in various contexts. Linguists have increasingly realized that the context of an utterance plays an important part in determining its meaning, as do beliefs that are shared by a speaker and a hearer. In "Pragmatics," Madelon E. Heatherington briefly describes three basic kinds of speech-act principles. Not unexpectedly, these principles interact, and like the other basic systems of language, they are rule-governed and part of what native speakers "know" about their language. Interestingly, damage to the brain's right hemisphere often disrupts normal functioning of both perception and production of various aspects of language involved in pragmatics. As Sid J. Segalowitz writes, "some subtle characteristics [of language] are disrupted more by right-sided brain damage than by left-sided damage: expression of emotion and feelings, inference of others' feelings and motivations, and a sense of humor." (*Two Sides of the Brain.* Englewood Cliffs, NJ: Prentice-Hall, 1983, p. 42.)

In the final selection, "Discourse Routines," Elaine Chaika offers specific examples of the ways in which social contexts often determine the meaning of what is said. In an abstract of "Discourse Routines," not included here, she writes:

> We control others and they control us by shared discourse routines. By saying certain things, the other party in a dialogue forces certain responses in us. Questions demand answers, and compliments elicit thanks, for instance. In order to understand these routines, one must understand the society in which they occur. Simply knowing the language is not suffi-

cient, for the true meaning often lies not in the actual words uttered but in a complex of social knowledge. Examining such routines can help us understand the unspoken assumptions on which a society is based (*Language: The Social Mirror* [Rowley, MA: Newbury House Publishers, 1982], p. 69).

1/The Meaning of A Word

GEORGE L. DILLON

Semantics—the analysis of the meaning of individual words and of such larger units as phrases and sentences—is one of the basic systems of language. It is also a controversial area, with many unresolved problems, and an area in which a lot of research is being done. In the following chapter from his book Introduction to Contemporary Linguistic Semantics, *Professor Dillon suggests a model to explain the kinds of semantic knowledge native speakers have. Speakers, he points out, know that some words are ambiguous and that their use can result in ambiguous sentences; that some combinations of words are anomalous or contradictory or redundant; that some words are related in meaning; and that sentences have certain kinds of logical relations to each other. He develops these central ideas with detailed examples, analyzing both the linguistic meaning of words (sometimes called* lexical semantics) *and the linguistic meaning of sentences* (sentence semantics).

The Domain of Semantics

Most writers on semantics would agree that it is the study of meanings. This is probably the only statement about the subject that all would subscribe to, and disagreement begins with what is properly meant by *meaning*. Nonetheless, a number of linguists have in recent years come to a shared understanding of what they would like to explain . . . . Essentially, they propose to explicate the knowledge speakers must have to be able to make the following judgments about words and sentences of the language:

(a) that many words are *ambiguous* over more than one *sense* and hence that some sentences containing them can be taken more than one way:

> He dusted the plants. ("put it on" or "took it off")
> She watered them. ("diluted" or "nourished")
> He is a tiger. (two- or four-legged)

(b) that various words in certain combinations are incongruous or *anomalous:*

> They amused the tulips.
> Green ideas sleep furiously.

(c) that certain combinations are *contradictory:*

> colorless red fabric
> accidentally chase

(d) that certain combinations are *redundant:*

> intentionally murder
> male uncle
> scrutinize carefully
> circumnavigate around

(e) that certain words share one or more elements of meaning—they are *related* in meaning:

> chase, follow, pursue
> embezzle, pilfer, filch, shoplift

(f) that a special case of relatedness exists where some words are more specific than more general words:

> parent—father
> cut—snip
> take—steal—embezzle

(g) that sentences have logical relations to other sentences—some *entail* other sentences:

> She killed him. He died.

some sentences are *equivalent* in truth-value:

> The book is underneath the pillow. The pillow is on top of the book.

(h) that an element of meaning, while not strictly part of the meaning of a word, is usually *associated* with it, or sometimes associated with it:

> Tigers are (usually) fierce.

One assumes that making these judgments draws on knowledge of the meanings of the words involved (plus knowledge about how these meanings are combined in sentences), and insofar as speakers agree in their judgments of particular cases (and they don't always) this knowledge is the same in the mind of each speaker.

Two facts about this knowledge are evident at the outset. First, word meanings cannot be unanalyzable wholes, each one arbitrarily different from every other, or judgments of relatedness and entailment could not be made. Second, judgments of anomaly and contradiction can be made with regard to whole classes of items: *colorless blue fabric* is as bad as *colorless red fabric, accidentally commit perjury* is as bad as *accidentally chase.* A major portion of modern linguistic semantics is devoted to finding the most general and explicit terms for analyzing this knowledge. A lot of it is represented in a scattered and implicit way in dictionaries—semantics aims at making it explicit and showing the general patterns. The most general and explicit analysis is not guaranteed to be psychologically the most real, however, for at least two reasons: one is that people undoubtedly differ in the degree to which they maximize the generality and simplicity of their codings of word meanings ("verbal aptitude" tests measure this); the other is that there may be alternative analyses that maximize generality in other areas of vocabulary, though not in the area in which we are looking. One person told me that she had always analyzed *telegraph* as "communicate a written message (electro)mechanically" (linking it with *write* and *telephone*) rather than "write at a distance" (linking it with *telephone, telescope, teletype*). Whether one analyzes *telegraph* her way or the other way does not affect the truth-value of *telegraph*. Both analyses, for example, can account for the contradiction in

I kept your location secret though I telegraphed it to the FBI.

Obviously one cannot make substantive claims about maximum generality and simplicity until whole vocabularies have been analyzed, and the accomplishment of this task lies very far in the future. The classic studies in descriptive semantics have been done in what appear to be fairly clearly bounded "fields" such as kinship terms, adjectival and prepositional meanings, causative and inchoative verbs, verbs of judging and verbs of cooking, and even with these there arise problems of psychological reality. Still, there is no question that the impulse to analyze and generalize is one very strong component in the human cognitive apparatus. . . .

Sameness and Difference of Meaning

When people speak of the meaning of a word, they are usually speaking about one of its senses (corresponding roughly to the numbered subdivisions of a dictionary entry), usually what they believe is the primary or central sense. They do not mean to generalize on what all the senses have in common. It is not always obvious, however, how many different senses should be discriminated for a word, or whether a word in two sentences is being used in the same or different senses (or whether, indeed, it is the same word. . . . Linguists have developed "gapping" and "pronominalization" tests based on the fact that words can be gapped and pronominalized in conjoined sentences only when they are used in the same sense. When they are used in different senses, the effect is that of a pun. For example,

John watered the plants, and Mary watered the lawn.

can be gapped to

John watered the plants, and Mary, the lawn.

but the effect of

John watered the plants, and Mary, the drinks.

is mildly humorous, giving rise to the conclusion that *water* in *water the drinks* is used in a different sense ("dilute by adding water to") from that of the first *water* ("nourish by applying water to"). On the other hand, using *paint* to mean "protect by applying paint to" and to mean "decorate by applying paint to" would seem to be using the word in the same sense:

Mary painted the hall, and John, the downspouts.

Rather than say *paint* has two senses ("decorate" and "protect") we should say that it has only one ("apply paint to") with a certain range of purposes. The intention of protecting or decorating must be present, however: if a baby wiped paint-covered hands on the wall, we would not say that it painted the wall, except ironically. Actually, one might try to apply a different sense of *paint* here—"to produce in lines and colors on a surface by putting paint on something"—but the Direct Object of *paint* for this sense must be an object of art (mural, water-color, etc.) or understood as a visual representation of the thing (*painted the tree in water-colors*—i.e., "a picture of the tree")—presumably the baby's smears would not amount to the representation of a wall, or anything else.

For another example, consider whether *suggest* has a different sense when used with a human Subject from the sense it has when used with a nonhuman Subject:

John suggested to Mary that she should get snow tires.
The skid suggested to Mary that she should get snow tires.

A slight variation of the gapping test yields the mildly humorous effect of a word being used in different senses:

> John suggested to Mary that she should get snow tires and so did the skid. . . .

The definition of a sense of a word is the representation of the sense in terms of other words. That is, the definition *paraphrases* the sense or is *synonymous* with the word in the relevant sense (or should be). To explicate this basic notion of "sameness of sense" it is necessary to introduce some logical terminology. Briefly, for S_1 to be said to be a paraphrase of S_2, it is necessary that S_1 and S_2 be truth-functionally equivalent (i.e., that S_1 logically entail S_2 and vice versa). Entailment is basically the notion "follows from" and will be defined as follows:

> S_1 *entails* S_2 if, over the whole range of possible situations truly described by S_1, S_2 would be true also.

For example, the sentence:

> S_1: John got out of bed at 10 o'clock.

entails the sentence:

> S_2: John was in bed immediately prior to 10 o'clock.

because there is no situation of which S_1 would be true but S_2 false. That is, if he got out of bed at 10 o'clock, then he *necessarily* was in bed to start with. Hence the conjunction of S_1 and *not-S_2* should be a contradiction (false in all possible worlds) (the X marks a contradiction):

> XJohn got out of bed at 10 o'clock though he wasn't in it then.

Other examples of entailment pairs (the arrow $\rightarrow$ indicates "entails") are:

> Jumbo is an elephant. $\rightarrow$ Jumbo is a mammal.
> John stopped beating his wife. $\rightarrow$ John was beating or used to beat his wife.
> John regrets beating his wife. $\rightarrow$ John beat his wife.

(Verbs like *stop* and *regret* are called "factive" verbs because they always entail the truth of their complements.)

Some reflection is often necessary to determine whether a relation between sentences is a true logical entailment. For example, the sentence:

S_1: He sharpened the knife.

might be said to entail:

S_2: The knife became sharp.

There are situations, however, of which S_1 would be true but not S_2, namely ones in which the knife became less dull but still not what one would want to call sharp.

If it happens also to be the case that S_2 entails S_1, then S_1 and S_2 are logically or truth-functionally *equivalent:*

S_1: John committed suicide.
S_2: John killed himself.

S_1: Not everyone came.
S_2: Some didn't come.

Again, the relation between two sentences may be close but fall short of full equivalence. *Forbid,* for example, entails *not permit,* but there are some cases where *not permit* does not entail *forbid*—where, that is, *not permit* would be true, but *forbid* false:

They didn't permit the crabgrass to spread.

One could argue, however, that there are really two senses of *permit,* one of which is equivalent to "grant permission to," the other equivalent to "allow to happen," and that, for the first of these, *not permit$_1$* is equivalent to *forbid.* This still will not work, however, since the following is not a contradiction:

They didn't *permit$_1$* him to leave, but they didn't forbid him to either.

Notice, by the way, that the *suicide* example is not quite right: suppose John were an anarchist who was working on a bomb and blew himself up by mistake—in that case, S_2 would be true but not S_1. If the word *deliberately* is added to S_2, however, the sentences are equivalent.

Logical entailment must be distinguished from what might be called factual entailment. As an example of the latter, S_1 might be said to factually entail S_2:

S_1: The batter hit a fly ball into center field which was caught.
S_2: The batter was out.

The "following" of S_2 from S_1 here depends on the rules of baseball rather than the meaning of *hit a fly ball* (and of course depends on the assumption that a game was in progress). This distinction is particularly hard to draw when the factual relation is one of natural cause and effect:

S_1: It began to rain.
S_2: The ground began to get wet.

This is a factual relation, however, not a logical one, because we can imagine circumstances in which the ground would not get wet when it rained (for instance, if it were covered with a tarpaulin).

Two Aspects of Extralogical Meaning

Sentences may convey more than their logical content. Two aspects of extralogical meaning are easily confused with logical meaning and must be distinguished from it: shadings associated with the grammatical relations Subject and Direct Object, and inferences arising from the pragmatics or "use" of sentences.

Shadings associated with what is Subject appear in the following sets:

(1) a. John met Harry.
    b. Harry met John.
    c. John and Harry met.
(2) a. The truck collided with the bus.
    b. The bus collided with the truck.
    c. The bus and the truck collided.
(3) a. The car is behind the bus.
    b. The bus is in front of the car.
(4) a. The devil used to be frightening to the ignorant.
    b. People used to be afraid of the devil before the age of science.

There seem to be three relevant properties we associate with Subjects: first, they are usually what the sentence is about (that is, the topic or *theme* under discussion). Thus (1a) seems to present the encounter as "what happened to John"—from his point of view, so to speak—but (1b) presents it from Harry's point of view and (1c) presents it as a mutual experience. So also in (3): one sentence is about the location of the car, the other about the location of the bus. Second, the Subject is often assumed to be the instigator or "doer" even when the verb does not clearly refer to an action performed by someone on someone or something. Thus in (2), (a) would be preferred if the bus were stationary, (b) if the truck were stationary, and (c) if neither were. The same considerations apply in (1) if we imagine situations where one or the other is stationary. Third, referentiality is preeminently a property of Subjects. Hence (4a) tends to suggest the existence (in at least the speaker's mind) of a referent for *the devil* more strongly than (4b) does.

The following sets have to do with what is the Direct Object:

(5) a. They loaded the truck with furniture.
    b. They loaded furniture onto the truck.
(6) a. They smeared the wall with paint.
    b. They smeared paint on the wall.
(7) a. I teach the little monsters arithmetic.
    b. I teach arithmetic to the little monsters.
(8) a. I am angry at Mary marrying that old man.
    b. I am angry at Mary's marrying that old man.
(9) a. I expected Mary to support me.
    b. I expected that Mary would support me.

One might say that the Direct Object is assumed to be the most directly and completely affected participant. (5a) more strongly suggests a full truck than (5b), (6a) a covered wall. (7a) suggests more strongly than (7b) success at the teaching (i.e., they learn). In (8a) and (9a) the anger and expectation seem more directed at Mary than in the (b) sentences. . . .

Certain inferences that can be made from sentences appear to be based on how the sentence functions in actual speech situations. These are generally called *conversational implicatures* to distinguish them from logical entailments. One assumes that a Speaker speaks in good faith, which means among other things that he is trying not to mislead his Hearer, is trying to convey information he things his Hearer wants to know or should know, and is not making unreasonable assumptions. For example, if you tell someone that something is possible, you conversationally implicate that it is not to your knowledge certain. If I said:

You may fail.

you would be justified in assuming that you have a chance to pass—such a statement from me after I had turned in an F would be highly misleading. . . .

Analysis into Components

The notion that the sense of a word can be expressed as a combination of the senses of other words is familiar to anyone who has used a dictionary. The goals of a semanticist and those of a lexicographer, however, differ considerably: one would like to make logical entailments and systematic relations of word senses clear, the other aims at giving clues to the common uses of words. In many cases it is possible to adapt a dictionary definition to semantic ends. For example, we can confirm the results of the gapping test with *water* by showing that the two different senses that the test indicated correspond to two different sets of entailments:

$water_1$: nourish by applying water to → nourish
  → put water on

$water_2$: dilute by adding water to → dilute
  → put water in

The senses of *water* here are not simply the sum of the two entailed parts, however, but include a causative or purposive relation between them. From here on, the term *component* will be used for these parts of meaning (other terms are *feature, sememe,* semantic *marker*), and they will be printed in block capitals to signify that they represent one sense of the word that they usually represent. The components may themselves abbreviate a complex of other components. . . .

The usefulness of componential analysis is perhaps most apparent when we consider the relations of words constituting an interlocking set, like kinship terms. With the components *male, female, parent* we can analyze the main senses of *father, mother, son, daughter, brother, sister.* For example:

X is father of Y: X parent Y & X male
X is brother of Y: A&B parent X&Y & X male. . . .

Taxonomic Hierarchies

It is not surprising that kinship terminology constitutes an inter-locking set of contrasts along certain parameters. In general, terms referring to human institutions, artifacts, and actions can be defined at least roughly in this manner. The human instinct to classify and differentiate is most at home here—much less so in regard to natural objects and processes (e.g., *pear, thunder, wither*). There seems to be a human ability and tendency to arrange things into genera-and-species groupings, usually called *taxonomic hierarchies,* and these can be directly translated into componential definitions. For example, rifles, pistols, and shotguns can be classified as sidearms, differing in how they are held and the nature of the bore of their barrels. These contrasts can be represented in a branching tree:

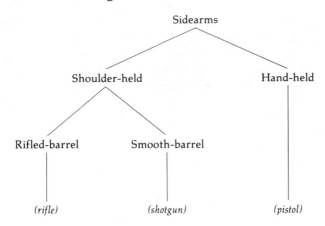

which translates into the analysis:

> *shotgun*: sidearm & shoulder-held & smooth-barrel
> *rifle*: sidearm & shoulder-held & rifled-barrel
> *pistol*: sidearm & hand-held

Notice that the components are entailed by the words:

> It is a shotgun.→ It is smooth-barreled.
> → It is shoulder-held.
> → It is a sidearm.*

There are other attributes of shotguns, however, not represented in the definition. These would include: *pellet-firing, double-barrel, short range,* and *for shooting game.* These attributes differ from the preceding ones, however, in that they are not necessary properties of things called shotguns. That is, they are not entailed by the sentence *It is a shotgun;* rather, they are only *associated* components. The phrase *rifled shotgun* is contradictory: there can be no object properly called a shotgun that is rifled. The phrases *slug-firing shotgun, single-barreled shotgun,* and so on are not contradictory: the modifiers block off components that are only associated. . . .

More on Associated Components

Speakers not only discriminate definitional and associated components—they discriminate between closely and loosely associated components. George Lakoff (1972) has pointed out that hedge-words

---

* Editor's note: These are treated as *definitional* components and, as such, are entailed by the words.

like *technically, strictly, loosely speaking, sort of, kind of, regular,* and *real* are sensitive to these discriminations. There are things that, while possessing the definitional attributes necessary to be referred to by an item, lack any of the associated attributes. In this case the hedge-word *technically* is appropriate:

Mae West is technically a spinster.

If the definitional attributes are present, and also some closely associated one or ones, but the more loosely associated ones are absent, the likely hedge-word is *strictly speaking*:

Strictly speaking, a whale is a mammal.

If we still want to refer to something that lacks the definitional attributes but has some of the associated ones, we can use *loosely speaking* or *in a manner of speaking:*

Loosely speaking, the whale is a fish.
In a manner of speaking, bats are birds.

Finally, if something has some attribute only loosely associated, and lacks the definitional and more tightly associated ones, the appropriate hedge is *real* or *regular:*

Harry is a regular fish.
Sam is a real tiger.

Notice that in the last examples the hedge-word can be omitted. . . .

How Children Learn Word Meanings

It is well known that younger children appear to overgeneralize the first words they learn, applying them to a wider range of things than they would be applied to in adult speech. A number of people, including Eve Clark (1973), have pointed out that these overgeneralizations can be viewed as underspecified senses. For example, if certain children use *apple* to refer to oranges, tennis balls, door knobs, and paper weights as well as apples, one can conclude from their uses that they have for the sense of *apple* [*spherical & small*] and not much else. Their learning to restrict the term to the range of things that adults call apples would involve adding definitional components to that sense, and perhaps in some cases demoting a component previously taken as definitional to associated status, or dropping an associated component altogether. Demotion appears to be involved in children's learning of kinship terms, where the component *adult* seems definitional for *uncle* for younger children but of course must be demoted to associated status to get an adult's sense of *uncle*.

There is a fairly good basis (surveyed in Clark, 1973) for supposing that the components children initially make use of for definitions are those that refer to perceivable qualities like shape, sound, and texture rather than those that refer to more abstract properties like function (what something is used for). Since, for very many nouns, what it is used for, or functions as, is important in its definition, children will have to considerably reorganize their vocabularies as they come to recognize that at times a functional definition, rather than a physical one, gives a more coherent generalization about the things people call, e.g., *polish*. Some research by Elaine Andersen (1975) concerning the terms *cup* and *glass* explores the specification that children of different ages have of these terms by asking them to name and sort an array of objects as cups, glasses, or neither. Not all of the objects would be called either glass or cup by adults (i.e., there are some glass bowllike things in the array). The observer can infer the bases of the naming and the specificity of the terms. It appears that younger children (up to six years) take the physical shape and material as the predominant definitional components, the older ones, like adults, rely more on probable function. Thus younger children will call a tall cylindrical plastic container a cup because it is made of plastic, especially if colored plastic, and a glass "bowl" a glass. There is a great deal more to be learned from this study, which the reader is urged to consult.

These terms are particularly tricky, because one term is also the name of a material (*glass*) but *cup* is not. This seems to induce us to call a thing that is a glass in shape and function a paper cup, though it may lack a handle. Having a handle is in general a good discriminator of a cup, but not perfect, and there are mugs to worry about as well as small bowls. In short, these terms "partition" the field of "drinking vessels" (notice the functionally defined term *drinking* has been smuggled in) but they do not constitute a discrete partitioning of the field—there are overlaps and conflicting criteria—and a taxonomic hierarchy like that set up for sidearms would be very difficult to construct. This situation is not uncommon: Adrienne Lehrer (1969) has noted that the set of verbs of cooking is not perfectly analyzable into a single hierarchy (*roast*, for example, overlaps *bake* and *broil*), and one might find similar results for *pot/pan*, etc. (and see Lehrer, 1974). Older children and adults come to accept that the most natural and useful senses of terms may be neither inclusive enough to refer appropriately to any object we come across or conclusive enough to decide whether a given thing should be called by one or another term (consider *anxiety, fear, appre-*

hension, uneasiness, . . .). They learn to modify and hedge their applications and even to explain them: "You could call it a cup since it is cuppy in shape—bowls are wider and shallower"; "It's sort of a bowl"; and so on.

The shift that Andersen found from components based on form (in the broad sense of "all physical characteristics") to those of function is most interesting in regard to adult definitions of instrument and artifact nouns generally. Dictionary definitions often mention both form and function, sometimes giving more weight to form, sometimes to function. Consider the definitions of *hammer* and *polish* given in [*Webster's New Collegiate Dictionary*].

> *hammer$_n$*: *1a.* A hand tool consisting of a solid head set crosswise on a handle and used for pounding.
> *polish$_n$*: *3.* A preparation that is used to produce a gloss and often a color for the protection and decoration of a surface.

Form and function are given about equal weight for *hammer*, but with *polish* function is the sole component. If children's definitions are heavy to the form side and weak to the function, one would expect them to generalize *hammer* to include axes and adzes and to have some trouble getting a stable sense for *polish*. I noticed both phenomena in my daughter's speech at age three, who insisted on calling shoe polish, applied with a brush, *paint*, but rejected the term for an unpigmented polish squeezed from a tube and applied with a rag, suggesting with question intonation: toof-paste?! I do not know the degree to which adults vary in the amount of redefinition they have performed for individual words and the relative weight they give to form and function, but I suspect that it may be fairly great. Georgia Green (1972: 86) observed that for her "anything which could be used to paste with is paste, but not everything that you could 'glue' with is glue." For me, it is roughly the opposite: *glue* is the more functionally defined term, *paste* the more formally defined.

There is an apparent contradiction between the claimed priority of formal to functional definition and recent work by Katherine Nelson (1974) discussed by Judith Kornfeld (1975), though this turns on what is meant by *function*. Nelson argues that very young children (12 to 15 months) appear to class items as similar that can be acted upon in the same way: they will, for example, pick a cylinder as "like a ball" rather than a fixed sphere held in a frame because they can roll the cylinder but not the fixed sphere. This is a dynamic or "motor"-oriented classification, which may be reanalyzed in terms of "static" properties of form later. Obviously, *function* as we have been using the term is a far more abstract kind of coding involving typical or canonical or intended uses. Kornfeld reports cases of retarded and learning-disabled children (mental age two and a half to four years) who seem still to be functioning on this level, responding to a direction to "put the book on the chair" by taking the book and sitting on the chair. In effect, *chair* seems to be coded "for sitting on" whenever it turns up. Nelson observes that this sort of primitive, preconceptual "knowledge" of things (and relations) is important even in adulthood.

A final point is that functional properties are inherently relational, while form properties are not, and that words that involve relational components in their definitions (e.g., kinship terms, many adjectives) are not mastered in the exact adult sense until quite late in childhood (9 to 11 years). This suggests that relational components involve greater cognitive complexity than formal components. The reanalysis of, e.g., *X brother Y* from [*X male & X not adult*] to [*X male & A&B parent X&Y*] is not merely the substitution of one definitional component for another: it is the substitution of a relational for a nonrelational one and as such reflects a major step in cognitive development. . . .

This [discussion] has been about the structure of word senses. Analyzing the senses of words into configurations of components enables one to predict for a given sentence what its entailments will be, what other sentences will be equivalent to it, what sentences will be redundant, and what contradictory. These components constitute the definitional core of a sense. Other components appear to be present also, though not so centrally as to affect the truth-value of sentences containing the word. Speakers vary somewhat in their sorting of components into definitional, closely and loosely associated groups, and some of the variation may be a residue of incomplete reanalysis of previously learned senses.

The judgments not yet discussed are those of ambiguity and anomaly. The meanings of words are also reflected in the potential of the word for combining with other words. One of the things that speakers know about *amuse*, for example, is that it requires the noun that functions as its Direct Object to refer to a thing of a certain class, namely, a human or animal. Otherwise the sentence will be anomalous (*They amused the tulips.*). This is called a *selectional* (or *co-occurrence*) *restriction* of the verb *amuse*. The operation of selectional restrictions is reflected in the fact that words are generally more determinate in meaning when used in sentences than when cited in isolation. The word *water*, in isolation, might be thought of as a noun or a verb. In

She watered them.

it is clearly a verb because of its construction with a noun and a pronoun, but it is still ambiguous over at least two senses. But if the Direct Object is further specified:

She watered the plants.

the possibility of the "dilute" sense is cancelled. . . .

References

Andersen, Elaine. "Cups and Glasses: Learning that Boundaries are Vague," *Journal of Child Language,* 2 (1975), 79–103.

Clark, Eve V. "What's in a Word? On the Child's Acquisition of Semantics in His First Language," in *Cognitive Development and the Acquisition of Language,* ed. T. E. Moore. New York: Academic Press, 1973.

Green, Georgia M. "Some Observations on the Syntax and Semantics of Instrumental Verbs," in *Papers From the Eighth Regional Meeting of the Chicago Linguistic Society,* ed. Paul M. Peranteau, Judith N. Levi, and Gloria C. Phares, 1972.

Kornfeld, Judith. "Some Insights into the Cognitive Representation of Word Meanings," in *Papers From the Parasession on Functionalism,* ed. Robin E. Grossman, L. James San, and Timothy J. Vance. Chicago Linguistic Society, 1975.

Lakoff, George. "Hedges: a Study in Meaning Criteria and the Logic of Fuzzy Concepts," in *Papers From the Eighth Regional Meeting of the Chicago Linguistic Society,* ed. Paul M. Peranteau, Judith N. Levi, and Gloria C. Phares, 1972.

Lehrer, Adrienne. "Semantic Cuisine," *Journal of Linguistics,* 5 (1969), 39–55.

———. *Semantic Fields and Lexical Structure.* New York: North Holland/American Elsevier, 1974.

Nelson, Katherine. "Concept, Word, and Sentence . . . ," *Psychological Review,* 81 (1974), 267–85.

FOR DISCUSSION AND REVIEW

1. **Make up an example of your own to illustrate each of the following points made by Dillon:**
    a. "[M]any words are *ambiguous* over more than one *sense* and hence . . . some sentences containing them can be taken more than one way. . . ."
    b. "[V]arious words in certain combinations are incongruous or *anomalous.*"
    c. "[C]ertain combinations [of words] are *contradictory.*"
    d. "[C]ertain combinations [of words] are *redundant.*"
    e. "[C]ertain words . . . are *related* in meaning."
    f. "[A] special case of relatedness exists where some words are more specific than more general words."
    g. Some sentences "*entail* other sentences."
    h. "[S]ome sentences are *equivalent* in truth-value. . . ."
    i. "[A]n element of meaning, while not strictly part of the meaning of a word, is usually [or sometimes] *associated* with it. . . ."

2. Using original examples, explain why "word meanings cannot be un-analyzable wholes" and why "judgments of anomaly and contradiction can be made with regard to whole classes of items."

3. Try to arrange the following terms in an age sequence (oldest to youngest or youngest to oldest), and then write a brief explanation of your reasons for choosing the order upon which you decided:

baby girl	young girl
woman	little girl
girl	young woman

(It may help to try each word or phrase in a context such as: *Yesterday I saw a _____ at the beach.*) Would you use the same terms if the individual referred to were present? (Adapted from Dwight Bolinger, *Aspects of Language,* 2nd ed. [New York: Harcourt Brace Jovanovich, 1975], p. 231.)

4. Create two sentences that illustrate the "gapping" test and two that illustrate the "pronominalization" test.

5. Explain the difference between *logical entailment* and *factual entailment,* and give an original example of each.

6. According to Dillon, two reasons that "sentences may convey more than their logical content" are "shadings associated with the grammatical relations Subject and Direct Object" and "inferences arising from the pragmatics or 'use' of sentences." Make up two sentences that illustrate each of these types of "extralogical meaning." Be prepared to explain how your examples work.

7. Explain the concept of "hedge words." Then make up a sentence in which each of the following hedge words could be used appropriately: *technically, strictly, loosely speaking, sort of, kind of, regular,* and *real.*

8. Explain what is odd or false about each of the following sentences. (Taken from George L. Dillon, *Introduction to Contemporary Linguistic Semantics.* Englewood Cliffs, NJ: Prentice-Hall, 1977, p. 24.)
   a. Strictly speaking the president is the chief executive.
   b. A beagle is sort of a dog.
   c. Loosely speaking, Peter is a skunk.
   d. A whale is a typical mammal.
   e. Strictly speaking, tomatoes are vegetables.

2/Automobile Semantics

MARK ARONOFF

Most Americans are familiar with the names of many car makes and lines and with the terms describing car sizes and models. In fact, we take these terms for granted; statements like "He bought a Cadillac convertible" or "She drives a Chevrolet Cavalier" convey information in an apparently uncomplicated way. However, as Professor Mark Aronoff of the State University of New York at Stony Brook makes clear in the following selection, an analysis of automobile semantics can demonstrate the validity of "the theory of semantic oppositions by showing that the senses of a number of words in one particular domain (i.e., automobile semantics) can be understood only in relation to one another." He also illustrates dramatically that "the systematic sense of any car name consists of the position which that car occupies in a semantic space relative to other kinds of cars." In other words, American car names do not have absolute values at all. They are part of a system in which different names can play the same role and the same names can play different roles. Therefore, the car manufacturer can mislead the public by "ringing the changes" on different sets of car names, each of which depends for its meaning on the other words in its semantic field (i.e., automobile semantics). In short, manufacturers deliberately manipulate the names of car makes and models— that is, change their meanings by shifting their relative position within automobile semantics—and Americans accept the new meanings because the overall conceptual framework remains constant. Although the exact meanings of individual words varies from person to person, automobile manufacturers can and do systematically downgrade the sense of car names, knowing that customers will notice the changes only slowly, if at all.

Chevrolet Monte Carlo and Malibu
Pontiac Grand Prix and Le Mans
Oldsmobile Cutlass Supreme and Cutlass Salon
Buick Regal and Century
These great GM car names offer a new dimension in value.
New car names crop up all the time. And quite often they disappear just as fast.
But when General Motors began redesigning the great cars you see listed here, we knew we had a tradition to uphold.

401

To provide as much value as we could while still delivering the excitement and styling these names are famous for . . .

So, look. If you want value in your car, you owe it to yourself to test drive some of the most popular names in automotive history.

GM ADVERTISEMENT (1978)

Saussure's theory of value rests on the insight that linguistic units cannot be defined independently, but must rather be treated within a system "où tout se tient," where everything holds together. The greatest impact of this insight has been in phonology, wherein the basic units, whether they be phonemes or features, are defined in terms of opposition or distinctiveness. At the underlying or phonemic level, it is only the distinctive units which count. In semantics, the theory of value is best represented by the various versions of semantic field theory, which are based on the notion that the senses of related words can be treated as covering distinct areas of a conceptual field. The sense of each word is not independent, but depends on the rest of the words in the field. A word will lose or gain territory through time, but this will always be reflected in the other words in the field.

Recent thought on the meanings of words has shied away from field theory and from related opposition-based theories, such as the semantic marker theory of Katz and Fodor (1963), because they seem to presuppose that the meanings of words are clear things. By contrast, linguistic research is concerned now with accounting for the observation that people do not really know exactly what a word means. Thus we have fuzzy semantics, which attempts (Lakoff (1972)) to account for the observation that people are less secure about calling a penguin a bird than they are about so categorizing a robin. Others (Berlin and Kay (1969), Labov (1978)) have adopted the notion of a prototype to explain the differences between central and peripheral instances of the same thing. Rosch (1973) has even provided good experimental evidence to support the psychological validity of prototype semantics for such things as color. Miller and Johnson-Laird (1976) have suggested that we view lexical semantics as lay theory, a view which allows a person to be mistaken or unsure about the concepts on which semantics rests, while both Putnam (1975) and Kripke (1972) have appealed to nature (in the guise of natural kinds) as a way out of some of our difficulties.

The goal of this article is integrative. On the one hand, as a simple study in lexical semantics, it seeks to demonstrate the validity of the theory of semantic oppositions by showing that the senses of a number of words in one particular domain can be understood only in relation to one another. On the other hand, it will show that these senses are

Thanks to P. A. and France for their continuing faith in the value of this article, and to N. G. for the Alfa and the rollerskates which made it possible.

elusive; they change so rapidly and imperceptibly that one person's idea of what a given word signifies may be markedly different from another person's. These changes, though, no matter how rapid, are very regular, and operate totally within the predetermined system of oppositions. Thus, even when we do not know what a word means, we can still discuss its sense in a systematic fashion, precisely because it is not the senses of words which are secure, but rather the conceptual frame within which the senses are arranged. . . .

Senses for Car Names

The semantic field which forms my example is distinctly mundane, that of the American automobile. I call the field *automobile semantics*. I will restrict it to the names of automobiles and will include no discussion of parts, which form a separate domain. The main object of my study is the meanings of these names. A typical question of automobile semantics is thus, What is the meaning of the word *Chevrolet*? or, equivalently, What is a Chevrolet?[1]

The system which I will outline is not a novel one, but is well known to most people who have any familiarity with the marketing classification of American cars. Nor is the knowledge of this system always tacit or unconscious. On the contrary, it is quite generally used in advertising at all levels, and assumed to be part of general American automobile culture. My goal, however, is not to enlighten the automotive industry, but rather to use this well-known classification to elucidate questions of language.

Before going on to semantics, I must give some syntactic information. First and most important, car names are not proper names, but rather common nouns. This can easily be shown by the fact that they readily allow determiners and adjectives:

(1) a blue Chevrolet
two big Cadillacs

In addition, they exhibit the characteristically English peculiarity (Levi (1978)) of appearing as attributives:

(2) a pink Cadillac coupe
a Chevrolet Impala sedan

This attributive construction is generally used to restrict the modified noun as to subtype, or kind, as the examples below demonstrate:

---

[1] *Meaning* for me is a broad term, including at least sense, reference, connotation, and level of usage. This article does not presuppose a position on the question of whether any of these is more purely linguistic than the others.

(3) city streets
Memphis blues
Chippendale chair
cobalt blue

Of course, cars can have proper names; there are many people who give their cars names. In my household, one car is named Scarface, the other Young Red. But examples like these only serve to underscore the fact that, though some car names may be etymologically derived from proper names, none are proper names synchronically. This means that—unlike proper names, whose semantics is relatively simple, consisting only of reference, and having no sense—car names, like all common nouns, must be possessed of both sense and reference.[2] To ask what a Chevrolet is is like asking what a table is.

It is clear from examples (2) and (3) that car names classify cars. The name specifies one or more of the following categories: *year, make, line, model,* and *body type.* When designating a car fully, all of these categories are specified in the order given:

(4)   1972 Chevrolet Chevelle Malibu sedan
       year make   line   model   body type

Less specific designations can be made by using fewer than all five categories, again in the fixed order:

(5)   Chevrolet sedan
       Chevrolet Malibu
       1972 Chevelle

As far as I can tell, all categories are optional, and the only restriction is that the year cannot stand alone:

(6)   Q: What kind of car do you drive?
       A: A Chevrolet; a Chevelle; a Malibu; a sedan; ??a 1972

This restriction is pragmatic; it can be traced to the fact that simply giving the model year of the car is not informative enough. We can therefore give the following phrase structure rule for American car names:

---

[2] It has been suggested to me that car names and other brand names, though they may function syntactically like common nouns, are still names semantically, having no sense. One might call this class *common names.* This claim may be valid for such brands as *Maytag* or *Kenmore,* which I discuss below. These denote nothing but the fact that they are marketed by a particular company and thus carry the reputation of that company. It is not valid, however, for American cars, because of the classification system for cars that I will describe below.

(7) car name → (year) (make) (line) (model) (body type)³

There is another category which is not represented in the name, but which is important semantically: *manufacturer*.

I will now discuss each category. The first and simplest category is that of *manufacturer*. Each car can be categorized according to its manufacturer, the major American ones being General Motors, Ford, and Chrysler. The name of the manufacturer may carry connotations, such as Chrysler's reputation for advanced engineering, but it does not have any systematic semantic properties beyond the purely referential one of naming a particular manufacturing company.⁴

Make is more complex than *manufacturer*. Each of the above three companies can be divided into divisions, which stem for the most part from the companies which merged to form the present ones. Originally, each division manufactured a particular car, so that *make* could be defined in the same way as *manufacturer*.⁵ This is no longer true, and the significance of the various makes is now much more complex. We will return to these complexities later. For the moment, the equation of *make* with *division* will suffice. This equation, I should note, is a common one. Most people think that if a car is called an *Oldsmobile*, then it must be made by the Oldsmobile division of General Motors.

---

³ There are various ways of treating the null expansion.

⁴ It is perhaps for this reason that the name of the manufacturer does not appear as part of the name of the car, as it does with most foreign cars (e.g. a Renault, a Volvo, a Fiat, a BMW). One cannot call a car made by GM *a GM*, nor could one speak of *a Ford Lincoln*. *Ford* and *Chrysler* do appear as car names, but each is a particular make manufactured by the respective company.

⁵ The similarity between the concepts of *make* and *manufacturer* is reflected syntactically. The manufacturer is generally called by its proper name.

(i) $\left\{ \begin{array}{l} \text{GM} \\ \text{Ford} \\ \text{Chrysler} \end{array} \right\}$ is putting out a new model.

Though the make is generally a [common] noun, it can also be used as a proper name:

(ii) $\left\{ \begin{array}{l} \text{Pontiac} \\ \text{Dodge} \\ \text{Lincoln} \end{array} \right\}$ is putting out a new model.

This is not true of *kind* or *model*:

(iii)   *$\left\{ \begin{array}{l} \text{Chevelle} \\ \text{Le Mans} \\ \text{Horizon} \end{array} \right\}$ is putting out a new model.

The reason for this pattern is the notion that each division is a separate entity, like the manufacturer, which markets automobiles.

Size	Line Name	Wheelbase	Weight of base 2-door coupe
subcompact	Vega	97"	2160 lb.
compact	Nova	111"	2950 lb.
mid-size	Chevelle	112" or 116"	3170 lb.
full-size	Chevrolet	122"	3864 lb.

Table 1.

The makes of American cars which we will be concerned with are as follows:

(8) General Motors: Chevrolet, Pontiac, Oldsmobile, Buick,
      Cadillac
   Ford: Ford, Mercury, Lincoln
   Chrysler: Plymouth, Dodge, Chrysler

Makes are ranked according to price category. There are three such categories: *lower-priced, mid-priced,* and *luxury.* Thus, of the Ford makes, Ford is lower-priced, Mercury is mid-priced, and Lincoln is luxury. Among GM makes, Chevrolet is lower-priced, while Pontiac, Buick, and Oldsmobile are mid-priced, though Pontiac is ranked somewhat lower, with Oldsmobile and Buick equal;[6] Cadillac is luxury.

It is important to note two things in regard to price category. First, it is a comparative scale or ranking, not an absolute one: the fact that Chevrolet is lower-priced does not mean that all Chevrolets will be less expensive than all Pontiacs; it means rather that a given Chevrolet will be less expensive than a comparably equipped Pontiac, and so on up the line. An expensive Chevrolet can easily be more expensive than an inexpensive Oldsmobile. It follows that the price ranking is related to prestige. One reason why a person buys a Pontiac rather than a similarly equipped Chevrolet is that the Pontiac carries more prestige. The higher the category, the greater the prestige. Rank is systematic, while prestige is a connotative value, dependent on a combination of rank and other less systematic factors. I therefore assume that prestige is determined by rank, rather than vice versa.

One of the results of the existence of ranks is that makes can be compared, regardless of manufacturer. Chevrolet and Ford are thus equivalent, as are Cadillac and Lincoln. Mercury is higher than Chev-

[6] At the low end, equivalent Oldsmobiles tend to be more expensive than equivalent Buicks, while the opposite is true at the high end. I have simplified matters by balancing the two ends and assuming that the makes are equal, even though they can usually be ranked in a given instance. Nothing of substance hinges on this balance.

rolet, etc. The ranks form a value system, and each make can be placed within this system.[7]

I will now show that the terms *line* and *model* also form value systems similar to the one constructed for *make*. The term *line* designates a car of a particular size marketed under a given make. The lines are conventionally categorized as *full-size, mid-size, compact,* and *subcompact,* and the categories are based on comparative weight and

---

[7] The importance of rank in the significance of a make cannot be underestimated. Two phenomena of recent years show this clearly. The first example is that of the Oldsmobile with the Chevrolet engine. Several years ago, it was discovered that some full-size Oldsmobiles were being sold with Chevrolet engines, without the customer's knowledge. The Chevy and Olds engines were approximately the same, the only major difference being the make. Many of the people who had bought these "hybrids" were furious. There were numerous court cases against GM for the deception, and the affair was finally settled with GM paying millions of dollars in compensation. All along, GM expressed puzzlement, for the interchange of components among different makes is standard practice and is becoming more and more widespread. There was no qualitative difference between the two engines, they said. But the customers and the courts would not buy this. After all, those of us who watched TV in the fifties knew all about being behind the wheel of a Rocket Oldsmobile with its famed Rocket V-8 engine. Chevrolet is OK, but a Chevy is not an Olds, nor is its engine. Since the incident, GM has explicitly indicated in its advertising that a car of a given make may, in some instances, be equipped with an engine manufactured by another division. The example demonstrates quite clearly that the public has certain ideas about what constitutes an Oldsmobile; a Chevrolet engine does not, because of its lower rank. No one but GM would object to an Olds with a Cadillac engine.

The second phenomenon is much more pervasive. In recent years it has become common for a manufacturer to market one basic automobile design under different names. Sometimes the differently named cars are identical in all but name, as with the *Plymouth Horizon* and the *Dodge Omni;* sometimes there are differences in trim, as with the *Chevy Vega* and *Pontiac Astre;* and sometimes there are differences in sheet metal and standard equipment. In fact, the practice has become so prevalent that very few designs are now marketed under only one name, and the practice has become common in Europe as well. Often, the different names under which a given design is marketed will be of different rank—Chevrolet and Pontiac, for example. Two essentially identical cars will then be sold at different prices, the more expensive one being of higher rank. This phenomenon is well exemplified in the following table of equivalent GM cars. Similar tables can be constructed for other designs and years: price and rank will always be closely correlated. The only explanation for the success of this practice is that customers are sensitive to the rank of a particular make. They are willing to pay more in order to have a higher-ranking car, even though they could have essentially the same car for less money with a different name.

Car	Price
Chevrolet Nova	$2798
Pontiac Ventura	$2873
Buick Apollo	$3024
Oldsmobile Omega	$3031

Table i. 1974 GM compact 2-door hatchback coupes with 250 CID/6 cyl. engine

The point of these two examples, that of the miscegenated Oldsmobile and that of the equivalent models, is to demonstrate that the perceived rank of a particular make of car is important to car buyers.

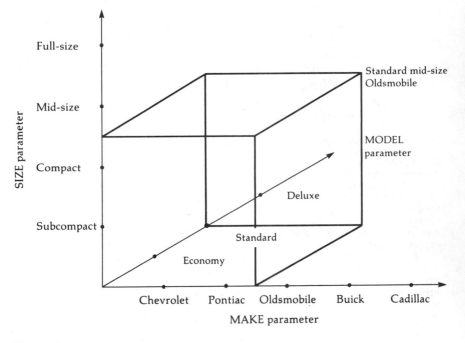

Figure 1

wheelbase.[8] The Chevrolet makes in 1972, for example, consisted of the lines shown in Table 1 (p. 406). Lines can be ranked in the same way as the makes: subcompact, compact, mid-size, and full-size, in ascending order. Prestige correlates directly with rank, as in the case of the categorization of makes. A Chevelle is more prestigious than a comparable Nova, and so on. As with price category, the size category allows for comparison across makes. A Vega is equivalent to a Pinto, and so on.[9]

The next term is *model*. Each line of car is produced in different models, with different standard and available equipment and accessories. There are usually three models of each line: *economy, standard,*

---

[8] These particular categories are even sanctioned by the Environmental Protection Agency of the United States Government, which uses them in its calculations of efficiency.

[9] The rank of a line, though it is usually based on size, can also become conventionalized. For example, the 1978 GM compacts were actually larger than the 1978 GM mid-size cars in external dimensions and in weight, because the latter had been downsized earlier. This discrepancy caused some consternation among buyers at first, and sales of the new mid-size cars lagged for a time, since one could buy a larger compact for less money. The problem did not last long though, for the public was soon convinced both that the mid-size cars were bigger inside and that they represented the way of the future.

and *deluxe*. The 1962 full-size Chevrolet, for example, consisted of the economy *Biscayne*, the standard *Bel Air*, and the deluxe *Impala*. Three is an average; the 1978 full-size Chevrolet had only two models, standard and deluxe, and the 1958 had four, the fourth being the special superdeluxe *Bel Air Impala*.

That the ranking of models forms a value system is self-evident. It is also clear that the ranking is correlated with price and prestige and that it is independent of make and line.

We now have three independent value systems according to which automobiles can be ranked, each of which goes from low to high. These are values for the categories of *make* (price category), *line*, and *model*. If we consider each ranking or value system as one dimension, we can construct a graph into which most American automobiles can be fit. Such a graph is given in Figure 1. The value of any given car can be determined by its distance from the origin. Equivalent cars will occupy the same place on the graph. The difference in value of any two is the distance between them.

I have still not discussed the categories of *body type* and *year*, and some readers may anticipate a similar ranking within these categories, culminating in the construction of a five-dimensional space. These latter two categories, however, are fundamentally different from the first three. In the case of body type, the category is not evaluative, but descriptive. This is clearly true in the case of body types such as *sedan, coupe, convertible, hardtop, station wagon*, etc. We can describe what each one is, and the relationship between a sedan and a convertible is not a relative one. Nor is it possible to construct a one-dimensional evaluative scale for body types.[10]

The category of year can easily be converted into a linear scale, but unlike make, line, and model, it is not basically evaluative. *Deluxe* and *standard* are defined purely in terms of one another, whereas 1962 ranks higher than 1957 on the year scale because it follows it in time, a dimension which is external to the world of automobiles. Year is, however, a very important category, and we will return to it shortly.

The graph of Figure 1 resembles closely the sort of diagrams one sees in discussions of semantic fields or componential analysis. The field is novel, however, in that it is purely relative. It seeks to represent the abstract value of types of automobiles in relation to each other. The scales of evaluation can be distinguished from one another, but the points on the scale have no external reference. It follows that knowing

---

[10] Certain body types are restricted to certain models (for example, convertibles are of high rank), but the body types themselves cannot easily be ranked. For example, is a station wagon higher or lower than a sedan?

what a particular term in the field means is simply knowing what its place is.[11]

Other Semantic Properties

Given that we have successfully depicted the senses of car names in Figure 1, why is it that these senses are so spare? Doesn't the name of a car mean more than this relativistic position in a field?

The answer to this question is yes; the rank of a car is not all there is to the meaning of its name. For one thing, a car name is a brand name, and brand names have interesting properties of their own. Syntactically, all brand names pattern like car makes, being either proper or common nouns, or occurring in attributive position:

(9) Maytag makes good washers. (proper noun)
   We've always had Maytags. (common noun)
   Maytag washers last. (attributive)

The semantics of brand names seems simple: the brand name refers to the manufacturer. An x (where x is a brand name) is therefore a y manufactured by x, where y ranges over the set of types of things manufactured by x. A *Maytag* is thus a washing machine or dryer manufactured by *Maytag*.

But there is more to this account. Consider the brand name *Kitchenaid*. Under this name are sold dishwashers, food mixers, garbage disposals, and trash compactors manufactured by *Hobart*. Hobart manufactures many other products, but reserves the name *Kitchenaid* for its household machines. *Kitchenaid* is thus not the name of the manufacturer, but a brand name used by the manufacturer. Another case is that of store brand names such as *Kenmore*. This brand is used on appliances sold by *Sears*. These appliances are manufactured by independent companies and are often identical in all but name to other brands. A *Kenmore* is therefore an appliance which is sold by Sears under the name *Kenmore*. A similar situation can hold for cars. Consider the *Opel*, whose most recent incarnation is sold by *Buick* dealers and manufactured by *Isuzu*. Yet it is called an *Opel*.

---

[11] Interestingly, this same sort of field cannot be constructed for European or Japanese cars, because there exists no comparable classification system. Some makes are more prestigious than others, and a given manufacturer may market different lines and models, but the value system is not conventionalized as the one for American cars is (at least it is not conventionalized for Americans: there may exist comparable systems for Europeans and Japanese). Though it may be possible to compare two cars, the comparison is a pragmatic one, not semantic. It is also reasonably possible that the present crisis in the American automobile industry will so radically alter the structure of the field that it will engender an entirely new value system for future American cars. This is an intriguing possibility.

The answer seems to lie in the etymology of the word *brand*. A brand, in one sense of the word, is a mark of a particular pattern burned into something to mark ownership. The brand is conventionally associated with the owner of the branded object. Brand names are similarly conventional, and their purpose is to associate a product with a particular firm. Because the association between a brand and what it labels is so conventional, brands are liable to be abused. They are therefore legally protected as trademarks. (*Trademark* is defined in Webster's Third as "a name or symbol used by a maker or seller to identify distinctively his products.")

Legally, a brand (name) can be legitimately applied to an object only by the company or person entitled to apply the brand. Conversely, the owner of the brand can legitimately apply it to anything he/she/it markets and, by doing so, identifies him/her/itself as the source of the object. The owner of a brand can thus be quite free with it, though no one else may use the brand, for that would constitute counterfeiting. An *Opel* can be sold by *Buick* and manufactured by *Isuzu* because *GM* owns all these brands. Similarly, *Kenmore* is owned by *Sears*, *Kitchenaid* by *Hobart*, *Ann Page* by *A & P*, etc.

Because a brand name is the property of an individual, that individual is free to label anything (which the individual is legally permitted to label) by that brand name. A *Chevrolet* is thus anything which GM chooses to call by the name *Chevrolet*. We must conclude that the fact that car names are brand names adds little to their meaning. What it does do, however, is allow the automobile manufacturers a certain liberty with the names, since they own them. We will see later how this liberty is taken.

One might ask whether kinds of cars have essential properties. Is there something about a *Cadillac Coupe de Ville*, for instance, without which it could not be called a *Cadillac Coupe de Ville*? The answer to this is no. One major reason for this lack of essential properties is a peculiarity of the American auto industry which was touched upon briefly above, the yearly model change. The practice of replacing all models yearly was popularized by A. P. Sloan (Sloan (1963)). It is simple, involving the annual replacement of all models by new models, usually bearing the same name, but differing somewhat in essentials. Sometimes the changes from one year to the next are merely cosmetic, but sometimes they are radical, as, for example, between the 1976 and 1977 full-size GM cars. For our purposes, the most important aspect of the yearly change is not the change, but the continuity: though the 1957 and 1958 *Chevrolet Bel Air* are very different looking cars, there is a sense in which they are the same car, only different versions of that car. What unites them is the fact that they have the same name and occupy the same spot in the field. In this respect they resemble the 5:38 train. This continuity in names and discontinuity in appearance make it very difficult for there to be any properties which one might select as being essential to any one kind of car.[12] The only property which is constant, besides the name, is the position which the car occupies in the field. That is why position in the field is so important in the semantics of automobiles.[13]

[12] Aware of this problem of discontinuity, the manufacturer will attempt to promote continuity by preserving certain small design features of a particular kind of car. The simplest of such features is the insignia. Curiously, few cars possess such insignia. There is the famous Rolls-Royce flying maiden, and the Mercedes-Benz emblem, but among American cars only the Cadillac V and Crest has any real significance. Not quite an insignia but similar are the three or four portholes on the front fenders of Buicks (the number depends on the rank of the model), which have been around on and off for a long time, though becoming more and more stylized. Another way of promoting continuity is to preserve a certain "look." Sometimes this will be done with an entire body style. Thus, the *Continental Mark* series of Lincolns has gone through four style changes since its reintroduction in 1956, but the particular "look" set by the 1956 model has persisted through the changes. At the opposite end of the spectrum, one aspect of a car can be selected. There are the Cadillac fins, which have persisted in one form or another from the early fifties to the present. Ford for a number of years had large round taillights. The full-size Chevrolet, since 1958, has had a string of small taillights, two or three on each side (depending on the rank of the model). Not all cars have persistent features of this type. Chrysler Corporation cars, for example, have fluctuated quite radically in design. There can also be aberrant years. The 1960 Ford was radically different in look from the 1959. This disturbed buyers enough that a more Ford-like design was (re)introduced in 1961. Changes in full-size Fords have been very gradual since then. These attempts to emphasize continuity in the face of yearly style changes are all quite conscious, and all reflect the semantic peculiarity of car names.

[13] The principle of continuity—keeping the same name for the same place in the field, regardless of essential changes in the car that bears the name—is so strong that it is sometimes followed with disastrous results for the manufacturer. I am thinking in particular of cases where a certain model has developed a bad reputation for one reason or another. When this model is replaced by another which occupies the same spot, if the second model is given the same name as the first, then the bad reputation of the first may accrue to the second. Consider the *Corvair*. The original Corvair, introduced in 1960, had severe problems with its suspension and was unsafe at any speed (Nader (1965)). The car was completely redesigned in 1965, retaining only the engine and its location in the rear. The safety of this second Corvair has never been impugned, and it is generally acknowledged to have been one of the best designed American cars of this quarter century. However, it could not bear the stigma of its name and died quietly in 1969. Nor do many ostensibly well-informed people realize even now that there were two Corvairs. Consider the following extract from an article by Peter Schuyten in the *New York Times* (Nov. 9, 1979, p. D1): "Introduced in 1960, the Corvair, with its rear-mounted engine, was said at the time to be highly innovative for an American automobile. Production was halted, however, ten years later following a series of fatal and near-fatal accidents believed to stem from engineering deficiencies in the car's rear suspension." Mr.Schuyten apparently believes that the 1960 Corvair (the car with engineering deficiencies) and the one whose production was halted in 1969 were one and the same car. This is true in name only.

GM management learned their lesson. Their next compact failure was the *Vega*, introduced in 1971, whose original four-cylinder engine was plagued with troubles because of its design. In 1973, GM attached the name *Monza* to a sport coupe built on the Vega chassis. In 1978, The Vega name and the original sedan model were discontinued, but the small station wagon which had been sold up to then as a Vega, and which resembled the Vega sedan very closely, continued to be sold except for one important change. It was now a Monza. This tale is just the opposite of that of the Corvair, but proves the same point with regard to names and roses.

It is important to note that though car names may be peculiar, they are not aberrant. The same problem of recognizing distinct instances of a given individual or type across time or events is one of the most persistent mysteries of philosophy and psychology. What makes car names peculiar is the institutionalization of the very factors which cause the greatest difficulty.

I set out at the beginning of this section to establish whether there wasn't more to automobile semantics than mere position in a field. I first looked at brand names in general and discovered very little in the way of meaning, finding instead that brand names are words which are owned by individuals. I then looked for essential properties of cars, properties which would always obtain for a particular type of car. I could not find such properties, and linked their absence to the practice of changing models yearly, a practice which makes it difficult to recognize instances of a given kind of car across years, except by the fact that they have the same name and the same position in the field. Finally, I noted that manufacturers are aware of this difficulty and sometimes attempt to remedy it by preserving continuity of style between adjacent model years.

This very awareness and the attempts to impose essential or characteristic properties on a kind of car demonstrate dramatically my main point, that the systematic sense of any car name consists of the position which that car occupies in a semantic space relative to other kinds of cars.[14]

[14] At this point, one might object that the field which has been described, though it may be valid, is irrelevant to linguistic semantics in the narrow denotational or conceptual sense, and that it is instead either a description of the real world or purely connotational. This is a difficult objection to counter. For one thing, I know of no infallible way to decide exactly what falls within the narrow domain of conceptual semantics. But this caveat aside, I still think that we can respond to the argument by showing that whatever the field is, it belongs neither to the real world nor to connotation, and that it has properties which are usually reserved for conceptual systems.

It is quite clear that the classification which I have described is conventionally discrete. For example, there is no reason why there should be four sizes of cars: full-size, mid-size, compact, and subcompact. There are in the real world cars of varying sizes running from small to large, but in that same world there are no discrete categories along this scale. Such a categorization depends on words having arbitrary senses.

From this we may conclude that the classification system which I have described is linguistic, and not part of the real world. If it is linguistic, then it can be either conceptual, connotative, or stylistic. Connotative meaning is closely tied to individual experience. One might argue that prestige is purely connotative, that a Mercedes is prestigious because of what we know about the Mercedes from experience and not because of some conceptual properties of the word *Mercedes*. This may be true of Mercedes, and to some extent it is true of such top-of-the-line American cars as Cadillac, but it cannot be true of Chevrolet and Pontiac. One may be more prestigious than the other, but that difference has nothing to do with experience. It is rather due to the fact that one is designated as being higher in value than the other, and this designation is conventional, not due to any physical properties of the cars. The connotation of prestige in this case follows from the linguistic categorization rather than vice versa.

There are other aspects of connotation which make it unlikely that we are dealing with a connotative system. Connotations are vague and do not form tight systems; they

Semantic Change

I will now turn to the second part of my task, a discussion of the elusiveness of the senses of car names. It is commonly said that the meanings of words are elusive, and many serious thinkers have objected to even attempting a systematic discussion of the meanings of words on the simple grounds that they are ineffable. But the elusiveness that I will describe is not so romantic as this. I will demonstrate first that the senses of car names change, and that this change is very quick, so quick that people cannot catch up with it and thus lag behind. Second, I will show that this change is of a very particular sort that can easily be understood within the semantic field which I have discussed in [the first two] sections. . . .

By way of setting the stage, let me first engage in a little naïve psychology, concerning how the semantic field which I have discussed is used by speakers of English who are knowledgeable about American cars. Let us assume that these speakers, using their knowledge of the field and additional information which is provided to them by the industry through advertising, construct hypotheses about the senses of particular brands of cars. For a given brand, this hypothesis consists of a place in the field. The speaker may have other ideas about the car, but these are either dependent on its position or are not systematic.

Thus, the speaker places a particular car name in the semantic field by using information provided by the manufacturer. Remember, however, that car names are proprietary brand names. The owner of the name has the right to apply it to whatever type of vehicle that individual wishes to apply it to. Thus, the owner of the name has the right to determine its place in the field. In short, there are two ways of determining the position of a given car in the field, each corresponding to one sense of *determine*. The first way is discovery: the speaker constructs a concept based on the information acquired through experience, which is what most of us do for most words (see Miller and Johnson-Laird (1976)). The second way, which stems from the fact that car names are trademarks, is by simple stipulation. The

are usually unstable; they vary from speaker to speaker within a community. None of these is true of the classification of American automobiles.

As for stylistic meaning, I cannot see how it is relevant to the matter at hand, unless we turn to such words as *Caddy*, *Chevy*, *Merc*, and *Gemmy*.

Thus, if only by elimination, we can conclude that we are dealing with a conceptual system. But surely we have stronger indications that this is the case, for I have shown that the meanings of car names can be described in terms of a small set of arbitrary discrete features, and such a description of meaning is the hallmark of a conceptual semantic system. I do not claim that this description exhausts all the meaning of a given car name. I purposely exclude connotation and extension, both of which are at least as important as sense in the entire semantics of automobiles. The purpose of this long excursus has been only to show that such an exclusion is possible and not to deny the importance of these other aspects of meaning.

owner of the trademark, by right of ownership, may apply the name as he/she/it will. This duality clearly allows for some discrepancy between the two groups, manufacturers and customers. The former may simply change the sense of a car name, so that the hypothesis of the latter is no longer true. This is precisely what happens in the case of model names within a given line, as I will now demonstrate.

It is possible to determine to a reasonable degree of certainty the rank which a manufacturer assigns to a given model name in a given year by examining the variety of body types and options available under that name. Any change in these factors signals a change in ranking. Close investigation of industry figures on body types and options reveals that manufacturers systematically change the position of model names by a process of downgrading or devaluation. A name which in a given year refers to a model of a particular rank will, in a later year, be applied to a model of the next rank down.

The change is usually effected by introducing a new model name ranked above the previous year's highest ranking model name, so that there will be no change in the relative positions of the existing names. The new name is almost always attached to a special model, outside the system, available only in a limited number of prestigious body types, such as convertible or sport coupe. Some time thereafter, often the next year, we find that the new model name has expanded its domain: it is now available in a wider range of body types. Concurrently, the former bottommost name has disappeared. In fact, by body type and option criteria, all names have simply dropped one rank, allowing the new name, previously outside the system, to enter it at the top. If this pattern repeats itself over an extended period, rather extensive changes can take place.

Consider the data in Table 2. In 1957, Chevrolet's top model was the *Bel Air*, available as a two- or four-door sedan, two- or four-door hardtop, two- or four-door station wagon, and convertible. In 1958, the *Bel Air Impala* was introduced, and was available only as a two-door hardtop and a convertible, both more expensive and better equipped than the corresponding Bel Air (the 1958 Impala had three taillights on each side as opposed to two on all other Chevrolets). The range of Bel Air body types for 1958 was essentially the same as for 1957. Turning to 1959, we find that Impala is now available as a two-door or four-door hardtop, a four-door sedan, a convertible, and a station wagon. The range of Bel Air contracts so that it is available only as a sedan or a station wagon (the range of body types in which the *Biscayne* was previously available). Concurrently, the lowest-ranking *Delray* disappears, so that the Biscayne, previously the middle-ranked model, is now at the bottom. This is a paradigm case of devaluation: between 1957 and 1959 all Chevrolet model names have dropped one

1957	One-Fifty	Two-Ten	Bel Air
	Utility Sedan	2-door Sedan	2-door Sedan
	2-door Sedan	Delray Coupe	4-door Sedan
	4-door Sedan	4-door Sedan	Sport Coupe
	2-door Wagon	Sport Coupe	Sport Sedan
		Sport Sedan	Convertible
		2-door Wagon	2-door Wagon
		4-door Wagon	4-door Wagon
		4-door Wagon (9p)	
1958	Delray	Biscayne	Bel Air
	Utility Sedan	2-door Sedan	2-door Sedan
	2-door Sedan	4-door Sedan	4-door Sedan
	4-door Sedan	4-door Wagon	Sport Coupe
	2-door Wagon	4-door Wagon (9p)	Sport Sedan
	4-door Wagon		Hardtop Impala
			Impala Convertible
			4-door Wagon
1959	Biscayne	Bel Air	Impala
	2-door Sedan	2-door Sedan	4-door Sedan
	4-door Sedan	4-door Sedan	2-door Hardtop
	2-door Wagon	4-door Wagon	4-door Hardtop
	4-door Wagon	4-door Wagon (9p)	Convertible
			4-door Wagon

Table 2. Chevrolet Models and Body Types, 1957–1959

rank; and this is accomplished by the introduction of a new model name at the top.

As a more systematic demonstration of the devaluation of car names, I offer the following cases. In Tables 3 and 4 are given the names and ranks of all full-size Chevrolet and Ford models from 1953 to 1978.[15] I have chosen these two makes because they have been the most popular over this extended period. I have chosen the period because it spans the greatest flourishing of American automobile culture before its recent disintegration in the face of economic constraints.

The two types of car are meant to be representative in their naming practices. They are certainly the most conservative; a perusal of similar tables for other makes and sizes would reveal much more change. These other changes, though, are not always so systematic, arising in many cases from attempts at gaining a more prominent place in the market.

[15] The rankings are based on price, but they are not purely comparative. The first three ranks are also correlated with certain body types. Rank 1 is reserved for models which are available only as basic sedans, and is the *economy* rank. Rank 3 is *deluxe*, in which is found the widest of variety of body types: sedan, two- and four-door hardtop, and convertible. Rank 2 is more variable. It does not contain a convertible, and it may or may not contain hardtops. I have designated this rank *standard*. Rankings above 3 are more fluid, containing as they do special and superdeluxe models, available only in limited body types. *Ford Galaxie 500 XL*, for example, was available only as a two-door hardtop or as a convertible, being a special "sport" model. What I have done for ranks 4 and above is simply to rank models by price.

Year	Rank:	1	2	3	4	5
1953		Special 1500	Deluxe 2100	Bel Air 2400		
1954		Special 1500	Deluxe 2100	Bel Air 2400		
1955		One-Fifty	Two-Ten	Bel Air		
1956		One-Fifty	Two-Ten	Bel Air		
1957		One-Fifty	Two-Ten	Bel Air		
1958		Delray	Biscayne	Bel Air	Bel Air Impala	
1959		Biscayne	Bel Air	Impala		
1960		Biscayne	Bel Air	Impala		
1961		Biscayne	Bel Air	Impala		
1962		Biscayne	Bel Air	Impala		
1963		Biscayne	Bel Air	Impala		
1964		Biscayne	Bel Air	Impala	Impala Sport	
1965		Biscayne	Bel Air	Impala	Impala S.S.	
1966		Biscayne	Bel Air	Impala	Impala S.S.	Caprice
1967		Biscayne	Bel Air	Impala	Impala S.S.	Caprice
1968		Biscayne	Bel Air	Impala	Caprice	
1969		Biscayne	Bel Air	Impala	Caprice	
1970		Biscayne	Bel Air	Impala	Caprice	
1971		Biscayne	Bel Air	Impala	Caprice	
1972		Biscayne	Bel Air	Impala	Caprice	
1973		Bel Air	Impala	Caprice		
1974		Bel Air	Impala	Caprice		
1975		Bel Air	Impala	Caprice		
1976			Impala	Caprice		
1977			Impala	Caprice Classic		
1978			Impala	Caprice Classic		

Table 3. Full-Size Chevrolet Models From 1953–1978.

The interpretation of the tables is quite straightforward. I have hypothesized that the sense of a given car name tends to be devalued over time. This shows in the charts as a diagonal path from upper right to lower left. A given name, if it shifts, will always shift in this direction. The Chevrolet table is paradigmatic in this respect. The only movement is in this direction. *Bel Air* is the name with the greatest longevity (23 years), and it moves all the way from 3 to 1 and out in that period. The Ford chart is no less consistent, but there are more names to follow, and the movement is faster. Good examples are *Fairlane* (1955–61), *Galaxie* (1959–63), and *LTD* (1965–present).

We can make some other general observations about the tables. For one, the rankings can be viewed as stacks with open ends and limited but variable capacity. Items can be inserted only at the top of the stack, as in a calculator's memory. The insertion of an item at the top of the stack will push down all the items already in the stack and push the bottom one out if the capacity of the stack is not increased. If the rank of a model is its position in the stack, then the insertion of a model at the top of the stack will lower the position of those already present, which is what we observe to happen. This stack model can also be used to express the fact that a given name, in changing, never drops more than one rank at a time: a name does not shift in a single

Year Rank:	1	2	3	4	5
1953	Mainline	Customline	Crestline		
1954	Mainline	Customline	Crestline		
1955	Mainline	Customline	Fairlane		
1956	Mainline	Customline	Fairlane		
1957	Custom	Custom 300	Fairlane	Fairlane 500	
1958	Custom	Fairlane	Fairlane 500		
1959	Custom 300	Fairlane	Fairlane 500	Galaxie	
1960	Custom 300	Fairlane	Fairlane 500	Galaxie	
1961	Fairlane	Fairlane 500	Galaxie		
1962	—	Galaxie	Galaxie 500	Galaxie 500XL	
1963	—	Galaxie	Galaxie 500	Galaxie 500XL	
1964	Custom	Custom 500	Galaxie 500	Galaxie 500XL	
1965	Custom	Custom 500	Galaxie 500	Galaxie 500XL	Galaxie 500LTD
1966	Custom	Custom 500	Galaxie 500	Galaxie 500XL	LTD
1967	Custom	Custom 500	Galaxie 500	XL	LTD
1968	Custom	Custom 500	Galaxie 500	XL	LTD
1969	Custom	Custom 500	Galaxie 500	XL	LTD
1970	Custom	Custom 500	Galaxie 500	XL	LTD
1971	Custom	Custom 500	Galaxie 500	LTD	LTD Brougham*
1972	Custom	Custom 500	Galaxie 500	LTD	LTD Brougham
1973	Custom 500	Galaxie 500	LTD	LTD Brougham	
1974	Custom 500	Galaxie 500	LTD	LTD Brougham	
1975		LTD	LTD Brougham	LTD Landau	
1976		LTD	LTD Brougham	LTD Landau	
1977		LTD	LTD Landau		
1978		LTD	LTD Landau		

Table 4. Full-Size Ford Models From 1953 to 1978
* LTD Brougham was introduced in 1970 as a special superdeluxe model, Rank 6.

change from 3 to 1, for example. One of the results of this gradualness in change is the enhancement of the illusion of continuity. Because shifts in ranking are never radical, they do not call attention to themselves and cause us to revise our hypotheses. If an Impala shifted two ranks in the course of one model change, we might become wary.

Downgrading is stipulative. It proceeds from the manufacturer. What about the customers, whose concept is rooted in experience? Quite clearly, their view cannot change so quickly, for a number of reasons. First, there is continuity, the fact that the name remains relatively stable despite yearly changes in the car to which it is attached. From 1959 to 1972, for example, the ranks of Chevrolet models did not change very much at all. Thus, customers do not expect changes in rank to occur. Second, though the introduction of a new model name at the top is heavily advertised, downgrading is not advertised at all; customers expect the rank of a model not to change, and they are not informed when it does change. The combination of strategies makes it unlikely that customers will notice these downgradings very readily. Furthermore, the individual changes, when they do take place, are small and systematic. This also renders them less noticeable. This is not to say that customers will never notice such changes at all, but only that their conceptions are likely to change much more slowly than the manufacturers' stipulations do. This is of course to the manufacturers' benefit.

Discussion

The phenomenon of downgrading is linguistically interesting for several reasons. First of all, the entire process is made possible in great part because of the arbitrariness of the linguistic sign. If manufacturers did not name their models but only described them, then there would be nothing to downgrade.

Second, though downgrading may be a conscious marketing strategy, it involves a very common type of semantic change, which is variously called *pejoration, devaluation,* or *depreciation* in the handbooks on semantic change. It is the historical process whereby the value of a word declines; it is often deplored by prescriptivists and academics, but it persists despite their best efforts. Again we see that the marketing strategy is designed to take advantage of basic properties of human language. . . .

References

Berlin, B. and P. Kay (1969) *Basic Color Terms: Their Universality and Evolution,* University of California Press, Berkeley and Los Angeles, California.

Dahlgren, K. (1978) "The Nature of Linguistic Stereotypes," in *Papers From the Parasession on the Lexicon,* Chicago Linguistic Society, University of Chicago, Chicago, Illinois.

Katz, J. and J. Fodor (1963) "The Structure of a Semantic Theory," in J. Fodor and J. Katz, eds., *The Structure of Language,* Prentice-Hall, Englewood Cliffs, New Jersey.

Kripke, S. (1972) "Naming and Necessity," in D. Davidson and G. Harman, eds., *Semantics of Natural Language,* Reidel, Dordrecht.

Labov, W. (1978) "Denotational Structure," in *Papers From the Parasession on the Lexicon,* Chicago Linguistic Society, University of Chicago, Chicago, Illinois.

Lakoff, G. (1972) "Hedges: A Study of Meaning Criteria and the Logic of Fuzzy Concepts," in P. Peranteau, J. Levi, and G. Phares, eds., *Papers From the Eighth Regional Meeting of the Chicago Linguistic Society,* University of Chicago, Chicago, Illinois.

Levi, J. (1978) *The Syntax and Semantics of Complex Nominals,* Academic Press, New York.

Miller, G. and P. Johnson-Laird (1976) *Language and Perception,* The Belknap Press of Harvard University Press, Cambridge, Massachusetts.

Nader, R. (1965) *Unsafe at any Speed: The Designed-in Dangers of the American Automobile,* Grossman, New York.

Nunberg, G. (1978a) *The Pragmatics of Reference,* Doctoral dissertation, City University of New York. Distributed by the Indiana University Linguistics Club, Bloomington, Indiana.

———. (1978b) "Slang, Use Conditions, and *l'arbitraire du signe,*" in *Papers From the Parasession on the Lexicon.* Chicago Linguistic Society, University of Chicago, Chicago, Illinois.

———. (1979) "The Non-Uniqueness of Semantic Solutions: Polysemy," *Linguistics and Philosophy* 3, 143–184.

Putnam, H. (1975) *Mind, Language, and Reality: Philosophical Papers,* volume 2, Cambridge University Press, Cambridge.

Rosch, E. (1973) "On the Internal Structure of Perceptual and Semantic Categories," in T. Moore, ed., *Cognitive Development and the Acquisition of Language,* Academic Press, New York.

Sloan, A. P. (1963) *My Years with General Motors,* Doubleday, Garden City.

FOR DISCUSSION AND REVIEW

1. On what basis does Aronoff argue that car names are common nouns, not proper names?

2. Consider the phrase structure rule that Aronoff suggests for car names—that is, the rule that describes possible answers to the question, What kind of car do you drive?:

car name → (year) (make) (line) (model) (body type)

What observations can you make about this rule? Consider especially the *order* in which the categories must appear and the fact that all categories (as indicated by the parentheses) are optional.

3. Aronoff discusses three automobile manufacturers and eleven car makes. Explain the relationship between *makes* and *price categories*. You may find it helpful to use diagrams. For example, acording to Aronoff:

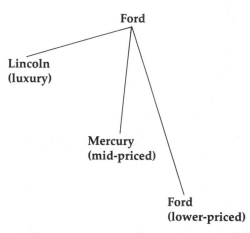

Ford

Lincoln
(luxury)

Mercury
(mid-priced)

Ford
(lower-priced)

Can one assume that a Ford will cost less than a Mercury? That a Mercury will cost less than a Lincoln? Why or why not?

4. Explain why Aronoff assumes that the prestige of any particular car "is determined by rank, rather than vice versa."

5. Explain the "three independent value systems," described by Aronoff, "according to which automobiles can be ranked, each of which goes from low to high."

6. Write a brief explanation of why the categories of body type and year are "fundamentally different" from the other three categories.

7. Describe what Aronoff calls the "interesting properties" of brand names, including the implications of their legal status.

8. Aronoff discusses the "continuity in names and discontinuity in appearance" of car models. Cite three specific examples of how car manufacturers are trying to give a sense of continuity to their products.

9. Explain Aronoff's statement that "the systematic sense of any car name consists of the position which that car occupies in a semantic space relative to other kinds of cars."

3/Pragmatics

MADELON E. HEATHERINGTON

Pragmatics, the study of speech acts or of how language is used in various contexts, is a relatively new subfield of linguistics. It is an important field because of the increasing recognition among linguists that the context of an utterance and the beliefs shared by a speaker and a hearer play an important role in determining meaning. Often people utter sentences that mean more than, or even something apparently different from, what they actually say and yet listeners understand the additional or altered meaning. In the following excerpt from her book How Language Works, *Madelon E. Heatherington discusses (1) the various types of illocutionary force, or the communicative intent of the speaker; (2) conversational principles, or expectations that are shared by all participants in a conversation; and (3) presuppositions, the surprisingly large number of assumptions made by all speakers about what their listeners know. Although it is difficult to analyze, this complex of social knowledge that constitutes the rules of pragmatics must be included in any complete description of language.*

This field of study [pragmatics] deals with particular utterances in particular situations and is especially concerned with the various ways in which the many social contexts of language performance can influence interpretation. Pragmatics goes beyond such influences as suprasegmental phonemes, dialects, and registers (all of which also shape interpretation) and looks at speech performance as primarily a social act ruled by various social conventions.

Anyone who is not a hermit lives in daily contact with other human beings, learns the explicit and implicit codes by which human beings usually manage to keep from doing violence to one another, and responds to alterations in those codes with greater or lesser good nature and skill. We drive on the right-hand side of the road and expect other drivers to do so. When we write checks, we have the money to cover them, and we expect the bank to honor them. We assume that food will be forthcoming in a restaurant, haircuts in a barber shop, gasoline—maybe—from a service station. We know these contexts so well that we do not think much about them, nor do we often stop to list the expectations we have about the behavior of people in such contexts. Ordinarily, there is no need to be explicit, because ordinarily, everybody else is behaving as we would expect them to. The "unspoken rules" governing behavior work very well, most of the time.

Occasionally, however, they do not work, or someone is not aware of them, or they are deliberately violated. Then it becomes important to be explicit about the "rules," the silent expectations and conventions, in order to discover what they ask of us and whether they are worth saving or not. For example, many people in the past decade or so have come to question certain "rules' about what gentlemen should do for ladies (open doors, light cigarettes, carry packages, etc.), asking whether those behaviors are fixed for all time by generic requirements or perhaps are signs, in the semiotic sense, of role-playing and strategies for coping with conflict. Similarly, pragmatics attempts to identify the "rules" underlying the performance of speech acts, or language as it is uttered in conjunction with the many social conventions controlling what speaker and auditor expect from one another.

Pragmatics theorists have identified three kinds of speech-act principles: illocutionary force, referring to the speaker as interpreted pragmatically by his auditors; conversational principles, referring to the auditors' expectations of the speaker; and presuppositions, referring to assumptions held by both the speaker and the auditors. Each of the three principles, of course, influences the others and therefore influences the significance of the speech act as a whole.

Illocutionary Force

This is the speaker's intention, so far as the auditors can discern it from the context. There are two major kinds of illocutionary force: implicit, below the surface and unstated, and explicit, on the surface and stated. The implicit forces are three: assertion, imperative, and question (sometimes called interrogative). Assertion is a statement about action or attitude ("He loves you," "He does not love you"). An imperative is a command for action ("Shut up!" "Will you please shut up!"). An interrogative is a request for information ("How much is that tie?" "What time is it?"). It is important to identify these implicit forces not only theoretically, but also as they appear in their various social contexts, for frequently the apparent intention of the speaker is not the same as the actual intent.

Social convention and good manners usually dictate, for instance, that a speaker will not use imperatives in polite company, perhaps at a party, at dinner, or when he is courting someone's favor. We are taught very early to say "please" as a way of disguising the illocutionary force of a command: "Please pass the biscuits"; "Give me the salt, please." It is even more polite to phrase the imperative as a question: "May I [or Can I] get through here?" "Would you like to go home now?" Most of us recognize that the implicit illocutionary force of these apparent questions is imperative, not interrogative, and we send the salt down or open a passageway without demur. We do not ordinarily respond to such implied commands by saying, "No" or by saying, "Yes" and not handing along the biscuits. We all understand that "May I have the biscuits?" is not a request for information, to be answered by "Yes" or "No," which would then have to be followed by another request for information—"Will you send them down here?"—which could then also be answered "Yes" or "No," and on and on while the biscuits stayed where they were and got cold.

Sometimes, however, the implicit illocutionary force of an utterance is not so clear, for it is often disguised by the surface-structure phrasing. When someone sitting outdoors on a cool evening says "I'm cold," that is phrased as a statement; it apparently requires neither information nor action. But if there is a wrap in the house, brought along for just this chilliness, and if the speaker's companion is attentive, the simple statement will probably be recognized as an implied command to bring the wrap out. Similarly, the statement "You're driving too fast" (assertion) may often carry the implicit illocutionary force of a command to slow down. "Do you love me?"—an apparent question—may carry many different implicit illocutionary forces: really a question, to be answered "Yes" or "No"; an assertion (perhaps "I love you" or perhaps "I am uncertain about your love for me"); or a command ("Tell me you love me"). Only context, linguistic or otherwise, will clarify this complex utterance.

It may be tentatively suggested that the more intimate the register, the more disguised the implicit illocutionary force in any given speech act. Conversely, the more formal is the register, the less disguised the force. Drill instructors in the armed forces do not suggest; they command. Their audience is presumed to be unfamiliar with the nuances of social convention that would instantaneously translate "Why don't we go for a walk?" into "Fifty-mile forced march, full packs, on the double!" Formalized situations tend to call for formalized utterances, so that an audience of varied backgrounds does not have to fumble with unfamiliar codes and levels of implied illocutions.

The other major kind of illocutionary force is explicit. Explicit illocutionary forces in speech acts take the form of statements in which the utterance itself is an action. "I tell you, it was awful!" performs the act of telling which the verb names. "I pronounce you man and wife" performs the act of pronouncing. "I promise I'll break your head" constitutes the act of promising. Statements like these, promising or pronouncing or telling (or asking or commanding), are called performative utterances; the utterance itself is the deed. There is an understood contract in such utterances, for assertions like these always carry the force of an unspoken command. The unspoken (implicit) command is that the auditor should believe the assertions to be true (should accept their truth value): it is true that something was awful; you are man and wife; your head will get broken.

Most of the time, we do accept such assertions as true, or we pretend to do so, but if the context is intimate enough, the implicit truth value may be questioned even here: "Oh, yeah? Who says it was awful? You wouldn't know 'awful' if it bit you!" Or "Oh, yeah? You and what army gonna break my head?" (But rarely "Oh, yeah? Who says you're married?" for the context here is formal, not intimate.) When explicit and implicit intentions clash over a performative utterance, the auditors are challenging the speaker's capacity, not to *tell* the truth, but to *verify* the truth of the statements. The speaker is challenged to match the truth value of the utterance to some external referent or some action.

Conversational Principles

This brings us to what the auditor can expect from a speaker, as opposed to the interpretive skills that a speaker can expect from his audience. In any speech act, the audience generally assumes that at least four conversational principles will apply to what a speaker says. The audience's first assumption is that the speaker is sincere, not saying one thing and meaning another, at least with no greater discrepancy between phrasing and intention than what we expect in the exercise of various illocutionary forces. The second assumption is that the speaker is telling the truth so far as he understands it, not deliberately telling lies. Third, the audience assumes that what the speaker has to say is relevant to the topic or general areas of concern. The final assumption is that the speaker will contribute the appropriate amount of information or commentary, not withhold anything important and not rattle on for an undue amount of time.

For example, if someone (speaker) asks, "What time is it?" we (auditors) usually assume that he does not know what the time is and that his request is a sincere one for information about the time. When we (now speakers) begin to reply, he (now auditor) will usually assume that we will answer with the correct time, not with a rambling discourse on the price of hamburger, nor with a scream of rage, nor with a lie. If any of those four assumptions prove incorrect, then discord immediately appears and one or the other of the conversants has to make a quick test of the assumptions, to discover which one has been violated and what the appropriate response should now be.

For example, should people be hurrying out of a burning building, a request for the correct time is presumed to be insincere and will elicit irritation or disgust: "You crazy? Keep moving!" But if someone begins a prepared speech on tax reform to the Lions Club with a joke about peanut butter, the audience will unconsciously recognize that the relevance of the joke is less to taxes than to the reduction of stress between strangers. It is understood here that the context of speech giving requires some preliminary establishment of shared concerns, even a sort of shared companionship, between the orator and the audience. Such a speaker is not expected to launch immediately into the technical points of his topic. But if that speaker's boss asks for a short telephone conversation on the same topic of tax reform, a joke would not be appropriate as an opening; it would be irrelevant in the context of a business discussion.

Presuppositions

Here, we move into what both speakers and auditors can expect of the content or information contained in an utterance,[1] that is, what a speaker and an auditor can suppose each other to know before a given speech act begins. For example, if I say, "But Jenny has never gone out with a married man before!" I presuppose (before I utter the sentence) that my listener knows at least these content items:

1. There is a person named Jenny.
2. Speaker and listener are both acquainted with Jenny.
3. Jenny goes out with men.
4. Jenny has just recently gone out with a married man.

Presumably, too, the listener and speaker both share the following bits of information, although these presuppositions are not so obvious nor so demonstrable from the utterance alone:

5. Jenny is female.
6. Jenny is not married.
7. Jenny does not usually go out with married men.
8. Jenny is adult.
9. Jenny is not so dependent upon speaker or listener that her behavior can be regulated by either of them.
10. Speaker and listener are surprised by Jenny's behavior.

Presupposition underlies a good deal of the unthinking adjustment we make from one speech situation to another, adjustment that helps en-

[1] Since each of the three speech-act principles influences the other, it will be recognized that to separate presupposition from the other two is to be somewhat arbitrary. Presupposition about content will vary from one speech situation to another, depending on the influence of intention and expectation.

sure we are not (as speech-communication teachers say) "talking over our audience's head" or not "insulting our audience's intelligence." Presupposition is operating when we mutter secrets in hallways so that outsiders will not understand. All codes, jargons, cants, and deliberate use of elliptical or confusing language make use of presupposition.

It is very easy to misjudge presupposition when one does not know one's audience well, or when one thinks one knows them all too well. A good many people seem to sense this principle, as evidenced by the frequency with which they intersperse phrases like "You know," "I mean," or "Know what I mean?" in their conversation. For instance, if I tell you that I will meet you on the corner of Third and Main at noon today, I assume that you know what noon is, where Third Street makes a corner with Main Street, and which of the four points of that intersection I will be waiting on. If you are new in town, I may wait a long time. Conversely, if my husband tells me he wants his favorite meal for dinner and presupposes I will cook it, because we have been married a long time and I always know and cook what he asks for, then he may wait a long time. Presuppositions always require testing from time to time, to be sure that what the speaker and what the auditor assume or know are really the same.

An attentiveness to the unspoken and often unconscious "rules" or expectations inherent in speech acts can help to sharpen our awareness of what is really going on as we speak. The illocutionary force implicit in certain contexts, the active nature of performative statements, the conversational principles applicable to most speech situations, and the presuppositions all of us bring to conversations: these pragmatic contexts of language use shape our performance all the time. The more we understand them, perhaps the better we can control them. The same may be said of our control over individual meanings as well.

FOR DISCUSSION AND REVIEW

1. Develop the many implications of Heatherington's statement that pragmatics "looks at speech performance as primarily a social act ruled by various social conventions."

2. One of the three basic kinds of speech act principles is *illocutionary force,* a term that refers to the speaker's communicative intention to the extent that the hearer(s) can discern it. It is divided into *implicit illocutionary force* and *explicit illocutionary force.* Define these three concepts in your own words.

3. The three implicit illocutionary forces are assertion, imperative, and question (interrogative). Why is it important, in actual conversations, that the hearer identify these implicit illocutionary forces? Give an ex-

ample from your own experience of an utterance or exchange involving a discrepancy between implicit and explicit illocutionary force. Did the social context make clear the actual intentions of the speaker? If so, describe how.

4. Heatherington suggests that "the more intimate the register, the more disguised the implicit illocutionary force in any speech act. Conversely, the more formal is the register, the less disguised the force." Do you agree? Support your answer with specific examples.

5. Define "explicit illocutionary force" and supply two examples of your own. Why are these speech acts called "performative utterances"? In what sense is there "an understood contract" in performative utterances?

6. Just as speakers expect certain behavior on the part of their audience, so too audiences have expectations about speaker behavior called conversational principles. In general, Heatherington says, audiences assume (1) that a speaker is sincere; (2) that a speaker is telling the truth; (3) that what a speaker says will be relevant to the topic under discussion; and (4) that the speaker will neither withhold important information nor monopolize the conversation. (Actually, all the participants in a conversation share these expectations.) Describe a situation in which all the conversational principles were observed and one in which one or more was violated. What conclusions can you draw?

7. Presuppositions involve both speakers and hearers; and all utterances, even the simplest, involve a number of presuppositions. Examine the following sentences and list the presuppositions for each:
   a. Mary's husband works for IBM.
   b. Even though Bob promised never to lie to me again, he told me today that he didn't go to the movies with Sherry.
   c. That C— I got on the Psych quiz you missed is really going to hurt my average.
   d. Nonsmokers have rights too!

4/Discourse Routines

ELAINE CHAIKA

In the following chapter from her book Language: The Social Mirror, *Professor Elaine Chaika examines a variety of ways in which the social rules of language, an aspect of pragmatics, control what we say and when and how we say it. We cannot fully understand the meaning of an utterance unless we understand its social context. And in order to understand the social context, we need to consider a complex set of interrelated rules, including speech events, intentions, speech acts, preconditions, presuppositions, utterance pairs, roles and social status, presequences, collapsing sequences, repairs by speaker or hearer, and more. All of these discourse routines play important roles in social interaction; all are rule-governed and largely unconscious behaviors, are learned as part of the language acquisition process, and are so important to people that "even when it makes no difference in a fleeting social contact . . . they demand that the right forms be chosen."*

A Paradox

Language makes us free as individuals but chains us socially. It has already been demonstrated that we are not mere creatures of conditioning when it comes to language. We can say things we never heard before, as well as understand what we have not previously heard.

When we consider discourse rules, however, we find a strange paradox. The social rules of language often force us into responding in certain ways. We are far from free in forming sentences in actual social situations. Frequently we must respond whether we want to or not. Furthermore, we must respond in certain ways (see Givon 1979; Schenkein 1978; Labov and Fanshel 1977).

Meaning and the Social Situation

The actual meaning of an utterance depends partially on the social context in which it occurs.

Rommetveit (1971) gives a classic example of this. He tells a story about a man running for political office who is scheduled to give a talk in a school auditorium. When he arrives, he sees that there are not enough chairs. He calls his wife at home. Then he goes to see the janitor. To each, the candidate says, "There aren't enough chairs." To the wife, this means "Wow! am I popular," but to the janitor it means "Go get some more chairs." The full meaning evoked by the statement "There aren't enough chairs" is largely a product of the context in which it is said, including the relative social statuses, privileges and duties of the speaker and listener. The remainder of this chapter is concerned with the obligations society places upon us in discourse, as well as the real meaning of utterances in a social context.

Speech Events, Genres, and Performances

A speech event is the situation calling forth particular ways of speaking (Gordon and Lakoff 1975). *Genre* refers to the form of speaking. Usually, it has a label, such as *joke, narrative, promise, riddle, prayer,* even *greeting* or *farewell.*

Members of a speech community recognize genres as having beginnings, middles, and ends, and as being patterned. "Did you hear the one about . . .", for instance, is a recognized opener for the genre *joke* in our society. "Once upon a time . . ." is a recognized opener for the genre *child's story,* and the ending is "They lived happily ever after." The end of *joke* is the *punch line,* often a pun, an unusual or unexpected response to a situation or utterance, or a stupid response by one of the characters in the joke. Typically the stupid response to a situation is one that reveals that the character is lacking in some basic social knowledge or one in which the social meaning of an utterance is ignored and its literal meaning is taken instead. For instance, an old Beetle Bailey cartoon shows Sarge saying to Zero "The wastebasket is full." Instead of emptying the basket, Zero responds "Even I can see that." The joke is that Zero took the words at their face value rather than interpreting them as a command, which was their actual social force.

Sometimes the genre is the entire speech event but not always. Church services are speech events, for instance. *Sermons* are a genre belonging to church, but sermons do not cover the entire speech event. Prayers, responsive readings, hymn singing, and announcements also constitute the speech events of church services.

The way that participants carry out the demands of a genre is their *performance.* In some communities, this is more important than others. Also, performance is more important in some speech events than others. A professor's performance, for instance, is far more important than that of the students in the classroom. The exception would be those classes in which students have been assigned special speaking tasks.

Perhaps *important* is not quite the right word. The professor's performance will be judged more overtly than a student's and judged according to different criteria. These are the criteria judged in public performance, such as clarity of diction, voice quality, logic of lecture, and coherence. Correct performance in less formal speech events is just as important, but in those judgment is often confined to how appropriate the speech was to the situation. Everyday discourse routines are as much performances as are preaching, joke-telling, and lecturing.

Linguists often use the word *performance* in a more general sense than here. They use it to refer to one's actual speech, which may contain errors, such as slips of the tongue. Since people often realize that they have made speech mistakes, linguists say that there is a difference between *competence* and performance. In this chapter, performance will refer specifically to one's ability to carry out the requirements of a speech event in a given social situation. This, too, may differ from one's competence in that one can be aware of errors in one's performance of a genre. A professor may realize with a sickening thud, for example, that a prepared lecture is boring a class to sleep, or a party goer may be unable to think of any of the small talk or repartee called for at a party.

Performances in discourse routines are strongly controlled by turn-taking rules that determine who speaks when. Co-occurrence restrictions . . . operate stringently on genres. Often the speech event itself determines them. The genre of sermons occurs in the speech event of church services. Therefore, only features that go with formal style are usually used in sermons. Jokes, in contrast, occur in informal, play situations or as a means of helping someone relax and become more informal. Therefore, formal style features are inappropriate in jokes, so that they are included usually only in the reported conversation of a character in the joke.

Intention

In all interaction, the parties assume that each person means what he or she says and is speaking with a purpose. Esther Goody (1978) points out that people impute intentions to others. In fact, she notes, they "positively seek out intentions in what others say and do." What people assume is another's intention colors the meaning they get from messages. How often has someone suspiciously said to a perfectly innocent comment of yours, "Now what did you mean by that?" The question is not asking for literal meaning but for your intention in saying what you did. Presequences rely heavily on our perceiving a speaker's intentions or thinking we do. The child who hears an adult's

"Who spilled this milk?" may rightly perceive the question as the precursor to a command "Wipe it up!"

Often, intentions are not perceived correctly, causing misunderstandings as harmless as hearing an honest question as a command or as serious as hearing an innocent comment as an insult. To illustrate the last, consider a man who, in front of his slightly plump wife, looks admiringly at a model, "Wow! what a body on that one!" The wife immediately bridles (or dissolves in tears, depending on her personal style) with a "I know I'm too fat. You don't have to rub it in."

The only time that we are freed from the obligation to carry out the socially prescribed roles in speech events is when the other party is incapable of acting with a purpose, as when drunk, stoned, or insane (Frake 1964). Perhaps one of the reasons that we get so angry when someone does not act or speak appropriately for the situation is that we cannot figure out his or her goals. Without knowing someone's goals, we do not know how to act ourselves when dealing with another person.

Speech Acts

People usually think of speech as a way of stating propositions and conveying information. Austin (1962) also stressed the functions of speech as a way of "doing things with words." Sociolinguists and anthropologists have been very concerned with how people use language to manage social interactions. Threatening, complimenting ("buttering someone up"), commanding, even questioning can all be manipulative. Another person's behavior may be affected quite differently from what one might expect from the actual words used. "See that belt?" may be sufficient to restrain a child from wrongdoing. The words themselves are an action. The child, of course, imputes intention to the words. They are heard as a threat of a spanking with the belt.

A Case in Point: The Telephone

The ritual nature of conversation as well as the role of social convention in determining meaning is easily seen in rules for the telephone (Schegloff 1968). The telephone has been common in American homes only for the past fifty or so years. Yet very definite rules surround its usage. Exactly how such rules arose and became widespread throughout society is not precisely known, any more than we know exactly how a new dialect feature suddenly spreads through a population. All we know is that whenever a social need arises, language forms evolve to meet the need.

The first rule of telephone conversation in the United States is that the answerer speaks first. It does not have to be so. The rule could as easily be that the caller speaks first. That makes perfectly good sense, as it means that the one who calls is identified at once. Of course, the American way makes equally good sense in that callers are ensured that the receiver is at someone's ear before they start to speak. There are often several equally logical possibilities in conversation rituals, but any one group may adopt just one of the possible alternatives. In other words, if we come across ways different from our own, we should not assume that "theirs" are any better or worse than "ours."

In any event, in the United States, the convention is that the answerer speaks first. If the call could conceivably be for the answerer because he or she is answering the phone in his or her home, the usual first utterance is "Hello."

In places of business or in a doctor's or lawyer's office, wherever secretaries or operators answer the phone, "Hello" is not proper. Rather, the name of the business or office is given, as in "E. B. Marshall Company," "Smith and Carlson," "Dr. Sloan's office" or "George West Junior High." Giving the name in itself means "This is a business, institution, or professional office." At one time it was appropriate for servants in a household or even neighbors or friends who happened to pick up the phone to answer "Jones' residence" rather than "Hello," unless the call might conceivably be for the answerer. Increasingly, however, it appears that people answer "Hello" to a residential phone even if the call might not be for them. This situation can lead to complications, especially since the callers seem to assume that whoever answers "Hello" belongs to that phone.

The British custom of answering with one's name, as "Carl Jones here" seems to be a very efficient solution. Many American callers get thrown off by such a greeting, however. Being impressed with the British rule, I have repeatedly tried to answer my own home phone with "Elaine Chaika here." The result is usually a moment of silence followed by responses like "Uh . . . uh. Elaine?" or "Uh . . . uh. Is Danny there?" The "Uh . . . uh" probably signifies momentary confusion or embarrassment, somewhat different from the "Uh" hesitation that precedes a request to a stranger for directions or the time, as in "Uh, excuse me . . .". Predictably, answering my office phone the same way does not elicit the "Uh . . . uh," although the moment of silence still often occurs.

Godard (1977) recounts the confusion on both her part and callers' in the United States because her native French routine requires that callers verify that the number called is the one reached. Violation of discourse routines, like violations of rules of style, hinders social interaction at least a little even when the violations otherwise fit the situation just fine.

After the answerer says "Hello" or another appropriate greeting, the caller asks, "Is X there?" unless he or she recognizes the answerer's voice as being the one wanted. If the caller recognizes the answerer's voice but wishes to speak to someone else, he or she might say, "Hi, X. Is Y there?" Some do not bother to greet the answerer first. Whether or not hurt feelings result seems to depend on the degree of intimacy involved. Students in my classes report that their mothers often feel hurt if a frequent caller does not say the equivalent of "Hi, Mrs. Jones. Is Darryl there?" Sometimes callers wish to acknowledge the existence of the answerer (phatic communication), but do not wish to be involved in a lengthy conversation so they say the equivalent of "Hi, Mrs. Jones. It's Mary. I'm sorry but I'm in a hurry. Is Darryl there?" On the surface, "I'm sorry but I'm in a hurry" seems to have no relevance. It does, though, because it is an acknowledgment that the caller recognizes acquaintance with the answerer and therefore, the social appropriateness of conversing with her or him.

Compulsion in Discourse Routines

In terms of social rules, perhaps what is most interesting is that the person who answers the phone feels compelled to go get the one the caller wants. This compulsion may be so great that answerers find themselves running all over the house, shouting out the windows if necessary to get the one called.

One student of mine, John Reilly, reported an amusing anecdote illustrating the strength of this obligation. He called a friend to go bowling, and the friend's sister answered the phone. She informed John that her brother was cutting logs but that she would go to fetch him. John, knowing that the woodpile was 100 yards away, assured her it was not necessary. All she had to do was to relay the message. Three times she insisted on going. Three times John told her not to. Finally, she said, confusedly, "Don't you want to talk to him?" John repeated that she could extend his invitation without calling the friend to the phone. Suddenly, she just left the phone without responding to John's last remarks and fetched her brother.

As extreme as this may sound, it is actually no more so than the person who leaps out of the tub to answer the phone and, still dripping wet with only a towel for protection, proceeds to run to another part of the house to summon the person for whom the caller asked. It is the rare person who can say, "Yes, X is here, but I don't see her. Call back later." Indeed, there are those who would consider such a response quite rude. It seems as if the person who picks up the phone has tacitly consented to go get whomever is called, regardless of inconvenience, unless the called one is not at home. The sense of obligation, of having to respond in a certain way, is at the core of all social routines, including discourse.

Meaning in Discourse Routines

Actually, if the one called on the phone is not at home or does not live there any more or never lived there at all, the semantically appropriate response to "Is X there?" should be "No." In fact, however, "No," is appropriate only if X does live there but is not now at home. For example:

If X once lived there, but does not now, an appropriate answer is

1. X doesn't live here any more.
2. X has moved.

or even

3. X lives at _____ now.

Although "no" has the correct meaning, it cannot be used if X no longer lives there.

If X has never lived there, one may answer

4. There is no X here.
5. What number are you calling?
6. You must have the wrong number.

Again "no" would seem to be a fitting response, but it cannot be used. "No" to "Is X there?" always means that X does belong there but is not there now. Notice that 4 semantically fits for a meaning of "X no longer lives here," but it never would be used for that meaning by someone socialized into American society.

In discourse routines, frequently an apparently suitable response cannot be used in certain social situations or the response will have a greater meaning than the words used.. For instance, one apparently proper response to:

7. Where are the tomatoes? (in a store)

is

8. I don't know.

Most people would find such an honest answer rude, even odd. More likely is

9. I'm sorry, but I don't work here.

or

10. I'm sorry, I'll ask the manager.

If the one asked is an employee, then 10 is appropriate. As with the telephone, the answerer feels obligated. In this instance, the obligation is to supply the answer if he or she is an employee.

Preconditions

The response 9 would be bizarre except that we all know it is not actually the answer to "Where are the tomatoes?" Rather, it is a response to the preconditions for asking a question of anyone (Labov and Fanshel 1977). These are:

I. The questioner has the right or the duty to ask the question.
II. The one asked has the responsibility or obligation to know the answer.

Preconditions for speech acts are as much a part of their meaning as actual words are. If one asks someone in a store where something is, one probably has categorized that person as an employee, and employees have an obligation to know where things are in their place of work. Hence 9 really means "You have categorized me erroneously. I don't work here, so I am not obligated to know the answer."

Sometimes people answer

11. "I don't work here, but the tomatoes are in the next aisle."

The giveaway here is the *but*. It makes no sense in 11 unless it is seen as a response to precondition II. When *but* joins two sentences, it often means "although," as in 11, which means "Although I don't work here I happen to know that the tomatoes are in the next aisle." That is, "Although I am not responsible for knowing or obligated to tell you, since I do not work here, I will anyhow." Note that the statement "I don't work here" really adds nothing to the pertinent information. It is frequently said anyhow as a way of letting the asker know that he or she miscategorized by assuming that the answerer was an employee.

Presupposition

Some meaning in discourse is also achieved by presupposition. This refers to meaning that is never overtly stated but is always presupposed if certain phrases are used. If one says "Even Oscar is going," the use of *even* is possible only if one presupposes that Oscar usually does not go, so that the fact of his going means that everyone is going. Both preconditions and presuppositions are part of the meaning of utterance pairs to be discussed shortly, and both may help constrain the kinds of responses people make to utterances.

Utterance Pairs

The phenomenon of responsibility which we have already seen as part of telephone routines and answering questions is part of a larger responsibility that adheres to the discourse rules that Harvey Sacks called *utterance pairs* (1968–72, 1970). These are conversational sequences in which one utterance elicits another of a specific kind. For instance,

- Greeting–greeting
- Question–answer
- Complaint–excuse, apology, or denial
- Request/command–acceptance or rejection
- Compliment–acknowledgment
- Farewell–farewell

Whoever is given the first half of an utterance pair is responsible for giving the second half. The first half, in our society, commands the person addressed to give one of the socially recognized appropriate responses. As with the telephone, these responses often have a meaning different from, less than, or greater than the sum of the words used.

Furthermore, the first half of the pair does not necessarily have to sound like what it really is. That is, a question does not have to be in question form nor a command in command form. All that is necessary for a statement to be construed as a question or a command is for the social situation to be right for questioning or commanding. The very fact that a speech event is appropriate for a question or a command may cause an utterance to be perceived as such, even if it is not in question or command form. As with proper style, situation includes roles and relative status of participants in a conversation. Situation, roles, and social status are an inextricable part of meaning, often as much as, if not more so, than the surface form of an utterance.

Questions and Answers

Let us consider questions and answers. Goody (1978) points out that questions, being incomplete, are powerful in forcing responses, at least in our society. . . . We have already seen that certain preconditions exist for questioning and that an answer may be to the pre-condition rather than to the question itself. In the following discussion, it is always assumed that the preconditions for questioning are fulfilled. We will then be able to gain some insights into how people understand and even manipulate others on the basis of social rules.

There are two kinds of overt questions in English, *yes–no* questions and *wh*-questions. The first, as the name implies, requires an answer of yes or no. In essence, if the *yes–no* question forms are used, one is forced to answer "yes," "no," or "I don't know." There is no way not to answer, except to pretend not to hear. If that occurs, the asker usu-ally repeats the question, perhaps more loudly, or even precedes the repetition with a tap on the would-be answerer's shoulder (or the equivalent). Alternatively, the asker could precede the repeated ques-tion with a summons, like "Hey, Bill, I said . . ." or any combination of the three.

It is because members of our society all recognize that they must answer a question and that they must respond "yes" or "no" to a *yes–no* question that the following question is a recognized joke:

12. Have you stopped beating your wife?/your husband?

Since you must know what you do to your spouse, "I don't know" cannot be answered. Only a "yes" or a "no" will do. Either answer condemns. Either way you admit to spouse-beating.

Yes–no questions can also be asked by tags:

13. You're going, *aren't you*?
14. It's five dollars, *right*?

If the preconditions for questioning are present, however, as Labov and Fanshel (1977) point out, a plain declarative statement will be con-strued as a *yes–no* question, as in

15. Q: You live on 114th Street.
   A: No, I live on 115th.

The *wh*- questions demand an answer that substitutes for the ques-tion word. An "I don't know" can also be given. The *wh*- words are *what, when, why, who, where,* and *how* appearing at the start of a ques-tion. These words are, in essence, blanks to be filled in.

What has to be answered with the name of a thing or event; *when* with a time; *where* with a location; *why*, a reason; *who*, a person; and *how*, a manner or way something was done. There is actually yet an-other *wh*- question, "Huh?" which asks in effect, "Would you repeat the entire sentence you just said?" That is, the "Huh" asks that a whole utterance be filled in, not just a word or phrase.

The answer to any question can be deferred by asking another, creating *insertion sequences* (Schegloff 1971, p. 76). For instance,

16.   A: Wanna come to a party?
        B: Can I bring a friend?
          A: Male or female?
          B: Female.
        A: Sure.
      B: O.K.

Note that these questions are answered in reverse order, but all are answered. Occasionally, insertion sequences can lead conversationalists "off the track." When this happens participants may feel a compulsion to get a question answered even if they have forgotten what it was. Hence, comments like:

17. Oh, as you were saying . . .
18. Oh, I forget, what were we talking about?

Note that the "oh" serves as an indicator that the speaker is not responding to the last statement, but to a prior one. Such seemingly innocuous syllables frequently serve as markers in conversation.

Using the Rules to Manipulate

It is easy to manipulate people subtly by plugging them into the presuppositions and preconditions behind statements (Elgin 1980; Labov and Fanshel 1977). For example, a wife might try to get her husband to go to a dance by saying "Even Oscar is going" (p. 436). The presupposition is that if Oscar is going, then everyone is. There is a further presupposition that if everyone else is doing something, then so should the person being spoken to. If Oscar is going then everyone is going, ergo, so should the husband. Readers may recognize in this rather common ploy the childhood "Everyone else has one" or "Everyone else is going."

Elgin (1980) also discusses manipulations of the "If you really loved me . . ." variety. There are actually subtle accusations. What they mean is "You should love me, but you don't. The guilt you feel for not loving me can easily be erased, though, by doing whatever I want."

Another manipulation is the "Even *you* should be able to do that" type. Here we have *even* again, the word that tells someone that he or she is alone in whatever failing is being mentioned. Its use with *should* is especially clever because it implies that the hearer is stupid or some sort of gross misfit, but it backgrounds that message so that it is not likely to be discussed. Rather, the hearer is made to feel stupid and wrong, so that he or she will be likely to capitulate to the speaker's demands in an effort to prove that if all others can do it, so can the hearer.

One can achieve both manipulation and insult by preceding a comment with "Don't tell me you're going to _____" or "Don't tell me that you believe _____!" Notice that these are questions in the form of a command. They are actually asking, "Are you really going to __?" or "Do you really believe . . . ?" However, the presuppositions behind these questions in command form are (a) "You are going to do _____" (or "You believe _____") and (b) "[your action or belief] _____ is stupid." For instance,

19. X: Don't tell me that you are going to vote for Murgatroyd!
    Z: Well, I thought I would, but now I'm not so sure.

The really clever manipulation is that Z is instantly made to feel foolish because of presupposition b. However, since X has not overtly accused Z of stupidity, argument is difficult. Z is not even allowed the luxury of anger at the insult, because the insult has not been stated. It is contained only in the presupposition. Z might become immediately defensive but still feel quite stupid because of the implied insult. Not only does X get Z to capitulate, but also X establishes that Z is the stupider of the two. As a manipulatory device, this one is a "double whammy."

Labov and Fanshel (1977) show that some people manipulate in even more subtle ways by utilizing common understanding of social and discourse rules. Using patient-therapist sessions which they received permission to tape, they describe the struggle of a woman named Rhoda for independence from a domineering mother. The mother finally leaves Rhoda at home and goes to visit Rhoda's sister Phyllis. Rhoda cannot cope, but neither can she ask her mother to come home, because that would be an admission that the mother is right in not giving Rhoda more freedom. Rather, Labov and Fanshel say that Rhoda employs an indirect request both to mitigate her asking her mother for help and to disguise her challenge to the power relationship between them. Rhoda calls her mother on the phone and asks,

20. When do you plan to come home?

Since this is not a direct request for help, Rhoda's mother forces an admission by not answering Rhoda's question. Instead, she creates an insertion sequence:

21. Oh, why?

This means "Why are you asking me when I plan to come home?" In order to answer, Rhoda must admit that she cannot be independent, that the mother has been right all along. Furthermore, as a daughter, Rhoda must answer her mother's question. Her mother has the right to question by virtue of her status, and Rhoda has the duty to answer for the same reason. So, Rhoda responds with

22. Things are getting just a little too much . . . it's getting too hard.

To which the mother replies:

23. Why don't you ask Phyllis [when I'll be home]?

Since, in our society, it is really up to the mother when she will come home, and also, since she has a prior obligation to her own household, "It is clear that Rhoda has been outmaneuvered," according to Labov and Fanshel. The mother has forced Rhoda into admitting that she is not capable, and she has, in effect, refused Rhoda's request for help.

It seems to me that this mother also has conveyed very cleverly to Rhoda that Phyllis is the preferred daughter and has said it so covertly that the topic cannot be discussed openly. Clearly it is the mother's right and duty to come home as she wishes. By palming that decision off on Phyllis, she is actually saying to Rhoda "No matter what your claim on me is, Phyllis comes first." That is, for Phyllis's sake, she will suppress her rights as a mother and allow Phyllis to make the decision. Notice that all of this works only because at some level both Rhoda and her mother know the rights and obligations of questioners and answerers.

Indirect Requests and Conflict With Social Values

All indirect requests do not arise from such hostile situations, although most are used when individual desires conflict with other social rules or values. Classic examples, spoken with an expectant lift to the voice, are:

24. Oh, chocolates.
25. What are those, cigars?

SACKS, 1968–72

Assuming that 24 and 25 are spoken by adults who have long known what *chocolate* denotes and are familiar with cigars, these observations are perceived as requests. This is shown by the usual responses to either:

26. Would you like one?
27. I'm sorry, but they aren't mine. (*or*, I have to save them for X.)

Young toddlers just learning to speak do practice by going about pointing at objects and naming them. Once that stage is past, people do not name items in the immediate environment unless there is an intent, a reason for singling out the item. All properly socialized Americans know that one should never directly ask for food in another's household or for any possibly expensive goods such as cigars. That would be begging. Therefore, one names the items in another's home or hands so that the naming is construed as an indirect request. There is rarely another reason for an adult to name a common object or food. The responses to 24 and 25 make sense only if the hearer construes those as really meaning "I want you to offer me some of those chocolates/cigars."

Commands

Requests for food are not the only discourse routines arising from conflicts between general social rules and the will of the individual. Both commands and compliments, albeit in different ways, run afoul of cultural attitudes.

Commands share virtually the same preconditions as questions.

I. The speaker who commands has the right and/or duty to command.
II. The recipient of the command has the responsibility and/or obligation to carry out the command.

The problem is that, even more than with questioning, the one who has the right to command is usually clearly of higher status than the one who must obey. The United States supposedly is an egalitarian society, but having the right or duty to command implies that some are superior to others. This runs counter to our stated ideals. Therefore, in most actual situations in American speech, commands are disguised as questions. The substitution of forms is possible because both speech acts share the same preconditions. Moreover, phrasing commands as questions maintains the fiction that the one commanded has the right to refuse, even when he or she does not. Consider.

28. Would you mind closing the door?

Even though it is uttered as a *yes–no* question, merely to answer "No" without the accompanying action or "Yes" without an accompanying excuse would either be bizarre or a joke. In the movie *The Return of the Pink Panther*, Peter Sellers asks a passerby if he knows where the Palace Hotel is. The passerby responds "Yes" and keeps on going. The joke is that "Do you know where X is?" is not really a *yes–no* question but a polite command meaning "Tell me where X is."

Direct commanding is allowed and usual in certain circumstances. For instance, parents normally command young children directly. For example,

29. Pick those toys up right away.

Intimates such as spouses or roommates often casually command each other about trivial matters, such as

30. Pick some bread up on your way home.

Often these are softened by "please," "will ya," "honey," or the like.

Direct commanding in command form occurs in the military from those of superior rank to those of inferior. During actual battle it is necessary for combatants to obey their officers without question, unthinkingly, and unhesitatingly. Direct commands yield this kind of obedience so long as those commanded recognize the social rightness of the command or the need. It is no surprise that direct commands are regularly heard in emergency situations, as during firefighting:

31. Get the hose! Put up the ladders!

A great deal of direct commanding is also heard in hospital emergency rooms:

32. Get me some bandages.
    Suture that wound immediately.

In situations that allow direct commands, the full command form need not always be invoked. Just enough has to be said so that the underling knows what to do, as in

33. Time for lunch. (meaning "Come in for lunch.")

34. Scalpel! Sutures! Dressings!

Note that such commands are contextually bound. They are interpretable as commands only if the participants are actually in a commanding situation. Similarly, Susan Ervin-Tripp's (1972) comment that

35. It's cold in here.

can be interpreted as a command works only in a specific commanding context. The speaker uttering 35 must somehow have the right to ask another to close a window, if that is the cause of the cold, or to ask another to lend his or her coat. In this situation, the fact that one person is closer to an open window may be sufficient reason for him or her to be responsible for closing it. The duty or obligation to carry out a command need not proceed only from actual status but may proceed from the physical circumstances in which the command has been uttered. That is why in the right circumstances ordinary statements or questions may be construed as commands, as in:

36. A: Any more coffee?
    B: I'll make some right away.
    A: No, I wanted to know if I had to buy any.

If it is possible to do something about whatever is mentioned, an utterance may be construed as a command. In 36, it was possible for B to make some coffee, and B must have been responsible for making it at least some of the time. Hence the question about coffee was misinterpreted as a command to make some. The same possibility of misinterpretation can occur in the question

37. Can you swim?

Said by a poolside, it may be interpreted as a command "Jump in," but away from a body of water, it will be heard merely as a request for information.

Although questions are often used as polite substitutes for commands, the question command can sometimes be especially imperious:

38. Would you mind being quiet?

Similarly, a command like the following may seem particularly haughty:

39. If you would wait, please.

I suspect that both 38 and 39 carry special force because the high formality signaled by "Would you mind" and "If you would . . . please" contrasts so sharply with the banality of keeping quiet and waiting that the effect of sarcasm is achieved.

Compliments

Compliments are another utterance pair type that create conflict. This is because of general social convention and the rule that the first part of an utterance pair must evoke a response. Compliments call for an acknowledgment. The acknowledgment can properly be acceptance of the compliment, as in "Thank you." The problem is that to accept the compliment is very close to bragging, and bragging is frowned upon in middle-class America. Hence, one typical response to a compliment is a disclaimer, like

40. This old rag?
41. I got it on sale.
42. My mother got it for me.

An exception is special occasions when compliments are expected, as when everyone is decked out to go to a prom or a wedding. Then, not only are compliments easily received with "Thank you," but not to compliment can cause offense or disappointment.

Except for such situations, complimenting can lead to social embarrassment. If one persists in complimenting another, the other person often becomes hostile, even though nice things are being said. At the very least the recipient of excessive praise becomes uncomfortable and tries to change the subject. Often he or she becomes suspicious and angry or tries to avoid the person who is heaping praise. The suspicion is either that the complimenter is being patronizing or is trying to get something, to "butter the person up."

Once, I ordered a class to persistently compliment their parents, spouses, or siblings. The most common response was "OK. What do you want this time?" One of the students received a new suit from a friend who owned a men's clothing store, with the friend practically shouting, "OK. If I give you a new suit will that shut you up?"

Many of those complimented became overtly angry. Others quickly found an excuse to leave, and several students found that those on whom they heaped praise shunned them the next time they met. I suspect that the anger results from the social precariousness of being complimented. As with style, when a person is put at a social disadvantage so that he or she does not know how to respond, anger results. It is very uncomfortable to receive too much praise. It is tantamount to continually being asked to tread the line between gracious acceptance and boasting. Most people prefer to ignore anyone who puts them in that situation.

Presequences and Saving Face

An interesting class of discourse rules is what Harvey Sacks called *presequences* (lecture, November 2, 1967), particularly preinvitations. Typically, someone wishing to issue an oral invitation, first asks something like

43. What are you doing Saturday night?

If the response includes words like *only* or *just*, as in

44. I'm just washing my hair.
45. I'm only studying.

the inviter can then issue an invitation for Saturday night. If, however, the response is

46. I'm washing my hair.
47. I'm studying.

the potential inviter knows not to issue the invitation. Following a response like 46 or 47, the inviter signals a change in conversation by saying "Uh—" and then speaks of something other than Saturday night (or whatever date was mentioned). Issuing of preinvitations is an ego saver like the use of style to signal social class. Having been spared overt refusal, the inviter is able to save face (Goffman 1955).

Collapsing Sequences

Sometimes utterance pairs are collapsed (Sacks, November 2, 1967) as in the following exchange at an ice cream counter:

48. A: What's chocolate filbert?
    B: We don't have any.

B's response is to what B knows is likely to come next. If B had explained what chocolate filbert is, then A very likely would have asked for some. Indeed, by explaining what it is, B would be tacitly saying that he or she had some to sell. In a selling situation in our society, explaining what goods or foods are is always an admission that they are available. Imagine your reaction, for instance, if you asked a waiter or waitress what some food was like, and he or she went into detail telling you about it. Then, if you said, "Sounds good. I'll have that," and the response were, "We don't have any," you would think you were being made a fool of.

Another common collapsing sequence is typified by the exchange:

49. A: Do you smoke?
    B: I left them in my other jacket.

Such collapsing sequences speed up social interaction by forestalling unnecessary explanations. They are used for other purposes as well, as when a newcomer joins a discussion in progress:

50. Hi, John. We were just talking about nursery schools.

This either warns John not to join the group or, if he is interested in nursery schools, gives him orientation so that he can understand what is going on.

Repairs

If a person uses the wrong style for an occasion, the other party(ies) to the interaction try to repair the error. Schegloff, Jefferson, and Sacks (1977) collected interesting samples of self-correction in discourse, people repairing their own errors. Sometimes this takes the form of obvious correction to a slip of the tongue, as in

51. What're you so *ha*—er un—un*ha*ppy about?

Sometimes speakers make a repair when they have made no overt error, as in

52. Sure enough ten minutes later the bell r—the doorbell rang.

Because such repairs do not show a one-to-one correspondence with actual spoken errors, Schegloff et al. preferred the term *repair* over *correction*. In both 51 and 52, for instance, neither repair was preceded by an error that actually occurred in speech.

Schegloff et al. found an orderly pattern in speech repair. Repairs did not occur just anywhere in an utterance. They occurred in one of three positions: immediately after the error, as in 51 and 52, or at the end of the sentence where another person would normally take the floor:

53. An 'en bud all of the doors 'n things were taped up—I mean y'know they put up y'know that kinda paper stuff, the brown paper.

or right after the other person speaks:

54. *Hannah:* And he's going to make his own paintings.
 Bea: Mm hm.
 Hannah: And—or I mean his own frames.

If the speaker does not repair an obvious error, the hearer will. Usually this is done by asking a question that will lead the speaker to repair his or her own error. Some examples:

55. A: It wasn't snowing all day.
 B: It *wasn't?*
 A: Oh, I mean it was.
56. A: Yeah, he's got a lot of smarts.
 B: *Huh?*
 A: He hasn't got a lot of smarts.
57. A: Hey, the first time they stopped me from selling cigarettes was this morning.
 B: From *selling* cigarettes?
 A: From buying cigarettes.

Often, the hearer will say "you mean" as in

58. A: We went Saturday afternoon.
 B: You mean Sunday.
 C: Yeah, uhnnn we saw Max . . .

In most of the repairs by hearers, it seems that the hearer knows all along what the intended word was. Still, it is rare, although not impossible, for the hearer actually to supply the word. This seems to be a face saver for the person who made the error. The hearer often offers the correction or the question leading to correction tentatively, as if he or she is not sure. That way, the speaker is not humiliated as he or she might be if the hearer in positive tones asserted that an error was made. Another reason that hearers offer corrections tentatively may be that in doing so, the hearer is in the position of telling someone else what must be going on in his or her mind.

Schegloff et al. (1977, p. 38) state that "the organization of repair is the self-righting mechanism for the organization of language use in social interaction." In other words, it maintains normal social interaction. We have already seen this in attempted repair of inappropriate style.

The importance of the self-righting mechanism is shown in the following almost bizarre interactions. These involve repairs in greetings and farewells collected as part of a participant observation by a student, Sheila Kennedy. While on guard duty at the door of a dormitory, she deliberately confounded greetings and farewells, with fascinating results.

To a stranger:
59. *Sheila:* Hi. [pause] Good night.
Stranger: Hello. [pause] Take it easy.

Note that the stranger also gave both a greeting and a farewell, even matching the pause that Sheila used between them. . . .

To a female friend:
60. *Friend:* Bye, Sheila.
Sheila: Hello.
Friend: Why did you say hello? I said goodbye. [pause] Hi.

Even though the friend questioned the inappropriateness of Sheila's response, she still felt constrained to answer the greeting with a greeting.

To a male friend:
61. *Friend:* Hi!
Sheila: So long.
[Both spoke at the same time, so Sheila starts again.]
Sheila: Hi!
Friend: Bye. [laughs] Wait a minute. Let's try that again. Hi!
Sheila: Hello.
Friend: Bye.
Sheila: So long.
Friend: That's better. [laugh and leaves]

What is interesting here is the lengths the subject went to in order that the appropriate pairs were given. Note that he had to get both greeting and farewell matched up before he would leave. The degree to which we are bound by the social rules of discourse is well illustrated in 59–61. The very fact that people go to so much trouble to repair others' responses is highly significant. It shows the importance of discourse routines to social interaction, that one cannot be divorced from the other. Not only must style and kinesics be appropriate for social functioning but so must the discourse itself. Even when people know what the other must mean, as in 55–58, they ask that the discourse be righted. And, even when it makes no difference in a fleeting social contact, as in 59–61, they demand that the right forms be chosen.

New Rules of Discourse

New situations may involve learning new discourse rules. Anthony Wooton (1975, p. 70) gives an example from psychotherapy. Psychiatrists typically do not tell patients what to do. Rather, by asking questions, they try to lead the patient into understanding. The problem is that the questions asked and the answers they are supposed to evoke are different from those already learned as part of normal routines. As an example, Wooton gives:

62. *Patient:* I'm a nurse, but my husband won't let me work.
    Therapist: How old are you?
    Patient: Thirty-one this December.
    Therapist: What do you mean, he won't let you work?

Here, the patient answers the psychiatrist's first question as if it were bona fide, a real-world question. The psychiatrist was not really asking her age, however, as we can see by his next question. What he meant by that question was "You are old enough to decide whether or not you wish to work." His question was aimed at leading her to that conclusion.

The patient in therapy has to learn new discourse routines in order to benefit from the therapeutic situation. The therapist uses modes of questioning different from everyday discourse. This is not surprising, since the aim of psychotherapy is for the psychiatrist to lead the patient into self-discovery. Some patients become very annoyed by the questioning, feeling that the therapist is refusing to tell them anything. In traditional psychoanalysis it was accepted that there had to be a period during which the patient "fought" the analyst by refusing to dredge up the answers from the murky subconscious. It has occurred to me that this period may actually represent a time during which the patient must learn to respond to the new question and answer routines demanded by analysis.

It is very hard to gain insights into oneself by sustained self-questioning, perhaps because questioning is rarely used that way outside the therapeutic situation. Furthermore, repeated questioning in it-self is threatening. In many societies, including our own, it is asso-ciated with accusation of wrongdoing and ferreting out the truth of one's guilt. It is used as a technique for teaching, to be sure, but even then it is often a way of ferreting out the pupil's lapses in learning.

Topic in Normal and Psychotic Speech

The first half of an utterance pair strongly limits what can come next. It limits both form and subject matter. These are intertwined virtually inseparably: a greeting is both a form and a subject matter. The response to a *wh-* question must use the same words as the ques-tion, filling in the missing word signaled by whichever *wh-* word was used. The answer to "Where did you go?" is "I went to [place X]." The answer to "Whom did you see?" is "I saw [person X]."

The larger conversation, beyond utterance pairs, is not so strongly constrained as to form. The entire syntax of the language can be drawn upon to encode new ideas, not just the syntax of greetings or com-pliments or invitation. The first sentence or so of an answer is pre-determined by the question just asked, but the speaker becomes free as soon as an answer is given that fills in the *wh-* word or supplies the *Yes, No,* or *I don't know.* The constraints upon topic, however, remain very strong.

In normal conversation, everything has to be subordinated to topic, whatever is being talked about (see Van Dijk 1977). Schegloff (1971) likens this to co-occurrence restrictions such as we saw in style. Once a topic is introduced, it must be adhered to unless some formal indication of change is made. Paradoxically, in American English, this often is "Not to change the subject, but . . .". This disclaimer always changes the topic. Other signals that change topic are "Oooh, that reminds me . . ." or "Oooh, I meant to tell you . . .". The "Oooh" in itself, uttered rapidly on a high pitch with a tense throat, is a warning that an announcement about topic change is coming.

Adherence to a topic is so important that failure to do so is evidence of mental incapacity. A person's mind is said to wander if his or her words wander off topics with no warning. Many observers of patients diagnosed as schizophrenic have noticed peculiarities in their speech, peculiarities traditionally called *thought disorder* (TD). Since not all schiz-ophrenics show these speech disorders, some are termed *nonthought disordered* (NTD). As a result of my own extensive analyses of speech termed TD, I think that such speech differs from normal or NTD speech mainly in that it does not stick to a topic. For instance,

63. My mother's name was Bill and coo. St. Valentine's Day was the start of the breedin' season of the birds.

CHAIKA 1974, 1977

64. Looks like clay. Sounds like gray. Take you for a roll in the hay. Hay day. May day. Help! I just can't. Need help. May day.

COHEN 1978

65. I had a little goldfish like a clown. Happy Hallowe'en down.

CHAIKA 1974, 1977

The greatest abnormality in such speech is that the patient is not sticking to a topic. Other than that, each part of the utterance is normal; grammar, word choice, and sounds are correctly used.

The words and phrases chosen do have a connection with one another in each of the samples just given. They are related on the basis of similarity of sound, especially rhyme, and on the basis of shared meaning. "Bill and coo" is an old metaphor for "love" based upon an image of lovebirds or doves, which bill and coo. Love is also associated with St. Valentine's Day. "Roll in the hay" means "(sexual) fun." "Hay day" not only rhymes with "hay," but if, as seems likely, the patient meant "heyday," it also refers to good times. "Hay day" rhymes with "May day," which is another way of saying "SOS" or "Help!" "Happy Hallowe'en" seems to be an association with "clown," with which "down" is a chance rhyme.

No matter how tightly such associations can be woven into the utterance, still 63–65 are obviously pathological speech. It is topic that determines normal speech, not other kinds of associations between words. Some people have suggested that schizophrenic speech is poetic, because, like poetry, it often rhymes. One major objection to this view is the high interjudge reliability when people are asked to distinguish schizophrenic utterances from others (Maher, McKeon and McLaughlin 1966; Rochester, Martin and Thurston 1977).

The schizophrenic rhyming and figurative speech occurs only because of chance association. Poetic rhyme and artistic language in general seem to be as constrained by a topic as any other kind of normal speech. Rhyming and other features of poetry, such as unusual associations and figurative language, are poetic when they are subordinated to a topic. . . .

In the twentieth century certain authors have deliberately set out to recreate stream of consciousness in their fiction, and some poetry is deliberately formless. Dr. Nancy Andreasen (1973) claims that James Joyce's *Finnegan's Wake* would appear to be schizophrenic to most psychiatrists. Even in such modern literature, however, form is usually subordinated to general topic.

What to Mention

Besides adhering to a topic, a speaker is constrained to follow another related rule: "Say only what needs saying." Personal and cultural knowledge that speakers share is not mentioned but is assumed. This is why the speech between two intimates is often obscure to outsiders. For instance:

66. A: Saw Mary today.
    B: She better?
    A: Yeah, she went to Bob's last night.
    B: When's the date?

This works if both know the one Mary, that she has just been sick, that she is engaged to Bob, but the wedding has been postponed because of her illness. To reiterate what each of the speakers knows would be boring or insulting or both.

One kind of bore is the person who insists on telling you more than you have to be told about something. Also, if someone insists on being overdetailed in an explanation, it implies that the hearer does not know those details. This is why people feel insulted if someone tells them obvious facts.

A difficulty that grown children have in dealing with their parents is that the parents persist in "treating them as if they were children"— that is, telling them things they already know. It is hard for the children not to feel insulted and defensive. Often repairmen are guilty of insulting by mentioning the obvious. For instance, when taking my computer in to be repaired, I felt very put out when the technician said "It's probably your diskette. They're very fragile." Since the first thing one learns about such equipment is that the diskettes are fragile, the effect was insultingly condescending.

In conversation it is assumed that all parties are cooperating (Gordon and Lakoff 1975). It is also assumed that they mean what they say. If something is mentioned that is known, therefore, unless it is taken as a putdown it will be construed to be newly important. Searle (1975) says that mentioning of extraneous matters leads listeners down false trails, as they try to figure out how those matters fit the topic at hand. It seems to me that this is why our courts of law have such strong rules against introducing irrelevant matters. To do so clouds the issue for the jury.

Mentioning too much, even if it is related to the topic, can be as distracting as actual departures from the topic itself. People assume that anything known to all parties in a given conversation will not be overtly stated unless there is some special reason for so doing.

References

Andreasen, N. 1973. "James Joyce, a portrait of the artist as a schizoid." *Journal of the American Medical Association.* 224:67–71.

Austin, J. L. 1962. *How to Do Things with Words,* 2nd ed. J. Urmson and M. Sbisa, eds. Cambridge, Mass.: Harvard University Press.

Chaika, E. 1974. "A linguist looks at "schizophrenic" language." *Brain and Language* 1:257–276.

———. 1977. Schizophrenic speech, slips of the tongue, and jargonaphasia: a reply to Fromkin and to Lecours and Vaniers-Clement." *Brain and Language* 4:464–475.

Cohen, B. D. 1978. "Referent communication disturbances in schizophrenia." In S. Schwartz, ed. 1978. *Language and Cognition in Schizophrenia.* Hillsdale, N.J.: Lawrence Erlbaum., pp. 1–34.

Ervin-Tripp, S. 1972. "On sociolinguistic rules: alternation and co-occurrence." In J. Gumperz and D. Hymes, eds. 1972. *Directions in Sociolinguistics.* New York: Holt, Rinehart, and Winston, pp. 213–250.

Frake, C. O. 1964. "How to ask for a drink in Subanum." *American Anthropologist* 66:127–32.

Givon, T., ed. 1979. *Syntax and Semantics,* vol. 12, *Discourse and Syntax.* New York: Academic Press.

Godard, D. 1977. "Same setting, different norms: Phone call beginnings in France and the United States." *Language in Society* 6:209–220.

Goffman, E. 1955. "On facework." *Psychiatry* 81:213–231.

Goody, E. N., ed. 1978. *Questions and Politeness.* New York: Cambridge University Press.

Gordon, D. and G. Lakoff. 1975. "Conversational postulates." In P. Cole and J. Morgan, eds. 1975. *Syntax and Semantics,* vol. 3, *Speech Acts.* New York: Academic Press, pp. 83–106.

Labov, W. and D. Fanshel. 1977. *Therapeutic Discourse.* New York: Academic Press.

Maher, B., K. McKeon, and B. McLaughlin. 1966. "Studies in psychotic language." in P. Stone, D. Dumphy, M. Smith, and D. Ogilvie, eds. 1966. *General Inquirer.* Cambridge, Mass.: M.I.T. Press, pp. 469–501.

Rochester, S., J. Martin, and S. Thurston. 1977. "Thought process disorder in schizophrenia: The listener's task." *Brain and Language.* 4:95–114.

Rommetveit, R. 1971. "Words, contexts and verbal message transmission." In E. A. Carswell and R. Rommetveit, eds. 1971. *Social Contexts of Messages.* New York: Academic Press, pp. 13–26.

Sacks, H. 1964–1972. Lecture notes. Mimeo.

———. 1970. Discourse anaylsis. Untitled manuscript. Mimeo.

———. 1972. "An initial investigation of the usability of conversational data for doing sociology." In D. Sudnow, ed., 1971. *Studies in Social Interaction.* New York: The Free Press. pp. 31–74.

Schegloff, E. A. 1968. Sequencing in conversational openings. *American Anthropologist* 70:1075–1095.

———. 1971. "Notes on a conversational practice: Formulating place." In D. Sudnow, ed. 1971. *Studies in Social Interaction.* New York: The Free Press, pp. 75–119.

Schegloff, E. A., G. Jefferson, and H. Sacks. 1977. "The preference for self-correction in the organization of repair in conversation." *Language* 53:361–382.

Schenkein, J., ed. 1978. *Studies in the Organization of Conversation.* New York: Academic Press.

Searle, J. 1975. "Indirect speech acts." In P. Cole and J. Morgan, eds. 1975. *Syntax and Semantics,* vol. 3, *Speech Acts.* New York: Academic Press, pp. 59–82.

Van Dijk, T. 1977. *Text and Context: Explorations in the Semantics and Pragmatics of Discourse.* New York: Longman.

Wooton, A. 1975. *Dilemmas of Discourse: Controversies about the Sociological Interpretation of Language.* London: Allen and Unwin.

FOR DISCUSSION AND REVIEW

1. Explain the paradox described by Chaika: "Language makes us free as individuals but chains us socially."

2. Explain the relationship among speech events, genres, and performance.

3. Summarize the rules of telephone conversation in the United States. Then describe the rules of another culture, and compare them with those of the United States.

4. Drawing on your own experience, describe a situation (like Chaika's telephone-call and grocery-store incidents) in which a semantically appropriate response would not actually be used.

5. Explain the concept of "preconditions for speech acts." Illustrate it by an original example of such a situation.

6. Give an example of each of the utterance pairs listed by Chaika on p. 437. Use examples in which the first half of the pair doesn't sound like what it really is.

7. Chaika states, "It is easy to manipulate people subtly by plugging them into the presuppositions and preconditions behind statements." Write a description of a real or imaginary instance of such manipulation.

8. Give two examples of conflicts between social rules and the wishes of an individual.

9. Test Chaika's description of people's reactions to persistent compliments by following the instructions she gave to her students (p. 445). Write a brief report summarizing your results.

10. Explain Chaika's statement, "In normal conversation, everything has to be subordinated to topic, whatever is being talked about."

Projects for "Semantics and Pragmatics"

1. In "The Meaning of a Word," George L. Dillon notes, "The classic studies in descriptive semantics have been done in . . . fairly clearly bounded 'fields' such as kinship terms, adjectival and prepositional meanings, causative and inchoate verbs, verbs of judging and verbs of cooking." Prepare a report summarizing some of the descriptive semantic work that has been done in one of these areas.

2. Study the table on p. 457 from Dwight Bolinger's *Aspects of Language,* 2nd ed. (New York: Harcourt Brace Jovanovich, 1975, p. 207). Try to develop a similar grid or matrix for another well-defined semantic area.

3. In "Automobile Semantics," Mark Aronoff states, "The importance of rank in the significance of a make cannot be underestimated," and then supports this assertion with examples and with Table i (p. 407). After checking actual prices with car dealers, prepare a similar table for the most recent model year. Analyze your findings in relation to Aronoff's. Do your data support Aronoff's assertion that "the perceived rank of a particular make of car is important to car buyers"?

4. Aronoff states, "Close examination of industry figures on body types and options reveals that manufacturers systematically change the position of model names by a process of downgrading or devaluation." He supports this assertion for Chevrolets in Tables 2 (1957–1959) and 3 (1953–1978) and for Fords in Table 4 (1953–1978) (see pp. 416–417). Choose a make of car, gather data for more recent years, and prepare comparable tables. You may want to use a time span that includes some years for which Aronoff has already provided data, but that introduces material from years after 1978.

5. In "Discourse Routines," Elaine Chaika briefly mentions certain peculiarities that often characterize schizophrenic speech (pp. 451–452). Using the references she cites, prepare a report on schizophrenic speech *(thought disorder,* or *TD).*

6. The *semantic differential* was developed originally by psychologists as a method for semantic differentiation and determination of the connotations of words, and was made well known, especially by Charles Osgood. Joseph S. Kess suggests marking your "impressions of a word on the [following] seven-point scale according to whether [you] view [it] as being, for example, extremely good, very good, good, neutral, bad, very bad, or extremely bad. Thus, if [you] had no feeling one way or the other about a word, [you] would mark the middle slot, indicating neutrality. Take, for example, the word *mother,* and mark it according to the way in which the word strikes you as being meaningful

	Nonfat liquid	Fat	Direct heat	Vigorous action	Long cooking time	Large amt. special substance	Kind of utensil	Special ingredient	Additional special purpose	Liquids	Solids
cook₃										+	+
boil₁	+	−								+	+
boil₂	+	−		+						+	+
simmer	+	−		−						+	+
stew	+	−		−	+				+ soften	−	+
poach	+	−		−					+ preserve shape	−	+
braise	+	−		−			+ lid			−	+
parboil	+	−			−					−	+
steam	+	−		+			+ rack, sieve, etc.			−	+
reduce	+	−		+					+ reduce bulk	+	−
fry	−	+					+ frying pan			−	+
sauté	−	+				−				−	+
pan-fry	−	+					+ frying pan			−	+
French-fry	−	+				+				−	+
deep-fry	−	+				+				−	+
broil	−	−	+							−	+
grill	−	−	+				?(griddle)			−	+
barbecue	−	−	+*					+ BarBQ sauce		−	+
charcoal	−	−	+*							−	+
plank	−	−	+				+ wooden board			−	+
bake₂	−	−	−							−	+
roast	−	−	±							−	+
shirr	−	−	−	−			+ small dish			−	+
scallop	−	−	−				+ shell	+ cream sauce		−	+
brown	−								+ brown surface	−	+
burn	−			+						−	+
toast	−	−	+						+ brown	−	+
rissoler	−	+		+					+ brown	−	+
sear	−	+		−					+ brown	−	+
parch	−	−	−						+ brown	−	+
flamber	−	−	+					+ alcohol	+ brown	−	+
steam-bake	−	−	−							−	+
pot-roast	+	−		−			(?) lid			−	+
oven-poach	+	−	−							−	+
pan-broil	−	−	+				+ frying pan			−	+
oven-fry	−	+	−							−	+

Culinary Semantics.
Source: Adapted from Adrienne Lehrer, "Semantic Cuisine," *Journal of Linguistics* 5 (1969): 39–55.
* "Hot coals."

on the following sample semantic differential" (*Psycholinguistics: Introductory Perspectives* [New York: Academic Press, 1976], p. 161).

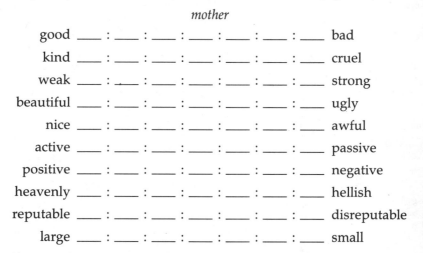

mother

good ___ : ___ : ___ : ___ : ___ : ___ : ___	bad
kind ___ : ___ : ___ : ___ : ___ : ___ : ___	cruel
weak ___ : ___ : ___ : ___ : ___ : ___ : ___	strong
beautiful ___ : ___ : ___ : ___ : ___ : ___ : ___	ugly
nice ___ : ___ : ___ : ___ : ___ : ___ : ___	awful
active ___ : ___ : ___ : ___ : ___ : ___ : ___	passive
positive ___ : ___ : ___ : ___ : ___ : ___ : ___	negative
heavenly ___ : ___ : ___ : ___ : ___ : ___ : ___	hellish
reputable ___ : ___ : ___ : ___ : ___ : ___ : ___	disreputable
large ___ : ___ : ___ : ___ : ___ : ___ : ___	small

Different informants will inevitably use different intuitive criteria when
making judgments about the same words. It follows, therefore, that a
high degree of subjectivity is inherent in the semantic differential,
which, paradoxically, is both its principal strength and its major lim-
itation.

Select two words, and ask two people to fill out a rating scale
similar to Kess's. After tabulating the results, see what conclusions you
can draw. For example, you could compare reactions to the words *sick*
and *ill*, or *woman* and *lady*. If this exercise is done as a class (rather
than individual) project, then class members themselves should fill out
rating scales. After the results are tabulated, discuss the results and
draw conclusions about the meanings of the words that were evaluated.

Selected Bibliography

*Note: The selections by Mark Aronoff and by Elaine Chaika both include extensive—
and helpful—bibliographies.*

Austin, J. L. *How to Do Things With Words.* Cambridge, MA: Harvard University
Press, 1962. (One of the classic works.)

Bierwisch, M. "Semantics." In John Lyons, ed., *New Horizons in Linguistics.*
Baltimore: Penguin Books, 1970.

———. "On Classifying Semantic Features." In D. D. Steinberg and L. A.
Jakobovits, eds., *Semantics.* Cambridge: Cambridge University Press,
1971.

Cole, Peter, and Jerry L. Morgan, eds. *Syntax and Semantics, Volume 3: Speech
Acts.* New York: Academic Press, 1975. (Excellent articles; see especially

"Logic and Conversation" by H. Paul Grice and "Conversational Postulates" by David Gordon and George Lakoff.)

Davidson, D. and G. Harman, eds. *Semantics of Natural Languages.* Dordrecht, The Netherlands: Reidel, 1972. (Another fine collection of essays.)

Fodor, J. D. *Semantics: Theories of Meaning in Generative Grammar.* New York: Crowell, 1977. (Important but difficult.)

Gumperz, John J., and Dell Hymes, eds. *Directions in Sociolinguistics: The Ethnography of Communication.* New York: Holt, Rinehart and Winston, 1972. (Explores the components of the social context that determine linguistic behavior.)

Jackendoff, R. *Semantic Interpretation in Generative Grammar.* Cambridge, MA: M.I.T. Press, 1972.

Katz, J. *Semantic Theory.* New York: Harper & Row, 1972.

———. *Propositional Structure and Illocutionary Force.* Cambridge, MA: Harvard University Press, 1980.

Kempson, R. *Semantic Theory.* Cambridge: Cambridge University Press, 1977.

Kess, Joseph S. *Psycholinguistics: Introductory Perspectives.* New York: Academic Press, 1976. (Good chapter on the relationship between the semantic differential and simpler versions of learning theory. Draws on the work of Charles Osgood.)

Leech, Geoffrey N. *Principles of Pragmatics.* New York: Longman, 1983. (Argues that "grammar (in its broadest sense) must be separated from pragmatics"; excellent bibliography.)

Lehrer, Adrienne. *Wine and Conversation.* Bloomington, IN: Indiana University Press, 1983. (Fascinating; excellent bibliography.)

Lyons, J. *Semantics.* Cambridge: Cambridge University Press, 1977. (An important two-volume work.)

Miller, George. "Semantic Relations Among Words." In M. Halle, J. Bresnan, and G. A. Miller, eds., *Linguistic Theory and Psychological Reality.* Cambridge, MA: M.I.T. Press, 1978.

Nilsen, Don L. F. and Alleen Pace Nilsen. *Semantic Theory: A Linguistic Perspective.* Rowley, MA: Newbury House Publishers, 1975. (Readable; excellent bibliographies, some of them annotated.)

Palmer, F. R. *Semantics: A New Outline.* Cambridge: Cambridge University Press, 1976. (A very good introductory work.)

Pratt, Mary Louise. *Toward A Speech Act Theory of Literary Discourse.* Bloomington, IN: Indiana University Press, 1977. (An essential synthesizing work.)

Rosenberg, Jay F. and Charles Travis, eds. *Readings in the Philosophy of Language.* Englewood Cliffs, NJ: Prentice-Hall, 1971. (Includes sections on "Theories of Meaning," "Semantics," and "Speech Acts.")

Sadock, Jerrold M. *Toward a Linguistic Theory of Speech Acts.* New York: Academic Press, 1974. (Detailed discussion of illocutionary force and performative verbs.)

Saville-Troike, Muriel. "Bilingual Children: A Resource Document." *Bilingual Education, Series 2, Papers in Applied Linguistics.* Washington, DC: Center for Applied Linguistics, 1973. (Includes interesting discussion of eight components of the social context that affect linguistic behavior [pp. 9–11].)

Searle, John R. *Speech Acts: An Essay in the Philosophy of Language.* Cambridge: Cambridge University Press, 1969. [A classic work.]

Steinberg, Danny G. and L. A. Jakobovits, eds. *Semantics: An Interdisciplinary Reader in Philosophy, Linguistics, and Psychology.* New York: Cambridge University Press, 1971. (Excellent but difficult collection of articles.)

Part Seven

Language Variation: Regional and Social

The language spoken in a country, or even in smaller areas—a town or city, for example—varies regionally and by social class. (It also varies over time, but chronological variation is the subject of Part Eight.) Regional and social dialects differ from one another because of (1) variations in vocabulary (*grinder, submarine, hoagie, hero, sub*); (2) pronunciation (/ˈgrisi/ or /grizi/, /krIk/ or /krik/, /ant/ or /ænt/); and (3) grammar ("It's quarter [*to, 'til, of*] four," "He is not [*to, at,* ∅] home now"). Some variations are primarily regional; others are primarily social. Still others have more to do with an individual's age, sex, occupation, or particular circumstances. To the trained listener, individuals' speech reveals many things about them, and even untrained people often can tell a great deal about people based on how they speak.

The first selection in Part Seven, Paul Roberts's "Speech Communities," explains that each of us belongs both successively and simultaneously to a number of different speech communities, some based on age, some on social class and education, and some on the places where we have lived. This article serves to introduce the concept of language variation.

The next selection, "Social and Regional Variation," reviews the study of regional and social dialects in the United States. The authors, Albert H. Marckwardt and J. L. Dillard, describe the first dialect research done in this country; it dealt with regional dialects and is best exemplified by works like the *Linguistic Atlas of New England* and the *Linguistic Atlas of the Upper Midwest*. They also identify a number of factors that have contributed to the various regional varieties of American English. And, explaining that in the 1960s the emphasis in dialect research shifted to the study of social dialects, they discuss some of the pioneering work that was done in this area. Next, Roger Shuy's "Dialects: How They Differ" focuses on regional dialects and examines examples of American regional variations in pronunciation, vocabulary, and grammar. Shuy also provides extensive samples of questionnaires used in regional dialect research.

With the next selection, "A Researcher's Guide to the Sociolinguistic Variable (ING)," Benji Wald and Timothy Shopen shift the focus to the study of social dialects, or identifying and analyzing dialect features that are significant indicators of social class. The methodology and reporting of social dialectologists differ noticeably from those of regional dialectologists in two ways: (1) social dialectologists rely heavily on population sampling techniques originally developed by sociologists, and (2) they tend to report their results in statistical format, using many tables, graphs, and charts. Although it has long been known that language differences are one manifestation of social class, the investigation of these differences and how people feel about them began in this country only in the late 1940s, with major studies not appearing until the 1960s, especially the pioneering work of William Labov. A brief look at two of his early studies will enhance our understanding of the selection by Professors Wald and Shopen.

Early in the 1960s, Labov (1963) became interested in the variations in pronunciation of /r/ among the people living on Martha's Vineyard, an island not far from Boston. Unlike the original settlers of Boston, the first English settlers of Martha's Vineyard pronounced /r/ before a consonant. In succeeding generations, many native Vineyarders continued to pronounce /r/ before consonants; others, however, adopted the Boston pronunciation. Wanting to know who used the Vineyard pronunciation and who used that of Boston, Labov conducted a survey in which subjects read passages aloud and answered questions that necessitated the use of words with many /r/ sounds. (Labov was also interested in the pronunciation of the diphthongs /a^i/ and /a^u/.)

The results of Labov's survey revealed that, rather than use one of the pronunciations all the time, the native Vineyarders varied in the way they pronounced these sounds. Significant was the percentage of times people used a Vineyard sound as opposed to a Boston sound. High frequency of Vineyard pronunciations correlated with certain attitudes of the speakers. Thus, long-time inhabitants, who may have resented the "invasion" of Boston vacationers, used the Vineyard /r/ and diphthongs most frequently. Younger inhabitants who planned to remain on the island, despite a scarcity of jobs, showed their loyalty by frequent use of the Vineyard pronunciations, as did the native Gay Head Indians. Interestingly, the attitudes and future plans of high-school students were reflected in their pronunciation: those who planned to leave the island used the Boston pronunciations; those who planned to remain on Martha's Vineyard spoke like Vineyarders. Elaine Chaika summarizes Labov's findings:

- Each social group used a key pronunciation a certain percentage of the time with no overlap from group to group.
- Attitude can be precisely correlated with fine points of pronunciation. Phonological variables, different ways of pronouncing the same sound, appeared to be a potent tool for sociological investigation.[1]

Labov's next work, done in New York City, led to the publication of *The Social Stratification of English in New York City* (Washington, D.C.: Center for Applied Linguistics, 1966), which profoundly affected the study of social variation in language. One chapter, "The Social Stratification of (r) in New York City Department Stores," describes a 1962 survey that was designed to test two ideas: "first, that the variable (r) is a social differentiator in all levels of New York City speech, and second, that casual and anonymous speech events could be used as the basis for a systematic study of language" (p. 63).

To conduct this now classic study, Labov visited three very different New York City department stores: Klein's, with primarily lower- and working-class customers; Macy's, with a middle-class clientele; and Saks Fifth Avenue, with upper-middle- and upper-class customers. First, he wanted to find out if the amount of constriction of postvocalic /r/ in the speech of the stores' employees would vary. As Lawrence M. Davis points out,

Labov's questionnaire was undoubtedly the shortest in history. He was, in every case, trying to elicit the response *fourth floor*, both in casual and in careful speech. Consequently, one of his interviews might have gone something like this:
    Fieldworker: "Where can I find ladies' dresses?"
    Informant: "Fourth floor."
    Fieldworker: "What did you say?"
    Informant: "Fourth floor!!"

[1] *Language: The Social Mirror.* Rowley, MA: Newbury House Publishers, 1982, p. 165.

Labov quite rightly reasoned that the informant would be somewhat more careful in the second response, and he was hence able to record the informants' behavior in essentially two different linguistic styles. The results, far from demonstrating that New Yorkers pronounce postvocalic /r/ haphazardly, showed that there is clear class differentiation.[2]

Use of constricted postvocalic /r/ varied: it was used by 30 percent of the informants at Saks, 20 percent at Macy's, and 4 percent at Klein's. In all the stores, the percentage of the constriction of postvocalic /r/ increased with the second utterance of "fourth floor."

According to Davis,

Perhaps the most important contribution of Labov's study is the notion that linguistic behavior is inconsistent but that the inconsistency is, paradoxically, ordered. What to earlier investigators of New York City speech appeared to be haphazard use of constricted postvocalic /r/, for example, was not so. But one has to count the occurrences of the variable before the systematic behavior can be discovered. . . . Just about every sociolinguistic study since Labov has employed the use of linguistic variables and has counted their occurrence. The introduction of quantitative methods, though used to some extent by Atwood in his *Verb Forms* [1953], must be credited to Labov, and in this sense, the changes he wrought for future studies have been truly remarkable.[3]

Professors Wald and Shopen's "A Researcher's Guide to the Sociolinguistic Variable (ING)" illustrates the use of linguistic variables and the kind of quantitative methods that Labov introduced. It does so by analyzing when and why people use one or another of the linguistic norms of -*ing*, primarily [iŋ] and [ən]. The selection also includes a number of suggestions for sociolinguistic projects that can be carried out by students.

The last two selections in this part address the subject of "nonstandard" English. First, in "The Study of Nonstandard English," William Labov discusses the close relationship between standard American English and nonstandard dialects, making the important point that the latter are rule-governed and not just "corrupt forms" of the standard language. Next, in "'It Bees Dat Way Sometime': Sounds and Structure of Present-Day Black English," Geneva Smitherman looks at Black English, analyzing its most significant phonological and syntactic rules and discussing their relationship to standard American English. Like Labov, she too stresses that all varieties of language are rule-governed. It should be understood that on the basis of linguistic criteria, Black English is one of the many dialects of English used in the United States. Although it shares many features with southern dialects,

---

[2] *English Dialectology: An Introduction.* University, AL: The University of Alabama Press, 1983, p. 87.
[3] Ibid., p. 94.

it is a distinct linguistic system and was recognized as such by a federal court in a July 1979 decision. The court ordered the Ann Arbor, Michigan, public schools to provide opportunities for teachers to learn about Black English so that they could incorporate this knowledge into their teaching methods in order to help children learn to read "standard" English.

1/Speech Communities

PAUL ROBERTS

The concept of speech communities is basic to an understanding of regional and social variation in language, or dialects. In the following excerpt from his book Understanding English, *Professor Paul Roberts introduces this concept and discusses the diverse factors that contribute to the formation of speech communities and to the kinds of variation that occur within those communities. Speech communities, he argues, "are formed by many features: age, geography, education, occupation, social position." He might well have added that an individual's racial or ethnic identity and his or her sex often lead to membership in additional speech communities. In addition to variations in speech attributable to membership in speech communities, all speakers of a language also use a variety of jargons and a range of styles, the latter varying in terms of levels of formality. (For a discussion of these kinds of variations, see Harvey A. Daniels's "Nine Ideas About Language" in Part One.) Finally, Professor Roberts emphasizes that language variation is a natural phenomenon, neither "good" nor "bad," and that value judgments about language are often really value judgments about people.*

Imagine a village of a thousand people all speaking the same language and never hearing any language other than their own. As the decades pass and generation succeeds generation, it will not be very apparent to the speakers of the language that any considerable language change is going on. Oldsters may occasionally be conscious of and annoyed by the speech forms of youngsters. They will notice new words, new expressions, "bad" pronunciations, but will ordinarily put these down to the irresponsibility of youth, and decide piously that the language of the younger generation will revert to decency when the generation grows up.

It doesn't revert, though. The new expressions and the new pronunciations persist, and presently there is another younger generation with its own new expressions and its own pronunciations. And thus the language changes. If members of the village could speak to one another across five hundred years, they would probably find themselves unable to communicate.

Now suppose that the village divides itself and half the people move away. They move across the river or over a mountain and form a new village. Suppose the separation is so complete that the people of New Village have no contact with the people of Old Village. The language of both villages will change, drifting away from the language of their common ancestors. But the drift will not be in the same direction. In both villages there will be new expressions and new pronunciations, but not the same ones. In the course of time the language of Old Village and New Village will be mutually unintelligible with the language they both started with. They will also be mutually unintelligible with one another.

An interesting thing—and one for which there is no perfectly clear explanation—is that the rate of change will not ordinarily be the same for both villages. The language of Old Village changes faster than the language of New Village. One might expect that the opposite would be true—that the emigrants, placed in new surroundings and new conditions, would undergo more rapid language changes. But history reports otherwise. American English, for example, despite the violence and agony and confusion to which the demands of a new continent have subjected it, is probably essentially closer to the language of Shakespeare than London English is.

Suppose one thing more. Suppose Old Village is divided sharply into an upper class and a lower class. The sons and daughters of the upper class go to preparatory school and then to the university; the children of the lower class go to work. The upper-class people learn to read and write and develop a flowering literature; the lower-class people remain illiterate. Dialects develop, and the speech of the two classes steadily diverges. One might suppose that most of the change would go on among the illiterate, that the upper-class people, conscious of their heritage, would tend to preserve the forms and pronunciations of their ancestors. Not so. The opposite is true. In speech, the educated tend to be radical and the uneducated conservative. In England one finds Elizabethan forms and sounds not among Oxford and Cambridge graduates but among the people of backward villages.

A village is a fairly simple kind of speech community—a group of people steadily in communication with one another, steadily hearing one another's speech. But the village is by no means the basic unit. Within the simplest village there are many smaller units—groupings based on age, class, occupation. All these groups play intricately on one another and against one another, and a language that seems at first a coherent whole will turn out on inspection to be composed of many differing parts. Some forces tend to make these parts diverge; other forces hold them together. Thus the language continues in tension.

The Speech Communities of the Child

The child's first speech community is ordinarily his family. The child learns whatever kind of language the family speaks—or, more precisely, whatever kind of language it speaks to him. The child's language learning, now and later, is governed by two obvious motives: the desire to communicate and the desire to be admired. He imitates what he hears. More or less successful imitations usually bring action and reward and tend to be repeated. Unsuccessful ones usually don't bring action and reward and tend to be discarded.

But since language is a complicated business it is sometimes the unsuccessful imitations that bring the reward. The child, making a stab at the word *mother*, comes out with *muzzer*. The family decides that this is just too cute for anything and beams and repeats *muzzer*, and the child, feeling that he's scored a bull's eye, goes on saying *muzzer* long after he has mastered *other* and *brother*. Baby talk is not so much invented by the child as sponsored by the parent.

Eventually the child moves out of the family and into another speech community—other children of his neighborhood. He goes to kindergarten and immediately encounters speech habits that conflict with those he has learned. If he goes to school and talks about his *muzzer*, it will be borne in on him by his colleagues that the word is not well chosen. Even *mother* may not pass muster, and he may discover that he gets better results and is altogether happier if he refers to his female parent as his ma or even his old lady.

Children coming together in a kindergarten class bring with them language that is different because it is learned in different homes. It is all to some degree unsuccessfully learned, consisting of not quite perfect imitations of the original. In school all this speech coalesces, differences tend to be ironed out, and the result differs from the original parental speech and differs in pretty much the same way.

The pressures on the child to conform to the speech of his age group, his speech community, are enormous. He may admire his teacher and love his mother; he may even—and even consciously— wish to speak as they do. But he *has* to speak like the rest of the class. If he does not, life becomes intolerable.

The speech changes that go on when the child goes to school are often most distressing to parents. Your little Bertram, at home, has never heard anything but the most elegant English. You send him to school, and what happens? He comes home saying things like "I done real good in school today, Mom." But Bertram really has no choice in the matter. If Clarence and Elbert and the rest of the fellows customarily say "I done real good," then Bertram might as well go around with three noses as say things like "I did very nicely."

Individuals differ of course, and not all children react to the speech community in the same way. Some tend to imitate and others tend to force imitation. But all to some degree have their speech modified by forces over which neither they nor their parents nor their teachers have any real control.

Individuals differ too in their sensitivity to language. For some, language is always a rather embarrassing problem. They steadily make boners, saying the right thing in the wrong place or the wrong way. They have a hard time fitting in. Others tend to change their language slowly, sticking stoutly to their way of saying things, even though their way differs from that of the majority. Still others adopt new language habits almost automatically, responding quickly to whatever speech environment they encounter.

Indeed some children of five or six have been observed to speak two or more different dialects without much awareness that they are doing so. Most commonly, they will speak in one way at home and in another on the playground. At home they say, "I did very nicely" and "I haven't any"; these become, at school, "I done real good" and "I ain't got none."

The Class as a Speech Community

Throughout the school years, or at least through the American secondary school, the individual's most important speech community is his age group, his class. Here is where the real power lies. The rule is conformity above all things, and the group uses its power ruthlessly on those who do not conform. Language is one of the chief means by which the school group seeks to establish its entity, and in the high school this is done more or less consciously. The obvious feature is high school slang, picked up from the radio, from other schools, sometimes invented, changing with bewildering speed. Nothing is more satisfactory than to speak today's slang; nothing more futile than to use yesterday's.

There can be few tasks more frustrating than that of the secondary school teacher charged with the responsibility of brushing off and polishing up the speech habits of the younger generation. Efforts to make *real* into *really*, *ain't* into *am not*, *I seen him* into *I saw him*, *he don't* into *he doesn't* meet at best with polite indifference, at worst with mischievous counterattack.

The writer can remember from his own high school days when the class, a crashingly witty bunch, took to pronouncing the word *sure* as *sewer*. "Have you prepared your lesson, Arnold?" Miss Driscoll would ask. "Sewer, Miss Driscoll," Arnold would reply. "I think," said Miss Driscoll, who was pretty quick on her feet too, "that you must mean 'sewerly,' since the construction calls for the adverb not the adjective." We were delighted with the suggestion and went about saying "sewerly" until the very blackboards were nauseated. Miss Driscoll must have wished often that she had left it lay.

Confronting the Adult World

When the high school class graduates, the speech community disintegrates as the students fit themselves into new ones. For the first time in the experience of most of the students the speech ways of adult communities begin to exercise real force. For some people the adjustment is a relatively simple one. A boy going to work in a garage may have a good deal of new lingo to pick up, and he may find that the speech that seemed so racy and won such approval in the corridors of Springfield High leaves his more adult associates merely bored. But a normal person will adapt himself without trouble.

For others in other situations settling into new speech communities may be more difficult. The person going into college, into the business world, into scrubbed society may find that he has to think about and work on his speech habits in order not to make a fool of himself too often.

College is a particularly complicated problem. Not only does the freshman confront upperclassmen not particularly disposed to find the speech of Springfield High particularly cute, but the adult world, as represented chiefly by the faculty, becomes increasingly more immediate. The problems of success, of earning a living, of marriage, of attaining a satisfactory adult life loom larger, and they all bring language problems with them. Adaptation is necessary, and the student adapts.

The student adapts, but the adult world adapts too. The thousands of boys and girls coming out of the high schools each spring are affected by the speech of the adult communities into which they move, but they also affect that speech. The new pronunciation habits, developing grammatical features, different vocabulary do by no means all give way before the disapproval of elders. Some of them stay. Elders, sometimes to their dismay, find themselves changing their speech habits under the bombardment of those of their juniors. And then of course the juniors eventually become the elders, and there is no one left to disapprove.

The Space Dimension

Speech communities are formed by many features besides that of age. Most obvious is geography. Our country was originally settled by people coming from different parts of England. They spoke different dialects to begin with and as a result regional speech differences existed from the start in the different parts of the country. As speakers of other languages came to America and learned English, they left their mark on the speech of the sections in which they settled. With the westward movement, new pioneers streamed out through the mountain passes and down river valleys, taking the different dialects west and modifying them by new mixtures in new environments.

Today we are all more or less conscious of certain dialect differences in our country. We speak of the "southern accent," "the Brooklyn accent," the "New England accent." Until a few years ago it was often said that American English was divided into three dialects: Southern American (south of the Mason-Dixon line); Eastern American (east of the Connecticut River); and Western American. This description suggests certain gross differences all right, but recent research shows that it is a gross oversimplification.

The starting point of American dialects is the original group of colonies. We had a New England settlement, centering in Massachusetts; a Middle Atlantic settlement, centering in Pennsylvania; a southern settlement, centering in Virginia and the Carolinas. These colonies were different in speech to begin with, since the settlers came from different parts of England. Their differences were increased as the colonies lived for a century and a half or so with only thin communication with either Mother England or each other. By the time of the Revolution the dialects were well established. Within each group there were of course subgroups. Richmond speech differed markedly from that of Savannah. But Savannah and Richmond were more like each other than they were like Philadelphia or Boston.

The Western movement began shortly after the Revolution, and dialects followed geography. The New Englanders moved mostly into upper New York State and the Great Lakes region. The Middle Atlantic colonists went down the Shenandoah Valley and eventually into the heart of the Midwest. The southerners opened up Kentucky and Tennessee, later the lower Mississippi Valley, later still Texas and much of the Southwest. Thus new speech communities were formed, related to the old ones of the seaboard, but each developing new characteristics as lines of settlement crossed.

New complications were added before and after the Revolution by the great waves of immigration of people from countries other than England: Swedes in Delaware, Dutch in New York, Germans and Scots-Irish in Pennsylvania, Irish in New England, Poles and Greeks and Italians and Portuguese. The bringing in of Negro slaves had an important effect on the speech of the South and later on the whole country. The Spanish in California and the Southwest added their mark. In this century movement of peoples goes on: the trek of southern Negroes to northern and western cities, the migration of people from Arkansas, Oklahoma, and Texas to California. All these have shaped and are shaping American speech.

We speak of America as the melting pot, but the speech communities of this continent are very far from having melted into one. Linguists today can trace very clearly the movements of the early settlers in the still living speech of their descendants. They can follow an eighteenth century speech community west, showing how it crossed this pass and followed that river, threw out an offshoot here, left a pocket there, merged with another group, halted, split, moved on once more. If all other historical evidence were destroyed, the history of the country could still be reconstructed from the speech of modern America.

Social Differences

The third great shaper of speech communities is the social class. This has been, and is, more important in England than in America. In England, class differences have often been more prominent than those of age or place. If you were the blacksmith's boy, you might know the son of the local baronet, but you didn't speak his language. You spoke the language of your social group, and he that of his, and over the centuries these social dialects remained widely separated.

England in the twentieth century has been much democratized, but the language differences are far from having disappeared. One can still tell much about a person's family, his school background, his general position in life by the way he speaks. Social lines are hard to cross, and language is perhaps the greatest barrier. You may make a million pounds and own several cars and a place in the country, but your vowels and consonants and nouns and verbs and sentence patterns will still proclaim to the world that you're not a part of the upper crust.

In America, of course, social distinctions have never been so sharp as they are in England. We find it somewhat easier to rise in the world, to move into social environments unknown to our parents. This is possible, partly, because speech differences are slighter; conversely, speech differences are slighter because this is possible. But speech differences do exist. If you've spent all your life driving a cab in Philly and, having inherited a fortune, move to San Francisco's Nob Hill, you will find that your language is different, perhaps embarrassingly so, from that of your new acquaintances.

Language differences on the social plane in America are likely to correlate with education or occupation rather than with birth—simply because education and occupation in America do not depend so much on birth as they do in other countries. A child without family connection can get himself educated at Harvard, Yale, Princeton. In doing so, he acquires the speech habits of the Ivy League and gives up those of his parents.

Exceptions abound. But in general there is a clear difference between the speech habits of the college graduate and those of the high school graduate. The cab driver does not talk like the Standard Oil executive, the college professor like the carnival pitch man, or an Illinois merchant like a sailor shipping out of New Orleans. New York's Madison Avenue and Third Avenue are only a few blocks apart, but they are widely separated in language. And both are different from Broadway.

It should be added that the whole trend of modern life is to reduce rather than to accentuate these differences. In a country where college education becomes increasingly everybody's chance, where executives and refrigerator salesmen and farmers play golf together, where a college professor may drive a cab in the summertime to keep his family alive, it becomes harder and harder to guess a person's education, income, and social status by the way he talks. But it would be absurd to say that language gives no clue at all.

Good and Bad

Speech communities, then, are formed by many features: age, geography, education, occupation, social position. Young people speak differently from old people, Kansans differently from Virginians, Yale graduates differently from Dannemora graduates. Now let us pose a delicate question: aren't some of these speech communities better than others? That is, isn't better language heard in some than in others?

Well, yes, of course. One speech community is always better than all the rest. This is the group in which one happens to find oneself. The writer would answer unhesitatingly that the noblest, loveliest, purest English is that heard in the Men's Faculty Club of San Jose State College, San Jose, California. He would admit, of course, that the speech of some of the younger members leaves something to be desired; that certain recent immigrants from Harvard, Michigan, and other foreign parts need to work on the laughable oddities lingering in their speech; and that members of certain departments tend to introduce a lot of queer terms that can only be described as jargon. But in general the English of the Faculty Club is ennobling and sweet.

As a practical matter, good English is whatever English is spoken by the group in which one moves contentedly and at ease. To the bum on Main Street in Los Angeles, good English is the language of other L.A. bums. Should he wander onto the campus of UCLA, he would find the talk there unpleasant, confusing, and comical. He might agree, if pressed, that the college man speaks "correctly" and he doesn't. But in his heart he knows better. He wouldn't talk like them college jerks if you paid him.

If you admire the language of other speech communities more than you do your own, the reasonable hypothesis is that you are dissatisfied with the community itself. It is not precisely other speech that attracts you but the people who use the speech. Conversely, if some language strikes you as unpleasant or foolish or rough, it is presumably because the speakers themselves seem so.

To many people, the sentence "Where is he at?" sounds bad. It is bad, they would say, in and of itself. The sounds are bad. But this is very hard to prove. If "Where is he at?" is bad because it has bad sound combinations, then presumably "Where is the cat?" or "Where is my hat?" are just as bad, yet no one thinks them so. Well, then, "Where is he at?" is bad because it uses too many words. One gets the same meaning from "Where is he?" so why add the *at*? True. Then "He going with us?" is a better sentence than "Is he going with us?" You don't really need the *is*, so why put it in?

Certainly there are some features of language to which we can apply the terms *good* and *bad*, *better* and *worse*. Clarity is usually better than obscurity; precision is better than vagueness. But these are not often what we have in mind when we speak of good and bad English. If we like the speech of upper-class Englishmen, the presumption is that we admire upper-class Englishmen—their characters, culture, habits of mind. Their sounds and words simply come to connote the people themselves and become admirable therefore. If we heard the same sounds and words from people who were distasteful to us, we would find the speech ugly.

This is not to say that correctness and incorrectness do not exist in speech. They obviously do, but they are relative to the speech community—or communities—in which one operates. As a practical matter, correct speech is that which sounds normal or natural to one's comrades. Incorrect speech is that which evokes in them discomfort or hostility or disdain. . . .

FOR DISCUSSION AND REVIEW

1. Identify the factors that, according to Roberts, bring speech communities into being and contribute to internal differences within each community. Trace the changing speech communities of an individual, considering age as the only variable.

2. Change has occurred less rapidly in American English than in British English; change also occurs more rapidly in both countries among the educated than among the uneducated. Identify three reasons why this is so.

3. Explain Roberts's statement that "Baby talk is not so much invented by the child as sponsored by the parent." Describe two examples of this phenomenon in your own family.

4. Roberts writes of the "enormous pressures" on people to conform to the speech of their age group and class, their speech community. Discuss the pressures that you felt while growing up.

5. Roberts believes that there are marked differences between the speech communities of one generation and the next. Observe and describe speech differences between students and faculty in your school. Compare your findings with those of your instructor. Is age the only factor here? What kinds of differences exist between your speech and that of your parents? Between your speech and that of your grandparents? What, in general, are people's attitudes toward these differences?

6. Explain the geographic basis from which American regional dialects originated. Do you agree with Roberts's statement: "If all other historical evidence were destroyed, the history of the country could still be reconstructed from the speech of modern America"? Why or why not?

7. Roberts writes that "Language differences on the social plane in America are likely to correlate with education or occupation rather than with birth." Discuss the implications of this statement. Do your experiences support it? Explain your answer.

(Note: Before answering questions 8 through 10, you should review Harvey A. Daniels's "Nine Ideas About Language" in Part One, pp. 18–36.)

8. Note three distinctive characteristics and/or functions of the consultative style.

9. In what ways does the casual style differ from the consultative?

10. Note five distinctive characteristics of the formal style. To what extent do you think most Americans have learned to speak in this style? Give specific examples—a professor lecturing to a class, for example, or an unrehearsed radio or television interview with a typical American.

11. Summarize M. A. K. Halliday's analysis of the seven principal purposes or uses of speech. Drawing upon your own experience, give an example of each use.

2/Social and Regional Variation

ALBERT H. MARCKWARDT
AND J. L. DILLARD

In the following chapter from American English *by Albert H. Marck-wardt, revised by J. L. Dillard, the authors present an overview of the study of regional and social dialects in the United States. Regional dialects were the first to be studied. The methodology used was based largely on that developed in France by Jules Gilliéron and in Italy, Sicily, Sardinia, and Switzerland by Karl Jaberg and Jakob Jud. Beginning in the late 1920s, under the leadership of Hans Kurath, the original North American project called for a linguistic atlas of the United States and Canada. The first actual research, done in New England in the early 1930s, resulted in the publication of the mul-tivolume* Linguistic Atlas of New England (LANE) *between 1939 and 1943 (reissued in 1972), the* Handbook of the Linguistic Ge-ography of New England *(1939, 1972), and* A Word Geography of the Eastern United States *(1949). Linguistic atlases for other parts of the United States have been published or are in progress (see pp. 571–572).*

In the 1960s, as Marckwardt and Dillard point out, emphasis shifted to the study of social dialects, the identification and analysis of dialect features that are significant indicators of social class. The authors describe some of the pioneering research in this area carried out by William Labov. Acknowledging the unique problems of working with dialects in the United States, they identify a few of the distinctive differences in the vocabulary, pronunciation, and grammar of various regional and social varieties of American English. As they write, "There is still some faith in the notion that understanding is the key to tolerance."

The English language is spoken natively in America by some two hundred million people, over an area of more than three million square miles, with a large number of minority subcultures offering proof that the "melting pot" was an ideal rather than a reality. For many groups found in all parts of the country, English is by no means the only—or even the first—language. Dialectologists are slowly coming to the

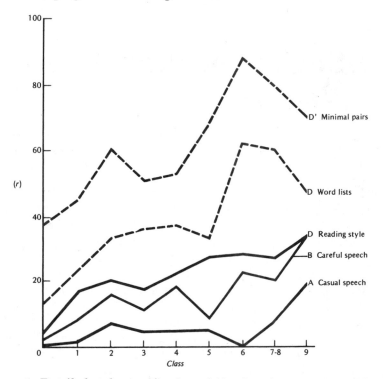

Figure 1. Detailed style stratification of (*r*): nine classes. From William Labov's *Social Stratification of English in New York City*. Reprinted by permission of the Center for Applied Linguistics.

realization that both class distribution of language variants, and prejudice against the users of "nonstandard" dialects are realities in twentieth-century America. Black English, the dialect of "disadvantaged" Black children, was recognized legally by a landmark Detroit court decision in July, 1979. Social dialect study was largely the product of the 1960s, but public awareness of social dialects may actually come about during the 1980s.

A pioneering sociologist, Glenna Ruth Pickford, began in 1956 to direct our attention to sociological factors like occupation and urban residence rather than to purely geographic factors in a paper published in that year but hardly noticed for ten years or so thereafter. The field of linguistics was, however, branching out into "hyphenated" disciplines like sociolinguistics, and works like William Labov's *Social Stratification of English in New York City* (1965) (though preceded by some important work on caste dialect in India), were perhaps most directly responsible for the new emphasis on social variation. [See Figure 1.]

Labov's influential work, although it contains much more highly technical data, is best known for its demonstration that certain variables of pronunciation like *that* and *dat* or *fourth floor* "with or without [r]" are socially and contextually distributed. Labov demonstrated that every speaker has some differing pronunciations: to do so, he ranked data collected in casual speech, in the reading of a paragraph, in the reading of lists of unrelated words, and in the reading of paired words with something like minimal contrasts (*guard* and *god*). Not only did everyone pronounce "r" more often in the last context, but floorwalkers at posh Saks' Fifth Avenue put more "r" into *fourth floor* than did those at middle-class Macy's. S. Klein's, the poor man's haberdashery, trailed in the amount of "r" as well as in rank on the social scale.

Even more interesting than relative frequency across class, however, was the greater variability evidenced by the lower-middle class. These sociologically insecure people also indulge extensively, Labov found, in hypercorrection. Insofar as class goes (ignoring, for now, such other factors as the greater likelihood that a new biological generation will make changes), not the highest or the lowest but the class in between is the one most likely to foment linguistic change.

Research by others, as well as by Labov himself, indicates that *Social Stratification* slightly underemphasized social factors like ethnic group membership. Black English, with many of the same features in New York and Detroit as in Shreveport, Louisiana, has become one of the most thoroughly studied dialects of all time. Especially prominent has been work on the so-called zero copula (*He my main man*), and the demonstration that all speakers who use the "zero" also realize the copula in some positions (*Yes, he is*), and that non-use of the verbs *is* and *are* is not categorical with any speaker. Labov's 1969 paper on this feature developed the theory of inherent variability, with variable rules becoming the indispensable new tool of variation studies. Almost overlooked, unfortunately, were the grammatical implications of Black English forms like preverbal *been* (*You been know dat; He been ate de chicken*) marking a strongly past time (longer ago, for example, than *He done ate de chicken*).

Dialectology, before the criticism expressed by sociologist Glenna Ruth Pickford, followed the reconstructive lead of the *Atlas Linguistique de la France* and the *Sprachatlas des Deutschen Reichs*. The approach still dominates publications like the *Journal of English Linguistics* and *American Speech*. The nineteenth century had seen the beginning of the English Dialect Society (and publications like the *English Dialect Dictionary*), and the American Dialect Society was organized in 1889. Beginning in 1928, a group of researchers under the direction of Professor Hans Kurath undertook the compilation of a *Linguistic Atlas of the United States and Canada*. The *Linguistic Atlas of New England* was published over the period from 1939 to 1943. Considerably more field work has been completed since that time.

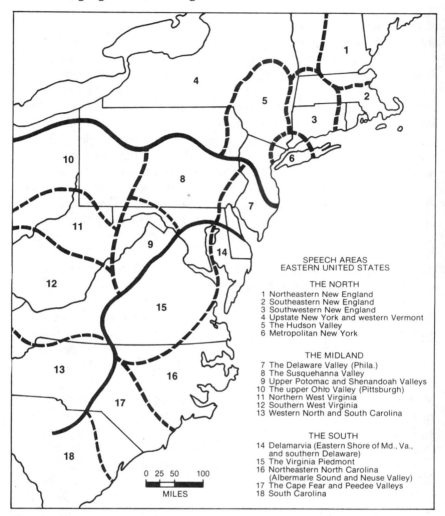

SPEECH AREAS
EASTERN UNITED STATES

THE NORTH

1 Northeastern New England
2 Southeastern New England
3 Southwestern New England
4 Upstate New York and western Vermont
5 The Hudson Valley
6 Metropolitan New York

THE MIDLAND

7 The Delaware Valley (Phila.)
8 The Susquehanna Valley
9 Upper Potomac and Shenandoah Valleys
10 The upper Ohio Valley (Pittsburgh)
11 Northern West Virginia
12 Southern West Virginia
13 Western North and South Carolina

THE SOUTH

14 Delamarvia (Eastern Shore of Md., Va., and southern Delaware)
15 The Virginia Piedmont
16 Northeastern North Carolina (Albermarle Sound and Neuse Valley)
17 The Cape Fear and Peedee Valleys
18 South Carolina

0 25 50   100

MILES

Figure 2.

Pickford strongly criticized this work for including only three social groups (five in the closely related *Dictionary of American Regional English*) and for limiting, in practice, the interviews almost exclusively to rural informants. In the 1960s, partly in response to Pickford's criticism, dialectologists began to conduct studies in Washington, D.C., Detroit, Chicago, and New York.

From the *Atlas* research procedures there seemed to emerge three major dialect boundaries, cutting the country into lateral strips and labeled by Kurath: Northern, Midland, and Southern. [See Figure 2.] This regional distribution had no place for either what Mencken had called the "American Vulgate" or for what others had called General

American. Standardizing practices, often associated with the concept of General American, were dismissed as not really part of the informants' "natural" language.

What emerged in the dialect research of the 1960s, however, was something other than a picture of regional distribution. The "neutral" dialect concept of General American was replaced, especially in the research of certain psycholinguists, by that of Network Standard, the speech of television newscasters on the major networks and the kind of English which Americans clearly admired more than any other. They tended, however inaccurately, to form mental pictures of their own speech in terms of that prestige form. This regionally and socially neutral dialect clearly emerged as the ideal, if not the actuality, for most speakers of American English. Television, becoming really important as a medium in the 1960s, would permit relatively "nonstandard" usage from comedians and sportscasters, but anyone else had to disguise his dialect in order to work regularly for the networks. A nationally oriented and highly mobile population substituted this concept of a standard dialect for the older notion of prestige centers.

The older, geographically oriented type of research identified dialect areas for the essentially rural population in terms of predominantly lexical materials. For example, characteristic Northern expressions that were current throughout the area include *pail, swill, whiffletree* or *whippletree, comforter* or *comfortable* for a thick quilt, *brook, co-boss* or *come-boss as a cow call, johnny-cake, salt pork,* and *darning needle* for a dragonfly. When one considers how few cattle are called in New York City, or how few Manhattanites see a dragonfly during the course of a day, one realizes how irrelevantly quaint and rustic some of this research came to seem.

In the Midland area one found *blinds* for roller shades, *skillet, spouting* or *spouts* for eaves, a *piece* for food taken between meals, *snake feeder* for dragonfly, *sook* as the call to calves, *armload* for an armful of wood; and one *hulled* beans when he took off the shells. A quarter *till* the hour was a typical Midland expression, as [was] the elliptical *to want off,* or *out,* or *in.* The South had *lightwood* as the term for kindling, a *turn* of wood for an armful; stringbeans were generally *snap beans; low* was used for the sound cows make at feeding time; *hasslet* was the term for the edible inner organs of a pig, and *chittlins* for the small intestines. The last item above has now, of course, achieved nationwide spread in connection with the Black institution of soul food.

Subdialect areas were also found to have their characteristic forms. In coastal New England, for instance, *pigsty* was the normal term for a pigpen, *bonny clapper* for curdled sour milk, *buttonwood* for a sycamore, and *pandowdy* for a cobbler type of dessert. Some Eastern Virginians still have *cuppin* for a cow pen, and *corn house* for a crib. *Lumber room* survives as the term for a storeroom. *Hopper grass* competed with the national term *grasshopper*, and *batter bread* was used for a soft cornbread containing egg.

As far as the domains of the American lexicon which reflect regional differences are concerned, the matter is summarized in Kurath's *Word Geography*, where the author points out first of all that the vocabularies of the arts and sciences, of industries, commercial enterprises, social and political institutions, and even many of the crafts, are national in scope because the activities they reflect are organized on a national basis. He then goes on to say:

> Enterprises and activities that are regionally restricted have, on the other hand, a considerable body of regional vocabulary which, to be sure, may be known in other parts of the country, even if it is not in active use. The cotton planter of the South, the tobacco grower, the dairy farmer, the wheat grower, the miner, the lumberman, and the rancher of the West have many words and expressions that are strictly regional and sometimes local in their currency.

> Regional and local expressions are most common in the vocabulary of the intimate everyday life of the home and the farm—not only among the simple folk and the middle class but also among the cultured. . . . Food, clothing, shelter, health, the day's work, play, mating, social gatherings, the land, the farm buildings, implements, the farm stocks and crops, the weather, the fauna and flora—these are the intimate concern of the common folk in the countryside, and for these things expressions are handed down in the family and the neighborhood that schooling and reading and a familiarity with regional or national usage do not blot out.

In other domains of the lexicon, social differences are more strikingly important. Americans have, from the first, identified themselves much more by occupation than by region, and early commentators made much of the "jargon" of groups like the trappers ("mountain men") and the cowboys. Groups as diverse as hoboes, prostitutes, and advertising men have their own peculiar terminology and phraseology. In particular, American Blacks have had African or Afro-Creole survivals; these survivals came to national attention beginning around 1920, through the vocabulary of jazz and blues musicians. White musicians and then American teenagers made a shibboleth of the use of Black-associated "slang," and British rock groups like the Beatles and the Rolling Stones propagated it among the English youth.

It is not only in the vocabulary that one finds regional differences in American speech; there are pronunciation differences as well. Throughout the Northern area, for example, the distinction between [o] and [ɔ] in such word pairs as *hoarse* and *horse, mourning* and *morning*, is generally maintained; [s] regularly occurs in *grease* (verb) and *greasy* and *root* is pronounced with the vowel of *wood*. Within the Northern area such subdialects as coastal New England and Metropolitan New

York also show many characteristic forms, although the extreme amount of variation found in the latter must not be forgotten. The treatment of the vowel of *bird* is only one of these, and words of the *calf, pass, path, dance* group constitute another. In the Midland area speakers fail to distinguish between *hoarse* and *horse* in many contexts. Rounding is characteristic of the vowels of *hog, frog, log, wasp,* and *wash,* and in the last of these words an *r* often intrudes in the speech of the rural and old-fashioned. The vowels of *due* and *new* will resemble that of *food* rather than that of *feud*. In the South and in eastern New England, there is a tendency to "lose" *r* except before vowels; but the former does not have the pronounced *Cuber* (for *Cuba*) and *idear of it* which John F. Kennedy carried from Massachusetts to the presidency. *R* is also "lost" in eastern New England and in New York City but not in the Northern area generally. Words like *Tuesday, due,* and *new* have a *y*-like glide preceding the vowel, and final [z] in *Mrs.* is the normal form. . . .

Regional variation in inflectional forms and syntax at the most superficial level can also be found, especially among older, relatively uneducated groups. *Hadn't ought* is a characteristic Northern double modal; *might could* and *may can* were perhaps exclusively Southern until Black speakers carried them into the Northern cities. Verb forms associated with the North have *been see* as a past tense form, *clim* for "climbed," *wa'n't* for "wasn't," uninflected *be* in such expressions as "How be you?" (much more limited syntactically than the superficially similar Black English form), and the choice of the preposition *to* in *sick to his stomach*. Associated with the Midlands were *clum* for "climbed," *seen* for "saw," *all the further,* and *I'll wait on you*. Characteristic Southern expressions, excluding Black English influence, were *belongs to be, heern* for "heard," *seed* as the past tense of "to see," and *holp* for "helped."

However quaint and rustic some of these forms may seem, and however unfamiliar to many other speakers of American English, they have been used, so far unsuccessfully, in attempts to trace the settlement history, particularly of the earliest immigrants. It has been hypothesized that, of ten families of settlers gathered in any one place, two might well have spoken London English, while three or four others spoke one of the southeastern county dialects. There might also have been a couple of families speaking northern English and another two or three employing a western dialect.

What would have happened to this hypothetical dialect mix is another matter. Recent studies emphasize the way in which children are influenced more strongly by the language of their peers than by that of their parents. Even if the parents retained the old regional dialect unchanged—and sociolinguistic research questions whether this is ever completely the case—children of the second generation would level the differences. Whatever compromises between British local dialects were worked out at various points on the Atlantic Seaboard would be supplemented by borrowings from the Indians and from other language groups. Other population groups which had extensive contacts with the children of the British immigrants, like the Black slaves of the Southern states, would also have strongly influenced their language.

Judging by the reports of observers, these influences became especially noticeable about the beginning of the nineteenth century. At about the same time, other changes occurred which were to have a profound effect upon the language situation in America. First, the industrial revolution resulted in the growth of a number of industrial centers, uprooting a considerable proportion of the farm population and concentrating it in the cities. The development of the railroad and other mechanical means of travel increased greatly the mobility of the average person. The large-scale migrations westward also resulted in some resettlement and shifting, even among those who did not set out on the long trek. All of this would have resulted in a general abandonment of narrowly local speech forms in favor of fewer, more accessible, varieties—even if there had not been prior forces leading toward the same end.

Some local speech forms have remained even to the present day. These are usually known as relics, particularly when they are distributed in isolated spots over an area rather than in concentration. *Open stone peach*, for example, is a relic for "freestone peach," occurring in Maryland. *Smurring up*, "getting foggy," survives as a relic in eastern Maine and more rarely on Cape Cod and Martha's Vineyard.

Even prior to the shifts in population and changes in culture pattern, certain colonial cities such as Boston, Philadelphia, and Charleston had acquired prestige by developing as centers of trade and immigration. They became socially and culturally outstanding, as well as economically powerful, thus dominating the areas surrounding them. As a consequence, local expressions and pronunciations peculiar to the countryside came to be replaced by new forms of speech emanating from these cosmopolitan centers. A fairly recent instance of this is to be found in the New England term *tonic* for soda water, practically coextensive with the area served by Boston wholesalers.

Little if anything of this sort has ever been observed for the influence of New York City on any large surrounding area. Nevertheless, Madison Avenue's influence on the advertising phraseology of the nation, along with the importance of New York City for radio, television, and publication, must have had a general, widely diffused influence. It has been suggested that the "Brooklyn" dialect of popular stereotype, particularly with its pronunciation of *bird, shirt, thirty-third*, etc. (imprecisely believed to be like "oy" of *Floyd*) resembles that of the same working-class people in New Orleans and elsewhere along the Atlantic and Gulf seacoasts because of the trade connections, particularly in cotton, between New Orleans and New York City.

Nor was the general process of dialect formation by any means completed with the settlement of the Atlantic seaboard. As the land to the west came to be taken up in successive stages (for example, western New York, Michigan, Wisconsin in the North; southern Ohio, Indiana, and southern Illinois in the Midland area), the same mixtures of speech forms among the settlers were present at first, and the same linguistic compromises had to be worked out. Although virtually every westward-moving group had to work out some way of dealing with the foreign-language groups in its language contact picture, the specific nature of the groups encountered varied at each stage.

The same processes occurred in the interior South, in Texas, and later on in the Far West. The complete linguistic history of the United States depends upon the formulation of what happened in each of those areas. We know, for example, from both surviving forms and historical sources that the Western cowboys used faro and poker terms (*in hock, pass the buck, deal from the bottom of the deck, four-flusher*), and occupational terms (*little dogies, break the string, hand* for "worker"), many of which moved back toward the East.

Such environmental factors as topography, climate, and plant and animal life also played their part in influencing the dialect of an area, just as they did in the general transplanting of the English language to America. The complexity and size of the network of fresh-water streams affect the distribution and meaning of such terms as *brook, creek, branch*, and *river*—not to mention *wash* and *bayou*. In parts of Ohio and Pennsylvania, for example, the term *creek* is applied to a much larger body of water than in Michigan. It is even more obvious that in those parts of the country where snow is a rarity or does not fall at all, there will be no necessity for terms to indicate coasting face down on a sled. It is not surprising that those areas of the country where cows can be milked outside, for at least part of the year, will develop a specific term for the place where this is done: witness *milk gap* or *milking gap* current in the Appalachians south of the James River. The wealth of terms for various types of fences throughout the country is again dependent, in part at least, on the material which is available for building them, be it stones, stumps, or wooden rails. It is equally obvious that nationwide technological terms for television, like *commercial, station break, prime time, talk show*, and *situation comedy* should be the same in all parts of the country. Neither is it surprising that the increasingly nationwide distribution of major sporting events should lead to uniformity in *Super Bowl, Number One* ("We're Number One!"), *playoff, World Series*, and a host of other terms.

Before the days of radio, television, and national magazine advertising, a new invention or development introduced into several parts of the country at the same time would acquire different names in various places. The baby carriage, for example, seems to have been a development of the 1830s and '40s, and this is the term which developed in New England. Within the Philadelphia trade area, however, the article became known as a *baby coach*. *Baby buggy* was adopted west of the Alleghenies and *baby cab* in other regions throughout the country.

Within the last four decades, the building of large, double-lane, limited-access automobile highways has been undertaken in all parts of the country. In the beginning, there were many regional differences: *parkways* in eastern New York, Connecticut, and Rhode Island; *turnpikes* in Pennsylvania, New Jersey, New Hampshire, Maine, Massachusetts, Ohio, and Indiana. (The fanciest highway in Florida, from Miami to Gainesville, is, however, now a turnpike.) In New York *thruway* is used for what are *expressways* in Michigan and *freeways* in California. For a while—in the late 1950s—these seemed like regionalisms in the making, but a generation of car travelers has learned them all and uses them now synonymously, now with some specialization.

It is of interest also to look at the dialect situation from the point of view of various words which are employed for the same concept in different parts of the country. One of the most interesting and instructive distributions is to be found in connection with the terms used for *earthworm*. This word is used by cultivated speakers in the metropolitan centers. *Angleworm* is the regional term in the North, *fishworm* in the Midland area, and *fishing worm* in the coastal South. *Fish bait* and *bait worm* occupy smaller areas within the extensive *fishworm* region, but are also distributed over a wide territory.

In addition, there have been a large number of local terms, many of them used principally by the older and less-educated inhabitants. The Merrimack Valley, in New Hampshire, and Essex County, Massachusetts, have *mud worm*. *Eace worm* is used in Rhode Island. *Angle dog* appears in upper Connecticut, and *ground worm* on the Eastern Shore of Virginia. *Red worm* is used in the mountains of North Carolina, and an area around Toledo, Ohio, uses *dew worm*. Scattered instances of *rainworm* appear on Buzzards Bay in Massachusetts, throughout the Pennsylvania German area, and in German settlements in North Carolina, Maine, and Wisconsin. We have, thus, a wealth of older local terms, three distinct regional words, and the cultivated *earthworm* appearing in addition as a folk word in South Carolina and along the North Carolina and Virginia coast. Where and how did the various terms originate, and what can be determined about their subsequent history?

Earthworm itself is not an old word; it appears to have been compounded only shortly before the earliest English migrations to America.

The earliest *Oxford English Dictionary* citation of the word in its present form is 1591; it appears also as *yearth worm* some thirty years earlier. The three regional terms all seem to have been coined in America; the dictionaries either record no British citations or fail to include the words at all.

The local terms have a varied and interesting history. *Mud worm* seems to occur in standard British English from the beginning of the nineteenth century on. *Eace worm*, as a combined form, goes back at least to Middle English; the first element was a term for "bait" as early as Aelfric; it is used today in a number of southern counties in England from Kent to Gloucester. *Angle dog* is used currently in Devonshire. *Ground worm*, though apparently coined in England, was transferred to North Carolina and Maryland in the eighteenth century. *Red worm* appears first in England in 1450 and continues through to the mid-nineteenth century, though chiefly in books on fishing, as does *dew worm*, which goes back even farther, to the late Old English period. *Rainworm*, though it appears in Aelfric as *renwyrm*, may be a reformation, even in British English, on the pattern of *Regenwurm* in German, for there is a gap of seven centuries in the citations in the *Oxford English Dictionary* and there is reason to believe that its revival in 1731 was influenced by the German form. Moreover, with but one exception, it has been cited for the United States only in areas settled by Germans.

Thus we have in the standard cultivated term one of relatively recent British formation. Apparently the regional terms were compounded in America, whereas the local terms represent survivals either of dialect usage or anglers' jargon and one loan translation. It is worth noting that the common Old English term, *angle twicce*, surviving as *angle twitch* in Cornwall and Devon, seems not to have found its way to America. There are, furthermore, such other English formations as *tag worm*, *marsh worm*, and *garden worm* which have not been recorded in America.

At times, too, changes in meaning seem to have entered into the dialect situation, as is illustrated by the development of the regional terms *skillet* and *spider*, the former current in the Midland and the Virginia Piedmont, the latter in the North and the Southern Tidewater area. *Frying pan* is the urban term and is slowly supplanting the others. *Spider*, once a nautical term for "the iron band around the mast to take the lower end of futlock rigging," was then applied to a cast-iron pan with short legs. It was later transferred to the flat-bottomed pan as well. The local term *creeper* is used in Marblehead, Massachusetts. *Skillet*, a term of doubtful etymology, first appears in English in 1403, when it was applied to a long-handled brass or copper vessel used for boiling liquids or stewing meat. It is still so used in dialects throughout England. The shift in meaning to a frying pan took place only in America, but an advertisement of 1790, offering for sale "bakepans, spiders, skillets," would suggest that even as late as this a distinction between the two was recognized.

The examples above have been offered only as a suggestion of the various language processes which have played a part in the distribution and meaning of some of our dialect terms. It is quite obvious that no definite conclusions about such matters can be reached on the basis of rather scant linguistic details. Such evidence as has been accumulated, however, seems to suggest that Kurath's original intuition was correct in that only home and farm terms give much evidence of regional or local distribution in the United States.

The question of social dialects or speech differences is quite another matter, with many scholars seeing much more profound grammatical differences between social—especially ethnic—groups. Black English, of which Gullah is the extreme case, comes immediately to mind; but the English of the Pennsylvania Germans also offers some grammatical constructions that are very strange to mainstream American English speakers.

Frequently, the matter of social dialect has been conceptualized in terms of "standard" and "nonstandard" dialects. H. L. Mencken believed in a so-called "American Vulgate" with reasonably uniform characteristics throughout the country—and with no special stated social distribution. Nonstandard dialects, however, do have many features in common, for whatever reason that may be.

One of the inflectional forms most characteristic of nouns in nonstandard American English is the unchanged plural after numbers: *six mile down the road, five foot tall*, and similarly applied to *month, year*, and *gallon*. In Black English it resembles the Afro-Creole nonredundant pluralization: *The boys* bears a plural inflection, but either *six boy* or *plenty boy* is plural without the final *s*. Any plural marking in the immediate environment, not just a numeral, may suffice, so that we sometimes find sentences like *Dem chair* for "Those are chairs."

The Mencken-type Vulgate may, in the case of some unmarked plurals, represent a preservation of linguistically older forms than those found in Standard English. It displays the opposite tendency, however, in the possessive pronoun in its so-called absolute form, which in the standard language represents a strange and inconsistent mixture of patterns. *Mine* and the archaic *thine* are derived from the adjectival form by adding -*n*. *Hers, ours, yours*, and *theirs*, on the other hand, add -*s* to the adjectival form. *His* and *its* are indistinguishable so far as their secondary and absolute forms are concerned. In contrast, the "Vulgate" possessive pronouns, *mine, yourn, hisn, hern, ourn, theirn*, present a perfectly regular pattern formed by an analogical extension of *mine* and *thine* to the third person singular and to the plural forms. The fact that Pidgin English probably had absolute *me one, you one, he one*, etc., may have contributed something to the leveling process of the Vulgate.

In the use of absolute possessives, Black English and other non-standard dialects part company. In the most extreme form, which William Stewart calls *basilect*, Black English has *he book, you friend, they uncle*. In the "exposed" position, *It he book* becomes neither *It he* nor *It hisn*. Instead, basilect *It he own* alternates with a Standard-English influenced *It his*.

The reflexive pronouns give us another instance of a more regular operation of analogy on the nonstandard level than on the standard. In Standard English, *myself, yourself, ourselves,* and *yourselves* are combinations of the genitive pronoun plus the singular or plural of the -*self* form; *himself* and *themselves* employ the object form of the pronoun, whereas *herself* and *itself* could be either. Nonstandard English, in substituting *hisself* and *theirself* in the third person and adhering to the singular of *self* in *ourself* and *yourself* (plural), is not only more consistent but more economical in that the latter combinations signal the plural only once and avoid the redundancy of the plural -*selves*. The only ambiguity is in the second person, but the second personal pronoun has lost its distinctions between singular and plural anyway, except for nonstandard formations like the Southern *you all*—which never figures in the reflexive.

One curious feature of the nonstandard pronoun is the substitution of the object for the subjective form in such sentences as *Us girls went home, John and her was married, Me and him was late*. The use of the object form for the subject is normal in Black English basilect (*Me help you?*) and in Pidgin English. In Cajun English, of Louisiana, it can be used at the end of the sentence for emphasis: *I was late, me*. In the "Vulgate," however, it seems to occur principally when the subject is compound or when the pronoun is syntactically a modifier of the subject, as in *us girls* above. The schools have made such emphatic use of *we girls* and *It is I* (or *he, she*), that the result is a lot of overcorrection on the order of *between you and I* (or even *between he and I*); *She gave it to Mother and I; She took all of we children*.

A few typical nonstandard inflectional forms deserve mention. *Them* as a demonstrative adjective (*them* books) probably harks back to the days when the English article and the demonstrative *that* (dative ðæm) were one and the same form. *Dem* is the regular demonstrative adjective and noun pluralizer (*dem man* = "men") in Gullah, but post-posed use as in Jamaican and other creoles (*man-dem*) is hinted at in the records of early Black English in one speech by newly imported African slaves and remembered by Frederick Douglass. The multiple negative was a regular and accepted feature of older English, but Black English negative concord (*It ain't no cat can't get in no coop*) has no such obvious earlier parallel. The adverb without the -*ly* suffix or other differentiation from the adjective (*He spoke quiet; You did real good*) may reflect very old practices in English.

The standard and nonstandard languages are undoubtedly far-thest apart with regard to verb forms. Black English nonpassive pre-verbal *been* (*He been rub me the wrong way*), and *be* in its negation by *don't*, and in contrast to "zero copula" are the most extremely different forms outside Gullah *de*. Less significantly, there is a tendency to dispose of the distinctive *-s* inflection for the third person singular, either by elim-inating it in such forms as *he want, she write*, etc., or by extending the peculiar form of the third person to the first and second—*I has some good friends; You is in lots of trouble*. Black English makes widespread, often hypercorrective, use of these forms; the records tend to indicate that older varieties used (also hypercorrectively) *he am*, etc.

The overwhelming tendency in English verb development throughout the last seven or eight centuries has been toward an ag-grandizement of the regular or weak inflection (*-ed* past tense) at the expense of the older minor conjugations. This is in effect a tendency toward a two-part verb, the infinitive or present stem opposed to an identical past tense and past participle. In general, this has been brought about through analogical processes. It is often impossible to know for certain whether nonstandard forms are the result of retention of an older preterite plural (*writ* as the past tense of *write*; or *begun* and *swum* in that function), or of analogies which have not operated in Standard English. Extension of the regular past inflections to such ir-regular verbs as *know* and *see* (*knowed, seed*) can only be analogical; as must the amalgamation of the strong preterite or past participle with the complementary form (*I taken, he done* as preterites; *have gave, have wrote, has went* as past participial forms).

The easy transition from one social class to another in the United States has resulted in a very hazy line of demarcation between what is acceptable and what is considered illiterate. According to the most rigorous textbook standard, some of the language employed in Amer-ican legislative councils and in business life would not pass muster; one could not even be sure that what is spoken in college faculty meet-ings would always meet those same criteria. The awareness of this, combined with an unrealistic treatment of language in our schools, has resulted at times in a defiance of these questionable standards, in what could be called "dramatic low status assertion." More often it has given people guilt complexes about the language they use. The puristic schoolteacher for whom nothing is good enough, has been attacked in linguistics courses and textbooks since the 1940s. Some changes may have been made, but the prescriptive attitude, in one guise or another, lives on in our school systems and in handbooks of usage. On tele-vision's Public Broadcasting System, groups consisting of actors, drama critics, newscasters, and occasionally even a linguistics professor meet to discuss the "deplorable" state of the English language in America.

Consequently, many Americans, especially those who are socially mobile, lack confidence and assurance of the essential aptness and correctness of their speech. Fewer members of any class are able to switch comfortably between a nonstandard dialect and the standard— although this is by no means rare in other countries. Those educational programs that have called for use of children's home and peer group dialects in such educational activities as initial or remedial reading have generally met with scorn, even from many dialectologists. The Ann Arbor, Michigan, school district became in July, 1979, the first U.S. school system ordered to take Black children's dialect into account in planning its curriculum. Lawsuits similar to the one that elicited this decision have already been filed in Tampa, Florida, and Houston, Texas, and many others may follow.

Within professional dialectology, new developments like variation theory and inherent variability provide an even more solid foundation for acceptance of and interest in dialect and speech pattern differences. Popularization of the variable rule may be more difficult to achieve than was the case of regional and local differences; but there also seems to be less chance that the popularized knowledge will form the basis for invidious comparisons and linguistic snobbery. There is still some faith in the notion that understanding is the key to tolerance.

FOR DISCUSSION AND REVIEW

1. Explain the difference between regional (geographical) and social dialectology. Why has a great deal of work been done in the latter field in the last twenty-five years?

2. Carefully examine Figure 1 on p. 478. The vertical axis indicates the percentage of respondents using (r); the horizontal axis indicates the frequency of occurrence of (r) by social class; the labels to the right of the chart show the increasing degrees of formality of speech. (The two top lines are broken rather than solid in order to indicate that these styles do not occur in normal connected speech.) Having studied the figure, explain Marckwardt and Dillard's statement: "Even more interesting than relative frequency across class, however, was the greater variability evidenced by the lower-middle class. These sociologically insecure people also indulge extensively, Labov found, in hypercorrection."

3. Identify the three major geographical dialect boundaries in the United States. How has the identification of these three areas modified earlier ideas about American regional dialects?

4. Explain the concepts of "General American" (dialect) and "Network Standard." Which, if either, is still important? Why or why not?

5. What, according to Marckwardt and Dillard, are the three aspects of American speech in which one finds regional differences? About which

aspect do we have the most information? Why? Give three examples of each kind of regional difference.

6. Identify three areas of the lexicon in which regional differences are most important, and explain why this is so.

7. Explain the effects on American regional dialects of (a) the industrial revolution, (b) the development of the railroad, and (c) the large-scale migration westward.

8. List four reasons for the difficulty of doing research on American regional dialects.

9. Using examples not cited by Marckwardt and Dillard, explain how four environmental factors have influenced American regional dialects.

10. Marckwardt and Dillard state that that the terms *parkway, turnpike, thruway, expressway,* and *freeway* for a while "seemed like regionalisms in the making, but a generation of car travelers has learned them all and uses them now synonymously, now with some specialization." Do you agree with their conclusion? Identify two other relatively recent inventions or developments that have acquired different names in various places.

11. Marckwardt and Dillard state that "Nonstandard dialects . . . have many features in common, for whatever reason that may be." Identify and describe four such features.

3/Dialects: How They Differ

ROGER W. SHUY

We all speak a dialect; dialects are not things spoken by other people in other places. One often quoted definition of a dialect is that of Raven I. McDavid, Jr., who describes a dialect as "simply a habitual variety of a language, regional or social. It is set off from all other such habitual varieties by a unique combination of language features: words and meanings, grammatical forms, phrase structures, pronunciations, patterns of stress and intonation." Professor McDavid then points out that "No dialect is simply good or bad in itself; its prestige comes from the prestige of those who use it. But every dialect is in itself a legitimate form of the language, a valid instrument of human communication, and something worthy of serious study."* In the following excerpt from Discovering American Dialects, *Roger W. Shuy discusses, with many examples, regional variations in pronunciation, vocabulary, and grammar, and provides extensive samples of dialect questionnaires. These questionnaires are shortened versions of those used by field investigators in preparing the* Linguistic Atlas of New England (LANE) *and other regional atlases. The LANE questionnaire, for example, contained about 750 items. Shuy also explains the methods used by fieldworkers to collect dialect data and the importance of the "personal data sheet," and warns the would-be investigator that people are usually more self-conscious about their grammar than they are about either their vocabulary or pronunciation.*

Speakers of one dialect may be set off from speakers of a different dialect by the use of certain pronunciations, words, and grammatical forms. The frequent first reaction of a person who hears an unfamiliar dialect is that the strange sounds and words are a chaotic mess. This is similar to the feeling an American has when he sees British motorists driving "on the wrong side of the street," or to the bewildered feeling

---

* "Sense and Nonsense About American Dialects" in *Dialects in Culture: Essays in General Dialectology by Raven I. McDavid, Jr.*, edited by William A. Kretzschmar, Jr. University, AL: The University of Alabama Press, 1979, p. 70; originally published in *PMLA* 81 (1966) 2:7–17.

we have upon hearing a foreign language for the first time. Surely, we feel, there is no system in that sort of behavior!

Mankind apparently views all unfamiliar human behavior as suspicious and unsystematic. If you have ever watched a bird build a nest on a window sill or in a bush within the range of any passing alley cat, you have probably not questioned the intelligence of the bird. Most people accept even apparently erratic animal behavior and assume that, no matter how foolish the act may seem, it probably makes sense to the animal. But as soon as a human being is seen to behave "differently," he is frequently considered foolish or uncooperative. Language, in this case a dialect, is also a form of behavior. That people speak different dialects in no way stems from their intelligence or judgment. They speak the dialect which enables them to get along with the other members of their social and geographical group.

Differences in Pronunciation

Differences in pronunciation are of two types: totally patterned and partially patterned. A totally patterned difference is one in which the sound behaves consistently in a particular situation. For example, in some parts of the country, particularly in eastern New England, the pronunciation of r is lost before consonants and in word-final position. Thus a Midwesterner's "park the car" becomes the New Englander's "pahk the cah." From the New Englander's point of view, it might be equally valid to say that Midwesterners insert r's before consonants (park) and following a vowel at the ends of words (car). That the words in question have r's in their spellings is really not important here, for spellings remain fixed long after pronunciations change, and letters may have different sound values in different dialects. But whether we say the New Englander *drops* an r or the Midwesterner *inserts* one, the fact remains that the difference is totally patterned in most speech styles. Recent dialect research has shown that a person may shift his pattern slightly, depending upon his relationship to his audience and on whether he is reading aloud or speaking impromptu. Professor William Labov of Columbia University has observed, for example, that New York working-class people tend to say *dis* for *this* and *dese* for *these* when they are talking about a bad accident or about a personal brush with death. They say *dis* and *dese* less frequently when talking with teachers and even less frequently when reading aloud.

The second kind of variation in pronunciation, a partially patterned difference, may occur in a few words or even in only one. The partially patterned sound is not consistent throughout the dialect. It

was mentioned above that the eastern New Englander "drops" an *r* before consonants and in word-final position in a totally patterned way. Now let us cite the Midwesterner who inserts an *r* in certain words but in no particular phonetic pattern. In most of Ohio, Indiana, and Illinois (except for a few northern counties), *wash* is pronounced *"worsh"* by a large number of speakers, particularly by those with no more than a high school education. If this were totally patterned, these speakers would also say *"borsh"* instead of *bosh* and *"jorsh"* instead of *josh* (many of them do say *"gorsh"* instead of *gosh*).

Other examples of partially patterned differences (still sticking with *r* problems) include "lozengers" for *lozenges*, "framiliar" for *familiar*, "quintruplets" for *quintuplets*, and "surpress" for *suppress*. This phenomenon, sometimes referred to as the "intrusive *r*," is most noticeable in someone else's dialect. Midwesterners are amused at the Bostonian's pronunciation of "Cuber" and "Asiar" for *Cuba* and *Asia* before words beginning with vowels, failing to hear their own intrusive *r* in *worsh* and *lozengers*. Likewise, the Bostonian tends to hear the Midwesterner's intrusive *r*'s but not his own.

Our standard alphabet cannot record the many sounds in American English pronunciation. The dialectologist uses a highly detailed phonetic alphabet to record the most minute audible features of speech. The student can easily learn and use a simpler set of symbols to record the variations he meets in his dialect studies. [Here the author supplies a resumé of the phonetic alphabet like that included by Edward Callary in "Phonetics" (Part Four). He then suggests that readers practice transcribing how various speakers pronounce certain words.]

Remember that a good ear for sounds is not developed right away. You may wish to practice with other transcription exercises, or you may simply write phonetically the words used by teachers, classmates, television performers, or members of your family. If classmates or friends from a different part of the country are willing to serve as informants, have them pronounce the following words:

Word	Northern	Midland	Southern
1. cr*ee*k	ɪ and i	ɪ (north Midland) i (south Midland)	i
2. p*e*nny	ɛ	ɛ	ɪ–(Southwest)
3. M*a*ry	ɛ e (parts of eastern New England)	ɛ	e
4. m*a*rried	æ (east of Appalachians) ɛ (elsewhere)	ɛ	ɛ
5. c*o*w	ɑʊ	æʊ	æʊ or ɑʊ
6. s*i*ster	ɪ	ɨ (eastern)	ɨ (eastern)
7. f*o*reign	ɔ	ɑ	ɑ
8. *o*range	ɑ (east of Alleghenies) ɔ	ɑ and ɔ	ɑ and ɔ
9. tomat*o*	o	ə	o or ə
10. c*oo*p	u	u (NM), ʊ (SM)	ʊ
11. r*oo*f	ʊ	u and/or ʊ	u
12. b*u*lge	ə	ə or ʊ	ə or ʊ
13. f*a*rm	ɑ	ɑ or ɔ	ɑ or ɔ
14. w*i*re	ɑɪ	ɑɪ or ɑ	ɑ
15. w*o*n't	ə o (urban)	o ɔ	o ɔ
16. f*o*g	ɑ (New England) ɑ and ɔ (Midwest)	ɔ	ɔ
17. h*o*g	ɑ (New England) ɑ and ɔ (Midwest)	ɔ	ɔ
18. *o*n	ɑ	ɔ	ɔ
19. l*o*ng	ɔ	ɔ	ɑ (eastern Virginia) ɔ (elsewhere)
20. car*e*less	ɨ	ə	ɨ
21. stom*a*ch	ə	ɨ	ə

The vowels of these words are pronounced differently in the various parts of our country. The major variants are listed beside the words along with their general distributions.

Consonants sometimes will give clues to the dialect a person speaks. The following generalizations may be helpful:

Word	Northern	Midland	Southern
1. *hu*mor	hɪumər	yumər	hɪumər or yumər
2. wa*sh*	waš or wɔš	wɔrš or wɔɪš	wɔš or wɔɪš or waš
3. wi*th*	wɪð and wɪθ (N.Y., Chicago, Detroit = wɪt working class)	wɪθ	wɪθ
4. grea*sy*	grisɪ	grizɪ	grizɪ
5. *ba*rn	barn (Eastern North = bɑn)	bɑrn	bɑrn (East Coast = bɑn)
6. *th*ese	ðiz (N.Y., Chicago, Detroit = diz working class)	ðiz	ðiz
7. *wh*ich	hwɪč	wɪč	wɪč
8. mi*ss*	mɪs	mɪs	mɪz
9. Mrs.	mɪsɫz	mɪsɫz	mɪzɫz or mɪz

With the mobility of the American population today, we are bound to discover exceptions to generalizations like these. Also, . . . settlement history has caused some curious mixtures of speech patterns in our country. On the whole, however, the generalizations may be useful in helping you to recognize the dialect of your informant.

One bit of advice as you get your informants to say these words— *try for a natural situation.* One way professional fieldworkers have done this is to ask, for example, for what the person calls a small stream of water that runs through a farm. *Creek* is a likely response. You can easily invent similar questions for other words. It might be interesting, furthermore, to compare a person's response in conversation with his pronunciation when he reads the word in a sentence or in a list of such words. You may discover that your classmates have different pronunciations for different occasions. . . .

Differences in Vocabulary

Words are interesting to almost everyone. Through his vocabulary a person may reveal facts about his age, his sex, his education, his occupation, and his geographical and cultural origins. Our first reaction may be to imagine that all speakers of English use the same words. Nothing could be further from the truth; our language contains a vast number of synonyms to show different shades of meaning or reveal as much of our inner feelings as we want to. Some of these vocabulary choices are made deliberately. We use other words, however, without really knowing that our vocabulary is influenced by our audience.

AGE

Certain words tell how old we are. For example, many people refer to an electric refrigerator as an *ice box* despite the fact that in most parts of our country ice boxes have not been in common use for many years. Older natives of some Northern dialect areas still may call a frying pan a *spider*, a term which remained in the vocabulary of the older generation long after the removal of the four legs which gave the descriptive title. Frying pans no longer look like four-legged spiders, but the name remains fixed in the vocabulary of certain people.

SEX

Our vocabulary may also identify whether we are male or female. Most high school boys, for example, are not likely to use *lovely*, *peachy*, *darling*, and many words ending in *-ie*. Adult males are not apt to know or use very many words concerned with fabrics, color shadings, sewing, or women's styles. Women of all ages are not likely to use the specialized vocabulary of sports, automobile repair, or plumbing.*

EDUCATION

A person also reveals his educational background through his choice of words. It is no secret that learning the specialized vocabulary of psychology, electronics, or fishing is necessary before one becomes fully accepted as an "insider," and before he can fully participate in these areas. Much of what a student learns about a course in school is shown in his handling of the vocabulary of the subject. It is also true, however, that a person's choice of words is not nearly as revealing of education as his grammar and pronunciations are.

OCCUPATION

The specialized vocabulary of occupational groups also appears in everyday language. Truck drivers, secretaries, tirebuilders, sailors, farmers, and members of many other occupations use such words. Linguists who interview people for *The Linguistic Atlas of the United States and Canada* have found that the calls to certain animals, for example, illustrate what might be called farm vocabulary, particularly for the older generation of farmers (city dwellers obviously have no particular way of calling sheep or cows from pasture). Even within farming areas, furthermore, vocabulary will reveal specialization. Recent Illi-

---

* Editors' note: Writing in 1967, Shuy could not have foreseen the many social changes that have occurred in the United States that necessitate some restriction of his generalizations in this area.

nois language studies showed that a male sheep was known as a *buck* only to farmers who had at some time raised sheep.

ORIGINS

It is common knowledge that certain words indicate where we are from. Northerners use *pail* for a kind of metal container which Midlanders refer to as a *bucket*. *Pits* are inside cherries and peaches of Northerners; *seeds* are found by some Midlanders. It is amusing to some people, furthermore, that as a general rule horses are said to *whinny* or *whinner* in Northern dialect areas, whereas they *nicker* in some of the Midland parts of our country.

Customs are also revealed in our vocabulary. The *county seat* is relatively unknown in rural New England, where local government is handled at the town meeting.

The special names for various ethnic or national groups, whether joking or derogatory, are an indication of the settlement patterns of an area. If a person has the terms *Dago, Kraut*, or *Polack* in his active vocabulary, it is quite likely that he lives among or near Italians, Germans, or Polish people. Sometimes the nickname of a specific immigrant group becomes generalized to include most or all newcomers. Such a case was . . . noted in Summit County, Ohio, where some natives refer to almost all nationality groups as *Hunkies*, regardless of whether or not they come from Hungary. That this practice has been with us for many years is shown in a comment by Theodore Roosevelt that anything foreign was referred to as *Dutch*. One nineteenth century politician even referred to Italian paintings as "Dutch daubs from Italy."[1]

VOCABULARY FIELDWORK

To show some of the ways a speaker's vocabulary may reveal his age, sex, occupation, or regional and cultural origins, let us do a dialect vocabulary project as it might be done by a linguist (called a fieldworker in this case) who interviews people (called informants) for *The Linguistic Atlas*.

The *Atlas* fieldworker gathers his information in face-to-face interviews. He may supplement his interview data, however, with questionnaires such as the one which follows. Sometimes these questionnaires are mailed; sometimes the fieldworker distributes them personally. Whatever method of distribution is used, one thing is certain: The questionnaires have been extremely helpful, reliable, and accurate indications of vocabulary in use.

---

[1] H. L. Mencken, *The American Language*, abridged and revised by Raven I. McDavid, Jr. (New York: Knopf, 1963), p. 371.

A Checklist of Regional Expressions

DIRECTIONS

1. Please put a circle around the word or words in each group which you ordinarily use (don't circle words you have heard—just those you actually use).
2. If the word you ordinarily use is not listed in the group, please write it in the space by the item.
3. If you never use any word in the group, because you never need to refer to the thing described, do not mark the word.

Example:
Center of a peach: pit, seed, (stone,) kernel, heart

HOUSEHOLD

1. *to put a single room of the house in order*: clean up, do up, redd up, ridd up, straighten up, tidy up, put to rights, slick up
2. *paper container for groceries, etc.*: bag, poke, sack, toot
3. *device found on outside of the house or in yard or garden*: faucet, spicket, spigot, hydrant, tap
4. *window covering on rollers*: blinds, curtains, roller shades, shades, window blinds, window shades
5. *large open metal container for scrub water*: pail, bucket
6. *of peas*: to hull, to pod, to shell, to shuck
7. *web hanging from ceiling of a room*: cobweb, dust web, spider's web, web
8. *metal utensil for frying*: creeper, fryer, frying pan, fry pan, skillet, spider
9. *over a sink*: faucet, hydrant, spicket, spigot, tap
10. *overlapping horizontal boards on outside of house*: clapboards, siding, weatherboards, weatherboarding
11. *large porch with roof*: gallery, piazza, porch, portico, stoop, veranda
12. *small porch, often with no roof*: deck, platform, porch, portico, step, steps, stoop, veranda, piazza
13. *devices at edges of roof to carry off rain*: eaves, eaves spouts, eavestroughs, gutters, rain troughs, spouting, spouts, water gutter
14. *rubber or plastic utensil for scraping dough or icing from a mixing bowl*: scraper, spatula, kidcheater, bowl scraper
15. *vehicle for small baby*: baby buggy, baby cab, baby carriage, baby coach
16. *to _____ the baby (in such a vehicle)*: ride, roll, wheel, push, walk, stroll

17. *furry stuff which collects under beds and on closet floors:* dust, bunnies, dust kittens, lint balls, pussies

FAMILY

18. *family word for father:* dad, daddy, father, pa, papa, pappy, paw, pop
19. *family word for mother:* ma, mama, mammy, maw, mom, mommer, mommy, mother
20. *immediate family:* my family, my folks, my parents, my people, my relatives, my relations, my kin, my kinfolks
21. *others related by blood:* my family, my folks, my kind, my kinfolks, my people, my relation, my relatives, my relations, my kin
22. of a child: favors *(his mother),* features, looks like, resembles, takes after, is the spitting image of
23. *of children:* brought up, fetched up, raised, reared
24. *the baby* moves on all fours *across the floor:* crawls, creeps

AUTOMOTIVE

25. *place in front of driver where instruments are:* dash, dashboard, instrument panel, panel, crash panel
26. *automobile device for making the car go faster*: accelerator, gas, gas pedal, pedal, throttle
27. *place where flashlight and maps may be kept*: glove compartment, compartment, shelf, cabinet
28. *automobile with two doors:* tudor, coupe, two-door
29. *the car needs* _____: a grease job, greased, lubrication, a lube job, to be greased, to be lubed, greasing, servicing, to be serviced
30. *large truck with trailer attached:* truck, truck and trailer, semi, rig, trailer-truck

URBAN

31. *new limited access road:* turnpike, toll road, freeway, parkway, pay road, tollway, thruway, expressway
32. *service and eating areas on no. 31:* service stop, service area, oasis, rest area
33. *grass strip in the center of a divided road:* median, center strip, separator, divider, barrier, grass strip, boulevard
34. *place where fire engines are kept:* fire hall, fire house, fire station
35. *place where scheduled airlines operate:* airport, port, terminal, air terminal (by proper name), air field, field

36. *place where train stops:* station, railway station, depot, train stop, train station, railroad station
37. *place where firemen attach hose:* fire hydrant, fire plug, plug, hydrant, water tap
38. *grass strip between sidewalk and street:* berm, boulevard, boulevard strip, parking, parking strip, parkway, sidewalk plot, tree lawn, neutral ground, devil strip, tree bank, city strip
39. *call to hail a taxi:* taxi!, cab!, cabbie!, hack!, hey!, (wave arm), (whistle)
40. *policeman:* cop, policeman, copper, fuzz, dick, officer, bull
41. *the road is:* slick, slippery
42. *place where packaged groceries can be purchased:* grocery store, general store, supermarket, store, delicatessen, grocery, market, food market, food store, supermart
43. *a piece of pavement between two houses on a city block:* gangway, walk, path, sidewalk
44. *place where you watch technicolor features in a car:* drive-in, drive-in movie, outdoor movie, outdoor theater, open-air movie, open-air theater, passion pit

NATURE

45. *animal with strong odor:* polecat, skunk, woodspussy, woodpussy
46. *small, squirrel-like animal that runs along the ground:* chipmunk, grinnie, ground squirrel
47. *worm used for bait in fishing:* angledog, angleworm, bait worm, eace worm, earthworm, eelworm, fish bait, fishing worm, fishworm, mudworm, rainworm, redworm
48. *larger worm:* dew worm, night crawler, night walker, (Georgia) wiggler, town worm
49. *dog of no special kind or breed:* common dog, cur, cur dog, fice, feist, mongrel, no-count, scrub, heinz, sooner, mixed dog, mutt
50. *insect that glows at night:* fire bug, firefly, glow worm, june bug, lightning bug, candle bug
51. *large winged insect seen around water:* darning needle, devil's darning needle, dragon fly, ear-sewer, mosquito hawk, sewing needle, snake doctor, snake feeder, sewing bug
52. *freshwater shellfish with claws; swims backward:* crab, craw, crawdad(die), crawfish, crayfish
53. *center of a cherry:* pit, seed, stone, kernel, heart
54. *center of a peach:* pit, seed, stone, kernel, heart
55. *hard inner cover of a walnut:* hull, husk, shell, shuck
56. *green outer cover of a walnut:* hull, husk, shell, shuck

57. *bunch of trees growing in open country (particularly on a hill):* motte, clump, grove, bluff
58. *web found outdoors:* cobweb, dew web, spider nest, spider's nest, spider web, web
59. *tree that produces sugar and syrup:* hard maple, rock maple, sugar maple, sugar tree, maple tree, candy tree, sweet maple

FOODS

60. *melon with yellow or orange insides:* muskmelon, melon, mush-melon, lope, cantaloup, mussmellon
61. *a spreadable luncheon meat made of liver:* liver sausage, braun-schweiger, liverwurst
62. *a carbonated drink:* pop, soda, soda pop, tonic, soft drink
63. *a glass containing ice cream and root beer:* a float, a root beer float, a black cow, a Boston cooler
64. *dish of cooked fruit eaten at the end of a meal:* fruit, sauce, dessert, compote
65. *peach whose meat sticks to seed:* cling, cling peach, clingstone, clingstone peach, hard peach, plum-peach, press peach
66. *food eaten between regular meals:* a bite, lunch, a piece, piece meal, a snack, a mug-up, munch, nash, nosh
67. *corn served on cob:* corn-on-the-cob, garden corn, green corn, mutton corn, roasting ears, sugar corn, sweet corn
68. *beans eaten in pods:* green beans, sallet beans, snap beans, snaps, string beans, beans
69. *edible tops of turnips, beets, etc:* greens, salad, salat
70. *a white lumpy cheese:* clabber cheese, cottage cheese, curd cheese, curd(s), dutch cheese, home-made cheese, pot cheese, smear-case, cream cheese
71. *round, flat confection with hole in center, made with baking powder:* crull, cruller, doughnut, fatcake, fried cake, cake doughnut, raised doughnut
72. *bread made of corn meal:* cornbread, corn dodger(s), cornpone, hoe cake(s), johnnycake, pone bread
73. *cooked meat juices poured over meat, potatoes, or bread:* gravy, sop, sauce, drippings
74. *ground beef in a bun:* hamburg, hamburger, burger
75. *large sandwich designed to be a meal in itself:* hero, submarine, hoagy, grinder, poor-boy

GAMES

76. *children's cry at halloween time:* trick or treat!, tricks or treats!, beggar's night!, help the poor!, Halloween!, give or receive!
77. *fast moving amusement park ride (on tracks):* coaster, roller coaster, rolly-coaster, shoot-the-chutes, the ride of doom

78. *call to players to return because a new player wants to join:* allie-allie-in-free, allie-allie-oxen free, allie-allie-ocean free, bee-bee bumble bee, everybody in free, newcomer-newcomer!

79. *call to passerby to return a ball to the playground:* little help!, ball!, hey!, yo!, ball up!

80. *to coast on sled lying down flat:* belly-booster, belly-bump, belly-bumper, belly-bunker, belly-bunt, belly-bust, belly buster, belly-down, belly-flop, belly-flopper, belly-grinder, belly-gut, belly-gutter, belly-kachug, belly-kachuck, belly-whack, belly-whop, belly-whopper, belly-slam, belly-smacker

81. *to hit the water when diving:* belly-flop, belly-flopper, belly-bust, belly-buster

82. *to stop a game you call:* time!, time out!, times!, pax!, fins!

SCHOOL

83. *to be absent from school:* bag school, bolt, cook jack, lay out, lie out, play hookey, play truant, run out of school, skip class, skip school, slip off from school, ditch, flick, flake school, blow school

84. *where swings and play areas are:* schoolyard, playground, school ground, yard, grounds

85. *holds small objects together:* rubber band, rubber binder, elastic binder, gum band, elastic band

86. *drinking fountain:* cooler, water cooler, bubbler, fountain, drinking fountain

87. *the amount of books you can carry in both arms:* armful, armload, load, turn

CLOTHING

88. *short knee-length outer garment worn by men:* shorts, bermuda shorts, bermudas, walking shorts, knee (length) pants, pants, knee-knockers

89. *short knee-length outer garment worn by women:* shorts, bermudas, walking shorts, pants

90. *outer garment of a heavy material worn by males as they work:* levis, overalls, dungarees, jeans, blue jeans, pants

91. *garment worn by women at the seashore:* swimsuit, swimming suit, bathing suit

92. *garment worn by men at the seashore:* swimsuit, swimming suit, bathing suit, swimming trunks, trunks, bathing trunks, swimming shorts

MISCELLANEOUS

93. *a time of day:* quarter before eleven, quarter of eleven, quarter till eleven, quarter to eleven, 10:45
94. *someone from the country:* backwoodsman, clodhopper, country gentleman, country jake, countryman, hayseed, hick, hoosier, hillbilly, jackpine savage, mossback, mountain-boomer, pumpkinhusker, railsplitter, cracker, redneck, rube, sharecropper, stump farmer, swamp angel, yahoo, yokel, sodbuster
95. *someone who won't change his mind is:* bull-headed, contrary, headstrong, ornery, otsny, owly, pig-headed, set, sot, stubborn, mulish, muley
96. *when a girl stops seeing a boyfriend she is said to:* give him the air, give him the bounce, give him the cold shoulder, give him the mitten, jilt him, kick him, throw him over, turn him down, shoot him down, give him the gate, brush him off, turn him off, break up with him
97. *become ill:* be taken sick, get sick, take sick, be taken ill, come down
98. *become ill with a cold:* catch a cold, catch cold, get a cold, take cold, take a cold, come down with a cold
99. *sick _____:* at his stomach, in his stomach, on his stomach, to his stomach, of his stomach, with his stomach
100. *I _____ you're right:* reckon, guess, figger, figure, suspect, imagine

The preceding vocabulary questionnaire, frequently called a checklist, is only suggestive of what might be asked for in a particular community. Of the hundred items in ten general fields, you may find some questions more interesting and useful to study than others. Furthermore, you may add other words to this list, or you may find other answers to questions listed here.

Let us suppose, however, that you wish to make a vocabulary survey of your community using this checklist. If your school has ample facilities and supplies, you could reproduce all or part of this questionnaire, distribute it to various neghbors, let them fill it out at their leisure, and then have them return it to you for tabulation and analysis.

One last matter of data must be included, however, if the checklist is to be meaningful. The dialectologist needs to know certain things about the people who fill out the checklists. The following questions should be answered if the data are to be interpreted meaningfully.

Let us look for a moment at the personal data sheet. We note that dialectologists think it important to keep a record of the informant's age, sex, race, education, mobility, travel, ancestry, language skills,

Personal Data Sheet

Sex _____ Race _____

Have you filled out this same   Age _____ Highest grade level

questionnaire before? Yes __ No __ reached in school _____

State _____ County _____ Town _____

How long have you lived here? _____ years

Birthplace _____
               (town)   (state)

Other towns, states, or nations you have lived in (please give
approximate years for each place)

_____
_____
_____

Have you traveled much outside your native state? ____ (Yes or No)
If so, where? _____
_____

Parents' birthplace (state or nation):

Father _____ Grandfather _____

                                      Grandmother _____

Mother _____ Grandfather _____

                                        Grandmother _____

Do you speak any non-English language? ____ If so, which? _____
                                       (yes or no)

Occupation _____

If retired, former occupation _____

If housewife, husband's occupation _____

Name (optional) _____

and occupation. People from the same general area may use different words, and this personal data sheet will help us find out why. In parts of Michigan, for example, the older generation may still use the term *spider* for what younger informants may call *frying pan*. This is an indication of current language change. It is never a surprise to us to hear that our parents' generation did things differently. Nor should we be surprised to note that they use different words.

There are any number of things you may be able to discover by making a vocabulary survey in your community. What you should remember as you gather your data is the principle of constants and variables, a principle familiar to you, no doubt, from mathematics. You may gather your data in any way you wish, but chances are you will not be able to get a representation of all ages, ethnic groups, religions, and occupations of the people in your area, especially if you live in an urban community. A somewhat narrower approach would be easier and more successful, for example:

1. *Age Contrast:* Collect checklists from three or four people who have lived all their lives in your community. This gives you two constants: the checklist and the native born residents. The most interesting variables will be their age and education along with, of course, their answers. If you select older people and younger people of roughly the same education and social status, chances are that any vocabulary differences will stem from the contrast in ages.

2. *Education Contrast:* Collect checklists from three or four people who have different educational backgrounds. College graduates, for example, may be contrasted with people who have had less than a high school education. If your informants are of roughly the same age, and if their personal data sheets are otherwise similar, the differences which you note may be attributable to their contrasting educations.

3. *Describe the Local Dialect Area:* Collect checklists from three or four people who have lived all their lives in your community. Try to get older, middle-aged, and younger people who have educational backgrounds characteristic of your community (in some parts of our country, for example, college graduates are simply not frequently found). Then note the responses of these informants to some or all of the following questions: 1, 2, 3, 5, 8, 9, 10, 13, 24, 45, 46, 47, 50, 51, 53, 54, 64, 67, 69, 70, 71, 72, 87, 93, 97, 98, 99. For each of these questions there is a response which research has shown to be characteristic of one side of the dialect map (of course, the term may be used elsewhere, too, but not as generally). The following chart will indicate some of the words you may expect to find *in certain parts* of the Northern, Midland, and Southern dialect areas:

Word	Northern	Midland	Southern
1. *to put room in order:*		redd up ridd up	
2. *paper container:*	bag	sack	sack
3. *on outside of house:*	faucet	spigot spicket hydrant	spigot spicket hydrant
5. *container:*	pail	bucket	bucket
8. *metal utensil:* (frying pan common everywhere)	spider	skillet	skillet spider
9. *over a sink:*	faucet	spigot spicket	spigot spicket
10. *boards:* (siding common everywhere)	clapboards	weatherboards	

Word	Northern	Midland	Southern
13. *devices at roof:*	gutters (ENE) eaves spouts eavestroughs	gutters spouting spouts	gutters
24. *baby moves:*	creeps	crawls	crawls
45. *animal:*	skunk	skunk polecat woodspussy woodpussy	polecat
46. *animal:* (note: for some people, chipmunk and ground squirrel are two different animals)	chipmunk	ground squirrel	ground squirrel
47. *worm:*	angleworm	fish(ing) worm	fish(ing) worm
50. *insect:*	firefly (urban) lightning bug (rural)	lightning bug fire bug	lightning bug
51. *insect:*	(devil's) darning needle sewing bug dragon fly	snake feeder snake doctor dragon fly	snake feeder snake doctor dragon fly mosquito hawk
53. *cherry:*	pit stone	seed stone	seed stone
54. *peach:*	pit stone	seed stone	seed stone
64. *dish:*	dessert sauce fruit	dessert fruit	dessert fruit
67. *corn:*	corn-on-the-cob green corn sweet corn	corn-on-the-cob sweet corn roasting ears	roasting ears sweet corn
69. *tops:*		greens	greens salad salat
70. *cheese:* (cottage cheese common everywhere)	dutch cheese pot cheese	smear-case	clabber cheese curds
71. *confection:*	doughnut fried cake	doughnut	doughnut
72. *bread:*	johnnycake corn bread	corn bread	corn bread corn pone
87. *to carry:*	armful	armload	armload
93. *quarter—:*	to of	till	till to
97. *become ill:*	get sick	take sick	take sick
98. *with a cold:*	catch a cold	take a cold	take a cold
99. *sick—:* (at his stomach common everywhere)	to his stomach	on his stomach in his stomach	

Many of the suggested checklist items have not been surveyed nationally (the automotive terms, for example), and so we cannot show their regional distributions. This should not prevent you from checking them in your own community to discover what term is characteristic there.

4. *Contrast Regional Dialects:* Have two natives of your area and two newcomers from other parts of the country fill out all or part of the checklist. Note the contrasts which are evidence of geographical differences. Your conclusions will be more certain if your informants are roughly the same age and have roughly the same educational background. This will help rule out age or education as the cause of the vocabulary difference.

Differences in Grammar

In addition to pronunciation and vocabulary differences in dialects, there are differences which involve matters of grammar. In grammar we include such things as past tenses of verbs, plural nouns, and word order (syntax) patterns. For example, many people use *dived* as the past tense of the verb *dive*. Others use *dove*. Still others use both forms. Likewise, some people say *this is as far as I go*. Others habitually say *this is all the farther I go*. These forms are used by educated and respectable people, and their English is considered equally educated and respectable. If one or two of the above examples sound strange or wrong to you, then you are probably living in an area which uses the alternative form. This does not mean that your way is better or worse—only that it is different.

On the other hand, some variants of grammatical items are used by relatively uneducated people. For the past tense of *dive* they might use the forms *duv* or *div*. For the distance statement they might say *this is the furtherest I go* or *this is the fartherest I go*.

Thus we can see that grammatical items may indicate place of origin or social level. Table 1 shows how people in two theoretical areas differ internally, because of social class, and externally, because of

Area X		Area Y	
Speaker	*Grammatical Item Used*	*Speaker*	*Grammatical Item Used*
higher social status	dove	higher social status	dived
middle social status	dove	middle social status	dived
lower social status	dove, duv	lower social status	dived, div

Table 1

where they live. Contrary to what some people think, even people of higher social classes do not make the same grammatical choices in different parts of our country. Well-educated natives of Wisconsin tend to say *dove;* their counterparts from Kentucky favor *dived.*

For determining social levels, grammatical choices are as important as pronunciation and vocabulary choices. Regional distributions of grammatical choice, however, are not as clearly marked as other differences. Of particular interest to American fieldworkers are the following items.[2]

1. *Prepositions*
    Trouble comes all _____ once. (to = N, at)
    It's half _____ six. (past, after)
    It's quarter _____four. (of, to = N, till = M, before, until)
    It's _____the door. (behind, hindside, in back of, back of)
    He isn't _____. (at home, to home, home)
    It's coming right _____you. (at , toward, towards)
    Guess who I ran _____. (into, onto, up against, upon, up with, against, again, afoul of = NE, across)
    They named the baby _____ him. (after, for, at, from)
    I fell _____the horse. (off, off of, offen, off from, from)
    I wonder what he died _____. (of, with, from, for)
    He's sick _____his stomach. (to = N, at = M, S, of, on = M, in = M, with)
    He came over _____tell me. (to, for to = SM, S, for = S)
    I want this _____of that. (instead, stead, in room, in place)
    We're waiting _____John. (on = M, for)
    The old man passed _____. (away, on, out, ϕ)
    He did it _____purpose. (on, a, for, ϕ)
    I want _____the bus. (off = M, to get off)
    He was _____(singing, a-singing) and _____. (laughing, a-laughing)
    How big _____(a, of a) house is it?
2. *Matters of agreement*
    Here _____your pencils. (is, are)
    The oats _____thrashed. (is = M, are = N)
    These cabbages _____(is, are) for sale.
3. *Plural formations*
    I have two _____of shoes. (pair = N, S, pairs = M)
    They had forty _____of apples. (bushel = N, bushels = M)
    He has two _____of butter. (pound = S, pounds = M)

---

[2] Whenever ϕ appears, it signifies that nothing is added to the statement. N stands for Northern, M for Midland, NM for North Midland, S for Southern, SM for South Midland, and NE for New England.

The fence has twenty _____. (posts, post, postis, poss)

He likes to play _____. (horseshoe, horseshoes)

Put your feet in the _____. (stirrup, stirrups)

Let's spray for _____. (moth, moths, mothis)

I bought two _____ of lettuce. (head, heads)

That's a long _____. (way = N, ways = M)

That's a short _____. (way = N, ways = M)

It's nine _____ high. (foot, feet)

We have three _____. (desks, desk, deskis, desses, dess)

4. *Pronouns*

It wasn't _____. (me, I)

This is _____. (yours, yourn)

This is _____. (theirs, theirn)

Are _____ (pl.) coming over? (you, youse, yuz, youns, you-all)

_____ boys are all bad. (those, them, them there)

He's the man _____ owns the car. (that, who, what, which, as, ɸ)

He's the boy _____ father is rich. (whose, that his, that the, his)

"I'm not going!" " _____." (Me either, Me neither, Neither am I, Nor I either, Nor I neither)

It is _____. (I, me)

It is _____. (he, him)

He's going to do it _____. (himself, hisself)

Let them do it _____. (themselves, themself, theirselves, theirself)

I'll go with _____. (ɸ, you)

5. *Adjectives*

The oranges are all _____. (ɸ, gone)

Some berries are _____. (poison, poisonous)

6. *Adverbs*

You can find these almost _____. (anywhere, anywheres, anyplace)

This is _____ I go. (as far as, as fur as, all the farther, all the further, the farthest, the furthest, the fartherest, the furtherest)

7. *Conjunctions*

It seems _____ we'll never win. (as though, like, as if)

I won't go _____ he does. (unless, without, lessen, thouten, douten, less, else)

I like him _____ he's funny. (because, cause, on account of, count, owing to)

Do this _____ I eat lunch. (while, whiles, whilst)

This is not _____ long as that one. (as, so)

8. *Articles*

John is _____university. (in, in the)

She is _____hospital. (in, in the)

I have _____apple. (a, an)

John has _____. (flu, the flu)

Do you have _____? (mumps, the mumps)

9. *Verbs*

Past tense forms:	began, begun, begin
	blew, blowed
	climbed, clim (N), clum (M)
	came, come, comed
	could, might could (SM, S)
	dived, dove (N)
	drank, drunk, drinked
	did, done
	drowned, drownded
	ate, et, eat
	gave, give (M)
	grew, growed
	learned, learnt, larnt, larnd
	lay, laid
	rode, rid
	ran, run
	saw, seen (M), seed (M), see (N)
	sat, set
	spoiled, spoilt
	swam, swim
	threw, throwed
	wore, weared
	wrote, writ
Past participles:	tore up, torn up
	wore out, worn out
	rode (M), ridden
	drank, drunk
	bit, bitten
Negative:	hadn't ought (N), ought not, oughtn't, didn't ought

Some of the preceding grammatical choices may seem appropriate to you; others may appear to be undesirable. But in unguarded moments you may find yourself using more than one of the choices. What is particularly interesting to linguists is the fact that many forces contribute to our shift from one variant to another.

GRAMMAR FIELDWORK

People tend to be much more self-conscious about their use of verb forms, prepositions, pronouns, and so on, than they are about their vocabulary or pronunciation. Consequently, no simple checklist will be given here. However, you can observe the above items in the casual conversations of your acquaintances, in the speech of television actors (especially those who portray Westerners, hillbillies, blue collar urbanites, farmers, well-heeled tycoons, and other special "types"), in the dialogue of novels or short stories, and in the speech of out-of-staters who have recently moved to your community. You must remember, however, that people are very sensitive about their grammar. The good fieldworker is tactful and objective. He does not ridicule the grammar of other areas or other social levels; in fact, he does not even seem to be especially interested in the grammar of his subject's responses. Much of the time he contents himself with getting details of grammar in conversation, without direct questioning.

FOR DISCUSSION AND REVIEW

1. As Shuy states, "That people speak different dialects in no way stems from their intelligence or judgment. They speak the dialect which enables them to get along with the other members of their social and geographical group." Despite this fact, many people consider dialects different from their own as "funny sounding," "strange," or even "wrong"—and these feelings about language are often transferred to the speakers of the different dialects. Drawing on your own experiences and attitudes, discuss the situation described above. For example, what are its implications for a family moving from, say, the South to New England?

2. Roberts describes two *types* of pronunciation differences. What are they, and how do they differ? Try to add to his lists of examples.

3. After reviewing the phonetic symbols provided by Callary (in "Phonetics," Part Four), carefully transcribe your pronunciation of each of the following words. Discuss any differences between your transcriptions and those of other members of the class.

a. calm   f. judgment
b. water   g. cushion
c. horse   h. roof
d. hoarse   i. parking
e. wharfs   j. scent

4. Discuss, using your own specific examples, how vocabulary can reveal facts about a person's age, sex, education, occupation, and geographical and cultural origins.

5. Complete the vocabulary questionnaire. Compare your responses with those of other members of the class and with those provided in the

article. Are the responses patterned? How do you account for any deviations from the patterns?

6. What is the importance of a "Personal Data Sheet" to a dialectologist?

7. Roberts states that "For determining social levels, grammatical choices are as important as pronunciation and vocabulary choices." Give three examples from your own experience that support or refute his assertion—that is, explain how grammatical constructions used by people, perhaps when you first met them, affected your opinion of them.

8. Why does Shuy believe that a checklist or questionnaire is inappropriate as the only means for determining the grammatical choices of informants? What are the alternatives to a direct questionnaire?

4/A Researcher's Guide to the Sociolinguistic Variable (ING)

BENJI WALD AND TIMOTHY SHOPEN

We turn now to social dialectology, the investigation of the relationships between social class and language variety. As W. Nelson Francis writes, "sociolinguistic dialectologists are primarily interested in language variation as a correlate or indicator of social variation and as a source of language change. . . . the focus shifts from the language itself to the people who use the language, their social orientation and contrasts." In the following selection, Benji Wald and Timothy Shopen illustrate the use of linguistic variables and of the kind of quantitative methods that William Labov introduced. Wald and Shopen focus on the linguistic variable (ING) and its two principal norms, -ing, referred to as G, and -in', referred to as N, and attempt to explain when and why people choose a particular variant. The two groups studied were native speakers of Australian English in Canberra and native speakers of American English in Los Angeles. In both studies, the research was carried out by students in introductory sociolinguistics courses. The findings of the studies are interesting, as are Wald and Shopen's suggestions for a number of small research projects that could readily be carried out by individual students or classes. Note that the authors, both social dialectologists, rely on population-sampling techniques, analyze their data statistically, and often report their results using many tables, graphs, and charts. In a part of the selection not reprinted here, the authors trace the historical development of (ING), making clear that "it is entirely a social matter which norm gains sway in a linguistic variable."*

This chapter [is] for readers who would like to do sociolinguistic research. [It is] also for those who might like to know something of the

* *Dialectology: An Introduction* New York: Longman, 1983, p. 193.
Thanks to Mike Heany for aid on the statistics in this chapter and to Mike, Frank Anshen, David Bradley, Bob Dixon, John Haviland, and Anna Wierzbicka for helpful comments.

interplay between data and theory in this kind of investigation, even if for the moment they only want to see how others do it.

To readers of English, the sociolinguistic variable (ING) is familiar in the spellings -ing and, in the representations of casual speech, -in'. It is one of our most widespread variables. Most, if not all, speakers display it (even if they do not want to own up to it), saying talking and nothing on some occasions and talkin' and nothin' on others. . . . [Here the authors provide an explanation of the historical development of -ing from Old English -unge and of -in' from either -ing or OE -inde.]

We find (ING) in our own social stereotypes and while their accuracy is not guaranteed, such stereotypes can demonstrate the values a community places on variant kinds of behavior. A good place to find them is in literature, especially comic strips. Hank Ketcham represents the preadolescent Dennis (the Menace) as always using -in', and his mother as always using -ing. The implication is that Dennis's use of -in' is "boyish" and socially immature. His friend Margaret's use of -ing is in character with her stereotype as a precocious little girl. Another instance is the invariant use of -in' by Reg Smythe's cockney characters, Andy Capp and his wife, with -in' as a part of a popular image of the British working class; outside Britain, the presence of -in' in this comic strip seems readily understood as symbolizing a lack of education and/or low job prestige.

The (ING) variable occupies a notable position in sociolinguistic studies: it was the first to be studied quantitatively in speech. In a study published in 1958, Fischer observed that preadolescent schoolchildren in a small New England town used both -ing and -in', but that females tended to use -ing more often than males; in addition, a "model" boy (well-behaved, school-oriented) used -ing more often than a "typical" boy, and changed the frequency of -ing to accord with different social situations. This frequency was highest in a test situation comparable to formal classroom recitation: the boy used -ing thirty-eight times and -in' once; on the other hand, in answers to questions read by the investigator from a questionnaire, he used -ing thirty-three times and -in' thirty-five times, and in a more relaxed interview the count was twenty-four for -ing and forty-one for -in'. Fischer also noted that for markedly "formal" words, he tended to use -ing and for markedly "informal" ones -in'. This same boy used -ing in criticizing, correcting, reading, visiting, and interesting, but -in' in punchin', flubbin', swimmin', chewin' and hittin', while for some common verbs such as play, go, and do, he alternated between -ing and -in'.[1]

Fischer's main observations have been replicated in studies elsewhere, all confirming that (ING) is sensitive to situations, the stylistic properties of words, and the social identity of speakers.

---

[1] J. L. Fischer, "Social Influences in the Choice of a Linguistic Variant," Word 14(1958):47–56.

The authors have both conducted research on (ING) with introductory sociolinguistics classes, first Wald in Los Angeles and then Shopen in Canberra, Australia.[2] The comparison of our results shows how linguistic variables can provide a useful index to social structures in different communities. In particular, our results with (ING) imply that Canberra is more conservative than Los Angeles in respect to the status and behavior of women. This kind of research is an excellent teaching instrument. It requires a minimum of apparatus (ears, pencil, and paper), and we suspect that it would be a feasible and revealing project for students in virtually any English-speaking community in the world.

In this chapter, we will first consider some concepts fundamental to the notion of (ING) as a sociolinguistic variable, and then we will proceed to the research project. In our conclusion, we will discuss the significance of the fact that -ing and -in' are both well entrenched and have long been in competition, a conflict many speakers may actually have encouraged.

Sociolinguistic Variables

LINGUISTIC NORMS

A linguistic norm is any linguistic feature that occurs regularly in the speech of more than one speaker in a community. It can be phonological, morphological, lexical, or syntactic. The spellings -ing and -in' represent two distinct linguistic norms; their decisive characteristics are phonological, but their choice is sensitive to several aspects of morphology and the lexicon.

In most dialects of English, the -ing norm is pronounced [iŋ], and its most important characteristic is the *velarity* of the final nasal, i.e. that the place of contact for the tongue is *velar*. We articulate velar consonants by raising the back of the tongue to the velum (soft palate), as in [ŋ], [k], or [g]. The -in' norm is pronounced in a variety of ways, all of which amount to closing the airstream through the mouth farther forward than for -ing, usually with an *alveolar* closure, with the tongue touching the gum ridge just behind the upper teeth, as in [n], [t], or [d]. The nasal may either stand by itself as a syllable, as in [kətn̩] for *cuttin'*, or follow a reduced central vowel, as in [rābən] for *robbin'*. There is also more extreme reduction, as in *some'm* [səmʔm] for *something*, with a glottal stop [ʔ] between two [m] sounds. We will refer to the

[2] T. Shopen, "Research on the Variable (ING) in Canberra, Australia," *Talanya* 5(1978):42–52.

Norm	Traditional Orthography	Phonetic Notation	Distinctive Feature
G	-ing	[iŋ]	Velar
N	-in'	[ən], etc.	Reduction, usually alveolar

-ing norm as G, a reminder of its velarity, and the -in' norm, in all its reduced variants, as N.[3]

LINGUISTIC VARIABLES

A linguistic variable is any linguistic unit realized by more than one norm. The test for a variable is that one norm can be substituted for another without any change in *meaning* (without any change in the semantic representation for utterances). One can, for example, say "He's working" with the pronunciation [wərkiŋ], and that sentence will mean the same as if one had said "He's workin'," with [wərkən]: it would in that sense be the same sentence. Since this would be true wherever this verb form was used, [wərkiŋ] and [wərkən] are variable realizations for the same word. Identical variation occurs in the articulation of many English words spelled -*ing*. In the range of pronunciations, what speakers regard as crucial is the presence or absence of *velarity*. From this we abstract the notion of the G and N norms and the (ING) variable.

Much work on linguistic variables depends on the unifying notion "same truth value"; that is, we justify including G and N in the same variable because we note "He's working" is true if and only if "He's workin'" is true. But only statements can be said to be true or false, and we are equally interested in other kinds of speech acts, including questions, commands, greetings, and insults: questions such as "Where are you going?", commands such as "Start walking!", greetings such as "Good morning," and insults such as "You blooming idiot!" We should also add "performative" sentences, a special kind

[3] Of the 1660 instances of (ING) in the Canberra study, 16 pronunciations were reported as [iŋk]. We had -INK on the research form along with -ING and -IN and were prepared to count it as a third norm, but so few instances of it were reported that we felt no valid judgments were possible on its social distribution or stylistic value and included the 16 in the total for -ING, 1332. These 16 were produced by three women and four men, 14 in the words *something, nothing,* and *anything,* and the remaining 2 in *hoping* and *going.* -INK would appear worth studying in its own right in Australia, if only because non-linguists find it noteworthy and report it. This pronunciation is also reported for native speakers in the British Isles. Wyld, writing in 1920 declared "Among very vulgar speakers—not in London alone—we sometimes hear *nothink* for *nothing* at the present time. . . ."

of statement that itself performs an action and does not have truth value, such as "I now declare this meeting closed." All these can have the relevant kind of variation, and can be studied appropriately under the notion "same meaning."

Now we should give careful scrutiny to the linguistic contexts that favor the variation of the (ING) variable. Note that G and N are interchangeable in *eating* and *something*, but not in *singer*, *sing*, or *Peking*, in which the syllable ending in *ing* is stressed. In these words a G pronunciation is invariant, so we cannot say they have the (ING) variable. It is essential to *exclude* contexts in which only one norm occurs. Thus we exclude:

(1) *Contexts which are not completely unstressed.* The word *thing*, made up of one stressed syllable, allows only the G norm. Compare *something*, *nothing*, and *anything* where *thing* occurs unstressed and allows both the G and N pronunciations. The word *Peking* illustrates that the syllable in question must be completely unstressed to accommodate the variation of (ING). Either syllable of *Peking* may receive primary stress, but even when the primary stress falls on the first syllable, the second one receives a reduced stress. The part of the word spelled *ing* is never fully unstressed, and we can infer that it is because of this that it is pronounced with just the G norm. Interestingly, there is an older variant *Pekin*, not in current use but found in the adjective *Pekinese*.

We also exclude:

(2) *De facto invariance.* This is any case which might appear to have the variation of (ING), but which was invariant in actual use with either the G or the N norm 100 percent of the time. One such case might be *gonna* [gənə] or *goin' ta* [gəntə] as pronunciation of the future auxiliary verb, as in "gonna leave." In some communities people never say things like "going to leave," or "going to eat" with a G pronunciation for the "going"; they always give one of the reduced pronunciations. This was the situation in Los Angeles and so Wald excluded this expression from his research. In Canberra, Shopen found some variation in the everyday use of this expression and so included it in his research. It favored the reduced pronunciation, but because there were some unreduced pronunciations, it was a part of variable behavior, and he counted the *gonna* and *goin' ta* pronunciations as N, the *going to* pronunciations as G.

There are other linguistic factors that are a part of variable behavior but show a *tendency* to influence the variable. Verbs tend to allow N more than nouns: for instance, *runnin'* is more likely than *ceilin'*. As

Fischer pointed out, everyday words of frequent use are more tolerant of N than learned specialized words: for example, *talkin'* is far more likely than *communicatin'*. Consider if one of these is easier to say than the other:

> He's givin' $10 to the Red Cross.
> He's donatin' $10 to the Red Cross.

Compare the stylistically neutral verb *moving* with the word derived from it in "That was a very moving speech" or "The prayer was even more moving than the sermon." This *moving* is an adjective. Its form is identical to the verb, but its meaning is narrowed to just one, the one in "The poem moved us" and not in "They moved the refrigerator." Because it has a "lofty" stylistic value, we tend to use it to describe art works, ceremonies, or love scenes more than motor repairs, auctions, or hockey matches. N turns out to be a good test against formality, elegance, and loftiness. The reader can confirm this by trying the following sentences with an N pronunciation each time:

> We're movin' out on Saturday.
> He composed a movin' epitaph for the slain hero.
> John and Bill are movin' the table over to our house.
> The concerto for flute and harp was especially movin'.

The comfort or discomfort one feels in consciously pronouncing N here reflects the different tendencies for N in everyday usage. Though the adjective will have an occasional N, the N/G ratio will be higher for the verb than the adjective. The adverb *movingly*, derived from the adjective, appears even more high-flown and resistant to N (try "It was a movin'ly delivered address"). How much the verb accommodates N seems surely to depend on its particular usage or meaning: instead of the sentences above, try N on the verb in "Her new symphony is moving the audience to tears." Ultimately, it is the full message of the speech act and intention of the speaker that most influences the style, the choice of words, and the choice of variant norms for their pronunciation. Even with its common meaning, the verb *moving* will be less likely to carry N if it is involved in a "lofty" message; but just because it carries that common meaning, it will often be involved in the kind of speech event where N is tolerated and indeed encouraged. Such observations are important because they tell us about factors inherent to individual words that influence variation and linguistic change. Little detailed research of this sort has been done on (ING) in present-day English.

Bona fide cases of (ING) occur only in unstressed syllables. Such syllables with (ING) are almost always *word final;* words such as *movingly* and *interestingly* are infrequent exceptions.[4] An unstressed syllable occurs only in words more than one syllable long, and words of one syllable are always stressed, e.g., *thing, ring, wing, king;* these words are never pronounced with N, and so do not express the (ING) variable. We can sum up: whenever G occurs in an unstressed syllable, you can expect N to occur at least sometimes; look for this variation at the end of words of two or more syllables. N is most likely to occur in everyday words and in some parts of speech more than others—especially in verbs such as *laughing, running, cooking, putting, studying, listening, borrowing, bothering,* and *establishing.* The next most likely hosts for N are the three pronouns *something, nothing,* and *anything.* Then there are nouns and adjectives that usually but not always derive from verbs, nouns such as *morning, railing, ceiling, writing, mining, boxing,* and *traveling,* and adjectives such as *boring, tiring, interesting,* and *exciting.*

One can find (ING) in virtually any English-speaking community, but its particular manifestation can vary. We have noted the different status of *going to,* a part of the variable in Canberra but not in Los Angeles; and in Canberra there is an -INK pronunciation, particularly in the words *something, nothing,* and *anything,* that appears to have a life of its own (see footnote 3). Researchers in other communities should be prepared to recognize special local features and take them into account in their research design.

SOCIOLINGUISTIC VARIABLES

A sociolinguistic variable is a linguistic variable sensitive to social context. We know we have a sociolinguistic variable when some feature of a social group or social situation allows us to predict which norms will be used from a variable. This is a phenomenon that gives us insight into both language and social structure.

Our task is to understand the linguistic inventories available to a conversation and how speakers choose among the variable norms. To do this, we look for the social characteristics that influence language behavior, characteristics of speakers and listeners, and situations and topics, as well as historical factors that might explain changes in lin-

---

[4] We suspect that the *-ly* suffix tends to resist N stylistically in all its occurrences. While we believe N *can* occur here, for instance, *borin'ly* for *boringly* in "He always makes his stories too long and he tells them borin'ly," it is not a place where much variation will occur. Quite apart from that, there is great advantage in the method of research if you set out to look for (ING) only at the ends of words. It is easier to hear. It is a small compromise that we made in our research projects, and it did much to make the observations more feasible.

guistic standards—whatever motivates people toward opposing linguistic variants.[5]

Consider the use of two languages in the same community. This is a choice between two sets of norms organized into distinct linguistic systems. There are communities where teenagers talk to each other in one language and to their parents in another. The topics they communicate about in the two languages vary; nevertheless, the great majority of meanings they express in one language they could express in the other, and that means that when they discuss most topics they can choose which language to use. The choices they make portend much for the future of the communities. In a report on a Puerto Rican community in New York City in the early 1970s, Wolfram describes how adolescents speak to their parents in Spanish but to their friends in English, even in some cases where the parents understand English and the peers Spanish. He notes that social forces operate so strongly that many parents insist on the use of Spanish, while peers may ridicule its use and demand English.[6] Similarly, Swahili is commonly used by Miji Kenda youth in urban coastal Kenya, but they report that their elders require them to use the home language, or risk being accused of disrespect or lack of ability in their cultural heritage.[7]

Bilingual systems that divide generations tend to be unstable. The language more prestigious among the young usually gains ground as that generation grows older, while the language favored by their parents fades away. In other situations two languages, or two varieties of

[5] To illuminate the theory and substance of sociolinguistic variables in a way ideal for students at the early stages of an introductory course on language and culture, sociolinguistics, English grammar, or style, we recommend a research project we learned about from the anthropologist Joel Sherzer. In situations where you have heard perfectly well what your interlocutors have said, ask them to repeat ("Huh?" "What's that?" "Would you say that again?"). If there is a difference between the initial utterance and the repetition, jot down as soon as possible the two versions, and brief notes on the social identity of the people involved in the speech event, their relationship to each other, the setting, the subject of the conversation, the apparent intention of the speaker, and anything else that might help explain the variation. When researchers have each recorded variation from a minimum of say twenty speakers, they write a report organizing their data and discussing the main tendencies. The teacher in turn gives a lecture based on all the observations by the class, using their data to illustrate concepts such as "variable, standard, stylistic level, hypercorrection, presupposition," etc., and pointing out the speech variation in the community that appears to have the greatest social significance.

When someone asks them to repeat something, speakers usually think there may have been something defective about the way they said it the first time. From this we have found two main tendencies: they can think the first version may have lacked *clarity*—presupposed too much common knowledge, or was inaccurate or too subtle—and they add more information, change to what they deem more accurate terms, or make a stronger statement. But at least as often they think they may have lacked *etiquette*, and then they shift to norms they consider more formal or more standard.

[6] W. Wolfram, *Sociolinguistic Aspects of Assimilation: Puerto Rican English in New York City* (Washington, D.C.: Center for Applied Linguistics, 1974).

[7] B. Wald, "Bilingualism," in B. Siegel, ed., *Annual Review of Anthropology*, 3(1974):301–21.

the same language, may be used in complementary social situations. In this case, the opposition tends to be more stable: the young may not command the same range of expressive forms as their parents, but they grow into them because they need them to fully participate in their culture. In the situation Ferguson calls *diglossia*, two varieties of a language, labeled "high" and "low," are used in complementary social situations.[8] Most norms are shared by the two varieties of the language, while smaller differences set them apart. The high variety of Greek (Katharevousa) refers to "water" as *idhór*, while the low variety (Dhimotiki) uses *néro*. The choice is a sensitive index to social situations. Katharevousa tends to be used on public, sometimes ceremonial occasions such as addresses through the mass media, while Dhimotiki tends to be used for private or intimate occasions such as conversations among friends.

Brown and Gilman discuss the variables to the second-person singular ("you" said to one person) in French, Italian, and German.[9] They conclude that the choice between the T and V forms (e.g., *tu* and *vous* in French) is predictable according to the relative status of the speakers, particularly whether they are equal or unequal in power and/or solidarity. Ervin-Tripp has done a similar study on terms of address in English asking under what circumstances a person is addressed by his first name, or by a title such as "mister" or "doctor."[10]

Sociolinguistic research usually uses well-recognized labels for participants in conversations, identifying speakers and listeners by sex, age, ethnic background, and socioeconomic status. Advances in sociolinguistics depend greatly on general social theory and its ability to offer an empirically supported and well-articulated view of the structure of society, one of the important sources of empirical support being linguistic data. But the linguistic data itself can also suggest lines of demarcation for social categories that might have been previously unsuspected. A study done by an undergraduate student at the Australian National University found an opposition between adult men under fifty on the one hand, and another group that consisted of both adult women and men fifty and over. The study concerned expressions for time. The men under fifty consistently used expressions for time that revealed a clock-governed perspective, while the other group used expressions that revealed a more intuitive and clock-free notion of time. This gives us a basis for saying that men fifty and over belong to a

[8] C. A. Ferguson, "Diglossia," *Word* 15:325–50.

[9] R. Brown and J. Gilman, "The Pronouns of Power and Solidarity," in T. A. Sebeok, ed., *Style in Language* (Cambridge, Mass.: The MIT Press, 1960), pp. 253–76. Reprinted in P. P. Giglioli, *Language and Social Context* (Baltimore: Penguin Books, 1972), pp. 252–82.

[10] S. Ervin-Tripp, "On Sociolinguistic Rules: Alternation and Co-occurrence," in J. J. Gumperz and D. Hymes, eds., *Directions in Sociolinguistics* (New York: Holt, Rinehart and Winston, 1972), pp. 213–50.

distinct social category from men under fifty, one which is likely to involve additional cultural traits besides time expressions, and one sharing at least some characteristics with adult women.[11]

As a phonological variable (ING) occurs in the pronunciation of many words and so pervades conversations in a wide range of social situations. It is sensitive to social groups and social situations, but as with many variables, we cannot make *absolute* predictions about which norm will be used in a given utterance. It has *inherent* variability that is embedded in the social context.

It is in this light that the notion of relative frequency has taken on such importance. In his study of English spoken in New York City, Labov demonstrated that the higher the socioeconomic class of the speaker, the more frequent the use of G. He showed further that different speakers in a community used different absolute frequencies of G but varied their frequency *in the same direction* according to the social situation: G was favored in spontaneous but guarded speech to a stranger-interviewer and less favored the more the speaker was involved in what he was saying.[12] These findings recurred in Trudgill's study of members of the Norwich community in the East Anglia area of England.[13]

In his work on sociolinguistic variation, Labov has contributed much to the theory of linguistic change, particularly on the workings of *linguistic change in progress*. Linguists have not always admitted that one could observe linguistic change in progress. In 1885 Schuchardt published a number of astute observations on sound change, arguing, as we would, that sound change spreads gradually through a language and through its community of speakers, with some vocabulary and some social contexts accommodating the new norms more than others. But his views were in direct opposition to those of a then more influential group, the *Junggrammatiker* (Neogrammarians), who held that sound changes were imperceptible, mechanical, and exceptionless.[14]

Even in 1933 the great Leonard Bloomfield wrote, "The process of linguistic change has never been directly observed; we shall see that such observation, with our present facilities, is inconceivable." He viewed sound change as a gradual replacement, by small steps, of

---

[11] A. Hazelwood, "Have You Got the Time?" Department of Linguistics, SGS, Australian National University, 1976.

[12] William Labov, *The Social Stratification of English in New York City* (Washington, D.C.: Center for Applied Linguistics, 1966). See also Labov, *Sociolinguistic Patterns* (Philadelphia: University of Pennsylvania Press, 1972).

[13] P. Trudgill, "The Social Stratification of English in Norwich:" (Cambridge: Cambridge University Press, 1974).

[14] Schuchardt's essay can be found in the original German and in English translation along with relevant essays by Wilbur and Vennemann, in T. Vennemann and T. H. Wilbur, *Schuchardt, the Neogrammarians, and the Transformational Theory of Phonological Change*, Linguistische Forschungen, Band 26 (Frankfurt: Athenäum Verlag, 1972).

certain phonetic features over others.[15] In his presidential address to the Linguistics Society of America in 1964, Charles F. Hockett expressed similar views.[16]

But recent work has demonstrated that sound change *can* be perceived in progress, with competing variants existing side by side in the same community, sometimes in the behavior of individual speakers. However little they can describe the variants, speakers often hear the differences, and the social values they place on opposing variants is a major influence on sound change. . . .

It may be that someday the opposition in (ING) will resolve itself. We can imagine a situation where the new norm has triumphed, while the few scattered G pronunciations that remain are viewed as quaint vestiges of the past. Spelling reformers might then demand that the modern character of the language be recognized and give us *nothin*, *negotiatin*, *talkin*, and *communicatin*. But we cannot know how or when—or even whether—the opposition will end. Both norms have had ups and downs: right now, G and N each have well-entrenched positions; in this sense (ING) is a stable variable.

Linguistic change has three phases: (1) a new norm appears, (2) the new and the old norm compete, and, if the change goes through, (3) the new norm displaces the old. (ING) is in a prolonged and stable phase (2). It provides a good opportunity to learn about this aspect of language because the variation (the competition) is so widespread in the speech of most native speakers. It is a typical situation: speakers tend to accord prestige to the older norm and view it as the only "correct" one (though N carried prestige among sections of the British aristocracy when the process of change might have been completed, but wasn't). Speakers tend to view the new norm as more casual and more intimate: some words accommodate it more easily than others. Some social gatherings welcome it while others resist it; speakers control the formality of their language as they play out different social roles.

Research on (ING)

THE PEOPLE AND THE CATEGORIES

The researchers who cooperated in our studies were students in introductory sociolinguistics classes, and we defined our projects so as to be feasible for them, people with good energy and motivation but no previous experience in sociolinguistic research. In Los Angeles, the population studied consisted entirely of speakers residing in and

---

[15] L. Bloomfield, *Language* (New York: Holt, Rinehart and Winston, 1933), p. 347.
[16] C. F. Hockett, "Sound Change," *Language*, 41, no. 2 (1965): 185–204.

usually native to Los Angeles, generally of middle-class status, and in contact with the students through work, family, or friendship. In Canberra, the population studied consisted entirely of native speakers of Australian English, most often *not* born in Canberra (Canberra being a community even younger than Los Angeles), but otherwise with a social definition similar to the one in Los Angeles.

An individual or group of any size could carry out research of the sort we describe here, and provided it is done with reasonable care, it is bound to be to good advantage. The size of the "sample" to be studied is of only relative importance. Small projects can help design later investigations of larger scale; their reliability can be checked by replicated studies. Social structure may be so uniform that basic patterns emerge out of a small study. The first study of (ING) by Fischer had a small sample population but found sexual differentiation and sensitivity to situations that agreed to a striking degree with the larger studies by Labov and Trudgill in other communities (Trudgill's on the other side of the Atlantic Ocean).

Don't wait to do a study large enough for statistical reliability, but if that is possible, so much the better. The number thirty is a good guide. If you are comparing men and women speakers, get data on at least thirty of each; if you are studying the effect of speaker and addressee sex in conversations among friends, then get counts of (ING) in at least thirty of each of the four kinds of conversations that are relevant: a man talking to a man friend, a man talking to a woman friend, a woman talking to a man friend and a woman talking to a woman friend.

We recommend the categories *man* and *woman* as a primary focus of study. It is an easy difference to identify, and it is likely to lead to interesting results anyplace. Previous linguistic research, including work on (ING), and factors other than language all lead us to expect sex to be important whenever status and degrees of formality are important, which is to say almost always.

Our research plan requires a population you can listen to, without intruding, in at least two conversations for each speaker with different addressees and that will let you interview them later. You are going to observe their use of (ING) in several conversations without telling them what you are doing; only afterwards will you explain the project and ask for an interview. You ought to be reasonably sure they will not mind being an object of study. If someone objects, discard the notes, make your apologies, and go on to someone else.

According to our research plan, you identify each speaker and addressee in a conversation by sex and then identify a relationship between them. If you do not know the relationship, you can ask afterwards. For our research we chose three categories, *friend, family,* and *other.*

Social Relationship	Typically Includes
Friend	boyfriend, girlfriend, co-worker, fellow student, etc.
Family	all kin, including by marriage
Other	boss, customer, salesperson, teacher, stranger, etc.

Categorize each conversation with just one of these labels. In particular, if the speaker and addressee are *family*, then categorize them as such along with whatever else you know about them, and then for those who are not *family* decide whether the relationship is *friend* or not. For people who are neither *family* nor *friend*, you put down *other*. Ask these interview questions:

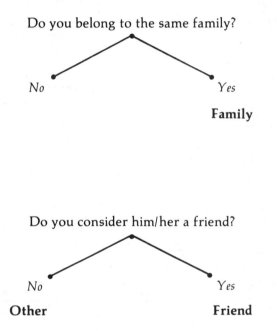

In a more extensive study more types of relationships could be distinguished, and one might want to apply more than one to a conversation, also recognizing different relationships for the same people in different situations. There is such a thing as a boss who is also a friend, and both *boss* and *friend* might be relevant categories, but it might also matter whether the speakers are conversing at their place of work in front of other employees or sharing a meal alone together after hours.

Using our three categories for relationships, you want to discover how the addressees affect the behavior of the speakers, with as little influence from you as possible. You should be like the proverbial fly on the wall.

Researcher _____*M. Morgan*_____ Speaker No. __27__

Sex of Speaker:
M(ALE) or F(EMALE)__*F*___

LANGUAGE USE

Conversation	1	2		
Date	Oct 10	Oct 12		
Sex of Addressee m(ale) or f(emale)	M	F		
Relationship FR(IEND), FAM(ILY) or O(THER)	FR	FR		
Variable Data (n/10): -ING	8	9		
-IN	2	1		

INTERVIEW

1. *Preference*
   Which pronunciation sounds better *somethING* or
   somethIN'? — Or have you no preference (n.p.)?
   Consider *working, swimming, nothing, morning,*
   etc. (Answer: -ING, -IN or n.p.) _____*- ING*_____

2. *Self-Report*
   Which pronunciation do you use when you
   talk, -ING, -IN or both? _____*- ING "Unless*____
   I was tired and made a mistake "

3. *Stereotype*
   What kind of people say -IN frequently? _*"Poorly educated*_
   people, people who don't care about the
   language, the kind with no ambition, no
   desire to better themselves . "

Figure 1. Completed research form of a sort to be used with each speaker studied. A group of researchers all use copies of the same form and compile them later for analysis. Here the researcher made observations on a speaker in two conversations (it could have been more), and then did the interview.

You are going to be studying people you know or are in contact with fairly regularly. You will not be doing a comprehensive study of your community, but rather a *pilot study,* a preliminary investigation the conclusions from which can be hypotheses for later research.

GATHERING DATA

You will be studying individual speakers and then comparing them according to social categories. Organize the study of each speaker in two parts, "Observations of Language Use," and "Interview." You do the interview *after* you have made all your observations of language use. It will be best to run off a form for each speaker, one that everyone cooperating on the project can use, with space to record observations on as many conversations as possible, as well as the results of the interview. You will correlate the G/N counts for particular speakers with their answers to interview questions (see Figure 1).

In the first part of the study, you are going to listen while a person talks to someone else. Count ten *consecutive* instances of the (ING) variable as we have defined it (unstressed *-ing* at the end of a word) and keep a running tally in your mind with the ratio of G to N pronunciations, e.g., "1–0, 2–0, 2–1, 3–1, 4–1, 5–1, 5–2, 5–3, 6–3, 7–3." You might find it difficult at first, but everyone reports being able to do it after only a little practice. It is important that the count be consecutive to guard against the possibility of a biased selection in which you might have picked one norm and ignored the other.

Note down your tally, together with your description of the situation, including the sex of the speaker, M(ale) or F(emale); the sex of the addressee, m(ale) or f(emale); and the relationship between the speaker and addressee, FR(iend), FAM(ily), or O(ther). We suggest making the counts when you are not the addressee because it is too difficult to both count (ING) and maintain a natural role in the conversation. Repeat this procedure with the same speaker and at least one other addressee. Take care the person does not know what you have been listening for until after you have finished this part of the study. Then do the interview.

Explain the purpose of your study. If necessary ask the person you are interviewing about his or her relationship with the addressee. Then ask three questions.

First ask a question about their preference for one of the (ING) norms: you can lead off with "Which pronunciation sounds better, *somethING* or *somethIN'*?" and then if you think it will help your speakers understand, elaborate with the variant pronunciations of other words such as *working, swimming, nothing,* and *morning.* Then add "Or have you no preference?" Indicate the answer as -ING, -IN, or n.p. (no preference). Note down that preference without distinction for the particular reasons. When one norm gets a preponderance of preferences, you have a basis for saying it is the prestige norm, or the *standard*.

The next question is "Which pronunciation do you use when you talk?" There are three possible answers, -ING, -IN, or BOTH. The most accurate answer for most people would be "both," but some will favor -ING because they are not aware that they vary their pronunciation. But they can also answer -ING because they interpret the question to mean "Which pronunciation is most typical of your speech?" In this case -ING would be accurate for most speakers. Try to get people to interpret -ING as meaning *only* -ING. The answer to this question is the speaker's *self-report*.

Finally, ask "What kind of people say -IN frequently?" A few speakers dislike this question because they may feel it demands they reveal a personal prejudice. Try to get the person to give a *personal* opinion: this question is intended to get an index of the attitudes of speakers. If they report what is said by others, what "people say," you should ask them whether they agree. See our discussion [under "Interviews," pp. 535–537) for how we have categorized the answers to this question.

Repeat this procedure with as many speakers as you can. The goal is to get data on as many speakers and as many different speaker-addressee combinations as possible, and that makes working in a group a big advantage. In an introductory course each student could set out to study at least two speakers, each one in at least two conversations with different addressees.

THE CANBERRA STUDY

Observations of Language Use. We will use the Canberra study for illustration.[17] The most important social distinction that emerged in the study was the one between men and women in their roles as both speakers and listeners; next most important was the distinction for men speakers between the relationship *friend,* as opposed to *family* and *other.* The results will be presented in a way to highlight these oppositions.

In the Canberra study forty-seven male speakers were observed in one hundred conversations, and thirty-three female speakers in sixty-six conversations, a total of 166 conversations. With 10 consecutive instances of (ING) having been observed in each, we have a total of 1660 observed instances of (ING). Of these 1660, 328 were N, or 1.98

---

[17] We will make several references to some statistical tests familiar to anyone with background in statistics. Readers with no background in statistics who would like to use such tests to check the validity of their findings should seek help, and in most places it should not be hard to find. If you compile your data neatly, there will usually be knowledgeable people around who would then be glad to give you help on the statistics.

N per 10 instances of (ING). The N per 10 (ING) for male and female speakers is as follows:

Male 2.44
Female 1.56

The standard deviations were M 2.04 and F 1.64. The variances of the two samples (the standard deviations squared) are "same" by a significant margin, and therefore the means can be meaningfully compared. By a standard test, the difference between the two means is large enough to make the possibility of error only 3.2 percent. See Figure 2 for the distribution of G and N pronunciations among male and female speakers.

Only in conversations between *friends* does the difference between M and F speakers become apparent, and as it happened, the great majority of conversations observed fell into this category. The sample collected on conversations between friends is quite large enough for the results to be statistically significant; the results from *family* or *other* conversations are based on a comparatively small sample and should be regarded as only suggestive. Table 1 reveals the oppositon between

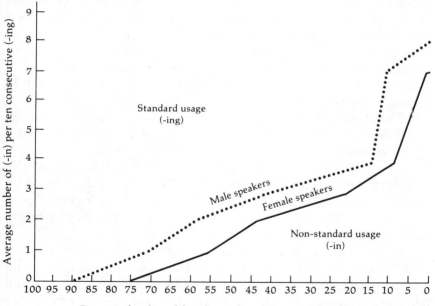

Figure 2. Nonstandard usage of the (ING) variable among men and women speakers in Canberra, Australia. In 100 conversations with men speakers and 66 with women speakers, a total of 166 conversations, each conversation with a count of 10 consecutive instances of (ING), a total of 1660 instances of (ING).

	Relation	Instances of (ING)	Occurrences of -IN	-IN % of Total
Male speakers	Friend	760	200	26
	Family	130	18	14
	Other	110	15	14
Female speakers	Friend	470	68	14
	Family	130	19	15
	Other	60	8	13

Table 1. Male and Female Speakers: Frequency of -IN per Relation Category in Canberra, Australia

friend and the other two relations for M speakers, the similarity between M and F speakers for the other two relation categories, and the similarity in the style level (the N/G ratio) for F speakers in all relation categories.

On the basis of these figures, we can see that only M speakers *shift* their style significantly according to their relation to the addressee. They shift to a significantly higher percentage of N when talking to friends as opposed to nonfriends. However, both the men and women in the Canberra study shift their style in another way, and here the women more than the men. If their addressee is male, both men and women use more N; if the addressee is female, both men and women use less N. The extent of the style-shifting is similar in absolute terms: in conversations between friends (the relation category where we have the most data), men speaking to men produced on average 2.90 N per 10 consecutive (ING), men speaking to women produced 2.29 N, a difference of .61; women speaking to men produced 1.88 N per 10 consecutive (ING), women speaking to women 1.20 N, a difference of .68. The absolute indices of style-shifting according to the sex of the addressee then are .61 for men speakers and .68 for women speakers. When we look at the matter in relative terms, we can see that the women shift their style more than men. Where men reduce their N by 21 percent when talking to women friends, women reduce theirs by 36 percent. Alternatively, we can say that when talking to men friends as opposed to women friends, women *increase* their N by 57 percent; the comparable figure for men is only 27 percent.

We have ranged the figures in Table 2 with the number of N per 10 (ING) going from highest to lowest. Men-to-men are at the top and women-to-women at the bottom. The differences between adjacent pairs on this scale were only suggestive statistically, but the difference between the outside pair, 2.90 for men-to-men, and 1.20 for women-to-women, was equivalent to *nine* standard deviations, which means the possibility for error was infinitesimally small. In other words, we can interpret that contrast as an index of a real social difference.

	Average Number of -IN per 10 (ING)	Style Shifting Depending on the Sex of the Addressee (a–b)
Men speaking		
(a) To men friends (M-m-FR) 420 (ING), 122 -IN	2.90	
		.61 (27% of 2.29)
(b) To women friends (M-f-FR) 340 (ING), 78 -IN	2.29	
Women speaking		
(a) To men friends (F-m-FR) 170 (ING), 32 -IN	1.88	
		.68 (57% of 1.20)
(b) To women friends (F-f-FR) 300 (ING), 36 -IN	1.20	

Table 2. Style Shifting and Absolute Frequency of -IN Forms in Conversations Between Friends in Canberra, Australia

The interview part of our research, which we will discuss next, shows that the G pronunciation is standard ("correct") and the N pronunciation nonstandard ("incorrect"). Using this interpretation of G and N, we can set forth the following conclusions about (ING) in this portion of the Canberra study:

1. Men use more nonstandard forms than women.
2. Men make a marked shift in style for friends as opposed to nonfriends, with the style for friends being a relatively nonstandard one.
3. Women do not shift style for any of the relationships categorized in this study, friend, family or other.
4. Both men and women speakers shift styles according to the sex of the addressee, using more standard forms talking to women than to men.
5. Women have a greater range of style-shifting according to the sex of the addressee than do men.

Table 3 presents all our data for the Canberra study in terms of categories of conversations, categories distinguished, according to the design of our research, by the sex of the speaker, the sex of the addressee, and the relationship between them. We compiled this table by combining our totals for all individual speakers. By contrast, the bases for the graph in Figure 2 are the totals for individual speakers, for instance where a particular male speaker was observed in 2 conversations, and of 20 instances of (ING) used N 7 times, or 3.5 N per 10 (ING). We used both kinds of totals in statistical tests, totals for individual speakers, and totals for categories of conversations.

	Category	Total (ING)	Number of - IN	% of Total
Conversation	M-m-FR	420	122	29
	M-f-FR	340	78	23
	F-m-FR	170	32	19
	F-f-FR	300	36	12
	M-m-FAM	50	9	18
	M-f-FAM	80	9	11
	F-m-FAM	80	13	16
	F-f-FAM	50	6	12
	M-m-O	70	3	4
	M-f-O	40	12	30
	F-m-O	40	6	15
	F-f-O	20	2	10
Speaker	Male	1000	233	23
	Female	660	95	14
Addressee	male	830	185	22
	female	830	143	17
Relationship	FRiend	1230	268	22
	FAMily	260	37	14
	Other	170	23	14
	Total	1660	328	20

Table 3. Percent of -IN Pronunciation, All Categories of Conversations, Relationships and Sex of Speaker and Addressee. *Sex of speaker,* M(ale), F(emale); *sex of addressee,* m(ale), f(emale); *relationship,* FR(iend), FAM(ily), O(ther).

Using the data in Table 3, you can make additional tables for other comparisons. For example, you might abstract figures from Table 3 to make another table like Table 2. That table focuses on the effect of speaker-addressee sex, but just for the relationship *friend.* You might do a similar table, one focusing again on speaker-addressee sex, but this time for all relationships, *friend, family,* and *other.* When you total all the figures for conversations labeled M-m (men speaking to men— there are such counts for each of the three relationships, M-m-FR, M-m-FAM, and M-m-O), you get a total of 540 (ING) and 134 N; dividing 134 by 54 gives 2.48 N per 10 (ING). Work out a similar figure for all M-f conversations (men speaking to women—again, there will be three kinds of conversation that will be relevant, M-f-FR, M-f-FAM, and M-f-O). According to generalization 4 above the combined totals for M-f should be lower than for M-m. Subtract the smaller number from the larger one to get the absolute index of style-shifting for men speakers according to the sex of the addressee, a figure comparable to the .61 in the righthand column of Table 2. Then you can divide that figure by either your M-m or M-f total to get a relative index of style-shifting, as in the parenthesized expressions in the righthand column of Table 2. Repeat the same procedure for the women speakers.

Other comparisons are less interesting because the data is sparse. For example, in Table 3 the counts for men speakers in conversation with *others* gives an index of style-shifting that is opposite to that entailed by generalization 4; however, the number of conversations studied is too small for the calculations to have statistical reliability, seven for M-m-O and four for M-f-O. Also, *other* is such a grab-bag of potentially distinctive social relationships that we should be wary of small undifferentiated samples. Another likely place to look for further differentiation relevant to speech behavior is within the category *family*. We might expect differences based on the relative *generations* of speaker and addressee within the same family (peer vs. parent-child vs. child-parent, etc.), and again between members of different families (it might turn out that peers speak to each other in the same style whether they belong to the same family or not, but that between members of different generations family membership is decisive, and so on).

Despite their limitations, our three categories proved useful for a research project of this scale. We have results that provide support for a compelling perspective on women and their status. Together all our generalizations are consistent with the view that of the two sexes women are both more constrained by, and more aware of, the conservative forces in our culture. There are fewer situations in which they vary their style, and fewer in which they speak in a relatively nonstandard, and we will argue, intimate way. (They can be intimate with men, but not so much with members of their own sex!) They use less nonstandard forms in absolute terms, but on the other hand in the social situations we have found where they do shift style, they show a greater range of style-shifting than men do, and we can explain this by saying that they have a greater awareness of the stylistic effect of the style-shifting.

Interviews. As in Los Angeles, the Canberra researchers conducted interviews with each speaker after they had observed him or her, usually in several conversations. Researchers asked speakers which variant sounded better, which pronunciation they thought they used, and stereotypes of the kind of people they thought used frequent nonstandard pronunciations of (ING). The G pronunciation emerged unquestionably as the standard, and N as a nonstandard variant. In their judgments about language usage, women emerged as more conservative than men, just as they did in their speech behavior. Because of additional evidence obtained after the data was compiled for Table 3, the sample considered for the interview was somewhat larger, 52 men (an increase of five) and 36 women (an increase of three).

In answer to the question about which pronunciation they preferred, *somethING* or *somethIN'*, 94 percent of the women said they believed G sounded better than N, as opposed to 82 percent of the

	All Speakers (88)		Male (52)		Female (36)	
Preference ("Which pronunciation sounds better?")						
-ING	77	(87%)	43	(82%)	34	(94%)
No Preference	8	(10%)	7	(14%)	1	(3%)
-IN	3	(3%)	2	(4%)	1	(3%)
Self-Report ("Which pronunciation do you use?")						
-ING	58	(66%)	33	(63%)	25	(69%)
Both	25	(28%)	15	(29%)	10	(28%)
-IN	5	(6%)	4	(8%)	1	(3%)

Table 4. Beliefs and Self-Reports of Men and Women Speakers.

men. Fourteen percent (7) of the men had no preference; only one woman (3 percent) gave that response. Two men (4 percent) and one woman (3 percent) said N sounded better.

There were discrepancies between self-report and actual performance, but they do not appear significant. When asked what pronunciation they used, 33 of 52 men (63 percent) said G, and only 15 (29 percent) reported both G and N. In fact all those reporting both *did* use both forms in the counts, but only 6 of the 33 reporting G used *only* G. However, the question may have been interpreted to mean "Which variant is most *characteristic* of your speech?"—in which case G would have been the appropriate answer.

Four men gave a self-report of N, and these men were indeed high N speakers, with counts of 9/20, 13/20, 8/10, and 3/10 respectively. No one produced only N.

A similar pattern emerged for women. Twenty-five (69 percent) gave self-reports of G when in fact just 6 of those used only G. Ten (28 percent) reported that they used both G and N, and in fact did so. One (3 percent) reported N, and she was a high N speaker, with 15/20. Table 4 summarizes the results of the interview.

The stereotypes ("What kind of people say -IN frequently?") provide some of the most interesting results, but also some of the most difficult to categorize. We imposed a three-way distinction to the answers, "personally negative," "socially lower," and "neutral."

Personally negative. These are stereotypes that denigrate the personal character of the N speakers. The most common comments referred to education, "not educated properly, uneducated," or "less educated." These expressions occurred seventeen times. The word "lazy" was used eleven times and "careless" six. The expression "Ockers" was used twice: this is an Australian term for Australian-style

	All Speakers (88)		Male (52)		Female (36)	
Personally negative	42	(48%)	23	(44%)	19	(53%)
Socially lower	24	(27%)	13	(25%)	11	(31%)
Neutral	20	(23%)	14	(27%)	6	(17%)
No opinion	2	(2%)	2	(4%)	—	

Table 5. Stereotypes of -IN Speakers Given by Men and Women.

boorish and uncouth behavior. Other negative expressions occurring once each were "less aware," "drunk," "sloppy," "lousy," "slack," and "not thinking." Almost half of the answers by our eighty-eight interviewees fell into the "personally negative" category.

Socially lower. These stereotypes say nothing about the intelligence, education, alertness, etc., of speakers, but rather are a comment on "lower" social origin. The most common expressions were "working class, lower class," and "blue collar." About 27 percent of the answers placed users of N in a social class lower than that of the respondents (who were middle class).

Neutral. These responses carried no obvious sense of "better" or "worse." It is a matter of inference that the expression "working class" means "socially lower," and in the world view of some people, "working class" is surely a neutral expression. Hence our distinction between "socially lower" and "neutral" is not reliable or valid in all cases. We grouped under the "neutral" category answers such as "Everyone tends to say -IN some of the time" (seven such responses), "It depends on the origin or environment one comes from" (two responses), and "average Australian" (two responses). We classed 23 percent of the answers as neutral. Two percent (two people) held no opinion.

Table 5 compares men and women speakers for their answers to the stereotype question. There is further suggestion here that women are more conservative in their judgments about the (ING) norms than men. And with both men and women speakers we see how strongly the community accords prestige to the G norm. What is left unsaid is why people feel motivated to use the N norm as well, for indeed it cannot be just the inherent variability of (ING) that accounts for the presence of N. The consistent tendencies for all speakers to produce more N in some social situations rather than others is proof that N has social motivation. Bringing to bear our general understanding of society we can interpret the language behavior and attitudes we have discovered. It can give us insight into social phenomena popularly referred to as "friendship," "women's place," "mateship" (an Australian term for males in group companionship), "polite behavior," "family upbringing," and the like.

EXTENSIONS

Comparing Communities. The Canberra study was patterned after one in Los Angeles. Canberra emerges from the study as the more linguistically conservative community, especially in regard to women. The linguistic structures in the two communities are identical, G and N. Speakers use them differently enough to imply differences in social structure. G was unquestionably the prestige norm in Los Angeles, N the nonstandard norm. Los Angeles speakers produced more N overall, 2.48 per 10 (ING), as opposed to the 1.98 in Canberra. Speakers of both sexes used more N talking to *friend* and *family* than to *other*, with similar frequencies of N for *friend* and *family*. But men used more N, and had a notably wider range of styles than women. With one exception, all speakers used less N speaking to women than to men. The one exception is important: In conversations among friends, Los Angeles women used more N speaking to women than to men. Recall that in Canberra, speech to women was always more conservative, even among women friends. It should be obvious how revealing similar research projects could be in other English-speaking communities.

The Los Angeles Family (ING) Study. The research design presented here can be expanded in two ways: one with respect to social structure, and the other with respect to the speech acts themselves.

Besides sex, one could easily control for the age of speakers and addressees: We could guess age by appearance, to the nearest number divisible by five, 20, 25, 30, 35, etc., or we could ask. While the criteria for sex and age are unequivocal, important social categories such as ethnic group and socioeconomic class are much more difficult to identify. Because they are so important, it is a challenge to define them in distinct, nonoverlapping, and reliable ways. Sociologists can give guidelines on how to gather and interpret information here. Socioeconomic class is typically identified on the basis of education, occupation, and income—information that must be obtained in interviews. As a somewhat rougher and more feasible method, one can do counts on (ING) in different *places* known to be frequented by people of distinct social groups, for example, among people in places of work with contrasting social status: factories vs. jewelry stores, banks vs. garages.

To understand (ING) better in relation to the internal structure of speech acts, we can control for several features, some of which require recording the speech acts to be studied. A number of things are of interest, from the specific words on which the G and N occur to topics and the styles in which they are discussed.

In Los Angeles we carried out a reasonably feasible project, one that can be done again without tape recorders, and one that expands the research design both for social structure and the internal workings of speech acts. We investigated the use of (ING) among family mem-

The Percentage of -IN from Total Occurrences of (ING)

Speaker	Joking Style	Arguing Style
Male	46	24
Female	28	21

Table 6. **The Effect of the Styles "Joking" and "Arguing" on the Percentage of -IN Pronunciations for Male and Female Speakers in Twelve Los Angeles Families (with 64 conversations in the joking style with male speakers and 51 with female speakers; 65 conversations in the arguing style with male speakers and 51 with female speakers)**

bers, controlling for generational as well as sexual differences. In addition, we controlled for the effect of *style* on (ING) by getting counts from at least two conversations for each pair of interlocutors studied, a "joking" conversation (a humorous one accompanied by good-natured smiles and laughter), and an "arguing" one (one where the predominant tone is one of disagreement, as can happen when people discuss politics, the death penalty, and other moral issues). In principle, one could find the same topic discussed in both a joking and an arguing style, but in practice joking is usually about small, personal things, and arguing about big issues.

Researchers sought to observe the same pair of family members conversing on at least two occasions that could be characterized as "joking" and "arguing." In each of these conversations, researchers made a count of *twenty* consecutive (ING) *for each interlocutor*, two counts of twenty in each conversation. The results were then compared for the influence of sex, generation, and style. The sample consisted of members of twelve middle-class families falling into two generations, a younger generation, under thirty (the age of most of the researchers and their siblings), and a generation over forty—as it turned out in all cases, the parents of the younger generation. For most of these families, the period of observation was the Thanksgiving holiday on which families share a traditional dinner.

The study of different generations produced interesting results. The older generation had the more standard usage, 24 percent N as opposed to 33 percent N for the younger generation. Both the younger and the older generation, especially female speakers, had more G and less N speaking across generations than to the same generation. An interesting difference in style shifting between the generations was that the younger generation used more G and less N when speaking across sex than to the same sex; the older generation had the same frequencies of G and N for both across sex and to the same sex.

The result of "joking" vs. "arguing" was as might be expected. Eleven of the twelve families used more G and less N when arguing than when joking. Table 6 shows the average frequency of N for all families by sex of the speaker. One can see style shifting by speakers of both sexes but a familiar pattern of contrast between the sexes. Male speakers use more N than female speakers, and, most notably, the male speakers have by far the wider shift between the two styles.

Conclusion: The Usefulness of Sociolinguistic Variables

It is significant that G and N have coexisted for so long without one driving out the other. It has been suggested that N would have taken over by now had it not been for the conservative force of the spelling -*ing*.[18] We should keep in mind that while spelling is indeed a conservative force, spelling norms have been overcome by change before. We have evidence of this in spellings that have been retained in spite of sounds that have disappeared or changed, for example, the silent *l* of *half, talk, salve, calm,* and *should,* pronounced until early modern English; the *k* of *knee* and *know,* lost in the seventeenth century; the *w* of *two, who, sword, wring, wreck, answer,* and *toward;* the *b* of *climb, comb, dumb, bomb,* and *womb;* the *gh* (from old [x]) of *through, daughter, high, dough, right, sight,* and *eight;* the *p* of *cupboard;* the *t* of *Christmas;* the *d* of *handsome;* and the *g* of *gnaw* and of many words like *sing.* The spelling *gn* is retained in words such as *sign, design, deign, reign,* and *champagne* borrowed from French. English speakers used to give this *gn the French palatal articulation (just as for the n* in the middle of *onion*), but now it has an alveolar pronunciation so the *reign* sounds just like *rain.* Last but not least there is the *r* at the end of syllables, standard pronunciation until the seventeenth century, but now absent for many speakers in the British Isles and for as many as a third of the speakers in North America, so that *farther* and *father* sound the same.[19] N could have displaced G entirely in spite of the spelling. That it came as close as it did at one point is evidence for this. N could also have retreated and disappeared—more needs to be said.

The longevity of the opposition between G and N is a sign of their usefulness. (ING) has endured in spite of the impulse language users have to resolve variable conflict and tidy up their language, their need for a standard in the form and meaning of each linguistic unit to which all members of their community can refer. Such a standard makes communication possible, and it is the stuff of group identity. But while people need a tidy, standardized language, they also appear to tolerate *some* variation to add to their expressive power.

[18] See also M. L. Samuels, "Linguistic Evolution," *Cambridge Studies in Linguistics* 5 (London and New York: Cambridge University Press, 1972).
[19] For sound change and spelling, see Jespersen, *A Modern English Grammar,* vol. 1, and H. Kurath, *A Phonology and Prosody of Modern English* (Ann Arbor, Mich.: University of Michigan Press, 1971).

Quite apart from the literal meaning of the utterance "He's working," it adds an extra social dimension to have both G and N available as possible pronunciations. If the speaker said G, it could have been N; and if N, it could have been G. Listeners can and will make social interpretations of the choice. The interpretations depend on a calculus of time, place, topic, and personae. But above all nowadays, N appears to convey or solicit a feeling of intimacy and G one of respect. We live in a culture with elaborate status distinctions. We tend to measure almost everything in terms of status, alternately signaling respect ("I give you respect," "I give respect to what I am talking about," "I want respect from you") or intimacy ("I am together with you: no status distinctions come between us," "I am close to what I am talking about," "I want you to be close to me"). We reveal this in our style of behavior as much as in what we explicitly say.

So there is more to the variation of speech sounds than sound change in progress. It is relevant that sound changes take different lengths of time to complete themselves, and that there can even be variables such as (ING), which for the moment appear to be stable. The opposition in (ING) could have led to definitive sound change, but community after community gave N vs. G a social interpretation, found it useful, nurtured it, and made it part of their culture. Just so, each time the process of linguistic change completes itself, we are seeing the propensity of communities for a single standard; but each time we see the process prolonged, we are seeing evidence for the social usefulness of variation.

Suggestions for Further Reading

Readers wishing to read further on the topic of sociolinguistic variables would do well to begin with the classic work introducing sociological techniques into urban dialectology:

Labov, William. *The Social Stratification of English in New York City.* Arlington, Va.: Center for Applied Linguistics, 1966.

Many of the findings in this work, together with a development of and refinement of the sociolinguistic issues are presented in:

————. 1972. *Sociolinguistic Patterns.* Philadelphia: University of Pennsylvania Press.

We also recommend:

————. 1972. *Language in the Inner City.* Philadelphia: University of Pennsylvania Press.

Here are the findings of the survey by Labov and co-workers of Black and Puerto Rican speakers in New York City with discussion of Black English speech communities elsewhere. Finally, for an application of Labov's techniques to the large British urban community of Norwich:

Trudgill, Peter. *Social Differentiation of English in Norwich.* Cambridge: Cambridge University Press, 1974.

FOR DISCUSSION AND REVIEW

1. What kinds of stereotypes does literature suggest we have about G and N? Find an example from literature that is not cited by Wald and Shopen, and explain what stereotype is involved.

2. The (ING) variable has been studied by many investigators. Give three reasons why it is such an attractive research subject.

3. Define, in your own words, the terms *linguistic norm, linguistic variable,* and *sociolinguistic variable.* Why are these concepts important?

4. Sometimes G and N are interchangeable, but sometimes they are not. Describe the situations in which only one of these variables is possible. Then describe the situations in which one or the other variable has a high probability of occurrence.

5. How can one account for the fact that "*-ing* and *-in'* are both well entrenched and have long been in competition"? Is it useful for speakers to have this choice? If so, how? Why?

6. Both pp. 525–530 of this article and footnote 5 suggest small research projects for individuals for a class. The instructions on pp. 525–530 are clear, and a project could be carried out by following them. In footnote 5, however, you would have to plan the project. What population would you sample? What relationships between people would you identify? Would only certain settings be appropriate? If so, which ones? And, most important, what variable would you study? (You could, of course, stay with (ING).)

5/The Study of Nonstandard English

WILLIAM LABOV

William Labov, a research professor at the Center for Urban Ethnography at the University of Pennsylvania, is well known for his many sociolinguistic studies, especially of New York City speech and of Black English. In this condensed version of "The Study of Nonstandard English," he explains the need, especially for teachers, to study and understand the various nonstandard dialects of English. He also clarifies the relationship between standard English and nonstandard dialects, showing the close relationship between a number of their phonological and syntactic rules. Most important, Labov emphasizes that nonstandard dialects of English, like all human languages, are rule-governed; they are not "corruptions" or "inferior versions" of standard English. In other studies, Labov has advocated functional bidialectalism for speakers of a nonstandard dialect and has attempted to show how linguistic knowledge about Black English can be used to improve the teaching of reading to BEV-speaking children.

Since language learning does take place outside of the classroom, and the six-year-old child does have great capacity for learning new language forms as he is exposed to them, it may be asked why it should be necessary for the teacher to understand more about the child's own vernacular. First, we can observe that automatic adjustment does *not* take place in all cases. Even the successful middle-class student does not always master the teacher's grammatical forms; and in the urban ghettos we find very little adjustment to school forms. Students continue to write *I have live* after ten or twelve years in school; we will describe below failures in reading the *-ed* suffix which show no advance with years in school. Second, knowledge of the underlying structure of the nonstandard vernacular will allow the most efficient teaching. If the teacher knows the general difference between standard negative attraction and nonstandard negative concord, he can teach a hundred different standard forms with the simple instruction: *The negative is attracted only to the first indefinite.* Thus by this one rule we can make many corrections

He don't know nothing → He doesn't know anything
Nobody don't like him → Nobody likes him
Nobody hardly goes there → Hardly anybody goes there
Can't nobody do it → Nobody can do it

Third, the vernacular must be understood because ignorance of it leads to serious conflict between student and teacher. Teachers in ghetto schools who continually insist that *i* and *e* sound different in *pin* and *pen* will only antagonize a great number of their students. The knowledge that *i* and *e* actually sound the same before *m* and *n* for most of their students (and "should" sound the same if they are normal speakers) will help avoid this destructive conflict. Teachers who insist that a child meant to say *He is tired* when he said *He tired* will achieve only bewilderment in the long run. Knowledge that *He tired* is the vernacular equivalent of the contracted form *He's tired* will save teacher and student from this frustration.

Granted that the teacher wishes to learn about the student's language, what methods are available for him to do so? Today, a great many linguists study English through their own intuitions; they operate "out of their own heads" in the sense that they believe they can ask and answer all the relevant questions themselves. But even if a teacher comes from the same background as his students, he will find that his grammar has changed, that he no longer has firm intuitions about whether he can say *Nobody don't know nothing about it* instead of *Nobody knows nothing about it.* He can of course sit down with a student and ask him all kinds of direct questions about his language, and there are linguists who do this. But one cannot draw directly upon the intuitions of the two major groups we are interested in, children and nonstandard speakers. Both are in contact with a superordinate or dominant dialect, and both will provide answers which reflect their awareness of this dialect as much as of their own. One can of course engage in long and indirect conversations with students, hoping that all of the forms of interest will sooner or later occur, and there are linguists who have attempted to study nonstandard dialects in this way. But these conversations usually teach the subject more of the investigator's language than the other way around. In general, one can say that whenever a speaker of a nonstandard dialect is in a subordinate position to a speaker of a standard dialect, the rules of his grammar will shift in an unpredictable manner towards the standard. The longer the contact, the stronger and more lasting is the shift. Thus adolescent speakers of a vernacular make very unreliable informants when they are questioned in a formal framework. The investigator must show considerable sociolinguistic sophistication to cope with such a situation, and indeed the teacher will also need to know a great deal about the social forces which affect linguistic behavior if he is to interpret his students' language.

Nonstandard Dialects as "Self-Contained" Systems

The traditional view of nonstandard speech as a set of isolated deviations from standard English is often countered by the opposite view: that nonstandard dialect should be studied as an isolated system in its own right, without any reference to standard English. It is argued that the system of grammatical forms of a dialect can only be understood through their internal relations. For example, nonstandard Negro English has one distinction which standard English does not have: there is an invariant form *be* in *He always be foolin' around* which marks habitual, general conditions, as opposed to the unmarked *is, am, are,* etc., which do not have any such special sense. It can be argued that the existence of this distinction changes the value of all other members of the grammatical system and that the entire paradigm of this dialect is therefore different from that of standard English. It is indeed important to find such relations within the meaningful set of grammatical distinctions, if they exist, because we can then *explain* rather than merely describe behavior. There are many cooccurrence rules which are purely descriptive—the particular dialect just happens to have X' *and* Y' where another has X and Y. We would like to know if a special nonstandard form X' *requires* an equally nonstandard Y' because of the way in which the nonstandard form cuts up the entire field of meaning. This would be a tremendous help in teaching, since we would be able to show what sets of standard rules have to be taught together to avoid confusing the student with a mixed, incoherent grammatical system.

The difficulty here is that linguistics has not made very much progress in the analysis of semantic systems. There is no method or procedure which leads to reliable or reproducible results–not even among those who agree on certain principles of grammatical theory. No one has yet written a complete grammar of a language—or even come close to accounting for all the morphological and syntactic rules of a language. And the situation is much more primitive in semantics; for example, the verbal system of standard English has been studied now for many centuries, yet there is no agreement at all on the meaning of the auxiliaries *have . . . ed* and *be . . . ing*. The meaning of *I have lived here*, as opposed to *I lived here*, has been explained as (a) relevant to the present, (b) past *in* the present, (c) perfective, (d) indefinite, (e) causative, and so on. It is not only that there are many views; it is that in any given discussion no linguist has really found a method by which he can reasonably hope to persuade others that he is right. If this situation prevails where most of the investigators have complete access to the data, since they are native speakers of standard English, we must be more than cautious in claiming to understand the meaning of *I be here* as opposed to *I am here* in nonstandard Negro English, and even more cautious in claiming that the meaning of nonstandard *I'm here* therefore differs from standard *I'm here* because of the existence of the other form. Most teachers have learned to be cautious in accepting a grammarian's statement about the meaning of their own native forms, but they have no way of judging statements made about a dialect which they do not speak, and they are naturally prone to accept such statements on the authority of the writer.

There is, however, [much] that we can do to show the internal relations in the nonstandard dialect as a system. There are a great many forms which seem different on the surface but can be explained as expressions of a single rule, or the absence of a single rule. We observe that in nonstandard Negro English it is common to say *a apple* rather than *an apple*. This is a grammatical fault from the point of view of standard speakers, and the school must teach *an apple* as the written, standard form. There is also a rather low-level, unimportant feature of pronunciation which is common to southern dialects: in *the apple*, the word *the* has the same pronunciation as in *the book* and does not rhyme with *be*. Finally, we can note that, in the South, educated white speakers keep the vocalic schwa which represents *r* in *four*, but nonstandard speakers tend to drop it (registered in dialect writing as *fo' o'clock*). When all these facts are put together, we can begin to explain the nonstandard *a apple* as part of a much broader pattern. There is a general rule of English which states that we do not pronounce two (phonetic) vowels in succession. Some kind of semiconsonantal glide or consonant comes in between: an *n* as in *an apple*, a "*y*" as in *the apple*, an *r* as in *four apples*. In each of these cases, this rule is not followed for nonstandard Negro English. A teacher may have more success in getting students to write *an apple* if he presents this general rule and connects up all of these things into a single rational pattern, even if some are not important in themselves. It will "make sense" to Negro speakers, since they do not drop *l* before a vowel, and many rules of their sound system show the effect of a following vowel.

There are many ways in which an understanding of the fundamental rules of the dialect will help to explain the surface facts. Some of the rules cited above are also important in explaining why nonstandard Negro speakers sometimes delete *is*, in *He is ready*, but almost always delete *are*, in *You are ready*; or why they say *they book* and *you book* but not *we book*. It does not always follow, though, that a grammatical explanation reveals the best method for teaching standard English.

Systematic analysis may also be helpful in connecting up the nonstandard form with the corresponding standard form and in this sense understanding the meaning of the nonstandard form. For example, nonstandard speakers say *Ain't nobody see it*. What is the nearest standard equivalent? We can connect this up with the standard negative "foregrounding" of *Scarcely did anybody see it* or, even more clearly, the literary expression *Nor did anybody see it*. This foregrounding fits in with the general colloquial southern pattern with indefinite subjects: *Didn't anybody see it*, nonstandard *Didn't nobody see it*. In these cases, the auxiliary *didn't* is brought to the front of the sentence, like the *ain't* in the nonstandard sentence. But there is another possibility. We could connect up *Ain't nobody see it* with the sentence *It ain't nobody see it*, that is, "There isn't anybody who sees it"; the dummy *it* of nonstandard Negro English corresponds to standard *there*, and, like *there*, it can be dropped in casual speech. Such an explanation is the only one possible in the case of such nonstandard sentences as *Ain't nothin' went down*. This could not be derived from *Nothin' ain't went down*, a sentence type which never occurs. If someone uses one of these forms, it is important for the teacher to know what was intended, so that he can supply the standard equivalent. To do so, one must know a great deal about many underlying rules of the nonstandard dialect, and also a great deal about the rules of English in general.

Nonstandard English as a Close Relative of Standard English

Differences between standard and nonstandard English are not as sharp as our first impressions would lead us to think. Consider, for example, the socially stratified marker of "pronominal apposition"— the use of a dependent pronoun in such sentences as

My oldest sister she worked at the bank.

Though most of us recognize this as a nonstandard pattern, it is not always realized that the "nonstandard" aspect is merely a slight difference in intonation. A standard speaker frequently says the same thing, with a slight break after the subject: *My oldest sister—she works at the bank, and she finds it very profitable*. There are many ways in which a greater awareness of the standard colloquial forms would help teachers interpret the nonstandard forms. Not only do standard speakers use pronominal apposition with the break noted above, but in casual speech they can also bring object noun phrases to the front, "foregrounding" them. For example, one can say

> My oldest sister—she worked at the Citizens Bank in Passaic last
> year.
> The Citizens Bank, in Passaic—my oldest sister worker there last
> year.
> Passaic—my oldest sister worked at the Citizens Bank there last
> year.

Note that if the foregrounded noun phrase represents a locative—
the "place where"—then its position is held by *there*, just as the persons
are represented by pronouns. If we are dealing with a time element,
it can be foregrounded without replacement in any dialect: *Last year,
my oldest sister worked at the Citizens Bank in Passaic.*

It is most important for the teacher to understand the relation
between standard and nonstandard and to recognize that nonstandard
English is a system of rules, different from the standard but not necessarily inferior as a means of communication. All of the teacher's social
instincts, past training, and even faith in his own education lead him
to believe that other dialects of English are merely "mistakes" without
any rhyme or rationale.

In this connection, it will be helpful to examine some of the most
general grammatical differences between English dialects spoken in
the United States. One could list a very large number of "mistakes,"
but when they are examined systematically the great majority appear
to be examples of a small number of differences in the rules. The
clearest analysis of these differences has been made by Edward
Klima (1964). He considers first the dialect in which people say sentences
like

> Who could she see?
> Who did he speak with?
> He knew who he spoke with.
> The leader who I saw left.
> The leader who he spoke with left.

What is the difference between this dialect and standard English? The
usual schoolbook answer is to say that these are well-known mistakes
in the use of *who* for *whom*. But such a general statement does not add
any clarity to the situation; nor does it help the student to learn standard English. The student often leaves the classroom with no more
than an uneasy feeling that *who* is incorrect and *whom* is correct. This
is the state of half-knowledge that leads to hypercorrect forms such as
Whom did you say is calling? In the more extreme cases, *whom* is seen
as the only acceptable, polite form of the pronoun. Thus a certain
receptionist at a hospital switchboard regularly answers the telephone:
"Whom?"

The nonstandard dialect we see here varies from standard English by one simple difference in the order of rules. The standard language marks the objective case—the difference between *who* and *whom*—in a sentence form which preserves the original subject-object relation:

Q—She could see WH-someone.

The WH-symbol marks the point to be questioned in this sentence. When cases are marked in this sentence, the pronoun before the verb receives the unmarked subjective case and the pronoun after the verb the marked objective case.

Q—She (subjective case)—could—see—WH-someone (objective case).

The combination of WH, indefinite pronoun, and objective case is to be realized later as *whom*. At a later point, a rule of WH-*attraction* is applied which brings the WH-word to the beginning of the sentence:

Q—Whom—she—could—see.

and finally the Q-marker effects a reversal of the pronoun and auxiliary, yielding the final result:

Whom could she see?

Here the objective case of the pronoun refers to the underlying position of the questioned pronoun as object of the verb.

The nonstandard dialect also marks cases: *I, he, she, they* are subjective forms, and *me, him, her, them* are objective. But the case marking is done after, rather than before, the WH-attraction rule applies. We begin with the same meaningful structure, Q—*She could see* WH-*someone*, but the first rule to consider is WH-*attraction*:

Q—WH someone—she—could—see.

Now the rule of case marking applies. Since both pronouns are before the verb, they are both unmarked:

Q—WH-someone (unmarked)—she (unmarked)—could see.

Finally, the question flip-flop applies, and we have

Who could she see?

The same mechanism applies to all of the nonstandard forms given above.

We can briefly consider another nonstandard grammatical rule, that which yields *It's me* rather than *It's I*. The difference here lies again in the rule of case marking. As noted above, this rule marks pronouns which occur after verbs; but the copula is not included. The nonstandard grammar which gives us *It's me* differs from standard English in only one simple detail—the case-marking rule includes the verb *to be* as well as other verbs. It is certainly not true that this nonstandard grammar neglects the case-marking rule; on the contrary, it applies the rule more generally than standard English here. But the order of the rules is the same as that for the nonstandard grammar just discussed: we get *Who is he?* rather than *Whom is he?* Like the other verbs, the copula marks the pronoun only after WH-attraction has applied.

In all of the examples just given, we can observe a general tendency towards simplification in the nonstandard grammars. There is a strong tendency to simplify the surface subjects—that is, the words which come before the verb. This is most obvious in pronominal apposition. The foregrounded part identifies the person talked about, *my oldest sister*; this person is then "given," and the "new" predication is made with a pronoun subject: *she worked at the Citizens Bank.*

A parallel tendency is seen in the nonstandard grammars which confine the objective marker to positions after the verb. But this tendency to simplify subjects is not confined to standard colloquial English. Sentences such as the following are perfectly grammatical but are seldom if ever found in ordinary speech:

For him to have broken his word so often was a shame.

Most often we find that the rule of "extraposition" has applied, moving the complex subject to the end of the sentence:

It was a shame for him to have broken his word so often.

In general, we find that nonstandard English dialects are not radically different systems from standard English but are instead closely related to it. These dialects show slightly different versions of the same rules, extending and modifying the grammatical processes which are common to all dialects of English.

Any analysis of the nonstandard dialect which pretends to ignore other dialects and the general rules of English will fail (1) because the nonstandard dialect is *not* an isolated system but a part of the sociolinguistic structure of English, and (2) because of the writer's knowledge of standard English. But it would be unrealistic to think that we can write anything but a superficial account of the dialect if we confine our thinking to this one subsystem and ignore whatever progress has been made in the understanding of [standard] English grammar.

FOR DISCUSSION AND REVIEW

1. According to Labov, why is it important for teachers to study "the child's own vernacular" (in this case, "the nonstandard vernacular")?

2. Granted that it is desirable for teachers to study the actual vernacular of children, what methods for doing so first suggest themselves? What, if any, are the problems with these methods? Explain your answer.

3. Labov argues that there is "a great deal that we can do to show the internal relations in the nonstandard dialect *as a system* [italics added]." Give some examples of what he means by this statement, and explain the importance of the phrase "as a system."

4. Labov argues that "nonstandard English is a system of rules, different from the standard but not necessarily inferior as a means of communication." What evidence does he present to support the first part of this claim? In your answer, explain some of the rules of nonstandard English and how they differ from those of standard English. What evidence does he present to support the second part? Do you agree or disagree? Defend your answer.

6/"It Bees Dat Way Sometime": Sounds and Structure of Present-Day Black English

GENEVA SMITHERMAN

Black English has been the object of intense interest and study since the 1960s. It has also been a center of controversy among linguists and among proponents of different theories of educational approaches to speakers of this dialect. In the following chapter from her book Talkin and Testifyin: The Language of Black America, *Professor Geneva Smitherman describes the sounds and grammatical structures of contemporary Black English. Like Labov in the preceding article, she argues that Black English is rule-governed, and she analyzes and illustrates a number of the most important phonological and syntactic rules, showing how they differ from those of standard American English. The list of Black proverbs and sayings at the end of this selection gives a sense of Black rhetorical style and the Black lexicon. Throughout the chapter, Dr. Smitherman shifts occasionally into Black idiom, showing how effectively this dialect can be used.*

Black Dialect consists of both language and style. In using the term "language" we are referring to sounds and grammatical structure. "Style" refers to the way speakers put sounds and grammatical structure together to communicate meaning in a larger context. Put another way, language is the words, style is what you do with the words.

Let's look first at the language of Black English. As we do so, it is important to keep in mind two facts. One is that, if blacks continue to be accepted into the American mainstream, many of the Africanized features of Black English may be sifted out of the language. Thus we are describing a form of speech which could, in, say, the twenty-first century, be in danger of extinction. (About all I will guarantee is that the patterns I'm describing were in regular and systematic use in the black community at the time of this writing!) Again, because of the process of decreolization, you should not expect Black English of today to be like that of the seventeenth century. All languages change over time; thus Black English of the twentieth century differs from early Black English just as White English of today is not identical to that of the founding fathers. The main linguistic differences between Black English and White English are cited below. In most other respects, the sounds and structure of the two dialects are generally the same.

The pronunciation system of Black English employs the same number of sounds as White English (ranging from 45–48 sounds counting stress and intonation patterns) but these sounds exist in a few different patterns of distribution. Of course, the real distinctiveness—and beauty—in the black sound system lies in those features which do not so readily lend themselves to concrete documentation—its speech rhythms, voice inflections, and tonal patterns. However, here we shall concern ourselves with those features of sound which are concrete and easily identified. For example, the *th* sounds in *then* and *with* are pronounced in black dialect as *den* and *wif*; that is, *th* [/ð/] may be pronounced as *d* or *f*, depending on position. (Of course it would be inaccurate to say that black language has no *th* sound simply bcause it's realized differently.) In linguistic environments where the initial *th* sound is voiceless [/θ/], it is pronounced the same way as in white speech, as in *thought*, which is always *thought* (not *dought*), or *thing*, which is *thing*, or more usually *thang* (not *ding* or *dang*). Many times, Black Dialect sounds tend to be generally similar to those of white speakers of any given region of the country. That is, some black speakers in Boston say *pahk the cah* (deleting *r*'s) in the same way as white speakers of that area, and Southern Black Speech sounds pretty much the same as Southern White Speech. As a matter of fact, when you talk about pronunciation, there is no national standard even among white speakers, since the different regional dialects of the country all have their own individual standards. The following list indicates the few different pronunciations in Black English that are used by large numbers of black speakers:

Initial /*th*/ [/ð/] = /d/
  them = *dem*; *then* = *den*
Final /*th*/ [/θ/] = /f/
  south = *souf*; *mouth* = *mouf*
Deletion of middle and final /r/
  during = *doing*; *more* = *mow*; *Paris* = *pass*; *star* = *stah*
Deletion of middle and final /l/
  help = *hep*; *will* = *wi*
  When the contracted form of *will* is used (/'ll/), you get a kind of /ah/ sound, as: *Iah be there in a minute* (for *I'll be there in a minute*).

Deletion of most final consonants
 hood = hoo; bed = be
 test = tes; wasp = was
 Pluralized forms ending in such double consonants add /es/, thus: *tests = tesses; wasps = wasses.* (One important exception to this rule involves words ending in /s/, such as the proper name *Wes.* Here the /s/ is *not* deleted.)
Vowel plus /ng/ [/ŋ/] in *thing, ring, sing* rendered as /ang/
 thing = thang; ring = rang; sing = sang
Contraction of *going to* rendered as *gon.* Here the *to* is omitted altogether, and the nasal sound at the end is shortened, producing a sound that is somewhat like an abbreviated form of *gone.*
 He was gon tell his momma good-by.
Primary stress on first syllable and front shifting
 police = PO-lice; Detroit = DEE-troit
Simple vowels
 nice = nahs
 boy = boah

While digging on the sights and sounds of the black community, here are some things you are likely to hear:

"Dem dudes always be doin day thang." (*Those dudes are always doing their thing* . . . Eighth grade student)
"Hur' up, the bell ranging." (*Hurry up, the bell is ringing* . . . Fourth grade student)
"Sang good, now y'all." (*Sing good* . . . Female adult in Baptist church)
"Doin the civil right crisis, we work hard." (*During the civil rights crisis, we worked hard* . . . College student)
"We are aware of the antagonism between the PO-lice and the black community." (Big city mayor)

Linguistically speaking, the greatest differences between contemporary Black and White English are on the level of grammatical structure. Grammar is the most rigid and fixed aspect of speech, that part of *any* language which is least likely to change over time. Couple this linguistic fact with the historical reality that only in recent years have there been concerted and intense pressures on the black masses to conform to the language standards of White America. Thus it is logical that the grammatical patterns of Black English have been the last component of Black Dialect to change in the direction of White English.

Black Idiom speakers throughout the United States have certain grammatical structures in common—despite the region of the country, and in some instances despite the social class level. Middle-class blacks from Detroit, for example, were found to delete -ed in verbs more frequently than middle-class whites from Detroit.

The most distinctive differences in the structure of Black Dialect are patterns using *be* (sometimes written and pronounced as *bees* or *be's*). These forms are mainly used to indicate a condition that occurs habitually. *Be* is omitted if the condition or event is not one that is repeated or recurring. For example, *The coffee bees cold* means *Every day the coffee's cold*, which is different from *The coffee cold* which means *Today the coffee's cold*. In other words if you the cook and *The coffee cold*, you might only just get talked about that day, but if *The coffee bees cold*, pretty soon you ain't gon have no job! The *be/non-be* rule operates with systematic regularity in the Black-English-speaking community.

Consider another example, this time from a young black Detroiter commenting on her father: *My father, he work at Ford. He be tired. So he can't never help us with our homework.* The *He be tired* here means *Every day my father is tired.* If the speaker had wanted to indicate that that fact applied to one day only, she would have left the *be* out of the sentence; thus, *My father, he work at Ford. He tired,* indicating that although he is tired today, this is generally not the case. (An unlikely situation, however, because if your father work at Ford Motor Company, on that Detroit assembly line where the Brothers bees humpin, he be tired all the time, believe me!) Here are a few other examples of *be* used to indicate habitual aspect:

They be slow all the time.
She be late every day.
I see her when I bees on my way to school.
By the time I go get my momma, it be dark.
The kid alway be messing up and everything.

Be is also used in combination with *do* to convey habitual conditions expressed in question form and for emphasis: *Do they be playing all day?* (in White English, *Do they play all day?*) and *Yeah, the boys do be messing around a lot* (in White English, *Yeah, the boys do mess around a lot*).

In addition to the use of *be* for habitual events, there is another important function of *be* that should be noted here. The Black English speaker can use *be* to convey a sense of future time, as in *The boy be here soon* and *They family be gone Friday.* Now keep in mind that these subtle distinctions in the meaning and use of *be* depend heavily on context. Thus the listener has got to heed the contextual cues in order to decode the speaker's meaning properly. For instance:

She be there later. (future *be*)
She be there everyday. (habitual *be*)

I be going home tomorrow. (future *be*)
I be going home all the time. (habitual *be*)

Future *be* may appear in combination with the contracted form of *will* ('ll). (Remember that due to the Black English sound rule of /l/ deletion, we get a kind of /ah/ sound for the letters /'ll/.) Thus you will hear: *He be looking for you next week*, as well as *He-ah be looking for you next week*. The explanation for both forms being used can be found in the process of language change [involved in] the transition from a more Africanized Black English to a more Americanized Black English. In the early stages of Black English, probably only *be* by itself was used to denote future time. Then, with the change in time and the collapsing of Black English structures toward those of White English, speakers of Black English began to indicate future time also with the use of *will* (pronounced, of course, according to rules for Black English sounds). However, since the process of language change is still incomplete, we find both ways of expressing future time in the black community and, indeed, within the speech of any one individual speaker of Black English.

Interestingly enough, forms of *be* (but not *be* itself) appear in places where they are needed for meaning, as in the past tense and in questions tacked on to sentences, so-called "tag" questions. For example, *He was my English teacher last year* rather than something ambiguous like *He my English teacher last year*. And *You ain't sick, is you?* rather than the unintelligible form, *You ain't sick, you?*

When the forms of *be* are used, they are simplified so that *is* and *was* usually serve for all subjects of sentences, whether the subjects are singular or plural, or refer to *I, you, we,* or whatever. For example, as above, we have *You ain't sick, is you?* as well as *She ain't home, is she?* And *He was my English teacher last year*, as above, as well as *They was acting up and going on*. The contracted form ('s) may also be used, as: *We's doing our book work and everythang when she start callin on us.*

As mentioned earlier, the Black English speaker omits *be* when referring to conditions that are fixed in time and to events or realities that do not repeat themselves. Applying the *non-be* rule, you get an absence of *be* before nouns: *He a hippie now;* before adjectives: *He too tall for me;* before adverbs: *They shoes right there;* before prepositional phrases: *My momma in the hospital;* and in auxiliary constructions: *They talking about school now.* Here are some additional examples of the absense of *be* to indicate a nonrecurring event or a fixed, static condition:

He sick today.
This my mother.
That man too tall for her little short self.
They daddy in the house.

The mens playing baseball and the womens cooking today.
Man, your ride really bad.

Black English speakers use *been* to express past action that has
recenty been completed. "Recently" here depends much more on the
particular words in the sentence that express the time, rather than the
actual amount of time itself. For example, it is correct Black English to
say: *She been tardy twice this semester* (which might have been several
weeks or months ago as long as it's what would be called "this semester"). But it is *not* correct Black English to say: *She been tardy twice
last semester* (although "last semester" might have just ended at the
time the speaker is stating the fact). In order to express the idea of two
tardinesses "last semester," the correct Black English statement would
be: *She was tardy twice last semester*. If this sounds confusing, remember
that White English has similar constraints upon the speaker's expression. Thus White English speakers can say: *I have been to New York this
year*, but they *cannot* say: *I have been to New York last year*. As a rule of
thumb, you can say that generally where Black English speakers use
been, White English speakers would use *have, has,* or *had* plus *been*.

Black English: He been there before.
White English: He has been there before.

Black English: They been there before.
White English: They have been there before.

Black English: She been there and left before I even got there.
White English: She had been there and left before I even got there.

Note that Black English uses only the verb form *been*, regardless of the
form of the subject or whether *have* is present or past tense.

Been is also used in combination with other verb forms to indicate
past action, which might be recently completed, or more distantly completed action (although again, it is structural expression that counts,
not the actual semantic reality). For example: *He been gone a year*, but
also: *He been gone a day*. The White English equivalents would be a form
of *have* plus *been* plus the verb, thus:

Black English: He been gone a year.
White English: He has been gone a year.

Black English: They been gone a year.
White English: They have been gone a year.

Black English: She been gone a year before anybody know it.
White English: She had been gone a year before anybody knew
                 it.

As mentioned, it is not the time itself that governs the verb choice, but the way the time is expressed. Keeping this in mind will help us distinguish betwen use of *been* plus the verb and the past tense of *be* plus the verb. Thus, *Tony been seen at her house today,* but not *Tony been seen at her house yesterday.* Instead, this latter statement would be rendered in correct Black English as *Tony was seen at her house yesterday.*

Now just when you think you got that all straight, I'm gon throw a tricky one in here because sometimes *been* is used to show emphasis, regardless of the time that has elapsed since an action took place. *She BEEN there,* uttered with stress on *BEEN,* means that the speaker wants to emphasize the fact that the individual has been wherever she is for a long enough period of time that it's an established fact. Now, she mighta just got there, or maybe she even been there for days, but the point here is not the amount of time but the intensity and validity of the fact. In other words, she been there long enough for me to be certain bout it, so ain no point in keepin on askin questions bout it!

In similar fashion, *been* patterns with other verb forms to suggest emphatic assertion, *He BEEN gone,* meaning I'm certain of the fact of his leaving (it might have taken place long ago, or the leaving might have just occurred; at any rate, the speaker is not concerned with the precise amount of time, just the real fact of the departure). Note that in both patterns of emphasis, *been* appears in the sentence without any other kind of qualifying expressions of time or emphasis. Thus while correct Black English would be *He BEEN gone,* if you added the words *a long time,* it would be incorrect Black English. If there is another word or words that convey the intensity or duration of time in the sentence, then the Black English speaker would not put any special stress on the *been.* Thus we would have simply *He been gone a long time,* not *He BEEN gone a long time.*

Done used by itself indicates past action, either recently completed or completed in the distant past. *I done my homework today* and *I done my homework yesterday* are both correct Black English statements. White English equivalents would be *I did my homework today* and *I did my homework yesterday.* When used in combination with another verb, *done* usually indicates only recently completed action (again "recently" depending on how it's expressed in the sentence). It is correct Black English to say *I done finish my work today,* but it is *not* correct Black English to say *I done finish my work yesterday.* The correct Black English here would be *I finish my work yesterday.* As explained earlier, White English has similar linguistic constraints. Thus White English speakers can say *I have finished my work today,* but they cannot say *I have finished my work yesterday.* The correct White English statement would be *I finished my work yesterday.*

What is important to keep in mind here is the distinction between *done* used by itself and *done* used in combination with other verbs. A

Black English statement containing only *done* can usually be understood to mean the White English *did*. However, when it is used with another verb, you cannot substitute the White English form *did*. Instead, the White English equivalent is a form of *have* (*have, has,* or *had*). The Black English *James done seen the show* is NOT White English *James did seen the show,* NOR *James did see the show,* BUT *James has seen the show.* Similarly, the Black English *I done did my hair* is not the White English *I did my hair,* but *I have done my hair,* as in *I have done my hair five times this week.* Note here that the Black English *did* actually translates into the White English *done.* But there are Black English uses of *did.* For example, if the Black English speaker wanted to express emphasis, he or she would use *did* in the same way as White English speakers, thus:

Black English: I DID do my hair five times this week!
White English: I DID do my hair five times this week!

Done can be found in Black English in combination with *been.* In such statements, *done* still functions like White English *have. He done been gone all night* (White English: *He has been gone all night*) and *They done been sitting there a hour* (White English: *They have been sitting there an hour*). Sentences like these can also be used without *done* and still be correct Black English. Just as the White English speaker has many different ways of expressing the same thing, so the Black English speaker has many linguistic options. Thus, the speaker of Black English could say any of the following:

He done been gone all night *or* He been gone all night.
They done been sitting there a hour *or* They been sitting there a hour.
She done been tardy twice this semester *or* She been tardy twice this semester.

Now here's a tricky one for you. This Black English use of *done* makes possible a tense that has pretty much gone out of white mainstream usage—that is, the future perfect, also referred to as past future. In White English, you used to get this kind of verb usage in sentences like the following:

He will have left by the time we get there.
I shall have finished before anyone arrives.

If those two expressions sound kinda stuffy, they should. Nowadays, you would more likely hear the following from White English speakers:

He will be gone by the time we get there.

I will be finished before anyone arrives.

Here's how Black English speakers render this future perfect: *be* plus *done* plus verb.

He be done left by the time we get there.
I be done finish before anyone arrive.

This usage is still very popular among Black English speakers and is found in the much-used Black Idiom expression "I be done ——— before you know it." Hip users of this Black English expression simply fill in whatever verb they want to use, according to context. Here are some examples of this use of future perfect from Black English speakers (for White English equivalents, simply substitute *will have* plus verb):

> "I *be done did* this lil' spot a hair fo' you know it." (middle age beautician)
> "If you mess wif me, *I be done did* you in fo' you know it." (young male about to git it on)
> "The Lord *be done call* me Home fo' you know it." (young church deacon)
> "If you ain mighty particular, yo' luck *be done run* out fo' you know it." (senior citizen to young black on the wild)
> "Look out, now! Fo' you know it, I *be done caught* you out there bluffin." (doctor at poker game)

Black Dialect relies on either the context of the immediate sentence or the context of an entire conversation to signal conditions of time. There is no *-ed* in either past tense or past participle constructions (*I look for him last night* and *This guy I know name Junior . . .*). Using context to signal time, the same verb form serves for both present and past tense, as: *The bus pass me up last week,* but also: *The bus pass me up every day.* The words *last week* and *every day* signal the time of these statements rather than a change in the verb form. Similarly, in the following statement from a black sermon, the preacher has already established the fact that he's talking about the past since he's talking about the life and sacrifice of Christ: "The man Jesus, He come here, He die to save you from your sins! He walk the earth, He go among the thieves and try to save the unrighteous. The Master say whosoever will, let him come!"

Most Black English verbs are not marked for person. The same verb forms serves for all subjects, whether singular or plural. The subject and number of the verb are marked by the context of the sentence or by some word in the sentence. Thus, *She have us say it.* Here the singular subject is indicated by *she,* with no change in the verb *have.*

Another example: *He do the same thang they do.* In this sentence, there is no need to alter the verb *do* because the subjects *he* and *they* in the context convey the meaning and notion of two different subjects.

Black Dialect obviously has the concepts of plurality and possession, but they are not indicated by the addition of *-s* or apostrophes with *-s*. *Two boys just left, two* indicates that *boy* is plural. *That was Mr. Johnson store got burn down,* the position of the noun, *Mr. Johnson,* signals who owns the store.

As a result of trying to conform Africanized patterns to Americanized ones, and doing so without the benefit of formal language instruction, blacks created in Black English a number of overly correct or hypercorrect forms, such as the addition of *-s* to already pluralized forms, as in *It's three childrens in my family* and *The peoples shouldn't do that.* We also find forms such as *they does.* Such hypercorrections are due to insufficient knowledge and instruction in the erratic rules of White English. For example, in White English, an *s* is added to a singular verb form (as in *He does*) but not to a plural form (as in *They do*). In learning the language without systematic formal instruction, the traditional Africanized English speaker tries to reconcile this paradox and may end up adding an *s* to a lot of forms, so we not only get attempts to be correct producing *They does* but such attempts also produce *I does.*

Black English speakers place stress on the subjects of sentences. In White English, this might be labeled the "double subject." Rather than being a duplicate subject as such, the repetition of the subject in some other form is used in Black English for emphasis. Two examples: *My son, he have a new car* and *The boy who left, he my friend.* Note that the emphasis is indicated without pronouncing the words in any emphatic way since this is accomplished by the "double subject." This feature of Black English is not a mandatory one, so you may hear it sometimes, other times not at all. As with White English speakers, there are many options open to the speaker of Black English. The repetition of subject is simply another such option.

The personal pronoun system of Black English is not as highly differentiated as that of White English. Thus, for example, with the third person plural pronoun, *they,* the same form serves for subject, possessive, and so-called reflexive as in *The expressway bought they house* and *They should do it theyselves.* In the case of the third person singular pronoun, *he,* we will hear both *He gone* and *Him cool,* and in the reflexive, *He did it all by hisself.* At an earlier stage in the development of Black English, forms like *he book* (for *his book*) and *she house* (for *her house*) were prominent, but these have gradually disappeared. You may hear them in very young preschool children. With many pronouns in White English, you have a somewhat similar rule that allows the same form to be used for subjects, objects, and possessives. Thus, White

English speakers say *James hit her* as well as *This is her book*. At one time in the early history of British-American English, there were different forms for all personal pronouns, but as the language changed, the English pronoun system was simplified to a reduced number of forms.

The pronoun *it* is used to refer to things and objects ("itsy" things) as in White English, but Black English adds an additional function for the pronoun. *It* can be used to introduce statements, and as such, has no real meaning. For example, *It's four boy and two girl in the family* and *It was a man had died*. The patterns of English sentences are such that they may require a "filler" word in some statements, even though the "filler" itself is empty in a semantic sense. Typically, American English uses the word *there* in such sentences. Thus, (White English) *There are four boys and two girls in the family* and *There was a man who had died*. Black English may also use the introductory *it* in question form.

Is it a Longfellow street in this city? (White English: Is there a Longfellow street in this city?)
Is it anybody home? (White English: Is there anybody home?)

As an adverbial demonstrative, *Here* or *There* plus *go* is used instead of *here/there* plus *is/are*. For example, *There go my brother in the first row* and *Here go my momma right here*. The speaker also has the option of expressing these two statements with *it* as explained above. Thus, *It's my brother in the first row* and *It's my momma right there*.

As with the deletion of final consonants in many Black English sounds, the dialect omits the final *'s* in adverbs, for example, *Sometime they do that* and *He alway be here*.

Whereas the old double negative goes back to Shakespeare and is in abundant use among whites today, triple and quadruple negatives are the sole province of Africanized English. Thus, *Don't nobody never help me do my work, Can't nobody do nothin in Mr. Smith class,* and *Don't nobody pay no attention to no nigguh that ain crazy!* Note that these are statements, not questions, despite the reverse word order. Now the rule for forming negatives in Black English is just a little bit tricky, so check it out closely. If the negative statement is composed of only *one* sentence, then *every* negatable item in the statement *must* be negated. Therefore, *Don't nobody never help me do the work,* which consists of only one sentence, has a negative in every possible place in the sentence. The White English translation is: *No one ever helps me do my work.* If, however, the negative statement involves *two* or more sentences combined together as one, a different rule operates. If every negatable item in the statement is negated, the White English translation would be a statement in the "positive." If, however, the statement contains all negatives plus one positive, the White English translation would be a statement in the "negative." Take the example mentioned above, the line from Lonne Elder's play, *Ceremonies in Dark Old Men: Don't nobody pay no attention to no nigguh that ain crazy!* Here, there are two sentences combined into one statement, and every item in the statement is negated, rendering the White English translation: *If you are a crazy nigger, you will get attention.* Now, suppose you wanted to convey the opposite meaning, that is, the White English, *If you are a crazy nigger, you will not get any attention.* The correct Black English would be expressed as all negatives plus one positive, thus: *Don't nobody pay no attention to no nigguh that's crazy!* (Keep in mind that this rule only applies to statements in which there are two or more sentences combined into one.)

To state the Black English negation rule more succinctly: if the statement consists of only *one* sentence, negate every item; if the statement consists of *two* or *more* sentences combined as one, all negatives indicate "positives," and all negatives, *plus one positive* indicate "negatives." Here are some other examples:

It ain nobody I can trust (White English: *I can trust no one.*)
It ain nobody I can't trust. (White English: *I can trust everyone.*)
Wasn't no girls could go with us. (White English: *None of the girls could go with us.*)
Wasn't no girls couldn't go with us. (White English: *All the girls could go with us.*)
Ain't none these dudes can beat me. (White English: *None of these dudes can beat me.*)
Ain't none of these dudes can't beat me. (White English: *All these dudes can beat me.*)

Another distinctive Black Dialect negation pattern occurs in statements which are only partly negative. These statements pattern with *but,* as in *Don't but one person go out at a time* and *Don't nobody but God know when that day gon be.*

The foregoing discussion of Black Dialect sound and structure patterns should prove useful to teachers and others who wish to understand black lingo so as to really dig where such speakers are comin from. Obviously this kind of understanding can help bridge the linguistic and cultural gap between blacks and whites and thus facilitate communication. However, certain cautions should be observed. First, do not expect *all* Black English speakers to use *all* these patterns *all* the time. The list is intended to be exhaustive of the range of patterns you might encounter in a given situation, but some Black Dialect speakers may be more bidialectal than others, preferring to use White English around whites, Black English around blacks. (For example, among school-age blacks, one would find a greater degree of bidialectalism among older adolescents than among younger black children, for adolescents have begun to get hip to the social sensitivities associated with different kinds of languages and dialects.) Second, no speaker of any hue uses the range of patterns in their language one hundred percent of the time. This caution is the more to be exercised in the face of the transition of Africanized English towards the direction of Americanized English. Thus, one may find in any Black English speaker both *he do* and *he does* although the *he do*'s will predominate. You will also find uses of *-ed* in some past tense forms and other features of White English. Again, this is due to dialect mixture and the transition of Black English to White English. . . . However, the Black English forms will prevail most of the time.

And with that, I'm going to close with a statement about "grammar and goodness" from my man, Langston Hughes, who often speaks through his folk hero, Jesse B. Simple—that beer-drinkin, rappin, profound thinkin Harlemite that Hughes first created for the pages of the well-known black newspaper, the *Chicago Defender*.

> "I have writ a poem," said Simple.
> "Again?" I exclaimed. "The last time you showed me a poem of yours, it was too long, also not too good."
> "This one is better," said Simple. "Joyce had a hand in it, also my friend, Boyd, who is colleged. So I want you to hear it."
> "I know you are determined to read it to me, so go ahead."
> "It is about that minister down in Montgomery who committed a miracle."
> "What miracle?" I asked.
> "Getting Negroes to stick together," declared Simple.
> "I presume you are speaking of Rev. King," I said.
> "I am," said Simple. "He is the man, and this is my poem. Listen fluently now! This poem is writ like a letter. It is addressed to the White Citizens Councilors of Alabama and all their members, and this is how it goes:

> Dear Citizens Councilors:
> In line of what my folks
> Say in Montgomery,
> In line of what they
> Teaching about love,
> When I reach out my hand,
> White folks, will you take it?
> Or will you cut it off
> And make a nub?
> Since God put it in
> My heart to love you,
> If I love you
> Like I really could,
> If I say, 'Brother,
> I forgive you,'

I wonder, would it
Do you any good?
Since slavery-time, long gone,
You been calling me
All kinds of names,
Pushing me down.
I been swimming with my
Head deep under water—
And you wished I would
Stay under till I drowned.
Well, I did not!
I'm still swimming!
Now you mad because
I won't ride in the
Back end of your bus.
When I answer, 'Anyhow,
I'm gonna love you,'
Still and yet, today
You want to make a fuss.

Now, listen, white folks:
In line with Rev. King
Down in Montgomery—
Also because the Bible
Says I must—
In spite of bombs and buses,
I'm gonna love you.
I say, I'm gonna LOVE you—
White folks, OR bust!"

"You never wrote a poem that logical all by yourself in life," I said.

"I know I didn't," admitted Simple. "But I am getting ready to write another one now. This time I am going to write a poem about Jim Crow up North, and it is going to start something like this:

In the North
The Jim Crow line
Ain't clear—
But it's here!
From New York to Chicago,
Points past and
In between,
Jim Crow is mean!
Even though integrated,
With Democracy
Jim Crow is *not* mated.
Up North Jim Crow
Wears an angel's grin—
But still he sin.
I swear he do!
Don't you?

"I agree that the sentiment of your poem is correct," I said. "But I cannot vouch for the grammar."

"If I get the sense right," answered Simple, "the grammar can take care of itself. There are plenty of Jim Crowers who speak grammar, but do evil. I have not had enough schooling to put words together right— but I know some white folks who have went to school forty years and do not do right. I figure it is better to do right than to write right, is it not?"

"You have something there," I said. "So keep on making up your poems, if you want to. At least, they rhyme."

"They make sense, too, don't they?" asked Simple.

"I think they do," I answered.

"They does," said Simple.

"They do," I corrected.

"They sure does," said Simple.

Some Well-Known Black Proverbs and Sayings[1]

1. You never miss yo water till yo well run dry.
2. Grits ain't groceries, eggs ain't poultry, and Mona Lisa was a man. (I must be telling the truth since grits *are* groceries, eggs *are* poultry and Mona Lisa sure wasn't a man!)
3. You ain't got a pot to piss in or a window to throw it out of. (you are in poor financial straits)
4. If I'm lying, I'm flying. (proving truth: I must not be lying, if I were, I'd be flying)
5. You so dumb you can't throw rain water out of a boot, and the directions say how.
6. The blacker the berry, the sweeter the juice. (he or she must be fine, he or she is so ripe and sweet; also suggestive of sexuality and sensual power)
7. What goes around comes around. (you reap what you sow)
8. If I tell you a hen dip snuff, look under its wing and find a whole box. (proving truth and claim of infallibility by speaker)
9. Study long, you study wrong. (listen to first impulses, because lengthy deliberations are liable to be inaccurate)
10. The eagle flies on Friday. (eagle, symbolizing money; statement commemorates payday)
11. Let the door hit you where the good Lord split you. (nasty command to leave, euphemism of "split you" avoiding profanity)

[1] For an outstanding collection and analysis of proverbs, see Jack L. Daniel. "Towards an Ethnography of Afro American Proverbial Usage," *Black Lines*, Winter 1972, pp. 3–12.

12. A hard head make a soft behind. (being stubborn, refusing to listen can make you pay a stiff price)
13. If you make yo bed hard, you gon have to lie in it.
14. It was so quiet you could hear a rat piss on cotton.
15. Pretty is as pretty does. (you are known by your actions)
16. Action speak louder than words. (same as above, this proverb is more common among younger blacks today)
17. You don't believe fat meat is greasy. (signifyin on fools who insist on adhering to certain beliefs or opinions in the face of logical evidence to the contrary)
18. Tight as Dick's hatband. (financially stingy, refusing to share or give)

FOR DISCUSSION AND REVIEW

1. Smitherman states that Black English uses the same sounds (phonemes) and the same number of sounds as does White English. Why, then, is the pronunciation of Black English so different from that of White English? Explain your answer, using specific examples.

2. Study the five sentences in Black English that follow. Identify the phonological rules of Black English that have affected each sentence (e.g., loss [or replacement] of interdental fricative).
"Dem dudes always be doin day thang."
"Hur' up, the bell ranging."
"Sang good, now y'all."
"Doin the civil right crisis, we work hard."
"We are aware of the antagonism between the PO-lice and the black community."

3. Grammatical (syntactic) differences between standard American English and Black English are very important, more so than phonological differences. Smitherman discusses a number of these syntactic differences in detail. Summarize her discussion of each of the following, giving examples to illustrate each point.
a. the use and non-use of the various forms of *be*
b. the use of *done*, both alone and in combination with other verbs
c. the past tense suffix *-ed*
d. subject-verb concord in the third person singular, present tense
e. plurality
f. possession
g. hypercorrection
h. subject repetition
i. the personal pronoun system
j. use of *it*
k. use of *go*
l. the effect of final consonant simplification or deletion on adverbs
m. double, triple, and quadruple negatives

4. List two words per rule that exemplify each of the following Black English (BE) pronunciation characteristics. Then transcribe each word phonemically to show its actual Black English pronunciation.
a. loss of medial and final /r/
b. final consonant deletion
c. monophthongization of SAE diphthongs /ay/ and /aw/
d. loss of interdental fricatives
e. loss of medial and final /l/

Projects for "Language Variation: Regional and Social"

1. Prepare a report on the purposes and methods of the *Linguistic Atlas of the United States and Canada* project. Use the library card catalogue, Hans Kurath's *Handbook of the Linguistic Geography of New England*, Lee Pederson's *A Manual for Dialect Research in the Southern States*, the *Newsletter of the American Dialect Society,*, the *PMLA Bibliography*, and the *Social Sciences Index* to locate materials for this project.

2. Collection of materials for the *Dictionary of American Regional English* (*DARE*) began in 1965; the goal was to produce by 1976 an American dictionary comparable to the *English Dialect Dictionary*. Prepare a report on the methodology and progress of the *DARE* project. A longer report could examine the similarities and differences in purposes and methods between the *Linguistic Atlas of the United States and Canada* and the *Dictionary of American Regional English*. As a starting point, read Frederic G. Cassidy's "The *Atlas* and *DARE*," in *Lexicography and Dialect Geography*, ed. Harold Sholler and John Reidy (Wiesbaden: F. Steiner, 1973).

3. The names of cities, towns, rivers, and mountains often provide clues to settlement and migration patterns. Using a map of your area, list three local place names and discuss their significance. For example, you may wish to find out the meaning of each name and whether or not any of the names appear elsewhere in the country (and, if so, whether or not they are related). You will find the following references useful: Kelsie B. Harder's *Illustrated Dictionary of Place Names* (1976) and George R. Stewart's *American Place-Names* (1970).

4. Study the history of your community so that you can write a report in which you discuss the ways in which settlement patterns, population shifts, and physical geography have influenced the speech of the area.

5. Bidialectalism is a highly controversial subject. Prepare a report (1) presenting the opposing views objectively or (2) after explaining the arguments, supporting one particular view. To start, reread Labov and consult O'Neil (1972), Pixton (1974), and Sledd (1969, 1972), plus more recent articles. Do you consider the sociologic and economic factors raised by the various authors important? What issues do not appear to be relevant? From an educational point of view, which argument is the strongest? Defend whatever position you take.

6. Prepare a report summarizing the history of Black English in America. (Note: Not all authorities agree on the origin and development of BE.) Consult Smitherman's book (from which the article in this section was taken) and Dillard (1972).

7. As evidenced by Roger Shuy's discussion of methodology, word geography is a fascinating aspect of dialect study. Read E. Bagby Atwood's "Grease and Greasy: A Study of Geographical Variation," *Texas Studies in English* 29 (1950), 249–60. Based on this reading, and using Shuy's "Checklist of Regional Expressions" and his "Personal Data Sheet," survey your class, your campus (or a random sample thereof), or your community (or a random sample). Before you actually collect any data, you will need to consider such matters as the size and nature of the population to be studied, the selection of reliable and representative informants, and possible significant influences in the history of the college or community. Tabulate your results. Do any local or regional patterns emerge? Do you find any other patterns (e.g., systematic differences by age, sex, educational level, etc.)?

8. In an article entitled "Sense and Nonsense About American Dialects" (*PMLA*, 81 [1966], 7–17), Raven I. McDavid, Jr., says that "the surest social markers in American English are grammatical forms." Collect examples of grammatical forms used in your community. What social classes are represented?

9. The concept of "standard English" has caused much misunderstanding and debate. For many Americans, "standard" implies that one variety of English is more correct or more functional than other varieties. Investigate the history of the concept of "standard English." How, for example, did the concept develop? How do various linguists define it? Is "standard English" a social dialect? What exactly is the power or mystique of "standard English"?

10. Select the work of an author whose characters speak a social or regional variety of English—e.g., William Dean Howells, *The Rise of Silas Lapham;* Mark Twain, *Roughing It* (particularly "Buck Fanshaw's Funeral"); Bret Harte, *The Luck of Roaring Camp and Other Sketches;* Sarah Orne Jewett, *The Country of the Pointed Firs;* Joel Chandler Harris, *Uncle Remus and Br'er Rabbit;* William Faulkner, *The Sound and the Fury;* Willa Cather, *My Antonia;* John Steinbeck, *The Grapes of Wrath;* or Henry Roth, *Call It Sleep.* Identify the dialect presented and discuss the devices that the author uses to represent dialect. Read a passage aloud; how closely does it approximate actual speech?

11. Dialect differences in pronunciation abound. Here are some words for which there are distinct regional pronunciations. Compare your pronunciation of these items with those of others in your class:

collar	cot	wash
car	apricot	paw
empty	dog	tomato
door	clientele	marry
garage	mangy	Mary

oil	house	roof
can	very	sorry
greasy	either	fog
lot	caller	water
caught	horse	almond
hurry	class	idea

What pronunciation differences do you note among the members of your class? Are any regional patterns of pronunciation evident? Compare your results with the regional pronunciations discussed by Roger Shuy.

12. Conduct one of the research projects suggested by Wald and Shopen and prepare a report summarizing your findings.

13. The Ann Arbor, Michigan, decision in July 1979 about Black English and the schools received national attention and has been the subject of controversy and misunderstanding (*Martin Luther King Junior Elementary School Children, et al.* v. *Ann Arbor School District Board*, 473 F. Supp. 1371 [1979]). Using your library resources, prepare a report analyzing (a) the causes of the litigation, (b) the findings of the court, or (c) the effects of the decision on the Ann Arbor schools. One useful reference is *Black English: Educational Equity and the Law*, edited by John W. Chambers, Jr. (Ann Arbor, MI: Karoma Publishers, Inc., 1983).

14. Study the following information about the status of various United States linguistic atlas projects.

LAGS   *Linguistic Atlas of the Gulf States.* Lee Pederson, ed. In progress.

LAMSAS   *Linguistic Atlas of the Middle and South Atlantic States.* Raven I. McDavid and R. K. O'Cain. Chicago: University of Chicago Press, 1980–

LANCS   *The Linguistic Atlas of the North-Central States.* University of Chicago Library, 1977. (Basic materials on microfilm and microfiche.)

LANE   *Linguistic Atlas of New England.* Hans Kurath et al. Providence: Brown University Press, 1939–43; reissued 1972.

LAO   *Linguistic Atlas of Oklahoma.* (Fieldwork completed.)

LAPC   *Linguistic Atlas of the Pacific Coast (California–Nevada).* (Fieldwork completed.)

LAPN   *Linguistic Atlas of the Pacific Northwest.* (Fieldwork completed for Washington.)

LARMS   *Linguistic Atlas of the Rocky Mountain States.* (Fieldwork completed for Colorado.)

LAUMW   *The Linguistic Atlas of the Upper Midwest.* Harold B. Allen. Minneapolis: University of Minnesota Press, 1973– 76.

Prepare two lists, one indicating states in which work is under way, the other indicating states in which no work has yet been done. What conclusions can you draw? Write a paragraph in which you argue for one of the following positions: (a) a *linguistic atlas of the United States* will probably be completed within the next twenty-five years or (b) the atlas will probably never be completed.

Selected Bibliography

The books by J. K. Chambers and Peter Trudgill, by Lawrence M. Davis, and by W. N. Francis contain excellent general bibliographies. Geneva Smitherman's book, from which the selection in this part was taken, contains an excellent bibliography of works dealing with Black English. The journal American Speech *and the monograph series* Publications of the American Dialect Society (PADS) *regularly publish material of interest.*

Allen, Harold B. *The Linguistic Atlas of the Upper Midwest.* Vol. 1, "Regional Speech Distribution." Minneapolis: University of Minnesota Press, 1973; vol. 2, "Grammar." Minneapolis: University of Minnesota Press, 1975; vol. 3. "Pronunciation." Minneapolis: University of Minnesota Press, 1976. (Invaluable reference for study of speech in the Upper Midwest.)

————. "The Linguistic Atlases: Our New Resource." *English Journal,* 45 (April 1956), 188–194. (A discussion of *Linguistic Atlas* data and their applications.)

————. "The Primary Dialect Areas of the Upper Midwest." *Studies in Language and Linguistics in Honor of Charles C. Fries.* Ed. Albert H. Marckwardt. Ann Arbor: The English Language Institute, The University of Michigan, 1964. (A study of the lexical, phonological, and morphological features of the speech in the Upper Midwest region.)

————. "Two Dialects in Contact." *American Speech* 48 (Spring–Summer 1973), 54–66. (A study of dialect boundaries in the Upper Midwest based on *Atlas* materials.)

Allen, Harold B., and Gary N. Underwood, eds. *Readings in American Dialectology.* New York: Appleton-Century-Crofts, 1971. (An anthology of essays dealing with important regional and social aspects of American dialectology.

Ann Arbor Decision. Washington, DC: Center for Applied Linguistics, 1979. (Landmark decision requiring the Ann Arbor schools to take BE into account in planning curricula; Civil Action No. 7–71861, United States District Court, Eastern District of Michigan, Southern Division; Martin Luther King Junior Elementary School Children, et al., Plaintiffs, v. Ann Arbor School District Board, Defendant.)

Atwood, E. Bagby. *A Survey of Verb Forms in the Eastern United States.* Ann Arbor: University of Michigan Press, 1953. (A fundamental work in linguistic geography.)

Bailey, R. W., and J. L. Robinson, eds. *Varieties of Present-Day English.* New York: Macmillan, 1973. (Excellent collection of articles.)

Bentley, Robert H., and Samuel D. Crawford, eds. *Black Language Reader.* Glenview, IL: Scott, Foresman and Company, 1973. (Good selection of articles, emphasizing education.)

Brasch, Ila Wales, and Walter Milton Brasch. *A Comprehensive Annotated Bibliography of American Black English.* Baton Rouge: Louisiana State University, 1974. (Invaluable bibliography on the subject of black English.)

Burling, Robbins. *English in Black and White.* New York: Holt, Rinehart and Winston, Inc., 1973. (Thorough introduction to dialects, with emphasis on black English; excellent for teachers.)

Cassidy, Frederic G. *Dictionary of American Regional English.* Cambridge, MA: Belknap Press, Harvard University, forthcoming. (A long-awaited reference and research work.)

————. "A Method for Collecting Dialect." *Publication of the American Dialect Society,* no. 20 (November 1953), 5–96. (Entire issue devoted to a discussion of field methods and the presentation of a comprehensive dialect questionnaire.)

Chambers, J. K. and Peter Trudgill. *Dialectology.* Cambridge: Cambridge University Press, 1980. (Very complete in its coverage; British orientation.)

Chambers, John W., Jr., ed. *Black English: Educational Equity and the Law.* Ann Arbor, MI: Karoma Publishers, 1983. (Collection of seven interesting essays plus a forward, an introduction, and the text of Judge Charles W. Joiner's "Memorandum Opinion and Order.")

Cullinan, Bernice E., ed. *Black Dialects & Reading.* Urbana, IL: National Council of Teachers of English, 1974. (Both theoretical and practical; all major positions are presented; includes an excellent 50-page annotated bibliography.)

Davis, A. L. "English Problems of Spanish Speakers," in *Culture, Class, and Language Variety,* ed. A. L. Davis, Urbana, IL: National Council of Teachers of English, 1972. (Detailed analysis of phonological contrasts between Spanish and English, with some discussion of grammatical contrasts.)

————. "Developing and Testing the Checklist." *American Speech* 46 (Spring–Summer 1971), 34–37. (Discussion of problems associated with developing a vocabulary questionnaire.)

————. "Dialect Distribution and Settlement Patterns in the Great Lakes Region." *The Ohio State Archeological and Historical Quarterly* 60 (January 1951), 48–56. (A study showing many interesting correlations between linguistic features and settlement patterns in the Great Lakes region.)

Davis, Lawrence M. *English Dialectology: An Introduction.* University, AL: The University of Alabama Press, 1983. (Intended as a text for courses in dialectology; surveys regional and social dialect work in the U.S. and Britain.)

Dillard, J. L. *American Talk.* New York: Random House, 1976. (Popular and interesting treatment of the development of a large variety of American expressions.)

————. *All-American English: A History of the English Language in America.* New York: Random House, 1975. (Stresses "Maritime English" and its influence on the American colonists.)

———. *Black English: Its History and Usage in the United States.* New York: Random House, 1972. (An investigation of the ways in which black English differs from other varieties of American English.)

Drake, James A. "The Effect of Urbanization Upon Regional Vocabulary." *American Speech* 36 (February 1961), 17–33. (A study of regional dialect items and urbanization in Cleveland, Ohio.)

Duckert, Audrey R. "The Second Time Around: Methods in Dialect Revisiting." *American Speech* 46 (Spring–Summer 1971), 66–72. (Methods for studying areas previously surveyed by the *Atlas* project—with emphasis on New England.)

Fasold, Ralph W. "Distinctive Linguistic Characteristics of Black English." *Linguistics and Language Study: 20th Roundtable Meeting.* Ed. James E. Alatis. Washington, DC: Georgetown University Press, 1970. (An examination of the distinctive differences between the nonstandard speech of poor blacks and the speech of whites.)

Fasold, Ralph W., and Walt Wolfram. *Teaching Standard English in the Inner City.* Washington, DC: Center for Applied Linguistics, 1970. (Discussion of the problems of teaching Standard English—interesting chapter on "Some Linguistic Features of Negro Dialect.")

Fischer, J. L. "Social Influences on the Choice of a Linguistic Variant." *Word* 14 (1958): 47–56. (The pioneering study that may have influenced Labov.)

Fishman, Joshua A. *Sociolinguistics: A Brief Introduction.* Rowley, MA: Newbury House Publishers, 1970. (Still a very good brief introduction to the field.)

Francis, W. N. *Dialectology: An Introduction.* New York: Longman, 1983. (An excellent introductory text.)

Grant, Steven A. "Language Policy in the United States," in *Profession 78.* New York: Modern Language Association of America, 1978. (Examination of both federal and state policies regarding, *inter alia*, foreign language training and use, bilingual education, cultural pluralism.)

Harder, Kelsie B., ed. *Illustrated Dictionary of Place Names: United States and Canada.* New York: Van Nostrand Reinhold Company, 1976. (Invaluable reference work for North American place names.)

Haskins, Jim, and Hugh F. Butts, M.D. *The Psychology of Black Language.* New York: Barnes & Noble Books, 1973. (A good, brief overview; extensive notes and bibliography, plus a glossary of BE words and phrases.)

Hoffman, Melvin J. "Bi-dialectalism Is Not the Linguistics of White Supremacy: Sense Versus Sensibilities." *The English Record* 21 (April 1971), 95–102. (An argument supporting the bidialectal approach to the teaching of Standard English and refuting James Sledd's position.)

Ives, Sumner. "Dialect Differentiation in the Stories of Joel Chandler Harris." *American Literature* 17 (March 1955), 88–96. (A study of the social implications of Harris's dialects.)

———. "A Theory of Literary Dialect." *Tulane Studies in English* 2 (1950), 137–182. (An essential reference for all students doing work in literary dialects.)

Kenyon, John S. "Cultural Levels and Functional Varieties of English." *College English,* 10 (October 1948), 31–36. (A classification of language that recognizes, first, levels having cultural or social associations and, second, formal and familiar varieties of language usage.)

Kretzschmar, William A., Jr., ed. *Dialects in Culture: Essays in General Dialectology by Raven I. McDavid, Jr.* University, AL: The University of Alabama Press, 1979. (A collection of 60 essays and reviews by one of America's best-known dialectologists.)

Kurath, Hans. *Studies in Area Linguistics.* Bloomington: Indiana University Press, 1972. (An examination of regional and social dialectology, American and foreign.)

————. *A Word Geography of the Eastern United States.* Ann Arbor: University of Michigan Press, 1949. (A basic book in linguistic geography.)

————, Miles L. Hanley, Bernard Block, et al. *Linguistic Atlas of New England.* 3 vols. in 6 parts. Providence RI: Brown University Press, 1939–1943; reissued New York: AMS Press, 1972. (Indispensable research and reference work for the study of speech in New England and for comparative studies. Should be used with companion *Handbook.*)

Labov, William. *Language in the Inner City: Studies in the Black English Vernacular.* Philadelphia: University of Pennsylvania Press, 1972. (A definitive work; detailed study of BE and of its social setting; bibliography.)

————. "The Logic of Nonstandard English." *Linguistics and Language Study: 20th Roundtable Meeting.* Ed. James E. Alatis. Washington, DC: Georgetown University Press, 1970. (Refutes theories that black English lacks logic and sophistication and reveals mental inferiority.)

————. *The Nonstandard Vernacular of the Negro Community: Some Practical Suggestions.* Washington, DC: Education Resources Information Center, 1967. (Some advice to teachers concerning bidialectalism for the speaker of a nonstandard dialect.)

————. *The Social Stratification of English in New York City.* Washington DC: Center for Applied Linguistics, 1966. (A landmark sociolinguistic study of New York City speech.)

————. "Stages in the Acquisition of Standard English." *Social Dialects and Language Learning.* Ed. Roger W. Shuy. Champaign, IL: NCTE, 1964. (An investigation of the acquisition of Standard English by children in New York City.)

Labov, William, Paul Cohen, Clarence Robins, and John Lewis. *A Study of the Non-Standard English of Negro and Puerto Rican Speakers in New York City.* Final Report, Cooperative Research Project no. 3288, vol. 1. Washington, DC: Office of Education, 1968.

Lamberts, J. J. "Another Look at Kenyon's Levels." *College English* 24 (November 1962), 141–143. (A reassessment of John S. Kenyon's classification of cultural levels and functional varieties of English.)

McDavid, Raven I., Jr. See Kretzschmar, 1979.

McDowell, Tremaine. "The Use of Negro Dialect by Harriet Beecher Stowe." *American Speech* 6 (June 1931), 322–326. (A study in literary dialect.)

McMillan, James B. *Annotated Bibliography of Southern American English.* Coral Gables: University of Miami Press, 1971. (A valuable reference work for the study of speech in southern states.)

Mencken, H. L. *The American Language: The Fourth Edition and the Two Supplements.* Abridged and ed. Raven I. McDavid, Jr. New York: Alfred A. Knopf, 1963. (A classic study of American English.)

Metcalf, Allan A. "Chicano English." *Language and Education: Theory and Practice* 2. Washington, DC: Center for Applied Linguistics, 1979. (Emphasizes that Chicano English is not an imperfect attempt by a native speaker of Spanish to master English.)

O'Neil, Wayne. "The Politics of Bidialectalism." *College English* 33 (1972), 433–438 (Argues that bidialectalism is aimed at maintaining the social status quo—the inequality of blacks in a predominantly white society.)

Pederson, Lee A. "An Approach to Urban Word Geography." *American Speech* 46 (Spring–Summer 1971), 73–86. (Presentation of vocabulary questionnaire suitable for urban testing—namely, in Chicago.)

———. "Negro Speech in *The Adventures of Huckleberry Finn*." *Mark Twain Journal* 13 (1966), 1–4. (An examination of the literary representation of Negro dialect in Twain's classic novel.)

Pixton, William H. "A Contemporary Dilemma: The Question of Standard English." *College Composition and Communication* 5 (1974), 247–253. (Argues for the use of Standard English by blacks.)

Pyles, Thomas, *Words and Ways of American English*. New York: Random House, 1952. (An introduction to American English from colonial times to the present.)

Reed, Carroll E. *Dialects of American English*. 2nd edition. Amherst: The University of Massachusetts Press, 1973. (An introduction to dialect study with units devoted to sectional atlas studies and to urban dialect studies.)

———. "The Pronunciation of English in the Pacific Northwest." *Language* 37 (October–December 1961), 559–564. (A description of the pronunciation of vowels and consonants by residents of the Pacific Northwest.)

Shopen, Timothy and Joseph M. Williams, eds. *Style and Variables in English*. Englewood Cliffs, N.J.: Winthrop Publishers, 1981. (An excellent collection of essays.)

———. *Standards and Dialects in English*. Englewood Cliffs, N.J.: Winthrop Publishers, 1980. (A companion volume to the preceding one; accompanying tapes are available.)

Shores, David L. and Carole P. Hines, eds. *Papers in Language Variation*. University, AL: The University of Alabama Press, 1977. (A collection of 29 papers, almost all originally presented at an ADS or SAMLA meeting.)

Shuy, Roger W. "Detroit Speech: Careless, Awkward, and Inconsistent, or Systematic, Graceful, and Regular?" *Elementary English* 45 (May 1968), 565–569. (A discussion of nonstandard speech in Detroit, Michigan.)

———. "Some Useful Myths in Social Dialectology." The *Florida FL Reporter* 11 (Spring–Fall 1973), 17–20, 55. (Identifies several myths that, though oversimplifications, are useful to social dialectologists.)

Sledd, James. "Bi-Dialectalism: The Linguistics of White Supremacy." *English Journal* 58 (1969), 1307–1315. (Argues against linguists and teachers who advocate bidialectal programs.)

———. "Doublespeak: Dialectology in the Service of Big Brother." *College English* 35 (January 1972). (A trenchant argument against bidialectalism; a classic.

Smith, Riley B. "Research Perspectives on American Black English: A Brief Historical Sketch." *American Speech* 49 (Spring–Summer 1974), 24–39. (A bibliographical essay with a historical perspective.)

Spolsky, Bernard, ed. *The Language Education of Minority Children*. Rowley, MA: Newbury House Publishers, 1972. (Fourteen essays; of interest especially to teachers.)

Stockton, Eric. "Poe's Use of Negro Dialect in 'The Gold-Bug.'" *Studies in Language and Linguistics in Honor of Charles C. Fries*. Ed. Albert H. Marckwardt. Ann Arbor: The English Language Institute, The University of Michigan, 1964. (An analysis of Jupiter's speech as an example of literary dialect used by pre-Civil War writers.)

Stoller, Paul, ed. *Black American English: Its Background and Its Usage in the Schools and in Literature*. New York: Dell Publishing Co., 1975. (Excellent collection of articles on the history and structure of BE, on BE and education, plus three literary excerpts illustrating use of BE; bibliography.)

Teschner, Richard V., Garland Bills, and Jerry R. Craddock. *Spanish and English of United States Hispanos: A Critical, Annotated, Linguistic Bibliography*. Washington, DC: Center for Applied Linguistics, 1975. (An invaluable research tool for studies in this area.)

Trudgill, Peter. *The Social Differentiation of English in Norwich*. Cambridge: Cambridge University Press, 1972. (A model study; basic.)

———. *Sociolinguistics: An Introduction*. Penguin Books, 1974. (An excellent introduction by a leader in the field.)

Underwood, Gary N. "Vocabulary Change in the Upper Midwest." *Publication of the American Dialect Society* 49 (April 1968), 8–28. (An investigation of language change that utilizes four generations of informants.)

Williamson, Juanita V., and Virginia M. Burke, eds. *A Various Language: Perspectives on American Dialects*. New York: Holt, Rinehart and Winston, 1971. (An anthology of essential articles dealing with American dialects.)

Wolfram, Walt. *A Sociolinguistic Description of Detroit Negro Speech*. Washington, DC: Center for Applied Linguistics, 1969. (Thorough and detailed.)

———. *Sociolinguistic Aspects of Assimilation: Puerto Rican English in New York City*. Washington, DC: Center for Applied Linguistics, 1974. (A thorough study of the language problems encountered by Puerto Ricans in New York City.)

Wolfram, Walt, and Donna Christian. *Sociolinguistic Variables in Appalachian Dialects*. National Institute of Education Grant Number NIE-G-74-0026, Final Report. Washington, DC: Center for Applied Linguistics, 1975. (Definitive and informative.)

Wolfram, Walt, and Ralph W. Fasold. *The Study of Social Dialects in American English*. Englewood Cliffs, NJ: Prentice-Hall, 1974. (An introduction to the linguist's view of social variation in language—special attention given to possible educational applications.)

Part Eight

Historical Linguistics and Language Change

Any living language is in a constant state of change. We are not usually aware of the changes taking place in our language because most of them occur slowly over time. But if we look back at earlier forms of English—Chaucer's *Canterbury Tales*, for example, or, going back even further, the epic poem *Beowulf*—we can see that many significant changes have occurred. The study of the history and development of languages, which often involves comparing different languages, is called *historical* or *comparative linguistics*, and it was the earliest of the diverse areas of linguistics that have developed as fields of study.

The first selection, in this part, "Comparative and Historical Linguistics," introduces some basic concepts of historical linguistics: for example, the idea that some languages share a common ancestor, and the concepts of reconstruction and the comparative method. Using Grimm's Law as an example, Jeanne H. Herndon illustrates the systematic nature of language change and the key role that phonology plays in understanding such change. Next, Professor Paul Thieme explains how the reconstruction of the Indo-European language has given us a great deal of information about many aspects of the Indo-European way of life and culture. Thieme's selection, "The Indo-

European Language," is followed by Herndon's chart of the Indo-European language family and its subdivisions, which details the large area over which these languages are now spoken. In "A Brief History of English," Professor Paul Roberts shows the relationship between historical events and the evolution of English, from the beginnings of Old English around A.D. 600, through Middle English to Early Modern English (1600), outlining the principal characteristics of the language during each of these periods.

The first four selections in this part emphasize the gradual, continuous changes that have taken place over the last six or seven thousand years in one language family, Indo-European, and during the last thirteen hundred years in English. In the last selection, "Language Change: Progress or Decay?" Professor Jean Aitchison concludes that language change is natural, inevitable, and continuous. Aitchison also discusses whether languages, as they change, are progressing or decaying, whether language change is evolutionary, and whether it is socially desirable and/or controllable.

1/Comparative and Historical Linguistics

JEANNE H. HERNDON

Our western grammatical tradition descends to us from the Greeks, via the Romans; and it was not until the late eighteenth century that language scholars broke away from traditional western grammar and began to look at language in a different way—to study similarities and differences among many languages and to identify patterns of relationships among languages. Their work was entirely descriptive, and it should be noted that such objectivity was something new in the western grammatical tradition. Unfortunately, the work of the great Indian grammarian Pānini (fourth century B.C.), who prepared a masterful descriptive grammar of Vedic Sanskrit, was unknown in the West until the beginning of the nineteenth century. In the selection which follows, excerpted from her book A Survey of Modern Grammars, *Professor Jeanne H. Herndon traces the beginnings of comparative and historical linguistics in the eighteenth century and, using Grimm's Law as an example, demonstrates the systematic nature of language change and that these changes can be most clearly traced through comparison of the sound systems of languages.*

In spite of the fact that most [of the early traditional] grammarians relied upon classical grammarians for method and classical languages for criteria of correctness, some new ideas were stirring in the field of language study in the eighteenth century. These new ideas were not to affect the work of school grammarians for several generations. But among these ideas are to be found the roots of a whole new approach to the problem of analyzing and describing language.

Many language scholars had noted similarities between various European languages; some languages had quite clearly developed from one variety or another of provincial Latin. It remained for an Englishman who was not primarily a language scholar to see relationships among the most widely dispersed of those languages that were later to be recognized as the Indo-European family of languages.

Sir William Jones had served in the colonial government of India and while there had studied Sanskrit. In 1786 he wrote of observing similarities between a remarkable number of vocabulary items in Sanskrit and their equivalents in European and Middle Eastern languages.

581

He suggested that all these languages might have "sprung from some common source, which, perhaps, no longer exists."

Investigation of similarities and differences among languages is called *comparative linguistics.* As language scholars began to establish patterns of relationships among languages, their work came to be called *historical linguistics.* (These scholars were interested primarily in relationships among languages; they were concerned with matters of grammar only insofar as these might indicate relationships among languages and not as a matter of establishing rules of correctness.) Their research was simply a matter of gathering data, sorting, and analyzing it. Their view of change was totally objective. They were interested only in what kinds of changes had occurred, not whether these changes were "right" or "wrong," "good" or "bad."

Among the first linguists to make important comparative studies was a Danish scholar named Rasmus Rask, who compared Icelandic and Scandinavian languages and dialects. Another, Jacob Grimm, carried Rask's studies still further and proposed a theory to account for [some of the regular differences in certain sounds which] he found among languages. Out of these and many other, similar studies grew the theory that languages not only change gradually, over long periods of time, but that they change systematically and that the changes are best traced through comparison of the sound systems of languages.

The single most sweeping statement of this kind of sound relationship is often referred to as Grimm's Law or the First Germanic Consonant Shift. It is a systematic comparison of the sound systems of Indo-European languages, which both demonstrates the validity of the theory that these languages sprang from a common source and gives a wealth of information about how they are related.

Grimm concentrated, as had his predecessors, on written forms of words. Actually, he had no choice since he dealt with stages of language development long past. The differences he noted and compared were letters and spellings, but the spelling differences came to be recognized as representative of pronunciation or sound differences. Grimm went even further and, in addition to a simple listing and comparing of differences, he proposed an explanation of the orderly nature of the shift.

According to this theory, three whole sets of sounds in an ancestor of the Germanic languages had shifted from their earlier Indo-European pronunciation. [The accompanying chart shows] the original sounds and how they changed:

1. The sounds *b*, *d*, and *g* became *p*, *t*, and *k*. (There is only one *kind* of change here—three voiced sounds became silent, or voiceless, sounds.)

2. The sounds that began as *p*, *t*, and *k* became *f*, *th*, and *h*. (Again only one kind of change occurred—three "stops" became three "spi-

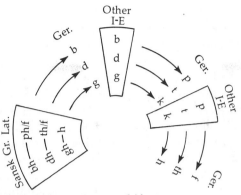

Chart of the first Germanic consonant shift.

rants," or sounds where the air is slowed down but not stopped completely.)

3. The history of the third set of sounds is more complex. These had begun as the breathy voiced stops *bh, dh,* and *gh* in early stages of Indo-European language development and still remain in Sanskrit. They had developed into similar, but not quite the same, sounds *ph* or *f, th,* and *h* in later stages of Indo-European language development represented by Latin and Greek. As a part of the Germanic Consonant Shift, this group of sounds shifted to become the voiced stop consonants *b, d,* and *g.* The shift of all three sets of consonant sounds—for speakers of the Germanic parent language only—can be seen as something very like a game of phonetic musical chairs.

The boxed letters [in the chart] represent the sounds that remained in other Indo-European languages; the letters outside the boxes represent the sounds found in Germanic languages as a result of the consonant shift. These correspondences figure prominently in setting the languages derived from this Germanic parent language apart as a distinct branch of the Indo-European family of languages.

These shifts, to repeat, occurred gradually, over very long periods of time. They can be demonstrated by comparing words in a Germanic language, English, which developed after the shift occurred, with items taken from Latin and Greek, languages in which the sounds of these consonants did not shift.

Latin *turba* ⟶ English *thorp*
Latin *dentum* ⟶ English *tooth*
Greek *agros* ⟶ English *acre*
Greek *pous* ⟶ English *foot*
Greek *treis* ⟶ English *three*
Latin *cor* ⟶ English *heart*

Greek *phrater* ⟶ English *brother*
Greek *thygater* ⟶ English *daughter*
Latin *hostis* ⟶ English *guest*

Many words in these languages do not show precisely the same correspondences, but these can be shown to be the result of other shifts or to be related to other factors. Scholars such as Karl Verner noted additional complexities in the nature of the shift and differences resulting from later shifts and proposed theories to explain the apparent "exceptions," until it was possible to trace, in great detail, the development of Indo-European languages over vast stretches of history.

More language samples were gathered, examined, and analyzed; more comparisons were made and new theories proposed. Each new theory could be tested by gathering still more language data and making still more comparisons.

The area of inquiry had been greatly expanded with investigation of Sanskrit and the languages of the Middle East. Sanskrit provided an especially rich body of material for these historical linguists because of the nature of the records open to them. Sanskrit, a literary language of India, had been the subject of grammatical study centuries before Western European scholars had undertaken such investigation of their own languages. As early as the fourth century B.C., an Indian grammarian named Pānini had analyzed Sanskrit and had organized his analysis into a masterful codification of the grammatical units and possible combinations in Sanskrit. For students of historical linguistics, discovery and study of this work were profoundly valuable for two reasons. First, it was a full-fledged grammatical analysis as compared to the fragmentary records of some of the earlier languages they had studied and, second, it represented by far the earliest stage of development of any Indo-European language available to them for study.

Through most of the nineteenth century, linguistic scholarship concentrated primarily on comparative and historical studies. Methods of gathering, classifying, and analyzing data were tested, improved, or discarded, and the improvements tested again.

Comparison of the sound systems of languages was seen to account for only a part of the systematic changes in language. Word forms, inflections, and syntactic differences came to be recognized as important considerations in comparing different stages of the development of languages.

This study of the historical development of a language or languages is sometimes called *diachronic linguistics*. *Diachronic* is a combination of Greek stems, *dia-* meaning *across*, and *chronos* meaning *time*. For linguists it means that single features of language are traced over long periods of time with changes noted and related to changes in other features of languages over the same periods.

Language researchers gathered data from every nook and cranny of Europe including many dialects peculiar to very small, isolated villages. This data led to a major shift of emphasis for some linguists. They moved from the study of historical developments into primary concentration on the similarities and contrasts between contemporary languages and dialects.

After two centuries of enormous amounts of language study, linguists have arrived at some very sweeping theories about the nature of the relationships among the many Indo-European languages. Stated in the simplest possible terms, the important points are these: (1) All these languages developed from a single language which no longer exists. (2) Differences developed when groups of people who spoke this language moved apart and were separated for long periods of time. That is, one group moved into India and their language developed and changed to become Sanskrit; another group moved into southeastern Europe and their language grew into the ancestor of Greek; another group broke off and moved into northern Europe and their language changed in some respects to become the parent language of German, English, Danish, and so on. (3) The fact that all these languages share a common heritage accounts for the fact that some similarities still exist in all of them.

FOR DISCUSSION AND REVIEW

1. What contribution to linguistics did Sir William Jones (1746–1794) make?

2. Describe the attitude of historical (or comparative) linguists toward language change. How does this attitude compare with that held by many popular contemporary writers about language usage (e.g., Edwin Newman and William Safire)?

3. What *kind* of change in language is the most useful to historical linguists? Why?

4. One of the most important characteristics differentiating the Germanic branch of Proto-Indo-European from the languages of all the other branches (see the chart on p. 583) is the set of sound changes called Grimm's Law. Its effects are most easily seen in word-initial sounds. Using the words *tooth, foot,* and *three,* show the effect of Grimm's Law in changing these words from their Latin equivalents.

5. Explain how the following sets of words do or do not illustrate Grimm's Law (note: do not consider *only* initial consonants):

	1	2	3
Sanskrit	pitar	bhinádmi	bhrátar
Greek	patĕr	pheídomai	phráter
Latin	pater	findō	fráter
English	father	bite	brother

6. Why was Sanskrit of special importance to early historical linguists?

7. What were the major conclusions of historical linguists concerning the relationships among the many Indo-European languages?

2/The Indo-European Language

PAUL THIEME

Except for Basque, Finnish, Hungarian, and Estonian, all of the languages currently spoken in Europe belong to the Indo-European family of languages. So too, almost all of the languages spoken in Canada, the United States, and Central and South America are of Indo-European origin. (The exceptions are such surviving indigenous languages as Navajo, Cherokee, Eskimo, Quechua [in Peru], and Mazatec [in Mexico].) Therefore, given the importance of the Indo-European languages in today's world, it is only natural to wonder, who were the original Indo-Europeans? When and where did they live? What was their culture like? How did it happen that so many languages developed from this one source? In the following selection, Professor Paul Thieme uses the methods of comparative linguistics or philology to show how it has been possible to reconstruct a large part of the sound system, grammar, and even vocabulary of the Indo-European language, and from this reconstruction to learn a great deal about Indo-European culture and the original Indo-European homeland.*

Every educated person knows that French and Spanish are "related" languages. The obvious similarity of these tongues is explained by their common descent from Latin; indeed, we could say that French and Spanish are two dialects of "modern Latin," forms of the ancestral language that have grown mutually unintelligible through long separation. Latin has simply developed somewhat differently in these two fragments of the old Western Roman Empire. Today these dialects are called Romance languages.

The other great family of European languages is of course the Germanic. It includes English, Dutch, German and the Scandinavian tongues, all descended from an ancient language—unfortunately unrecorded—called Teutonic [or Proto-Germanic].

Romance languages and Teutonic, plus Greek—these were once the center of our linguistic universe. During the past 200 years, how-

---

* Editor's note: Additional information about the Indo-European culture and homeland has become available since the original publication of this selection. See, for example, Calvert Watkins' "Indo-European and the Indo-Europeans" in *The American Heritage Dictionary*.

ever, linguistics has been undergoing a kind of prolonged Copernican revolution. Now the familiar European tongues have been relegated to minor places in a vaster system of languages which unites Europe and Asia. Known collectively as the Indo-European languages, this superfamily is far and away the most extensive linguistic constellation in the world. It is also the most throroughly explored: while other language families have remained largely unknown, the Indo-European family has monopolized the attention of linguists since the 18th century. The modern discipline of linguistics is itself a product of Indo-European studies. As a result of these intensive labors we have come to know a great deal about both the genealogy and the interrelationships of this rich linguistic community.

If we look at the family as a whole, several questions spring to mind. Where did these languages come from? Every family traces its descent from a common ancestor: what was our ancestral language? What did it sound like? What manner of men spoke it? How did they come to migrate over the face of the earth, spreading their tongue across the Eurasian land mass?

Linguistics can now provide definite—if incomplete—answers to some of these questions. We have reconstructed in substantial part the grammar and sound-system of the Indo-European language, as we call this ultimate forebear of the modern Indo-European family. Although much of the original vocabulary has perished, enough of it survives in later languages so that we can contrive a short dictionary. From the language, in turn, we can puzzle out some characteristics of Indo-European culture. We can even locate the Indo-European homeland.

We can never hope to reconstruct the Indo-European language in complete detail. The task would be immeasurably easier if the Indo-Europeans had only left written records. But the Indo-Europeans, unlike their Egyptian and Mesopotamian contemporaries, were illiterate. Their language was not simply forgotten, to be relearned by archaeologists of another day. It vanished without a trace, except for the many hints that we can glean and piece together from its surviving daughter languages.

The Discovery of the Language

The first clue to the existence of an Indo-European family was uncovered with the opening of trade with India. In 1585, a little less than a century after Vasco da Gama first rounded the Cape of Good Hope, an Italian merchant named Filippo Sassetti made a startling discovery in India. He found that Hindu scholars were able to speak and write an ancient language, at least as venerable as Latin and Greek. Sassetti wrote a letter home about this language, which he called *San-*

scruta (Sanskrit). It bore certain resemblances, he said, to his native Italian. For example, the word for "God" (*deva*) resembled the Italian *Dio;* the word for "snake" (*sarpa*), the Italian *serpe;* the numbers "seven," "eight" and "nine" (*sapta, ashta* and *nava*), the Italian *sette, otto* and *nove.*

What did these resemblances prove? Sassetti may have imagined that Sanskrit was closely related to the "original language" spoken by Adam and Eve; perhaps that is why he chose "God" and "snake" as examples. Later it was thought that Sanskrit might be the ancestor of the European languages, including Greek and Latin. Finally it became clear that Sanskrit was simply a sister of the European tongues. The relationship received its first scientific statement in the "Indo-European hypothesis" of Sir William Jones, a jurist and orientalist in the employ of the East India Company. Addressing the Bengal Asiatic Society in 1786, Sir William pointed out that Sanskrit, in relation to Greek and Latin, "bears a stronger affinity, both in the roots of verbs and in the forms of grammar, than could possibly have been produced by accident: so strong, indeed, that no philologer could examine them all three without believing them to have sprung from some common source, which, perhaps, no longer exists; there is similar reason, though not quite so forcible, for supposing that both the Gothick and the Celtick, though blended with a very different idiom, had the same origin with the Sanskrit."

Sir Williams's now-famous opinion founded modern linguistics. A crucial word in the sentence quoted is "roots." Jones and his successors could not have done their work without a command of Sanskrit, then the oldest-known Indo-European language. But they also could not have done it without a knowledge of traditional Sanskrit grammar. Jones, like every linguist since, was inspired by the great Sanskrit grammarian Panini, who sometime before 500 B.C. devised a remarkably accurate and systematic technique of word analysis. Instead of grouping related forms in conjugations and declensions—as European and U.S. school-grammar does to this day—Panini's grammar analyzed the forms into their functional units: the roots, suffixes and endings.

Comparative grammar, in the strict sense, was founded by a young German named Franz Bopp. In 1816 Bopp published a book on the inflection of verbs in a group of Indo-European languages: Sanskrit, Persian, Greek, Latin and the Teutonic tongues. Essentially Bopp's book was no more than the application to a broader group of languages of Panini's technique for the analysis of Sanskrit verbs. But Bopp's motive was a historical one. By gathering cognate forms from a number of Indo-European languages he hoped to be able to infer some of the characteristics of the lost language—the "common source" mentioned by Jones—which was the parent of them all.

In the course of time Bopp's method has been systematically developed and refined. The "affinities" which Jones saw between certain words in related languages have come to be called "correspondences," defined by precise formulas. The "Indo-European hypothesis" has been proved beyond doubt. And many more groups of languages have been found to belong to the Indo-European family: Slavonic, Baltic, the old Italic dialects, Albanian, Armenian, Hittite and Tocharian. The "family tree" of these languages has been worked out in some detail. It should be borne in mind, however, that when it is applied to languages a family-tree diagram is no more than a convenient graphic device. Languages do not branch off from one another at a distinct point in time; they separate gradually, by the slow accumulation of innovations. Moreover, we cannot be sure of every detail in their relationship. The affinities of the Celtic and Italic languages, or of the Baltic and Slavonic, may or may not point to a period when each of these pairs formed a common language, already distinguished from the Indo-European. Some Indo-European languages cannot be placed on the family tree because their lineage is not known. Among these are Tocharian and Hittite. These extinct languages (both rediscovered in the 20th century) were spoken in Asia but descend from the western branch of the family.

Reconstruction

Let us see how a linguist can glean information about the original Indo-European language by comparing its daughter tongues with one another. Take the following series of "corresponding" words: *pra* (Sanskrit), *pro* (Old Slavonic), *pro* (Greek), *pro* (Latin), *fra* (Gothic), all meaning "forward"; *pitā* (Sanskrit), *patēr* (Greek), *pater* (Latin), *fadar* (Gothic), all meaning "father." Clearly these words sprang from two words in the original Indo-European language. Now what can we say about the initial sounds the words must have had in the parent tongue? It must have been "p," as it is in the majority of the languages cited. Only in Gothic does it appear as "f," and the odds are overwhelmingly in favor of its having changed from "p" to "f" in this language, rather than from "f" to "p" in all the others. Thus we know one fact about the original Indo-European language: it had an initial "p" sound. This sound remains "p" in most of the daughter languages. Only in Gothic (and other Teutonic tongues) did it become "f."

Now let us take a harder example: *dasa* (Sanskrit), *deshimt* (Lithuanian), *deseti* (Old Slavonic), *deka* (Greek), *dekem* (Latin), *tehun* (Gothic), all meaning "ten"; *satam* (Sanskrit), *shimtas* (Lithuanian), *suto* (Old Slavonic), *he-katon* (Greek), *kentum* (Latin), *hunda-* (Gothic), all meaning "hundred." (The spelling of some of these forms has been altered for purposes of exposition. The hyphen after the Gothic *hunda-* and certain other words in this article indicates that they are not complete words.)

Certainly the "s," "sh," "k" and "h" sounds in these words are related to one another. Which is the original? We decide that "k" changed into the other sounds rather than *vice versa*. Phoneticians tell us that "hard" sounds like "k" often mutate into "soft" sounds like "sh." For example, the Latin word *carus* ("dear") turned into the French word *cher*; but the reverse change has not occurred.

Reconstruction would be much easier sailing but for two all-too-common events in the history of language: "convergence" and "divergence." In Sanskrit the three old Indo-European vowels "e," "o" and "a" have converged to become "a" (as in "ah"). In the Germanic languages the Indo-European vowel "e" has diverged to become "e" (as in "bet") next to certain sounds and "i" (as in "it") next to others.

Like most procedures in modern science, linguistic reconstructions require a certain technical skill. This is emphatically not a game for amateurs. Every step is most intricate. Some people may even wonder whether there is any point to the labors of historical linguists—especially in view of the fact that the reconstructions can never be checked by immediate observation. There is no absolute certainty in the reconstruction of a lost language. The procedure is admittedly probabilistic. It can only be tested by the coherence of its results.

But the results in the reconstruction of ancestral Indo-European are heartening. By regular procedures such as those I have illustrated, we have reconstructed a sound system for Indo-European that has the simplicity and symmetry of sound systems in observable languages. We have discovered the same symmetry in our reconstructions of roots, suffixes, endings, and whole words. Perhaps even more important, the Indo-European words we have reconstructed give a convincing picture of ancient Indo-European customs and geography!

The Indo-European Culture

Consider the words for "mother," "husband," "wife," "son," "daughter," "brother," "sister," "grandson," "son-in-law," "daughter-in-law," all of which we can reconstruct in Indo-European. As a group they prove that the speakers lived in families founded on marriage—which is no more than we might expect! But we obtain more specific terms too: "father-in-law," "mother-in-law," "brother-in-law," "sister-in-law." Exact correspondences in the speech usage of the oldest daughter languages which have been preserved lead to the conclusion that these expressions were used exclusively with reference to the "in-laws" of the bride, and not to those of the groom. There are no other words that would designate a husband's "father-in-law," and so on. The inference is unavoidable that the family system of the old Indo-Europeans was of a patriarchal character; that is, that the wife married into her husband's family, while the husband did not acquire an official relationship to his wife's family as he does where a matriarchal family system exists. Our positive witnesses (the accumulation of designations for the relations a woman acquires by marriage) and our negative witnesses (the complete absence of designations for the relations a man might be said to acquire by marriage) are trustworthy circumstantial evidence of this.

The Indo-Europeans had a decimal number system that reveals traces of older counting systems. The numbers up to "four" are inflected like adjectives. They form a group by themselves, which points to an archaic method of counting by applying the thumb to the remaining four fingers in succession. Another group, evidently later arrivals in the history of Indo-European, goes up to "ten" (the Indo-European *dekmt-*). "Ten" is related to "hundred": *kmtom,* a word which came from the still earlier *dkmtom,* or "aggregate of tens." In addition to these four-finger and ten-finger counting systems there was a method of counting by twelves, presumably stemming from the application of the thumb to the twelve joints of the other four fingers. It is well known that the Teutonic languages originally distinguished a "small hundred" (100) from a "big hundred" (120). The latter is a "hundred" that results from a combination of counting by tens (the decimal system) and counting by twelves (the duodecimal system). Traces of duodecimal counting can also be found in other Indo-European languages.

Reconstruction yields an almost complete Indo-European inventory of body parts, among them some that presuppose the skilled butchering of animals. The Indo-European word for "lungs" originally meant "swimmer." We can imagine a prehistoric butcher watching the lungs float to the surface as he put the entrails of an animal into water. There is no reference in the word to the biological function of the lungs, which was presumably unknown. The heart, on the other hand, appears to have been named after the beat of the living organ.

So far as tools and weapons are concerned, we are not quite so lavishly served. We obtain single expressions for such things as "arrow," "ax," "ship," "boat," but no semantic system. This poverty is due partly to an original lack of certain concepts, and partly to the change of usage in the daughter languages. It is evident that new terms were coined as new implements were invented. We do find words for "gold" and perhaps for "silver," as well as for "ore." Unfortunately we cannot decide whether "ore" was used only with reference to copper or to both copper and bronze. It is significant that we cannot reconstruct a word for "iron," which was a later discovery. In any case we need not picture the people who spoke Indo-European as being very primitive. They possessed at least one contrivance that requires efficient tools: the wagon or cart. Two Indo-European words for "wheel" and words for "axle," "hub" and "yoke" are cumulative evidence of this.

The Indo-European Homeland

Especially interesting are the names of animals and plants, for these contain the clue to the ancient Indo-European homeland. It is evident that our reconstructed language was spoken in a territory that cannot have been large. A language as unified as the one we obtain by our reconstruction suggests a compact speech community. In prehistoric times, when communication over long distances was limited, such a community could have existed only within comparatively small boundaries.

These boundaries need not have been quite so narrow if the people who spoke Indo-European had been nomads. Nomads may cover a large territory and yet maintain the unity of their language, since their roamings repeatedly bring them in contact with others who speak their tongue. The Indo-Europeans, however, were small-scale farmers and husbandmen rather than nomads. They raised pigs, which kept them from traveling, and they had words for "barley," "stored grains," "sowing," "plowing," "grinding," "settlement" and "pasture" (agros), on which domesticated animals were "driven" (ag).

We cannot reconstruct old Indo-European words for "palm," "olive," "cypress," "vine," "laurel." On the strength of this negative evidence we can safely eliminate Asia and the Mediterranean countries as possible starting points of the Indo-European migrations. We can, however, reconstruct the following tree names: "birch," "beech," "aspen," "oak," "yew," "willow," "spruce," "alder," "ash." The evidence is not equally conclusive for each tree name; my arrangement follows the decreasing certainty. Yet in each case at least a possibility can be established, as it cannot in the case of tree names such as "cypress," "palm" and "olive."

Of the tree names the most important for our purposes is "beech." Since the beech does not grow east of a line that runs roughly from Königsberg (now Kaliningrad) on the Baltic Sea to Odessa on the northwestern shore of the Black Sea, we must conclude that the Indo-Europeans lived in Europe rather than in Asia. Scandinavia can be ruled out because we know that the beech was imported there rather late. A likely district would be the northern part of Middle Europe, say the territory between the Vistula and Elbe rivers. It is here that even now the densest accumulation of Indo-European languages is found—languages belonging to the eastern group (Baltic and Slavonic) side by side with one of the western group (German).

That the Indo-Europeans came from this region is indicated by the animal names we can reconstruct, all of them characteristic of the region. We do not find words for "tiger," "elephant," "camel," "lion" or "leopard." We can, however, compile a bestiary that includes "wolf," "bear," "lynx," "eagle," "falcon," "owl," "crane," "thrush," "goose," "duck," "turtle," "salmon," "otter," "beaver," "fly," "hornet," "wasp," "bee" (inferred from words for "honey"), "louse" and "flea." We also find words for domesticated animals: "dog," "cattle," "sheep," "pig," "goat" and perhaps "horse." Some of these words are particularly significant. The turtle, like the beech, did not occur north of Germany in prehistoric times.

The Importance of the Salmon

It is the Indo-European word for "salmon" that most strongly supports the argument. Of all the regions where trees and animals familiar to the Indo-Europeans live, and the regions from which the Indo-Europeans could possibly have started the migrations that spread their tongue from Ireland to India, it is only along the rivers that flow into the Baltic and North seas that this particular fish could have been known. Coming from the South Atlantic, the salmon ascends these rivers in huge shoals to spawn in their upper reaches. The fish are easy to catch, and lovely to watch as they leap over obstacles in streams. Without the fat-rich food provided by the domesticated pig and the salmon, a people living in this rather cold region could hardly have grown so strong and numerous that their migration became both a necessity and a success.

The Indo-European word for "salmon" (*laks*-) survives in the original sense where the fish still occurs: Russia, the Baltic countries, Scandinavia and Germany (it is the familiar "lox" of Jewish delicatessens). In the Celtic tongues another word has replaced it; the Celts, migrating to the West, encountered the Rhine salmon, which they honored with a new name because it is even more delectable than the Baltic variety. The Italic languages, Greek and the southern Slavonic tongues, spoken where there are no salmon, soon lost the word. In some other languages it is preserved, but with altered meaning: in Ossetic, an Iranian language spoken in the Caucasus, the word means a large kind of trout, and the Tocharian-speaking people of eastern Turkestan used it for fish in general.

Several Sanskrit words echo the importance of the salmon in Indo-European history. One, *laksha*, means "a great amount" or "100,000," in which sense it has entered Hindustani and British English with the expression "a lakh of rupees." The assumption that the Sanskrit *laksha* descends from the Indo-European *laks-* of course requires an additional hypothesis: that a word meaning "salmon" or "salmon-shoal" continued to be used in the sense of "a great amount" long after the Indo-European immigrants to India had forgotten the fish itself. There are many analogies for a development of this kind. All over the world the names of things that are notable for their quantity or density tend to designate large numbers. Thus in Iranian "beehive" is used for 10,000; in Egyptian "tadpole" (which appears in great numbers after the flood of the Nile) is used for 100,000; in Chinese "ant," for 10,000; in Semitic languages "cattle," for 100; in Sanskrit and Egyptian "lotus" (which covers lakes and swamps), for "large number." Several words in Sanskrit for "sea" also refer to large numbers. In this connection we may recall the words in *Hamlet:* ". . . to take arms against a sea of troubles, and by opposing end them."

A second Sanskrit word that I believe is a descendant of the Indo-European *laks-* is *lākshā*, which the dictionary defines as "the dark-red resinous incrustation produced on certain trees by the puncture of an insect (*Coccus lacca*) and used as a scarlet dye." This is the word from which come the English "lac" and "lacquer." *Lākshā*, in my opinion, was originally an adjective derived from the Indo-European *laks-;* meaning "of or like a salmon." A characteristic feature of the salmon is the red color of its flesh. "Salmonlike" could easily develop into "red," and this adjective could be used to designate "the red (substance)," *i.e.*, "lac."

There is even a third possible offshoot: the Sanskrit *laksha* meaning "gambling stake" or "prize." This may be derived from a word that meant "salmon-catch." The apparent boldness of this conjecture may be vindicated on two counts. First, we have another Indo-European gambling word that originally was an animal name. Exact correspondences of Greek, Latin and Sanskrit show that the Indo-Europeans knew a kind of gambling with dice, in which the most unlucky throw was called the "dog." Second, in Sanskrit the gambling stake can be designated by another word, a plural noun (*vijas*) whose primary meaning was "the leapers." The possibility that this is another old word for "salmon," which was later used in the same restricted sense as *laksha*, is rather obvious.

By a lucky accident, then, Sanskrit, spoken by people who cannot have preserved any knowledge of the salmon itself, retains traces of Indo-European words for "salmon." Taken together, these words present a singularly clear picture of the salmon's outstanding traits. It is the fish that appears in big shoals (the Sanskrit *laksha*, meaning "100,000"); that overcomes obstacles by leaping (the Sanskrit *vijas*, meaning "leapers," and later "stake"); that has red flesh (*lākshā*, meaning "lac"); that is caught as a prized food (*vijas* and *laksha,* meaning "stake" or "prize").

The Age of the Language

If we establish the home of our reconstructed language as lying between the Vistula and the Elbe, we may venture to speculate as to the time when it was spoken. According to archaeological evidence, the domesticated horse and goat did not appear there much before 3000 B.C. The other domesticated animals for which we have linguistic evidence are archaeologically demonstrable in an earlier period. Indo-European, I conjecture, was spoken on the Baltic coast of Germany late in the fourth millennium B.C. Since our oldest documents of Indo-European daughter languages (in Asia Minor and India) date from the second millennium B.C., the end of the fourth millennium would be a likely time anyhow. A thousand or 1,500 years are a time sufficiently long for the development of the changes that distinguish our oldest Sanskrit speech form from what we reconstruct as Indo-European.

Here is an old Lithuanian proverb which a Protestant minister translated into Latin in 1625 to show the similarity of Lithuanian to Latin. The proverb means "God gave the teeth; God will also give bread." In Lithuanian it reads: *Dievas dawe dantis; Dievas duos ir duonos.* The Latin version is *Deus dedit dentes; Deus dabit et panem.* Translated into an old form of Sanskrit, it would be *Devas adadāt datas; Devas dāt* (or *dadāt*) *api dhānās.* How would this same sentence sound in the re-constructed Indo-European language? A defensible guess would be: *Deivos ededōt dntns; Deivos dedōt* (or *dōt*) *dhōnās.*

FOR DISCUSSION AND REVIEW

1. What do Filippo Sassetti and Sir William Jones have in common?

2. Thieme states that "a crucial word" in Sir William Jones's 1786 statement is *roots.* Explain (a) why this is so and (b) why the work of Pānini has been so important to historical linguists.

3. Summarize what the Indo-European vocabulary tells us about the way its speakers lived.

4. According to Thieme, where was the original Indo-European home-land? What evidence does he use to support this conclusion? Find this area on a map. In what country or countries is it now located?

5. The following are reconstructed Indo-European roots (as indicated by the asterisks) from which English words and words in cognate languages

have developed: *māter -, *agh-, *eis-, *nekwt-, *dhē-, *kwon-. Identify one English word and at least one cognate word in a contemporary language that have developed from each of these roots. (Note: You will find *The American Heritage Dictionary* especially useful in doing this exercise.)

3/Relationships of Some Indo-European Languages with Detail of English Dialects

JEANNE H. HERNDON

The Indo-European family of languages, of which English is a member, is descended from a prehistoric language, Proto-Indo-European, or Indo-European, which was probably spoken in the fourth millennium B.C. *in a region that has not been positively identified. However, we have been able, through the comparative method, to learn a great deal about the phonology, morphology, syntax, and semantics of Indo-European, and—because language is an aspect of culture—about the kind of society that its speakers created. The following chart lists the principal branches of the Indo-European family and indicates the new languages that developed in each branch. The branches of Indo-European that are still represented today by one or more living languages are Celtic, Germanic, Italic, Hellenic, Balto-Slavic, Armenian, Albanian, and Indo-Iranian. In the lower left-hand corner of the chart, note the list of the various dialects of Old English (i.e., Mercian, Northumbrian, Kentish, and West Saxon) and the development of Mercian into some dialects of Middle English, Early Modern English, and finally Modern English.*

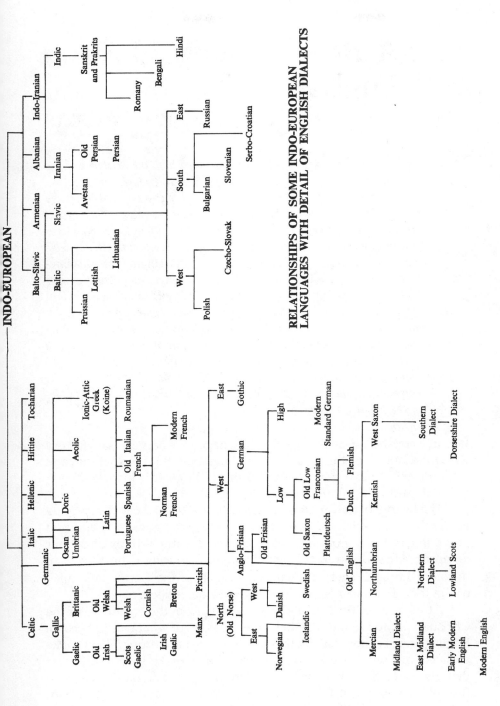

RELATIONSHIPS OF SOME INDO-EUROPEAN
LANGUAGES WITH DETAIL OF ENGLISH DIALECTS

4/A Brief History of English

PAUL ROBERTS

Earlier selections in this part have discussed how the existence of the Proto-Indo-European language was established through historical reconstruction, and have described the major branches of that language family. In this selection, the late Paul Roberts narrows the focus still more and traces briefly the history of the English language. He places its development in the context of historical events, showing their effects on the language. In general, the grammatical changes from Old English to Modern English have resulted in a change from a synthetic or highly inflected language (like Latin or Russian) to an analytic language, with few inflectional endings and heavy reliance on word order and function words to signal grammatical meaning. Roberts also discusses some of the major changes in pronunciation and vocabulary from Old English through Middle English to Modern English, commenting especially on the effects of the Great Vowel Shift and on the borrowing of large numbers of foreign words that increased the size of the English vocabulary.

No understanding of the English language can be very satisfactory without a notion of the history of the language. But we shall have to make do with just a notion. The history of English is long and complicated, and we can only hit the high spots.

The history of our language begins a little after A.D. 600. Everything before that is pre-history, which means that we can guess at it but can't prove much. For a thousand years or so before the birth of Christ our linguistic ancestors were savages wandering through the forests of northern Europe. Their language was a part of the Germanic branch of the Indo-European Family (see the previous selection).

At the time of the Roman Empire—say, from the beginning of the Christian Era to around A.D. 400—the speakers of what was to become English were scattered along the northern coast of Europe. They spoke a dialect of Low German. More exactly, they spoke several different dialects, since they were several different tribes. The names given to the tribes who got to England are *Angles, Saxons,* and *Jutes.* For convenience, we can refer to them as Anglo-Saxons.

Their first contact with civilization was a rather thin acquaintance with the Roman Empire on whose borders they lived. Probably some of the Anglo-Saxons wandered into the Empire occasionally, and certainly Roman merchants and traders traveled among the tribes. At any rate, this period saw the first of our many borrowings from Latin. Such words as *kettle, wine, cheese, butter, cheap, plum, gem, bishop, church* were borrowed at this time. They show something of the relationship of the Anglo-Saxons with the Romans. The Anglo-Saxons were learning, getting their first taste of civilization.

They still had a long way to go, however, and their first step was to help smash the civilization they were learning from. In the fourth century the Roman power weakened badly. While the Goths were pounding away at the Romans in the Mediterranean countries, their relatives, the Anglo-Saxons, began to attack Britain.

The Romans had been the ruling power in Britain since A.D. 43. They had subjugated the Celts whom they found living there and had succeeded in setting up a Roman administration. The Roman influence did not extend to the outlying parts of the British Isles. In Scotland, Wales, and Ireland the Celts remained free and wild, and they made periodic forays against the Romans in England. Among other defense measures, the Romans built the famous Roman Wall to ward off the tribes in the north.

Even in England the Roman power was thin. Latin did not become the language of the country as it did in Gaul and Spain. The mass of people continued to speak Celtic, with Latin and the Roman civilization it contained in use as a top dressing.

In the fourth century, troubles multiplied for the Romans in Britain. Not only did the untamed tribes of Scotland and Wales grow more and more restive, but the Anglo-Saxons began to make pirate raids on the eastern coast. Furthermore, there was growing difficulty everywhere in the Empire, and the legions in Britain were siphoned off to fight elsewhere. Finally, in A.D. 410, the last Roman ruler in England, bent on becoming emperor, left the islands and took the last of the legions with him. The Celts were left in possession of Britain but almost defenseless against the impending Anglo-Saxon attack.

Not much is surely known about the arrival of the Anglo-Saxons in England. According to the best early source, the eighth-century historian Bede, the Jutes came in 449 in response to a plea from the Celtic king, Vortigern, who wanted their help against the Picts attacking from the north. The Jutes subdued the Picts but then quarreled and fought with Vortigern, and, with reinforcements from the Continent, settled permanently in Kent. Somewhat later the Angles established themselves in eastern England and the Saxons in the south and west. Bede's account is plausible enough, and these were probably the main lines of the invasion.

We do know, however, that the Angles, Saxons, and Jutes were a long time securing themselves in England. Fighting went on for as long as a hundred years before the Celts in England were all killed, driven into Wales, or reduced to slavery. This is the period of King Arthur, who was not entirely mythological. He was a Romanized Celt, a general, though probably not a king. He had some success against the Anglo-Saxons, but it was only temporary. By 550 or so the Anglo-Saxons were firmly established. English was in England.

Old English

All this is pre-history, so far as the language is concerned. We have no record of the English language until after 600, when the Anglo-Saxons were converted to Christianity and learned the Latin alphabet. The conversion began, to be precise, in the year 597 and was accomplished within thirty or forty years. The conversion was a great advance for the Anglo-Saxons, not only because of the spiritual benefits but because it reestablished contact with what remained of Roman civilization. This civilization didn't amount to much in the year 600, but it was certainly superior to anything in England up to that time.

It is customary to divide the history of the English language into three periods: Old English, Middle English, and Modern English. Old English runs from the earliest records—i.e., seventh century—to about 1100; Middle English from 1100 to 1450 or 1500; Modern English from 1500 to the present day. Sometimes Modern English is further divided into Early Modern, 1500–1700, and Late Modern, 1700 to the present.

When England came into history, it was divided into several more or less autonomous kingdoms, some of which at times exercised a certain amount of control over the others. In the century after the conversion the most advanced kingdom was Northumbria, the area between the Humber River and the Scottish border. By A.D. 700 the Northumbrians had developed a respectable civilization, the finest in Europe. It is sometimes called the Northumbrian Renaissance, and it was the first of the several renaissances through which Europe struggled upward out of the ruins of the Roman Empire. It was in this period that the best of the Old English literature was written, including the epic poem *Beowulf*.

In the eighth century, Northumbrian power declined, and the center of influence moved southward to Mercia, the kingdom of the Midlands. A century later the center shifted again, and Wessex, the country of the West Saxons, became the leading power. The most famous king of the West Saxons was Alfred the Great, who reigned in the second half of the ninth century, dying in 901. He was famous not only as a military man and administrator but also as a champion of learning. He founded and supported schools and translated or caused to be translated many books from Latin into English. At this time also much of the Northumbrian literature of two centuries earlier was copied in West Saxon. Indeed, the great bulk of Old English writing which has come down to us is in the West Saxon dialect of 900 or later.

In the military sphere, Alfred's great accomplishment was his successful opposition to the viking invasions. In the ninth and tenth centuries, the Norsemen emerged in their ships from their homelands in Denmark and the Scandinavian peninsula. They traveled far and attacked and plundered at will and almost with impunity. They ravaged Italy and Greece, settled in France, Russia, and Ireland, colonized Iceland and Greenland, and discovered America several centuries before Columbus. Nor did they overlook England.

After many years of hit-and-run raids, the Norsemen landed an army on the east coast of England in the year 866. There was nothing much to oppose them except the Wessex power led by Alfred. The long struggle ended in 877 with a treaty by which a line was drawn roughly from the northwest of England to the southeast. On the eastern side of the line Norse rule was to prevail. This was called the Danelaw. The western side was to be governed by Wessex.

The linguistic result of all this was a considerable injection of Norse into the English language. Norse was at this time not so different from English as Norwegian or Danish is now. Probably speakers of English could understand, more or less, the language of the newcomers who had moved into eastern England. At any rate, there was considerable interchange and word borrowing. Examples of Norse words in the English language are *sky, give, law, egg, outlaw, leg, ugly, scant, sly, crawl, scowl, take, thrust*. There are hundreds more. We have even borrowed some pronouns from Norse—*they, their,* and *them*. These words were borrowed first by the eastern and northern dialects and then in the course of hundreds of years made their way into English generally.

It is supposed also—indeed, it must be true—that the Norsemen influenced the sound structure and the grammar of English. But this is hard to demonstrate in detail.

A SPECIMEN OF OLD ENGLISH

We may now have an example of Old English. The favorite illustration is the Lord's Prayer, since it needs no translation. This has come to us in several different versions. Here is one:

Fæder ure,
þu þe eart on heofonum,
si þin nama gehalgod.
Tobecume þin rice.
Gewurþe ðin willa on eorðan swa swa on heofonum.

Urne gedœghwamlican hlaf syle us to dæg.
And forgyf us ure gyltas, swa swa we forgyfað urum gyltendum.
And ne gelæd þu us on costnunge,
ac alys us of yfele. Soþlice.

Some of the differences between this and Modern English are merely differences in orthography. For instance, the sign œ is what Old English writers used for a vowel sound like that in modern *hat* or *and*. The *th* sounds of modern *thin* or *then* are represented in Old English by þ or ð. But of course there are many differences in sound too. *Ure* is the ancestor of modern *our*, but the first vowel was like that in *too* or *ooze*. *Hlaf* is modern *loaf*; we have dropped the *h* sound and changed the vowel, which in *hlaf* was pronounced something like the vowel in *father*. Old English had some sounds which we do not have. The sound represented by *y* does not occur in Modern English. If you pronounce the vowel in *bit* with your lips rounded, you may approach it.

In grammar, Old English was much more highly inflected than Modern English is. That is, there were more case endings for nouns, more person and number endings for verbs, a more complicated pronoun system, various endings for adjectives, and so on. Old English nouns had four cases—nominative, genitive, dative, accusative. Adjectives had five—all these and an instrumental case besides. Present-day English has only two cases for nouns—common case and possessive case. Adjectives now have no case system at all. On the other hand, we now use a more rigid word order and more structure words (prepositions, auxiliaries, and the like) to express relationships than Old English did.

Some of this grammar we can see in the Lord's Prayer. *Heofonum*, for instance, is a dative plural; the nominative singular was *heofon*. *Urne* is an accusative singular; the nominative is *ure*. In *urum gyltendum* both words are dative plural. *Forgyfaþ* is the first person plural form of the verb. Word order is different: "urne gedæghwamlican hlaf syle us" in place of "Give us our daily bread." And so on.

In vocabulary Old English is quite different from Modern English. Most of the Old English words are what we may call native English: that is, words which have not been borrowed from other languages but which have been a part of English ever since English was a part of Indo-European. Old English did certainly contain borrowed words. We have seen that many borrowings were coming in from Norse. Rather large numbers had been borrowed from Latin, too. Some of these were taken while the Anglo-Saxons were still on the Continent (*cheese, butter, bishop, kettle,* etc.); a large number came into English after the conversion (*angel, candle, priest, martyr, radish, oyster, purple, school, spend,* etc.). But the great majority of Old English words were native English.

Now, on the contrary, the majority of words in English are borrowed, taken mostly from Latin and French. Of the words in *The American College Dictionary* only about 14 percent are native. Most of these, to be sure, are common, high-frequency words—*the, of, I, and, because, man, mother, road,* etc.; of the thousand most common words in English, some 62 percent are native English. Even so, the modern vocabulary is very much Latinized and Frenchified. The Old English vocabulary was not.

Middle English

Sometime between the years 1000 and 1200 various important changes took place in the structure of English, and Old English became Middle English. The political event which facilitated these changes was the Norman Conquest. The Normans, as the name shows, came originally from Scandinavia. In the early tenth century they established themselves in northern France, adopted the French language, and developed a vigorous kingdom and a very passable civilization. In the year 1066, led by Duke William, they crossed the Channel and made themselves masters of England. For the next several hundred years, England was ruled by kings whose first language was French.

One might wonder why, after the Norman Conquest, French did not become the national language, replacing English entirely. The reason is that the Conquest was not a national migration, as the earlier Anglo-Saxon invasion had been. Great numbers of Normans came to England, but they came as rulers and landlords. French became the language of the court, the language of the nobility, the language of polite society, the language of literature. But it did not replace English as the language of the people. There must always have been hundreds of towns and villages in which French was never heard except when visitors of high station passed through.

But English, though it survived as the national language, was profoundly changed after the Norman Conquest. Some of the changes—in sound structure and grammar—would no doubt have taken place whether there had been a Conquest or not. Even before 1066 the case system of English nouns and adjectives was becoming simplified; people came to rely more on word order and prepositions than on inflectional endings to communicate their meanings. The process was speeded up by sound changes which caused many of the endings to sound alike. But no doubt the Conquest facilitated the change. German, which didn't experience a Norman Conquest, is today rather highly inflected compared to its cousin English.

But it is in vocabulary that the effects of the Conquest are most obvious. French ceased, after a hundred years or so, to be the native language of very many people in England, but it continued—and continues still—to be a zealously cultivated second language, the mirror of elegance and civilization. When one spoke English, one introduced not only French ideas and French things but also their French names. This was not only easy but socially useful. To pepper one's conversation with French expressions was to show that one was well-bred, elegant, *au courant*. The last sentence shows that the process is not yet dead. By using *au courant* stead of, say, *abreast of things*, the writer indicates that he is no dull clod who knows only English but an elegant person aware of how things are done in *le haut monde*.

Thus French words came into English, all sorts of them. There were words to do with government: *parliament, majesty, treaty, alliance, tax, government*; church words: *parson, sermon, baptism, incense, crucifix, religion*; words for foods: *veal, beef, mutton, bacon, jelly, peach, lemon, cream, biscuit*; colors: *blue, scarlet, vermilion*; household words: *curtain, chair, lamp, towel, blanket, parlor*; play words: *dance, chess, music, leisure, conversation*; literary words: *story, romance, poet, literary*; learned words: *study, logic, grammar, noun, surgeon, anatomy, stomach*; just ordinary words of all sorts: *nice, second, very, age, bucket, gentle, final, fault, flower, cry, count, sure, move, surprise, plain*.

All these and thousands more poured into the English vocabulary between 1100 and 1500 until, at the end of that time, many people must have had more French words than English at their command. This is not to say that English became French. English remained English in sound structure and in grammar, though these also felt the ripples of French influence. The very heart of the vocabulary, too, remained English. Most of the high-frequency words—the pronouns, the prepositions, the conjunctions, the auxiliaries, as well as a great many ordinary nouns and verbs and adjectives—were not replaced by borrowings.

Middle English, then, was still a Germanic language, but it differed from Old English in many ways. The sound system and the grammar changed a good deal. Speakers made less use of case systems and other inflectional devices and relied more on word order and structure words to express their meanings. This is often said to be a simplification, but it isn't really. Languages don't become simpler; they merely exchange one kind of complexity for another. Modern English is not a simple language, as any foreign speaker who tries to learn it will hasten to tell you.

For us Middle English is simpler than Old English just because it is closer to Modern English. It takes three or four months at least to learn to read Old English prose and more than that for poetry. But a week of good study should put one in touch with the Middle English poet Chaucer. Indeed, you may be able to make some sense of Chaucer straight off, though you would need instruction in pronunciation to make it sound like poetry. Here is a famous passage from the *General Prologue to the Canterbury Tales*, fourteenth century:

> Ther was also a nonne, a Prioresse,
> That of hir smyling was ful symple and coy,
> Hir gretteste oath was but by Seinte Loy,
> And she was cleped Madame Eglentyne.
> Ful wel she song the service dyvyne,
> Entuned in hir nose ful semely.
> And Frenshe she spak ful faire and fetisly,
> After the scole of Stratford-atte-Bowe,
> For Frenshe of Parys was to hir unknowe.

Early Modern English

Sometime between 1400 and 1600 English underwent a couple of sound changes which made the language of Shakespeare quite different from that of Chaucer. Incidentally, these changes contributed much to the chaos in which English spelling now finds itself.

One change was the elimination of a vowel sound in certain unstressed positions at the end of words. For instance, the words *name, stone, wine, dance* were pronounced as two syllables by Chaucer but as just one by Shakespeare. The *e* in these words became, as we say, "silent." But it wasn't silent for Chaucer; it represented a vowel sound. So also the words *laughed, seemed, stored* would have been pronounced by Chaucer as two-syllable words. The change was an important one because it affected thousands of words and gave a different aspect to the whole language.

The other change is what is called the Great Vowel Shift. This was a systematic shifting of half a dozen vowels and diphthongs in stressed syllables. For instance, the word *name* had in Middle English a vowel something like that in the modern word *father; wine* had the vowel of modern *mean; he* was pronounced something like modern *hey; mouse* sounded like *moose; moon* had the vowel of *moan.* Again the shift was thoroughgoing and affected all the words in which these vowel sounds occurred. Since we still keep the Middle English system of spelling these words, the differences between Modern English and Middle English are often more real than apparent.

The vowel shift has meant also that we have come to use an entirely different set of symbols for representing vowel sounds than is used by writers of such languages as French, Italian, or Spanish, in which no such vowel shift occurred. If you come across a strange word—say, *bine*—in an English book, you will pronounce it according to the English system, with the vowel of *wine* or *dine.* But if you read *bine* in a French, Italian, or Spanish book, you will pronounce it with the vowel of *mean* or *seen.*

These two changes, then, produced the basic differences between Middle English and Modern English. But there were several other developments that had an effect upon the language. One was the invention of printing, an invention introduced into England by William Caxton in the year 1475. Where before books had been rare and costly, they suddenly became cheap and common. More and more people learned to read and write. This was the first of many advances in communication which have worked to unify languages and to arrest the development of dialect differences, though of course printing affects writing principally rather than speech. Among other things it hastened the standardization of spelling.

The period of Early Modern English—that is, the sixteenth and seventeenth centuries—was also the period of the English Renaissance, when people developed, on the one hand, a keen interest in the past and, on the other, a more daring and imaginative view of the future. New ideas multiplied, and new ideas meant new language. Englishmen had grown accustomed to borrowing words from French as a result of the Norman Conquest; now they borrowed from Latin and Greek. As we have seen, English had been raiding Latin from Old English times and before, but now the floodgates really opened, and thousands of words from the classical languages poured in. *Pedestrian, bonus, anatomy, contradict, climax, dictionary, benefit, multiply, exist, paragraph, initiate, scene, inspire* are random examples. Probably the average educated American today has more words from French in his vocabulary than from native English sources, and more from Latin than from French.

The greatest writer of the Early Modern English period is of course Shakespeare, and the best-known book is the King James Version of the Bible, published in 1611. The Bible (if not Shakespeare) has made many features of Early Modern English perfectly familiar to many people down to present time, even though we do not use these features in present-day speech and writing. For instance, the old pronouns *thou* and *thee* have dropped out of use now, together with their verb forms, but they are still familiar to us in prayer and in Biblical quotations: "Whither thou goest, I will go." Such forms as *hath* and *doth* have been replaced by *has* and *does;* "Goes he hence tonight?" would now be "Is he going away tonight?"; Shakespeare's "Fie, on't, sirrah" would be "Nuts to that, Mac." Still, all these expressions linger with us because of the power of the works in which they occur.

It is not always realized, however, that considerable sound changes have taken place between Early Modern English and the English of the present day. Shakespearian actors putting on a play speak the words, properly enough, in their modern pronunciation. But it is very doubtful that this pronunciation would be understood at all by Shakespeare. In Shakespeare's time, the word *reason* was pronounced like modern *raisin; face* had the sound of modern *glass;* the *l* in *would, should, palm* was pronounced. In these points and a great many others the English language has moved a long way from what it was in 1600.

Recent Developments

The history of English since 1700 is filled with many movements and countermovements, of which we can notice only a couple. One of these is the vigorous attempt made in the eighteenth century, and the rather half-hearted attempts made since, to regulate and control the English language. Many people of the eighteenth century, not understanding very well the forces which govern language, proposed to polish and prune and restrict English, which they felt was proliferating too wildly. There was much talk of an academy which would rule on what people could and could not say and write. The academy never came into being, but the eighteenth century did succeed in establishing certain attitudes which, though they haven't had much effect on the development of the language itself, have certainly changed the native speaker's feeling about the language.

In part, a product of the wish to fix and establish the language was the development of the dictionary. The first English dictionary was published in 1603; it was a list of 2,500 words briefly defined. Many others were published with gradual improvements until Samuel Johnson published his *English Dictionary* in 1755. This, steadily revised, dominated the field in England for nearly a hundred years. Meanwhile in America, Noah Webster published his dictionary in 1828, and before long dictionary publishing was a big business in this country. The last century has seen the publication of one great dictionary: the twelve-volume *Oxford English Dictionary*, compiled in the course of seventy-five years through the labors of many scholars. We have also, of course, numerous commercial dictionaries which are as good as the public wants them to be if not, indeed, rather better.

Another product of the eighteenth century was the invention of "English grammar." As English came to replace Latin as the language of scholarship, it was felt that one should also be able to control and dissect it, parse and analyze it, as one could Latin. What happened in practice was that the grammatical description that applied to Latin was removed and superimposed on English. This was silly, because English is an entirely different kind of language, with its own forms and signals and ways of producing meaning. Nevertheless, English grammars on the Latin model were worked out and taught in the schools. In many schools they are still being taught. This activity is not often popular with schoolchildren, but it is sometimes an interesting and instructive exercise in logic. The principal harm in it is that it has tended to keep people from being interested in English and has obscured the real features of English structure.

But probably the most important force on the development of English in the modern period has been the tremendous expansion of English-speaking peoples. In 1500 English was a minor language, spoken by a few people on a small island. Now it is perhaps the greatest language of the world, spoken natively by over a quarter of a billion people and as a second language by many millions more. When we speak of English now, we must specify whether we mean American English, British English, Australian English, Indian English, or what, since the differences are considerable. The American cannot go to England or the Englishman to America confident that he will always understand and be understood. The Alabaman in Iowa or the Iowan in Alabama shows himself a foreigner every time he speaks. It is only because communication has become fast and easy that English in this period of its expansion has not broken into a dozen mutually unintelligible languages.

FOR DISCUSSION AND REVIEW

1. Roberts describes in some detail the relationships between historical events in England and the development of the English language. Summarize the most important events and comment on their relationship to or effect on the English language.

2. What are the three major periods in the history of English? What are the approximate dates of each? On what bases do linguists make these distinctions?

3. During what period was the epic poem *Beowulf* written? Does Roberts suggest why this period was propitious for the creation of such a work?

4. How did the pronouns *they, their,* and *them* come into English? What is unusual about this occurrence?

5. List four important ways in which the grammar of Old English differed from that of Modern English. What was the principal difference between the vocabulary of Old English and that of Modern English?

6. When the Anglo-Saxons invaded England, their language became the language of the land, almost completely obliterating the Celtic which had been spoken by the earlier inhabitants. How do you account for the fact that French did not become the language of England after the Norman Conquest? Explain Roberts's statement that "English . . . was profoundly changed after the Norman Conquest."

7. How would you characterize in social terms the French words that were brought into English by the Norman Conquest? In what areas of life did French have the greatest influence?

8. Describe the changes the English language underwent as a result of the Great Vowel Shift. What is the importance of this linguistic phenomenon for modern English?

9. Identify two significant effects that the invention of printing had on the English language.

10. Early English grammars—indeed, almost all English grammars published before 1950—were modeled on Latin grammars. Why was this the case? List four of the erroneous assumptions included in these Latin-based grammars.

5/Language Change: Progress or Decay?

JEAN AITCHISON

In this chapter from her book Language Change, *Professor Jean Aitchison of the London School of Economics asserts that language change is "natural, inevitable and continuous, and involves interwoven sociolinguistic and psycholinguistic factors which cannot easily be disentangled from one another." It is not, she points out, in any sense "wrong for human language to change." In view of these facts, Professor Aitchison raises three questions: "First, is it still relevant to speak of [language] progress or decay? Secondly, irrespective of whether the move is a forwards or backwards one, are human languages evolving in any detectable direction? Thirdly, even though language change is not wrong in the moral sense, is it socially undesirable, and, if so, can we control it?" In the following pages, she describes the difficulties of answering these questions and suggests some reasonable answers: (1) language is constantly changing, but it is neither progressing nor decaying; (2) languages are slowly changing (not "evolving" in the usual sense of the word) in different—indeed, sometimes opposite—directions; (3) language change is not wrong, but it may sometimes lead to situations in which speakers of different dialects of the same language have difficulty understanding one another; and (4) although it is impossible to halt such change by passing laws or establishing monitoring "academies," careful language planning can often help.*

If you can look into the seeds of time,
And say which grain will grow and which will not. . . .
WILLIAM SHAKESPEARE, *Macbeth*

Predicting the future depends on understanding the present. The majority of [the many objectors to language change, from the purists of the eighteenth century to today's self-proclaimed experts,] had not considered the complexity of the factors involved in language change. They were giving rise to a purely emotional expression of their hopes and fears.

A closer look at language change [indicates] that it is natural, inevitable and continuous, and involves interwoven sociolinguistic and psycholinguistic factors which cannot easily be disentangled from one another. It is triggered by social factors, but these social factors make use of existing cracks and gaps in the language structure. In the circumstances, the true direction of a change is not obvious to a superficial observer. Sometimes alterations are disruptive, as with the increasing loss of *t* in British English, where the utilization of a natural tendency to alter or omit final consonants may end up destroying a previously stable stop system. At other times, modifications can be viewed as therapy, as in the loss of *h* in British English, which is wiping out an exception in the otherwise symmetrical organization of fricatives.

However, whether changes disrupt the language system, or repair it, the most important point is this: it is in no sense wrong for human language to change, any more than it is wrong for humpback whales to alter their songs every year (Payne, 1979). In fact, there are some surprising parallels between the two species. All the whales sing the same song one year, the next year they all sing a new one. But the yearly differences are not random. The songs seem to be evolving. The songs of consecutive years are more alike than those that are separated by several years. When it was first discovered that the songs of humpbacks changed from year to year, a simple explanation seemed likely. Since the whales only sing during the breeding season, and since their song is complex, it was assumed that they simply forgot the song between seasons, and then tried to reconstruct it the next year from fragments which remained in their memory. But when researchers organized a long-term study of humpbacks off the island of Maui in Hawaii, they got a surprise. The song that the whales were singing at the beginning of the new breeding season turned out to be identical to the one used at the end of the previous one. Between breeding seasons, the song had seemingly been kept in cold storage, without change. The songs were gradually modified as the season proceeded. For example, new sequences were sometimes created by joining the beginning and end of consecutive phrases, and omitting the middle part—a procedure not unlike certain human language changes.

Both whales and humans, then, are constantly changing their communication system, and are the only two species in which this has been proved to happen—though some birds are now thought to alter their song in certain ways. Rather than castigating one of these species for allowing change to occur, it seems best to admit that humans are probably programmed by nature to behave in this way. As a character in John Wyndham's novel *Web* says: "Man is a product of nature. . . . Whatever he does, it must be part of his nature to do—or he could not do it. He is not, and cannot be *un*natural. He, with his capacities, is as much the product of nature as were the dinosaurs with theirs. He is an *instrument* of natural processes."

A consideration of the naturalness and inevitability of change leads us to . . . three final questions which need to be discussed. . . . First, is it still relevant to speak of progress or decay? Secondly, irrespective of whether the move is a forwards or backwards one, are human languages evolving in any detectable direction? Thirdly, even though language change is not wrong in the moral sense, is it socially undesirable, and, if so, can we control it?. . .

Forwards or Backwards?

"Once, twice, thrice upon a time, there lived a jungle. This particular jungle started at the bottom and went upwards till it reached the monkeys, who had been waiting years for the trees to reach them, and as soon as they did, the monkeys invented climbing down." The opening paragraph of Spike Milligan's fable, *The Story of the Bald Twit Lion*, indicates how easy it is to make facts fit one's preferred theory.

This tendency is particularly apparent in past interpretations of the direction of change, where opinions about progress or decay in language have tended to reflect the religious or philosophical preconceptions of their proponents, rather than a detached analysis of the evidence. Let us briefly deal with these preconceptions before looking at the issue itself.

Many nineteenth-century scholars were imbued with sentimental ideas about the "noble savage," and assumed that the current generation was by comparison a race of decadent sinners. They therefore took it for granted that language had declined from a former state of perfection. Restoring this early perfection was viewed as one of the principal goals of comparative historical linguistics: "A principal goal of this science is to reconstruct the full, pure forms of an original stage from the variously disfigured and mutilated forms which are attested in the individual languages," said one scholar (Curtius, 1871, in Kiparsky, 1972: 35).

This quasireligious conviction of gradual decline has never entirely died out. But from the mid-nineteenth century onward, a second, opposing viewpoint came into existence alongside the earlier one. Darwin's doctrine of the survival of the fittest and ensuing belief in inevitable progress gradually grew in popularity: "Progress, therefore, is not an accident, but a necessity. . . . It is a part of nature," claimed one nineteenth-century enthusiast (Herbert Spencer, *Social Statics*, 1850). Darwin himself believed that in language "the better, the shorter, the easier forms are constantly gaining the upper hand, and they owe their success to their inherent virtue" (Darwin, 1871, in Labov, 1972: 273).

The doctrine of the survival of the fittest, in its crudest version, implies that those forms and languages which survive are inevitably better than those which die out. This is unfortunate, since it confuses the notions of progress and decay in language with expansion and decline. [But] expansion and decline reflect political and social situations, not the intrinsic merit or decadence of a language. For example, it is a historical accident that English is so widely spoken in the world. Throughout history, quite different types of language—Latin, Turkish, Chinese, for example—have spread over wide areas. This popularity reflects the military and political strength of these nations, not the worth of their speech. Similarly, Gaelic is dying out because it is being ousted by English, a language with social and political prestige. It is not collapsing because it has got too complicated or strange for people to speak, as has occasionally been maintained.

In order to assess the possible direction of language, then, we need to put aside both religious beliefs and Darwinian assumptions. The former leads to an illogical idealization of the past, and the latter to the confusion of progress and decay with expansion and decline.

Leaving aside these false trails, we are left with a crucial question: what might we mean by "progress" within language?

The term "progress" implies a movement towards some desired endpoint. What could this be, in terms of linguistic excellence? A number of linguists are in no doubt. They endorse the view of Jespersen, who maintained that "that language ranks highest which goes farthest in the art of accomplishing much with little means, or, in other words, which is able to express the greatest amount of meaning with the simplest mechanism" (Mühlhaüsler, 1979: 151).

If this criterion were taken seriously, we would be obliged to rank pidgins as the most advanced languages. . . .[However,] true simplicity seems to be counterbalanced by ambiguity and cumbersomeness. Darwin's confident belief in the "inherent virtue" of shorter and easier forms must be set beside the realization that such forms often result in confusing homonyms, as in the Tok Pisin *hat* for "hot," "hard," "hat," and "heart."

A straightforward simplicity measure then will not necessarily pinpoint the "best" language. A considerable number of other factors must be taken into account, and it is not yet clear which they are, and how they should be assessed. In brief, linguists have been unable to decide on any clear measure of excellence, even though the majority are of the opinion that a language with numerous irregularities should be less highly ranked than one which is economical and transparent. Note, however, that preliminary attempts to rank languages in this way have run into a further problem.

A language which is simple and regular in one respect is likely to be complex and confusing in others. There seems to be a trading relationship between the different parts of the grammar which we do not fully understand. This has come out clearly in the work of one researcher who has compared the progress of Turkish and Yugoslav children as they acquired their respective languages (Slobin, 1977). Turkish children find it exceptionally easy to learn the inflections of their language, which are remarkably straightforward, and they master the entire system by the age of two. But the youngsters struggle with relative clauses (the equivalent of English clauses beginning with *who*, *which*, *that*) until around the age of five. Yugoslav children, on the other hand, have great problems with the inflectional system of Serbo-Croatian, which is "a classic Indo-European synthetic muddle," and they are not competent at manipulating it until around the age of five. Yet, they have no problems with Serbo-Croatian relative clauses, which they can normally cope with by the age of two.

Overall, we cannot yet specify satisfactorily just what we mean by a "perfect" language, except in a very broad sense. The most we can do is to note that a certain part of one language may be simpler and therefore perhaps "better" than that of another.

Meanwhile, even if all agreed that a perfectly regular language was the "best," there is no evidence that languages are progressing towards this ultimate goal. Instead, there is a continuous pull between the disruption and restoration of patterns. In this perpetual ebb and flow, it would be a mistake to regard pattern neatening and regularization as a step forwards. Such an occurrence may be no more progressive than the tidying up of a cluttered office. Reorganization simply restores the room to a workable state. Similarly, it would be misleading to assume that pattern disruption was necessarily a backwards step. Structural dislocation may be the result of extending the language in some useful way.

We must conclude therefore that language is ebbing and flowing like the tide, but neither progressing nor decaying, as far as we can tell. Disruptive and therapeutic tendencies vie with one another, with neither one totally winning or losing, resulting in a perpetual stalemate. As the famous Russian linguist Roman Jakobson said fifty years ago: "The spirit of equilibrium and the simultaneous tendency towards its rupture constitute the indispensable properties of that whole that is language" (Jakobson, 1949: 336; translation in Keiler, 1972).

Are Languages Evolving?

Leaving aside notions of progress and decay we need to ask one further question. Is there any evidence that languages as a whole are moving in any particular direction in their intrinsic structure? Are they, for example, moving towards a fixed word order, as has sometimes been claimed?

It is clear that languages, even if they are evolving in some identifiable way, are doing so very slowly—otherwise all languages would be rather more similar than they in fact are. However, unfortunately for those who would like to identify some overall drift, the languages of the world seem to be moving in different, often opposite, directions.

For example, over the past two thousand years or so, most Indo-European languages have moved from being SOV (subject-object-verb) languages, to SVO (subject-verb-object) ones. . . . Certain Niger-Congo languages seem to be following a similar path. Yet we cannot regard this as an overall trend, since Mandarin Chinese seems to be undergoing a change in the opposite direction, from SVO to SOV (Li and Thompson, 1974).

During the same period, English and a number of other Indo-European languages have gradually lost their inflections, and moved over to a fixed word order. However, this direction is not inevitable, since Wappo, a Californian Indian language, appears to be doing the reverse, and moving from a system in which grammatical relationships are expressed by word order to one in which they are marked by case endings (Li and Thompson, 1976).

A similar variety is seen in the realm of phonology. For example, English, French and Hindi had the same common ancestor: nowadays, Hindi has sixteen stop consonants and ten vowels, according to one count. French, on the other hand, has sixteen vowels and six stops. English, meanwhile, has acquired more fricatives than either of these two languages, some of which speakers of French and Hindi find exceptionally difficult to pronounce. Many more such examples could be found.

Overall, then we must conclude that "the evolution of language as such has never been demonstrated, and the inherent equality of all languages must be maintained on present evidence" (Greenberg, 1957: 65).

Is Language Change Socially Undesirable?

Let us now turn to the last two questions. Is language change undesirable? If so, is it controllable?

Social undesirability and moral turpitude are often confused. Yet the two questions can quite often be kept distinct. For example, it is certainly not "wrong" to sleep out in the open. Nevertheless, it is fairly socially inconvenient to have people bedding down wherever they want to, and therefore laws have been passed forbidding people to camp out in, say, Trafalgar Square or Hyde Park in London.

Language change is, we have seen, in no sense wrong. But is it socially undesirable? It is only undesirable when communication gets disrupted. If different groups change a previously unified language in different directions, or if one group alters its speech more radically than another, mutual intelligibility may be impaired or even destroyed. In Tok Pisin, for example, speakers from rural areas have great difficulty in understanding the urbanized varieties. This is an unhappy and socially inconvenient state of affairs.

In England, on the other hand, the problem is minimal. There are relatively few speakers of British English who cannot understand one another. This is because most people speak the same basic dialect, in the sense that the rules underlying their utterances and vocabulary are fairly much the same. They are likely, however, to speak this single dialect with different accents. There is nothing wrong with this, as long as people can communicate satisfactorily with one another. An accent which differs markedly from those around may be hard for others to comprehend, and is therefore likely to be a disadvantage in job-hunting situations, as a number of recent immigrants have found. But a mild degree of regional variation is probably a mark of individuality to be encouraged rather than stamped out.

A number of people censure the variety of regional accents in England, maintaining that the accent that was originally of one particular area, London and the southeast, is "better" than the others. In fact, speakers from this locality sometimes claim that they speak English *without* an accent, something which is actually impossible. It is, of course, currently socially useful in England to be able to speak the accent of so-called Southern British English, an accent sometimes spoken of as Received Pronunciation (RP), which has spread to the educated classes throughout the country. But there is no logical reason behind the disapproval of regional accents. Moreover, such objections are by no means universal. In America, a regional accent is simply a mark of where you are from with no stigma attached, for the most part.

Accent differences, then, are not a matter of great concern. More worrying are instances where differing dialects cause unintelligibility, or misunderstandings. In the past, this often used to be the case in England. Caxton, writing in the fifteenth century, notes that "comynenglysshe that is spoken in one shyre varyeth from another" (Caxton, preface to *Erydos* [1490]). To illustrate his point, he narrates an episode concerning a ship which was stranded in the Thames for lack of wind, and put into shore for refreshment. One of the merchants on board went to a nearby house, and asked, in English, for meat and eggs. The lady of the house, much to this gentleman's indignation, replied that she could not speak French! In Caxton's words, the merchant "came in to an hows and axed for mete and specyally he axyd after eggys.

And the goode wyf answerde that she coude speke no frenshe. And the marchaut was angry for he also coude speke no frenshe, but wolde haue, hadde egges and she vnderstode hym not." The problem in this case was that a "new" Norse word *egges* "eggs" was in the process of replacing the Old English word *eyren*, but was not yet generally understood.

Unfortunately, such misunderstandings did not disappear with the fifteenth century. Even though, both in America and England, the majority of speakers are mutually intelligible, worrying misunderstandings still occur through dialect differences. Consider the conversation between Samuel, a five-year-old [black] boy from West Philadelphia, and Paul, a white psychologist who had been working in Samuel's school for six months:

> Samuel: I been know your name.
> Paul: What?
> Samuel: I been know your name.
> Paul: You better know my name?
> Samuel: I *been* know your name. (Labov, 1972a: 62).

Paul failed to realize that in Philadelphia's black community *been* means "for a long time." Samuel meant "I have known your name for a long time." In some circumstances, this use of *been* can be completely misleading to a white speaker. A [black] Philadelphian who said *I been married* would in fact mean "I have been married for a long time." But a white speaker would normally interpret her sentence as meaning "I have been married, but I am not married any longer."

Is it possible to do anything about situations where differences caused by language change threaten to disrupt the mutual comprehension and cohesion of a population? Should language change be stopped?

If legislators decide that something is socially inconvenient, then their next task is to decide whether it is possible to take effective action against it. If we attempted to halt language change by law, would the result be as effective as forbidding people to camp in Trafalgar Square? Or would it be as useless as telling the pigeons there not to roost around the fountains? Judging by the experience of the French who have an academy, the Académie Française, which adjudicates over matters of linguistic usage, and whose findings have been made law in some cases, the result is a waste of time. Even though there may be some limited effect on the written language, spoken French appears not to have responded in any noticeable way.

If legal sanctions are impractical, how can mutual comprehension be brought about or maintained? The answer is not to attempt to limit change, which is probably impossible, but to ensure that all members of the population have at least one common language, and one common variety of that language, which they can mutually use. The standard language may be the only one spoken by certain people. Others will retain their own regional dialect or language alongside the standard one. This is the situation in the British Isles, where some Londoners, for example, speak only standard British English. In Wales, however, there are a number of people who are equally fluent in Welsh and English.

The imposition of a standard language cannot be brought about by force. Sometimes it occurs spontaneously, as has happened in England. At other times, conscious intervention is required. Such social planning requires tact and skill. In order for a policy to achieve acceptance, a population must *want* to speak a particular language or particular variety of it. A branch of sociolinguistics known as "language planning" or, more recently, "language engineering" is attempting to solve the practical and theoretical problems involved in such attempts (Bell, 1976; Würm, Mühlhäusler, and Laycock, 1977).

Once standardization has occurred, and a whole population has accepted one particular variety as standard, it becomes a strong unifying force and often a source of national pride and symbol of independence.

Great Permitters

Perhaps we need one final comment about "Great Permitters"—a term coined by William Safire, who writes a column about language for the *New York Times* (Safire, 1980, from whom the quotations in this section are taken). These are intelligent, determined people, often writers, who "care about clarity and precision, who detest fuzziness of expression that reveals sloppiness or laziness of thought." They want to give any changes which occur "a shove in the direction of freshness and precision," and are "willing to struggle to preserve the clarity and color in the language." In other words, they are prepared to accept new usages which they regard as advantageous, and are prepared to battle against those which seem sloppy or pointless.

Such an aim is admirable. An influential writer-journalist can clearly make interesting suggestions, and provide models for others to follow. Two points need to be made, however. First, however hard a "linguistic activist" (as Safire calls himself) works, he is unlikely to reverse a strong trend, however much he would like to. Safire has, for example, given up his fight against *hopefully,* and also against *viable* which, he regretfully admits, "cannot be killed." Secondly, and perhaps more importantly, we need to realize how personal and how idiosyncratic are judgments as to what is "good" and what is "bad," even when they are made by a careful and knowledgeable writer, as becomes clear from the often furious letters which follow Safire's pronouncements in the *New York Times*. Even a Safire fan must admit that he holds a number of opinions which are based on nothing more than a subjective feeling about the words in question. Why, for example, did he give up the struggle against *hopefully*, but continue to wage war on *clearly*? As one of his correspondents notes, "Your grudge against clearly is unclear to me." Similarly, Safire attacks ex-President Carter's "needless substitution of encrypt for encode," but is sharply reminded by a reader that "the words 'encrypt' and 'encode' have very distinct meanings for a cryptographer." These, and other similar examples, show that attempts of caring persons to look after a language can mean no more than the preservation of personal preferences which may not agree with the views of others.

Summary and Conclusion

Continual language change is natural and inevitable, and is due to a combination of psycholinguistic and sociolinguistic factors.

Once we have stripped away religious and philosophical preconceptions, there is no evidence that language is either progressing or decaying. Disruption and therapy seem to balance one another in a perpetual stalemate. These two opposing pulls are an essential characteristic of language.

Furthermore, there is no evidence that languages are moving in any particular direction from the point of view of language structure—several are moving in contrary directions.

Language change is in no sense wrong, but it may, in certain circumstances, be socially undesirable. Minor variations in pronunciation from region to region are unimportant, but change which disrupts the mutual intelligibility of a community can be socially and politically inconvenient. If this happens, it may be useful to encourage standardization—the adoption of a standard variety of one particular language which everybody will be able to use, alongside the existing regional dialects or languages. Such a situation must be brought about gradually, with tact and care, since a population will only adopt a language or dialect it *wants* to speak.

Finally, it is always possible that language is developing in some mysterious fashion that linguists have not yet identified. Only time and further research will tell. There is much more to be discovered.

But we may finish on a note of optimism. We no longer, like Caxton in the fifteenth century, attribute language change to the domination of man's affairs by the moon:

> And certaynly our langage now vsed varyeth ferre from that which was
> vsed and spoken whan I was borne. For we englysshe men ben borne

vnder the domynacyon of the mone, which is neuer stedfaste but euer wauerynge wexynge one season and waneth and dycreaseth another season. (Caxton, preface to *Erydos* [1490])

Instead, step by step, we are coming to an understanding of the social and psychological factors underlying language change. As the years go by, we hope gradually to increase this knowledge. In the words of the nineteenth-century poet, Alfred Lord Tennyson: "Science moves, but slowly slowly, creeping on from point to point."

References

Bell, R. (1976), *Sociolinguistics: Goals, Approaches, and Problems*. London: Batsford.

Greenberg, J. H. (1957), *Essays in Linguistics*. Chicago: University Press; Phoenix Books edition, 1963.

Keiler, A. R., ed. (1972), *A Reader in Historical and Comparative Linguistics*. New York: Holt, Rinehart & Winston.

Kiparsky, P. (1972), "From paleogrammarians to neogrammarians." *York Papers in Linguistics* 2, 33–43.

Labov, W. (1972), *Sociolinguistic Patterns*. Philadelphia: University of Pennsylvania Press.

————. (1972a), "Where do grammars stop?" In R. W. Shuy, ed., *Sociolinguistics: Current Trends and Prospects*, 23rd Annual Round Table Meeting, Georgetown University School of Languages and Linguistics. Georgetown: University of Georgetown Press.

Li, C. N. and Thompson, S. A. (1974), "Historical change of word order: A case study of Chinese and its implications." In Anderson, J. M., and Jones, C., eds. (1974), *Historical Linguistics*. Amsterdam: North Holland.

————. (1976), "Strategies for signaling grammatical relations in Wappo." *Papers From the Twelfth Regional Meeting*. Chicago: Chicago Linguistic Society.

Mühlhäusler, P. (1978), "Samoan plantation pidgin English and the origin of New Guinea Pidgin." *Papers in Pidgin and Creole Linguistics*, I, 67–119.

Payne, R. (1979), "Humpbacks: their mysterious songs." *National Geographic* 155, 1, January, 18–25.

Safire, W. (1980), *On Language*. New York: Times Books.

Slobin, D. I. (1977), "Language change in childhood and history." In J. Macnamara, ed., *Language Learning and Thought*. New York: Academic Press, 1977.

Wurm, S. A., Mühlhäusler, P., and Laycock, D. C. (1977), "Language planning and engineering in Papua New Guinea." In S. A. Wurm, ed., *New Guinea Area Languages and Language Study*, vol. 3. Canberra: Pacific Linguistics, C–40.

FOR DISCUSSION AND REVIEW

1. What point about human language does Aitchison make by describing the songs of humpback whales?

2. What was the attitude of the early historical linguists toward language change? How did Darwin's doctrine of survival of the fittest affect linguists' attitudes?

3. Explain three criteria that might be used to measure "progress" in language. Are these criteria completely satisfactory? Why or why not?

4. Describe four of the very slow changes that are occurring in the world's languages, noting especially instances in which languages seem to be evolving in different or opposite directions. In your description, consider such things as word order, inflections, and phonology.

5. Drawing upon your own experience, describe an instance in which "differing dialects cause[d] unintelligibility, or misunderstandings."

6. Summarize Aitchison's conclusions about the "Great Permitters."

Projects for "Historical Linguistics and Language Change"

1. The articles in Part Eight have dealt primarily with genetic classification of languages. Another type of classification, typological, was formerly popular and, much refined, is still useful. Prepare a report on typological classification that includes discussion of its earlier problems and its present status. You will want to read "A Quantitative Approach to the Morphological Typology of Language" by Joseph H. Greenberg and consult a text such as *Introduction to Historical Linguistics* by Anthony Arlotto (both are listed in the bibliography).

2. Prepare a report summarizing the development of the English dictionary. One useful source is the workbook *Problems in the Origin and Development of the English Language* by John Algeo (listed in the bibliography).

3. The *Oxford English Dictionary* (*OED*) is probably the finest historical dictionary ever prepared. Prepare a report describing its preparation and explaining the kinds of information that it contains.

4. The following passages are versions of the Lord's Prayer as they were written during different periods in the history of the English language. (a) Analyze the forms that the various words have in common, and consider how each word changes from the first to the last version and, also, from one version to the next (e.g., Faeder, fadir, father, Father). (b) Do the same kind of analysis on the various syntactical (i.e., word-order) changes that you discover (e.g., Tōcume þīn rīce; Thy kyngdom cumme to; Let they kingdom come; Thy kingdom come). (c) Write an essay in which you comment on the changes that you have discovered in these excerpts. Give as many examples of the various changes as you believe are necessary to support your conclusions. Finally, draw some conclusions about the evolution of the English language as it is revealed in the passages.

1. Eornostlīce gebiddaþ ēow þus Fæder ūre þū be eart on heofonum, sie þin nama gehālgod.
2. Tōcume þīn rice. Gewurþe þīn willa on eorþan swā swā on heofonum.
3. Ūrne daeghwæmlīcan hlāf syle ūs tōdæg.
4. And forgyf ūs ure gyltas swā swā we forgyfaþ ūrum gyltendum.
5. And ne gelæd þū ūs on costnunge ac ālys us of yfele.
6. Witodlice gyf gē forgyfaþ mannum hyra synna, þonne forgyfþ ēower sē heofonlīca fæder ēow ēowre gyltas.
7. Gyf gē sōþlīce ne forgyfaþ mannum, ne ēower fæder ne forgyfþ ēow ēowre synna.

Old English (ca. 1000)

1. Forsothe thus ȝe shulen preyen, Oure fadir that art in heuenes, halwid be thi name;
2. Thy kyngdom cumme to; be thi wille don as in heuen and in erthe;
3. ȝif to vs this day oure breed ouer other substaunce;
4. And forȝeue to vs oure dettis, as we forȝeue to oure dettours;
5. And leede vs nat in to temptacioun, but delyuere vs fro yuel. Amen.
6. Forsothe ȝif ȝee shulen forȝeuve to men her synnys, and ȝoure heuenly fadir shal forȝeue to ȝou ȝoure trespassis.
7. Sothely ȝif ȝee shulen forȝeue not to men, neither ȝoure fadir shal forȝeue to ȝou ȝoure synnes.

Middle English (Wycliffe, 1389)

1. After thys maner there fore praye ye, O oure father which arte in heven, halowed be thy name;
2. Let thy kingdom come; they wyll be fulfilled as well in erth as hit ys in heven;
3. Geve vs this daye oure dayly breade;
4. And forgeve vs oure treaspases, even as we forgeve them which trespas vs;
5. Leede vs not into temptacion, but delyvre vs ffrom yvell. Amen.
6. For and yff ye shall forgeve other men there trespases, youre father in heven shal also forgeve you.
7. But and ye wyll not forgeve men there trespases, no more shall youre father forgeve youre trespases.

Early Modern English (Tyndale, 1526)

1. Pray then like this: Our Father who art in heaven, Hallowed be thy name.
2. Thy kingdom come, Thy will be done, On Earth as it is in heaven.
3. Give us this day our daily bread;
4. And forgive us our debts, As we also have forgiven our debtors;
5. And lead us not into temptation, But deliver us from evil.
6. For if you forgive men their trespasses, your heavenly Father also will forgive you;
7. but if you do not forgive men their trespasses, neither will your Father forgive your trespasses.

Modern English (1952)

5. Roberts mentions that there was at one time interest in establishing an "academy" to monitor and purify the English language. One of those interested was Jonathan Swift (1667–1745). Prepare a report

on the history of interest in such an academy and of the arguments for and against it.

6. A number of artificial languages have been developed with the aim of providing a universal language that would be acceptable to everyone and easily learned. The best known of these languages are Volapük, Esperanto, and Interlingua. Basic English is also sometimes included in this group. Prepare a report on one of these languages; be sure to include samples of it, and argue for or against the concept of a universal language. The following works will be helpful: (1) Connor, George Alan, D. T. Connor, and William Solzbacher. *Esperanto: The World Inter-Language.* New York: Bechhurst Press, 1948. (2) Pei, Mario. *One Language for the World.* New York: Devin-Adair, 1961. (3) White, Ralph G. "Toward the Construction of a Lingua Humana." *Current Anthropology* 13 (1972), 113–23. (4) Hayes, Curtis W., Jacob Ornstein, and William W. Gage. *ABC's of Languages and Linguistics.* Silver Spring, MD: Institute of Modern Languages, Inc., 1977, especially Chapter X, "One Language for the World?"

7. The following words have interesting etymologies: *algebra, anaesthetic, assassin, caucus, crocodile, tawdry,* and *zest.* Look at their entries in the *Oxford English Dictionary* and then write a brief statement about each. If you have difficulty understanding the abbreviations and designations in the *OED,* consult the frontmatter.

8. Aitchison mentions the possibility and the importance of "language planning." A great deal has been written about this subject in recent years, and the material deals with a number of different countries (e.g., India, the Sudan, various African countries, Haiti, Papua-New Guinea, and the Scandinavian countries). Using the resources in your college library, investigate the particular problems faced in one country and the kinds of "language planning" that have been done. Evaluate the success (or lack of success) of the planning.

9. Modern English developed from the East Midland dialect of Middle English (1100–1500). Chaucer wrote in this dialect, which is one reason why his poetry is relatively easy to read. But *why* did Modern English develop from the East Midland dialect? Based on library research, write a brief paper explaining the various reasons for this development.

10. After briefly discussing the "Great Permitters" (pp. 620–621), Aitchison concludes that "attempts of caring persons to look after a language can mean no more than the preservation of personal preferences which may not agree with the views of others." After reading at least three articles or book chapters by such "Great Permitters" as William Safire, Edwin Newman, and John Simon, write a short paper in which you analyze the validity of Aitchison's statement. You may find two books particularly helpful: (a) Harvey A. Daniels, *Famous Last Words: The American Language Crisis Reconsidered* (Carbondale: Southern

Illinois University Press, 1983) and (b) Jim Quinn, *American Tongue and Cheek* (New York: Pantheon, 1981).

11. As we have seen, English is a member of the Germanic branch of the Indo-European language family. Prepare a report on either the Indo-Iranian, Balto-Slavic, or Italic branch, indicating what contemporary languages have developed from it, where they are spoken, and, if possible, by how many people.

12. Of the world's approximately five thousand living languages, only seventy are Indo-European. Some of the major non–Indo-European language families are the Afro-Asiatic, Altaic, Dravidian, Malayo-Polynesian, Niger-Congo, and Sino-Tibetan. Each of these families contains a number of different languages, each of which has more than a million native speakers. Choose one of these six non–Indo-European language families, and prepare a report describing it. For example, does the language family have subfamilies? What are they? What languages belong to it? Where are they spoken? By how many people? What features characterize these languages?

Selected Bibliography

Algeo, John. *Problems in the Origin and Development of the English Language*, 3d. ed. New York: Harcourt Brace Jovanovich, 1982. (An outstanding workbook; interesting and careful problems.)

Anttila, Raimo. *An Introduction to Historical and Comparative Linguistics*. New York: The Macmillan Company, 1972. (Excellent text; many examples; difficult but comprehensive.)

Arlotto, Anthony. *Introduction to Historical Linguistics*. Boston: Houghton Mifflin Company, 1972. (Very clear, readable, brief [243 pp.] introductory text.)

Baugh, Albert C., and Thomas Cable. *A History of the English Language*, 3rd ed. Englewood Cliffs, NJ: Prentice-Hall, 1978. (Long a standard, nontechnical text, the third edition is largely unchanged from the second.)

Bender, Harold H. *The Home of the Indo-Europeans*. Princeton: Princeton University Press, 1922. (The standard work on the subject.)

Bolton, W. F. *A Living Language: The History and Structure of English*. New York: Random House, 1982. (An excellent text; uncommon linking of the history of the language and the development of its literature.)

Dillard, J. L. *All-American English: A History of the English Language in America*. New York: Random House, 1975. (Emphasizes influence of maritime English on American colonists and the later imports of Yiddish, Pennsylvania Dutch, and "Spanglish.")

Gordon, James D. *The English Language: An Historical Introduction*. New York: Thomas Y. Crowell Company, 1972. (A good text; useful bibliography.)

Greenberg, Joseph H. "A Quantitative Approach to the Morphological Typology of Language." *International Journal of American Linguistics* 26 (1960),

178–194. (Presents a number of criteria for typological classification of languages; an important article.)

Greenough, James B., and George L. Kittredge. *Words and Their Ways in English Speech.* New York: Crowell-Collier and Macmillan, 1901; paperback by Beacon Press, 1962. (An older book but still valuable especially on meaning changes and slang.)

Haas, Mary. *The Prehistory of Languages.* The Hague: Mouton, 1969. (The title of an earlier version describes the contents: "Historical Linguistics and the Genetic Relationship of Languages.")

Jeffers, Robert J., and Ilse Lehiste. *Principles and Methods for Historical Linguistics.* Cambridge, MA: The MIT Press, 1979. (An excellent advanced text; numerous examples.)

Keiler, Alan R., ed. *A Reader in Historical and Comparative Linguistics.* New York: Holt, Rinehart and Winston, 1972. (Twenty essays, from 1902 on.)

King, Robert D. *Historical Linguistics and Generative Grammar.* Englewood Cliffs, NJ: Prentice-Hall, 1969. (A pioneering work; not for the beginner.)

Krapp, George Philip. *Modern English: Its Growth and Present Status.* Rev. by Albert H. Marckwardt. New York: Charles Scribner's Sons, 1969. (First published in 1909, it became a classic; now updated by the late Professor Marckwardt.)

Lass, Roger, ed. *Approaches to English Historical Linguistics: An Anthology.* New York: Holt, Rinehart and Winston, 1969. (Thirty articles of general interest.)

Lehmann, Winfred P. *Historical Linguistics: An Introduction,* 2nd ed. New York: Holt, Rinehart and Winston, Inc., 1973. (An excellent standard text; annotated bibliography.)

Lloyd, Donald J., and Harry R. Warfel. *American English in Its Cultural Setting.* New York: Alfred A. Knopf, 1956. (Includes an excellent short history of the American dictionary plus sections ["Our Land and Our People" and "Our Language"] interesting for the history of American English.)

Lodwig, Richard R., and Eugene F. Barrett. *The Dictionary and the Language.* New York: Hayden Book Companies, 1967. (Good section on the making of a modern dictionary.)

Markman, Alan M., and Erwin R. Steinberg, eds. *English Then and Now: Readings and Essays.* New York: Random House, 1970, (Collection of essays and excerpts arranged by language period.)

Marckwardt, Albert H. *American English,* 2nd ed. Rev. by J. L. Dillard. New York: Oxford University Press, 1980. (Fine revision and updating of a classic work.)

Myers, L. M. *The Roots of Modern English.* Boston: Little, Brown and Company, 1966. (See especially Myers's specimens of OE.)

Nunberg, Geoffrey. "The Decline of Grammar." *The Atlantic* (December 1983), pp. 31–46. (Excellent and entertaining essay about attitudes toward change in the English language.)

Pedersen, Holger. *The Discovery of Language: Linguistic Science in the Nineteenth Century.* Trans. by John Webster Spargo. Bloomington: Indiana University Press, 1962. (Readable discussion of the principles of historical linguistics; many examples; originally published in Copenhagen in 1924.)

Pyles, Thomas. *Words and Ways of American English.* New York: Random House, 1952. (An introduction to American English from colonial times to the present.

Pyles, Thomas and John Algeo. *The Origins and Development of the English Language*, 3rd ed. New York: Harcourt Brace Jovanovich, 1982. (An outstanding revision of an already fine text; the Algeo workbook [*supra*] accompanies this text.)

Roberts, Paul. "How to Find Fault With a Dictionary." *Understanding English.* New York: Harper & Row, 1958. (Useful on both the history of dictionaries and how to use them.)

Sledd, James, and Wilma R. Ebbitt. *Dictionaries and THAT Dictionary.* Glenview, IL: Scott, Foresman and Company, 1962. (A casebook on the controversy concerning the publication of *Webster's Third New International Dictionary, Unabridged;* introductory section on the history of dictionaries.)

Watkins, Calvert. "The Indo-European Origin of English," "Indo-European and the Indo-Europeans," "Indo-European Roots," in *The American Heritage Dictionary of the English Language.* Ed. William Morris. Boston: American Heritage Publishing Co. and Houghton Mifflin Company, 1969. (The first two items are essays and are somewhat technical; the third item is an Indo-European root dictionary to which items in the dictionary proper are cross-referenced.)

Weinreich, Uriel. *Languages in Contact: Findings and Problems.* The Hague: Mouton, 1967. (A classic work; a revision of the original 1953 edition.)

Whitehall, Harold. "The Development of the English Dictionary," in *Webster's New World Dictionary of the English Language.* New York: The World Publishing Company, 1958. (A basic historical survey.)

Williams, Joseph M. *Origins of the English Language: A Social and Linguistic History.* New York: The Free Press, 1975. (Contains especially fine and numerous problems.)

Wilson, Kenneth G., R. H. Hendrickson, and Peter Alan Taylor. *Harbrace Guide to Dictionaries.* New York: Harcourt, Brace & World, 1963. (Thorough, but does not treat recently published dictionaries; good historical section.)

Part Nine

Beyond Speech: Broader Perspectives

As linguistics as a discipline has developed and changed during the twentieth century, the number and variety of its subdivisions and areas of study have steadily increased. In this final part, we will examine four different topics, all of which have attracted a great deal of attention from linguists in recent years.

The first selection, George A. Miller's "Nonverbal Communication," discusses the significant role of nonverbal signals in the communication process. When people think of language, they generally consider it in terms of the words they say or write—or, on a more sophisticated level, in terms of phonology, morphology, syntax, semantics, and pragmatics. To look at language in this way, however, is to ignore the importance of the role played by nonverbal communication. Ray L. Birdwhistell estimates that in a typical two-person conversation, more than sixty-five percent of the social meaning is conveyed by nonverbal signals. He also estimates that the average person spends only about ten or eleven minutes a day actually talking. Given the importance to communication of nonverbal cues, it behooves us to study them carefully. But nonverbal signals differ from culture to culture at least as much as one language differs from another. Thus, as Miller points out, knowledge of a language is woefully incomplete unless it extends to the nonverbal system of the culture in which the language is spoken.

One reason why linguists study nonverbal communication is in order to understand the fundamental properties of human language. For the same reason, other linguists are working in the field of artificial intelligence (AI), as Gary C. Hendrix and Earl D. Sacerdoti explain in the second selection, "Natural-Language Processing: The Field in Perspective." Using examples of several computer programs, they make clear how difficult it is to understand all that is involved in human communication—and in particular, how difficult it is to provide computers with the kinds of information that human participants in a conversation take for granted. As Hendrix and Sacerdoti state, "The fluent use of natural language is an information-processing activity of great complexity."

In the third selection, "Animal Communication: A Survey of Recent Research," William Kemp and Roy Smith turn to a fascinating topic. Animal communication systems are interesting in themselves; in addition, by studying them we may learn more about how human language evolved. But of more immediate interest to many readers will be the question of human attempts to communicate with various animals, especially chimpanzees. The early 1970s brought what many people, scientists and nonscientists alike, believed was a real breakthrough: a number of chimpanzees had apparently learned forms of human language, ranging from American Sign Language, to a keyboard linked to a computer and used to make requests and respond to questions, to the rearrangement of plastic symbols so as to produce meaningful utterances. By the 1980s, however, some skeptics suggested that the problem of uncontaminated human-animal experiments designed to teach some form of human language to animals might be insoluble. Kemp and Smith survey the evidence thoroughly and objectively, concluding that the chimpanzee research achieved less than its extreme advocates claim but more than its severest critics allow.

With the final selection, John P. Hughes's "Languages and Writing," we shift our focus to a "secondary" form of language. By *secondary*, we mean that, whereas all normal children learn to speak their native language(s) without formal instruction, this is not the case with writing. We have to be taught to read and write; we are not genetically predisposed to acquire this form of language. Furthermore, many millions of the world's inhabitants are illiterate, and there are some languages that do not have a writing system. Nevertheless, the alphabet has been called the greatest invention since the wheel, and Hughes explains why. In doing so, he traces the variety of ways in which human beings, over the centuries, have attempted to represent the spoken language. He concludes that the alphabetic system is truly unique.

1/Nonverbal Communication

GEORGE A. MILLER

The famous linguist Edward Sapir once described nonverbal behavior as "an elaborate and secret code that is written nowhere, known by none, and understood by all." His statement is to a great extent still true. Nonverbal behavior has been studied extensively, but our understanding of it is far from complete. Unfortunately, most of the popular books and articles about nonverbal communication—usually referred to as "body language"—have drastically oversimplified the subject, suggesting that one can easily learn to "read" the nonverbal signals unconsciously "sent" by other people. In fact, however, the study of nonverbal communication is complex and subtle, far more than a kind of game that anyone can play. Returning to Sapir's phrase, "understood by all," the "all" refers to members of the same culture. Cross-culturally, people continue to misunderstand one another because they have different nonverbal systems—different acceptable postures, ways of moving, gestures, facial expressions, eye behavior, and use of space and distance. In the following article, Professor George A. Miller uses a variety of examples to explain how necessary it is to understand the nonverbal systems as well as the languages of other cultures.

When the German philosopher Nietzsche said that "success is the greatest liar," he meant that a successful person seems especially worthy to us even when his success is due to nothing more than good luck. But Nietzsche's observation can be interpreted more broadly.

People communicate in many different ways. One of the most important ways, of course, is through language. Moreover, when language is written it can be completely isolated from the context in which it occurs; it can be treated as if it were an independent and self-contained process. We have been so successful in using and describing and analyzing this special kind of communication that we sometimes act as if language were the *only* kind of communication that can occur between people. When we act that way, of course, we have been deceived by success, the greatest liar of them all.

Like all animals, people communicate by their actions as well as by the noises they make. It is a sort of biological anomaly of man—

something like the giraffe's neck, or the pelican's beak—that our vocal noises have so far outgrown in importance and frequency all our other methods of signaling to one another. Language is obviously essential for human beings, but it is not the whole story of human communication. Not by a long shot.

Consider the following familiar fact. When leaders in one of the less well developed countries decide that they are ready to introduce some technology that is already highly advanced in another country, they do not simply buy all the books that have been written about that technology and have their students read them. The books may exist and they may be very good, but just reading about the technology is not enough. The students must be sent to study in a country where the technology is already flourishing, where they can see it first hand. Once they have been exposed to it in person and experienced it as part of their own lives, they are ready to understand and put to use the information that is in the books. But the verbal message, without the personal experience to back it up, is of little value.

Now what is it that the students learn by participating in a technology that they can not learn by just reading about it? It seems obvious that they are learning something important, and that whatever it is they are learning is something that we don't know how to put into our verbal descriptions. There is a kind of nonverbal communication that occurs when students are personally involved in the technology and when they interact with people who are using and developing it.

Pictures are one kind of nonverbal communication, of course, and moving pictures can communicate some of the information that is difficult to capture in words. Pictures also have many of the properties that make language so useful—they can be taken in one situation at one time and viewed in an entirely different situation at any later time. Now that we have television satellites, pictures can be transmitted instantaneously all over the world, just as our words can be transmitted by radio. Perhaps the students who are trying to learn how to create a new technology in their own country could supplement their reading by watching moving pictures of people at work in the developed industry. Certainly the pictures would be a help, but they would be very expensive. And we don't really know whether words and pictures together would capture everything the students would be able to learn by going to a more advanced country and participating directly in the technology.

Let me take another familiar example. There are many different cultures in the world, and in each of them the children must learn a great many things that are expected of everyone who participates effectively in that culture. These things are taken for granted by everyone who shares the culture. When I say they are taken for granted, I mean that nobody needs to describe them or write them down or try self-consciously to teach them to children. Indeed, the children begin to learn them before their linguistic skills are far enough developed to understand a verbal description of what they are learning. This kind of learning has sometimes been called "imitation," but that is much too simple an explanation for the complex processes that go on when a child learns what is normal and expected in his own community. Most of the norms are communicated to the child nonverbally, and he internalizes them as if no other possibilities existed. They are as much a part of him as his own body; he would no more question them than he would question the fact that he has two hands and two feet, but only one head.

These cultural norms can be described verbally, of course. Anthropologists who are interested in describing the differences among the many cultures of the world have developed a special sensitivity to cultural norms and have described them at length in their scholarly books. But if a child had to read those books in order to learn what was expected of him, he would never become an effective member of his own community.

What is an example of the sort of thing that children learn nonverbally? One of the simplest examples to observe and analyze and discuss is the way people use clothing and bodily ornamentation to communicate. At any particular time in any particular culture there is an accepted and normal way to dress and to arrange the hair and to paint the face and to wear one's jewelry. By adopting those conventions for dressing himself, a person communicates to the world that he wants to be treated according to the standards of the culture for which they are appropriate. When a black person in America rejects the normal American dress and puts on African clothing, he is communicating to the world that he wants to be treated as an Afro-American. When a white man lets his hair and beard grow, wears very informal clothing, and puts beads around his neck, he is communicating to the world that he rejects many of the traditional values of Western culture. On the surface, dressing up in unusual costumes would seem to be one of the more innocent forms of dissent that a person could express, but in fact it is deeply resented by many people who still feel bound by the traditional conventions of their culture and who become fearful or angry when those norms are violated. The nonverbal message that such a costume communicates is "I reject your culture and your values," and those who resent this message can be violent in their response.

The use of clothing as an avenue of communication is relatively obvious, of course. A somewhat subtler kind of communication occurs in the way people use their eyes. We are remarkably accurate in judging the direction of another person's gaze; psychologists have done experiments that have measured just how accurate such judgments are.

From an observation of where a person is looking we can infer what he is looking at, and from knowing what he is looking at we can guess what he is interested in, and from what he is interested in and the general situation we can usually make a fairly good guess about what he is going to do. Thus eye movements can be a rich and important channel of nonverbal communication.

Most personal interaction is initiated by a short period during which two people look directly at one another. Direct eye contact is a signal that each has the other's attention, and that some further form of interaction can follow. In Western cultures, to look directly into another person's eyes is equivalent to saying, "I am open to you—let the action begin." Everyone knows how much lovers can communicate by their eyes, but aggressive eye contact can also be extremely informative.

In large cities, where people are crowded in together with others they neither know nor care about, many people develop a deliberate strategy of avoiding eye contacts. They want to mind their own business, they don't have time to interact with everyone they pass, and they communicate this fact by refusing to look at other people's faces. It is one of the things that make newcomers to the city feel that it is a hostile and unfriendly place.

Eye contact also has an important role in regulating conversational interactions. In America, a typical pattern is for the listener to signal that he is paying attention by looking at the talker's mouth or eyes. Since direct eye contact is often too intimate, the talker may let his eyes wander elsewhere. As the moment arrives for the talker to become a listener, and for his partner to begin talking, there will often be a preliminary eye signal. The talker will often look toward the listener, and the listener will signal that he is ready to talk by glancing away.

Such eye signals will vary, of course, depending on what the people are talking about and what the personal relation is between them. But whatever the pattern of eye signals that two people are using, they use them unconsciously. If you try to become aware of your own eye movements while you are talking to someone, you will find it extremely frustrating. As soon as you try to think self-consciously about your own eye movements, you do not know where you should be looking. If you want to study how the eyes communicate, therefore, you should do it by observing other people, not yourself. But if you watch other people too intently, of course, you may disturb them or make them angry. So be careful!

Even the pupils of your eyes communicate. When a person becomes excited or interested in something, the pupils of his eyes increase in size. In order to test whether we are sensitive to these changes in pupil size, a psychologist showed people two pictures of the face of a pretty girl. The two pictures were completely identical except that in one picture the girl's pupil was constricted, whereas in the other picture her pupil was dilated. The people were asked to say which picture they liked better, and they voted in favor of the picture with the large pupil. Many of the judges did not even realize consciously what the difference was, but apparently they were sensitive to the difference and preferred the eyes that communicated excitement and interest.

Eye communication seems to be particularly important for Americans. It is part of the American culture that people should be kept at a distance, and that contact with another person's body should be avoided in all but the most intimate situations. Because of this social convention of dealing with others at a distance, Americans have to place much reliance on their distance receptors, their eyes and ears, for personal communication. In other cultures, however, people normally come closer together and bodily contact between conversational partners is as normal as eye contact is in America. In the Eastern Mediterranean cultures, for example, both the touch and the smell of the other person are expected.

The anthropologist Edward T. Hall has studied the spatial relations that seem appropriate to various kinds of interactions. They vary with intimacy, they depend on the possibility of eye contact, and they are different in different cultures. In America, for example, two strangers will converse impersonally at a distance of about four feet. If one moves closer, the other will back away. In a waiting room, strangers will keep apart, but friends will sit together, and members of a family may actually touch one another.

Other cultures have different spatial norms. In Latin America, for example, impersonal discussion normally occurs at a distance of two or three feet, which is the distance that is appropriate for personal discussion in North America. Consequently, it is impossible for a North and a South American both to be comfortable when they talk to one another unless one can adopt the zones that are normal for the other. If the South American advances to a distance that is comfortable for him, it will be too close for the North American, and he will withdraw, and one can chase the other all around the room unless something intervenes to end the conversation. The North American seems aloof and unfriendly to the South American. The South American seems hostile or oversexed to the North American. Hall mentions that North Americans sometimes cope with this difference by barricading themselves behind desks or tables, and that South Americans have been known literally to climb over these barriers in order to attain a comfortable distance at which to talk.

Within one's own culture these spatial signals are perfectly understood. If two North Americans are talking at a distance of one foot or less, you know that what they are saying is highly confidential. At a distance of two to three feet it will be some personal subject matter.

At four or five feet it is impersonal, and if they are conversing at a distance of seven or eight feet, we know that they expect others to be listening to what they are saying. When talking to a group, a distance of ten to twenty feet is normal, and at greater distances only greetings are exchanged. These conventions are unconscious but highly reliable. For example, if you are having a personal conversation with a North American at a distance of two feet, you can shift it to an impersonal conversation by the simple procedure of moving back to a distance of four or five feet. If he can't follow you, he will find it quite impossible to maintain a personal discussion at that distance.

These examples should be enough to convince you—if you needed convincing—that we communicate a great deal of information that is not expressed in the words we utter. And I have not even mentioned yet the interesting kind of communication that occurs by means of gestures. A gesture is an expressive motion or action, usually made with the hands and arms, but also with the head or even the whole body. Gestures can occur with or without speech. As a part of the speech act, they usually emphasize what the person is saying, but they may occur without any speech at all. Some gestures are spontaneous, some are highly ritualized and have very specific meanings. And they differ enormously from one culture to another.

Misunderstanding of nonverbal communication is one of the most distressing and unnecessary sources of international friction. For example, few Americans understand how much the Chinese hate to be touched, or slapped on the back, or even to shake hands. How easy it would be for an American to avoid giving offense simply by avoiding these particular gestures that, to him, signify intimacy and friendliness. Or, to take another example, when Khrushchev placed his hands together over his head and shook them, most Americans interpreted it as an arrogant gesture of triumph, the sort of gesture a victorious prize fighter would make, even though Khrushchev seems to have intended it as a friendly gesture of international brotherhood. Sticking out the tongue and quickly drawing it back can be a gesture of self-castigation in one culture, an admission of a social mistake, but someone from another culture might interpret it as a gesture of ridicule or contempt, and in the Eskimo culture it would not be a gesture at all, but the conventional way of directing a current of air when blowing out a candle. Just a little better communication on the nonverbal level might go a long way toward improving international relations.

Ritualized gestures—the bow, the shrug, the smile, the wink, the military salute, the pointed finger, the thumbed nose, sticking out the tongue, and so on—are not really nonverbal communication, because such gestures are just a substitute for the verbal meanings that are associated with them. There are, however, many spontaneous gestures and actions that are unconscious, but communicate a great deal. If you take a moving picture of someone who is deeply engrossed in a conversation, and later show it to him, he will be quite surprised to see many of the gestures he used and the subtle effects they produced. Sometimes what a person is saying unconsciously by his actions may directly contradict what he is saying consciously with his words. Anthropologists have tried to develop a way to write down a description of these nonverbal actions, something like the notation that choreographers use to record the movements of a ballet dancer, but it is difficult to know exactly what the significance of these actions really is, or what the important features are that should be recorded. We can record them photographically, of course, but we still are not agreed on how the photographic record should be analyzed.

Finally, there is a whole spectrum of communication that is vocal, but not really verbal. The most obvious examples are spontaneous gasps of surprise or cries of pain. I suspect this kind of vocal communication is very similar for both man and animal. But our use of vocal signals goes far beyond such grunts and groans. It is a commonplace observation that the way you say something is as important as what you say, and often more important for telling the listener what your real intentions are. Exactly the same words may convey directly opposite messages according to the way they are said. For example, I can say, "Oh, isn't that *wonderful*" so that I sound enthusiastic, or I can say, "Oh, isn't *that* wonderful" in a sarcastic tone so that you know I don't think it is wonderful at all. Because the actual words uttered are often misleading, lawyers and judges in the courtroom have learned that it is sometimes important to have an actual recording and not just a written transcript of what a person is supposed to have said.

Rapid and highly inflected speech usually communicates excitement, extremely distinct speech usually communicates anger, very loud speech usually communicates pomposity, and a slow monotone usually communicates boredom. The emotional clues that are provided by the way a person talks are extremely subtle, and accomplished actors must practice for many years to bring them under conscious control.

A person's pronunciation also tells a great deal about him. If he has a foreign accent, a sensitive listener can generally tell where he was born. If he speaks with a local dialect, we can often guess what his social origins were and how much education he has had. Often a person will have several different styles of speaking, and will use them to communicate which social role he happens to be playing at the moment. This is such a rich source of social and psychological information, in fact, that a whole new field has recently developed to study it, a field called "sociology of language." . . .

One of the most significant signals that is vocal but nonverbal is the ungrammatical pause. . . . In careful speech most of our pauses are grammatical. That is to say, our pauses occur at the boundaries of grammatical segments, and serve as a kind of audible punctuation. By calling them "grammatical pauses" we imply that they are a normal part of the verbal message. An ungrammatical pause, however, is not a part of the verbal message. For example, when I . . . uh . . . pause within a . . . uh . . . grammatical unit, you cannot regard the pause as part of my verbal message. These ungrammatical pauses are better regarded as the places where the speaker is thinking, is searching for words, and is planning how to continue his utterance. For a linguist, of course, the grammatical pause is most interesting, since it reveals something about the structure of the verbal message. For a psychologist, however, the ungrammatical pause is more interesting, because it reveals something about the thought processes of the speaker.

When a skilled person reads a prepared text, there are few ungrammatical pauses. But spontaneous speech is a highly fragmented and discontinuous activity. Indeed, ungrammatical pausing is a reliable signal of spontaneity in speech. The pauses tend to occur at choice points in the message, and particularly before words that are rare or unusual and words that are chosen with particular care. An actor who wanted to make his rehearsed speech sound spontaneous would deliberately introduce ungrammatical pauses at these critical points.

Verbal communication uses only one of the many kinds of signals that people can exchange; for a balanced view of the communication process we should always keep in mind the great variety of other signals that can reinforce or contradict the verbal message. These subtleties are especially important in psychotherapy, where a patient tries to communicate his emotional troubles to a doctor, but may find it difficult or impossible to express in words the real source of his distress. Under such circumstances, a good therapist learns to listen for more than words, and to rely on nonverbal signals to help him interpret the verbal signals. For this reason, many psychologists have been persistently interested in nonverbal communication, and have perhaps been less likely than linguists to fall into the mistaken belief that language is the only way we can communicate.

The price of opening up one's attention to this wider range of events, however, is a certain vagueness about the kind of communication that is occurring—about what it means and how to study it. We have no dictionaries or grammars to help us analyze nonverbal communication, and there is much work that will have to be done in many cultures before we can formulate and test any interesting scientific theories about nonverbal communication. Nevertheless, the obvious fact that so much communication does occur nonverbally should persuade us not to give up, and not to be misled by our success in analyzing verbal messages.

Recognizing the great variety of communication channels that are available is probably only the first step toward a broader conception of communication as a psychological process. Not only must we study what a person says and how he says it, but we must try to understand why he says it. If we concentrate primarily on the words that people say, we are likely to think that the only purpose of language is to exchange information. That is one of its purposes, of course, but certainly not the only one. People exchange many things. Not only do they exchange information, but they also exchange money, goods, services, love, and status. In any particular interaction, a person may give one of these social commodities in exchange for another. He may give information in exchange for money, or give services in exchange for status or love. Perhaps we should first characterize communication acts in terms of what people are trying to give and gain in their social interactions. Then, within that broader frame of reference, we might see better that verbal messages are more appropriate for some exchanges and nonverbal messages for others, and that both have their natural and complementary roles to play in the vast tapestry we call human society.

FOR DISCUSSION AND REVIEW

1. According to Miller, why is reading about some advanced technology developed in another country not enough? Why must students actually *go* to the country? In answering this question, try to use specific, original examples.

2. Miller asserts that along with their language, children also learn certain nonverbal "cultural norms" that "are communicated to the child nonverbally." Drawing from your own experience, describe three of the cultural norms that American children learn.

3. Keep track for a day of the way people you meet use their eyes to make or avoid eye contact. Write a brief description of the behavior you have observed. Do your findings agree with Miller's statements about the way Americans use their eyes? If not, what are the differences?

4. Miller uses two examples of the use of clothing to communicate. Based on your own experience, give two additional examples.

5. Spatial norms vary from culture to culture. Describe any differences between American norms and those of other countries that you have noticed while traveling abroad. If you haven't had such experiences, ask two or three of your friends about theirs.

6. Miller states that "ungrammatical pausing is a reliable sign of spontaneity in speech." Compare this statement with what Jean Aitchison says about pauses in speech in "The Cheshire Cat's Grin," pp. 341–363. Do Miller and Aitchison agree? Explain your answer.

2/Natural-Language Processing: The Field in Perspective

GARY G. HENDRIX
AND EARL D. SACERDOTI

On a typical day, all of us take part in a number of conversations with different people about a wide range of topics. We take for granted our ability to do this. If, however, you want to design a natural-language processing system that will permit a human being and a computer to have a conversation, you learn very quickly, as Professors Gary G. Hendrix and Earl D. Sacerdoti state, that "the fluent use of natural language is an information-processing activity of great complexity." The "fluent use of natural language" is not an isolated intellectual activity; it involves our total intellect—our own goals, beliefs, knowledge of the world, and plans—plus our knowledge about the goals, beliefs, and so on, of other participants in the conversation. It also depends upon our ability to make inferences and upon our lexical, syntactic, semantic, and pragmatic knowledge. Steven K. Roberts uses the following example to illustrate the complexity of human language behavior:

> Consider the following conversation:
>
> He: "Hungry?"
> She: "I have a coupon for McDonald's."
> He: "Have you seen my keys?"
> She: "Look on the dresser."
>
> There are some very sophisticated information-processing operations going on here. In this dialogue, most of the real meaning—the real communication—is not explicitly stated. He opens by inquiring whether she is hungry and, in the process, is probably implying that he is hungry as well. She processes this and issues a very cryptic response. Not only does she inform him that she is either hungry or willing to go along for a ride, but also suggests a specific place to eat and, further, hints at economic realities by weighting the selection of

We wish to express our thanks to SRI International and Machine Intelligence Corporation for supporting the preparation of this article and acknowledge the helpful critiques of early drafts that were provided by Barbara Grosz, Norman Haas, Robert Moore, Jane Robinson, and Donald Walker.

642

a restaurant on the basis of a discount coupon. Her statement assumes that he will understand what a coupon is as well as what a McDonald's is. His next question indicates even deeper communication: he has agreed with her about the choice of restaurant and suggests a specific mode of transportation. This suggestion, however, is made in a round-about fashion: he asks if she knows where his keys are at the moment, assuming that she knows not only what keys are but that they are linked with transportation. She, of course, understands that the keys he's talking about are those of his automobile and suggests a course of action that will solve the transportation problem—correctly assuming that he will not only know which dresser she means, and that a dresser is a piece of furniture, but that he will deduce that the keys must be there.

The implication is that communication between two people involves substantially more than the lexical meanings of the words. The conversation above would not have been so succinct if he had approached a stranger on the street with the same question. The difference suggests the existence of a special relationship between he and she: they share certain aspects of their internal models of the world.

This highlights a crucial truth: language has to be considered as only one part of a much more complex communication process, one in which the knowledge and states of mind of the participants are as much responsible for the interpretation of verbal utterances as are the words from which those utterances are formed. As a conversation progresses, the internal state of each participant continually changes to represent the modified reality that is the result of the communication. ("Artificial Intelligence," Byte, *September 1981, pp. 172, 174.)*

By studying what humans know that makes such apparently simple but actually very complex conversations possible, researchers in artificial intelligence hope to design computers that have humanlike communication skills. Although the final goal remains to be achieved, a large number of surprisingly capable systems already exist. These programs, their problems, and their capabilities are described in the following selection.

Through a process spanning thousands of years, natural languages have evolved to meet the manifold needs of people to communicate and record a diversity of information in a wide variety of circumstances. Natural language is the medium of the butcher, the baker, and the candlestick maker; the poet and the lover; the politician and the preacher; the parent and the child. Even for the scientist and computer programmer, it is the mother tongue—the language resorted to when formal expressions and intuition fail.

Natural languages stand in marked contrast to formal languages, such as BASIC and Pascal, which were designed to be easily understood by computers and are intended for the specialized task of expressing algorithms and data structures. The fluent use of natural language is an information-processing activity of great complexity. Endowing computers with this ability has long been a major goal of research in *artificial intelligence* (also called *machine intelligence*), a branch of experimental computer science that studies the nature of knowledge and its manipulation.

Understanding the computational mechanisms that underlie the use of natural language is the central objective of *computational linguistics*, a science at the juncture of artificial intelligence, philosophy, linguistics, and psychology.* The two primary goals of this field are:

- to understand how humans communicate
- to create machines with human-like communication skills

The first is a scientific goal pursued to help us understand ourselves. In particular, although we all are implicitly expert in the *use* of natural language, we have only vague notions of the mental processes involved. A clearer insight into their essential nature and functioning might enable us to be better communicators, to train our children better in language skills, and even to design more efficient intercomputer communications.

The second goal is an engineering one pursued for a practical purpose—to create machines that can communicate with people in languages they already know. At present, only a small segment of the population, computer programmers, can communicate with computers. The advent of machines that understand natural languages will make it possible for virtually anyone to make direct use of powerful computational systems.

Progress in computational linguistics is facilitated by pursuing both of the above goals simultaneously. Creation of mechanical schemes for dealing with some aspect of natural-language processing sheds light on how it might actually be performed by the human brain. Similarly, evidence derived from observing how people use language suggests prospective computational mechanisms or, more often, provides valuable insights into the reasons particular mechanical processes fail.

To create computer systems that deal with certain significant subsets of natural-language phenomena, it is probably not necessary to perform the task in a way closely simulating computational processes

* The Association for Computational Linguistics is a professional society for people interested in this subject; it publishes the *American Journal of Computational Linguistics*. For information, contact Donald Walker, SRI International, Menlo Park CA 94025. Readers are also referred to the American Association for Artificial Intelligence (contact Bruce Buchanan, Computer Science Department, Stanford University, Stanford CA 94305), and the Cognitive Science Society, which publishes the journal *Cognitive Science* (contact Donald Norman, Center for Human Information Processing, C-009, University of California at San Diego, La Jolla CA 92093).

in the human brain. This should not be surprising. Mechanical dishwashers use a nonhuman technique to produce a result equivalent to that of a human dishwasher. For interactions about very limited subject areas, we can hope to employ thoroughly nonhuman techniques in dealing with natural language. Nevertheless, machines concerned with any but the most mundane aspects of human language will probably have to deal with human psychology. After all, natural language has evolved as an efficient tool for conveying information between human minds. One of the participants in a man-machine dialogue operates with all the constraints and richnesses of the human psyche; the other has to take these into account.

The ultimate goal of creating machines that can interact in a facile manner with people remains far off, awaiting both improved information-processing algorithms and alternative computing architectures. However, progress in the last decade has demonstrated the feasibility of employing today's computers to deal with natural-language input in highly restricted contexts. Furthermore, microcomputer implementation of these limited language-processing techniques is leading to more practical, cost-effective systems.

In this article, we offer an overview of the potential applications, experimental systems, existing techniques, research problems, and future prospects in this rapidly evolving field. We will address major issues in natural-language processing by focusing on several representative systems, necessarily leaving much important work unmentioned. For example, we will not discuss the complex issues involved in understanding spoken (as opposed to typed) language. Our intentions are to demonstrate that natural-language processing techniques are useful *now*, to reveal the richness of the computations performed by human natural-language communicators, and to explain why the fluent use of natural language by machines remains an elusive aspiration.

Applications of Natural-Language Processing

To motivate our discussion about how to approach the technological goal of creating a machine with human-like communication skills, let us consider some potential areas for the application of natural-language processing:

- *Machine translation*—The oldest dream of computational linguistics is of a mechanical device that can read documents written in one natural language and produce corresponding documents written in other languages, but with equivalent meanings. In fact, the birth of computational linguistics occurred in 1946, when Warren Weaver and A. Donald Booth first suggested the use of a digital computer to create such a device. The Association for Computational Linguistics, the professional organization in this discipline, was originally named the Association for Machine Translation and Computational Linguistics.

- *Document understanding*—Beyond simply translating a document from one language to another, a device might read and *understand* documents, fitting their information into a larger framework of knowledge. A practical device of this sort would read and assimilate a document much as a person would. The device might subsequently produce abstractions of the document, alert people likely to be interested in it, or answer specific questions based on its information. If such a device had read many documents, it might be able to act as a librarian, directing users to pertinent references.

- *Document generation*—A task related to document understanding is document generation. We can envisage a device that translates information stored in a formal language in a computer's memory into ordinary language. For example, the designer of an automobile engine might describe repair procedures in a formal language. (After all, we expect that the designing of mechanical devices will someday be done principally by computer systems, which may *prefer* formal languages.) From this formal description, instruction manuals in various languages could be generated.

A more sophisticated system could generate special manuals for particular groups or individuals. Taking into account that mechanics know much about auto repair, a smart system would generate a different manual for mechanics than for automobile owners, but on the basis of the same underlying information. Information on elementary mechanical tasks would be included in manuals for less knowledgeable individuals. An ultimate system would tailor a manual to the background of each individual.

It is worth noting that a repair manual need not be written in linear sequence in a typical book format. Using a computer, advice about how to proceed on any particular problem could be dynamically generated to apply specifically to the task at hand. We will return to this topic later in the article.

- *As part of a system*—An interesting use of natural-language processing is as part of a larger computer-based system. For example, imagine devices that not only communicate in English, but also:

  - provide answers to questions by accessing large data bases

Figure 1. The typical nontechnical user confronts a "black box" that contains large amounts of knowledge on a given subject.

- control complex equipment such as industrial robots, power generators, or missile systems
- furnish expert advice about medical problems, mechanical repairs, how to buy stocks, or what to cook for supper
- teach courses in a broad range of subjects

An extreme example of a computer-based system that would use natural-language processing as an integral component is a robot that communicates in English. Such a robot might be expected to perform as many tasks involving the use of natural language as might be done by a human assistant.

The importance of these potential applications and the basic science needed to make them possible has long been appreciated by scientific-funding agencies of the United States government. Current progress in the field is due largely to support from the Defense Advanced Research Projects Agency, the National Science Foundation, and the Office of Naval Research.

What Existing Systems Can Do

One of the most important and feasible areas for the application of natural-language processing is accessing data in data bases. Billions of dollars have been spent in collecting and encoding such data. However, this information is generally not readily available to the people who need it. The situation is illustrated by Figure 1.

An executive in the widget business wants to direct a simple question to his black box. He wants to know, "How many widgets did we sell in August?" He knows the information is in the black box, but he lacks the expertise to make the box understand him.

As shown in Figure 2, he must find an interpreter (computer programmer) who can translate his question into a formal query to give to the machine. Unfortunately, programmers are out drinking coffee when you need them, or they are working on a project more important than your project—so they cannot help you this week. When a programmer *is* available, misunderstandings often occur and there are problems in creating proper code. By the time an answer is extracted from the computer, it may no longer be timely and may not even be relevant!

The LADDER System

To produce timely answers to questions and quickly clear up problems as to how a decision-maker's question is to be interpreted, the turnaround time must be cut from hours or days to seconds.

Research groups around the world are attempting to do this by automating the programmer in Figure 2. For example, the LADDER system developed at SRI International (see references 11 and 12 at the end of this article) is capable of translating a question such as:

TO WHAT COUNTRY DOES THE FASTEST SUB BELONG?

into [code that can be processed by a computer]. An explanation of [this] code is unnecessary here. The point is that systems exist that are capable of accepting simple English queries specifying *what* information a user wants, then generating fairly complex programs specifying *how* the computer is to retrieve the information.

Two problems are being confronted together:

Problem 1: The system must translate from English into a formal language.
Problem 2: The system must convert a statement of what is wanted into a statement of how to get it.

Problem 2 is concerned with automatic programming, an artificial-intelligence problem currently receiving much attention (see reference 2). (Fortunately, most work on natural-language processing needs to consider only a highly restricted subset of this general problem.)

What it's like to use a system such as LADDER is suggested by the transcript, shown in Listing 1, of an actual interaction. The system prompts users with a transaction number followed by a hyphen. The user then types in a question or command. (In this and future listings, we refer to the question half as a *query* and to the question/response

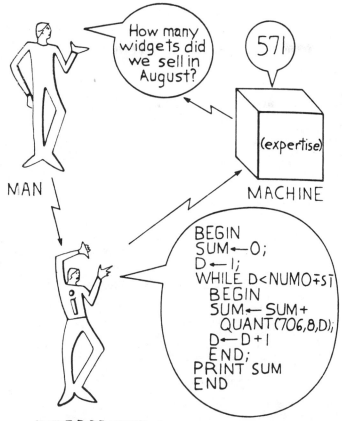

INTERPRETER

Figure 2. The nontechnical user obtains information from the computer through the use of an interpreter (computer programmer), who translates the English question into a form the machine understands.

pair as an *interaction*.) Query 1, "Give me the length of the Kenedy," contains a misspelled word. LADDER corrects this automatically, typing a note to the user directly below the input line. Once LADDER has corrected the spelling error and completed an analysis of the input, it types the message "PARSED!", and displays its interpretation of the user's query. The system then calls a remote data base to retrieve the answer—in this case, the length (abbreviated to LEN) of the *Kennedy* is 1072 (feet).

Query 2 is not a complete sentence. In fact, it makes no sense when considered in isolation. But in the context of the preceding query, it is clear that the intended meaning is, "Give me the width and draft of the Kennedy." Leaving out pieces of a sentence is called *ellipsis*. Processing such elliptical inputs is more difficult than it may seem. The system has to avoid such interpretations as, "Give me the length of

1—Give me the length of the Kenedy.
    spelling → KENNEDY
PARSED!
Give the length of the ship KENNEDY JF

LEN = 1072
2—width and draft
PARSED!
Trying Ellipsis: GIVE ME WIDTH AND DRAFT OF THE KENEDY
Give the beam and draft of the ship KENNEDY JF
(BEAM 130 DFT 36)
3—Who is her commander?
Give the rank and name of the commander of the ship KENNEDY JF
(RANK CAPT NAME MOFFETT P)
4—What about the Fox?
PARSED!
Trying Ellipsis on: THE FOX
  WHO IS THE FOX COMMANDER
Give the rank and name of the commander of the ship FOX
(RANK CAPT NAME EVERETT J)
5—What U.S. merchant ships carrying vanadium ore are within 500 miles of the Kimlow?
PARSED!
Give the position of and time at position for the ship KIMLOW T
Give the name of merchant American ship S
  where the type of cargo on S is VNAD
    the great-circle distance from the position of S to
      15-33N, 30-10W, is less than or equal to 500
SHIP = GREENVILLE VICTORY, CRAIN ME, TOTOR
6—How fast are the U.S. subs with lengths greater than 150 feet?
PARSED!
Give the maximum cruising speed for and name of American ship S
  where the first character of the type of S is S
    the second character of the type of S is S
    the length of S is greater than 150
[A long table relating the names and maximum cruising speeds of American submarines is printed.]
7—What French ships are at readiness status 1?
PARSED!
Give the name of French ship S
  where the state of readiness of S is 1

There is no French ship S
NONE

Listing 1. *An actual conversation with the LADDER system. Boldface words represent user input. Material in square brackets replaces lengthy material not relevant to this article.*

the width and draft," or even, "Give width and draft the length of the Kennedy."

    Query 3 illustrates the use of a pronoun, another linguistic construct that cannot be interpreted in isolation.

    Query 4 demonstrates a more sophisticated form of ellipsis in which the analysis involves more than just grammatical substitution of the new input into the old one. (This is accomplished in LADDER by looking for "WHAT ABOUT" at the beginning of an input, and then applying the standard elliptical technique to what follows.)

Query 5 illustrates a major benefit of natural-language processing: the user can interact with the system in terms of the job being done, letting the system be concerned with what is required from the data base. Though this is only one question from the user's perspective, it requires two questions of the data base. First, the location of the *Kimlow* must be determined, and then the appropriate ships within 500 miles of that location must be retrieved. The process of translating from the user's terms to those of the data base obstructs the user's decision-making job. It is therefore an appropriate process to automate.

Interaction 6 causes a large body of information to be retrieved from the data base. Although omitted from the listing to save space, a table summarizing the answer is displayed to the user.

Interaction 7 shows an example of a cooperative response to the user's question. The user asks a question about the readiness of French ships. However, the base contains no information about French ships. Therefore, the literal answer to the user's question, NONE, is inappropriate by itself, since it leads the user to believe all French ships are unready. To provide a more informative response, LADDER presents additional information showing the rationale for producing the NONE response. . . .

Summary of LADDER-Like Systems

In a later section, we will say more about what systems like LADDER can do. For now, it is sufficient to note the following:

- The computer capability shown in the transcript of Listing 1 is of considerable practical utility.
- LADDER deals with a relatively large and complex data base that includes over 100 fields in fourteen files and has records for 40,000 ships.
- LADDER has been performing at this level of capability since 1976 (except for the cooperative responses such as those in interaction 7, which are relatively new—see reference 14).
- There are several systems in laboratories around the world that are capable of essentially the same level of performance as shown in Listing 1. These include the systems described in references 10, 14, 24, 25, 26, and 31.

For restricted classes of applications, systems such as LADDER provide language-processing capabilities that are very useful. Never-

A: HOW DO I REMOVE THE FLYWHEEL?
E: FIRST LOOSEN THE TWO SMALL ALLEN HEAD SETSCREWS HOLDING IT TO THE SHAFT THEN PULL IT OFF.
A: THE TWO SETSCREWS ARE LOOSE BUT I'M HAVING TROUBLE GETTING THE WHEEL OFF.
E: USE THE WHEEL PULLER. DO YOU KNOW HOW?
A: NO.
E: LOOSEN THE SCREW IN THE CENTER AND PLACE THE JAWS AROUND THE HUB OF THE WHEEL; THEN TIGHTEN THE SCREW.
A: THE LITTLE METAL SEMICIRCLE FELL OFF WHEN I TOOK THE WHEEL OFF.

Listing 2: *A dialogue between an expert and an apprentice repairman showing definitely determined noun phrases (underlined).*

theless, LADDER falls far short of being an ideal system, both conceptually and linguistically.

LADDER's concept of the world is based on the underlying conventional data-base management system to which it provides access. Data-base management systems can effectively store large numbers of individual, concrete facts, such as:

THE KENNEDY IS OWNED BY THE US

But they are incapable of dealing in a general way with more logically complex notions, such as disjunction, quantification, implication, causality, and possibility. They act as if they were dealing with information about a world containing a fixed number of objects and relationships among them, with the objects and relationships being immutable.

Perhaps LADDER's most important linguistic deficiency is its limited notion of linguistic context. With minor (though useful) exceptions, LADDER treats each input as if it were given in isolation. To perceive the problem, let's consider the question:

WHO ARE THE CAPTAINS OF THE US TANKERS?

Isolated from all contexts, this question should be interpreted as a request for the names of the commanding officers of all US tankers in the data base. But if a user has just asked the question, "What is the status of convoy C86?" and has received information on a number of ships in the convoy, including two US tankers, the sample question should elicit the captains' names for only the two tankers in the convoy. LADDER ignores the context, however, answering the question as if it had been asked in isolation.

The ability to follow a changing context and make accurate references to prominent objects is a fundamental characteristic of human communication. In fact, about half the words used in ordinary speech are found in DEF NPs (*definitely determined noun phrases*), the linguistic constructions most often used to refer to objects in context. Note, for example, all the definitely determined noun phrases underlined in the dialogue shown in Listing 2.

The need to understand context throws considerable doubt on the idea of building natural-language interfaces to systems with knowledge bases independent of the language-processing system itself. This is because the information in the knowledge base may be needed simply for comprehension of a question. For example, to understand the phrase "the filter" in:

IF I CHANGE THE OIL IN MY CAR, WHERE SHOULD I LOOK FOR THE FILTER?

it is necessary to know that automobiles use oil cleaned by a filter. Such knowledge makes possible the assumption that such a filter, the one on the user's car, is the referent of "the filter." We cannot translate the question into a formal query to an auto-maintenance system unless the translation system also has some information about the nature of auto maintenance. . . .

Systems With Knowledge of Ordinary Situations

One of the more interesting attempts to deal with ordinary human situations, in contrast to interfacing with a data base or a model of a microworld, was made by Roger Schank and Robert Abelson, aided by their students at Yale University. Their system, SAM (for Script Applier Mechanism), as described in reference 22, was built to cope with certain kinds of everyday problems. For example, the system is told the following story:

John went to a restaurant.
He ordered the lamb.
He paid the cashier and
left the restaurant.

Then the system is asked:

What did John eat?

It might seem trivial for a system to answer that John ate the lamb— but nowhere in the story is this explicitly stated. Nor is it directly deducible from what was said. To understand the story, the system must have both knowledge of what usually happens in restaurants and an ability to apply that knowledge to particular situations.

Schank and Abelson encoded SAM's knowledge about everyday situations in formal constructs called *scripts*. The information contained in a script about restaurants is shown in Table 1. It includes a list of players who participate in the normal routine of a restaurant, a list of

Players: customer, server, cashier
Props: restaurant, table, menu, food, check, payment, tip
Actions:
  1. Customer goes to restaurant
  2. Customer goes to table
  3. Server brings menu
  4. Customer orders food
  5. Server brings food
  6. Customer eats food
  7. Server brings check
  8. Customer leaves tip for server
  9. Customer gives payment to cashier
 10. Customer leaves restaurant

Table 1: *A restaurant script for the SAM program.*

props supporting the action, and a sequence of generic actions that characterize what usually happens when a customer visits a restaurant.

The information in this script can be used to support a variety of commonsense-reasoning tasks, including a reply to the question, "What did John eat?" The processing is as follows: the system identifies "John went to a restaurant" with action 1 from the script. In doing this, John is assigned the role of the customer. The system identifies "He ordered the lamb" with action 4, assigning the role of food to "the lamb." (Notice that with "he" referring to John, the customer is the same in both actions 1 and 4.) "He paid the cashier" is identified with action 9 and "[he] left the restaurant" with action 10.

Although not all the actions in the script were explicitly mentioned, it is reasonable (but not strictly necessary) to assume that they happened nonetheless. In particular, action 6, the customer eating the food, probably did happen. Moreover, because the entities playing the various parts in the script remain constant throughout its enactment, the system assumes that, for this particular visit to the restaurant, the customer in each action is John and the food is "the lamb." Therefore, action 6 particularizes to "John ate the lamb," providing the answer to the original question.

Information in scripts can be used for more than just answering questions; it can also be used to produce "paraphrases" of a story. For example, SAM can convert the original story:

John went to a restaurant. He sat down. He got mad. He left.

into the "paraphrase":

John was hungry. He decided to go to a restaurant. He went to one. He sat down in a chair. A waiter did not go to the table. John became upset. He decided he was going to leave the restaurant. He left it.

This restatement is not a true paraphrase because it adds many details based on speculation about what happened. But such an ability to speculate on the basis of knowledge about how our everyday world is structured is the very feature that makes SAM interesting.

Much of SAM's knowledge is not about natural language at all, but about our everyday world. SAM demonstrates that understanding natural-language stories about mundane actions requires more than a knowledge of language—it requires a knowledge of the world. The more language is studied, the more apparent it becomes that fluent communication in natural language is a process of the total intellect. Language, thought, and knowledge are inextricably intertwined.

Limitations of SAM

SAM's scripts provided one of the first mechanisms in a language processor for dealing with the structured sequences of actions that make up much of ordinary life, but they suffer from a number of limitations:

- Only a single object can serve the role of player or prop. This makes it impossible to handle stories about restaurants with many tables, customers, or servers. The problem of figuring out what the phrase "the customer" refers to becomes trivial because there can be only one customer.
- The actions in a script follow a strict linear sequence, making it impossible to deal with alternative possibilities, simultaneous or overlapping actions, or a repetition of actions.
- It is difficult to determine which particular script or scripts are appropriate for understanding a given story.

The TDUS System

. . . The SAM example showed how inference (i.e., filling in the blanks regarding what was implied, as well as what was explicitly stated) is essential in understanding natural language. To determine how knowledge-based inference and dialogue management interact, as well as work toward solving a problem of practical value, a group of researchers at SRI International investigated cooperative, task-oriented, man-machine dialogue (see reference 19). They developed a system called TDUS (Task-Oriented Dialogue Understanding System), which had the goal of communicating with a human apprentice about repair operations on electromechanical equipment. The key research problems considered concerned how to encode knowledge about the repair operations and how to follow the context of a dialogue as the

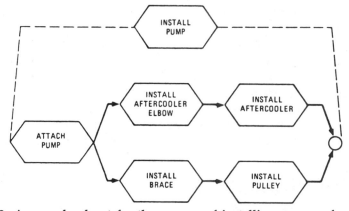

Figure 3. A procedural net for the process of installing a pump for an air compressor.

apprentice moved from task to task in the course of performing a repair operation.

In TDUS, information about how various tasks can be performed is recorded in data structures called *procedural networks* (see reference 21), which can be viewed as generalizations of scripts. Simplified procedural nets are shown in Figures 3, 4, and 5. For example, the net of Figure 3 indicates how installing a pump for an air compressor can be divided into a number of subtasks. The first subtask is to attach the pump to the platform. Once this is done, either the aftercooler elbow or the brace is installed. Once the aftercooler elbow is installed, the aftercooler is installed. Once the brace is installed, the pulley is installed. When both the aftercooler and pulley have been installed, regardless of the order accomplished, the task of installing the pump is complete.

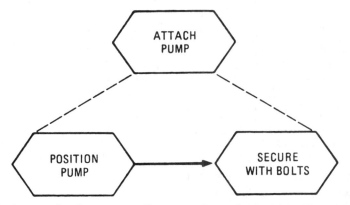

Figure 4. A procedural net expanding an action referenced in Figure 3.

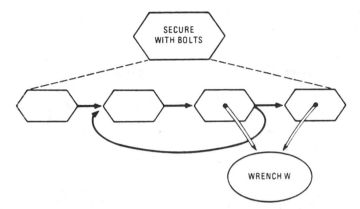

Figure 5. A procedural net that contains actions repeated in a loop.

Much like a script, the procedural net associates an action with a number of subactions. However, as opposed to the strict sequence of actions in a script, the procedural net imposes only a partial ordering on subactions. Moreover, subactions are usually associated with procedural nets of their own, which specify in yet greater detail how tasks are divided. For example, the "attach pump" action referred to in Figure 3 is described further in Figure 4, while the "secure with bolts" action referred to in Figure 4 is described further in Figure 5. The net of Figure 5 contains a loop specifying the repeated procedure of using a wrench to tighten each bolt.

As mentioned earlier, a major problem for natural-language processing systems is following the dialogue context and being able to ascertain the referents of noun phrases by taking the context into account. In preparing to build the TDUS system, Barbara Grosz collected a number of dialogues between human experts and apprentices performing repair tasks (see reference 8). After constructing procedural nets for the tasks, it was discovered that, as a general rule, the structure of task-oriented dialogues closely follows the structure of the nets representing the division of the task itself. As shown in Figure 6, if a task divides into subtasks A and B, the dialogue tends to start with general information about the overall task, then enters a subdialogue about subtask A followed by a subdialogue about subtask B.

Of greater interest is the fact that referential expressions tend to refer to objects salient in the current subtask or higher in the task hierarchy, but generally do not refer to objects in sibling subtasks. For example, if in the dialogue of Figure 6 a wrench W_1 is mentioned in one of the initial utterances before entering subdialogue A, and if a second wrench W_2 is mentioned within subdialogue A, the phrase "the wrench" uttered in subdialogue B more likely refers to W_1 than to W_2—even though W_2 was mentioned more recently. . . . In this regard,

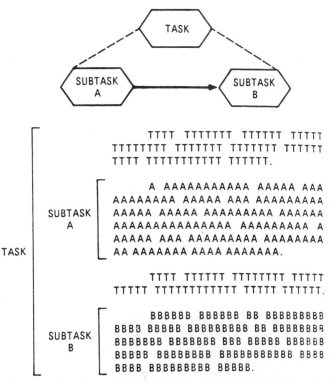

Figure 6. The structure of a task (*top*) is reflected in the structure of an English dialogue about the task (*bottom*). When discussing the task, descriptions referring to the overall task (the two paragraphs of the letter *T*) are interspersed with the paragraphs of text referring to subtask A and subtask B.

referential expressions in natural languages tend to follow much the same conventions as do variable references in block-structured programming languages such as ALGOL and Pascal. But the block structure of natural language is not indicated explicitly.

TDUS's ability to follow real-world tasks and deal with shifts in both the linguistic and physical context is illustrated in the transcript of Listing 3, which relates to information contained in the nets of Figures 3 through 5.

In interaction 1, the apprentice sets the stage by specifying what action is being done. This allows TDUS to pinpoint the location in the INSTALL-PUMP net where the apprentice appears to be. In interaction 2, the apprentice refers to a bolting action and a wrench used in that action. Neither of these is in the top-level representation of the AT-TACH-PUMP net, but they both occur in the subordinate net of Figure 5. TDUS finds this subnet and determines that no other relevant subnet refers to a different bolting action. Therefore, the system responds by specifying the wrench mentioned in the net shown in Figure 5.

1—**I AM ATTACHING THE PUMP.**
  OK.
2—**WHICH WRENCH SHOULD I USE TO BOLT IT?**
  USE THE BOX-END WRENCH.
3—**WHERE ARE THE BOLTS?**
  I DON'T KNOW.
4—**I FOUND THEM.**
  OK.
5—**WHERE IS THE WRENCH?**
  THE BOX-END WRENCH IS ON THE TABLE.
6—**I FOUND IT.**
  OK.
7—**I ATTACHED THE PUMP.**
  OK.
THE FOLLOWING HAS BEEN ASSUMED.
  YOU PUT THE PUMP AT THE PLATFORM. YOU BOLTED THE PUMP TO THE
  PLATFORM WITH THE BOLTS.
8—**SHOULD I INSTALL THE PULLEY NOW?**
  NO.
THE NEXT STEP IS:
  INSTALL THE AFTERCOOLER ELBOW ON THE PUMP
  OR
  INSTALL THE BRACE ON THE PUMP.
9—**I'M DOING THE BRACE NOW.**
  OK.
"DO" IS ASSUMED TO MEAN:
  YOU ARE INSTALLING THE BRACE.
10—**I'VE DONE IT.**
  OK.
"DO" IS ASSUMED TO MEAN:
  YOU INSTALLED THE BRACE.
THE FOLLOWING HAS BEEN ASSUMED:
  YOU PUT THE BRACE AT THE PUMP.
  YOU SECURED THE BRACE.
11—**I'VE INSTALLED THE PULLEY.**
  OK.

Listing 3. *An actual conversation with the TDUS system. With this system, the computer supervises a task performed by a human apprentice. Human input is shown in boldface.*

In interaction 3, the apprentice asks for the location of the bolts. TDUS does not operate under the closed-world assumption and realizes that there are some things it does not know. Luckily, the user finds the bolts in interaction 4.

In interaction 5, the apprentice refers to "the wrench." TDUS determines that the reference is to the wrench mentioned in interaction 2 and tells the apprentice its location. In interaction 6, TDUS resolves "it" as pertaining to the same object.

In interaction 7, the apprentice tells TDUS that the pump-attaching operation is completed. The system infers from this that all the constituent subtasks have also been done. To make sure, it reviews these assumptions for the apprentice. This filling in of intermediate steps is much like that in the SAM examples.

In interaction 8, the apprentice poses a logically complex question involving the modal concept "should." TDUS's rudimentary notion of "should" interprets the question as asking whether the action mentioned is compatible with one of the possible next steps in the procedural-net model of the task at hand. Since it is not, TDUS answers in the negative, but goes on to outline the range of acceptable alternatives at this point in the process.

Interaction 9 is of considerable interest in that it contains the proverb "do." This is a reference to some action involving the apprentice and the brace. But the action is not completely specified. By examining the procedural net, TDUS determines that the likely thing to do with a brace in this context is to install it—so TDUS makes that assumption and reports it to the apprentice.

Interaction 10 demonstrates TDUS's ability to comprehend an extreme case of contextually dependent use of language. Neither "done" nor "it" conveys much information. Here, "it" refers not to some object in the world, but to an action previously alluded to by the phrase "doing the brace."

Limitations of TDUS

TDUS exhibits a reasonable understanding of the interplay among various types of possible real-world actions, and it can follow the evolution of particular instantiations of those actions. However, it has little understanding of the goals and motivations of the apprentice with whom it holds conversations.

An exchange well beyond the capability of TDUS is shown in the following actual dialogue between a novice and an expert mechanic:

1. **WHAT DO I DO NEXT?**
REMOVE THE BOLT.

2. **HOW DO I GET IT OFF?**
USE THE RATCHET WRENCH.

3. **WHAT'S A RATCHET WRENCH?**
IT'S ON THE TABLE.

The key point to note here is that, in interaction 3, the response is not a *direct* answer to the question. If TDUS could answer this question at all, it would likely respond with a dictionary definition such as: "a tool for grasping and turning the head of a bolt, consisting of fixed or adjustable jaws mounted on a pawl that is engaged by the toothed end of a gripping bar." The person who answered query 3 understood the motivation behind the question. It was asked so the inquirer would know the description of a ratchet wrench, so he could find it, so he could grasp it, and so he could use it to remove the bolts. Understand-

Figure 7. A sentence that conveys different information to different people.

ing the inquirer's hierarchy of goals, the respondent addresses one of the goals closer to the end of the chain (finding the wrench). The co-operative respondent saves the inquirer the trouble of taking the step of locating the wrench from its description.

Beyond Current Systems

Researchers in computational linguistics have only recently begun to appreciate the impact on natural-language communication of what the participants in a conversation know about each other's knowledge, beliefs, plans, and goals. To appreciate the importance of such knowledge, consider the situation illustrated in Figure 7.

A young mother is giving a birthday party for Junior, and Grandma has come to help. Grandma's task is to light the candles on the cake, so she asks, "When shall I light the candles?" The mother replies, "We'll have the cake as soon as the children wash their hands," which informs Grandma that it will be about five minutes. The mother knows that the big-eared kids are listening, so she phrases her response to serve multiple purposes for multiple audiences. With her one statement, she tells Grandma when the candles need to be lit, and, in a nice, indirect way, tells the children to get their dirty hands washed. She knows that her response to Grandma will serve this purpose because she knows that:

- the children want the cake

USER: **THE TOOLBOX IS LOCKED.**
SYSTEM: (WHY IS HE TELLING ME THIS? I ALREADY KNOW THE BOX IS LOCKED.)
(I KNOW THE USER NEEDS TO GET IN. PERHAPS HE IS TELLING ME THE BOX IS LOCKED BECAUSE HE BELIEVES I CAN SOMEHOW HELP.)
(TO GET IN TAKES A KEY. THE USER KNOWS THIS AND KNOWS I KNOW IT. THE KEY IS IN THE DRAWER. IF THE USER KNEW THIS HE WOULD JUST UNLOCK THE BOX. THEREFORE, HE MUST NOT KNOW IT.)
(I CAN MAKE HIM COME TO KNOW IT BY SAYING "THE KEY IS IN THE DRAWER." I AM SUPPOSED TO HELP. I WILL SAY IT.)
THE KEY IS IN THE DRAWER.

Listing 4. *An imaginary conversation with a TDUS-like system showing the possible behavior of a computer system that reacts to human needs in a way not currently possible by existing systems.*

- her response to Grandma will convey to them the information that all that stands in the way of their getting it is to wash their hands
- if they know that all that stands in the way of their getting cake is to wash their hands, they will perform the ritual forthwith
- it takes them about five minutes to wash their hands

Similarly, Grandma now knows that she should light the candles in five minutes because she knows that the mother knows all the circumstances just outlined and that the mother knows Grandma knows that the mother knows it. Thus, Grandma infers that the mother expects her to understand that the children are being told to wash their hands, that they are motivated to do it right away, and the result five minutes later will presumably be washed hands reaching avidly for cake.

No system is currently capable of handling language with this level of sophistication, but a number of researchers are actively engaged in studying the various problems involved; see references 3, 5, 6, 7, 13, 14, 16, 18, 23, and 27. Much of this work is concerned with the difficulties of interpreting not just what is literally said, but also of establishing the underlying intention. Should this work succeed, systems may be capable of the kind of reasoning indicated in Listing 4.

The examples of the locked toolbox and the birthday party support a central point: communicating in natural language is an activity of the total intellect. Seen in broad perspective, the use of natural language can be placed in a general framework that seeks to account for all human activity. Within this framework, humans are seen as intelligent beings motivated by complex sets of goals they seek to fulfill by planning, executing, and monitoring sequences of actions—some of which are physical, some linguistic. That is, uttering a sentence is just as much an action as taking a step or taking a bath. Whereas the usual purpose of a physical action is to alter the physical world, the usual purpose of a linguistic action is to alter the mental states of the hearers. In the latter case, the desired modification may be to add knowledge, change a mood, or establish a new goal for the hearers.

A speaker may plan and execute linguistic actions to change some aspect of a hearer's mental state, not as an end in itself, but as part of an overall plan to achieve some more ambitious end. Just as a child might push over the first domino of a long row to make them all tumble in sequence, a lifeguard at the beach may yell "Shark!" at swimmers to set off a chain of reasoning in their minds that will result in a mad dash for the shore, which is the lifeguard's intended mechanism for accomplishing the primary goal of preserving life.

Given this view of how language works, it becomes less important to ask what a given utterance means (what does "Shark!" mean?) and more important to ask about the effect it produces. People in advertising have an explicit understanding of this concept, but all of us use it implicitly when we understand the agony conveyed by the string of curses uttered by the handyman who smashes his finger, and when we realize that our friend's question, "Do you know the time?," deserves more than a "yes" or "no" answer.

The understanding of poetry can even be cast in this mold. The poet deliberately triggers certain chains of inference in readers. Indeed, an important element in the appreciation of poetry is the reader's awareness of the interplay among the inference chains followed, the chains followed partway that turn out to be not quite appropriate, and the surface meanings of the sentences comprising the poem itself. To experience this, just consider the title of T. S. Eliot's poem, "The Love Song of J. Alfred Prufrock."

The Nature of Natural-Language Research

The previous sections discussed the capabilities and limitations of specific natural-language processing systems. But it must be recognized that these systems are merely spin-offs of the underlying science. In essence, most researchers in this field do not think of themselves as engineers seeking to evolve better natural-language processing systems, but rather as scientists concerned with the following related problems:

- identification of sources of knowledge necessary for understanding or generating natural language
- discovery or devising of mechanisms for encoding and applying such knowledge in a mechanical device

- creation of integration frameworks to control and coordinate the application of a variety of knowledge sources

Once sources of knowledge have been identified, whole subdisciplines come into being to study the associated bodies of knowledge, their structure, and methods for their computerization. Some of the major knowledge sources are discussed below.

Lexical knowledge concerns individual words, the parts of speech they belong to, and their meanings.

Syntactic knowledge has to do with the grouping of words into meaningful phrases. For example, syntactic knowledge distinguishes between the following two sentences:

NAME THE PARTS OF THE PUMP THAT *WAS* FIXED BY JOE.
NAME THE PARTS OF THE PUMP THAT *WERE* FIXED BY JOE.

In particular, it is the syntactic number distinction between WAS and WERE that indicates whether the pump or the parts were fixed.

Syntactic ambiguity is a common source of trouble in natural-language processing systems. For example, decisions about where to associate the prepositional phrase "on the table" in:

PUT THE HAMMER IN THE TOOLBOX ON THE TABLE.

can lead to any one of the interpretations:

PUT THE HAMMER THAT IS IN THE TOOLBOX ONTO THE TABLE.
PUT THE HAMMER INTO THE TOOLBOX THAT IS ON THE TABLE.
WHILE YOU STAND ON THE TABLE, PUT THE HAMMER INTO THE TOOLBOX.

Compositional semantics is the knowledge of how to compose the literal meaning of large syntactic units from the semantics of their subparts. Its utility is illustrated by the pair of sentences:

THE MAN HELD THE NUT (with a wrench).
THE WRENCH HELD THE NUT.

These two sentences are syntactically identical, but the subject of the first sentence is the agent of the action "hold," whereas the subject of the second is the instrument used by the agent. The lexical entry for the verb HOLD indicates that it is used to refer to actions in which an agent (usually a person) using an instrument exerts a force on some physical object. The syntactic subject of the verb might refer either to the agent or the instrument. But the semantics of HOLD indicate that these roles must be filled by objects of mutually disjoint classes of objects. Utilization of this knowledge allows a system to assign the role of agent to THE MAN, but assign the role of instrument to THE WRENCH.

Discourse knowledge concerns the way clues from the current context are used to help interpret a sentence. For example, if we have just been talking about this month's issue of *BYTE*, the noun phrase "the magazine" in:

I'VE ALREADY READ MY COPY OF THE MAGAZINE.

is easily understood *in this context* as referring to this month's issue of *BYTE*. Yet, we often have personal knowledge of hundreds of issues of various magazines. The ability to pick the one of current interest is based on specific knowledge of the current situation.

World knowledge is concerned with information about how the world is currently configured and about physical constraints upon possible configurations. For example, we understand:

PRESIDENT REAGAN FLEW TO CALIFORNIA.

to mean that he *was flown* to California as a passenger in an airplane. Had the sentence been about a bird, we might have taken the sentence to mean that the bird did the flying.

As an example of how knowledge about the current physical situation can be of aid in understanding sentences, consider again the sentence:

PUT THE HAMMER IN THE TOOLBOX ON THE TABLE.

discussed in the earlier paragraph on syntax. If we know that the hammer is currently in a toolbox on the floor, the only interpretation of the sentence is to lift the hammer out of the toolbox and place it onto the table. The other interpretations are ruled out because they are impossible in the current state of the world.

Knowledge of mental states relates to comprehending the knowledge and goals of other participants in the dialogue. The use of such knowledge is shown in the locked-toolbox example in Listing 4. . . .

Conclusion

Considerably more research in computational linguistics will be required before mechanical devices can be created that are fluent in the use of natural language. However, current research efforts are shedding new light on the types of knowledge required for communication in human languages, as well as on prospective mechanisms for encoding and applying that knowledge in computers. These efforts are showing that language use is not an isolated intellectual activity; it also involves our basic facilities for commonsense reasoning and planning. A computer system fluent in a natural language will be a genuinely intelligent machine.

Although the fluent use of natural language by machines remains a long-term goal, a number of practical mechanisms have been developed to deal with significant fragments of language in specialized application areas. For many applications, an ability to communicate within such fragments is both sufficient for the task at hand and clearly preferable to forcing users to learn machine-oriented languages. In coming years, we expect to see natural-language processing employed in an increasing number of practical applications, enabling more and more people to interact directly and effectively with computer systems.

References

1. Appelt, D. E. "A Planner for Reasoning About Knowledge and Action." *Proceedings of the First Annual National Conference on Artificial Intelligence,* August 1980, pages 235–239.
2. Biermann, A. B. "Approaches to Automatic Programming," *Advances in Computers,* volume 15, 1976, pages 1–63.
3. Bruce, B. "Pragmatics in Speech Understanding." *Advance Papers of the Fourth International Joint Conference on Artificial Intelligence,* 1975, pages 461–467.
4. Burton, R. R. "Semantic Grammar: An Engineering Technique for Constructing Natural Language Understanding Systems." BBN Report 3453, Bolt, Beranek, and Newman Inc., Cambridge MA, December 1976.
5. Carbonell, J. "Politics." *Inside Computer Understanding* (reference 23), pages 259–317.
6. Cohen, P. R. and C. R. Perrault. "Elements of a Plan Based Theory of Speech Acts." *Cognitive Science,* volume 3, number 3, 1979, pages 177–212.
7. Grosz, B. J. "Utterance and Objective: Issues in Natural Language Communication." *Sixth International Joint Conference on Artificial Intelligence,* 1979, pages 1067–1076; also in *AI Magazine,* volume 1, number 1, 1980, pages 11–20.
8. Grosz, B. J. "Focusing and Description in Natural Language Dialogues." *Elements of Discourse Understanding: Proceedings of a Workshop on Computational Aspects of Linguistic Structure and Discourse Setting,* A. K. Joshi, I. A. Sag, and B. L. Webber (editors), Cambridge: Cambridge University Press, 1981.
9. Haas, N. and G. G. Hendrix. "An Approach to Acquiring and Applying Knowledge." *Proceedings of the First Annual National Conference on Artificial Intelligence,* August 1980, pages 235–239.
10. Harris, L. R. "User Oriented Data Base Query with the ROBOT Natural Language Query System." *Proceedings of the Third International Conference on Very Large Data Bases,* October 1977.
11. Hendrix, G. G. "The LIFER Manual: A Guide to Building Practical Natural Language Interfaces." AI Center Technical Note 138, SRI International, Menlo Park CA, February 1977.
12. Hendrix, G. G., E. D. Sacerdoti, D. Sagalowicz, and J. Slocum. "Developing a Natural Language Interface to Complex Data." *Association for Computing Machinery Transactions on Database Systems,* volume 3, number 2, June 1978.

13. Hobbs, J. R. and D. A. Evans. "Conversation as Planned Behavior." AI Center Technical Note 203, SRI International, Menlo Park CA, 1979.
14. Kaplan, S. J. "Cooperative Responses From a Portable Natural Language Data Base Query System." Ph.D. Dissertation, University of Pennsylvania, Philadelphia, 1979.
15. Lewis, W. H. "TED: A Transportable English Datamanager." *Proceedings of the Principal Investigators' Meeting of the ACCAT Program*, October 1979.
16. Mann, W. "Toward a Speech Act Theory for Natural Language Processing." ISI/RR-79-75, USC/Information Sciences Institute, Marina del Ray CA, 1980.
17. Moore, R. C. "Reasoning About Knowledge and Action." AI Center Technical Note 191, SRI International, Menlo Park CA, October 1980.
18. Perrault, C. R. and J. F. Allen. "A Plan-Based Analysis of Indirect Speech Acts." *American Journal of Computational Linguistics*, volume 6, number 3–4, July–December 1980, pages 167–182.
19. Robinson, A. E., *et al.* "Interpreting Natural-Language Utterances in Dialog About Tasks." AI Center Technical Note 210, SRI International, Menlo Park CA, 1980.
20. Robinson, J. J. "DIAGRAM: A Grammar for Dialogues." AI Center Technical Note 205, SRI International, Menlo Park CA, February 1980.
21. Sacerdoti, E. D. *A Structure for Plans and Behavior*. New York: Elsevier North-Holland, 1977.
22. Schank, R. and R. Abelson. *Scripts, Plans, Goals, and Understanding*. Hillsdale NJ: Lawrence Erlbaum, 1977.
23. Schank, R. and C. Riesbeck. *Inside Computer Understanding*. Hillsdale NJ: Lawrence Erlbaum, 1981.
24. Templeton, M. "EUFID: A Friendly and Flexible Frontend for Data Management Systems." *Proceedings of the 1979 National Conference of the Association for Computational Linguistics*, August 1979.
25. Thompson, F. B. and B. H. Thompson. "Practical Natural Language Processing: The REL System as Prototype." *Advances in Computers 13*, M. Rubinoff and M. C. Yovits (editors), New York: Academic Press, 1975.
26. Waltz, D. "Natural Language Access to a Large Data Base: An Engineering Approach." *Proceedings of the Fourth International Joint Conference on Artificial Intelligence*, September 1975, pages 868–872.
27. Wilensky, R. "Meta-Planning." *Proceedings of the First Annual National Conference on Artificial Intelligence*, 1980, pages 334–336.
28. Wilks, Y. "Natural Language Understanding Systems Within the AI Paradigm: A Survey and Some Comparisons." *Linguistic Structures Processing*, A. Zamplolli (editor), Amsterdam: North-Holland, 1977, pages 341–398.
29. Winograd, T. *Understanding Natural Language*. New York: Academic Press, 1972.
30. Woods, W. A. "Transition Network Grammars for Natural Language Analysis." *Communications of the Association for Computing Machinery*, volume 13, number 10, October 1970, pages 591–606.
31. Woods, W. A., R. M. Kaplan, and B. Nash-Webber. "The Lunar Sciences Natural Language Information System." BBN Report 2378, Bolt, Beranek, and Newman Inc. Cambridge MA, 1972.

FOR DISCUSSION AND REVIEW

1. Hendrix and Sacerdoti identify two primary goals of computational linguistics. Explain each goal in your own words. Does one seem to be more important than the other? If so, why? Has more progress been made toward achieving one than the other? Explain your answer.

2. What do the authors mean by the term "natural-language processing"?

3. Identify two possible applications of a natural-language processing system. Try to go beyond those suggested by the authors.

4. Study Listing 1, p. 650. Then explain in your own words what LADDER can do (for example, spelling, incomplete sentences, and pronoun reference).

5. Despite its impressive capability, Hendrix and Sacerdoti state that "LADDER falls far short of being an ideal system, both conceptually and linguistically." Explain, being as specific as possible.

6. What is a *definitely determined noun phrase* (DEF NP)? Why are DEF NPs important in designing natural-language interfaces with computers?

7. Explain the concept "script" as developed by Roger Schank and Robert Abelson. How is SAM different from LADDER? (Consider, for example, SAM's ability to "speculate on the basis of knowledge about how our everyday world is structured.") What are SAM's limitations?

8. Describe TDUS—what were its goals? What major problems did its designers face?

9. Explain the relationship between *scripts* and *procedural networks*.

10. What do the authors mean by saying that "TDUS does not operate under the closed-world assumption"?

11. Explain what Hendrix and Sacerdoti mean when they state: "Researchers in computational linguistics have only recently begun to appreciate the impact on natural-language communication of what the participants in a conversation know about each other's knowledge, beliefs, plans, and goals."

3/Animals, Communication, and Language

WILLIAM KEMP
AND
ROY SMITH

For many years human beings have studied a variety of animal communication systems—and for many reasons. Just as the possibility of life somewhere in space has long fascinated people, so too has the possibility of finding that some animal here on earth can learn a form of human language. People have studied "talking" horses, dolphins, bees, whales, monkeys, and chimpanzees, all in an effort to discover if we alone possess language. Other researchers, especially ethologists, have studied animal communication systems because of their intrinsic interest and because such study helps us to understand both the similarities and differences between animal communication and human language. This research has revealed a great deal about the complexity of animal communication systems; it has also shown that human beings "share with other species an impressive degree of nonlingual communication." In the following selection, Professors William Kemp and Roy Smith, both of Mary Washington College, survey the research on animal communication. They explain the difficulties of such research, as well as its importance to understanding human language. They also describe the elaborate communication systems of bees, birds, and mammals, especially the nonhuman primates. Discussing the extensive work with chimpanzees and gorillas that was done in the 1970s and early 1980s, they argue convincingly that these experiments have "demonstrated that apes can learn to use semantically a large number of arbitrary symbols. That achievement is more than the most hostile critics will allow. But it is also considerably less than human semantic abilities."

Research for this article was generously supported by the graduate council of Mary Washington College. Figure graphics are by Donna Grasso.

> The sound of the waterfall
> has for a long time
> ceased,
> yet with its name
> we can hear it still.
> FUJIWARO NO KINTO (d. 1041)

Haiku are instances of human language at its peak; they create stunning images with a few carefully chosen syllables. Despite claims for remarkable communication and even language among the many animals around us, no one has offered an example of a haiku from a humpback whale or a chimpanzee. This is not to say that nonhumans do not communicate effectively; they certainly do. Still, most humans use language as something qualitatively different from other forms of communication, at least some of the time.

What are the differences between human language and nonhuman communication? This seemingly simple question has been the subject of considerable research and discussion among linguists and ethologists (specialists in animal behavior). An easy answer might be that language is the form of communication humans use, while animal communication is what nonhumans use. Unfortunately, this implies that a loving glance from your mother is part of language while a loving glance from your dog is not. Humans use language layered atop other forms of communication, and sometimes, the nonlanguage signals contain more important messages. At the very least, we share with other species an impressive degree of nonlingual communication. Examining the types of animal communication allows us to see the important ways in which language differs from communication in other animals. It also suggests that language is not an aberration that appears suddenly, without evolutionary precursors, in humans.

Ethologists have made the greatest advances in understanding animal communication. Their analysis, clearly presented by W. John Smith (1977a), treats it under three headings. The first of these is *form*. For an animal's behavior to have value as a signal, it must be in a constant form that others can recognize and connect reliably to some future behavior by the signaler. Ethologists call such stereotyped behavior a *display*. The second part of animal communication is *context*; it includes the general environment in which an animal is displaying as well as simultaneous displays it sends through other sensory modes or channels. Thus, a dog's bark conveys one message about future behavior when its tail is wagging, another when its tail is stiff. Context usually resolves such ambiguities. The third part of animal communication is the *response* to the signal. Communication is valuable because it increases the likelihood of one animal's choosing behavior that fits the behavior of others. We must see the choice by the receiving animal to be sure communication has actually occurred. Otherwise, we can't tell the difference between ruffling feathers to get them straight and ruffling feathers to signal an impending conflict.

Distinctive behavior that reliably indicates what an animal will do promotes cooperation and reduces conflict, because it allows neighbors to adjust their actions according to what the display predicts. For example, very few creatures seriously injure one another in disputes over territory, food, or mates, because displays allow rivals to establish which animal is dominant without resorting to real combat. Crudely put, the meaning of an agonistic display is, "I feel like attacking you ferociously very soon." The individual whose display is more convincing will usually win. To understand such interchanges of information we need not imagine animals computing the odds as they respond to each other, or planning their own displays. Sending and comprehending displays are part of each animal's (and human's) automatic behavior. In human interactions smiling usually elicits a responding smile and a frown prompts a frown, without any planning by anyone.

In discussing human language, linguists use concepts similar to ethologists' form, context, and response. They work with *syntax*, which emphasizes form; *semantics*, which emphasizes meaning (defined partly by context); and *pragmatics*, which emphasizes how context modifies or replaces the meaning of an utterance. Linguists also analyze human speech into *morphemes* and *phonemes*, units that seem unique to spoken language. But the particular manifestations of phonemes (called *allophones*) share with displays an invariant form guided by a central neural program; hence the persistence of social, regional, and national pronunciations across a lifetime. Both allophones and displays are examples of unvarying sets of motor movements that ethologists call *fixed action patterns* (Hinde, 1970). Any animal or species has a limited set of these patterns, and depending on the species, a predictable capacity for learning new ones. According to whether the pattern is genetically programmed or learned, "any particular movement of this type may be characteristic of a genus . . . , a species, or merely one individual" (Hinde, 1970, p. 22).

As displays become language, several things change. The form of communication shifts from a limited number of lengthy, stereotyped displays to a very large number of very short displays (allophones) that can be combined in many ways according to hierarchical rules. The importance of context also changes. Displays begin as indications of an animal's probable response to its environment or context; they are more about the animal itself than about the world. For example, most adult birds vocalize as they are deciding what to do next, so the fundamental meaning of the sound might be, "I'm about to do something!" Their neighbors can then deduce from context what they are likely to do. In contrast, humans frequently use language to describe environment(s), while their displays signal much of the accompanying affective content. Although the context in which a sentence appears usually colors its meaning, the sentence has its own meaning independent of context. Displays do not have this independent meaning.

While the response to a display is often the best indication of the display's meaning, the response of others to language may be unimportant. Although Fujiwaro wrote his haiku for others to read, and would probably have been delighted to know that people would be reading and appreciating it nine hundred years after his death, he must have written it partly, or perhaps chiefly, for the delight of capturing his experience in words. We have no clear evidence that nonhumans play with their communication systems simply to revel in the workings of the system itself.

Language is also capable of abstraction, a power that seems to have no natural parallel in animal communication. Of course, many animals can create general concepts (Griffin, 1981); many dogs understand that *all* cars are to be chased. And some higher primates, having learned artificial sign systems from humans, clearly use and understand some abstract signs (Walker, 1983). But even in the cleverest animals, natural displays have no way of presenting abstract propositions about either the animal or its world. The abilities conferred by language to plan for the future and control our environment are without parallel in other species. Language is far removed from the simple fixed action patterns of affective displays. A hierarchy of rule systems, from phonetics to semantics, transforms language from a set of environmental responses to a self-referencing symbol system operating simultaneously on several independently structured levels. Thus our thoughts are at least partly dissociated from our feelings.

Comparing animal and human communication seems a fairly straightforward task, but it is full of wrong turns, and poses a number of perplexing questions. Do we think without language, or is language so completely the medium of thought that we can have no thoughts without a language to articulate them? Do animals with reasonably complex communication systems and clear cognitive skills have anything like human awareness? And how did language evolve in humans? Unanswered questions all.

Despite our present inability to resolve these questions, animal communication systems have a lot to tell us about language. For one thing, in every other species displays have evolved out of environmental demands and animals' adaptations to meet those demands. The more carefully we study how other animals exchange signals, the more clearly we see how closely communication systems connect to other elements of behavior. We also find that many animals are a good deal more clever than we suppose.

For example, whereas we usually regard insects as just barely sentient, doing their business by instinct and incapable of significant mental activity, we marvel at the architectural achievements of social insects (ants, bees, termites, and wasps). In fact, the architecture of a termite mound or an ant nest is genetically designed; these insects are no more likely to change the plans of their nests than they are to grow eight legs apiece. Each insect responds to the chemical and tactile signals around it with a set of fixed action patterns programmed into its simple brain. In a real sense no member of this miniature corps of engineers has any plan at all; the genetic repository of the whole community contains the blueprint for building the nest, and for other activity besides. More marvelous still are the systems of communication by which social insects manage their collective lives, using chemicals (called *pheromones*), sound, and physical activity to exchange information and coordinate their behavior.

The best understood insect communication system is the dance of the honeybee (*Apis mellifera*). Because honey is delicious, humans have been interested for centuries in the bees that make it, and from ancient times whole libraries have been devoted to beekeeping. But until the 1920s, no one noticed that bees returning from a successful foray convey to hivemates important information which concentrates hive activity on the best nectar sources. In 1919, Karl von Frisch set out to discover how hundreds of foraging bees could arrive as if by magic at a rich food source discovered only a short while before by a single bee. The result of his experiment was striking:

> I attracted a few bees to a dish of sugar water, marked them with red paint and then stopped feeding for a while. As soon as all was quiet, I filled the dish again and watched a scout which had drunk from it before after her return to the hive. I could scarcely believe my eyes. She performed a round dance on the honeycomb which greatly excited the marked foragers around her and caused them to fly back to the feeding place. (von Frisch, 1967, pp. 72–73)

In a series of elegant experiments over the next twenty years, von Frisch established that the round dance conveys three pieces of information: the presence of a food source, its richness, and the type of food available (see Figure 1). The scent clinging to the dancer's body, along with droplets of nectar regurgitated from her honey stomach, tell nearby bees of her find. If she dances vigorously, displaying her agitation at a rich find, other recruits follow her dance, then promptly leave the hive and search busily for the odors she carries, completely ignoring all other food sources. They may also be guided by a "Here it is!" pheromone that the scout releases as she visits the source a second time. Returning to the hive, the recruits will also dance vigorously and

Figure 1. Round dance.

spread the odor. Soon, hundreds of hivemates will be exploiting the recently discovered treasure.

In 1944, more than twenty years after his initial discovery, von Frisch began a series of experiments to explore how honeybees deal with food sources far from the hive. The results were even more exciting, for he discovered that bees use a "tail-wagging" dance to communicate the distance and direction of remote food sources (see Figure 2). "In the tail-wagging dance," he reported (1967), "they run in a straight line wagging their abdomen to and fro, then return to the starting point in a semicircle, repeat the tail-wagging run, return in a semicircle on the other side, and so on." Bees responding to this dance, he found, would completely ignore food sources near the hive—even those with identical odors—in their flight to the distant goal.

Even more startling was von Frisch's discovery that the tail-wagging dance told the recruit bees which direction to go in and how far to fly before starting their search. The scout bee does her dance on a vertical comb inside the dark hive. The angle between an imaginary vertical line running up the comb surface and the tail-wagging run of her dance corresponds to the angle between the sun and the food source (see Figure 3, p. 676). So if the food source is twenty degrees to the left or right of the sun as seen from the opening of the hive, her waggle run will be offset twenty degrees to the left or right of the vertical. If the food source is directly toward the sun, she will start her

Figure 2. Tail-wagging dance.

waggle run at the bottom of the comb and dance straight up. If the source is directly away from the sun, she will start at the top of the comb, dancing straight down, and so on. Later experiments established that this directional information is extremely accurate. In a typical trial lasting fifty minutes, 42 of 54 bees (78%) found the target food source, 7 missed by an angle of fifteen degrees to the right or left, 4 by thirty degrees, and 1 by forty-five degrees. The scout bees also compensate for detours, directing hivemates to fly straight toward the goal. Having a reasonably accurate internal clock, they can even adjust their waggle dance for the sun's movement across the sky (von Frisch, 1971).

While the angle of the waggle run indicates the direction of the goal, its tempo indicates the distance; the farther the source, the more waggle runs the dancer makes per unit of time. In fact, the tail-wagging dance is a ritualized reenactment of flying to the food source (Wilson, 1971), displaying how much energy the dancer expended; a prevailing head or tail wind will increase or decrease the dance's tempo for a given destination.

Not all honey bees use exactly the same language. Von Frisch's Austrian bees (*Apis mellifera carnica*) use the round dance for food

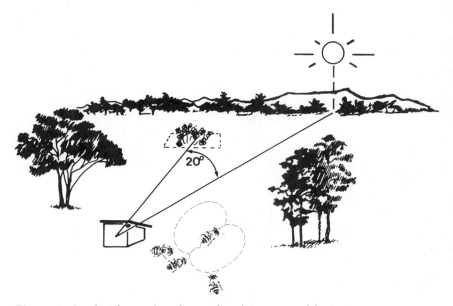

Figure 3. Angle of wagging dance showing sun position.

within twenty meters of the hive, the pure tail-wagging dance for food over eighty meters away, and gradual transitional forms between those distances. Five related strains show a clear third form, the sickle dance, for varying portions of the intervening distance. Von Frisch's students have established that different honeybee strains also set the boundaries between the round and tail-wagging dances at different distances, and encode like distances by different tempos. For example, Italian bees (*Apis m. ligustica*) dance slower for any given distance than do Austrian ones. When Boch put both kinds of bees into one hive, miscommunication ran rampant. In response to Italian bees, the Austrian ones flew too far; in response to Austrian scouts, Italian bees did not fly far enough (Lindauer, 1961). One can accurately say that the bee "language" has genetic dialects.

But is the bee dance really language? It certainly conveys information in an arbitrary code about parts of the world outside the bee herself and remote from where she dances. To understand it, one must share her code, particularly the tempo scale indicating distance. The dance thus satisfies several of the design features by which Hockett and Altmann (1968) attempted to distinguish between animal communication and human language. But von Frisch himself found significant limits to the bee's communication system. He put a hive beneath a radio tower, placed a very rich sugar water solution fairly high up in the tower, and showed several scouts where it was. They returned to the hive and danced heroically. Their mates then searched busily all around the hive—but not up the tower (von Frisch, 1966). Evolved to make foraging across horizontal planes efficient (von Frisch, 1971; Wilson, 1971), the powerful communication system of honeybees has no way of indicating up or down; as von Frisch explains (1966, p. 139), "there are no flowers in the clouds." Unlike human language, bee displays are not productive; they do not permit recombining bits of the code to produce novel messages. Bee messages are essentially the same message, differing only in a few details, uttered almost mechanically, over and over again in response to a narrow band of stimuli. This rigidity prevents the bees in mixed hives from learning each others' dialects, despite repeated attempts to communicate.

Assessing not only the honeybees' communication system but their ability to create mental maps of the territory around their hive and remember what flower they are seeking, Gould and Gould (1983) observe, "these hard-working insects appear simply to be well-programmed learning machines, attending only to the cues deemed salient by evolution (and then only in well-defined contexts and often during precise critical periods)—and then filing the information thus obtained in pre-existing arrays." Of course, as Gould and Gould conclude, much the same can be said of humans.

Because birds are larger and interact over longer distances, one might suppose they use even more complicated communication systems. Their behavior certainly seems more varied than that of insects, and more vocal. Calls and songs are embedded in a rich context of elaborate visual displays; no bird sits like a lump and sings. Its message to mate, rival, or neighbor arises from a coordinated package of activities, not any single element within the package (Smith, 1977b). Still, to linguists birds' sounds are the most interesting part of their behavior because, like humans, birds are physiologically and behaviorally specialized to produce and respond to streams of meaningful sound.

Ornithologists divide bird vocalizations into two categories: calls and songs. Calls tend to be brief, simple in structure, and confined to a particular context. As a result, some calls elicit sharp reactions from nearly every bird hearing them. The contrasting alarm and mobbing calls that many birds produce when they spot a predator, usually an owl or a hawk, are often shared across species; many birds make similar acoustic distinctions between the two calls. Alarms, given when the predator is airborne and thus able to strike promptly, are often high-frequency pure tones with no sharp beginnings or endings. Such tones make it difficult for the predator to find the bird emitting them (Marler, 1955, 1957; Konishi, 1973). In contrast, mobbing calls, which summon neighbors to attack a stationary predator, often have a wide frequency range, begin sharply, and end abruptly. These acoustic features make the sound easy to locate, so that every bird responding will know where to attack. The survival value of such a system is obvious.

But only a predator, rival, or a prospective mate shows any interest in the information contained in a bird's song. Song is usually loud, sustained, complex in structure, seasonal, confined to males, and prompted by mating or territorial concerns. Some species, of course, sing no songs at all, and use calls for territorial and breeding information; in strictest terms a song is simply an especially elaborate call. Still, the distinction between the two has a practical value because song seems musical to us and calls do not. Certainly, if a male songbird is to breed, he must learn to sing the right tune. It attracts females and keeps rival males away. And if a female is to breed, she must know the tune a proper male should sing. Regarded as speech (song?) acts, bird songs indicate the singer's species, gender, approximate age (mature instead of immature), and readiness to breed. Neither immature males nor females sing. In all these features, bird song is like other forms of animal display. Much of what it conveys simply repeats information stated by the bird's size, plumage, or other behavior.

A major function of bird song is to establish and maintain breeding territories. Each resident male spends much of his time patrolling his boundaries and declaring his presence in song. The "message" of the song indicates the singer's probable behavior. Roughly translated, a territorial song says that the singer will attack any adult male of the same species entering his territory. But as the singer's probable behavior changes across the spring, so does the meaning of the song. Early in the season, when pairs are still forming, a male chaffinch (*Fringilla coelebs*) will not attack adult females entering his territory. At that time of year, his song contains no threat message for them; it is all invitation. But later on, when eggs are incubating, he will attack strange females. The song does not change, but its meaning does (Nottebaum, 1975). Other birds know the meaning from the time of year.

Of even greater interest to linguists than what birds sing about is how they learn to repeat sometimes long and complex songs with great precision. In fact, most do not *learn* their songs in the strict meaning of the word. Only four of the twenty-nine avian orders (Passeriformes [sparrow or sparrowlike], Psittaciformes [parrots], Toucants, and Hummingbirds) have complex song repertoires or dialects and clearly must acquire their songs after birth (Nottebaum, 1975). In the other twenty-five orders, the appropriate calls or songs appear to be part of each bird's genetic inheritance. Even within passerine birds, learning strategies differ sharply from one species to the next. Young song sparrows (*Melospiza melodia*), for example, must hear themselves—but not adults—sing to produce their full repertoire. Individuals deafened when young fail to develop normal song, unlike individuals merely isolated when young (Konishi and Nottebaum, 1969). In contrast, young finches of several species learn the song of the adult male who helps care for them, even if he is of another species (Immelmann, 1969).

White-crowned sparrows (*Zonotrichia leucophrys*) and chaffinches must in the first spring of their lives hear adults of their own species sing. Individuals raised in isolation until their second spring never perform properly, even after they have heard adult song (Thorpe, 1958; Marler and Tamura, 1964). In some species, each male appears to be born with a generalized template for his species song. The length and timing of his critical learning period differ according to species, but the general pattern is similar (Konishi and Nottebaum, 1969; Nottebaum, 1975). During his first spring, the young male must hear adults of his species sing, although he makes no effort to sing himself. When his second spring arrives, he begins singing, usually imperfectly, but soon develops the full range of adult repertoire. The point of crystallization, when the template has become rich enough to support full adult song during the coming year, varies with the species. But the necessity of a passive learning period does not. The analogy between this template and Chomsky's hypothesis of a genetically supported universal grammar in humans is obvious.

While the dialect differences in bees are genetically fixed, learning appears to produce regional dialects in birds just as it does in human speech. In many species, birds of one area will develop shared variations on the species song (Thielke, 1969). These variations persist for several generations at least, and are clearly differences in learning rather than in the genetic template; fledglings from one area transported to another will sing the new dialect, not that of their parents. And although analogies between bird song and human speech are intriguing, we should remember that the variety of adaptation in birds is immense. Many do not sing at all (vultures, for instance, only croak and hiss). Of those that do, some sing as their genes conduct, others as their father or foster-father does, others as conspecific adult males around them do, and a few are exceptional mimics of everything from sewing machines to foul-mouthed sea captains.

Are we right in supposing that because birds are more like us than bees they are closer in communicative ability as well? Probably not. Insect communication and behavior are in many ways as complex as our own. The impressive achievements of insect communities depend on reliable communication systems coordinating the behavior of thousands, even millions. Bees rely on long fixed action patterns, available in the nervous system of each individual, released by a small range of stimuli. In contrast, bird vocalizations seem ambiguous. It may even be useful to see bird song as a simpler form of communication than either the stereotyped, meaning-packed movements and chemical signals of bees or the more variable multichannel displays of mammals. While some birds rely on learning to establish the form of the fixed action pattern, the displays are long and generally limited in number. Mammals, pushed by changes in reproductive strategy and social structure, have expanded on learning as a source of displays while shortening the length of individual fixed action patterns. These shorter displays can be arranged through learning in a wide variety of sequences, producing a communication system of greatly increased flexibility and complexity.

Your dog may display his claim for territory by scent-marking your favorite rosebush, erecting his hair and posturing when he sees another dog next door, and barking when your best friend tries to come into his (your) yard. Each display has several variations and levels of intensity. Despite all this complexity, humans easily identify and interpret their pets' signals. Does that mean that people, as apprentice Dr. Doolittles, have learned to speak dog language? Do dogs have a language? Although we are not foolish enough to say that *your* dog doesn't talk to *you*, we can suggest a simpler way of explaining human ability to understand other mammals easily. The complexity and variability of mammalian signaling may disguise the rather limited range of subjects about which mammals signal (Smith *et al.*, 1977; Peters, 1980). If most mammals communicate about the same limited set of subjects, and if those subjects are part of an environment shared by humans, it is not really surprising that humans understand their mammalian pets—or that the pets appear to understand humans. (It would be somewhat more difficult to share the world of a pet slime mold.)

Four activities account for almost all the displays seen in mammals: mating, rearing young, resolving conflict, and maintaining group organization. In many species, from insects to birds, elaborate courtship rituals supplement the basic chemical signals of sexual readiness. Still, the rituals give only redundant information about the sexual condition and identity of the displaying animal. Mammals are no different, although their sexual displays are rather ordinary compared to the courtship of ducks. In contrast, the other three display categories show extensive expansion, reflecting specific mammalian adaptations.

Communication between mother and offspring is unimportant in sea turtles, which abandon their newly laid eggs and return to the sea. Even birds, many of which are good and faithful parents, communicate with their young through a simple set of calls and several kinds of specialized physical contact until the young are ready to fly. Then the fledgling is on its own to find food, avoid predators, and maybe even navigate from Great Britain to central Africa without ending up in Iowa by mistake. Young turtles are genetically programmed to run for the sea as soon as they hatch. In ways we are only beginning to understand, migratory birds are programmed to find their way accurately across immense distances. Neither turtles nor birds learn much from their parents. So it is hardly surprising that all turtles and most birds produce multiple offspring as insurance; although the casualty rate may be high, some are bound to solve their life tasks successfully and keep the species going.

In contrast, mammalian parents invest a truly remarkable amount of energy and time in a few offspring, so maternal care over a long period involves elaborate and sustained interaction between mothers and their young. The displays guiding this interaction are no more complex than those controlling mating. In fact, to a casual human observer they may not seem to be displays at all, because we behave very similarly in caring for our own infants: feeding, cleaning, restraining, warning, punishing, and petting.

All young mammals must learn a good deal, so they spend much time imitating adults and playing with each other. Imitation is a way of acquiring complex skills such as finding food, reproducing, or caring for offspring. Adult nonhumans don't deliberately describe the environment to their offspring in symbolic terms or offer lessons in infant care, but nearly all young mammals watch closely and copy diligently what their elders do. Long-lived social mammals in particular must learn not only skills but a large number of individual identities and interaction signals. Wolves (Mech, 1970), lions (Schaller, 1972), chimpanzees (Goodall, 1971), and gorillas (Schaller, 1963), for example, form relatively stable social groups in which each individual must know and recognize the other members. Youngsters inherit the status of their mothers, but as they mature through a long adolescence they will rise or fall in the dominance system according to their own efforts. A young male must find safe ways to spend time with occasionally dangerous adult males while working his way into their hierarchy. Simultaneously, the dominance relationship between him and his mother will slowly alter. All these changes will occur over several years during thousands of encounters in which messages are conveyed by details of posture and expression as well as more obvious displays. Encounters will be highly reciprocal, consisting of very rapid interchanges; and although the messages will be about very few things, they will come frequently and in great numbers. Because the individuals involved will also have distinctive personalities, each youngster must learn not only the group members' identities but their temperaments; different adults will respond in different ways. Adult gorillas in repose tolerate young ones climbing all over them, but some adults are more tolerant than others. It is well for young gorillas to learn tolerance levels rapidly.

Still, the fundamental feature of animal communication persists in even the most highly social mammals: the value of displays does not depend on a desire to tell another animal something. Perhaps you have seen one of the elaborate prairie dog cities on the western plains. Your approach is announced by alarm calls that send the animals nearest you scurrying to their holes, from which they examine you. Can there be any doubt that sentries are telling their comrades about the intruder? Patient observation and careful analysis have shown that this alarm display, like other prairie dog vocalizations, is just that—a display about the state of alarm of the caller (Smith et al., 1977). Prairie dogs apparently give this signal whenever they are aroused enough to stop their activity and scan the environment, but not so scared as to run for cover immediately. They give the same call during territorial disputes when the caller is unsure whether to attack or retreat. Other prairie dogs, upset by the signaler, give their own version of the display and spread agitation through the colony. The alarm system works very effectively; knowing that your neighbor is aroused is important. But the prairie dog's behavior is a display containing information about the caller, not a word or sentence about the source of the alarm. Each prairie dog must sit up and look for himself.

And even the most highly social mammals send messages with great redundancy. Your dog growls, erects the hair on his shoulders, stiffens his tail and legs, and faces the intruder. All the components of this display reinforce the same aggressive message. Such redundancy, together with a fairly limited number of messages, perhaps only a couple of dozen, is important because it means that pulling one sensory channel from the display for some other purpose need not seriously disrupt the message. Humans appear to have done exactly that with the acoustic channel in developing language. But the original display system still functions in human behavior, as the expanding literature on kinesics testifies.

Two other groups of mammals—bats and cetaceans (whales and porpoises)—have separated sound for special purposes. Lilly (1975) believes dolphins have a complex vocal language. Certainly dolphins are active, highly social, and very intelligent animals, but humans are at a tremendous disadvantage in studying them. Their environment is so foreign and their adaptation to it so complete that we have not even begun to analyze or understand their behavior in their natural habitat; in fact, we know very little about how they spend their time (Caldwell and Caldwell, 1977). The absence of a natural behavioral context in which to analyze cetacean signals makes conclusions about their communication and their possession of language exceedingly tenuous.

We are safer studying our closest surviving biological relatives, the other primates. While we can examine the bones, artifacts, tracks, and markings left by extinct species of *Homo*, spoken language has left no traces in the archaeological record. So investigators from many disciplines have turned to nonhuman primates for answers to questions about the evolutionary origin of human physical and behavioral traits, including language. Others have looked to primate communication for a suitable yet simple analogy to the cognitive basis of human language. And those interested in the development of language in children have seen in primates possible models for separating heritable from acquired components. Although communication among primates is important in and of itself, many who study primates do so implicitly or explicitly to exploit their physical and behavioral similarities to humans.

This likeness to humans makes research with primates difficult. Ann Premack (1976, p. 17) writes, "Aside from a human baby, I can think of no creature which can arouse stronger feelings of tenderness than an infant chimpanzee. It has huge round eyes and a delicate head and is far more alert than a human infant of the same age. When you pick up a young chimp, it encircles your body with its long, trembling arms and legs, and the effect is devastating—you want to take it home!" Being objective about any experimental work with such an appealing animal is extremely difficult, and the study of language capacity in primates presents a special problem. While any visit to a local zoo will suggest that monkeys are often quite vocal, and while careful observations in zoos and the wild have shown that primates can make a wide variety of sounds, our closest relatives do not share our tendency toward constant chatter. Human social gatherings are noisy compared to those of other higher primates, and most of the noise is spoken language. Early studies, some using human infants as controls, investigated whether raising chimpanzees in a completely human environment (*cross-fostering*) would produce more human behavior, including spoken language. While chimps learned rapidly to respond to a variety of spoken commands, none acquired speech, or even clearly intelligible word sounds (Hayes, 1951; Kellogg, 1980).

The possibility that primates are physically incapable of producing and controlling the speech sounds of human language led investigators to reconsider the problem of defining language for the purpose of their studies: Is speech itself necessary for us to say that a human has language? Allen and Beatrice Gardner decided that American Sign Language (Ameslan or ASL) was not only a true language, but an appropriate way to test the language capability of chimps. Ameslan is a complex, flexible system of hand signs developed for the deaf using the shape of the hand(s), their relative position, and their movement to convey ideas; it is not a facsimile of English, but a language in its own right, with a distinctive grammar. Since previous home-raised chimps had shown excellent motor control at an earlier age than human infants, the Gardners felt confident that chimps could master Ameslan.

They began their work in 1966 with a female chimp about one year old whom they named Washoe, after the Nevada county where their lab was located. Certain that a chimpanzee could readily learn arbitrary signs to obtain food, drink, and other things, they set a larger goal: ". . . we wanted Washoe not only to ask for objects but to answer questions about them and also to ask us questions. We wanted to develop behavior that could be described as conversation" (Gardner and Gardner, 1969). Reasoning that an environment rich in stimulation and emotional support was important for human language learning, they deliberately created one for Washoe. She lived in a furnished, though chimp-proofed trailer, with numerous toys, books, and magazines to provide topics for signing. She also had human companions during her waking hours, all trained to some degree in Ameslan. To avoid uncertainty about what Washoe was responding to, vocal communication with and around her was prohibited.

The Gardners taught Washoe signs in several ways. Early in the experiment they made regular activities such as bathing, going to bed, and using the potty highly ritualized events involving specific signs. This provided Washoe with plentiful material to imitate, but these efforts produced few signs. Using the instrumental technique of shaping, in which successive approximations to the desired sign were rewarded, the Gardners began helping Washoe acquire a stable vocabulary. Later on, they deliberately taught her some signs by physically molding her hands into the desired conformation. Before recording data on how frequently Washoe used a given sign, they required reports from three different observers that she had used it spontaneously and in an appropriate context. After Washoe had done so on each of fifteen successive days, they regarded the sign as a stable part of her vocabulary. Just under two years into the project, Washoe had acquired 34 signs. By the end of the third year, she knew 85 signs. Her current vocabulary, at age 17, is approximately 180 signs. (See Figure 4.)

In later years the Gardners acquired other animals and offered them similar training, with similar results. Changes in funding transported this small colony of signing chimpanzees from Nevada to the University of Oklahoma for several years and finally to Central Washington University, where Roger Fouts, who began working with the animals as a graduate student of the Gardners, presides over five chimps living in a laboratory approximation of a natural group. Independently of the Gardners, though inspired by their work, Patterson (1978; Patterson and Linden, 1981) carries on a similar project with two gorillas, Koko and Michael, as does Miles (1983) with an orangutan named Chantek.

Even before the Gardners' first reports, Ann and David Premack (1972) had begun training a chimp named Sarah to answer simple questions using plastic tokens instead of words, and their first publications nearly coincided with the Gardners'. Sarah's tokens were completely arbitrary shapes and colors (a blue triangle meant "apple," for instance), and the Premacks gave her very elaborate, step-by-step training in both definitions and sequence of tokens within a statement. (See Figure 5.)

Figure 4. Washoe signing "tickle."

Inspired by both the Gardners and the Premacks, Rumbaugh (1980) developed an arbitrary language called Yerkish (after the Yerkes Primate Center in Atlanta) to communicate first with a female chimp named Lana, then with two males named Sherman and Austin. Its symbols, called lexigrams, are arbitrary designs displayed on the back-lit keys of a large, computer-controlled keyboard. (See Figure 6.) They

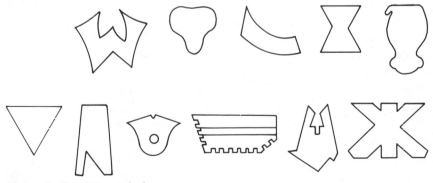

Figure 5. Sarah's symbols.

Figure 6. Yerkish: sample lexigrams.

are moved from key to key randomly so the animals will learn to select the designs rather than locations on the board. The lexigrams of the current message appear on a screen above the board, and all input is recorded by the computer.

Terrace (1979) directed a Gardner-like program with one animal, Nim Chimsky. The Gardners themselves no longer work with chimps. The Premacks' project continues, focused on the cognitive rather than linguistic abilities of their animals. Rumbaugh has extended his lexigram system to work with profoundly retarded humans and has achieved interesting initial results (Romski and Rumbaugh, 1981). Fouts, Patterson, and Miles continue their Ameslan research programs. Fouts has given Washoe an adopted son, Loulis, and studies the transfer of signing from one generation to the next (Fouts, Hirsch, and Fouts, 1982).

Each of these experimenters wrestled with the problem Ann Premack explained: the animals are so engaging that workers may emphasize their human qualities, interpreting results according to extensive informal interaction as well as formal tests. Science, however, requires the results of an experiment to be always the same, even if it is repeated by someone who does not share the theoretical position of the original observer, in this case someone not already enamored of primates. To avoid allowing their expectations or their affection for their subjects to influence the outcome of their experiments, these researchers borrowed an experimental design developed by social psychologists to control the influence of extraneous information on the behavior of human subjects.

This influence arises because subjects often try to "help" the experimenter, modifying their behavior to fit the experimenter's expectations. Even if the experimenter tries to avoid revealing the study's hypothesis, subjects can usually detect from contextual or unintentional kinesic signals what behavior the experimenter expects to find. Animals too detect kinesic cues, and intelligent, observant animals may do it very well. This ability to respond to unintentional signals rather than to the intended stimuli of an experiment has been dubbed the *Clever Hans effect*, after a horse which seemed to do arithmetic. Given a problem, Hans would count out the answer by tapping his hoof the appropriate number of times. Careful testing revealed that he could answer correctly only when he could see people who knew the answers. He would faithfully tap his hoof until he saw a nearly imperceptible relaxation in his trainer; then he would stop tapping. The trainer, of course, would unconsciously relax just as Hans got to the right answer. When his trainer was not present, Hans would read his cues from any human who was paying attention. Oskar Pfungst (1911), the psychologist who unraveled Hans's behavior, found that he himself could not avoid cuing the horse, even after he had figured out what was going on. In other words, Hans was reading fixed action patterns, which are normally unconscious and nearly unalterable. Both sending and receiving nonverbal signals is so fundamental a part of behavior that experiments with living subjects can be seriously distorted by inevitable kinesic communication between researcher and subject.

The experimental design by which most social scientists control cuing of subjects is called a *double-blind*. In this method, neither the person running the experiment nor the one recording data can cue the subject because both are blind to stimuli the subject receives. Consider for example a study to test for the effects of hypnosis on suggestibility. The experimenter decides on the design of the experiment but does not interact with the subjects. Having been told for example that the experiment is about pain perception, the person who actually hypnotizes subjects is blind to the hypothesis. Neither the hypnotized nor the control subjects can gather relevant cues from someone who does not know what behavior the experiment is measuring. The person recording data, not knowing which of the subjects have been hypnotized, is also blind to the experimental manipulation and cannot provide distorting cues.

Obviously, the double blind design can minimize both unconscious cuing and the tendency to anthropomorphize of anyone who works with higher primates. However, double blinds are more difficult to use than other experimental designs. Either more than one person must help with the experiment, or the experimenter must develop a mechanical way of presenting stimuli, recording responses, or both. In any case, those involved must restrain their natural tendencies to interact freely with each other and with their very engaging subjects. Those who do not use such cumbersome methods are not attempting to mislead us with their reports on primate communication; in fact, few studies of language development in children have satisfied the requirements of objectivity that lead experimenters to use the double-blind method. But researchers working in an area as controversial as the language capability of primates must anticipate skepticism from those who have not had contact with young primates of the sort nearly everyone has with human infants. Our own limited experience with nonhuman primates leads us to treat studies that use a double-blind design as more reliable than those that do not.

Figure 7. Washoe's double-blind test.

As the Gardners and others began publishing accounts of symbol-learning experiments with chimpanzees, critics attacked their results as arising from the Clever Hans effect (see de Luce and Wilder, 1983). No one has doubted that the animals perform clearly arbitrary behavior, whether making gestures, manipulating plastic tokens, or punching computer keys. But several critics (Umiker-Sebeok and Sebeok, 1980; Pettito and Seidenberg, 1979; Seidenberg and Pettito, 1979) have charged that the animals are responding to unconscious cues rather than doing anything even remotely languagelike. This interpretation can be answered by successful double-blind tests; and the Gardners early established a reliable double-blind system for testing Washoe's vocabulary. (See Figure 7.) The chimp was enticed to sit in front of a rear-projection screen while one experimenter (E1 in the diagram) sat beside the enclosure, able to see Washoe but not the screen. As images flashed onto the screen in random order, the experimenter asked Washoe to name them, recorded the meaning of her sign on a slip of paper, and dropped the record into a slot. At the same time, a second observer (E2) watched Washoe's signs through a one-way mirror and recorded each meaning. Although located in the same room with the slide projector, this second observer could see neither the slide being shown nor the first observer. A third experimenter (E3) determined the sequence of slides. The Gardners (1980) report that in a typical trial Washoe correctly named 91 (according to E1) or 92 (according to E2) of 128 items.

The obvious meaning of these experiments, confirmed by the Premacks and Rumbaugh using different symbol systems, is that chimpanzees can make the conceptual link between an arbitrary sign and a referent. While some other animals can perform the same kind of feat, only another higher primate, the gorilla, has thus far mastered anything like the sheer quantity of arbitrary signs reported in the various chimp experiments (Walker, 1983).

Critics have rejected even this limited conclusion, arguing that the animals are simply using a learned manuever—whether making a gesture, selecting a plastic token, or punching a computer key—to get something they want from the experimenters (Chomsky, 1980; Umiker-Sebeok and Sebeok, 1980). The charge, in other words, is that the animals are not performing a cognitive function even vaguely analogous to naming familiar objects and actions; they are simply doing tricks for reward, just as a pet mynah bird will say "come in" when it hears a knock on the door. But workers on all the primate language projects report spontaneous signaling that sometimes names, instead of soliciting. The Gardners (1969) describe Washoe's simply naming a toothbrush, an object she disliked, on entering a room and seeing one. Patterson and Linden (1981) report the gorilla Koko signing to herself while flipping through magazines. Even Terrace, who counts as a critic of the chimp work, reports (1979) that only 40% of Nim's signs were imitations or reductions of a teacher's signs; some of Nim's signs were spontaneous, unprompted, and unsolicited. Finally, Savage-Rumbaugh, Rumbaugh, and Boysen (1978) have run elaborate experiments requiring Sherman and Austin to exchange information through lexigrams so they could use appropriate tools to extricate food from various containers. The animals were placed in different rooms, and one was allowed to watch a human put food into one of six different kinds of container. After the human left, whichever animal knew where the food was hidden could use the keyboard to ask his comrade for the appropriate tool. If they completed the transaction successfully, they could share the prize. Allowed to use lexigrams, each would readily ask for or give the appropriate tool; deprived of lexigrams, each would present the available tools in random order, or persistently offer the same tool. Having or not having access to the arbitrary symbols of Yerkish completely changed how they solved their problem. In a reductive sense, of course, Sherman and Austin were doing tricks, but so is any student who takes a test. Their different ways of solving the problem indicate that one trick they have is using a shared set of arbitrary symbols to represent things. The Premacks (1983) also found that Sarah's language training improved her problem-solving ability, even when word symbols were not involved. Whatever tricks Sarah performs, learning to represent things by arbitrary symbols has improved her cognitive skills.

The symbol systems used by Rumbaugh and the Premacks impose sequence on the signs—left to right for Rumbaugh, top to bottom for Premack. Lana, for example, had to begin each request with a lexigram interpreted as "start," end it with another interpreted as "stop," and use English active-voice word order for the symbols in between. Typical commands (transcribed) are, *"start give banana stop"*; *"start trainer tickle Lana stop"*; and *"start machine make window open stop."* Analogous arbitrary sequence rules governed the Premacks' token system; both projects treated misordered sign sequences as errors. So when Washoe began stringing Ameslan signs together, it became possible to ask whether the animals had learned something like syntax in human language. Initially, David Premack (1971) and the Gardners (1975) argued that they had. The Premacks' claim was based on Sarah's ability to carry out instructions such as these (reading top to bottom):

Sarah	Sarah	Sarah	Sarah
banana	chocolate	apple	cracker
		cracker	candy
			yellow
dish	dish	dish	dish
apple	chocolate	cracker	cracker
			blue
pail	pail	pail	pail
insert	insert	insert	insert

The commands required Sarah to put the first item(s) into the first receptacle and the second item(s) into the second receptacle. First the Premacks taught her the simple type of command in the left column, then the progressively more complicated ones. Her high degree of success in carrying out these instructions—80%, even for the most complex instruction involving grouped items and colored receptacles— indicates that she understood the importance of symbol sequence in the commands. And sequence, or word order, is certainly important in the grammars of many languages—including English, the native language of these researchers. But in every human language, a sentence has hierarchical as well as linear structure. The sentence "Sebastian has bound books," for instance, has two different meanings, each described by a different way of grouping words (*immediate constituent analysis*). If *has bound* is the verb phrase, the sentence means that Sebastian has worked at binding books. If *has* is the verb phrase and *bound* an adjective modifying *books,* the sentence means that Sebastian owns books that are bound. Our ability to recognize such ambiguity demonstrates that we know something more about the possible structures of this sentence than the order of its words tells us. Because the rigidity of the arbitrary systems invented by the Premacks and Rumbaugh prohibits structurally ambiguous sentences, their animals' success does not indicate mastery of syntax.

In fact, a much simpler explanation is available. Straub (1979) trained pigeons to peck four colors in rigid sequence to obtain food. Labeling the four colors with words to produce English sentences like "please give me corn," "start give corn stop," "dammit, where's the corn," does not mean that pigeons have learned syntax. Although critics have argued that the chimpanzees have simply learned to put one symbol after another, the comparison to pigeons is unfair in the sense that Sarah and the Rumbaugh chimps learned to insert a variety of signs into the slots provided by their symbol systems. In fact, Sherman and Austin can reliably identify a number of lexigrams as belonging to the tool or the food classes, and Sarah clearly grasps the concept "name of." Still, the systems themselves preclude any evidence of the hierarchical structure that is essential to syntax.

The Gardners (1980) have offered a similar analysis of the Premacks' and Rumbaugh's work, and argued that because they themselves did not deliberately teach word order to Ameslan-signing chimps, the evidence for sequence rules in Washoe and her companions is significant. They claim, in fact, that the chimps' acquisition of sign-sequence regularities is analogous to that of very young children learning spoken or sign language. But one can tell little about syntax rules from two- and three-symbol utterances, even in children; the sequences are too short to indicate the hierarchical structure essential in syntax (Limber, 1980). No reliable evidence indicates that the two-word utterances of children have genuine syntax; only when children begin overgeneralizing inflection rules to produce forms they have never heard, such as *mans instead of *men*, can we be certain they are using any linguistic rules at all. We see firm evidence of syntax only with the development of telegraphic speech.

In addition, Terrace (1979, 1983) found as he analyzed videotapes of Nim's signing sequences that often a query or prompt from the human teacher would intervene between Nim's signs. Because Ameslan is a visual language, two people can be "talking" simultaneously with much less confusion than arises in a verbal language. Terrace observed that Nim's teachers would often hold their first sign or begin another while Nim was making his first one. If Nim then made a second sign, his total performance could be transcribed as either a two-sign combination or as two unconnected signs, each responding to a different prompt from the teacher. The usual sort of written transcript, in which words represent the kinetic signs of Ameslan, disguises such overlap. Terrace also noticed that Nim's utterances did not steadily get longer; instead, they fluctuated in average length between 1.1 and 1.6 signs. While all the signing apes do occasionally produce long strings of signs, they do so by simple repetition. Nim's longest string, for example, was *give orange me give eat orange me eat orange give me eat orange give me you*. The string contains sixteen signs but is clearly not a syntactic unit. In contrast, as children progress from the two-word stage to telegraphic speech, the mean length of their utterances grows very rapidly, reaching about 4.0 by 43 months of age in hearing children

(Brown, 1973) and somewhat less (2.8–3.1 by 50 months of age) in deaf children learning Ameslan (Klima and Bellugi, 1972; Terrace, 1979, p. 211). These numbers come from very small samples (two children in each category), and *mean length of utterance* is an extremely crude measure of development. It favors speaking over signing subjects because it counts morphemes, in which spoken language is much richer than Ameslan. Even so, Nim's utterances did not increase significantly in average length, while those of children get longer and longer as the children master morphemics and syntax.

Terrace's project suffered from clear limitations. Because Nim worked long hours in a comparatively sterile environment with a parade of more than fifty teachers, his performance may well be inferior to that of animals enjoying happier circumstances (Fouts, 1983; Terrace, 1983). Still, Walker (1983) seems right in rejecting the arguments for even elementary syntax in trained apes. Experimental designs such as those of the Premacks and Rumbaugh, which insist on a rigid sequence of symbols, cannot avoid the strong implication that the animals have simply learned arbitrary sequence. The Ameslan experiments are only slightly less susceptible to the same argument, and their sign sequence data is cloudy. Even if it were not, two-sign units do not contain enough material to imply hierarchical syntax.

What then have all the signing ape projects accomplished? They seem to have shown that apes do not have a latent capacity for human language, but that is hardly a significant finding. As Chomsky (1980, p. 433) observes, "it would be something of a biological miracle . . . to discover that some other species had a [language] capacity but had never thought to put it to use, despite the remarkable advantages it would confer, until instructed by humans." Only Patterson and to a lesser degree Fouts continue to claim that the animals have even quasi-human language capacity. Criticisms of the signing ape research are not groundless. Sometimes the animals did respond to inadvertent cuing. Every time the Premacks, for example, introduced some variation in procedure to decrease Sarah's access to cues, her performance declined, and David Premack (1976) faithfully reported that development. But speculation (Umiker-Sebeok and Sebeok, 1980) about the possibility of cuing does not negate the results (summarized in Fouts and Rigby, 1980; Gardner and Gardner, 1980) of experiments that control for it, such as the Gardners' double-blind vocabulary tests. Clearly, a number of animals have learned the meanings of a large number of symbols.

Again, some of the animals' performance can be attributed to their learning an arbitrary string of actions that elicits prizes. If we think of vocabulary testing for these animals as a game, we can never be sure that they are always playing exactly the same game we are; ours may involve word meanings while theirs involves blue triangles, scratching the top of one's left hand, or picking out the three wavy lines. The very strong implication is that the early stages of training consist of exactly such parallel games. But later developments suggest with equal clarity that the animals master the notion of symbolic meaning. The total body of experiments with plastic tokens, Yerkish, and Ameslan has demonstrated that apes can learn to use semantically a large number of arbitrary symbols. That achievement is more than the most hostile critics will allow. But it is also considerably less than human semantic abilities. No ape seems to have anything like the rich, interlocked network of semantic relationships characteristic of human vocabulary. The name of the waterfall does not appear to evoke its sound for them.

The strongest critics of work on language capabilities in primates would agree with Chomsky (1980, p. 436) that "the analogies observed between human language and the systems taught to apes are not particularly suggestive, at least in the domains where something nontrivial is known about human language." Since he defines those domains as the structural principles and ontogenetic development of language in humans, his statement can hardly be faulted; he simply reasserts that human language is species specific. The work with symbolizing apes does provide experimental support for that claim, which was previously grounded on evolutionary theory alone; and since the ways of evolution are devious at best, the support is worth having. But Chomsky goes on to argue that even if we had discovered latent language capacity in apes, the discovery would be meaningless because it would "leave the scientific problems concerning human language exactly where they now stand. We would . . . face a dual problem, replacing the single problem to which research is currently addressed: what is the nature of human language in its mature and initial stage" (p. 439). His definition of the single problem to which research is currently addressed no doubt came as a surprise to everyone studying animal communication, and to most people studying how language fits into other systems of human communication, since it omits entirely the subjects of their research.

The expanding body of information on animal communication in general and the acquisition of symbol systems by primates in particular is in fact valuable to students of human language. First, it helps us to understand, however vaguely, the mental worlds of animals we often consider mindless if not senseless. And for linguists particularly, the study of ape signing provides a rare contrast to normal human language competence. Parallels between teaching signs to chimps and to severely retarded humans have already proved instructive (Romski and Rumbaugh, 1981). Last, because language does not leave fossils in the ground, we are unlikely to resolve completely all our questions about how it evolved. But we might resolve some of them by examining the closest thing to language fossils we have: the communicative and cognitive capacities of our nearest relatives.

Whereas careful study has shown how much human communication takes place on the level of affective displays using fixed action patterns, the same studies have shown just how great a gap separates animal use of symbols from our own. Human language is an additional symbolic layer, extremely rich in hierarchical rule systems, superimposed on an existing pattern of communication that we share with other animals. This new layer has led to rapid alteration of every facet of our social structure and even to changes in the way we perceive the world. Only another human can understand the symbolic levels in the statement, "you can make a monkey out of a man, but you can't make a man out of a monkey."

References

Brown, R. (1973), *A First Language: The Early Stages*. Cambridge, MA: Harvard University Press.

Caldwell, D. K., and M. C. Caldwell (1977), "Cetaceans," in T. A. Sebeok, (ed.), *How Animals Communicate*. Bloomington: Indiana University Press.

Chomsky, N. (1980), "Human Language and Other Semiotic Systems," in T. A. Sebeok, and J. Umiker-Sebeok (eds.), *Speaking of Apes: A Critical Anthology of Two-Way Communication With Man*. New York: Plenum Press.

De Luce, J. and H. T. Wilder (1983), "Introduction," in J. de Luce and H. T. Wilder (eds.), *Language in Primates: Perspective and Implications*. New York: Springer-Verlag.

Fouts, R. (1983) "Apes and Language: The Search for Communicative Competence," in J. de Luce and H. T. Wilder (eds.), *Language in Primates: Perspective and Implications*. New York: Springer-Verlag.

Fouts, R., A. D. Hirsch, and D. H. Fouts (1982), "Cultural Transmission of a Human Language in a Chimpanzee Mother-Infant Relationship," in H. E. Fitzgerald et al. (eds.), *Child Nurturance 3*. New York: Plenum Press.

Fouts, R. and R. Rigby (1980), "Man-Chimpanzee Communication," in T. A. Sebeok, and J. Umiker-Sebeok (eds.), *Speaking of Apes: A Critical Anthology of Two-Way Communication With Man*. New York: Plenum Press.

Gardner, B. T. and R. A. Gardner (1969), "Teaching Sign Language to a Chimpanzee." *Science* 165:664–672.

———. (1975), "Evidence for Sentence Constituents in the Early Utterances of Child and Chimpanzee." *Journal of Experimental Psychology: General* 104(3):244–276.

Gardner, R. A., and B. T. Gardner (1980), "Comparative Psychology and Language Acquisition," in T. A. Sebeok and J. Umiker-Sebeok (eds.), *Speaking of Apes: A Critical Anthology of Two-Way Communication With Man*. New York: Plenum Press.

Goodall, J. (1971) *In the Shadow of Man*. Boston: Houghton Mifflin.

Gould, J. L. and C. G. Gould (1983), "Can a Bee Behave Intelligently?" *New Scientist* 98:84–87.

Griffin, D. R. (1981) *The Question of Animal Awareness: Evolutionary Continuity of Mental Experience*, 2nd ed. New York: Rockefeller University Press.

Hayes, C. H. (1951) *The Ape in Our House*. New York: Harper & Row.

Hinde, R. A. (1970) *Animal Behaviour: A Synthesis of Ethology and Comparative Psychology*, 2nd ed. New York: McGraw-Hill.

Hockett, C. F. and S. A. Altmann (1968), "A Note on Design Features," in T. A. Sebeok (ed.), *Animal Communication*. Bloomington: University of Indiana Press.

Immelmann, K. (1969), "Song Development in the Zebra Finch and Other Estrildid Finches," in R. A. Hinde (ed.), *Bird Vocalizations*. Cambridge: Cambridge University Press.

Kellogg, W. N. (1980), "Communication and Language in the Home-Raised Chimpanzee," in T. A. Sebeok and J. Umiker-Sebeok (eds.), *Speaking of Apes: A Critical Anthology of Two-Way Communication With Man*. New York: Plenum Press.

Klima, E. S. and U. Bellugi (1972), "The Signs of Language in Child and Chimpanzee," in T. Alloway, et al. (eds.), *Communication and Affect*. New York: Academic Press.

Konishi, M. (1973), "Locatable and Non-Locatable Acoustic Signals for Barn Owls." *American Naturalist* 107:775–785.

Konishi, M. and F. Nottebaum (1969), "Experimental Studies in the Ontogeny of Avian Vocalizations," in R. A. Hinde (ed.), *Bird Vocalizations*. Cambridge: Cambridge University Press.

Lilly, J. C. (1975), *Lilly on Dolphins*. Garden City, N.Y.: Anchor Books.

Limber, J. (1980), "Language in Child and Chimpanzee?" in T. A. Sebeok and J. Umiker-Sebeok (eds.), *Speaking of Apes: A Critical Anthology of Two-Way Communication With Man*. New York: Plenum Press.

Lindauer, M. (1961), *Communication Among Social Bees*. Cambridge, MA: Harvard University Press.

Marler, P. (1955), "Characteristics of Some Animal Calls." *Nature* 176:6–7.

———. (1957), "Specific Distinctiveness in the Communication Signals of Birds." *Behaviour* 11:13–39.

Marler, P. and M. Tamura (1964), "Culturally Transmitted Patterns of Vocal Behavior in Sparrows." *Science* 146:1483–1486.

Mech, L. D. (1970), *The Wolf: The Ecology and Behavior of an Endangered Species*. Garden City, NY: Natural History Press.

Miles, H. L. (1983), "Apes and Language: the Search for Communicative Competence," in J. de Luce and H. T. Wilder (eds.), *Language in Primates: Perspectives and Implications*. New York: Springer-Verlag.

Nottebaum, F. (1975), "Vocal Behavior in Birds," in D. S. Farner, et al. (eds.), *Avian Biology V*. New York: Academic Press.

Patterson, F. (1978), "The Gestures of a Gorilla: Sign Language in Another Pongoid Species." *Brain and Language* 5:72–97.

Patterson, F., and E. Linden (1981), *The Education of Koko*. New York: Holt, Rinehart and Winston.

Peters, R. (1980), *Mammalian Communication: A Behavioral Analysis of Meaning*. Monterey, CA: Brooks/Cole.

Pettito, L. A. and M. S. Seidenberg (1979), "On the Evidence for Linguistic Abilities in Signing Apes." *Brain and Language* 8:162–183.

Pfungst, O. (1911), *Clever Hans, the Horse of Mr. von Osten.* New York: Holt. (ed. R. Rosenthal. New York: Holt, Rinehart and Winston, 1965).

Premack, A. (1976), *Why Chimps Can Read.* Harper & Row: New York.

Premack, D. (1971), "Language in Chimpanzee?" *Science* 172:808–822.

———. (1972), "Teaching Language to an Ape." *Scientific American* 227:92–99.

———. (1976), *Intelligence in Ape and Man.* Hillsdale, N.J.: Lawrence Erlbaum.

Premack, D. and A. Premack (1983), *The Mind of an Ape.* New York: W. W. Norton.

Romski, M. A. and D. M. Rumbaugh (1981), "Computer Based Language Training." *Education and Training of the Mentally Retarded,* 16:193–200.

Rumbaugh, D. M. (1980), "Language Behavior in Apes," in T. A. Sebeok and J. Umiker-Sebeok (eds.), *Speaking of Apes: A Critical Anthology of Two-Way Communication With Man.* New York: Plenum Press.

Savage-Rumbaugh, S., D. M. Rumbaugh, and S. Boysen (1978), "Linguistically Mediated Tool Use and Exchange by Chimpanzees, (*Pan troglodytes*)." *Behavioral and Brain Sciences* 1:539–54.

Schaller, G. B. (1963), *The Mountain Gorilla: Ecology and Behavior.* Chicago: University of Chicago Press.

———. (1972), *The Serengeti Lion.* Chicago: University of Chicago Press.

Seidenberg, M. S. and L. A. Pettito (1979), "Signing Behavior in Apes: A Critical Review." *Cognition* 7:177–215.

Smith, W. John (1977a), *The Behavior of Communicating.* Cambridge, MA: Harvard University Press.

———. (1977b), "Communication in Birds," in T. A. Sebeok (ed.), *How Animals Communicate.* Bloomington: Indiana University Press.

Smith, W. John, S. L. Smith, E. C. Oppenheimer, and J. G. DeVilla (1977), "Vocalizations of the Black-Tailed Prairie Dog *Cynomys ludovicianus.*" *Animal Behaviour,* 25:152–164.

Straub, R. O. (1979), "Serial Learning in the Pigeon." *Journal of the Experimental Analysis of Behavior,* 32:137–48.

Terrace, H. S. (1979), *Nim: A Chimp Who Learned Sign Language.* New York: Alfred A. Knopf.

———. (1983), "Apes Who 'Talk': Language or Projection of Language by Their Teachers?" in J. de Luce and H. T. Wilder (eds.), *Language in Primates: Perspective and Implications.* New York: Springer-Verlag.

Thielke, G. (1969), "Geographic Variation in Bird Vocalizations," in R. A. Hinde, (ed.), *Bird Vocalization.* Cambridge: Cambridge University Press.

Thorpe, W. H. (1958), "The Learning of Song Patterns by Birds, With Especial Reference to the Song of the Chaffinch *Fringilla coelebs.*" *Ibis* 100:535–570.

Umiker-Sebeok, J. and T. A. Sebeok (1980), "Introduction: Questioning apes," in T. A. Sebeok and J. Umiker-Sebeok (eds.), *Speaking of Apes: A Critical Anthology of Two-Way Communication With Man.* New York: Plenum Press.

Von Frisch, K. (1966), *The Dancing Bees.* New York: Harcourt, Brace & World.

———. (1967), *A Biologist Remembers.* Trans. Lisbeth Gombrich. Oxford: Pergamon Press.

———. (1971) *Bees: Their Vision, Chemical Senses, and Language,* rev. ed. Ithaca, N.Y.: Cornell University Press.

Walker, S. (1983) *Animal Thought.* London: Routledge and Kegan Paul.

Wilson, E. O. (1971) *The Insect Societies.* Cambridge, MA: Harvard University Press.

FOR DISCUSSION AND REVIEW

1. Explain why ethologists and linguists believe that studying different kinds of animal communication is important.

2. In analyzing animal communication, ethologists use the terms *form, context,* and *response.* Define each term, and give an original example illustrating each.

3. Kemp and Smith state that "distinctive behavior that reliably indicates what an animal will do promotes cooperation and reduces conflict, because it allows neighbors to adjust their actions according to what the display predicts." Drawing on your own experience, write brief descriptions of three situations involving animals that illustrate this principle.

4. Explain the relationship between the *allophones* of human speech and animal *displays.*

5. Review Hockett's "design features" discussed by W. F. Bolton (pp. 4–6). To what extent does animal communication embody these features? Be specific; you may wish to consider only bees, or birds, or mammals, etc.

6. Explain the differences between bird *calls* and *songs;* be sure to consider the functions of each.

7. Review the articles by Neil Smith and Deirdre Wilson (pp. 325–339) and Frank Heny (pp. 294–323). Then write a short explanation of William Kemp and Roy Smith's statement that "the analogy between this template [in the males of some species of birds] and Chomsky's hypothesis of a genetically supported universal grammar in humans is obvious."

8. Explain the implications for comparisons of human language and animal communication of Kemp and Smith's statement that "the fundamental feature of animal communication persists in even the most highly social mammals: the value of displays does not depend on a desire to tell another animal something."

9. Why are specialists from many disciplines especially interested in studying nonhuman primate communication?

10. Write a short description of a *double-blind* experimental design. Why is this an important technique?

11. In all human languages, sentences have both hierarchical and linear structure. What is the significance of this fact to conclusions based on the work done with nonhuman primates?

4/Languages and Writing

JOHN P. HUGHES

*Most Americans take mass literacy for granted; they find it difficult
to imagine not being able to read and write, and they are surprised
to learn that even today a significant proportion of the world's currently spoken three thousand to five thousand languages lack writing
systems. In the following chapter from his book* The Science of Language, *Professor John P. Hughes suggests the limitations that the
lack of a writing system can impose. He traces in detail the evolution
of writing systems, sometimes logical and sometimes not, from the
earliest Cro-Magnon cave drawings to present-day systems. Important
to note is his explanation of the advantages of alphabetic systems, and
the unique nature of their origin.*

It has been said that the two oldest and greatest inventions of man
were the wheel and the art of controlling fire. This is probable enough:
and if one wished to make a group of three, surely the development
of writing must claim the third place. Without a system of writing, no
matter how wise or sublime the thought, once uttered it is gone forever
(in its original form, at least) as soon as its echoes have died away.

Indeed, it would seem that without a means of preserving wisdom
and culture, civilization, which depends on the passing on of a heritage
from generation to generation, could not develop. The facts, however,
are otherwise: noteworthy civilizations *have* arisen and flourished without possession of any form of writing, usually by forming a class of
society whose duty and profession it was to keep in memory what we
write down in books (and, too often, subsequently forget). Even the
average citizen in such a society took as a matter of course demands
upon his memory which we today would consider beyond human
capacity.

All the same, one may question whether a really complex civilization—one capable of governing large areas, for instance—could be
supported by such a system. If there ever was one, we may be sure it
has been grossly slighted by history—which, after all, depends almost
entirely on written records. Who, for example, has ever heard the
Gaulish version of Caesar's campaigns?

698

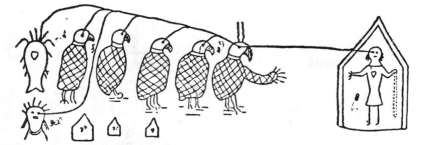

Figure 1. An Indian pictographic message. This message of friendship was sent from an American Indian chief to the president of the United States— the figure in the White House. The chief, identified by the lines rising from his head, who is sending the message, and the four warriors behind him, belong to the eagle totem; the fifth warrior is of the catfish totem. The figure at lower left is evidently also a powerful chief. The lines joining the eyes indicate harmony, and the three houses indicate the willingness of the Indians to adopt white men's customs. (From Henry R. Schoolcraft, *Historical and Statistical Information Respecting the Indian Tribes of America*, I, 418.)

Ideographic Writing

There seems to be no reason to doubt that the many systems of writing which have been developed at different times by various peoples during mankind's long history all grew, by steps which we can and shall trace, out of man's ability to draw pictures.

Suppose you wish to preserve a record of your catching a twenty-pound trout, but happen to be illiterate. The obvious thing to do would be to draw and hang a picture of yourself catching the big fish. It was, apparently, an equally obvious thing to do some fifty thousand years ago, for the caves which yielded us the remains of the Cro-Magnon man first attracted attention because of their beautifully drawn pictures of a procession, perhaps a hunt, of animals. We shall never know whether this was a mere decoration or a record.

Given the ability to draw well enough so that your representations of persons and objects can be readily recognized, it is, of course, not difficult to tell a complete story in one panoramic picture, or in a series of uncaptioned sketches. The range of information that can be conveyed in this way can be greatly extended if a few simple conventions are agreed upon between the artist and his prospective audience: the use of a totem-sign for a certain tribe; considering a prone man to be sick or wounded if his eyes were open, dead if they are closed, and so on. Several tribes of North American Indians made use of this kind of communication (Figure 1).

In these circumstances, it will be noted, pictures act as a means for the communication of thought, and thus are somewhat like a language in themselves. Indeed, some authorities include this kind of

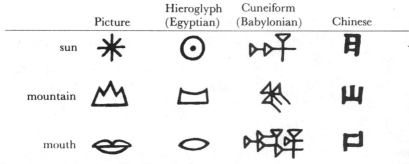

Figure 2. Conventionalized symbols.

communication among various forms of "language," but we have deliberately excluded it from our definition. It is common and conventional to call this kind of writing *ideographic writing*, and while the term is convenient, this is properly in no sense either language or writing, as we shall proceed to show.

Note, first, that the kind of communication achieved in Figure 1 is totally independent of the language or languages of the persons who make the drawing and of those who read it. The "text" may be correctly "read" in any language. It is not an effort to record the *language* in which the event is described, but, like language itself, to record the *original events:* we might even say it is a system alternative to language for symbolizing events. And therefore it is not strictly writing; for writing is always a *record or representation of language.*

Ideographic "writing" cannot be strictly language either, for it has two limitations which would make it unworkable as a system for expressing human thought. First, it is not within everyone's competence: some of us have no talent for drawing. This, however, could be offset by conventionalizing the characters to a few simple strokes, not immediately recognizable as the original picture except by previous knowledge of the convention (See Figure 2).

But then the second, more serious objection still remains: even with such conventionalization, the system cannot adequately express the whole range of human thought; and to do so even partially will require thousands of characters and a system of such complexity that exceedingly few in the society could master it.

The Chinese people have an ancient and beautiful script which was originally, and still is largely, ideographic. The characters have been conventionalized, but it is still quite easy to recognize their origin, as was shown in Figure 2. Although there are many mutually unintelligible dialects of Chinese, the same written text can be read by any native (each in his own dialect), and the gist can even be made out by one who knows the principles of the system, but little of the language.

Chinese writing is thus one of the strongest forces toward Chinese cultural unity. . . . But it is estimated that 70,000 to 125,000 characters exist (not all, of course, used with equal frequency), and it is said that a scholar takes seven years to learn to read and write Chinese if he already speaks it, while over 80 percent of the native speakers of Chinese are illiterate in their own language.

Where there is considerable divergence between a language and its written representation, as in the case of Chinese or Italian, where many different dialects are written with the same spelling, or in French or English, where the language has changed considerably since the stage for which the writing was devised, a tendency may arise to consider the written language the "correct" language, of which the spoken language is a deformation which should be "corrected" to agree with the writing. This is particularly true when the writing either records, or once recorded, or is believed to record, the speech of a class of society which enjoys prestige, to which many native speakers would like to assimilate themselves.

This, however, always obscures things and puts the cart before the horse. Actually, the prestige class of any society probably least conforms its speech consciously to writing: sure of their status, its members do not worry about betraying an inferior origin in speech or behavior. It is said that if a man's table manners are absolutely disgusting, he is either a peasant or a duke. Writing is, in its essence, nothing but a means of recording language with some degree of efficiency. Whether one form or another of the language is "good" or "correct" is an entirely different question; a system of writing is good or bad according as it records, accurately or otherwise, whatever form of the language it is aiming to record.

However, because of the prestige of letters in largely illiterate populations (which is so great that *gramarye* has even been thought to have magic power), the opposite tendency to "correct" language according to written forms has been so strong as to lead to such things as the creation of a word like "misle" from a misreading of the word "misled."[1] Many similar examples could be given.

Pictographic Writing

Any nation which finds occasion to use a form of ideographic writing with any regularity, even if all the writing is the job of one relatively small social group, will probably sooner or later take the simple and logical step to *pictographic writing.* In this case, the written

---

[1] This is an extreme case of what is called "spelling pronunciation." More typical examples are the pronunciation, by Americans in England, of words like *twopence* and *halfpenny* as written.

sign, which in ideographic writing is the symbol for an *idea*, becomes the symbol of a *word*. For example, a device like

┌◻

which represents the floor-plan of a house, now becomes a sign for *per*, the Egyptian word for "house," or of *beyt'*, the Hebrew word for "house." Another example: the picture

conventionalized to

which of course represented the snout of an ox, now becomes a sign for *alep*, the ancient Hebrew word for "ox."

The advantages of this step for the improvement of communication are evident. The written sign now symbolizes, not an idea, but a word, and a word is a far more precise symbol of a mental concept than any other which can be devised. With a sufficient stock of symbols of this new type, the writer can distinguish among a house, a stable, a barn, a shed, and a palace; whereas with ideographic writing he is pretty well limited to "house" vs. "big house" or "small house" (as there is no separate symbol for the adjective, the bigness or smallness cannot be specified and can range from "largish" to "enormous"). Much ambiguity is avoided: if you have tried to convey messages ideographically . . . you know how easy it is for an intended message "the king is angry" to be interpreted "the old man is sick."

Pictographic writing is, moreover, true writing, since it is a means of recording language, not just an alternative way of expressing the concepts which language expresses.

All pictographic writing systems that we know have developed from ideographic systems, and show clear traces of this, notably in their tendency to preserve ideographic symbols among the pictographic. Thus, the ancient Egyptians had an ideograph for water, a representation of waves or ripples:

〜〜〜

Eventually they derived from this a sign

〜〜〜
〜〜〜
〜〜〜

standing for the *mu*, which meant "water." But they often wrote the word *mu* as follows:

And in writing of a river, the word for which was *atur*,

they also added the water sign: *atur* was written

The purpose of these ideographic "determinants" was probably to help the reader who did not know the particular word or sign by giving an indication of its general connotation. Nouns denoting persons were usually given the "determinant" of a little man—

or a little woman—

For, despite the noteworthy increases in efficiency which pictographic writing represents, thousands of characters are still necessary; and one advantage of the ideographic system has been lost—the characters are no longer self-explanatory. (This is only a theoretical advantage on behalf of ideographic script, since, while the ideographic character for a bird should presumably be readily recognized as a bird, in practice the characters have to be conventionalized for the sake of those who do not draw well.)

A considerable number of pictographic writing systems have been developed at different times in different parts of the world, but, Sunday-supplement science to the contrary notwithstanding, quite independently of one another, so that we have no ground for talking about the "evolution" by man of the art of writing. There is no evidence whatever for a First Cave Man who sat with hammer and chisel and stone and figured out how to chisel the first message, after which man made improvement after improvement, until the peak (represented, of course, by English orthography of the present day) was reached. Actually, nations once literate have been known to lapse into illiteracy as a result of ruinous wars and social disorganization.

Syllabic Writing, Unlimited and Limited

The step from pictographic to syllabic writing is an easy, logical and, it might very well seem, self-evident one; yet there have been several nations which developed the first without ever proceeding to the second. It would probably be safe to say, however, that a majority of those who came as far as pictographic writing took the step to syllabic script.

In pictographic writing it is, of course, as easy to develop a stock of thousands of characters as in ideographic; yet, strange as it might seem, there is still always a shortage. This shortage arises because it is extremely difficult or impossible to represent some words in pictures. Take "velocity," for example. Is there any picture you could draw to express this that might not be read as, say, "the man is running"? Or, if you think you could picture "velocity," how would you handle "acceleration"? If you still think you could manage this one, what sort of picture, pray, would you draw for the word "the"?

The first step toward syllabic writing is taken when you permit youself to cheat a little and take advantage of homophones. There is, let us say, a good pictograph for "the sea"; you use it to express the Holy "See," or "I see" (writing, perhaps, the characters for *eye* and *sea*).

When you have expressed the word "icy" by the characters for *eye* and *sea*, or *belief* by the characters for *bee* and *leaf*, you have turned the corner to syllabic writing. Any relationship whatever between the character and the *meaning* of the syllable it stands for is henceforth entirely irrelevant. The character expresses nothing but a sequence of sounds—the sounds making up one of the syllables of the language.

The first result of this is a gain of efficiency: a decrease in the number of possible characters (since more than one word or syllable can be written with the same syllabic character—in fact a great number can be written with varying sequences and combinations of a rather small number of characters). This gain is largely theoretical, however, for there will still be several thousand characters. The superiority of syllabic writing over pictographic from the point of view of efficiency will largely depend on the structure of syllables in the language using it. If syllables are generally or always simple in structure, a syllabic system of writing may work extremely well.

In every type of language, however, ambiguity and duplication are likely to be discovered in this kind of *unlimited syllabic* writing. It is often uncertain which of various homonymous readings is intended (e.g., does a character for "deep" joined to one for "end" mean "deep end" or "depend"?). And conversely, there are almost always two or more ways to say the same thing.

If the users of a syllabic system have a sense of logic, they will soon tend to adopt the practice of always writing the same syllable with the same character. The immediate result of this is for the first time to reduce the number of signs to manageable proportions: the sequence *baba* will always be expressed by signs expressing BA BA— never by signs for syllables such as BAB HA, BA ABA, 'B AB HA. Hence the number of signs is not so great as not to be within the capacity of the more or less average memory.

Since many languages have only one syllable-type—CV (i.e., consonant followed by vowel)—application of the principle above to the syllabic writing of such a language results in a very simple, logical and efficient system, next to alphabetic writing the most efficient writing possible.

The simplicity and efficiency are likely to prove elusive, however, when applied to languages of more complex syllabic structure. Even so, one almost inevitably arrives at the idea of having a series of signs representing syllables in which each consonant of the language is paired with each vowel: BA, BE, BI, BO, BU; DA, DE, DI, DO, DU; FA, FE, FI, FO, FU; and so on. A list of such signs is called a *syllabary*.

Some time after this stage of *limited syllabic writing* has been reached, the thought may occur that the inventory of signs can be further reduced by taking one form, without any specification, as the form for, say, BA; and then simply using diacritic marks to indicate the other possible syllable structures: something like the following:

△ BA	⟁ BI	⟁ BU
⟁ BE	⟁ BO	

This brings us very close to alphabetic writing. The last step in syllabic writing and the first in alphabetic writing might come about by accident; suppose a class of words ends in a syllable *-ba*, and in the course of time the vowel ceases to be pronounced. Now the syllabic sign △ stands for B alone, not BA; and some sign (in Sanskrit *virāma*, in Arabic *sukūn*) is invented to express this situation: e.g., △ will express BA, and △ will express B. By use of this sign the vowel of any syllabic sign can be suppressed, and any sign in the syllabary can be made alphabetic.

A situation like that just described is seen in the Semitic writing systems (Arabic, Hebrew), of which it is often said that they "write only the consonants." Actually, all the Arabic and Hebrew letters were originally syllabic signs, representing the consonant *and* a vowel (see Figure 3).

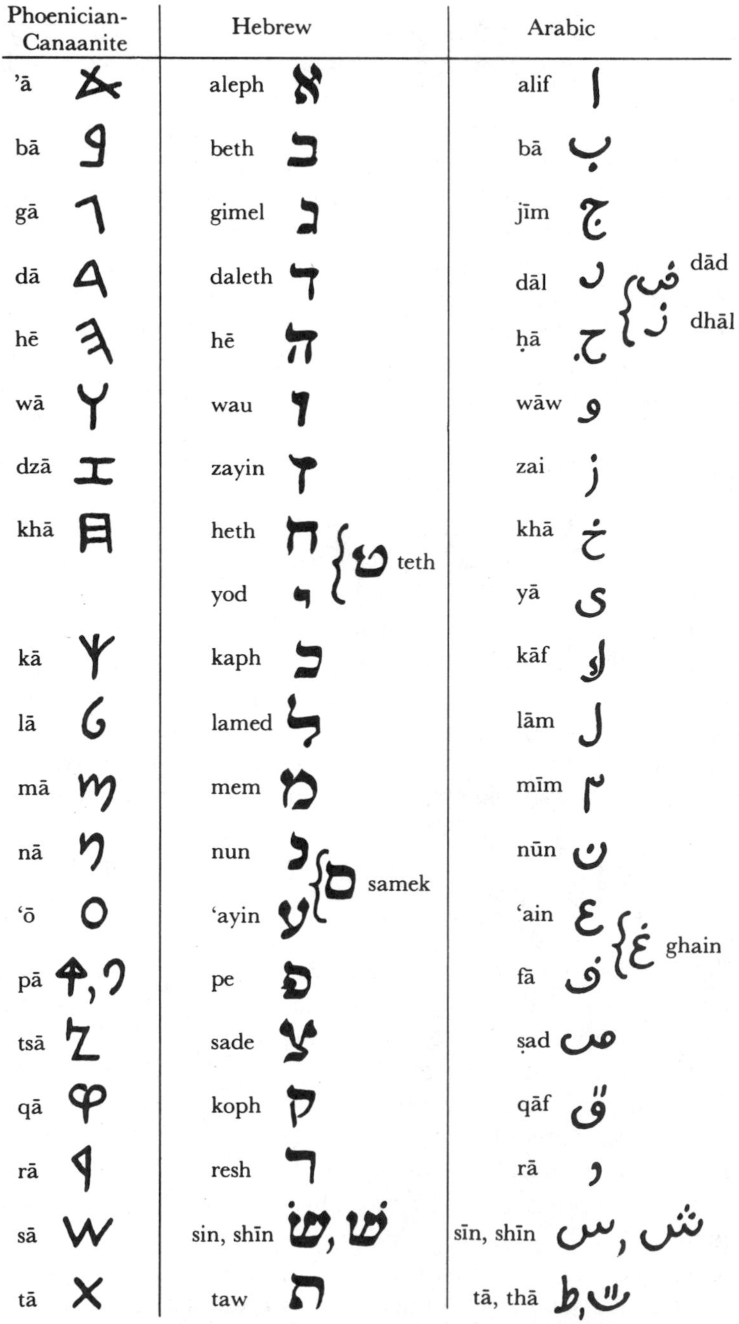

Phoenician-Canaanite		Hebrew		Arabic	
'ā	𐤀	aleph	א	alif	ا
bā	𐤁	beth	ב	bā	ب
gā	𐤂	gimel	ג	jīm	ج
dā	𐤃	daleth	ד	dāl	د dād / dhāl
hē	𐤄	hē	ה	ḥā	ح
wā	𐤅	wau	ו	wāw	و
dzā	𐤆	zayin	ז	zai	ز
khā	𐤇	heth	ח {teth	khā	خ
		yod	י	yā	ى
kā	𐤊	kaph	כ	kāf	ك
lā	𐤋	lamed	ל	lām	ل
mā	𐤌	mem	מ	mīm	م
nā	𐤍	nun	נ	nūn	ن
'ō	𐤏	'ayin	ע samek	'ain	ع {ghain
pā	𐤐,𐤐	pe	פ	fā	ف
tsā	𐤑	sade	צ	ṣad	ص
qā	𐤒	koph	ק	qāf	ق
rā	𐤓	resh	ר	rā	ر
sā	𐤔	sin, shīn	שׂ, שׁ	sīn, shīn	س, ش
tā	𐤕	taw	ת	tā, thā	ت, ث

Figure 3. Semitic alphabets. The names of the letters of the Phoenician-Canaanite (Old Semitic) alphabet are surmises. Letters in one alphabet which do not have correlatives in the others are set off to the side. The traditional order of the Arabic letters has been modified slightly to stress parallels.

Alphabetic Writing

As will be clear by now, true alphabetic writing consists in having a sign for each *sound* (technically each phoneme) of the language, rather than one for each *word* or one for each *syllable*. This is the most efficient writing system possible, since a language will be found to have some thousands of words and at least a couple of hundred different syllables, but the words and syllables are made up of individual speech sounds which seldom exceed sixty to seventy in number, and sometimes number as few as a dozen. Hence an alphabetic writing system can, with the fewest possible units (a number easily within anyone's ability to master), record every possible utterance in the language.

It would seem that the different stages we have traced, from drawing pictures to ideographs, to pictographic and syllabic writing, so logically follow each other as inevitably to lead a nation or tribe from one to the next until ultimately an alphabetic writing would be achieved. But such is simply not the case. Many great nations, for example the Japanese, have come as far as syllabic writing, and never seemed to feel a need to go beyond it. Indeed, in all the history of mankind, alphabetic writing has been invented only once, and all the alphabets in the world that are truly so called are derived from that single original alphabet. It seems likely that but for a certain lucky linguistic accident, man would never have discovered the alphabetic principle of writing. Had that been the case, the history of mankind would certainly have been very, very different.

There is a strong probability that it was the ancient Egyptians who first hit on the alphabetic principle; but we cannot prove it, for we cannot show that all or even a majority of the characters which ultimately became the alphabet we know were used in Egyptian texts of any period (though an apparently sound pedigree can be made for a few of them).

Of course, the hieroglyphic writing had a stock of thousands of characters, and might well have included the ones we are looking for in texts which have disappeared or not yet been discovered. What is harder to explain, however, is that when the Egyptians wrote alphabetically, they gave alphabetic values to an entirely different set of characters (Figure 4). Yet the Egyptians had been using a writing system for literally thousands of years, and had gone through all the stages. It does not seem likely that some other nation came along just as the Egyptians were on the point of discovering the alphabetic principle, snatched the discovery from under the Pharaohs' noses—and then taught *them* how to write alphabetically! There is certainly a mystery here which is still to be solved, and much fame (in learned circles) awaits him who solves it. If the Egyptians did indeed fail, after three thousand years, to discover the principle of alphabetic writing, it is

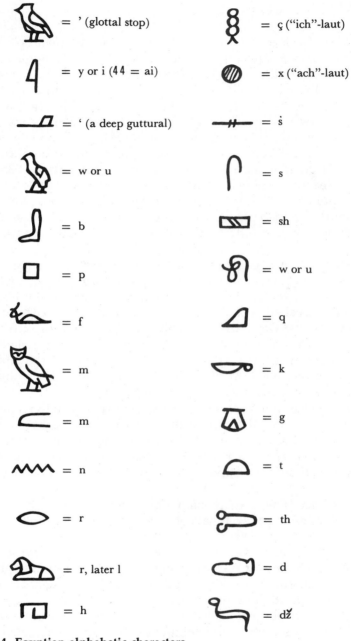

Figure 4. Egyptian alphabetic characters.

striking evidence that man might never have had this art except for the lucky accident which we shall now proceed to describe.

Not being able to prove a connection between the alphabet and Egyptian writing, for the present we have to say that the oldest known genuine alphabet was the Old Semitic, ultimate ancestor of the scripts used today to write Arabic and Hebrew. This alphabet had, of course, been a syllabic script. How had it turned that all-important corner into alphabetic writing? It seems probable that it was prompted in this direction by the structure of the Semitic languages.

To us, the "root" of our verb *ask* is the syllable *ask*, to which various other syllables are prefixed or suffixed to make the various verbal forms, for example the past tense (*ask-ed*), the progressive present tense (*is ask-ing*), the third person singular present (*ask-s*), and so on.

With verbs like *drive* or *sing*, however, we might say that the root is a syllable *dr-ve* or *s-ng*, where the dash indicates some vowel, but not always the same vowel, since we have *drive, drove, driven, sing, sang, sung*. Something is expressed by the alternation of these vowels, to be sure . . . , but the root of the verb is still a *syllable*, even with a variable vowel.

It was probably some kind of [alternating vowel] system like this which led to the situation now characteristic of Semitic languages (which is really just a further step in this direction), whereby the meaning of "driving" would inhere in the consonants D-R-V, that of "asking" in '-S-K. In Semitic languages the "root" of a word is really a *sequence of consonants* (usually three), modifications of the root being effected by kaleidoscopic rearrangements of the vowels intervening.

Thus, anything to do with writing shows the consonants K-T-B, but "he wrote" = *KaTaBa*, "it is written" = *meKTūB*, "he got it written" = *KaTtaBa*, "scribes" = *KuTtaBūn*, and so on. Words which seem to us quite unrelated turn out to be, in this system, derived from each other, like *SaLāM*, "peace," *iSLāM*, "the Mohammedan religion," *muSLiM*, "a Mohammedan." (From *salām* we get *'aslāma*, "he pacified, subjugated"; *islām* is "subjugation, submission" to God, and *muslim* is "one who has submitted.")

Obviously, no other type of language is better adapted to suggest to its speakers that there is a unit of word structure below the syllable; that BA is in turn composed of B- and -A. This is precisely what other nations might never have guessed. In Semitic, where BA alternates constantly with BI and BU, and sometimes with B- (the vowel being silenced), it is almost inevitable that every user of the language should develop a concept of the phoneme—a notion which is fundamental to the development of true alphabetic writing.

The structural nature of the Semitic languages is, therefore, in all probability the happy accident which became the key that unlocked for mankind, for the first and only time, the mystery of how to record speech by the method of maximum efficiency—one which does not have so many characters as to make learning it a complex art demanding years of training nor require a skill in drawing which few possess, nor consume large volumes of material for a relatively small amount of recorded message.

The consequences of this lucky accident are truly tremendous. If we did not have the alphabet, it would be impossible to hope for universal literacy, and therefore (if Thomas Jefferson's view was correct) for truly representative government. Writing could have been kept a secret art known only to a privileged few or to a particular social class which would thus have an undue advantage over the others. Information could not nearly so easily be conveyed from nation to nation, and the levels of civilization achieved by the Romans and ourselves might still be only goals to strive for. Truly, Prometheus did not do more for human progress than the unnamed scribe who first drew an alphabetic sign.

The Wanderings of the Alphabet

Let us here stress again that as far as can be ascertained from the available records, the principle of alphabetic writing has only been discovered once—hence, in the whole world *there is only one alphabet*. It follows that any people which writes in alphabetic signs has learned and adapted the use of the alphabet from another people who, in turn, had done the same. When the wanderings of this most potent cultural innovation are plotted, it makes an impressive odyssey. But the same would no doubt be true of every other discovery which has figured in an advance of civilization, if the same means existed for following its trail.

The earliest preserved inscriptions in alphabetic script date to about 1725 B.C. and were found in and around Byblos, in the country then known as Phoenicia (now Lebanon). It would seem that an alphabetic script which we might call Old Semitic was fairly familiar in that region at that time, though, as we have said, we cannot establish precisely where this script was invented, or by which Semitic tribe. It has been suggested that several Semitic peoples might have hit on the alphabetic principle at around the same time; but, if so, they seem to have soon adopted a common set of symbols.

This Old Semitic alphabet is of course the ancestor of the Hebrew, Phoenician, and Aramaic systems of writing. From these northern Semites, the knowledge of the alphabet appears to have passed, on the one hand, to the Greeks of Asia Minor, and on the other, to the Brahmans of ancient India, who developed from it their *devanagari*, the sacred script in which the religious rituals and hymns of the ancient Hindus were recorded.

With this exception, it seems that the genealogy of every other alphabetic system of writing goes through the Greeks. And it was because of the structure of *their* language that the Greeks were responsible for the greatest single improvement in the system: the origination of signs for the vowels.

The Semitic dialects had certain sounds which did not exist in Greek. The symbols for some of these, such as *qoph* (Q), the sign for the velar guttural which had existed in Indo-European but had everywhere been replaced by *p* in Attic Greek, were simply discarded by the Greeks (except in their use as numbers, but that is a different story). In other cases, however, the Greeks kept and used the symbol for a syllable beginning with a non-Greek sound, but pronounced it *without the foreign consonant*—so that the symbol became a sign for the syllable's vowel.

Thus, the first sign in the alphabet originally stood for the syllable '*A*, where the sign ' represents the "glottal stop," a contraction and release of the vocal chords—not a phoneme in English, but used often enough as a separator between vowels (e.g., oh-'oh), and you have heard it in Scottish dialect as a substitute for T: *bo'le* for *bottle*, *li'le* for *little*. Some dialects of Greek had this sound, and others did not. Those which did ultimately lost it, so that the sign ∀ (by now written in a different direction, A) everywhere became the sign, not for '*A*, but for the vowel *A*.

Other Semitic gutturals had had the tendency to influence adjacent vowels in the direction of O or U, and they accordingly, by the process just described, became the signs for those vowels.

A rather good illustration of what was going on is found in the sign H, standing for the syllable HE. In Ionic Greek, where the sound *h* was eventually eliminated, H became the sign for the vowel *e*. In Sicilian Greek, however, where syllables beginning with *h* still remained, the same H became the sign for *h*—which is our usage also, because we got the alphabet from the Romans, who got it from the Greeks, who followed the Sicilian tradition.

This fact explains deviations in *our* values for the alphabetic signs as compared with those of the standard (Attic) Greek alphabet (see Figure 5). Since the alphabet had not been invented as a tool for writing Greek, each Greek dialect which adopted it had to modify it a little—to assign different values to some of the signs, and discard the excess signs or use them in new ways, according to the phonology of their own speech.

While practically all modern nations which have alphabetic writing got it directly or indirectly from the Romans, there are a few to whom the tradition passes directly from the Greeks, in some cases concom-

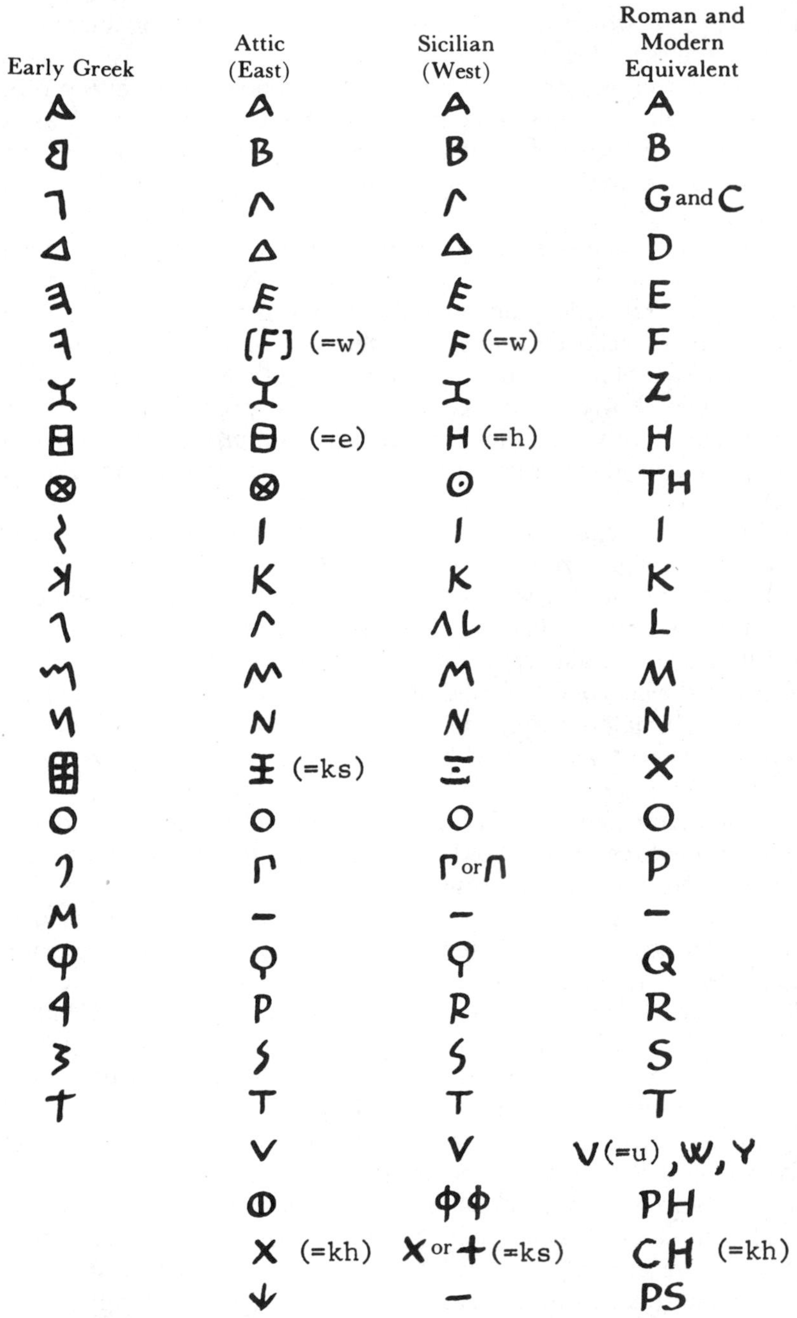

Early Greek	Attic (East)	Sicilian (West)	Roman and Modern Equivalent
A	A	A	A
B	B	B	B
⌐	Λ	Γ	G and C
◁	△	△	D
Ǝ	E	E	E
٦	[F] (=w)	F (=w)	F
X	I	I	Z
⊟	⊟ (=e)	H (=h)	H
⊗	⊗	⊙	TH
⌇	I	I	I
⋊	K	K	K
⌐	Λ	ΛL	L
⌇	M	M	M
⋈	N	N	N
⊞	Ξ (=ks)	Ξ	X
O	O	O	O
⌐	Γ	Γ or Π	P
M	—	—	—
Φ	Q	Q	Q
٩	P	R	R
ξ	)	)	S
✝	T	T	T
	V	V	V (=u), W, Y
	Φ	ΦΦ	PH
	X (=kh)	X or + (=ks)	CH (=kh)
	↓	—	PS

Figure 5. Greek alphabets. Note changes in direction of writing and variation of values between Attica and Sicily (after E. M. Thompson).

itantly with direct northern Semitic influence. Between the third and fifth centuries A.D., the spread of Christianity occasioned the devising of the ornamental and highly efficient Armenian, and the intriguing, delicate Georgian alphabets. And when the feared Goths were marauding throughout Latin Christendom, Ulfilas, child of a Gothic father and a Greek mother, became the St. Patrick of the Goths, Christianizing them and translating the Bible into their language, writing it with an alphabet which, according to repute, he invented, basing it on Greek. Ulfilas' lucky bilingualism not only gave us our oldest extensive records of any Germanic language, but also, it is believed, served as the basis of the Scandinavian "runic" writing, although some think it was the other way around.

Later, in the ninth century, when Christianity reached the Slavic peoples, two principal alphabets, the "glagolitic" and the "Cyrillic" (the latter named in honor of one of its reputed inventors, St. Cyril, who died 869 A.D.; the other inventor was his brother, St. Methodius, d. 885 A.D.), were devised to represent the then most generally used Slavic dialect. From these developed in the course of time the national alphabets of those Slavic peoples who were evangelized from Byzantium—the Russians, the Ukrainians, the Bulgarians, and the Serbs (Figure 6). (In contemporary Russia the Cyrillic alphabet has in turn been adapted for writing many non-Indo-European languages of the Soviet Union.)

Slavs who got their religion from Rome had to struggle to put their complex Slavic phonology into the Latin alphabet, with what often seem (to English speakers) jaw-breaking results, as seen in names like Przmysl, Szczepiński and Wojcechowic. The name Vishinsky, as a rough transcription from the Cyrillic, is identical with the Polish name Wyszinski.

From the great Roman empire the art of alphabetic writing passed, by inheritance or adoption, to virtually all the peoples who know it today. They were responsible for many interesting and important innovations in the basic system which there is not space to detail here, but which may be found in any thorough and complete history of the alphabet. We shall just point out a few of the most significant ones.

The Romance-speaking peoples simply inherited their alphabet; in many cases, they did not realize that they were not still speaking, as well as writing, genuine but perhaps rather careless Latin. When they made an effort to write Latin more correctly, only then did they realize that theirs was actually a different language.

It was during the time when Latin was still spoken, however, that the first modifications had to be made in the alphabet—leading to the first diacritic signs. The sound *h* became silent in colloquial Latin in the first century B.C. and in standard Latin by the second century A.D. Thereafter the letter was a zero, expressing nothing, and hence could

Cyrillic	Russian	Equivalent	Cyrillic	Russian	Equivalent
Ⰰ	а	a	Ȣ	у	u
Б	б	b	Ф	ф	f
В	в	v	Ѳ	ѳ*	f (originally th)
Г	г	g	Х	х	kh
Д	д	d	Ѡ		ō
Є	е	ye	Ш	ш	sh
Ж	ж	zh	Ⱛ	щ	shch
Ѕ		dz	Ч	ц	ts
Ꙁ	з	z	Ⴣ	ч	ch
Н	и	i	Ъ	ъ*	"hard sign"
І	і*	i	Ы	ы	ÿ
Ћ		d', t'	Ь	ь	"soft sign"
К	к	k	Ѣ	я	ya
Λ	л	l	Ю	ю	yu
М	м	m	Ѥ	ѣ*	ye
N	н	n	Ꙗ, Ꙗ		ĕ, yĕ
О	о	o	Ѫ Ѭ		ō, yō
П	п	p	Ѯ		ks
Р	р	r	Ѱ		ps
С	с	s	Ѵ		ü
Т	т	t			

*These letters were abolished in 1918.

Figure 6. Slavic alphabets. Some of the Modern Russian letters are given out of standard order for purpose of matching.

be used with other letters to express variations: TH for something like T that was not quite a T; GH for something like G that was not a G, and so on.

Another early diacritic, perhaps the earliest, was the letter G. Words like *signum* had shifted in pronunciation at a very early period from SIG-NUM to SING-NUM to, probably, [seɲo] (where the sign ɲ stands for what is technically a "palatalized n," as *gn* in French *mignon* or *ñ* in Spanish *cañón*). This made the G, in this particular position, another zero: and the idea logically arose that any sound could be distinguished from a palatalized correlative by prefixing G to the latter: N/GN; L/GL. Hence Romance languages blossomed with forms like *egli, Bologna, segno, Cagliari*. But Portuguese used the faithful H to express these sounds (*filho, senhor*), and Spanish, which had divested itself of doubled consonants, used a doubled letter (*castillo, suenno*), and later used an abbreviation for a doubled *n* (*sueño*)—for the Spanish *tilde* is nothing other than the well-known medieval Latin MS. abbreviation for an M or N (*tā, dōinū, ītētiōē*). Thus, the American who reads the Italian name *Castiglione* as *Cas-tig-li-o-ni* is murdering the harmonious genuine sound, since the spelling stands for *Ca-sti-lyo-ne*.

When the practice ceased of using as names of the letters the names of the objects they had pictured (or some meaningless derivative thereof, like *alpha, beta*), there arose the custom of naming a letter by giving (in the case of a vowel) its *sound*, or (in the case of a consonant), its sound *preceded or followed by [e]*. (In English this latter sound has uniformly shifted to [i], so we say the letters of the alphabet [e], [bi], [si], but Frenchmen say [a], [be], [se].) In some exceptional cases, however, phonetic shift has eliminated the letter's sound from its name. Our name for R is [ar] (from earlier [er] by the same change which gives us *heart, hearth, sergeant*). In English pronunciation, however, R is silent after a vowel, so the name of the letter R is *ah*—with no R in it.

Again, our name for *h* is *aitch*, a meaningless word in English but a preservation of French *la hache* "the hatchet"—suggested by the letter's appearance, to be sure

$$\text{₣} = h$$

—but originally containing its sound; no [h] has been pronounced in French, however, for over a century, so the name of this letter, too, fails to contain its sound . . .

Our present letters J and W are known to have been invented in the sixteenth century. In Latin, since all W's had become V's by the second century A.D., the letter U, however written (V, U), expressed that sound—the choice between the rounded and the angular form being purely a matter of calligraphy. The English language, however, had both the V sounds and the W sounds; so, to express the latter, English printers of the sixteenth century "doubled" the former, writing *vv* (or *uu*).

Latin also lacked any sound like English J; but this sound appeared in Old French in words where Latin had had *i*, either as *ee* or as *y* (*Fanuarius* > *janvier; iuvenis* > *jeune*), and printers traditionally used *i* for it. Medieval scribes often extended this letter downwards in an ornamental flourish at the end of a number (thus: xiiij), and no doubt it was this which suggested the adoption in English printing of this alternative form of *i* for the *j*-sound. For quite a while, however, many printers continued to regard i/j and u/w/v as interchangeable and to print *Iohn, starres aboue, A VVinter's Tale, Fnterlude*, and so on.

We have been able to mention here only a few of the vicissitudes undergone by the alphabet—*the* alphabet, only one, always the same— in its long journey through space and time from the eastern shores of the Mediterranean to the far islands of the Pacific.

FOR DISCUSSION AND REVIEW

1. According to Hughes, "ideographic writing" is "properly in no sense either language or writing." How does he support this statement? Do you agree or disagree? Defend your answer.

2. The characters of written Chinese each represent, in general, one morpheme or one word. Explain the advantages of such a system, which does not involve any linking of sound to the written characters, to the Chinese as a nation. What are the disadvantages of such a system?

3. Justify Hughes's statement that "Pictographic writing . . . is true writing."

4. Describe the development of syllabic writing systems from pictographic systems. What are the advantages of the former? How might a limited syllabic system develop into an alphabetic system? Is such a logical progression more or less inevitable? Why or why not?

5. Why is alphabetic writing "the most efficient writing system possible"?

6. Explain how the structure of the Semitic languages and the development of the concept of the phoneme led to the development of the alphabet.

7. Summarize chronologically what Hughes calls "the wanderings of the alphabet." In doing so, be sure to explain the important contribution made by the Greeks and how the structure of their language made this improvement possible.

8. What is a diacritic sign? Give three examples (draw them from at least two languages). Describe the development of diacritic signs as part of alphabetic writing.

9. Hughes describes the development of an alphabetic writing system as a "lucky accident" and as "truly tremendous." Describe the kind(s) of cultures that might have developed had an alphabetic writing system not evolved. (Consider, for example, Ray Bradbury's *Fahrenheit 451* or George Orwell's *1984.*)

Projects for "Beyond Speech: Broader Perspectives"

1. Obtain the book *Gender Advertisements* by Erving Goffman (New York: Harper Colophon Books, 1979). Read the excellent introduction by Vivian Gornick, and then examine at least one section of text and illustrative advertisements. Prepare a report of your findings, indicating to what extent the way you look at advertisements in the future will be affected by what you have learned.

2. Most of our feelings of territoriality are unconscious unless and until "our territory" is violated. Prepare a report in which you describe the reactions of another person when you do some or all of the following: (a) after a class has been meeting for at least three weeks, deliberately sit in a seat that you know has regularly been occupied by someone else; (b) in your library or snack bar, move someone else's books or food and sit down while the person is temporarily away; (c) in an uncrowded library or classroom, deliberately sit right next to another individual; (d) in your dorm room or at home, deliberately sit (in a chair, at a desk, etc.) where you know someone else "belongs."

3. Individually or in small groups, prepare answers to the following questions for a class discussion: (a) What are your three most common gestures? What are your instructor's three most common gestures? What conclusions (about personality, setting, etc.) can you draw from these? (b) In a conversation, how do you know when someone is losing interest? Is not losing interest? (c) What aspects of a person's appearance cause you to feel (at least initially) friendly? Hostile? (d) In what ways do you act differently at home from the way you do at a friend's? Why?

4. Study the illustration (on p. 718) of a typical buyer-seller relationship; the buyer is on the left and the seller on the right. Discuss the interaction between the buyer and the seller in terms of their gestures, their personal appearances, and their proxemic arrangement. What general statements can you make about the buyer? About the seller?

5. Using the following diagrams of common classroom seating arrangements, devise an experiment that will test the effects on behavior of the various arrangements. You may wish to poll the feelings of members of a number of classes and elicit reasons for their feelings. Which arrangement was judged most comfortable? Least comfortable? Why? Is there any relationship between seating arrangements and class size? Between seating arrangements and class or grade level? Between seating arrangements and types of classroom activities or subject matter? Explain.

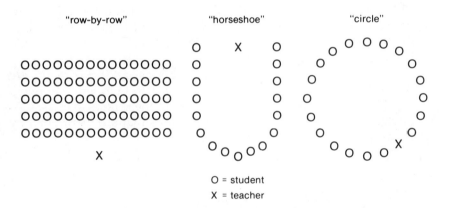

6. Study a short movie while the sound is turned off. Make notes on your observations of proxemics and body language and what you learn from these aspects of behavior. Turn on the sound and make notes on your findings once again. Write a paper that discusses the quantitative and qualitative differences in what you learned from both viewings. Ideally, you should try to determine the relative importance of body language, verbal communication, and proxemics.

7. If you know Russian, prepare a comparison of the Cyrillic and Roman alphabets. Which alphabet is a better fit for Russian? For English? Why?

8. Hendrix and Sacerdoti specifically exclude speech synthesizers from their discussion of artificial intelligence. Prepare a report on the development and applications of speech synthesizers.

9. A number of "expert systems" are currently available and being used in a variety of situations. Prepare a report describing one of the

following systems: DENDRAL, MYCIN, PROSPECTOR, KAS, TEI-RESIAS, MOLGEN, GUIDON, TATR, CATS-1, PUFF, ONCOCIN.

10. A good deal of interesting work has been done with the systems of communication of animals other than chimpanzees. Using items included in the bibliography for this section, write a paper in which you review the research that has been done with bees, birds, or dolphins. You should supplement your research materials by looking in the *Reader's Guide to Periodical Literature* and the *Social Sciences and Humanities Index*.

11. Prepare a report describing the work with one or more of the chimpanzees involved in communication experiments described in this section. A good starting place is Eugene Linden's paperback book *Apes, Men, and Language* (Pelican Books, 1976) and its bibliography, but be sure to go beyond this single source. An interesting variation would be to have the class divide into groups, with each group responsible for preparing an oral or written report on a particular experiment.

12. The story of "Clever Hans," the extent of the belief in his near-human abilities, the variety of those abilities, and the long struggle to reveal the truth is a fascinating one. Prepare a report in which you review the events chronologically.

13. A number of films of the various chimpanzee experiments are available. Your media librarian should be able to help you compile a reasonably complete list. Watch at least one of these films in class. Can you detect any of the flaws in the experiments that are mentioned by Kemp and Wilson? If so, describe them.

Selected Bibliography

NONVERBAL COMMUNICATION

Ardrey, Robert. *The Territorial Imperative.* New York: Atheneum, 1966. (An examination of the concept of territoriality, the relationship of men and animals to space.)

Ashcraft, Norman, and Albert E. Scheflen. *People Space: The Making and Breaking of Human Boundaries.* Garden City, NY: Anchor Books, 1976. (Two distinguished scholars, an anthropologist and a psychiatrist, examine the hidden rules that govern our use of space.)

Birdwhistell, Ray L. *Introduction to Kinesics.* Louisville: University of Louisville Press, 1952. (Introduction to the field of kinesics, with kinegraphs and what they symbolize.)

———. "Kinesics." *International Encyclopaedia of Social Sciences.* Ed. David L. Sills. New York: Macmillan and The Free Press, 1968. (A brief but technical introduction.)

———. *Kinesics and Context: Essays on Body Motion Communication.* Philadelphia: University of Pennsylvania Press, 1970. (An interesting collection of Bird-

whistell's essays on nonverbal human communication; excellent bibliography.)

Davis, Flora. *Inside Intuition: What We Know About Nonverbal Communication.*
New York: New American Library (A Signet Book), 1975. (Despite its
popular title, a good summary of recent research; complete bibliography;
readable.)

Goffman, Erving. *Gender Advertisements.* New York: Harper Colophon Books,
1979. (Goffman is a widely recognized social scientist; here he investigates
advertisements and the way in which they do and do not reflect reality;
highly recommended.)

————. *Behavior in Public Places.* New York: The Free Press of Glencoe, 1963.
(A psychiatrist's analysis of public behavior.)

————. *The Presentation of Self in Everyday Life.* Edinburgh: University of Edinburgh, Social Sciences Research Center, 1956. (An analysis of an individual's impressions of himself when appearing before others.)

Hall, Edward T. *Beyond Culture.* Garden City, NY: Doubleday, 1976. (A study
of how some of the basic cultural systems such as time and space are used
to organize human behavior.)

————. "Proxemics." *Current Anthropology,* 9 (April–June 1968), 83–104. (A
good introduction to proxemics with charts, comments by authorities, and
bibliography.)

————. *The Hidden Dimension.* Garden City, NY: Doubleday, 1966. (A fascinating discussion of human and animal use of space.)

————. *The Silent Language.* Garden City, NY: Doubleday, 1959. (A pioneer
work on space and language.)

Harris, Christie, and Moira Johnston. *Figleafing Through History: The Dynamics
of Dress.* New York: Atheneum, 1971. (An entertaining historical discussion of clothes and how they affect the self-conceptions of individuals in
different societies.)

Henley, Nancy M. *Body Politics: Power, Sex, and Nonverbal Communication.* Englewood Cliffs, NJ: Prentice-Hall, 1977. (A very important book; crucial
to an understanding of the full impact of nonverbal communication.)

Hewes, Gordon W. "World Distribution of Certain Postural Habits." *American
Anthropologist,* 57 (April 1955), 231–244. (Distribution and significance of
certain standing and sitting positions.)

Hinde, Robert A., ed. *Non-Verbal Communication.* Cambridge: Cambridge University Press, 1972. (An informative collection of fifteen essays on the
nature of communication, communication in animals, and nonverbal communication in man.)

Knapp, Mark L. *Nonverbal Communication in Human Interaction.* 2nd ed. New
York: Holt, Rinehart and Winston, 1978. (Very thorough survey of research; excellent notes and comprehensive bibliography.)

Michael, G. and F. N. Willis, Jr. "The Development of Gestures as a Function
of Social Class, Education, and Sex." *Psychological Record,* 18 (October
1968), 515–519. (A study of eight groups of children differing in social
class, education, and sex.)

Morris, Desmond. *The Human Zoo.* New York: McGraw-Hill, 1969. (A zoolo-
gist's analysis of the sociological implications of population clusters.)

Pittenger, Robert E., Charles F. Hackett, and John J. Danehy. *The First Five Minutes: A Sample of Microscopic Interview Analysis.* Ithaca, NY: Paul Martineau, 1960. (An in-depth analysis with emphasis on paralinguistic features of a five-minute interview between a psychiatrist and a young female patient.)

Scheflen, Albert E. *How Behavior Means.* Garden City, NY: Anchor Press/Doubleday, 1974. (A pioneer in kinesics examines nonverbal communication, territoriality, the environment, and cultural context; highly recommended.)

————. *Body Language and the Social Order: Communication as Behavior Control.* Englewood Cliffs, NJ: Prentice-Hall, 1972. (A discussion of the uses of body language for purposes of social control.)

————. "The Significance of Posture in Communications Systems" *Psychiatry*, 27 (November 1964), 316–331. (A psychiatrist's analysis of the significance of postural activities and markers in interview and group situations; illustrated.)

ARTIFICIAL INTELLIGENCE

Note: Much of the literature in this field is highly technical. The books listed below represent a small selection from the available material. The article in this part by Hendrix and Sacerdoti also contains a useful bibliography.

Barr, Avron and Edward A. Feigenbaum, eds. *The Handbook of Artificial Intelligence.* Volumes I, II, and III. Los Altos, CA: William Kaufman, 1982.

Bobrow, D. G. and Allan Collins, eds. *Representation and Understanding: Studies in Cognitive Science.* New York: Academic Press, 1975.

Boden, Margaret. *Artificial Intelligence and Natural Man.* New York: Basic Books, 1977.

Campbell, Jeremy. *Grammatical Man: Information, Entropy, Language, and Life.* New York: Simon & Schuster, 1982.

Feigenbaum, Edward A. and Pamela McCorduck. *The Fifth Generation.* Reading, MA: Addison-Wesley, 1983.

Hanson, Dirk. *The New Alchemists.* New York: Avon, 1982.

Hofstadter, Douglas. *Godel, Escher, Bach: An Eternal Golden Braid.* New York: Basic Books, 1979.

McCorduck, Pamela. *Machines Who Think.* New York: W. H. Freeman and Company, 1979.

Schank, Roger C., ed. *Conceptual Information Processing.* New York: American Elsevier, 1975.

Simon, Herbert A. *The Sciences of the Artificial.* 2nd ed. Cambridge, MA: MIT Press, 1981.

Winograd, Terry. *Understanding Natural Language.* New York: Academic Press, 1972.

Winston, Patrick. *Artificial Intelligence.* Reading, MA: Addison-Wesley, 1977.

ANIMAL COMMUNICATION

Fleming, Joyce D. "Field Report: The State of the Apes." *Psychology Today*, 7 (January 1974), 31–38, 43–44, 46, 49–50. (Summary of research with Washoe, Lucy, Sarah, and other chimps.)

Ford, Barbara. "How They Taught a Chimp to Talk." *Science Digest*, 67 (May 1970), 10–17. (A discussion of the chimpanzee Washoe's sign language, with illustrations.)

Gardner, Beatrice T. and R. Allen Gardner. "Teaching Sign Language to a Chimpanzee." *Science*, 165 (August 15, 1969), 664–672. (Teaching the infant chimpanzee Washoe the gestural language of the deaf.)

———. "Teaching Sign Language to a Chimpanzee. VII: Use of Order in Sign Combinations." *Bulletin of the Psychonomic Society*, 4 (1974), 264. (More technical; Washoe at a later stage.)

———. "Early Signs of Language in Child and Chimpanzee." *Science*, 187 (1975), 752–753. (Comparison of Washoe's acquisition of signs with child language acquisition.)

Hayes, Catherine. *The Ape in Our House*. New York: Harper & Brothers, 1951. (The story of the Hayes family's experiences with the chimpanzee Viki.)

Krough, August. "The Language of the Bees." *Scientific American Reader*. New York: Simon & Schuster, 1953. (A summary of Karl von Frisch's classic study of communication among bees.)

Lilly, John C. *Man and Dolphin*. New York: Pyramid Publications, 1969. (The story of man's attempt to communicate with another species.)

———. *The Mind of the Dolphin: A Nonhuman Intelligence*. New York: Avon Books, 1969. (An introduction to the controversial world of communication among dolphins.)

Linden, Eugene. *Apes, Men, and Language*. New York: Pelican Books, 1976. (A chatty survey of most of the research then being done in this country with chimpanzees.)

Patterson, Francine. "Conversations With a Gorilla." *National Geographic* (October 1978), 438–465. (Excellent photographs.)

Premack, David, "The Education of Sarah: A Chimp Learns the Language." *Psychology Today*, 4 (September 1970), 54–58. (Teaching a chimpanzee a nonvocal language.)

Riopelle, A. J., ed. *Animal Problem Solving*. Baltimore: Penguin Books, 1967. (A collection of reports on problem-solving experiments with animals.)

Sebeok, Thomas A., and Jean Umiker-Sebeok, eds. *Speaking of Apes: A Critical Anthology of Two-Way Communication With Man*. New York: Plenum Press, 1980. (Indispensable and totally comprehensive. Very complete bibliography.)

Terrace, Herbert S. *Nim: A Chimpanzee Who Learned Sign Language*. New York: Alfred A. Knopf, 1979. (Book-length study detailing Terrace's four-year work with Nim.)

Terrace, H. S., L. A. Petitto, R. J. Sanders, and T. G. Bever. "Can an Ape Create a Sentence?" *Science*, 206 (November 1979), 891–902. (A more technical and complete account than that which appeared in *Psychology Today*; extensive bibliography.)

Wilson, Edward O. "Animal Communication." *Scientific American*, 227 (1972), 52–60. (From insects to mammals, animals communicate—but man's language is unique.)

WRITING

Diringer, D. *The Alphabet*. New York: Philosophical Library, 1948. (Detailed history.)

Gelb, I. J. *A Study of Writing*. Rev. ed. Chicago: University of Chicago Press, 1963. (Highly recommended study of the origin and evolution of writing systems.)

Pyles, Thomas and John Algeo. *The Origins and Development of the English Language*. 3rd ed. New York: Harcourt Brace Jovanovich, 1982. (See Chapter 3, "Letters and Sounds: A Brief History of Writing," which traces the origin and development of English writing.)

Glossary

acoustic phonetics. The study of the properties of human speech sounds as they are transmitted through the air as sound waves.

affix. In English, a prefix or suffix (both are bound morphemes) attached to a base (either bound or free) and modifying its meaning.

affricate. A complex sound made by rapidly articulating first a stop and then a fricative. Affricates appear initially in the English words *chin* and *gin*.

allophone. A nonsignificant variant of a phoneme.

alveolar. A sound made by placing the tip or blade of the tongue on the bony ridge behind the upper teeth (e.g., the initial sounds of the English words *tin*, *sin*, *din*, *zap*, *nap*, and *lap*); also, a point of articulation.

alveolar ridge. The bony ridge just behind the upper front teeth.

ambiguity. Having more than one meaning; ambiguity may be semantic or syntactic.

American Sign Language (ASL, Ameslan). A system of communication used by deaf people in the United States, consisting of hand symbols that vary in the shape of the hands, the direction of their movement, and their position in relation to the body. It is different from finger spelling, in which words are spelled out letter by letter, and Signed English, in which English words are signed in the order in which they are uttered, thus preserving English morphology and syntax.

aphasia. The impairment of language abilities as a result of brain damage (usually from a stroke or trauma).

articulatory phonetics. The study of the production of human speech sounds by the speech organs.

aspiration. An aspirated sound is followed by a puff of air; the English voiceless-stop consonants /p, t, k/ are aspirated in word-initial position (e.g., *pot*, *top*, *kit*).

assimilation. A change that a sound undergoes to become more like another, often adjacent, sound.

back formation. A process of word formation that uses analogy as a basis for removing part of a word; *edit* was formed by back formation from *editor*.

base. In English, a free or bound morpheme to which affixes are added to form new words; *cat* is a free base, *-ceive* is a bound base.

bilabial. A sound made by constriction between the lips (e.g., the first sound in *pet*, *bet*, and *met*).

Black English. A vernacular variety of English used by some black people; more precisely divided into Standard Black English and Black English Vernacular.

blending. A process of word formation, combining clipping and compounding, that makes new words by combining parts of existing words that are not morphemes (e.g., *chortle* and *galumphing*).

borrowing. A process in which words, and sometimes other characteristics, are incorporated into one language from another.

bound morpheme. A morpheme that cannot appear alone. In English, prefixes and suffixes are bound morphemes, as are some bases.

Broca's area. One of the language centers in the left hemisphere of the brain.

caretaker speech. Used by parents in talking to children who are beginning to speak, it is characterized by simplified vocabulary, systematic phonological simplification of some words, higher pitch, exaggerated intonation, and short, simple sentences.

central. A sound, usually a vowel, made with the tongue body neither front nor back.

clipping. A process of word formation, common in informal language, in which a word is shortened without regard to derivational analogy (e.g., *dorm* from *dormitory*, *bus* from *omnibus*).

coinage. A rare process of word formation in which words are created from unrelated, meaningless elements.

comparative linguistics. The study of similarities and differences among related languages.

complementary distribution. A situation in which two allophones of a phoneme each occurs in a position or positions in which the other does not. See also *free variation*.

compounding. A process of word formation in which two or more words or bound bases are combined to form a new word.

consonant. A kind of speech sound produced with significant constriction at some point in the vocal tract.

conversational principles. What an auditor can expect from a speaker: that the speaker is sincere, is telling the truth, is being relevant, and will contribute an appropriate amount of information.

creole. A language that developed from a pidgin and that has a complex structure and native speakers.

derivation. A process of word formation in which one or more affixes are added to an existing word or bound base.

diachronic linguistics. Historical linguistics; the study of changes in languages over long periods.

dialect. A variety of a language, usually regional or social, set off from other varieties of the same language by differences in pronunciation, vocabulary, and grammar.

dichotic listening. A research technique in which two different sounds are presented simultaneously, through earphones, to an individual's left and right ears.

diphthong. Complex vowel sounds having one beginning point and a different ending point. The English words *hoist* and *cow* contain diphthongs.

dissimilation. A change in one or more adjacent sounds that serves to make a string of similar sounds less similar.

downgrading. A historical process in which the value of a word declines. Also known as *pejoration, devaluation,* and *depreciation.*

Early Modern English. The English spoken in England from about A.D. 1450 to 1700.

ethnocentricity. The belief that one's culture (including language) is at the center of things, and that other cultures (and languages) are inferior.

free variation. A situation in which two or more allophones of a phoneme can occur in a particular position. See also *complementary distribution.*

fricative. A sound produced by bringing one of the articulators close enough to one of the points of articulation to create a narrow opening; a manner of articulation.

front. A sound, usually a vowel, articulated with the body of the tongue set relatively forward.

function words. Function words (e.g., articles, prepositions, conjunctions), having little reference to things outside of language, indicate some grammatical relationship; the function-word class is small and closed.

functional shift. A process of word formation in English (made possible by the gradual loss of most inflectional affixes) in which a word is shifted from one part of speech to another without changing its form.

glide. Sounds that provide transitions to or from other sounds; they are vowel-like sounds, but sometimes act more like consonants. The English words *yet* and *wet* begin with a glide; the English words *my* and *cow* end with a glide.

glottal. A sound made by constriction of the vocal cords (e.g., English *uh-uh* has a glottal stop in the middle).

glottis. The space, within the larynx, between the two vocal cords.

Great Vowel Shift. A set of sound changes that affected the long vowels of English during the fifteenth century A.D., and that resulted in many discrepancies between the spelling and pronunciation of modern English words.

Grimm's law. A statement of the regular sound changes that took place in Proto-Germanic but not in other Indo-European languages.

high. A sound, usually a vowel, that is articulated with the body of the tongue set relatively high (i.e., close to the roof of the mouth).

historical linguistics. The study of change in languages over time.

holophrastic speech. The stage of language acquisition in which children use one-word utterances.

ideograph. A character in a writing system that stands for an idea and is, or was, pictorial.

ideolect. The variety of language spoken by one person. See also *dialect*.

illocutionary force. The intentions of a speaker, as far as those listening can discern from the context. *Implicit* illocutionary force is unstated; *explicit* illocutionary force is stated.

Indo-European. A group of languages descended from a common ancestor and now widely spoken in Europe, North and South America, Australia, New Zealand, and parts of India.

interdental. A sound made by placing the tongue tip between the teeth (e.g., the initial sounds of the English words *thin* and *then*).

International Phonetic Alphabet (IPA). A set of symbols and diacritical marks that permits the unambiguous recording of any perceivable differences in speech sounds; an alphabet with a different symbol for every different sound in the world's languages.

labial. A manner-of-articulation term under which are included the bilabials and the labiodentals.

labiodental. A sound made by bringing the lower lip into contact with the upper teeth (e.g., the first sound of the English words *fat* and *vat*).

larynx. The structure that contains the vocal chords.

liquid. A sound in which the vocal tract is not closed off, nor is there sufficient constriction to produce friction; in English, the liquids are [1] and [r], both consonant sounds.

low. A sound, usually a vowel, articulated with the body of the tongue set relatively low, away from the roof of the mouth.

manner of articulation. The way in which the flow of air from the lungs is modified, usually in the mouth, to produce a speech sound. See also *place of articulation*.

mean length of utterance (MLU). A measure of morphemes in the speech of young children; often used to determine the progress of language acquisition.

mid. A sound, usually a vowel, articulated with the body of the tongue set midway between the roof of the mouth and the bottom of the mouth.

Middle English. The English spoken in England from approximately A.D. 1100 to 1450.

minimal pair. Two words with different meanings that are distinguished only by having a different phoneme in the same position in both words; e.g., in English, *bat* and *pat* are a minimal pair.

morpheme. A morpheme is the smallest unit in a language that carries meaning; it may be a word or part of a word.

morphology. The study of the composition or structure of words.

nasal. A sound made with the velum lowered so that air resonates in the nasal as well as in the oral cavity and the airstream flows out of the vocal tract through the nose. A manner of articulation.

native speaker. One who has learned a language as a child and therefore speaks it fluently.

Old English. The ancestor of Modern English, Old English was the language spoken in England from about A.D. 450 to 1100.

orthography. Any writing system that is widely used in a society.

palatal. A sound made by bringing the tongue into contact with the front part of the roof of the mouth (e.g., the initial sounds of the English words *church*, *ship*, *judge*, *rim*, and *yet*, and the medial sound of *measure*).

palate. The hard front part of the roof of the mouth.

perceptual phonetics. The study of the perception and identification of speech sounds by a listener.

phoneme. A speech sound that is a single mental unit but that usually has one or more physical representations (i.e., allophones).

phonetics. The study of speech sounds.

phrase-structure rule. A rule that expands a single symbol into two or more symbols (e.g., S → NP VP).

pictograph. A character in a writing system that stands for a word. See also *ideograph*.

pidgin. A rudimentary language with a simplified grammar and limited lexicon, typically used for trading by individuals who do not speak the same language. Pidgins are auxiliary languages; people do not learn them as native speakers.

place of articulation. The place in the vocal tract where the airflow is modified, usually by constriction, in the production of speech sounds; also called *point of articulation*. See also *manner of articulation*.

pragmatics. The study of speech acts or of how language is used in various social contexts.

presuppositions. Those things that the speaker and the listener in a conversation can suppose each other to know; meanings that are presupposed but not overtly stated.

semantics. The analysis of the meaning of individual words and of such larger units as phrases and sentences.

sociolinguistics. The study of social dialects; the identification and analysis of dialect features that are significant indicators of social class.

spectrogram. A visual representation of speech made by a *sound spectrograph*, indicating the frequency, duration, and intensity of speech sounds.

speech community. A group of people who regularly communicate with one another and who share certain speech characteristics.

stop. A sound produced by completely blocking the airstream; a manner of articulation.

syntax. The study of the structure of sentences and of the interrelationships of their parts.

telegraphic speech. Speech that follows the two-word stage in language acquisition. It lacks function words and morphemes and is characterized by short, simple sentences made up primarily of content words.

trachea. The tubal area extending from the larynx through the back of the mouth as far as the rear opening of the nasal cavity.

velar. A sound made by bringing the tongue into contact with the velum (e.g., the final sounds of the English words *sick, rig,* and *sing*). See also *velum.*

velum. The soft, back part of the roof of the mouth.

vocal cords. Muscular, elastic bands within the larynx that, in speech, are either relaxed and spread apart (for voiceless sounds) or tensed and drawn together so that there is only a narrow opening between them (for voiced sounds).

vocal tract. The vocal tract includes the pharynx, the nasal cavity, and the mouth cavity. It is located above the vocal cords and used for the production of speech sounds.

voice-onset-time (VOT). The time between moving the lips and vibrating the vocal cords. In English, /b/ has a VOT of 0 milliseconds; /p/ has a VOT of +40 milliseconds.

voiced sound. A sound made with the vocal cords tensed and vibrating.

voiceless sound. A sound made with the vocal cords relaxed, spread apart, and relatively still.

vowel. A speech sound produced with a relatively free flow of air; vowel sounds are "open" sounds made by varying the shape of the vocal tract.

Wernicke's area. One of the language centers in the left hemisphere of the human brain.

Acknowledgments (continued from page iv)

"The Rules of Language" by Morris Halle. Reprinted with permission from *Technology Review*, copyright 1980, and with permission of the author.

"The Minimal Units of Meaning: Morphemes" from *Language Files* by The Ohio State University Department of Linguistics, published by Advocate Publishing Group, 6810 East Main St., Reynoldsburg, Ohio 43068. Copyright © 1978, 1979, 1982 by The Ohio State University Department of Linguistics and used with their permission.

"The Identification of Morphemes" by H. A. Gleason. From *An Introduction to Descriptive Linguistics*, Revised Edition by H. A. Gleason, Jr. Copyright © 1955, 1961 by Holt, Rinehart and Winston, Inc. Reprinted by permission of CBS College Publishing.

"Morphology: Three Exercises" by H. A. Gleason. From *Workbook in Descriptive Linguistics* by Henry Allan Gleason, Jr. Copyright © 1955 by Holt, Rinehart and Winston, Inc. Reprinted by permission of CBS College Publishing.

"Word-Making: Some Sources of New Words" by W. Nelson Francis. Selection is reprinted from *The English Language: An Introduction* by W. Nelson Francis, with permission of W. W. Norton & Company, Inc. Copyright © 1963, 1965 by W. W. Norton & Company, Inc.

"What Do Native Speakers Know About Their Language?" by Roderick A. Jacobs and Peter S. Rosenbaum. Reprinted by permission of the authors.

"Sentence Structure" by Frank Heny. Copyright 1985 by Frank Heny.

"What Is a Language?" by Neil Smith and Deirdre Wilson. From *Modern Linguistics: The Results of Chomsky's Revolution*. Indiana University Press, 1979.

"The Cheshire Cat's Grin: How Do We Plan and Produce Speech?" by Jean Aitchison. From *The Articulate Mammal: An Introduction to Psycholinguistics*, Second Edition by Jean Aitchison. Copyright 1976, 1983 by Jean Aitchison. Reprinted by permission of Universe Books, New York, and Hutchison Publishing Group Ltd., London.

"An Interview with Noam Chomsky" by John Gliedman. Copyright 1983 by John Gliedman and reprinted with permission of Omni Publications International Ltd.

"The Meaning of a Word" by George L. Dillon. *Introduction to Contemporary Linguistic Semantics*, © 1977, pp. 1–25, 99–117, 137–146. Reprinted by permission of Prentice-Hall Inc., Englewood Cliffs, NJ.

"Automobile Semantics" by Mark Aronoff. Reprinted from *Linguistic Inquiry* 12: 3 (1981) by permission of The MIT Press, Cambridge, Massachusetts.

"Pragmatics" by Madelon E. Heatherington. From *How Language Works*, pp. 153–157. Copyright 1980 by Little, Brown and Company. Reprinted by permission.

"Discourse Routines" by Elaine Chaika. From *Language: The Social Mirror* by Elaine Chaika. Copyright 1982 Newbury House Publishers, Inc., Rowley, Mass. 01969. Reprinted by permission of the publisher.

Figure, p. 457. From "Semantic Cuisine" by Adrienne Lehrer in the *Journal of Linguistics*. Cambridge University Press.

"Culinary Semantics" chart from "Semantic Cuisine" by Adrienne Lehrer in *The Journal of Linguistics*. Cambridge University Press.

Excerpt and rating scale from *Psycholinguistics: Introductory Perspectives* by Joseph F. Kess. New York: Academic Press, Inc. 1976. Reprinted by permission of publisher and Joseph F. Kess.

"Speech Communities" by Paul Roberts. From *Understanding English* by Paul Roberts. Copyright 1958 by Paul Roberts. Reprinted by permission of Harper & Row, Publishers, Inc.

"Social and Regional Variation" by Albert H. Marckwardt and J. L. Dillard. From *American English*, Second Edition, by Albert H. Marckwardt, revised by J. L. Dillard. Copyright © 1980 by Oxford University Press, Inc. Reprinted by permission. Map, "Speech Areas, Eastern United States," from *Social Stratification of English in New York City* by William Labov. Washington: Center for Applied Linguistics, 1982. Reprinted by permission of the Center for Applied Linguistics. "Detailed style stratification" chart from Hans Kurath, *Word Geography of the Eastern United States*. Ann Arbor: University of Michigan Press, 1949. Copyright by The University of Michigan; renewed 1976.

"Dialects: How They Differ" by Roger W. Shuy. From *Discovering American Dialects* by Roger W. Shuy. Copyright 1967 by the National Council of Teachers of English. Reprinted by permission of the publisher and author.

"A Researcher's Guide to the Sociolinguistic Variable (ING)" by Benji Wald and Timothy Shopen. From *Styles and Variables in English*, edited by Timothy Shopen and Joseph M. Williams; Winthrop Publishers, 1981. Reprinted by permission of the author.

"The Study of Nonstandard English" by William Labov. From *The Study of Nonstandard English* by William Labov. Copyright 1970 by the National Council of Teachers of English. Reprinted by permission of the publisher and the author.

"'It Bees Dat Way Sometime': Sounds and Structure of Present-Day Black English," Geneva Smitherman. From *Talkin' and Testifyin'* by Geneva Smitherman. Copyright 1977 by Geneva Smitherman. Reprinted by permission of Houghton-Mifflin Company.

731

Index

THE BRUMBACK LIBRARY
OF VAN WERT COUNTY
VAN WERT, OHIO